THE
CAMBRIDGE EDITION OF
THE WORKS OF
JOSEPH CONRAD

'TWIXT LAND AND SEA

THE WORKS OF JOSEPH CONRAD

JOSEPH CONRAD

'TWIXT LAND AND SEA

TALES

A SMILE OF FORTUNE
THE SECRET SHARER
FREYA OF THE SEVEN ISLES

EDITED BY
J. A. Berthoud
Laura L. Davis
S. W. Reid

ASSISTANT EDITOR
Raymond T. Brebach

CAMBRIDGE
UNIVERSITY PRESS

CAMBRIDGE UNIVERSITY PRESS
Cambridge, New York, Melbourne, Madrid, Cape Town, Singapore, São Paulo, Delhi

Cambridge University Press
The Edinburgh Building, Cambridge CB2 2RU, UK

Published in the United States of America by
Cambridge University Press, New York

www.cambridge.org
Information on this title: www.cambridge.org/9780521871266

First published 2008

Printed in the United Kingdom at the University Press, Cambridge

An Approved Edition
Committee on Scholarly Editions

A catalogue record for this publication is available from the British Library

ISBN 978-0-521-87126-6 hardback

In Memoriam

BRUCE HARKNESS

1923–2004

Published in association with

CENTER FOR CONRAD STUDIES
INSTITUTE FOR BIBLIOGRAPHY AND EDITING
KENT STATE UNIVERSITY

Preparation of this volume has been supported by

RESEARCH AND GRADUATE STUDIES, KENT STATE UNIVERSITY
THE KENT STATE UNIVERSITY FOUNDATION
PROGRAM FOR EDITIONS
NATIONAL ENDOWMENT FOR THE HUMANITIES
AN INDEPENDENT FEDERAL AGENCY

CONTENTS

ILLUSTRATIONS

Figures

xiii

Maps

PREFACE

JOSEPH CONRAD'S place in twentieth-century literature is now firmly established. His novels, stories, and other writings have become integral to modern thought and culture. Yet the need for an accurate and authoritative edition of these works remains. Owing to successive rounds of authorial revision, transmissional errors, and deliberate editorial intervention, Conrad's texts exist in various unsatisfactory and sometimes confused forms. In his last years he attempted to have his works published in a uniform edition that would fix and preserve them for posterity. But though trusted by scholars, students, and general readers alike, the received texts in the British and American editions published since 1921 have proved to be at least as defective as their predecessors. The Cambridge Edition, grounded in thorough research on the original documents, is designed to reverse this trend by presenting Conrad's novels, stories, and other prose in texts that are as trustworthy as modern scholarship can make them.

The present volume contains critical texts of 'The Secret Sharer', based on Conrad's manuscript, and of 'A Smile of Fortune' and 'Freya of the Seven Isles', based on his revised typescripts, which restore passages excised in the early magazines and incorporate revisions drawn from these and other authoritative documents, as well as editorial emendations. The Cambridge text of the 'Author's Note' is based on the revised typescript. The survival of these manuscripts and typescripts has made possible the recovery of numerous and often significant words, phrases, sentences, and even paragraphs lost to his many readers since Conrad's day and finally published in this volume for the first time.

The 'Introduction' included in this volume provides a literary history of the work focused on its genesis, development, and reception in the twentieth century and describing its place in Conrad's life and art. The essay on 'The Texts' traces its textual history, examining the sources of the texts and explaining the policies followed in editing them. The apparatus records basic textual evidence, documenting the discussion of genealogy and authority in 'The Texts' as well as other editorial decisions. The various appendices include a version of the first tale rejected for this edition and further information on matters discussed in the 'Introduction' and 'The Texts'. The 'Notes' comment on specific readings that require glosses or involve particular textual problems. Two sets of illustrations either supplement the descriptions of documents given in the editorial matter (pp. 190–202) or help clarify the references to places made there or found in the texts themselves (pp. 530–39). Although they may interest the great variety of readers, the 'Introduction' and 'Notes' are written primarily for an audience of non-specialists, whereas the textual essay, apparatus, and appendices are intended for the scholar and specialist.

This volume follows certain policies and conventions observed throughout the Cambridge Edition. The pages of the text contain line numbers in their margins to facilitate reference to the 'Notes' and other editorial matter. References to Conrad's other works cite volumes of the Cambridge Edition already published, or else the Doubleday collected edition in its Sun-Dial printing (1921) and in the Dent printings (1923 and subsequently). Superior letters (e.g., 'M^r') in the original documents have been lowered (i.e., to 'Mr'). The beginnings of paragraphs are represented by standard modern indentation regardless of the various conventions of the documents, and Conrad's '_"' is reduced to simple inverted commas. Dashes of variable lengths are normally printed as one-em dashes. Other typographical elements in the texts and titles of the original documents (e.g., display capitals, chapter heads, running titles) have been standardized.

The texts and apparatus in this volume were prepared by computer. Those interested in data and documentation not published here should contact the Chief Executive Editor.

In addition to those named in the Acknowledgements, the editors wish to thank the Trustees and beneficiaries of the Estate of Joseph Conrad and Doubleday and Company and J. M. Dent and Company for permission to publish these new but old texts of Conrad's works. The support of the institutions and individuals listed on p. ix has been essential to the success of the series and is gratefully acknowledged.

CHIEF EXECUTIVE EDITOR

ACKNOWLEDGEMENTS

L IKE MOST critical editions, this volume has benefited from the support and numerous kindnesses of individuals and institutions during its preparation. Thanks are due to the following libraries and professional staff for facilitating access to manuscripts and other unpublished materials: the Beinecke Rare Book and Manuscript Library at Yale University and Vincent Giroud, Timothy Young, and Anne Marie Menta; the Berg Collection, The New York Public Library, and Isaac Gewirtz and the late Lola S. Szladits; the Free Library of Philadelphia, and William F. Lang and Joël Sartorius, as well as William M. Brown; the Imaging and Photographic department of the Wilson Library at the University of North Carolina, Chapel Hill, and Jane Daley Witten; and, finally, Elizabeth E. Fuller and Najia Khan of the Rosenbach Museum and Library for helpful answers to queries.

For their support of the Edition we also wish to express gratitude to present and former administrators of Kent State University, including (in alphabetical order) Rudolph O. Buttlar, Carol A. Cartwright, Ronald J. Corthell, Joseph H. Danks, Susanna G. Fein, Suzanne B. Fitzgerald, Paul L. Gaston, Charlee Heimlich, Myron S. Henry, E. Thomas Jones, Dean H. Keller, Gordon W. Keller, Michael Schwartz, F. S. Schwarzbach, Carol M. Toncar, Darrell R. Turnidge, Eugene P. Wenninger, and John L. West. Gratitude for special support goes to the staffs of Kent State University's Libraries and Media Services, and Nancy Birk, Cara L. Gilgenbach, Don L. Tolliver, Jeanne M. Somers, and Mark W. Weber, and particularly to the Systems staff, including Thomas L. Hedington, Thomas E. Klingler, Todd M. Ryan, and Richard A. Wiggins.

As always it is a pleasure to acknowledge the aid of colleagues associated with the Cambridge Edition as well as other scholars who have given advice or answered queries: Stephen Donovan on the *London Magazine*, Jeremy Hawthorn on circuses, J. H. Stape for various counsel on the explanatory notes, Susan Jones and Ernest W. Sullivan, II, for checking manuscripts and typescripts at libraries, and Andrea White on 'A Smile of Fortune'. We wish especially to thank Laurence Davies, Owen Knowles, and J. H. Stape, the editors of Cambridge University

Press's *Letters* for 1916–21, for their cooperation and permission to consult texts of the letters prior to publication.

The explanatory notes to 'Freya of the Seven Isles' have benefited immensely from information given by the late Hans van Marle in a 1994 letter to the late Bruce Harkness. We wish to acknowledge the generosity of both in sharing this information as well as the extraordinary research of the former. The latter began this volume early in his tenure as one of the General Editors of the series. His work on one of its stories during much of his professional career is evidenced at various points; less evident are his contributions to the foundations of the volume, including examination of the early documents and numerous other details. In a unique exception to the policies of the series, the editors express on a separate page their debt to a scholar, a gentleman, and our quiet collaborator.

CHRONOLOGY

JOSEPH CONRAD'S life may be seen as having several distinct stages: in Poland and in Russian exile before his father's death (1857–69); in Poland and the south of France under the care of his maternal uncle (1870–78); in the British merchant marine, mainly as junior officer sailing in the Far East (1878–90); after a transitional period (early 1890s), as writer of critical esteem (1895–1914); as acclaimed writer, though perhaps with his greatest work achieved (1914–24). After 1895 the history of his life is essentially the history of his works. Publication dates given below are those of the London editions, unless otherwise specified.

1857 December 3	Józef Teodor Konrad Korzeniowski (Nałęcz coat-of-arms) born in Berdyczów in the Ukraine to Apollo and Ewelina (or Ewa), née Bobrowska, Korzeniowski
1862 May	Korzeniowski, his wife, and son forced into exile in Russia
1865 April	Ewa Korzeniowska dies
1867	Conrad visits Odessa with his uncle Tadeusz Bobrowski, perhaps his first view of the sea
1868	Korzeniowski permitted to leave Russia
1869 February	Korzeniowski and Conrad move to Cracow
May	Korzeniowski dies
1870	Conrad, under care of Bobrowski, begins study with tutor, Adam Pulman
1873 May	Visits Switzerland and northern Italy
1874 October	Takes position in Marseilles with Delestang et Fils, wholesalers and shippers
1875	Apprentice in *Mont-Blanc*
1876–7	In *Saint-Antoine*
1878 February or March	Attempts suicide
April	Leaves Marseilles in British steamer *Mavis*

1878 June	Lands at Lowestoft, Suffolk; first time in England
July–September	Sails as ordinary seaman in *Skimmer of the Sea*
1878–80	In *Duke of Sutherland* (voyage to Sydney), *Europa*
1880	Meets G. F. W. Hope, Adolf Krieger
June	Passes examination for second mate
1880–81	Third mate in *Loch Etive* (voyage to Sydney)
1880 August	*Cutty Sark* incident
1881–4	Second mate in *Palestine, Riversdale, Narcissus* (eastern seas)
1881	*Costa Rica* affair
1884 December	Passes examination for first mate
1885–6	Second mate in *Tilkhurst*
1886	Submits perhaps his first story, 'The Black Mate', to *Tit-Bits* competition
August	Becomes a British subject
November	Successfully passes examination for master and receives 'Certificate of Competency'
1886–7	Second mate in *Falconhurst*
1887–8	First mate in *Highland Forest*, in *Vidar* (Malayan waters)
1888–9	Captain of barque *Otago*: Bangkok to Singapore, to Sydney, to Melbourne, to Sydney, to Port Louis (Mauritius), to Melbourne and Australian ports
1888	Proposes marriage to Eugénie Renouf
1889 autumn	Begins *Almayer's Folly* in London
1890 February–April	In Poland for first time since 1874
May–December	To Congo as second-in-command, then temporarily as captain, of *Roi des Belges*
1891	Manages warehouse of Barr, Moering, London
1891–3	First mate in *Torrens*
1893	Meets John Galsworthy, Edward L. Sanderson

1893 autumn	Visits Bobrowski
November	Signs on as second mate in *Adowa*, which never makes voyage
1894 January	Ends career as seaman
February	Bobrowski dies
	Meets Edward Garnett, Jessie George
1895 April	*Almayer's Folly*
1896 March	*An Outcast of the Islands*. Marries Jessie George
September	Settles in Stanford-le-Hope, Essex, after spending six months in Brittany
1897	Begins friendship with R. B. Cunninghame Graham; meets Henry James, Stephen Crane
December	*The Nigger of the 'Narcissus'*
1898	Meets Ford Madox (Hueffer) Ford, H. G. Wells
January	Alfred Borys Leo Conrad born
April	*Tales of Unrest*
October	Moves house to Pent Farm, Postling, Nr Hythe, Kent, sub-let from Ford
1900	Begins association with J. B. Pinker
October	*Lord Jim*
1901 June	*The Inheritors* (with Ford)
1902 November	*Youth: A Narrative and Two Other Stories*
1903 April	*Typhoon and Other Stories*
October	*Romance* (with Ford)
1904 October	*Nostromo*
1905 June	*One Day More* staged in London
1906	Meets Arthur Marwood
August	John Alexander Conrad born
October	*The Mirror of the Sea*
1907 September	*The Secret Agent*. Moves house to Someries, Luton, Bedfordshire
December	Begins 'Razumov' (later *Under Western Eyes*)
1908	Continuing 'Razumov'
August	*A Set of Six*
September–December	Writes first four instalments of 'Some Reminiscences' (later *A Personal Record*)

1910 December 26	Has begun 'Freya of the Seven Isles'
1911 February 25	'A Smile of Fortune' in *London Magazine*
February 28	Finishes 'Freya of the Seven Isles'
March	Revises 'The Partner' and perhaps 'Prince Roman' for serialization, defers *Chance*
March 2	Acknowledges receipt of cheque for £60 from Pinker for 'Freya of the Seven Isles'
March 28	Asks Warrington Dawson to have Mrs Demachy return the 'MS' of *Freya* if she still has it in her possession
April 29	Resumes *Chance*
August–September	Writes 'A Familiar Preface' for book form of *Some Reminiscences* (*A Personal Record*)
August 24	Sends John Quinn two mss: *An Outcast of the Islands* and 'Freya of the Seven Isles'
October 5	*Under Western Eyes* in England (19 October in America)
November 1	'The Partner' in *Harper's*
November 21	*Blackwood's* refuses 'Freya of the Seven Isles'
December 8	Has learned Pinker has placed 'Freya of the Seven Isles' with an American magazine
1912 January 21	Serialization of *Chance* begins in *New York Herald*
ca. January 22	*Some Reminiscences* in England, as *A Personal Record* in America (*ca.* 3 January)
January 28	Sends Quinn the manuscripts of 'The Secret Sharer', 'The Partner', 'Il Conde'
February	Resumes accustomed working methods, ending two-year breach with Pinker
March 25	Finishes *Chance*
April	'Freya of the Seven Isles' in New York's *Metropolitan Magazine*; rewrites ending of *Chance*
April 18	Knows *English Review* has rejected *Chance*
April 22	Has begun story called 'Dollars' (*Victory*) and suggests that Pinker offer *English Review* an article on the *Titanic*

1912 April 24–25	Writes 'Some Reflexions', which appears in May number of *English Review*
May 10	Requests of Davray the 'typescript' of 'Freya of the Seven Isles'
May 19	Returns to Pinker 'corrected proof' of 'Freya of the Seven Isles' for *London Magazine*
ca. June 6	Moots book titles ''Twixt Land and Water' and 'Tales of Hearsay' to Pinker
June 18	Finishes 'Certain Aspects', probably in two days, for July number of *English Review*
June 28	Tells Galsworthy that Dent's will publish book edition of his stories on 'best terms' he has ever had
July	'Freya of the Seven Isles' in *London Magazine*
July 6	Sends Pinker revised printer's copy for Dent's edition and requests proofs
July 23	Has settled title of book with Dent
July 29	Sends Quinn sheet of Symons's epigraph, returned from Dent's printer
September 17	Returns proofs of Dent's edition
October 10	British Museum depository copy of Dent's edition of *'Twixt Land and Sea* received
October 14	Dent's edition of *'Twixt Land and Sea*
November	Second printing of Dent's edition
November 28	*'Twixt Land and Sea* has had 'a very good reception'
December 3	Doran's edition of *'Twixt Land and Sea* in America
December 24	Demurs at Edith Wharton's idea of translating 'The Secret Sharer' into French
1913 September	*Chance*, with 'main' publication date of January 1914
1914 July–November	Visits Poland with family; delayed by outbreak of First World War; returns via Austria and Italy
1915 February	*Within the Tides*
September	*Victory*

1917 March	*The Shadow-Line*
1919 March	Moves house to Spring Grove, Wye, Kent
April	Writes 'Author's Note' for *'Twixt Land and Sea*
August	*The Arrow of Gold*
October	Moves house to Oswalds, Bishopsbourne, Near Canterbury, Kent
1920 June	*The Rescue*
1921	Collected editions begin publication in England (Heinemann) and America (Doubleday)
February	*Notes on Life and Letters*
1922 November	*The Secret Agent* staged in London
1923 May–June	Visits America, guest of F. N. Doubleday
December	*The Rover*
1924 May	Declines knighthood
August 3	Dies at Oswalds (Roman Catholic burial, Canterbury)
September	*The Nature of a Crime* (with Ford)
October	*The Shorter Tales*
1925 January	*Tales of Hearsay*
September	*Suspense*
1926 March	*Last Essays*
1928 June	*The Sisters*

ABBREVIATIONS

[London is the place of publication unless otherwise indicated]

Allen	Jerry Allen, *The Sea Years of Joseph Conrad.* New York: Doubleday, 1965
Baines	Jocelyn Baines, *Joseph Conrad: A Critical Biography.* Weidenfeld and Nicolson, 1960
Barnwell	P. J. Barnwell, 'Conrad, Joseph (1857–1924)', in *Dictionnaire de Biographie Mauricienne: Dictionary of Mauritian Biography.* Société de L'Histoire de L'Ile Maurice, 1941–3
Bibliography	William R. Cagle and Robert W. Trogdon, 'A Bibliography of Joseph Conrad'. Typescript, unpublished
CA	*Joseph Conrad: Critical Assessments*, ed. Keith Carabine. 4 vols. Mountfield, East Sussex: Helm Information, 1992
Carabine	Keith Carabine, *The Life and the Art.* Amsterdam and Atlanta: Rodopi, 1996
CEW	Norman Sherry, *Conrad's Eastern World.* Cambridge University Press, 1966
CH	*Conrad: The Critical Heritage*, ed. Norman Sherry. Routledge & Kegan Paul, 1973
Chronology	Owen Knowles, *A Conrad Chronology.* Macmillan, 1989
CHW	Norman Sherry, *Conrad and His World.* Thames and Hudson, 1972
Enc. Brit.	*Encyclopaedia Britannica.* 11th edn. Cambridge University Press, 1910–11
Furnivall	J. S. Furnivall, *Netherlands India: A Study in Plural Economy.* Cambridge University Press, 1939, 1967
Jean-Aubry	Gérard Jean-Aubry, *The Sea Dreamer: A Definitive Biography of Joseph Conrad.* New York: Doubleday, Page, 1957. Trans. by Helen Sebba of *Vie de Conrad* (Paris: Gallimard, 1947)

Karl   Frederick R. Karl, *Joseph Conrad: The Three Lives*.
                    New York: Farrar, Straus and Giroux, 1979
Larabee   Mark D. Larabee, '"A Mysterious System":
                    Topographical Fidelity and the Charting of
                    Imperialism in Joseph Conrad's Siamese Waters'.
                    Studies in the Novel, 32 (2000), 348–68
Letters   *The Collected Letters of Joseph Conrad*, ed. Frederick R.
                    Karl, Laurence Davies, *et al.* 7 vols. Cambridge
                    University Press, 1983–
Lettres   *Lettres françaises de Joseph Conrad*, ed. G. Jean-Aubry.
                    Paris: Gallimard, 1929
LL   *Joseph Conrad: Life and Letters*, ed. G. Jean-Aubry.
                    2 vols. Heinemann, 1927
Lubbock   Basil Lubbock, *The Log of the 'Cutty Sark'*. Glasgow:
                    Brown, Son & Ferguson, 1974; rpt of Glasgow:
                    James Brown & Son, 1924 / Boston: Charles E.
                    Lauriat Co., 1924
Najder   Zdzisław Najder, *Joseph Conrad: A Chronicle*. New
                    Brunswick, NJ: Rutgers University Press,
                    1983
Nautical Terms   *The Country Life Book of Nautical Terms Under Sail*.
                    Trewin Copplestone Publishing, 1978; New York:
                    Crown Publishers, as *The Visual Encyclopedia of
                    Nautical Terms Under Sail*
OED   *Oxford English Dictionary*. 2nd edn. Oxford
                    University Press, 1989
Portrait in Letters *A Portrait in Letters: Correspondence to and about
                    Conrad*, ed. J. H. Stape and Owen Knowles.
                    Amsterdam: Rodopi, 1996; *The Conradian*, 19, nos.
                    1–2 (1995)
Ships and the Sea *The Oxford Companion to Ships and the Sea*, ed.
                    Peter Kemp. Oxford University Press, 1976,
                    1990
Stape   J. H. Stape, 'Topography in "The Secret Sharer"'.
                    The Conradian, 26, no. 1 (2001), 1–16
Toussaint   Auguste Toussaint, *History of Mauritius*. Trans.
                    W. E. F. Ward. Macmillan, 1977

Turnbull   C. M. Turnbull, *A History of Singapore 1819–1988*.
                  Singapore: Oxford University Press, 1977
Vlekke   Bernard H. M. Vlekke, *Nusantara: A History of
                  Indonesia*. Revised edn. The Hague and Bandung:
                  W. van Hoeve, 1959; Chicago: Quadrangle Books,
                  1960
Wallace   Alfred Russel Wallace, *The Malay Archipelago*.
                  Macmillan, 1890–

Locations of Unpublished Documents

Berg   Berg Collection, The New York Public Library, Astor,
                  Lenox and Tilden Foundations
BL   British Library
HRHRC   Harry Ransom Humanities Research Center,
                  University of Texas at Austin
NYPL   Rare Books and Manuscripts Division, The New York
                  Public Library
Philadelphia   Free Library of Philadelphia
Yale   Beinecke Rare Book and Manuscript Library, Yale
                  University

INTRODUCTION

THE THREE NOVELLAS that Conrad composed between December 1909 and February 1911, and that were published in October 1912 under the title *'Twixt Land and Sea: Tales*, followed (with a slight overlap) the creation of three of his greatest novels, *Nostromo* (1903–4), *The Secret Agent* (1906–7), and *Under Western Eyes* (1907–10). What the three tales may have owed to these mighty predecessors has not yet been determined, perhaps because the debt is indirect; but what is beyond doubt is that had Conrad, desperate as he was to bring *Under Western Eyes* to a conclusion, not received an unexpected visit, *'Twixt Land and Sea* would not have been written. Captain C. M. Marris, a merchant sea-captain from Penang, Indonesia, who had come to England for medical treatment, called on Conrad in Aldington, Kent, on Monday, 13 September 1909, the day before his return to the East, and informed him that his earlier sea narratives evoking the old trading life in the Malay Archipelago had become the favourite reading of the surviving merchant mariners out there, that they had identified the figure behind the pseudonym 'Conrad' as the Captain Korzeniowski they knew, and that they were eager for more such stories from him.[1]

The conditions of Conrad's current life in England, where the novels which are now read in every part of the world were respected only by fellow specialists, and where he and his family had been reduced to living in four tiny rooms above a butcher's shop, had begun to demoralize him. His friendship with Ford Madox (Hueffer) Ford, who had supported his work since 1898, had collapsed at the end of June. His 'gout' – a condition in him teeming with stress symptoms – had become chronic.[2] He was struggling to complete the disastrously overdue 'Razumov' (the working title of *Under Western Eyes*) – a task which was forcing him to confront his deepest insecurities as an orphaned

---

[1] Born in New Zealand, Carlos Murrell Marris (1875–1910) had traded in the Malay Archipelago, married a Malay 'princess', and settled in Penang in the Straits Settlements. His letters to Conrad on 18 July 1909, 6 September 1909, and 11 January 1910, which he signed 'Carlos. M. Marris' or 'C. M. Marris', together with three of Conrad's about his visit, provide the evidence we have about the substance of their conversation. See *Portrait in Letters*, pp. xxvi, 66–70, 71–2, and *Letters*, IV, 273, 277–8, 469–70.
[2] On this question and Conrad's complicated illnesses, see Martin Bock, *Joseph Conrad and Psychological Medicine* (2002), esp. pp. 39–40, 59–60.

and *émigré* Pole. Finally, he owed his agent, James B. Pinker, a staggering £2,566 (or roughly seven times the annual earnings in the professions),[1] which only the product of his pen could repay. Under such conditions Marris's visit came upon him like an act of grace. As he heard what Marris had to tell him, his sense of paralysis apparently began to lift, and it eventually yielded to a run of creative energy which, by the end of January 1910, had enabled him not only to generate the 46,000 words required to complete a great novel, but also to produce, in a faultless two weeks, the 16,400 words of 'The Secret Sharer' – a story which converted into a comic key the novel's tragic narrative, and which also opened the door to two further tales inspired by memories of his final year's maritime service in eastern waters.

SOURCES

CAPTAIN MARRIS'S visit, then, proved to be massively productive. But does that make it a 'source' of Conrad's three tales? The answer to that question, which is by no means straightforward, requires us to recognize a distinction between the general and the particular uses of this term. When, for example, John Locke invokes the 'Source of Ideas' that 'every Man has wholly in himself',[2] he invites us to seek the origins of a text in the creative energy that brings it into existence, and for which the quality of that text is the sole evidence. To enquire, however, into the sources of a piece of writing would seem to ask us to relate it less to the author than to the world available to him. But this distinction is misleading, for the production of source – that is to say, the absorption of a piece of the world into a text – presupposes creative power. An event in the world is not a source until it has ceased to be merely itself, until it has been adapted to the requirements of its new environment.

---

[1] That is, by one measure, of the average lawyer, doctor, and dentist; it represented approximately eighteen years' earnings for a qualified teacher and twenty-seven for a male clerk at 1913 money levels. At the end of the century, by other measures, Conrad's debt would have amounted to about £900,000 as compared to per-capita gross domestic product, or £160,000 in purchasing power (for goods and services). See Guy Routh, *Occupation and Pay in Great Britain 1906–60* (1965), pp. 63–4, 69, 104, and Lawrence H. Officer, 'What Is Its Relative Value in UK Pounds?', *Economic History Services* (www.EH.net, 2004). See also 'Purchasing Power of the British Pound 1600–2000', compiled by the Librarian of the House of Commons, as well as *The Consumers' Price Index* (brought out by the Treasury between 1900 and 1938) and *The Economist* for the period 1938 to 2003, which together indicate that during the period 1900–2003 the purchasing power of the pound sterling fell to 1.3 pence (i.e., by a factor of 75).

[2] *An Essay Concerning Human Understanding*, ed. Peter H. Nidditch (1975), II.i.§4 (p. 105).

The criterion for the identification of a source, therefore, remains its creative function, whether that source originates as an episode in another text, or as a person in life, or as an event in time. In this perspective, the Marris who called on Conrad in September 1909, indispensable as his visit may have been in restoring Conrad's faith in himself, cannot be regarded as a source unless he himself acquires some textual presence, as he arguably does in 'Freya of the Seven Isles'. Until then (like Edward Garnett and Ford Madox Ford, who for years fostered Conrad's writing without featuring in it), he should be understood in relation to Conrad's talent – that 'Source of Ideas that every Man has wholly in himself' – rather than to those 'sources' by means of which the outside world enters narrative fiction.

The Secret Sharer

ONE OF the most commanding of Conrad's shorter works, 'The Secret Sharer' owes much of its power to the interaction of two sources. The first is autobiographical, and draws on his experience of his first command, which he assumed in Bangkok on 24 January 1888. The second is historical, and is centred on the killing of a seaman by the first mate of the legendary clipper, *Cutty Sark*, in early August 1880. The novella is also significantly indebted to Conrad's extraordinary visual memory, the major effects of which are indicated in the 'Notes' to this edition.

The circumstances connected with Conrad's first and only appointment to a command deserve to be recalled, for they form the autobiographical context of 'The Secret Sharer'. On 19 January 1888,[1] the Singapore Harbour Office offered him charge of the *Otago*, a barque immobilized in Bangkok (today also called Krung Thep) by the death at sea of her captain. Conrad left at once by steamer, assuming his post four days later. He found the *Otago* to be a small but elegant commercial sailing ship of 367 tons gross, measuring 147 × 26 × 14 feet, and equipped with the standard barque rigging (sails set square on the fore and main masts, and fore-and-aft on the mizzen mast). Apart from the captain, her complement consisted of two officers (the first mate, a German called Charles Born, and the second mate, probably an Englishman, named Jackson), together with six ordinary sailors

---

[1] *CEW*, p. 213; Owen Knowles and Gene M. Moore, *The Oxford Reader's Companion to Conrad* (2000), p. 350 (hereafter *Oxford Companion*). Najder, p. 103, dates the actual offer to the previous month.

comprising two Englishmen, one Scot, one German, and two Norwegians, with one of these doubling as steward. After Conrad joined her, the *Otago* was detained in Bangkok for a further sixteen days. The reasons for this delay remain unclear, but it offered an opportunity for acquaintance with a city that provided settings for two other tales of first command, 'Falk' (1903) and, more incidentally, *The Shadow Line* (1917). On 9 February, however, having loaded a cargo of teak, the *Otago* was taken down the winding twenty-five or so miles of the River Meinam (today, the Chao Phraya), over the sand-bar at the river's entrance, and into the head of the Gulf of Siam, known to the British merchant marine as the Bight of Bangkok. Although Captain Korzeniowski (to give him his contemporary title) was eager to prove his mettle, prevailing calms, ruffled only by occasional faint breezes, turned the southern route to Singapore past the south-east corner of the Bight of Bangkok into a three-week ordeal.[1] When the *Otago* finally reached Singapore on the evening of 1 March, three ordinary sailors stricken with fever (malaria) were hospitalized, while a fourth resigned his berth. These had to be replaced before the barque was able to resume her voyage to Sydney via the Sunda Straits and Western Australia.[2]

How much of this found its way into the tale? The magnificent opening description of land and sea as perceived some distance from the shore is generally an accurate impression;[3] so is, at the climax of the narrative, the evocation of the craggy island landscape of the south-east coast of the Bight of Bangkok. The depiction of the barque, her officers and men, and her sailing qualities as it unfolds through the narrative confirms what is known of the *Otago*'s design, performance, and complement – except perhaps for the disposition of the officers' cabins around the cuddy under the poop deck, which has to reflect the requirements of the plot rather than the facts of memory. Conrad's treatment of the handling of the barque, from her initial immobilization outside the mouth of the river to the dangerous manœuvre required to drop Leggatt as near the shore as safety permits, exhibits the authority and precision (if not the wisdom) of professional experience. Furthermore, his representation of the effects of the failure of the wind on the psychology of the Captain and the crew retains the concreteness of remembered events. However, the illness which

---

[1] See Map 4; see 81.13n, 81.20n. References to the 'Notes' in this volume take this form.

[2] See Najder, pp. 102–6; *CEW*, pp. 211–49.

[3] As expected in a broadly fictional description, some details have been slighted or modified; see, e.g., 81.2–82.23n, 81.2n, 81.13n, 81.14n, 81.20n, 81.23n, 81.33n.

had disabled two-thirds of the *Otago*'s men disappears from the tale –
though it will return no later than in 'A Smile of Fortune'. Nor does
the tale's treatment of the Captain's relations with his crew show
any sign that he had, like Conrad, already spent nearly a fortnight
in harbour with them, especially when many of them had required
treatment for fever (malaria). And finally, least of all does the story's
central incident – the protection and release of a fugitive from justice – derive from any incident known or suspected in its author's
life.

The difficulty of relying on biographical evidence in interpreting
a text is shown by the Captain's connivance in Leggatt's escape from
prosecution. This episode originates in an incident recorded in the
essay 'Emblems of Hope' published in the earliest collection of his
reminiscences *The Mirror of the Sea* (1905). Referring to his vigilant and
irascible first mate 'Mr B.' ('Mr Born' in life, 'Mr Burns' in fiction),
he writes: 'then, on our first leaving port (I don't see why I should
make a secret of the fact that it was Bangkok), a bit of manœuvring
of mine amongst the islands of the Gulf of Siam had given him an
unforgettable scare'.[1] This is a source for 'The Secret Sharer' that
is as firm as anything one receives from the horse's mouth; but it
does not, of course, have any bearing on the meaning it acquires by
its transplantation. For that, we must go to one of Conrad's very last
essays, 'Geography and Some Explorers' of November 1923,[2] which
evokes briefly Conrad's second deep-sea voyage as master of the *Otago*,
from Sydney to Mauritius to collect a cargo of sugar. Conrad decided
against the safer but allegedly slower route via southern Australia, and
instead took his ship through the rock- and wreck-strewn Torres Straits
dividing northern Australia from New Guinea. Zdzisław Najder, the
only biographer to link this decision with the dangerous self-testing
manœuvre that concludes 'The Secret Sharer', attributes Conrad's
recklessness to his need to exorcise his less-than-distinguished Trinity
House examination record, which included two failures in navigation
that had to be made good before the master's certificate could be
awarded. Be that as it may, there is little to suggest that Conrad's opting
for the riskier route betrays an inferiority complex. With hindsight –
that is, with some awareness of the cultural impact achieved by 'The
Secret Sharer' – one is tempted to say that, like the gamble required
to release Leggatt near enough to the coast to ensure his safe escape,
the magnificent twelve-hour passage through the 'windswept, sunlit

[1] *The Mirror of the Sea*, p. 19.   [2] *Last Essays*, pp. 1–21.

empty waters'[1] of the Torres Straits, within sight of wrecks old and new, reveals Conrad's mistrust of those who, like the captain of the *Sephora*, fetishize the rule book – that is to say, believe that the act of following a rule requires the relinquishment of moral independence.

However, it is from the tale's use of historical sources – public events which bear directly on its plot or action – that the power of its action derives. By far the most significant of these are associated with the *Cutty Sark*'s disastrous outward-bound voyage of 1880 to the Far East. This voyage has been fully documented by Basil Lubbock in Chapter 5 of *The Log of the 'Cutty Sark'* (1924) and in that book's Appendix VII, which reports on the trial of the ship's first mate at London's Central Criminal Court in 1882.[2] Lubbock's appendix takes into account contemporary reports which appeared in *The Times* of 5 July and 4 August, but he seems also to have had access to information that the reporters disregarded or did not have.

Under the celebrated Captain J. S. Wallace, who had been appointed master of the already legendary clipper at the exceptionally young age of twenty-seven, the *Cutty Sark* sailed from Cardiff's port of Penarth on 4 June 1880 with a full complement of twenty-eight (officers, men, and apprentices), carrying a cargo of coal for the American fleet anchored in Yokohama, Japan. The first mate, a 'hard-fibred, despotic character' named John Anderson, alias Sidney Smith, but also known as 'Bucko' Smith, early acquired an aggressive dislike for John Francis, one of the three black sailors on board – a physically powerful man and well-liked by his fellows, but 'incapable and clumsy' in his handling of ropes and tackle. In an attempt to ease the tension between the two, Wallace got them to fight out their aggression, but the contest proved inconclusive. Meanwhile, the ship, which had rounded the Cape of Good Hope and descended to latitude 42° 30′ South to catch the winds of the 'roaring forties', drove eastward before gales which gradually intensified into a hurricane that eventually reduced her storm canvas to shreds. The wave troughs that threatened to becalm her as she sank into them exposed her to the fearful phenomenon of 'pooping' (being overtaken by a following sea). The men struggled for two hours to 'bend' (attach to a yard) a fresh top-sail, while the decks remained continuously awash. However, the sail was finally set, and the ship went on to make over 1,000 miles in three days, until it reached about longitude 90° East, when it became necessary to alter her

[1] 'Geography and Some Explorers', p. 20.   [2] Lubbock, pp. 142–92, 324–5.

course north-north-east towards the Sunda Straits and Anjer.[1] At that point John Francis, who was on the look-out forward, twice ignored Anderson's order to release a line to the foresail to allow the men aloft to make the required adjustment to the foremast yard. Losing his temper, the mate attacked him; Francis retaliated with a heavy capstan bar, and a struggle ensued during which Anderson got hold of it and brained his opponent. Three days later, Francis died and was buried at sea. Anderson, now seriously vulnerable, was retired to his cabin and not seen again on deck for the rest of the voyage, which lasted another seven days. On 14 August the ship dropped anchor off Anjer, among half-a-dozen international vessels, to await orders by telegraph from John Willis, the owner of the *Cutty Sark*, whom Conrad affectionately recalled eleven years later in his 'Author's Note' to *'Twixt Land and Sea*. Meantime, Wallace was persuaded by Anderson to let him escape to an American ship moored near the *Cutty Sark*, which, knowing herself beyond the reach of British law, was only too eager to get hold of a man-handler of his reputation.

Willis's orders, when they at last arrived, were to proceed directly to Yokohama. On 5 September, therefore, Wallace took the *Cutty Sark* and her increasingly resentful crew northwards into a becalmed Archipelago. There ensued four days of continuous struggle to make headway, at the end of which, seeing nothing but disgrace before him, Wallace walked off his ship into the shark-infested waters. After a hopeless search, the *Cutty Sark* returned to Anjer, which she reached on the 14th. On the 20th she was instructed to proceed under pilot to Singapore, a voyage which with better winds she was able to accomplish in a week – only to discover that the population was agog with the news of the *Jeddah* scandal. (That ship's officers had abandoned her 900 pilgrims off Aden under the mistaken assumption that she was about to sink – an event which Conrad would eventually turn into *Lord Jim*, drawing for good measure Wallace's suicide into the novel.) The *Cutty Sark*'s cargo was ignominiously transferred to a steamer, and she was subjected to an official inquiry, which appointed a new master called Bruce. He was a 'fat little man with an uneasy look' who proved boastful ashore, timid on the water, prone to bouts of drinking, and sanctimonious with his crew, whom he forced into prayer meetings conducted

---

[1] Anjer, or Anger, on the Java side of the Sunda Straits dividing Java and Sumatra, with its large anchorage, was the port of reception of the Dutch East Indies for western sea traffic before the opening of the Suez Canal. It was destroyed by the explosion of the volcanic island of Krakatoa in August 1883. See Map 4, and 92.15*n*.

by himself. He was also pedantic, literal-minded, ultra-cautious, and legalistic – traits which, aided by his terror of landfalls, turned him into an excellent navigator, but also bred endless hesitations that made him a very bad handler of men. His first port of call out of Singapore was not Bangkok on the Meinam but, next door as it were, Bombay on the Houghley River. His career ended a year later when, after an atrocious voyage to New York, his first officer made a formal complaint against him which was upheld by the consular inquiry that ensued.[1]

That Conrad would have been familiar with every detail of these events is beyond dispute. In his 'Author's Note' of 1920, he alludes to the 'basic fact of the tale' (the mate's killing of a seaman) as 'the common possession of the whole fleet of merchant ships trading to India, China and Australia' (p. 6), and claiming, too, that 'I had heard of it before, as it were privately' (p. 6). There he also evokes 'the great wool fleet in which my first years in deep water were served' (p. 6). The vessel in which he made his first voyage as an officer to the East was the *Loch Etive*, an iron clipper of 1,287 tons with a crew of twenty-eight, which brought it into the same class as the *Cutty Sark*. It left London for Sydney on 21 August 1880, about a fortnight after the Francis homicide, and almost three weeks before Wallace's suicide. By the time Conrad reached Sydney, on 24 November, the whole of the maritime East was awash with these scandals[2] – which additionally now included the desertion of the *Jeddah*'s pilgrims. Thus Conrad's voyage to Sydney – memorable enough to be recalled in another essay in *The Mirror of the Sea*, 'Cobwebs and Gossamer', the title of which describes what happens to heavy canvas sails when they encounter the winds of the southern latitudes – provides a double foundation for his rendering of the *Sephora*'s tribulations in 'The Secret Sharer': direct experience of a passage to the East in a similar vessel, and the scandalous news of the *Cutty Sark*'s doom-laden voyage.

In composing 'The Secret Sharer', Conrad's relationship with his sources ranges from the near literal to the near independent. The second mate's account of the arrival of the big vessel beyond the bar guarding the entrance to the River Meinam – 'She draws over twenty feet. She's the Liverpool ship *Sephora* with a cargo of coal. Hundred and twenty-three days from Cardiff' (p. 83) – could be applied almost without alteration to the *Cutty Sark*. As for their respective voyages, they differ only in incidentals. With the *Sephora* the hurricane and the

[1] Lubbock, pp. 160–61.   [2] Najder, pp. 67–8.

killing are not separate incidents, as they were for the *Cutty Sark*, but parts of a single event which occurs in the Southern Ocean deducibly south of Cape Augulhas (the southernmost part of Africa). However, in both cases the mate is confined to his cabin until he escapes, though – since Conrad has removed Wallace from 'The Secret Sharer', replacing him with a socially improved version of the *Cutty Sark*'s sanctimonious Bruce – Leggatt's detention does not last ten days, but for the duration of the *Sephora*'s voyage from a point south of Africa – 'thirty nine south', he tells the Captain-narrator (p. 88) – to the northernmost reach of the Gulf of Siam. The exact time taken by that long final leg would have depended on wind and weather, but of the 123 days taken by the *Sephora* to reach the mouth of the Meinam from Cardiff, sixty-three days, or nine weeks, were required from the point where Leggatt killed the sailor. Leggatt tells the Captain that he spent 'six weeks' in detention before the *Sephora* reached Java Head, i.e., Anjer (p. 91); he then states that faltering winds prolonged the voyage between Java Head and the Meinam anchorage by another three weeks (p. 93), a total of nine weeks from the killing of the sailor (p. 95).[1] The 'completely muddled' Archbold estimates the time as 'just over two months' (p. 100), which more or less confirms Leggatt's computation. This very minor wobble is not fatal to the integrity of a text that seeks to reflect the subjectivities of experience. Conversational memory is less reliable than a ship's log; but it is only the detained Leggatt, and certainly not the self-gratifying Archbold, who would have counted the days.

Conrad's narrative, however, begins to draw away from its source when it deals with Leggatt's 'crime' and Archbold's response to it. There are radical differences between the *Sephora*'s Leggatt, whose strangling of the uncooperative sailor as the ship is 'pooped' is presented as an unavoidable reflex attending the effort to set the saving sail in monstrous seas, and the *Cutty Sark*'s testosterone-charged 'Bucko' Smith Anderson, whose racism had already vented itself on the uncooperative and truculent black sailor, Francis, before he finally killed him in an explosion of rage. Although Anderson was highly rated by his employers for his authority over a crew – these admirers included Wallace, who helped him escape, and indeed John Willis, who spoke for Anderson at his trial and re-employed him after he had

---

[1] On the misunderstanding of these matters by the story's first editor and its consequent muddling in the book editions, see 91.25n.

served his sentence[1] – he has absolutely nothing in common with the *Conway*-trained, self-possessed, and up-market Leggatt, except for the circumstances of his crime.

As for Archbold, Conrad has derived him from Wallace's successor, the evangelical hypocrite Bruce, though he took his ship not up the Gulf of Siam, as Conrad's Archbold does the *Sephora*, but up the Gulf of Bengal parallel to it. In Conrad's tale, Archbold (like Leggatt in relation to Anderson) is an eminently respectable Bruce, without Bruce's emotionalism and vulgarity and instability, and with a much more self-confident sanctimoniousness, secured in a literalist conception of the law that disdains the very idea of the mitigating circumstance and in a conception of religion that recognizes no intermediate space between salvation and damnation. As the gale turns into a hurricane, the *Sephora*'s captain takes cover in his cabin, leaving Leggatt to deal with the crisis. The mate is able to rally the hands to hoist a storm-sail, even as a following sea overtakes the ship, sending the men scrambling up the shrouds. When the ship rises again, Leggatt is found grasping a dead man's throat. Far from feeling any gratitude, Archbold strips the apparently compromised Leggatt, to whom he and the crew owe their lives, of all credit, attributing the saving of the ship to the Almighty (as if God and man were in competition), and withdrawing into an inflexible legalism. Conrad's Captain, of course, variously undoes this scenario, by identifying with Leggatt, by repudiating legal and religious orthodoxy, by accepting risk as a condition of life, and by demonstrating that leadership requires a good deal more than managerial competence.

Hence Conrad's villain in 'The Secret Sharer' is not the mate – i.e., Anderson, alias 'Bucko' Smith, whom he writes out of his scenario – but Archbold, whose interview with the Captain forms the central episode of the undivided tale. However, if Anderson disappears, out of what source is Leggatt created? No individual precedent has been found, nor is one likely to be, for he has, as it were, been summoned into being out of Conrad's struggle with *Under Western Eyes*, the political novel he allowed 'The Secret Sharer' to interrupt, despite all his legal, financial, moral, and indeed human obligations to his agent not to do so. Yet at a subtler level, 'The Secret Sharer' does not turn away from *Under Western Eyes*. In that novel, the protagonist, a St Petersburg student named Razumov, finds Victor Haldin, a political

---

[1] Lubbock, p. 325.

idealist who has just assassinated the State Minister of Public Order, hiding in his rooms. This discovery turns the life of Razumov, who betrays Haldin to the authorities, into an agony of divided loyalties – a condition not unknown to his creator, who had himself, in fact if not in spirit, left his hapless country to make a career for himself in the West. Everything conspires to suggest that 'The Secret Sharer' – where Leggatt, in flight from authority for a crime of which he is and is not guilty, is protected and set free by the Captain – represents a re-negotiation of the tragic contradictions of *Under Western Eyes*. This feat is achieved by means of a highly original revaluation of the ethics of leadership which implicitly calls into question Archbold's inflexible segregation of right from wrong through the young Captain's demonstration that there is more to leadership than the laws that define it – that is to say, that there is more to following a rule than activating a conditioned reflex, just as the existence of sources, whether or not they can be traced, indicates that there is more to art than the rules of art.

A survey of the major sources of 'The Secret Sharer' shows that the autobiographical material sustaining Conrad's Captain is massively enriched by the historical material invested in Leggatt, and that together they permit an exhilarating inquiry into the complex interdependence of private affection and public duty. Moreover, this inquiry (if the term is not too cold-blooded) is enriched by a number of minor sources, two of which deserve mention. The first, which centres on Leggatt, is Biblical and is evoked as early as the opening sentence and as late as the concluding one (pp. 81, 119). In Genesis, chapter iv, verses 5 to 19, God's 'mark' is set upon Cain, murderer of his brother Abel, as a sign of his expulsion from the community of mankind. But it is also the signature of divine protection accorded to 'a fugitive and a vagabond' upon earth 'lest any finding him, should kill him'. Cain's crime of fratricide is, of course, decidedly more transgressive than Leggatt's, whose offence an impartial court might have classified, if not as self-defence, then as 'manslaughter' – that is, 'the unlawful killing of a human being without malice aforethought'. What this source provides, however, is a context which broadens the ethical perspectives on the central action. For example, it calls into question a sanctimonious moralism which the narrative by no means confines to Archbold, but extends to our Captain's officers and steward. It also raises questions about the limits of private morality, such as what being one's 'brother's keeper' (the phrase is of course Cain's) might mean – questions that become markedly unorthodox when one recalls Poland's, and Conrad's, notion of brotherhood as 'solidarity'.

The second such source is cultural rather than religious. It is explicitly signalled by the title of the tale which, according to Conrad's letter of 18 December 1909 to his agent, could have been 'The Secret Self' or 'the Other Self'.[1] The notion of the self as double, which varies and qualifies the Christian notion of the self as fallen, pervades the literature of the nineteenth century, from Jean Paul Richter's *Doppelgänger* to W. B. Yeats's *anti-self*. Conrad's major writing, in which doubleness of identity is always latent and frequently explicit, is rooted in this tradition. For him, however, the double is never a ghostly other, summoned by a hyperactive subjectivity, or else an *angst* fished out of the subconscious. Instead, it is produced by the tension between the self and the condition of plurality into which it is born, and which indeed requires it to act. Thus in his work the double is always summoned at moments of crisis, or more precisely by the protagonist's need to decide what to do, whether politically as with the Razumov of *Under Western Eyes*, or professionally as with the new Captain of 'The Secret Sharer', whose story demonstrates that the successful performance of a public role requires that the claims of the private self should not be disregarded or repressed by it, as the Stoic ideal demands, but disentangled from it.

A Smile of Fortune

ACCORDING TO Jessie Conrad, 'A Smile of Fortune', unlike 'The Secret Sharer' which was mostly 'pure fiction', was inspired by two episodes from her husband's 1888 visit to Mauritius: 'Joseph Conrad's one and only bargain' (the potato deal that gives the story its penultimate ironic twist), and his entanglement with Alice Jacobus, of whom, Jessie adds, 'He used to accuse me of being jealous'.[2] We know, of course, that 'A Smile of Fortune' is closer to the facts of biography than 'The Secret Sharer' which predates it, for Conrad's seven-week visit to Mauritius generated a surprising number of testimonies, whereas only two elements of the earlier tale – the *Otago* itself, and the coasts and weather of the Bight of Bangkok (the upper part of the Gulf of Siam

---

[1] Conrad to Pinker, [18 December 1909] (*Letters*, IV, 300); see also Conrad to Pinker, [15 December 1909] (*Letters*, IV, 299), where 'The Second Self' is the title first floated. On the development of these concepts and titles through composition and revision of the text, see 'The Texts', pp. 208, n.3, 209, and also Appendix B, 'The Titles of the Tales'.

[2] Jessie Conrad, *Joseph Conrad As I Knew Him* (1926), pp. 139–40.

which replicates the main part in little) – can be recognized from the records. Nevertheless, despite the accuracy of Conrad's observation of Mauritius, and despite the sometimes irascible candour of his writing, 'A Smile of Fortune' has something to hide.

What that has turned out to be is an unsuccessful offer of marriage he made two days before his departure from Mauritius. Moreover, contrary to what Jessie Conrad was encouraged to believe, the object of this offer was not the nubile Alice with whom the novella's Captain is drawn into decidedly ambiguous relations, and whose historical reality is by no means secure, but the second daughter of a well-to-do Port Louis family, who turned out to be already engaged, and whom the master-mariner turned master-novelist continued to feel compelled, twenty-one years later, to write out of his script. Thus the central event of 'A Smile of Fortune' – the Captain's three-week dalliance with the sensuous Alice Jacobus – turns out to be perhaps nearly as imaginary as the Leggatt episode in 'The Secret Sharer', though psychologically much more evasive and complicated.

There are, therefore, two kinds of source material in 'A Smile of Fortune'. The first bears witness to a vividness of observation in its author that seems, yet again, to have been unaffected by the passage of time and that generated flawlessly focussed writing. The second, which acquires its energy at least in part from the need to recode rather than record the past, is sustained by what it represses and conceals, often with help from other writers. That Conrad is able to combine these two sources to create an integrated new text shows that repression may be no less potent than inspiration in the achievement of classic fiction.

The island of Mauritius imprinted itself so vividly on Conrad's memory that it seems to have lost nothing of its freshness over the near quarter-century it had to wait before its transformation into fiction. Conrad's treatment of the approaches to the island, of its port and shipping, of the small capital city with its public buildings, gardens, and suburbs against a backdrop of volcanic mountains, of its socially and racially mixed population, of its history, politics, and commerce, of its tropical climate and vegetation, and above all of its isolation in the midst of a vast ocean – all this, and much more, demonstrates not only the distinctness of his original perceptions, but the degree to which they continued to live within him during the intervening years.[1] Conrad sailed for Port Louis from Sydney on 7 August 1888,

---

[1] For example, see 17.21n, 25.32n, 33.7n, 33.12n, 39.31n, 40.9n, 45.5n, 45.12–13n, 56.7–8n, 58.35–36n.

some seven months after assuming command of the *Otago*. He carried a cargo of fertilizer,[1] a commodity required by the sugar-cane on which the island's prosperity depended. Taking a route through the Torres Strait,[2] he reached Mauritius on 30 September and delivered his cargo to his 'consignees' – the term for receivers of goods sent by public carrier. The unloading seems to have been done quickly; however, he encountered problems with the return loading, which took seven weeks to resolve. During this delay he was able to get to know Port Louis and some of its inhabitants. Indeed, as a master-mariner with a romantic background, fastidious manners, an excellent command of French, and an extensive culture, he proved sufficiently striking to be remembered nearly half a century later. Most of these recollections were gathered at the beginning of the 1930s by one Auguste Esnouf, citizen of Curepipe, Mauritius' second town. Esnouf was enough of a litterateur to value his island's association with a world-famous author. His inquiries proved remarkably successful, and he published his findings in an article, 'Joseph Conrad et Nous', under the nom-de-plume of 'Savinien Mérédac', in the 15 February 1931 number of *L'Essor* ('Uplift'), the periodical of the Port Louis Literary Circle. Further findings appeared in a later and shorter article, 'Joseph Conrad chez Nous' in the Port Louis daily *Le Radical* of 7 August 1931.[3]

Esnouf discovered that Conrad's consignees were a firm called Blyth Brothers, and that through one Krumpholtz, the only freight agent in the Mauritius of those days, he was able to find a business house, Langlois and Co., willing to charter the *Otago* to transport a cargo of sugar to Melbourne. This information came from Paul Langlois, at the time a young director of the firm of that name, who recorded his recollections in a letter published by Esnouf in his first article. Langlois vividly remembered Captain Korzeniowski's appearance and manners, his punctilious dress sense, his multilingual culture, his aloofness among his rough fellow captains, and his intense, volatile personality. To be sure, all these traits could be deduced from a careful reading of 'A Smile of Fortune'; but Langlois' account is distinctive enough (e.g., Conrad's fellow captains called him 'the Russian count',

---

[1] Najder, p. 107. According to the *Sydney Morning Herald* of 5 August 1888, the *Otago*'s cargo comprised not only 1,180 bags of fertilizer, but also 1,093 bags of ammonium sulphate, 600 boxes of soap, seven casks of tallow, and 853 empty casks.

[2] See the discussion of 'The Secret Sharer', pp. xxxv–xxxvi.

[3] See Jean-Aubry, pp. 139–48, 306–7.

he had 'a nervous tick in the shoulder and the eyes') and is sufficiently fallible (he thought, for example, that Conrad 'never made any contact with fashionable society') to confirm his independence. Further research by Esnouf into Conrad's business affairs established that the reason why the 550 tons of sugar he had secured could not be loaded was the contamination of the *Otago*'s hold by the fertilizer she had brought to Mauritius, and that the jute matting (not the 'bags' that delay the tale's protagonist) required to insulate the boards was currently unobtainable because a fire in the factory of Valaydon & Co., a firm which held the monopoly for the manufacture of the matting, had destroyed their stock.[1] Moreover, although Conrad was forced by increasing competition from steam-ships to accept freight at the lowest rates, he remained (unlike his counterpart in the novel) sufficiently self-possessed to persuade his charterers, Langlois & Co., to pay for the costs of pilotage up the River Melbourne, and apparently to purchase a small cargo of potatoes on his own account.[2] He left Mauritius for Melbourne on 22 November.

The tale's version of these events, which it focusses on and around the Jacobus brothers (about whom we have no independent information), is much sourer. Having laboriously secured his sugar cargo, the Captain quickly falls foul of his business contact, one Ernest Jacobus, a truculent and rapacious merchant who is also a member of the Council (the ruling body of Mauritius under the Governor), and whose wealth rests on his influence over the island's law-enforcement system. He controls the sugar bag supply, and thus the price of Mauritius' principal export; and he refuses to help the Captain on the spurious grounds that supplies of this commodity have run out. It is only through a decidedly louche deal with Ernest's brother, the ship-chandler Alfred – a man who is generally despised because he hawks for himself – that the Captain is able to prise the bags out of Ernest and make his ignominious departure.

It is in the nature of literary fiction to transform its origins in life (or indeed in fantasy) in order to serve a determinate idea. What is unusual about 'A Smile of Fortune' is that one of its major autobiographical sources has been suppressed by the narrative, and thus driven into covert activity. This source is Conrad's relations with a leading Mauritian family, the Schmidt-Renoufs, which lasted from just after

---

[1] Jean-Aubry, p. 142.
[2] Najder, pp. 109–11; Jean-Aubry, pp. 142, 145; Jessie Conrad (1926), p. 139.

his arrival till just before his departure. According to Auguste Esnouf's on-the-spot investigations, the story's claim that he gained access to that household (or rather, as it turns out, to an extremely abbreviated and contemptuous version of it) through a chance encounter derives from fact. Esnouf reports that the day after his arrival in Port Louis Conrad, who was calling on his consignees, Blyth Bros., ran into a Mauritian captain in the French merchant marine, Gabriel Renouf by name, whom he had met in India four years earlier and to whom he had been of financial service. The circumstantial support for this story is compelling. Relations between India and Mauritius were very close (Mauritius imported from India the indentured labour on which its production of sugar depended); Conrad had spent a month in Bombay in May 1884 (indeed 'four years' before his arrival in Mauritius), waiting for the departure of the *Narcissus* on which he had enrolled as second mate; finally, this Gabriel's elder brother, Henri Renouf, was an employee of Blyth's. Through such a contact Conrad would have been invited into one of the more exclusive households of Port Louis, located on the corner of the still fashionable Rue de la Bourdonnais and the Rue Saint-Georges.

Its head was Louis Edouard Schmidt, who was not only a member of the Council but also Receiver-General, or Collector of Taxes and Revenues, for Mauritius, and who had married the senior Renouf girl.[1] With them lived her two sisters and two brothers. During his stay in Mauritius, Conrad visited the house regularly, participating in drawing-room games (such as answering indiscreet questionnaires, one of which has survived in Conrad's hand to tell us that the virtue he thought he most lacked was 'self-confidence', and the vice he most despised, 'false pretences'), and reciprocating with invitations for tea on board the *Otago*, and a carriage ride to the then magnificent 'Jardin des Pamplemousses' (Garden of Grapefruits) about seven miles north of Port Louis.[2] During these visits he fell for the second Renouf sister, Eugénie. Two days before he was due to return to Australia, he proposed marriage through her brother Gabriel, only to be told that she was already engaged to her cousin – a pharmacist fifteen years her senior called Loumeau, whom she married on 14 January 1889,[3] less than two months after Conrad's departure. Conrad's last act before leaving was to write to Gabriel asking him to convey his respect to the

---

[1] Barnwell, p. 110. Schmidt died in 1898.
[2] Jean-Aubry, p. 144; Najder, pp. 108–9.   [3] Barnwell, p. 110.

family and to assure him he would never return to Mauritius.[1] Nor did the after-shocks of Conrad's amatory blunder end there. After some desultory sailing between Melbourne, Minlacowie (Melaton), and Adelaide, he received a letter dated 19 January 1889 from the *Otago*'s owners proposing a voyage to Cape Town and Algoa Bay (Port Elizabeth), and adding: 'you will, no doubt, return to Mauritius from So: Africa'. The next surviving letter from these employers was a testimonial referring to their earlier acceptance of his resignation from the command of the *Otago*.[2]

This major episode has not been entirely excised from the tale (otherwise the notion of an 'absent source' could scarcely get a foothold), but it converts its representation of the Schmidt-Renoufs to satire, reducing them to a clan marked by domestic narrowness, bilingual vacuity, and provincial smugness (see p. 39). Even worse, they lionize the rich and squalid merchant Ernest Jacobus (who in the fiction seems to have displaced the distinguished Louis Edouard Schmidt), while turning their noses up at his ship-chandler brother Alfred for daring to bring up his illegitimate daughter in a reputable Port Louis district, and for looking after her godless mother – a travelling circus-performer for whom he had conceived an abject *amour fou* and for whom, to the town's immense scandal, he had hired a bungalow after she turned up (damaged by the kick of a horse), where she died, impenitent and raving to the last. Thus in the tale the Schmidt-Renouf episode is explicitly reduced to a mere illustration of reactionary colonial snobbery. However, Conrad's elimination of a romantic idyll (if such a term could ever be associated with Józef Korzeniowski) ending in a humiliation which – as his life-long silence about it indicates – he never forgot should be regarded not simply as an absent source, but as a repressed one. As such, it drains the story inspired by his visit to Mauritius of much of its original responsive zest, spreading over portions of the narrative a tone of sardonic disenchantment.

This repressed source, however, is more creative than the epithet suggests. It generates a substitute narrative which becomes the central movement of the tale: the narrator's ambiguous dalliance with

---

[1] Jean-Aubry, p. 145. Jean-Aubry had access to eleven letters from Esnouf, two letters from Mme [Eugénie] L[oumeau] dated 16 June and 7 July 1931, and summaries (by Esnouf) of his two interviews with her on 4 and 11 July 1931, as well as much supplementary material. Mme Loumeau died on 15 May 1939, aged seventy-seven (Barnwell, p. 110).

[2] *Portrait in Letters*, pp. 4, 5.

Alice Jacobus in her *hortus conclusus* (the enclosed garden of courtly love). Such an argument assumes, of course, that this episode is not a reflection or transformation of a biographical event. That assumption, however, must overcome a serious difficulty. In 1942 P. G. Barnwell reported the discovery that in 1888 there lived near Port Louis' commercial centre a stevedore of English descent named James Horatio Shaw, who possessed a rose-garden unique in Port Louis, who was married, and who had a daughter named Alice aged nearly seventeen when Conrad was in Mauritius. Although Barnwell's supporting evidence takes the form of a bibliography only, the detail he gives about these people's subsequent lives commands respect. It is likely that Conrad, living for two months on board his ship, would have got to know an English dock-hand and been taken to admire his garden, and even his daughter. The question, however, is whether, since at that time he was regularly visiting the socially desirable Renoufs, he did more than notice her attractions. The fact that when he was writing the story he teased his wife about the attractions of Alice while remaining as silent as the grave about the debacle of Eugénie, does not augur well for Barnwell's thesis that Conrad enjoyed a 'highly charged idyll' among the stevedore's flowers.[1]

Another reason to suspect the autobiographical importance of this episode is the fact that Conrad had to resort to a major literary source in order to flesh it out. This is Guy de Maupassant's 'Les Sœurs Rondoli'[2] a story of 11,000 words written in 1884 for the delectation of the male readers of the racy newspaper *L'Echo Parisien*. In this exuberant and cynical narrative, a young Parisian, Pierre Jouvenel, persuades a philandering friend to join him for a fortnight's dalliance in Genoa. After an uncomfortable night in the train the young men awaken to the radiant beauty of early summer in Provence. At Marseille station a magnificent young woman, who eventually identifies herself as Francesca Rondoli, enters their compartment. Although she is in due course persuaded to devour the provisions the young men offer her, she remains truculently unresponsive to Jouvenel's attempts at flirtatious conversation. Reaching Genoa too late for her to get home, she agrees without fuss to share one of the young men's hotel rooms, spending an

---

[1] Barnwell, p. 110. Alice Shaw married a Mauritian sea-captain, and following his death in Denmark re-married a German commercial traveller; she died in the Far East in 1936 or 1937.

[2] See Paul Kirschner, *Conrad: the Psychologist as Artist* (1968), pp. 220–29, and especially Yves Hervouet, *The French Face of Joseph Conrad* (1990), pp. 112–17.

uninhibited night with Jouvenel to the envy and mortification of his friend. Francesca proves, however, to be no one-night stand and shares with pleasure the young men's sightseeing in her native city. A fortnight later, just before their return to Paris, she calls at last on her mother, who lives in a working-class district, but fails to rejoin the young men. After a vain search, they return to France. The next spring Jouvenel, unable to forget her, goes back to Genoa alone where he tracks down the mother's address, is welcomed by her with open arms, and learns that Francesca, who had pined for him for some weeks, had met a French painter and was now happily established with him in Paris. Jouvenel's disappointment, however, does not last long. Another and even more splendid Rondoli daughter appears, and after her another two, still growing up but highly promising. Jouvenel discovers, finally, that Francesca's original truculence, when she had boarded the train at Marseille the previous year, was owing to her frustration at parting from an original lover, who had decided to resume his profession as painter in Paris (where else?), and whom she had accompanied on the first leg of his journey from Genoa.

Conrad's twenty-four significant verbal borrowings from Maupassant's text bear almost wholly on his presentation of Alice Jacobus and the Captain's response to her. Her jet-black hair, the sensuality of her body under her light garments, her indifference to the young man's attentions, her lack of self-consciousness, her pagan innocence, and even her petulant 'shan't', 'won't', 'don't care', and so on all derive from 'Les Sœurs Rondoli'. More generally, Conrad owes to Maupassant rather than Mauritius the juxtaposition of an innocent exhibitionist and a not-so-innocent voyeur. This whole scenario suggests that Conrad's memory, usually the engine of his creative work, needed supplementation. Thus the tale's 'absent' or 'repressed' source returns to the text by the back door, transforming Maupassant's amoral erotic farce, whose message is 'You don't have to go to Tahiti, or even Mauritius, in order to find sex free of charge', into a narrative riven with emotional and moral discomfort. In Maupassant's Mediterranean paradise, mothers bring up daughters to do what comes naturally. In Conrad's equivocal garden, whose very blooms have been transplanted from Baudelaire's Fleurs du Mal,[1] who can tell whether a father is seeking

---

[1] Compare such phrases as 'the garden was one mass of gloom . . . Only whiffs of heavy scent passed like wandering, fragrant souls' (p. 53) and 'the garden an enormous censer swinging before the altar of the stars' (p. 701), with Baudelaire's 'Harmonie du Soir' (Les Fleurs du Mal, no. 47), lines 1–8, which deploys these very metaphors.

to save his daughter from a life of solitary and sterile excommunication in hypocritical Mauritius, or is treating her as bait to promote a profitable deal in potatoes?

Returning in imagination to Mauritius some twenty-two years after an experience of humiliation, magnified of course by his patrician pride and emotional insecurity, Conrad was able to wrest a final meaning out of his visit. To judge from his depiction of Mauritian society, and especially of the 'Renouf' family, the fiasco of his proposal seems to have opened his eyes to the ferocity of colonial snobbery and its effects on the island's underclasses. The tale offers several examples of bullying and exploitation, from Ernest Jacobus' treatment of his illegitimate mulatto son to the condition of the negro dockers of Port Louis's harbour, but it is the ostracism of Alfred Jacobus and his daughter Alice that fully exposes the cynicism of the island's social establishment. The family that Conrad has virtually written out of the script remains in it as an example of the decay of the patrician values of the pre-revolutionary French colonists. They cannot see anything reprehensible in Ernest Jacobus, the visibly squalid, politically corrupt, and racist tycoon of Mauritius; on the other hand, they warn the Captain against associating with his brother, the *déclassé* Alfred, who sells his wares himself, refuses to go to church, and above all takes in the disreputable, indeed godless, mother of his child when she seeks his protection after an irremediable circus accident. To be sure, Conrad's narrative shows no special awareness of the general exploitative scandal of Mauritius: that the source of its wealth, the production of the sugar justifying a trading ship's trip to Port Louis, is rendered profitable only by the importation of a sub-population of indentured labourers who, at the time of Conrad's visit, were still slaves in all but name. Be that as it may, his Captain defies the family's threat of ostracism. Thus the absent source – Conrad's 22-year suppression of his failed marriage proposal – finally reappears, in a politicized guise, in the Captain's choice of the socially untouchable Alfred over the courted, even toadied, Ernest. This represents a commitment of sorts to the island's despised social classes. But Conrad is too keen a psychologist to try to raise the red flag over his text. In choosing Alfred, the Captain does not choose revolution; he chooses ambiguity, for he continues (as we do) to find him unreadable. Is marriage to the sensuous Alice, whom her father seems to throw at him, the price he will have to pay the merchant for procuring the unobtainable sugar bags? And when the bags finally materialize and his response to her collapses, is the purchase of the potato crop the fine he has to pay the father for having compromised the daughter? Confronted by these conundrums, all that remains for him is to return to the sea.

The sea narrative that frames the Captain's misadventures in Mauritius also grows out of an autobiographical source. The voyage to and from Mauritius is rendered in terms of the Captain's sea-relationship with his 'chief-officer', Mr Burns. This figure is based on the *Otago*'s first mate, the German Charles Born, who was in life three (not five) years older than Conrad. He is described in *The Mirror of the Sea* as a man with 'a red moustache, a lean face, also red, and an uneasy eye', who fulfils to the letter two essential qualities in a naval officer: 'the sense of insecurity . . . so invaluable in a seaman', and 'an absolute confidence in himself'. Conrad's lapses in navigational caution persuade Born that his Captain is utterly reckless, but the grip of his hand at parting at 'the end of two years and three months' (in fact one year and two months) tells a friendlier tale.[1] When the newly promoted Captain Korzeniowski joined the ship which Born had hoped to command, he found, as the 'Physician of Her Majesty's Legation of Siam' testified, that the crew of the *Otago* had 'suffered severely . . . from tropical diseases, including Fever, dysentery and Cholera';[2] but there is no evidence at all that Born was himself seriously affected, let alone hospitalized, as Burns is in 'A Smile of Fortune'. On the contrary, in 'The Secret Sharer' – the story that concludes with the most memorable example of the recklessness that earned Born's disapproval in *The Mirror of the Sea* – the first mate is in excellent health.

'A Smile of Fortune', therefore, seems to juggle history. Mr Burns is rescued by the new Captain in the teeth of the protests of the British Consulate Doctor in Bangkok, is brought back to the ship on the point of death, and is restored to health by the Captain's 'six weeks of anxious nursing' (p. 14). Two years later, they are both, each in his own way, in excellent spirits as they approach the 'Pearl of the Indian Ocean'. Burns is the first to spot the island on the remotest horizon, and he rouses his Captain. The ship reaches the island at nightfall, too late to enter the port – but not too late for its master to perform a 'reckless' act, which recalls the release of Leggatt at the end of 'The Secret

---

[1] *The Mirror of the Sea*, pp. 18–19. See above, pp. xxxiv–xxxvi.   [2] *Portrait in Letters*, p. 2.

Sharer', by shooting the ship 'in so close to the cliffs as almost to frighten' himself, then checking it over the anchorage only at the last moment.[1] No such exuberance marks their departure, with a cargo of sugar, to be sure, but also with a supply of rotting potatoes exuding the contamination of shore life. It is now Burns's turn to look after his Captain, who is prostrate in his cabin. This he does in his own way, by nursing the Captain's investment back to health with a devotion equal to the Captain's refusal two years before to leave him to die in Bangkok. It would appear, then, that in the frame narrative, the solidarity of life at sea displaces the ambiguities of life on shore, and an unsavoury deal is converted into a magnificent profit.

The evidence is that this smile of fortune was as true of Conrad's life as it is of his story. To be sure, the Australian press does not confirm that the *Otago* carried more than sugar. Najder, however, rightly points out that the potatoes were transported on the captain's account and, as a private transaction, would have had no public record. We also possess, as already noted, Jessie Conrad's testimony that they represented Conrad's 'one and only bargain'.[2] There is the strongest circumstantial support from the weather, a ten-month drought in 1888, ending in torrents of rain, which destroyed all root vegetables in south-east Australia. Finally, the other circumstantial details are consistently plausible: on a forty-four day voyage, with the first half spent in the tropics, potatoes would certainly have required the ventilation they receive in the tale. We should take it that, like his Captain, Conrad was manipulated into buying a lottery ticket, and then won. For both, however, the solidarity of sea-life offers no protection from the island. The very devotion of Burns, and presumably of Born, too, is mired in the logic of gain. The Captain resigns at once, and Conrad some weeks later, when a return to Mauritius seems inevitable. Even the sources get into the act: in the tale, the Captain recommends Burns as his successor; in life, Born was once again overlooked.[3]

It seems, then, that the virtues of service at sea cannot salvage the vices of self-interest on land, for the latter have been shown to disrupt

[1] See pp. 14, 17. Conrad's description of this action appears only in his revised version of the prologue (see 'The Texts', pp. 236–7). Cf. Jasper Allen's thoroughly romantic act in 'Freya of the Seven Isles', p. 127.

[2] Najder, p. 111; Jessie Conrad (1926), p. 139.

[3] While serving as first mate under Conrad, Born took his Master's certificate in Melbourne on 29 June 1888. He failed, however, to secure the command Conrad had vacated, which went to a Captain Edward Trivett. See *CEW*, pp. 268–9.

and destabilize the former, as the Captain apprehends while contemplating the island at the end of his sea passage (pp. 15–16). It looks as if Conrad can no longer sustain the hard optimism of *The Nigger of the 'Narcissus'*, a narrative which opens out a space, as it were, between the ship and her cargo by allowing her temporarily to transcend the 'sordid inspiration of her pilgrimage' (p. 30). Conrad's sexual humiliation in Mauritius may have been repressed; but it has not been wasted. Relocated as it is from Eugénie Renouf's Rue de la Bourdonnais to Alice Jacobus' prison garden, it generates what is perhaps Conrad's most radical study of the irreconcilability of sex and money – radical enough indeed to close the ideal gap between the word 'merchant' and the word 'marine'.

Freya of the Seven Isles

OF THE three tales prompted by the visit of their dedicatee, Captain Marris, it is only the third, 'Freya of the Seven Isles', that is indebted to him for its content. The first two are autobiographical fictions built on episodes from the days of Conrad's command of the *Otago*. 'Freya of the Seven Isles', however, marginalizes the autobiographical Conrad into a passive spectator–narrator who with his small steamer trades in the regions frequented by Conrad when he was first mate of the *Vidar*, plying regularly between Singapore and north-east Borneo, with occasional deviations to the Seven Isles some thirty-five miles due north of Bangka in order to call on old Nelson (or Nielsen) and his daughter Freya. But this narrator, who sees and understands much, has no effect at all on the action. Well before the narrative crisis, he withdraws to a dreary London where, in the end, he is sought out by the bereaved old Nelson, who tells him the story of Freya's humiliation of Lieutenant Heemskirk, captain of a Dutch police-boat, of its consequences in the destruction of the sensitive Jasper Allen to whom Freya is secretly betrothed, and of her own ensuing death.

The action of 'Freya of the Seven Isles', then, is largely confined to those parts of the Malay Archipelago that Conrad had known at first hand: Bangka, to which he had been taken in March 1883, when the *Palestine* on which he was serving had foundered in its vicinity; Singapore, where Conrad spent in all more than five months over several visits between 1883 and 1888; and the entrance of the River Berau off north-east Borneo, to which Conrad made four trading voyages between 22 August 1887 and 2 January 1888.[1] Although Conrad never set foot on the Seven Isles, he would have passed near them whenever he travelled between the Sunda Straits and Singapore. As for Macassar, where the novella's tragic climax is located but in which Conrad never set foot, his astonishingly exact and vivid description of it as it was some forty years before the date of the novella's action is owed entirely to A. R. Wallace's account of it in his masterpiece *The Malay Archipelago*. Moreover, the 1890 edition, which Conrad owned, contains a map in which the Seven Isles (to-day the 'Pulau Tujuh' or 'Islands Seven') are identified as the 'Toojoo Islands'.[2]

Yet, even if the main action of the tale mostly derives from Conrad's first-hand knowledge of the Archipelago, his narrative evokes the whole of that immense area, which covers over 3,400,000 square miles. The reasons for this will be touched on later. Its origins, however, are to be found in Captain Marris's self-introductory letter of 18 July 1909, which – to judge from Conrad's subsequent correspondence with Pinker (11 October 1909) and with Edward Garnett (4 August 1911) – effectively set the agenda for their meeting on Monday 13 September, the day before Marris embarked in Southampton on his return to Penang.[3] Of Marris's three letters to Conrad, his first should be regarded as a comprehensive source for a tale that highlights geographical space, as early as its opening page, with an image that embraces the entire expanse of the East Indies. Nelson's tracks, we are told, 'if plotted out would have covered the map of the Archipelago like a cobweb – all of it, with the sole exception of the Philippines' (p. 123): an exception that serves to keep them on the map. Conrad's narrative goes on to do just that. Its geographical allusions cover the whole of Indonesia, from Manila in the north-east to New Guinea

[1] Jasper's brig is ambushed by Heemskirk in a jungle-lined estuary of a great river, with a town upstream, where Jasper has delivered a cargo of rice to a hungry population and Schultz has exchanged the *Bonito*'s supply of defensive rifles for silver. The town is riven by 'troubles', and 'there's no trade there now' (see p. 171). In *The Sea Years of Joseph Conrad* (1965), p. 231, Jerry Allen quotes the official Dutch shipping history for the period, *Een Halve Eeuw Paketvaart*, on the Berau region: 'Almost everywhere along the coast there was smuggling of guns and gunpowder'. Between 1886 and 1892 the contested successor of the deceased ruler of the Gunung Tabor sultanate, whose upstream river-port was Berau, inflicted endemic fighting on the region.

[2] Wallace, facing the 'Preface' (p. viii). See Map 4.

[3] For details, see above, p. xxxi. In his letter of 6 September 1909, Marris told Conrad that he would be sailing on the 'Prinzess[in] Alice', which departed from Southampton on Saturday, 14 September, the day after his visit to Aldington. His third letter, of 11 January 1910, from Penang, more subdued, and asking Conrad to look at his writing, probably reached Conrad as he was trying to finish *Under Western Eyes*.

(which divides the Archipelago from the Pacific), then westwards to Ternate (the Moluccas) and Celebes (Macassar) and along the southern border from Flores and Sumbawa to Sumatra, then northwards to Chantabun (Chantaburi, on the eastern edge of the Gulf of Siam), and finally to Hong Kong (where Freya goes to die). And this list is limited to the localities on the periphery.

This spatial restlessness correlates with perhaps the most remarkable moment in Marris's long letter of self-introduction. In what is in effect a single sentence of over 200 words, he evokes his escape from Macassar following the arrest of the *Costa Rica* (see below), first to Deli, on the island of Timor, then (having acquired an Australian ketch) on a headlong course of contraband and 'trade' stretching from the north-eastern tip of Celebes to Ternate, then back to Macassar, then northwards to the southern Philippines, then westwards through the treacherous north Borneo passage to the great Meinam River and Bangkok, then down the eastern side of the Malay Peninsula, round Singapore, and up the western side, with excursions in the dangerous Atjeh of northern Sumatra, then pushing further north to the fabled Nicobar Islands – only to be 'smashed up on the Lys shoal between Mergui & Tavoy, losing everything & so ended sailing days'. This résumé scarcely does justice to the headlong excitement of Marris's trajectory, which names twenty-one identifiable places; nor does it convey what the letter certainly does: a nostalgia for an age not yet subdued into the predictabilities of law and order, when the Archipelago was not yet fully dominated by the high imperialism in place at the beginning of the 1880s.

When Marris refers to ending his 'sailing days', he does not mean giving up seafaring but taking up 'steam'. He lists the nine coast boats he commanded after writing off his 'Ketch' (a two-masted sailing boat), among which is Conrad's *Vidar*. Thus Marris's letter becomes a lament for the passing of the age of sail: 'There is not now I suppose a square topsail to be met with between the Yangtze & Batavia, & the days of shipping & harbor crowded with sail, in Bangkok, Singapore and Sourabaya are done'. Now, he adds, 'there is nothing to be met with but steam . . . where of old we saw nothing but the 6 weekly Packetvaart boat from Java . . . & the Dirty little Dutch Kapal prang [= man-of-war] that used to cruise about in Caramata & Macassar Straits'.[1] The area

---

[1] *Portrait in Letters*, p. 66. Caramata was the refuelling island between Borneo and the Seven Isles. The Packetvaart boat was the postal-route boat. The 'Dirty little Dutch Kapal prang' is surely the ancestor of Heemskirk's gunboat.

patrolled by this gunboat exactly covers Conrad's itinerary with the *Vidar*. How strongly Marris's headlong sentences would have revived Conrad's memories of 1888–9, the period of his life revisited in the three tales that comprise *'Twixt Land and Sea*, can be seen in the last, which not only turns Jasper's brig into a symbol of the beauty of sail at the moment of its passing, but makes 'progress', in the guise of a 'Dirty little Dutch' steamer, the agent of its destruction.

Marris's first letter expresses an aversion for England: 'I . . . am disgusted with the climate, customs, & language', he writes. His second letter, dated 'September 6ᵗʰ / 09', confirms this, though more positively: 'the East is calling too strongly, & I must return'.[1] Conrad's tale responds powerfully to these feelings. When the narrator suddenly removes himself from the action in Indonesia, just as it begins to accelerate to the catastrophe, and returns to England, the East seems to drop out of his life. London's 'winter days composed of the four devilish elements: cold, wet, mud and grime, combined with a particular stickiness of atmosphere that clings like an unclean garment' (pp. 185–6) obliterate the past. But old Nelson's visit, like Marris's to Conrad, reawakens in him a visionary nostalgia for the tropical beauty of virgin forests with their rivers 'opening their sombre forest-lined estuaries amongst a welter of pale green reefs and dazzling sand-banks', and far-away glimpses of Jasper's brig, 'a tiny dazzling white speck flying across the brooding purple masses of thunder-clouds piled up on the horizon' (p. 140).

When Marris, the day before returning to Penang, travelled down to the Conrads' cramped and uncomfortable quarters in Aldington to make what Jessie Conrad describes as a 'never to be forgotten visit', Conrad was able to see for himself Marris's 'partial paralysis', worse than that of old age, 'that obscured his recollection' and to understand his eagerness to return to his 'Malay princess' and his little daughter.[2] When *'Twixt Land and Sea* came out in October 1912, all three stories were dedicated to 'Captain C. M. Marris late master and owner of the *Araby Maid*' though it was only the third for which Marris was the direct source. The thought that the man who had urged him to 'give us some more tales of the East, & weave some further romances about Rajah Laut & the old times of the 70's and 80's', or to 'write the story of the *Costa Rica*',[3] was now gone as irretrievably as Conrad's own past helps

[1] *Portrait in Letters*, pp. 68, 69.   [2] Jessie Conrad, *Joseph Conrad and His Circle* (1935), p. 137.
[3] *Portrait in Letters*, p. 68; *Letters*, IV, 469. Marris apparently died in 1910 (*Portrait in Letters*, p. xxvi).

account for the sometimes piercing sadness that haunts this tale, and it legitimates the sense of dissolution that concludes it, despite the reservations expressed by Garnett, who felt that the tragedy was 'too "willed" & led up to'.[1]

Marris's intervention was crucial not only in reawakening Conrad's creative interest in the maritime East from Bangkok and Port Louis to Sydney and Melbourne, but also, and specifically, in Indonesia proper, the tropical setting of his first novels, to be sure, but more originally the arena for intensely confrontational politics, both native and colonial, which play so important a part in this tale's catastrophe. The rivalry between the Netherlands and Great Britain had become endemic since the gifted and audacious but less-than-scrupulous James Brooke, in contemptuous disregard of the spirit if not the letter of the convention limiting British interests in Indonesia to north of the Malacca Straits, had been confirmed Rajah of Sarawak by the Sultan of Brunei and thus 'completed the encirclement of the South China Sea by British dependencies'.[2] As a result, imperialist tensions between the British and the Dutch remained high until the Second World War. In his tale Conrad plants this conflict deep in the psychology of old Nelson/Nielsen, who with his divided self – a symptom not only of fear (Danish or Nordic nationality being much less provocative than a British passport in the Seven Isles), but also of a kind of paralyzing neurosis – comes through as being more politically receptive than Marris, secure with his Malaysian wife in the British–Malay Federation. Yet, once he has settled in his Dutch-held island, his anxieties become disastrous as they discourage his daughter from confiding in him about her English lover, Jasper Allen, or indeed from revealing to Jasper himself the danger represented by the rebuffed Dutch naval lieutenant, Heemskirk.

Still, Marris's letter of self-introduction to Conrad has a final card to play. It is represented by the sentence 'I finished up with Sail with Carpenter in Macassar, in the old "Costa Rica Packet" when he got into the big smuggling trouble with the Dutch there'. This could have been passed over as a simple association of Marris with an international *cause célèbre*. In 1881 John Bolton Carpenter, skipper of the *Costa Rica*, was stopped by the Dutch authorities over disputed casks of gin that Carpenter had allegedly retrieved from a derelict prau. The Dutch

---

[1] Edward Garnett, quoted in Carolyn Heilbrun, *The Garnett Family* (1961), pp. 113–14. See also *Letters*, v, 127–8, and Appendix G, 'The Garnett Controversy'.

[2] See Vlekke, pp. 297–8, an indispensable study. Sarawak comprised nearly a fifth of the territory of Borneo, along its north-western coast.

took him, but not his ship, to Macassar where, the following year, he was charged with theft and the smuggling of arms. Carpenter maintained that the original offences had occurred in waters outside Dutch jurisdiction. A diplomatic row ensued between Great Britain and the Netherlands; the matter was submitted to international arbitration, and in 1895 the Russian arbiter found in favour of Great Britain. Evidently this episode offered Conrad, at the end of 1910, a political context supercharged with Dutch–British rivalry which forms the political–psychological foundation of the novella.

Conrad, however, seems to have found more than that in this 'source'. Writing on 4 August 1911 to Garnett in defence of a tale about which his former mentor had reservations, he explained:

It is the story of the *Costa Rica* which was not more than five years old when I was in Singapore. The man's name was Sutton. He died in just that way – but I don't think he died of Slav temperament. He was just about to go home to marry a girl (of whom he used to talk to everybody and anybody) and bring her out there when his ship was run of[f] a reef by the commander of a Dutch gunboat whom he had managed to offend in some way. He haunted the beach in Macassar for months and lies buried in the fort there.

Only 18 months ago Charles Marris master and owner of the *Araby Maid* island-trader, came to see me in Aldington . . . He said: "You ought to write the story of the *Costa Rica*. There's a good many of us left yet who remember Sutton." And I said I would, before long.[1]

There is no mention of Sutton in Marris's initial letter to Conrad, but Conrad is clearly referring to their conversation during Marris's visit to Aldington – which of course is irrecoverable. The problem with this explanation is not Sutton's story, about which there is no reason to doubt that Marris and Conrad talked to each other, but its connection with the *Costa Rica* affair, since surviving accounts of that do not mention him.[2] What the episode nevertheless offered Conrad was a sensational case of 'firearms' smuggling – though one which went in favour of the accused, whereas in Conrad's novella the man formally charged with that infraction (Jasper) cannot defend himself

[1] *Letters*, IV, 469. The correspondence between Conrad, his agent Pinker, and his former mentor Garnett, is worth sorting out, if only because it reveals Conrad's emotional investment in 'Freya of the Seven Isles': see Appendix G for a summary.
[2] In the best research on the subject, neither G. J. Resink, 'Jozef Korzeniowski's voornaamste lectuur betreftende Indonesië', *Bijdragen tot de taal-, land-, en Volken Kunde*, 117 (1961), 209–37, nor H. A. van Karnebeek's Utrecht LLD dissertation, *De 'Costa Rica Packet' – Arbitrage* (1900), refers to a Sutton. The editors owe these two references, and much else, to that peerless researcher, the late Hans van Marle.

in court because the man who has committed it (Schultz, the first mate who steals to pay for his alcoholic bouts) cannot be believed.

However, another precedent for Jasper's tragic end does exist – indeed was already in existence in 1898. This is not the real-life Sutton that Marris and Conrad remembered – though that does not prove that such a figure never existed. This precedent is to be found in the first-draft version of Conrad's *The Rescue*, Part II, Chapter 5, which Garnett had seen twelve years earlier, for he returned Part II to Conrad, who confirmed its receipt on 29 March of that year (*Letters*, II, 49). The following extract from the manuscript now in the British Library differs only incidentally from the revised form Conrad gave it after 1916, when he returned to a project that had been mothballed for nearly twenty years. One Jörgenson, an old drop-out loner, who years before had been obliged to burn his prized barque *The Wild Rose* to prevent her confiscation by the Dutch, tells the shocked Lingard, in explanation, that he did not wish to follow the example of 'Dawson' (whose name, if similar, is still not quite 'Sutton'): 'I wasn't going to let her rot to pieces in some Dutch port.' Lingard then asks: 'He died – didn't he?', to which Jörgenson replies:

"Cut his throat on the beach below fort Rotterdam" said Jörgenson. He seemed to waver in the unsteady moonshine as though his gaunt figure had been made of mist. "Yes. He broke some trade regulation or other and talked big about law-courts and of legal trials to the lieutenant of the "Komet." "Certainly" says the hound. "Jurisdiction of Macassar; I will take your schooner there." Then coming into the roads he tows her full tilt on a ledge of rocks on the north side. Smash! When she was half full of water he takes his hat off to Dawson. "There's the shore" – says he – go and get your legal trial you damned Englishman. . . ." He lifted a long arm and shook his fist at the moon which dodged suddenly behind a cloud. "All was lost. Poor Dawson walked the streets for months barefooted and in rags. Then one day he begged a knife from some charitable soul, went down to take a last look at the wreck, and". . . .

Dawson obviously anticipates Jasper Allen, though it is Schultz who cuts his throat; Allen loses his wits and gradually fades away. The hounding lieutenant with his *Komet* plainly prefigures Heemskirk and his *Neptun*. This does not, of course, resolve the question of a real-life precedent for the fate of Jasper's *Bonito*: the first cause, as such causes do, continues to elude capture. But it does provide a literary source which casts some light on the psychology of the tale. In his debate with Lingard, Jörgenson's point is that it is better to destroy your vessel yourself than to have it destroyed for you by others, for sailing ships – like human beings – are not machines, and awaken in their owners a commitment usually reserved for living things.

The source material determining the catastrophe of Conrad's third land-and-sea narrative also determines the location of that climax – a town that Conrad never visited. He was not at liberty to choose a site in a part of the Archipelago he knew, such as Mintok, for the politics of his story; and indeed its sources required that the catastrophe occur in the Dutch naval headquarters of the Eastern Archipelago. When he reached the final section of his tale, he was obliged to seek help. This he found, as already noted, in Wallace's *The Malay Archipelago*. On his first visit to Macassar in September 1856, his contact in Macassar was a Mr Mesman, a hospitable merchant and botanist established in the district, whom Conrad had already used as a source for Stein in *Lord Jim* and whom he brought back into 'Freya of the Seven Isles' under his own name (p. 178). The town itself Wallace found to be 'prettier and cleaner than any I had yet seen in the East' (p. 162). It consists, he added, 'of one long narrow street, along the sea-side . . . principally occupied by the Dutch and Chinese merchants' and lined by 'native shops or bazaars'. Two short streets parallel to the sea edge formed the old Dutch town with its fort and church. The long beach-front extended beyond the fort, lined with 'native huts and many country houses of the tradesmen and merchants' (p. 163). Conrad follows this description closely, and he owes many further significant details to Wallace. For example, on his arrival Wallace notices in 'the road-stead of Macassar' not only a '42-gun frigate' but, more significantly, 'a small war steamer' (p. 162). He then puts up at 'a kind of club-house, in default of any hotel' (p. 162). Old Nelson books into the 'Oranje House' (named after the royal house of the Netherlands), which evokes all the atmosphere and amenities of a colonial club.

Conrad's need to provide a geographical as well as a historical foundation for his fiction, whether in the form of documentary or of first-hand evidence, is a legacy of the later nineteenth-century tradition of French realism where he went to school as a novelist. And yet, like other works in that tradition, 'Freya of the Seven Isles' remains art, not reportage, and retains all the disciplined plenitude of Conrad's characteristic style. The current of events that determines the catastrophe of the novella owes very little to fantasy or improvisation. Like the grand inclusive sweep of islands and seas it evokes, it represents Conrad's farewell to the East he had known at the moment of its transformation under the onslaught of European progress. The glamour (his word) of the East had made itself felt as early as his first deep-water voyage to Australia in 1878–9.[1] During the four months his ship remained moored at Sydney's Circular Quay, he became (in the words of his guardian–uncle Tadeusz Bobrowski) 'acquainted with some captain famous for his knowledge of the trade with that Archipelago' and devoted to 'the Sunda Isles, the beauty and the wealth of which he describes with the greatest enthusiasm'.[2] This delight remained intermittently with him until he resigned his command of the *Otago* in 1889. To be sure, after 'Freya of the Seven Isles' Conrad's fiction revisited the East at least five times. But of these works, it is this tale that expresses most deeply the exploitative menace of modernity which hangs over the Archipelago, and without which its elegy of love and youth would dwindle into merely private grief.

This collaboration between the personal and the political Conrad owes to a genuinely unexpected source: the music of Richard Wagner, with which he associates his heroine. Conrad's Freya bears the name of the Nordic goddess of love and youth who reaches her nineteenth-century apotheosis in Wagner's *Das Rheingold* (1852–4). There Wotan, ruler of the gods, exchanges his daughter Freia for possession of the world's gold – a choice which will eventually bring about the destruction of the gods. Conrad draws Wagner's *Ring of the Nibelungen* into his novella not only through his heroine's Nordic physique and bearing, but also, more literally, in the power of her performance of Wagner's music on the pianoforte. Wagner, whose fame had spread to the East by the early 1880s, not only contributes a realistic touch to Conrad's narrative; his music is also a constitutive part of the power of Freya's glamour. Offenbach and Franz Lehár were at least as popular in Singapore, but neither would have provided the piano scores required to turn Heemskirk from clown to monster. At the end of the nineteenth century the acquisition of pianos in the remoter parts of the world was a statement of prestige – though even here realism has not been banished: Conrad's account of the efforts required to unload Freya's 'Steyn and Ebhart' upright grand (125.37n) has been graphically corroborated by Jane Campion's 1998 film *The Piano*, set in the New Zealand of the same period.

Broader formal resemblances between Conrad's novella and Wagner's *Ring* could be and have been proposed. It is just possible,

[1] See 'Youth', in *Youth: A Narrative, and Two Other Stories*, p. 42.
[2] Tadeusz Bobrowski to Stefan Buszczyński, 18/30 May 1879, in Zdzisław Najder, ed., *Conrad's Polish Background* (1964), pp. 179–80.

for instance, to establish links between old Nelson's failure to see, let alone to face, the menace of Heemskirk's infatuation with his daughter and Wotan's incapacity in *Die Walküre* (1854–6) to check the murderous jealousy which his son-in-law Hunding (physically a Nordic Heemskirk, if such a thing can be imagined) vents on her blond lover Siegmund. But there would be no end to such comparisons. Instead, it is more profitable to pause, in conclusion, over Conrad's justification of his art in a crucial letter written on 31 May 1902 to William Blackwood, editor of *Blackwood's Edinburgh Magazine* and publisher of *Lord Jim*, 'Youth', and other narratives of that period (*Letters*, II, 418). In this letter, Conrad defended himself against the charge of commercial unsuccess 'in a time when Sherlock Holmes looms so big' with the claim that 'I am <u>modern</u>, and I would rather recall Wagner the musician and Rodin the Sculptor who . . . had to suffer for being "new" . . . My work shall not be an utter failure because it has the solid basis of a definite intention – first: and next because . . . in its essence it is action'.

COMPOSITION

THE COMPOSITION OF a literary work is distinguishable from its sources as a verb is distinguished from a noun. Captain C. M. Marris's visit to Conrad at Aldington on 13 September 1909 not only reminded him of his past in the eastern seas: it also energized him. Returning to 'Razumov' (the working title of *Under Western Eyes*), he produced, between mid-September 1909 and the first few days of December, 302 pages, or 32,000 words, of a novel that had been labouring, even seizing up, since December 1907. He then interrupted this run, but only to double his rate of production by generating the some 16,400 words of 'The Secret Sharer' in about ten days. This extraordinary spurt of inspiration was partly driven by his guilt at stealing time from Pinker, who was dependent on the novel to recoup his enormous investment in its author. Once delivered of his tale, Conrad returned headlong to 'Razumov', finishing the novel with a final burst of over 14,000 words.[1]

---

[1] For details of the writing and revision of 'The Secret Sharer', see below, pp. lxv–lxviii, and 'The Texts', pp. 207–13. On the composition of 'Razumov', see Carabine, Appendix, pp. 49–58, Table Three; on the composition of the last chapter, Roger S. Osborne, 'For Art and Money: A Textual History and Annotated Scholarly Edition of Joseph Conrad's *Under Western Eyes*' (2000), pp. 158–60; on the work of these last months, the batches of manuscript, and

Conrad's productiveness, part-cause of his breakdown in late January 1910, became the instrument of his recovery. After six weeks of prostration, which had begun to ease only with the revision of 'Razumov', he set about doggedly writing himself back into the world of the living. Over the next three-and-a-half months (from mid-May to the end of August), at first falteringly and inadequately, then with rising confidence, he coaxed out of himself the nearly 28,000 words of 'A Smile of Fortune'. On its completion he almost at once turned to 'Prince Roman', a minor 8,000-word masterpiece of patriotic hagiography which consumed the month of September.[1] Thereupon, in complete contrast, over a period of ten weeks punctuated by the shortening of 'A Smile of Fortune' for serial publication, he produced 'The Partner', a tale in which the profit motive of capitalist England turns the louche deals of colonial Mauritius into the murderous brutality of the Edwardian underworld. Thus, it was only in late December, and probably in response to the news of Marris's death, that he fulfilled his promise to him to return to the Archipelago they both had known by writing 'Freya of the Seven Isles', a task which required nine weeks and nearly 29,000 words to complete.

This episode in a literary career at a major turning-point is a striking example of the degree to which the act of writing can generate self-recovery. Progress on 'Razumov' was held up by the anxiety of an ever-increasing debt to Pinker, by the demands of a novel which was forcing him to envisage the possibility that his life in England rested on a betrayal of his origins, and by his estrangement from Ford Madox Ford, who had been a source of support and stimulus to him since 1898. Thus Conrad's breach with Pinker represented the climax of a long-incubating crisis, advanced by such local trespasses as the writing of *A Personal Record* and of 'The Secret Sharer', and finally brought

the number of words, *Under Western Eyes*, ed. Keith Carabine, Paul Eggert, and Roger S. Osborne (forthcoming), esp. 'The Texts' and Appendix A. The precise date of Marris's visit is somewhat inferential, but the evidence of Conrad's September 1909 letters, particularly that to Perceval Gibbon (*Letters*, IV, 272–3), and of departures from Southampton (*Letters*, IV, 272, n. 3) strongly indicates the 13th. (Cf. *Chronology*, p. 76; Baines, pp. 354–5; Najder, p. 353; Karl, pp. 674–5.) Conrad's early October letter to Pinker (*Letters*, IV, 276–8) justifying the writing of 'The Silence of the Sea' for the *Daily Mail* (18 September) reveals something of the tone of their relationship well before the last explosions.

[1] On the relation of this tale to the writing of his autobiographical reminiscences, themselves involved with the intermittent composition of *Under Western Eyes*, see the 'Introduction', in *A Personal Record*, ed. Zdzisław Najder and J. H. Stape (2007), p. xxii. The composition of 'A Smile of Fortune' itself entailed interruption by four reviews for the *Daily Mail* (see 'The Texts', p. 233).

to a head by the 'completion' of *Under Western Eyes*. Yet the long process of recovery only reversed the paradox that writing had destroyed
Conrad's capacity to write: for it was by writing that he was able to overcome his paralysis. What he struggled to produce, as he fought for the
recovery of his creative talent, was the second of three tales he would
eventually dedicate to Captain Marris, and that itself would demand
nearly four months of effort.

The Secret Sharer

THE MEMORIES awakened by Captain Marris's visit found their initial expression in what many regard as Conrad's finest novella, 'The
Secret Sharer'. But as already noted, its writing, like its subject, was an
act of transgression. Since 3 December 1907, Conrad had been struggling with 'Razumov', which Pinker, over and above other occasional
advances, was sponsoring at the rate of £6 per week. By June 1909,
Conrad owed the man whose business was wagered heroically on the
success of the novel no less than £2,250.[1] Driven by the prospect of his
own ruin, and perhaps Pinker's too, Conrad spent part of an August
recess with a younger friend, the novelist Perceval Gibbon, trying to
work out some kind of strategy for completing 'Razumov'. Although
this exercise was not very successful,[2] from the time he saw Marris he
was able to settle down to completing the last third of the novel; and
during the following three months he worked steadily at it, even while
revising proofs of a French translation of *The Nigger of the 'Narcissus'*
in November.[3] However, around 5 December, having posted the latest
manuscript batch to Pinker, he abruptly broke off once again – this
time to launch himself into a new tale, which would find enduring
celebrity under the name of 'The Secret Sharer'. With an unprecedented concentration and fluency driven at once by elation and anxiety he completed the manuscript on the 14th.

The external evidence for these dates comes from Pinker's archives
and Conrad's correspondence. The extant typescript of *Under Western*

---

[1] Najder, p. 352. In end-of-century terms, this would have amounted to about £138,550 in
purchasing power; see above, p. xxxii, n. 1, for other equivalent values and for bases of
computation.

[2] Early in August, he mentioned to Pinker consulting Gibbon's 'Russian notes' (*Letters*, IV,
269). On 7 September 1909 Conrad wrote to Galsworthy: 'In Trosley I could not write'
(*Letters*, IV, 271). Trosley (Trottiscliffe), West Malling, near Maidstone, was where Gibbon's
new home was.

[3] For Marris's visit, see above, p. xxxi; for mention of the proofs, see *Letters*, IV, 283, 287–94.

Eyes has now been thoroughly analysed.[1] This document consists of the typewritten copies of the manuscript batches received by Pinker's office from December 1907 to January 1910, when the novel was at last 'completed'. The usefulness of this record consists in the dating of almost every batch of manuscript or typescript from March 1909, when, after moving to Aldington from Luton, Conrad resumed 'Razumov' under increasing concern about his relationship with Pinker. The record shows that Conrad's determination to complete the novel flagged only once in late 1909, between the 5th and the 31st of December, when Pinker received no further manuscript. Moreover, a letter by Conrad dated 19 December to the particularly supportive Gibbon indicates that on the previous day Pinker had warned Conrad that if the novel was not completed within a fortnight (i.e., by 2 January) he would suspend the weekly subsidy (*Letters*, IV, 301–2). The letter also reveals that Conrad's own page-count of 'Raz' on 19 December showed only four pages beyond the batches of twenty and twelve pages sent the first week of December.

Conrad's correspondence for December is unusually informative about the progress of his work, though a bit imprecise about when he began the tale.[2] Yet he was well into the central episode of the narrative, the interview with the captain of the *Sephora*, before he showed his hand.[3] On Friday the 10th, he sent Pinker the incomplete manuscript of 'a short story of say 8 thou, which could be reduced to 6 if necessary', together with the request: 'Pray have these 64 pages typed and sent back to me say on Sat – as I have Sunday post. The last 15 pp will be sent by to-night's mail if I can get them ready by six o'clock. If

---

[1] See 'The Texts' in *Under Western Eyes* (forthcoming); and Carabine, pp. 51–2 and Appendix, Table Three.

[2] The 3rd, 4th, 5th, and 6th have of late been proposed as possible dates. On the basis of the 'Razumov' typescript, Keith Carabine has argued for the 4th or the 3rd, Conrad's fifty-second birthday, exactly two years since he had begun *Under Western Eyes*, and a date with additional appeal because 'Conrad seems to have been fond of symbolic gestures'; in that view Conrad's '10 days' (*Letters*, IV, 296), like his word count, is a slight exaggeration in the interest of brevity, if not simply a round number, or a poetic truth. But further analysis of that typescript and the two batches of *Under Western Eyes* from early December yields a later date, probably the 5th (though a Sunday), in precise accord with Conrad's 14th December reference to '10 days', which he repeated five days later (*Letters*, IV, 301). See Keith Carabine, '"The Secret Sharer": A Note on the Dates of Its Composition', *Conradiana*, 19 (1987), 209–13, esp. p. 212, n. 8; Carabine, p. 51, n. 6; S. W. Reid and Robert W. Trogdon, '"The Secret Sharer": A Further Note on the Dates of Its Composition', *Conradiana* 38 (2006), 169–73. See also p. lxx, n. 1.

[3] For details, including the coincidence between the number of leaves dispatched and the evidence of marks on the manuscript, see 'The Texts', pp. 207–8.

not then you won't get them till Monday.' The bustling tone does not wholly conceal the underlying unease: plainly, there is no prospect of catching the evening mail-train. Conrad concludes: 'With them I'll send you a title and a letter explaining why the thing came to be written' (*Letters*, IV, 294). But the explanation is already there: the story is the product – as Wordsworth once put it – of 'a paramount impulse not to be withstood'.

On the same day, Conrad addressed Galsworthy in a very different key: 'I have been working rather well of late. I took off last week to write a short story. *Raz* is really nearing the end. The French *Nigger* has been made to look like an original work – almost.' (*Letters*, IV, 294). Now the balance sheet looks and feels good: Conrad is on the point of completing a full-scale novel and a long story (both of which posterity would rate as masterpieces). And in addition, he has recently corrected and enhanced the proofs of Robert d'Humières' French translation of *The Nigger of the 'Narcissus'* for the *Mercure de France*.[1] He was riding the crest of a creative wave; but, as waves do, it was moving towards the shore.

On the following day, Saturday the 11th, having been forced by a delay in the publication of the 'French *Nigger*' to accept the offer of a loan from Galsworthy to tide him over, he concluded his letter of thanks with: 'I've been working all day and feel horribly stiff and discouraged' (*Letters*, IV, 295). Evidently, 'The Secret Sharer' needed much more attention than he had led Pinker to understand the day before. But at last, on Tuesday the 14th – one day later than he had promised a now ominously silent Pinker – he announced to Galsworthy: 'I've just finished the short story – 12000 words in 10 days. Not so bad. I had to lay aside Razumov for a bit tho' I didn't think it would take 10 days' (*Letters*, IV, 296). In fact, the 'last 15 pages' or 'say 1200' words which on 10 December he had told Pinker he might be able to post 'by to-night's mail' had taken four days and had grown to 7,800 words, and by 6,000 words – or perhaps even more than that, since it was only on Wednesday the 15th that Conrad was finally able to separate himself from his manuscript.

With the end of the story at last on its way to London, Conrad concocted a letter of explanation to Pinker that managed to blend

---

[1] On 29 October, Conrad acknowledged (or anticipated) receipt of the proofs. On 11 November (or perhaps the 18th), he wrote to d'Humières about reading them. On the 15th, he complained to Galsworthy that 'the French proofs of the Nigger coming in for correction complicate matters . . . And how can I let it pass?' On the 27th he reported: 'The French proofs of the N of the N are finished' (*Letters*, IV, 283, 286, 288, 292).

deliberate nonchalance with devious self-justification. He justified breaking his promise to remain with 'Razumov' until its completion by having had to hospitalize the suddenly stricken 'faithful maid' Nellie Lyons between 10 November and about 9 December at a guinea a week, and he minimized his neglect of 'Razumov' with the explanation that the story, which he had just posted to Pinker, had initially been conceived as a sketch for the *Daily Mail* in response to an invitation by its literary editor, Lindsay Bashford, but had spontaneously grown into something which he 'hadn't the heart to throw . . . away'. He added, somewhat disingenuously, that 'we may call it 10,000 words', and that it had been 'written in 8 days'. He then offered it to Pinker as collateral for a loan to cover the cost of Nellie's illness (six guineas) and, for good measure, the cost of his son Borys's change of schools (5 pounds), though making 'no demand whatever' with respect to the latter.[1] To reassure Pinker that 'Razumov' was now back on course, he described a return of energies he had not known since writing *Lord Jim* ten years earlier. The literary quality of 'The Secret Sharer', and indeed of what finally became *Under Western Eyes*, suggests that this claim was more than manipulative. However, it was also *that*, for before signing off Conrad had to come clean about yet another contractual breach: that he had borrowed yet more of Pinker's time to revise the French translation of 'the Nigger' – to the point of transforming it into 'a French work'. His uneasiness, moreover, persisted after he had signed off, for he added a postscript designed to draw his agent into a collaborative stance: 'What do you think for title of the story *The Second Self. An episode from the sea*.'

By this time presumably, Conrad was already at work revising the early typescript pages of the new tale.[2] Two days later, still having heard

---

[1] Conrad to Pinker, [15 December 1909] (*Letters*, IV, 297–9). Although undated, this letter was almost certainly written and sent on 15 December. On the 11th apparently, he had told Galsworthy, who had offered to help with the hospital costs, that he had already paid the hospital, but still needed £18 to pay for Borys's schooling (*Letters*, IV, 295).

[2] For the dates and the logistics of processing the typescript, see 'The Texts', pp. 208–9. The revisions Conrad made were quite substantial, and not least so at the end, where, for instance, 'the sharer of my cabin' became 'the secret sharer of my cabin' (p. 119), where important words regarding Leggatt's escape – 'to take his punishment, a free man –' (p. 119) – expanded the last sentence, and where Conrad added whole sentences and numerous phrases to enhance the description of the final manœuvre. Other revisions made earlier had already introduced new wording important to the themes and atmosphere of the tale, to clarifying action aboard ship, and to characterizing Leggatt, Captain Archbold, and the Captain–narrator through their speech. For a summary, see 'The Texts', pp. 209–13; for details see the 'Apparatus'.

nothing from Pinker himself, he must have received from his office by the morning mail the rest of the typescript and set about revising it almost instantly, for he returned the whole the next day or the following one, with a covering note to which he anxiously appended a prompt, 'For titles I suggest *The Secret Self* or *The Other Self*', and then added: 'It could be also *The Secret Sharer* but that may be too enigmatic.'[1] On the morning of the 18th, he had at last received Pinker's reply (*Letters*, IV, 304). Although all of Conrad's allusions to the new story were, at the very least, uneasy, he had utterly underestimated the effect this latest breach of his contract would have on his agent and patron, whose already massive debt on Conrad's behalf, secured by no fewer than four mortgages, would according to his accountants shortly reach the catastrophic sum of £2,702.19.9.[2]

The effect on Pinker, and thus on Conrad, of the discovery that Conrad had yet again marginalized the novel on which his firm's viability now depended can be recovered from Conrad's correspondence between 19 and 27 December. Echoes of Conrad's first reaction to Pinker's letter can be picked up in a letter to Gibbon of the following day, Sunday the 19th. He began by summarizing his productivity over the past twenty-four months – or, more exactly, sixteen months, since eight months had to be written off on grounds of illness. It came to a total of 187,000 words in all, comprising the still incomplete novel 'Razumov', which required only another 20,000 words, two long stories ('The Black Mate' and 'The Secret Sharer', as yet untitled), and the 35,000-word autobiographical manifesto which Ford's *English Review* had serialized as 'Some Reminiscences' the past year and which Eveleigh Nash and Harpers would publish in 1912 (in America as *A Personal Record*). And what was Pinker's response to that performance? – That Conrad had given him nothing to sell for two years, and that he would cut off his weekly retainer 'if he don't get the end of R. in a fortnight'. If that happened, however, Conrad would burn the autograph of 'Razumov' – an empty threat, at best.[3]

---

[1] *Letters*, IV, 300; the stroke beneath 'too' in Conrad's letter appears to be a rule dividing its paragraphs, rather than an underline, as the editors of the Cambridge *Letters* tentatively infer. Galsworthy made a rare visit to Conrad on the 17th which must have limited his work on the typescript; see 'The Texts', p. 209, n. 1. On the question of the titles, see Appendix B, 'The Titles of the Tales'.

[2] As of 9 February 1910 (see *Letters*, IV, 298, n. 5). For equivalent values, see p. xxxii, n. 1.

[3] *Letters*, IV, 301–2. Here Conrad genuinely underestimated his output not only for 'The Secret Sharer', but for his 'Reminiscences' as well, which amounted to about 42,500 words. Conrad would add just over 14,000 words to the novel by the end of January.

On the following day (Monday the 20th) Conrad fired off his response to Pinker. He vigorously defended his assiduity over 'the last $23\frac{1}{2}$ months', despite 'severe attacks of gout', and despite Pinker's contemptuous dismissal of the 'Reminiscences' (to-day regarded as one of Conrad's monuments); and he peremptorily told him, in a pointed reference to his reminder that Conrad had given him nothing to sell for two years, 'You have the story', written 'for the very purpose to ease the strain': 'Sell it' (*Letters*, IV, 303–4). This was, of course, not strictly true: 'The Secret Sharer' had demanded to be born. Two days later (Wednesday the 22nd), driven frantic by Pinker's continuing silence, Conrad sent a letter to Galsworthy with an explanation of why he had written the tale (to pay for the maid's hospital expenses) and a summary of what he had told Pinker in defence of his lapse; he then abandoned himself to an outburst of fear, rage, despair, resentment, and humiliation, pathetically concluding with: 'One must secure a certain detachment which is beyond me. I can hardly sit still' (*Letters*, IV, 305–6).

Soon after posting this letter Conrad's suspense, which during the seven days had risen to a kind of frenzy, was over. Although the letter he received from Pinker has not surfaced, it is clear from his response to it later that day that Pinker (who had surely had time to realize that nothing could be gained by ending Conrad's contract) had broached the question of where to place the new story. This abrupt fall in the emotional temperature is confirmed, though more pathetically, in a surviving letter by Conrad to his medical doctor. It discloses that he proposes to tackle at once 'the last chapters of that interminable novel', but that, since the 'only thing which lags a bit yet is the brain. It isn't steady', he would be 'grateful' for something to help him 'to more continuous working'.[1] Thus Conrad prepared himself for the last stage of the ascent of a literary summit he would not attempt again.

The compositional history of a substantial literary text must distinguish between 'immediate' and 'deep' causes. The story was propelled into existence by the coincidence of the *Daily Mail*'s request for literary sketches and the sudden illness of 'the faithful maid Nellie'.[2] These

---

[1] *Letters*, IV, 306. The doctor in question was Robert Mackintosh, a Scot with ambitions as a playwright, who practised in Barnes, West London, and whom Conrad first consulted in March 1909. See Bock, p. 209, and Janet Jellard, 'Joseph Conrad to His Doctor: Nine Unpublished Letters 1909–1921', *Conradiana*, 19 (1987), 87.

[2] See Conrad's letters to Galsworthy of 10 November and 11 December (*Letters*, IV, 285–6, 295).

two events certainly qualify as its immediate causes even though they have absolutely no bearing on the tale's meaning and merit. But there is also, as there must be, a more general if equally efficient cause without which 'The Secret Sharer' would not have come about: the visit of Captain Marris, some two-and-a-half months earlier, with its news of the success of Conrad's sea-fiction in the Malay Archipelago. Such a cause, of course, is not yet a source, for 'The Secret Sharer' does not use any of the material evoked by the voluble Marris; but it qualifies as a deep cause in that it resurrected Conrad's artistic self-confidence, which the technical and psychological demands of 'Razumov' had undermined, by associating it with his successful initiation in a profession that offers no second chance.

If, however, we attend to the actual writing of 'The Secret Sharer' we are immediately struck by an unerring fluency and control quite at variance with Conrad's usual struggle for forceful articulation. The writing of the 'Razumov' manuscript, agonizingly dragged out over a total of two years and two months and repeatedly interrupted by bouts of illness and French leave, averaged about 167 words a day; the tale of 16,400 words that interrupted the novel's final run was produced in a mere ten days of elated inspiration at roughly ten times that rate.[1] The sense of moral release perceptible in every sentence of the tale becomes a kind of *felix culpa*, for it is owed to Conrad's defection from a double burden of accountability represented by 'Razumov' – a text driven by his confrontation with the meaning of his apparent defection from a cause for which his parents had given their lives, yet also weighed down by the enormous sum his agent and patron had invested in its author. When, therefore, on about 5 December 1909 Conrad dropped 'Razumov' in order to write 'The Secret Sharer', he performed an act of defiant self-expression evident not only in its insolent plot, but also in the elated confidence of its style.[2]

It would be naive to claim, however, that this declaration of Conradian independence merely entailed a set of substitutions – of

---

[1] To Galsworthy he reported '12000 words in 10 days' (14 December); to Gibbon '10 000 or perhaps 12 000 words . . . in 10 days' (19 December); to Pinker he shrunk his transgression to '10 000 words' in '8 days' (15 December): *Letters*, IV, 296, 301, 298.

[2] The other side of this defiance is revealed in Conrad's need for moral reassurance and material help, both of which were unstintingly provided by John Galsworthy. Twice during the period when Pinker – himself desperate to recover his investment in Conrad – assumed that he was hard at work, Conrad met with Galsworthy, first in London, on 14 September (the day after Marris's visit), as he was about to resume 'Razumov', and then at Aldington, on 17 December, when he was revising 'The Secret Sharer'. See *Letters*, IV, 273, 296, 303.

intruders (Leggatt for Haldin), or of values (service at sea for individualism on land), or of outcomes (self-affirmation for self-submission).
The young Captain's achievement of command, which overrides nautical legalism, is a response to and therefore dependent on Razumov's
discovery that there are no gratuitous acts. Although 'The Secret
Sharer' is in every formal respect an independent achievement able
to yield a reading on its own terms, it remains indebted to the novel
it defies, very much as its creator, however remote his sea-voyages may
have been, could not cease to be a child of the land-locked nation
that gave him his being. This is not to say, of course, that 'The Secret
Sharer' is ultimately a mere pendant of *Under Western Eyes*. Nearly three
years later, still able to relive the elation of its composition, he himself
told his first and best mentor, Edward Garnett: 'The Secret Sharer,
between you and me, is <u>it</u>. Eh? . . . Every word fits and there's not a
single uncertain note.'[1]

A Smile of Fortune

IF THE two-week trespass of 'The Secret Sharer' and Pinker's reaction
to it significantly contributed to Conrad's breakdown at the end of
January, he owed his return to independent health to the support of
his wife and his friends, to be sure, but also to his four-month struggle
to write 'A Smile of Fortune'. The pre-history of that novella thus
becomes part of its compositional record.

Having recovered from an attack of influenza during the first week
of 1910, Conrad resumed his supply of 'Razumov' copy to Pinker. On
10 January he sent him 20 pages; on the 12th he proposed, for the first
time, to call the novel *Under Western Eyes*. On the 13th, still pleading
the effects of an attack of 'flu' for the delay, he promised to come up to
London on the 17th 'with the last pages'. On Wednesday the 19th he
cited an unexpected visitor (the scholar Sidney Colvin) as the reason
for having failed to appear two days earlier, and enclosed 'the pages
up to 1300'.[2] On the 26th, having written an astonishing fifty pages
in sixteen days, he telegraphed Pinker to announce his arrival with
the completed novel for Thursday the 27th. On that day, author and
agent, tied together by a fearful debt and divided by the existence of
'The Secret Sharer', had a furious row about which we know only that
Pinker, going for the jugular, complained that Conrad 'did not speak

[1] 5 November 1912 (*Letters*, v, 128).   [2] See *Letters*, IV, 318–20.

English to him'.[1] Conrad spent the night in London with Galsworthy, returning to Aldington the following morning in a very overwrought condition, and he collapsed on Sunday, 30 January. His doctor diagnosed 'a complete nervous breakdown' which 'has been coming on for months'.[2] The attack kept Conrad delirious and paranoiac for over a fortnight, and incapacitated until deep into April; and when it finally lapsed, he remained enfeebled for several months.

The disintegration of Conrad's relations with Pinker – his agent, paymaster, and friend – left him hugely exposed. A necessary condition for his return to health and creativity was the establishment of an alternative support system. His wife Jessie, who had always run the household, nursed him night and day and became his typist; his wealthy and generous fellow-novelist John Galsworthy opened and re-opened his purse; and Robert Garnett, the lawyer–brother of Conrad's first mentor, Edward, took over Conrad's legal and financial affairs and negotiated a new contract with Pinker.[3] A major effect of this solidarity was that on 21 June the Conrads were able to move from their cramped Aldington quarters to Capel House, a seventeenth-century farmstead near Ashford. Moreover, on 9 August, following a two-year campaign by Galsworthy, Conrad was awarded an annual Civil List pension of £100. Yet even this concerted help, indispensable as it was, would have remained insufficient without Conrad's own determination, sustained for over six months, to work himself back into creativity. The result of this effort of self-repair was not only the major revision of *Under Western Eyes*, but also the production of 'A Smile of Fortune' – a tale which might lack the explosive mastery of 'The Secret Sharer', but which by its very existence embodies a deeper understanding of the interdependence of living and writing.

At 27,700 words, 'A Smile of Fortune' is 11,300 words longer than 'The Secret Sharer', but its composition took almost four months, not ten or twelve days. The reason, of course, is that it was a work of convalescence – or, more precisely, of forced recovery, since, notwithstanding the Civil List award, Conrad's pen continued to stand between his family and penury. His initial prostration, as we have noted, lasted

---

[1] Conrad to Pinker, 23 May 1910 (*Letters*, IV, 334).
[2] Telegrams from Jessie Conrad to Pinker, 3 and 6 February 1910 (see *Letters*, IV, 321, n. 1).
[3] Conrad to Galsworthy, mid-March 1910 (*Letters*, IV, 321–2, and 321, n. 2). On 17 May he told Galsworthy that Robert Garnett was negotiating with Pinker for '3 pounds per thousand words', but 'on delivery of MS' (i.e., fair typed copy), 'since he won't have it otherwise' (*Letters*, IV, 329). On the implications of this arrangement, see 'The Texts', pp. 231–2.

six weeks. When he was finally able to write his first letter – to John Galsworthy – it was movingly to express his gratitude to him and to Robert Garnett: 'I don't know what to say to you my dearest Jack. Without you I would have perished morally and materially. I daren't ask what has been done by Robert'.[1] When, at the very end of March, he felt at last capable of undertaking a preliminary task, the 'correction' of the *Under Western Eyes* typescript, he was unable to sustain attention for more than a few minutes at a time;[2] and it was only three and a half weeks later, on 24 April, that he found himself able to give the task the concentration it required; and only on 11 May, nearly six weeks after his first attempt, that he was able to bring it to a conclusion.[3]

Several days before this minor triumph, he had intimated to Henry-Durand Davray, the French translator of *The Secret Agent*, that he would 'recuperate by the sea' for a while, adding that he planned 'Nothing technical. Dramatised experience'.[4] He meant that the merit of the story would consist in the conversion of a remembered episode of his life into narrative fiction. Writing to Galsworthy a fortnight later he was even more down-to-earth: 'I am going to begin to-morrow a short story – if the devil's in it. It's to be comical in a nautical setting and its subject is (or <u>are</u>) potatoes. Title: A Smile of Fortune'.[5]

Conrad, however, found the prospect of writing even more daunting than the task of revising, and in part re-shaping, the typescript of *Under Western Eyes*. His correspondence with Galsworthy in particular, virtually a diary of his progress, continued to betray the seriousness of his recent breakdown. Struggling to begin, he complains of periods of 'a sort of queerness'[6] and that he 'can't concentrate for more than $\frac{1}{2}$ hour at a time' (20 May); he refers to a 'relapse or check in the slow improvement' though 'the new story moves on halting a little' (27 May); then, three days later, suddenly wiping the slate clean, he exclaims: 'All that went before is a mere trial run' (31 May). After another fortnight, he is forced to confess: 'I haven't yet finished my

---

[1] Conrad to Galsworthy, inscribed 'Thursday evening' and dated by the Cambridge editors 'mid March?' 1910 (*Letters*, IV, 321–2).

[2] Conrad to Galsworthy, 31 March (*Letters*, IV, 322).

[3] Conrad to Davray, 17 May (*Letters*, IV, 324); Conrad to Galsworthy, 17 May (*Letters*, IV, 328): 'I finished the revise of Raz. on the night of Wednesday last.'

[4] 3 May (*Letters*, IV, 324–5).

[5] 17 May (*Letters*, IV, 329). On the basis of this letter, the 18th is generally taken as the date Conrad began the tale.

[6] This was probably two days after starting the tale and on the same day as the 20 May letter to Rothenstein. See *Letters*, IV, 331, n. 4.

story. It's no use worrying. What can't be can't be and there's an end of it' (18 June). But a week later, now settling into the secluded and relatively spacious Capel House, he allows himself a note of cautious optimism: 'The hot spring boils somewhere deep within. There's no doubt of that; but if uncovered nothing would come out but a little vapour – a thin mist of words' (26 June). On the same day, he confirms this glimpse of hope: 'I am still not myself . . . Not so much empty-headed as just unable to keep up any sort of mental pace . . . But I am not depressed'.[1]

At last, on 13 July, nearly two months after his first frail attempts, he was able to report a measurable achievement: 'I have 70 pp of the short story written <u>and typed</u>' he told Galsworthy; 'Mentally I am not empty – the trouble is that after an hour or so I grow confused. But that's improving since I can by an effort of will get over that queer sensation and continue at work in six cases, say out of ten' (*Letters*, IV, 347). Twenty-three days later, on 5 August, having thoroughly revised and partly rewritten those seventy pages, he informed the same correspondent, almost in the style of his former self: 'I've 14 000 words of a long short-story ready. Another 6 will finish it'.[2] And although the story would, in the event, demand as many words again before Conrad deemed it complete, his sense of returning self-possession is confirmed by his covering note to Pinker, written almost certainly by the 15th – and the first to deal with new work since the fracas: 'Herewith pp 1 to 39 roughly 9000, first half of a story, ready for <u>clean</u> copy. Great part of other half is already written but . . . I must request you to forward me against the enclosed MS £20 = half the agreed advance on short stories'.[3] The agreement referred to was, of course, the new one secured by Robert Garnett. Finally, on the 27th, he was able to tell Galsworthy that he could see the winning post: 'Another couple of thousand which I <u>must</u> do by next Monday [29 August] will end it. This will mean over 20 thou. words in two months because I did not really start till July. June's work was mere fooling . . . But I certainly can

---

[1] Conrad's letters of 20 May to 26 June 1910 – all to Galsworthy except for one of 20 May to William Rothenstein and one of 26 June to Stephen Reynolds (*Letters*, IV, 331–42).

[2] Conrad to Galsworthy, 5 August (*Letters*, IV, 354). On this complex process, see 'The Texts', pp. 234–8. In the same letter Conrad reports, with dissatisfaction, the publication of the first of two instalments of 'The Secret Sharer' in *Harper's*.

[3] Conrad to Pinker, early August (*Letters*, IV, 355). For the dating of this letter, which involves not only those of the 5th and 15th (*Letters*, IV, 359) to Galsworthy but Conrad's reviews for the *Daily Mail*, see 'The Texts', p. 235, n. 3; *Letters*, IV, 355, n. 1; and 'The Texts' in *Notes on Life and Letters*, ed. J. H. Stape with Andrew Busza (2004), p. 257.

write in this place' (*Letters*, IV, 362). And Conrad was able to be as good as his word, for he dated the finished typescript '30 Augst 1910', and his letter to Pinker of 3 September states: 'Dear Sir, I beg to acknowledge the receipt of £40 against MS *Smile of Fortune*'.[1] Pinker must have received those final pages – in fact two-thirds of the total – during the intervening days.

After an initial sterile struggle with the new tale that lasted forty-two days, during which Conrad could do nothing except try again and again to ignite his imagination, he suddenly started writing consecutively. On the informed inference that this breakthrough occurred about the beginning of July, the 27,700 words of the novella got themselves on paper in sixty days, at a daily average of just over 460 words. Indeed, this matches the speed he had achieved over the four months preceding his breakdown, when he produced the 46,000 words required to complete *Under Western Eyes* and the 16,400 words of 'The Secret Sharer' at a rate of about 420 words a day.

Conrad was back in business – except for a final hitch. In November, about two and a half months after he had sent the tale to his long-suffering agent, Pinker was able to place it with the *London Magazine* on condition that it be curtailed. Whether what its editor required was specifically that the prologue, which described the rescue of Mr Burns from an eastern hospital and the brig's voyage to Mauritius, should be eliminated or drastically reduced is not certain. Conrad's reply began by opposing any alteration for 'any person whatever' on artistic, if not ethical, grounds; but it soon modulated into conceding that the prologue might be severely shortened for serialization, despite the fact that it '"establishes" our principal character – gives his "note" as: – impressionable, impulsive, humane' in his treatment of the ailing Burns, and 'susceptible to mystery, imaginative' in his 'vision of the Island'.[2] Moreover, that letter indicates that during his convalescence Conrad had not only recovered his powers as a self-conscious artist, but also regained his diplomatic skills in placating his agent and his editor by offering them the much shorter first-draft of the prologue. Thus on the 22nd Conrad telegraphed Pinker to say that he did not 'care much for *London Magazine*' but that 'if terms allow you make it up to 55 for me' he would 'deliver altered MS by

---

[1] *Letters*, IV, 365. See 'The Texts' on the logistics involved in these circumstances.
[2] See Appendix E, 'Correspondence with the *London Magazine*', for complete transcriptions of the letters from Conrad and the editor, and 'The Texts', pp. 241–4, for a more detailed analysis of this complicated episode.

Friday'.[1] And indeed two or perhaps three days later he returned the amputated manuscript with the comment: 'I am disgusted at the silly job but what has been agreed to is performed'.[2] What he did not anticipate, however, was that nearly a century would have to pass before his final versions of the prologue and the related ending would be published.

The compositional dynamics of the second tale destined for *'Twixt Land and Sea* are not primarily reactive – as they were for 'The Secret Sharer', a story that derived its momentum, and indeed its nonconformity, from its interruption of 'Razumov' – but generative. As a study of its sources indicates (see above), 'A Smile of Fortune' is more autobiographical than its famous predecessor. It responds, of course, to Marris's invitation to return to eastern themes, though less to satisfy an eastern fan club than to resurrect an imperfect former self in order to repair a damaged present self. This attempt receives support from the tale's realism. We have noted that 'A Smile of Fortune' stands out among Conrad's eastern tales for the vividness and comprehensiveness of its depiction of Mauritius. Thus the resurrection of Conrad's 22-year-old recollections of the island and the struggle to recover his writing powers should be regarded as complementary aspects of a single-minded attempt to return to creative life.

Conrad's struggle against illness affected not only the tale's composition but also its substance. Its expanded but suppressed prologue would appear to owe little to autobiography. When Conrad joined the *Otago* in Bangkok, his first mate, a German called Born, was probably the fittest member of the ship's company. His fictional equivalent, Burns, is seriously ill, terrified to be left to die in a local hospital, and pitifully grateful to be taken on board to recover at leisure. It is difficult to believe that Conrad's wholesale alteration of the history of 1888 owes nothing to the history of 1910. His own terror and despair as he sank into delirium at the end of January 1910, and the depth of his gratitude to his wife and friends which surfaced in his first letter after his collapse (to Galsworthy in mid-March) and was still audible a month and a half later in a letter (to Davray on 3 May), where he said of Jessie 'Elle m'a soigné toute seule jour et nuit'[3] – these are *both* transposed into the relations of the Captain and the Mate, where Conrad's identification with the latter is nearly as close as with the former.

---

[1] Telegram to Pinker, 22 November (*Letters*, IV, 389).
[2] Conrad to Pinker, [24 or 25? November 1910] (*Letters*, IV, 391).
[3] 'She nursed me by herself day and night' (*Letters*, IV, 322, 324).

Conrad's breakdown invaded the writing of 'A Smile of Fortune' by other routes. The letters marking the very first stage of his recovery powerfully express the humiliation of his collapse. It is therefore unsurprising that Conrad should have covertly recalled, in planning his new story, the unforgotten mortification of his proposal of marriage in Mauritius, some twenty-one years earlier, to Eugénie Renouf, who was already engaged and indeed on the point of marrying her fiancé.[1] The shame of this self-exposure, which most of us would have learned to live with sooner rather than later but which marked him for life, reveals how deeply it had engaged his pride and his diffidence. He suppressed it from a narrative composed twenty-two years later as thoroughly as he had concealed it from everybody else – not excluding his wife, to judge by her references to the tale in her first memoir of her life with her husband, where she reports that he used to tease her for being jealous of 'Alice', the fictional and far less respectable cover for the fiasco with Eugénie.[2] But repressed feelings do not consent to lie low for ever: they returned disguised to Conrad's text twenty-two years later, in the intense moral and sexual ambiguities of the narrator's dalliance with Alice.

However, art, like memory, has its own logic. The narrative of Conrad the mature writer achieves a much more complex and self-critical response to hurt pride than Conrad the master-mariner would have been capable of. What it does is to complicate the experience of humiliation by raising the question of the lover's responsibility. At the climax of the story, the protagonist becomes aware of his role in bringing the humiliation not only on himself but also on the defenceless Alice. At thirty-two years of age Conrad was capable of shame; at fifty-two he acknowledged guilt. Guilt, of course, was far from a new experience to him – as *Under Western Eyes*, as profound an exploration of the meaning of an act of moral and political betrayal as any we possess – had recently revealed. But what was new was Conrad's confessional intimacy, which he owed to an illness that revealed to him how dependent he was on his wife and his friends for his return to life.

Finally, Conrad's illness entered the composition of 'A Smile of Fortune' through the open-handed generosity of these friends – which stands in sharpest contrast to the commercialism implicit in the tale's title. The mercantile reality which underpins the Captain's

---

[1] See above, pp. xliii, xlvi–xlvii.
[2] Jessie Conrad (1926), pp. 139–40. See 'The Texts', p. 239, for Jessie Conrad's especially intrusive alterations to this part of the text when typing it.

voyage to Mauritius and which spoils every aspect of Mauritian life for him – from its louche business and social establishments to the unreadable private agenda of the ship's chandler – turns the island into a moral maze from which in the end all he can do is to extricate himself. Just as the voyage to Mauritius had been marked by the Captain's kindness to the physically ailing Burns, so the return journey to Melbourne is defined by the grateful Burns's preservation of the rotting potato investment which Jacobus had foisted on his demoralized guest. But neither Burns's gratitude nor indeed the caprice of the Australian weather which, as the ship reaches harbour, turns the potatoes into a phenomenal bargain, is able to dissuade the Captain from resigning his commission and returning to Europe. As the full maritime context of 'A Smile of Fortune' recovered in this edition shows, Conrad's misgivings about the profit motive that drove the merchant fleets of the world could no longer be overridden or ignored. The man who in 1897 had celebrated the voyage of the *Narcissus* as transcending the 'sordid inspiration of her pilgrimage' (p. 30) was unable fourteen years later to recover that confidence. This was, of course, partly because he was now an older and sadder man; but it was also because he was recalling his life as master of a commercial vessel who, as such, was responsible not only for her navigation but for her profitability – and thus vulnerable to such temptations as trading for himself. Now that the tale's narrative framework has been fully restored, the tension between sea and land values stands disclosed, and the complexity of its moral psychology can no longer be underplayed.

Freya of the Seven Isles

CONRAD FINISHED 'A Smile of Fortune' on 30 August 1910 and started 'Freya of the Seven Isles' on or about 26 December. During the three-and-a-half intervening months he completed, as already noted (p. lxiii), two narratives – 'Prince Roman' with its *noblesse oblige* commitment to the idea of Poland, and 'The Partner', with its exposure of the criminal underside of Edwardian capitalism – which together anticipated the collision in 'Freya of the Seven Isles' of nostalgic romance and colonial realism.

Conrad was, of course, fully aware that with 'Freya of the Seven Isles' he was at last embarking on the substantial story of colonial life in the Malay Archipelago which he had promised Marris some fifteen months earlier. After his return to Penang, Marris had written to him on 11 January 1910 to report that his 'owners' (the owners of the ships he was employed to sail) had not thought him sufficiently recovered from his stroke to let him have a command.[1] By the time this letter reached him, Conrad would have been working day and night on the very last sections of 'Razumov'; and stricken by his breakdown at the end of January, he would not have been able to reply to it. Whether or not he heard again from Marris before the latter's death, which occurred some time in 1910,[2] is not known, but it is unlikely, for he preserved Marris's letters, and none dated after January has been found. However, if the evidence of 'Freya of the Seven Isles', which he apparently began to write the day after Christmas that year, can be relied on, he would by then have been in possession of the fact, for that novella's relentless inevitability is full of it. We can assume, therefore, that Conrad's promise to Marris that he and his eastern friends would receive 'more of the stories they liked'[3] was carried out, but only after Marris was no longer able to know anything about it.

Unlike several of his endlessly productive contemporaries such as John Galsworthy or H. G. Wells, Conrad did not usually start a piece of fiction with a clear idea of what the finished product would look like. His method of composition, with its large-scale alterations and end-lessly retreating horizons, meant that most of his longer pieces started life as short stories. For him writing was a form of thinking rather than a technique of articulation – which is one of the reasons why he could not keep to deadlines. So it was with 'Freya of the Seven Isles'. On 'Monday evening' (26 December 1910) Conrad told Galsworthy: 'I've begun another story and moiling over the foolish stuff I forgot the time' (*Letters*, IV, 400). Seventeen days later, on 12 January 1911, he wrote to Edward Garnett to explain why he could not read his *Joan of Arc* at once: 'The straight truth of it is that I am now writing a silly story (being near the end of it) and as soon as I am done with the truck and have got over the disgust my writing leaves behind I shall drop you a postcard asking for that play' (*Letters*, IV, 407). After another eleven days, he responded to a letter from Joseph de Smet, a Belgian priest and writer, who had asked him how he had learnt English. 'In writing

---

[1] *Portrait in Letters*, pp. 71–2.

[2] *Oxford Companion*, s.v. 'Marris'. This date was obtained from the late Hans van Marle; for a selection of his papers, see *A Joseph Conrad Archive*, ed. Gene M. Moore, *The Conradian*, 30, no. 2 (2005), esp. 126–31.

[3] Conrad to Pinker, 11 October 1909 (*Letters*, IV, 278).

I wrestle painfully with that language which I feel I do not possess but which possesses me', Conrad replied, adding: 'Pardon delay in answering but I am trying to finish a longish story' (*Letters*, IV, 409). However, sixteen days later, on 8 February, he felt able to announce to Pinker that he would be 'sending a longish story in a day or two' (*Letters*, IV, 412).

Yet with another week gone, on the 15th Conrad was still not done, as two letters written that day demonstrate. The first was a response to a note from the young American journalist Warrington Dawson alerting him to the prospect of a new Parisian magazine: Conrad assured him that he was 'putting the finishing touches to a story, (which I think I'll call *Freya of the Seven Isles*), length about 20 000 words (3 or four instalments) of which I could send her the typescript in say fortnight' (*Letters*, IV, 413). The second, in complete contrast, was addressed to Galsworthy: 'I expect to finish a longish story in a day or two – but the devil only knows. I have been fooled too often by such expectations to put my trust in them' (*Letters*, IV, 414). A couple of days later, he told Davray, translator into French of some of the best contemporary English fiction: 'I am in the process of finishing a novella (24000 words)'.[1] But it was only on the final day of February, after sixty-six days at his desk, that Conrad was able to tell Pinker: 'Herewith Freya: say 27000. Eastern seas tale – quite a novel in character and quite suitable for serialising' (*Letters*, IV, 417). In sober truth, the story had consumed something over two months. However, still smarting from Pinker's treatment of 'A Smile of Fortune', which had had its initial framing episode virtually cancelled and its final one therefore altered, Conrad was exerting pressure to ensure that his new text would remain intact: 'Whatever happens, I beg to say at once that no suggestion of alteration or curtailment will be entertained. Not a single word.'

This combative note reflects Conrad's changed relationship with Pinker which, since their quarrel, he had kept on the chilliest register. But his letters to his other correspondents, being far less guarded, expressed the full range of his authorial anxieties. They continue to reveal his inability to meet his own deadlines as he struggles to control a constantly expanding text. They also sound the usual litany of complaints about the inadequacy of his writing, and for the first time express fears of a loss of creative power. To Garnett he refers to feeling 'as if I had smashed myself' (12 January); to de Smet he complains

---

[1] *Letters*, IV, 416: 'Je suis en train de finir une nouvelle (24000 mots)'.

about being 'so tired at the end of the day' (23 January); to Symons he suspects that 'my days of fine things are done' (7 February); to Galsworthy he even invokes martyrdom: 'I had . . . no consecutive ideas, no six consecutive words to be found anywhere in the world. I would prefer a hot gridiron to that cold blankness' (15 February).[1]

Conrad had of course always felt acutely the stress of composition, partly because of his native volatility, partly because of his struggles with the English language, but mostly because of his uncompromising commitment to the demands of high art. And it is this last which comes to the surface in his two revelatory letters to Arthur Symons, mediator to the English 1890s of French *symbolisme*, who (like Conrad during the first months of the previous year) was struggling to recover from a nervous collapse which, in his case, had required a period in a mental hospital.[2] What Conrad's letters to a fellow-sufferer reveal is that his writer's anguish, far from being symptomatic of a 'Slav temperament', or merely an expression of the traumas of an infancy spent in political detention, or of the loss of a mother at the age of six and of a father at the age of eleven, was largely a product of the effort demanded by the creation of masterpieces. Even if he is right to claim that his 'days of fine things are done', he tells Symons on 7 February: still 'we must go on.' It is not success but defeat that measures resolve: 'Don't look back', he tells him on the 14th, 'for indeed the only way to overcome injustice whether of man or fate is to disregard it' (*Letters*, IV, 411, 415). On such principles 'Freya of the Seven Isles', which in so many respects seems to look back, does so in order to go forward.

The composition of 'Freya of the Seven Isles' was nourished by Conrad's relationship with its material. The integrity of the collection of tales gathered under the title *'Twixt Land and Sea* derives from the fact that they were all, in one way or another, inspired by Conrad's meeting with Marris. 'Freya of the Seven Isles', however, being the only tale of the three written after Marris's death, possesses a distinctive sub-text. This sub-text is variously present in the story, but it becomes most visible in a composite narrative structure: whereas the narrators of 'The Secret Sharer' and 'A Smile of Fortune' control the stories they tell from start to finish, the narrator of 'Freya of the Seven Isles' does not. In an action that properly belongs to old Nelson, Freya, Jasper, and

---

[1] *Letters*, IV, 407, 409, 411, 414.
[2] See Karl Beckson, *Arthur Symons: A Life* (1987), chs. 17 and 18.

Heemskirk, his sole contributions are to land a piano on Nelson's isle for Freya's use, and to assent to Jasper Allen's decision to sign on the disastrous Schultz. To be sure, both these are links in the causal chain that will destroy Jasper and Freya; but otherwise the narrator (like Conrad in his relation to Marris) remains a mere spectator or recipient of the events of the first two acts. Thereafter, he abruptly removes himself from the scene of the action to return 'home', where in the fullness of time he will become merely the auditor of the tragic finale of a story long over and done with. Should we conclude, therefore, that 'Freya of the Seven Isles' has diverted or even checked the autobiographical current which 'A Smile of Fortune', and indeed 'The Secret Sharer', sustain to the end?

Attention to the compositional dynamics of 'Freya of the Seven Isles' supports the view that it is the most autobiographical of the three tales in that it offers the most literal rendering of its author's relationship to his material. Its narrator, like Conrad, having spent some time trading between Singapore and north-east Borneo – though of course, unlike him, calling at the Seven Isles, which Conrad only by-passed – returns to England, where he loses touch with his former life in the tropics until it suddenly returns to him in the form of a letter from an old trader–mariner. This man reminds the narrator, as Marris had Conrad, of the freedom and beauty of the East. But in both instances he also reveals that he has himself been damaged: Marris exhibits the symptoms of a stroke which will kill him in under a year, old Nelson of a catastrophic bereavement that deprives him of his future.

Thus for the author, as for the narrator of this tale, the prison door of the past, having momentarily half-opened to offer a glimpse of a young and beautiful world, slams shut again. And that it will remain shut is guaranteed by the fact that the man who opened it is himself now no more. It is to the brutality of this effect, present in the story in the remorseless destruction of the young couple, that Conrad's earliest and best reader, Edward Garnett, responded when he complained of 'a certain weakness in the manipulation of the tragedy at the close', and advised Pinker to get Conrad to 'have another look at the MS'. But Conrad indignantly rejected this advice,[1] for in his new story the young lovers' fate is an expression of his most searching fears and griefs. Marris's death, to be sure, once again puts the East out of Conrad's

---

[1] *Letters*, IV, 469–70 and 470, n. 1.

reach. But it does so not only by depriving Conrad of the youthful memories Marris had reawakened: it does so because Marris revealed to him how far the East had changed behind his back, so to speak, in the course of his twenty-two years of absence.

The novella's composition was a product of the tension between Conrad's memories of the relatively unexploited and unspoilt Indonesia of the 1880s and Marris's reports (despite his loathing of England and his longing for Penang) of its modernization. It is this discontinuity that transforms the love of Freya and Jasper into a dysfunctional idyll, poisoned by a father's political neurosis and a rival's nationalistic paranoia. More generally, it opens out the story's narrative fault-line which, as noted, disjoins the first-person narrator from the third-person narrative. After the narrator's return to England, for example, Conrad does not hesitate, when describing events which his narrator could not have witnessed himself or even deduced from old Nelson's testimony, to resort to the third-person narrative, or indeed to revert to the first-person narrative when, for instance, old Nelson brings him the intolerable news of Freya's death and Jasper's ruin.

First-person narrative, of course, exhibits the voice of the self; third-person assumes impersonality and tends to project objectivity. Thus, when the gap between the two is highlighted – for example through physical distance, as when the narrator learns of the fate of the young couple 10,000 miles away – the pathos of that tragedy is deepened by a separation which increases helplessness without diminishing grief. This effect Conrad must have felt himself when he received the news of Marris's disappearance on the other side of the globe. But such effects become even more poignant when they extend over time rather than space to reveal that 'there is no greater pain than to recall past happiness in present misery'.[1] Marris's visit to Conrad reawakened, in the midst of his sedentary toil, the exhilaration of his first command. And the news of his death, which followed Conrad's own long, slow recovery from breakdown, prompted the requiem for lost youth which brings 'Twixt Land and Sea to a close.

But it did more. The juxtaposition of a remembered past with a reported present permitted Conrad to perceive these deaths as products of the commercial-imperialist rivalries now firmly installed in and

---

[1] Dante, *Inferno*, V, 121–3: 'Nessun maggior dolore, / che recordarsi del tempo felice / nella miseria.'

around the Archipelago, and which were even then beginning to rav-age and pollute a virginal world. Conrad's awareness of the threatened beauty of Indonesia is everywhere apparent in his narrator's evocation of its seas, islands, forests, and distances, especially when recalled from within the dank and stifling thickness of a London pea-souper. In this we now know that 'Freya of the Seven Isles' has proved prophetic. However, even in 1911, such warnings were not premature. In the final page of the last revised edition of Conrad's favourite bedside book, Wallace's *The Malay Archipelago* (1890), Conrad would have read – and to judge by his work read again and again – the following warning: 'And if we continue to devote our chief energies to the utilizing of our knowledge of the laws of nature with the view of still further extending our commerce and our wealth, the evils which necessarily accompany these when too eagerly pursued may increase to such gigantic dimen-sions as to be beyond our power to alleviate.'

RECEPTION

THE MANUSCRIPT OF 'The Secret Sharer' was completed by the middle of December 1909, that of 'A Smile of Fortune' by the end of August 1910, and that of 'Freya of the Seven Isles' by the end of February 1911. Pinker was able to place 'The Secret Sharer', with the subtitle 'An Episode from the Sea', in the August and September 1910 issues of New York's prestigious *Harper's Monthly Magazine*, which pub-lished on both sides of the Atlantic. After he and Conrad agreed to cuts in its prologue, the *London Magazine* brought out 'A Smile of Fortune' in February 1911. But it was only a full year later, just before its appear-ance in book form, that 'Freya of the Seven Isles' achieved magazine publication, first in New York's rather down-market *Metropolitan Mag-azine* of April 1912, and three months later in the *London Magazine* of July 1912, where it carried a dedication to 'Captain C. M. Marris'.

More than eight months after he had completed the composition of the final tale of *'Twixt Land and Sea,* Conrad told Pinker, on 10 November 1911, that he 'would very much like to have *Sharer – Smile & Freya* published in one vol', adding: 'These three stories are a set of which I am not ashamed. They have a common character – some-thing slightly different from any short stories I ever wrote' (*Letters*, IV, 503–4). Methuen would have been the natural choice for such a book: that firm had handled virtually all his work since 1906, and in 1911 they were still owed two novels. But Conrad's feeling that the projected volume represented a new departure together with his growing dissatisfaction with Methuen prompted him to seek a different publisher. Pinker therefore eventually sold the stories in London to J. M. Dent and Sons and in New York to George H. Doran, and the collection was issued on 14 October and on 3 December 1912, respectively. The volume turned out to be Conrad's first unqualified commercial success.[1] As a result, he at once sought to sever his links with Methuen, who, Conrad maintained, had failed to make him any money over the previous seven years; but, perhaps sensing a turn for the better, that firm understandably held to their legal contract, and Conrad was obliged to publish *Chance* (1914) and *Victory* (1915) with them. In the event, both those novels generated a small fortune.

In planning the volume, Conrad had briefly entertained the possibility of including 'The Partner' on the grounds that it might otherwise look a bit thin. But on 6 July 1912 he told Pinker: 'if there's enough copy I would dearly like to have the *Partner* thrown out. It doesn't match . . . Please ask Dent' (*Letters*, v, 83). Although 'The Partner' qualified as a land–sea story, it dealt with a ruffianly attempt to wreck a ship off the Somerset coast for the insurance money: as such it had nothing to do with Conrad's autobiographical East, and even less with Captain Marris, to whose visit the collection was partly indebted. The *'Twixt Land and Sea* we now possess relates its central tale of achievement of command to two surrounding narratives of resignation from command – in the 'Mauritius' tale from a sense of self-disgust, in the 'Seven Isles' tale from feelings of personal and historical irrelevance. Moreover, by dedicating the collection to the 'late' Captain Marris 'in memory of those old days of adventure', Conrad unobtrusively emphasized its underlying effect of 'family resemblance'. And, finally, by choosing as an epigraph 'a few lines' which Arthur Symons, at the time recovering from a serious breakdown, had written after reading 'Freya of the Seven Isles' ('Life is a tragic folly / Let us mock at life and be jolly . . .'), Conrad suggested to readers opening the collection for the first time that the 'affirmation' its stories propose is no more (and no less) than self-generated defiance of mortality.[2]

---

[1] For more detail on these matters, see 'The Texts', pp. 203, 280–84.
[2] See Conrad to Quinn, 29 July 1912 (*Letters*, IV, 90).

Early Reception

CONRAD'S CONFIDENCE in the artistic integrity of his new volume was vindicated by its reception in England from mid-October and in America from the end of December. As a happy augury, on the day of the book's publication in England there appeared an exceptionally perceptive review in the *Daily News* by its literary critic Robert Lynd, who was obviously taking advantage of his pre-publication review copy. Invoking 'Typhoon', Lynd identified the Conradian narrative style as 'visionary realism'. Though quieter than 'Typhoon' in its power to project the reality of the seas we know, 'The Secret Sharer' shared the intensity of such works as Coleridge's 'Ancient Mariner'. Conrad's art revealed a 'sense of life . . . far richer' than Kipling's. It showed the impersonal power of nature to be greater than the moral power at the disposal of those who have to face it, despite the 'miracles of endurance' they perform. This is the reason why Conrad's characters tend to have the quality of victims – as with 'Freya of the Seven Isles', a 'wonderful pitiless story of revenge in the Dutch East Indies', in which a man (Jasper) is struck down not by his vices but by his virtues (his generosity to Schultz). The 'intense imaginative excitement' that Conrad generates is free from melodrama or rhetoric, even at the story's climax, when 'Jasper Allen's beautiful white ship' is manœuvred by an enemy 'to its doom upon the reef where it would lie long afterwards, a grey ghost, haunting the insane eyes of its owner as he watched it from the shore'. 'A Smile of Fortune', set in tropical seas, is also 'a study of a spell cast on the captain of a ship by a mysterious outcast, shy, untamed, animal of a woman' – though it is not quite as good as 'Freya of the Seven Isles', or indeed as 'The Secret Sharer'. 'The great elation of [the latter] story', Lynd concludes, 'does not arise from its study of the psychology of fascination', or of self-identity, but in what it generates: the concluding episode, when 'the captain compels his crew, almost still with horror, to bring the ship right up under the shadow of the land ... That scene gives us one of the great thrills of modern literature'. And he concludes: 'The elation that we get from this story is the elation which all great literature, even tragic literature, ought to give.'[1] Thus, on the very day of its publication, *'Twixt Land and Sea* received its near definitive response from a Belfast-born journalist–critic who, employed between 1908 and 1947 by the *Daily News* (originally a Liberal London paper founded by Charles

[1] Lynd, *Daily News*, 14 October 1912, p. 8 (rpt *CH*, pp. 251–3).

Dickens in 1845), managed to turn out 'every week an impeccable essay . . . about anything or everything or nothing' – to cite Leonard Woolf's rather snide formulation.[1]

A sample of other English reviews confirms the critical success of Conrad's new book. John Masefield, writing for the *Manchester Guardian* of 16 October, regarded Conrad, with his 'old colours of mystery, romance, and the strangeness of life' as a master of the long story in 'A Smile of Fortune' (which he thinks re-writes 'Heart of Darkness' with Alfred Jacobus in the role of Kurtz) and in 'Freya of the Seven Isles', which begins with 'its movement rather clogged . . . until the tragedy is at its height'.[2] The anonymous reviewer in the *Times Literary Supplement* of 17 October found that the three stories are 'each a masterpiece'. On 19 October the *Athenaeum* found Conrad's stories 'tragic, vivid and penetrating', but warned readers that sometimes 'he explains too much'. The following day, the *Observer* opined that the three stories were 'as good as anything Conrad has ever written, tales as good as any man might hope to write'. The *Standard* of 25 October offered an unsigned piece which identified Conrad's originality in his blending of 'the sense of life proclaimed by the great Victorians with the sense of form discovered here in England somewhere about 1890', and declared that this 'welding' of 'vision and matter-of-fact' in the stories leaves us with a 'haunting . . . conviction that in the heart of the darkest . . . things there is a great light shining'. The *Spectator* congratulated Conrad on 16 November for throwing off the evil influence of Henry James which (it claimed) had rendered *The Secret Agent* indigestible, and for producing a collection which, mingling the 'comic and psychological', included the purely 'tragic' 'Freya of the Seven Isles', which it dubbed 'Conrad's greatest success'. And – to conclude this sample – the London *Bookman* for December 1912 announced that ' '*Twixt Land and Sea* is as good as the best of Conrad's early works in its combination of adventure and psychology: the narrator does not have to go on "a Pateresque search" for new impressions which come to him unbidden'.[3] In Britain other reviews appeared in the *Scotsman* (17 October), the *Outlook* (2 November), the *Sketch* (6 November), the

---

[1] Quoted in *The Oxford Companion to English Literature*, ed. Margaret Drabble (2000), s.v. 'Lynd, Robert Wilson'.

[2] Masefield, *Manchester Guardian*, 16 October 1912, p. 7 (rpt *CH*, pp. 254–6).

[3] *Times Literary Supplement*, 17 October 1912, p. 443; *Athenaeum*, 19 October 1912, p. 446; *Observer*, 20 October 1912, p. 5; *Standard*, 25 October 1912, p. 7 (rpt *CH*, pp. 256–8); *Spectator*, 16 November 1912, pp. 815–16 (rpt *CH*, p. 258); W. E., *Bookman*, December 1912, p. 187.

English Review (for November), the *Nation* (26 October), the *Evening Standard* (18 October), and the *Glasgow Evening News* (14 November). Reviews also surfaced in Germany in the *Zeitschrift für Französichen und Englischen Unterricht* (1914), and in France in the *Mercure de France* on 1 January 1913 (by Henry-Durand Davray, one of Conrad's literary associates).[1]

This chorus of approbation, which contained more than a hint of relief at the return of the 'traditional Conrad', was repeated at a much more leisurely pace in New York, following the issue of the American edition on 3 December. Conrad's young American admirer, Warrington Dawson, journalist and aspiring novelist, provided a review-essay on Conrad, Hardy, and Meredith for the *New York Times Review of Books* of 2 February 1913, in which he claimed that the three tales of Conrad's *'Twixt Land and Sea* 'rank with the most mature and romantic of his work', and argued that his 'principle is to unfold a tale just as we ourselves might observe it if we were thrown into intimate touch with the characters', for 'he knows that the straight line does not exist in nature'.[2] Frederick Taber Cooper, in the March issue of the *Bookman*, noted that Conrad, having written about 'nihilism and dynamite' (in *The Secret Agent*) returned to 'exotic lands and waters' with 'A Smile of Fortune' in the lead, a story that remains untouched by 'the new flamboyance' – whatever that may be. An anonymous article in the *Outlook* of 15 March 1913 identified Conrad's three 'tales of Eastern lands and waters' as the 'very best' of Conrad – better especially than his 'book-romances', spoilt by his 'tendency to involution' – the reason being that they allowed 'passion, fate, and character' to 'play their part in human life mercilessly but with exactness of truth'. In *America* (New York) of 22 March 1913, the anonymous reviewer praised the power of the stories, but in a sudden recoil of *pudeur* found Alice in 'A Smile of Fortune' 'as impossible as she is unpleasant'. In the *Nation* of 10 April 1913, another reviewer discovered that the 'odd fascination' of these stories comes from 'Mr Conrad's faculty in creating . . . the atmosphere of a strange enchantment, or a deadly fear, or an imminent catastrophe'. Finally, in June 1913 the *Review of Reviews*,

---

[1] *Scotsman*, 17 October 1912, p. 3; *Outlook*, 2 November 1912, p. 599; *Sketch*, 6 November 1912, p. xiv; Richard Curle, *English Review*, 11 (1912), 668–9; *Nation*, 26 October 1912, pp. 187–8; *Evening Standard*, 18 October 1912, p. 11; *Glasgow Evening News*, 14 November 1912, p. 2; Julie Sotteck, *Zeitschrift für Französichen und Englischen Unterricht*, 13 (1914), 180; *Mercure de France*, 101 (1913), 208. Theodore G. Ehrsam, *A Bibliography of Joseph Conrad* (1969), p. 318, reports other notices, including one in *Das Literatur* not verified.

[2] Dawson, *New York Times Review of Books*, 2 February 1913, p. 51.

still from New York, ushered Conrad into immortality by announcing
that the three tales have a 'delicacy and truth' that 'rivals Dickens and
Thackeray'.[1]

If the American reviews exhibited a rather dispiriting sameness of
approval, it is perhaps because they perforce appeared by up to six
months after the English chorus of marginally livelier and more eccentric praise.[2] But on both sides of the Atlantic, responses to *'Twixt Land
and Sea* added up to a statement that the unremunerative *succès d'estime*
that had been Conrad's fate throughout his middle career was now
over. On 11 February Conrad told Pinker that 'Dent without lying
advtis¹' had 'managed to sell nearly 5000 copies of a vol of Short Stories
in something under six months' (*Letters*, v, 348); and there is no reason
to believe that the volume fared less well under its American imprint.
Moreover, although the majority verdict was that the stories owed their
success to Conrad's reversion to his earlier mode of sea adventure, two
of them, 'A Smile of Fortune' and 'Freya of the Seven Isles', contained enough cultural and political ballast to require contemporary
readers to confront their views of their own world. For that matter,
so would Conrad's next full-scale novel, *Chance*, which by mixing land
and sea in the story of the conflict between an Edwardian capitalist
swindler, the 'Great de Barral', and an other-worldly merchant-navy
captain, Anthony, over the possession of the emotionally and socially
orphaned Flora de Barral, decisively turned Conrad into an international celebrity.

Critical Reception

THE INITIAL and popular reception of *'Twixt Land and Sea* was followed by about three decades of critical neglect.[3] During that period,

---

[1] Cooper, *Bookman*, March 1913, p. 85; *Outlook*, 15 March 1913, p. 596; *America*, 22 March
1913, p. 571; H. W. Boynton, *Nation*, 10 April 1913, pp. 360–61; *Review of Reviews*, June 1913,
pp. 762–3.

[2] Other American reviews included those in the *Chicago Evening Post*, 27 June 1913, p. 8; the
Critic, January 1913, pp. 57–8; the *Boston Evening Transcript*, 29 January 1913, p. 22; the
New-York Tribune, 8 February 1913, p. 12; the *Newark Evening News*, 15 March 1913, p. 26;
the *Springfield Republican*, 20 February 1913, p. 5; *Current Opinion*, January 1913, pp. 57–8;
McClure's Magazine, May 1913, p. 212; *Publishers' Weekly*, 15 February 1913, p. 563; also the
Canadian Magazine, July 1913, p. 319.

[3] For comprehensive and selective lists as well as critical surveys, please see, in addition
to Ehrsam (cited above), Bruce E. Teets and Helmet E. Gerber, *Joseph Conrad: An Annotated Bibliography of Writings About Him* (1971), rev. edn; Teets, *Joseph Conrad: An Annotated
Bibliography* (1990), which concludes with the year 1975; Owen Knowles, *An Annotated Critical
Bibliography of Joseph Conrad* (1992); *Oxford Companion*, p. 376.

to judge by the number of prestige and popular editions of his work that appeared, Conrad continued to be read variously and widely, though without yet having acquired the *cachet* of election to the 'great tradition'. In the wake of the astounding commercial success of *Chance*, which dwarfed even that of '*Twixt Land and Sea*, critical discussion tended to focus on Conrad's novels and either to ignore or, at best, make only brief mention or use of his shorter fiction. To be sure, Richard Curle's appreciative survey (1914), which soon followed his 1912 review of the volume, gave its tales frequent and sometimes sustained attention; identified an 'underworld', an 'undertone', an 'undercurrent' throughout the collection; often cited the stories (especially the first and last) in its attempt to portray the general nature of Conrad's achievement; and found 'Freya of the Seven Isles' Conrad's 'most painful' work, 'The Secret Sharer' absolutely compelling, and 'A Smile of Fortune' the best example of 'the close-knit fabric of his later style', a point that he illustrated by quoting several pages from the Captain's first encounter with Alfred Jacobus. But the tales' almost total absence from Wilson Follett's otherwise penetrating and judicious study (1916) presaged the silence that would increasingly greet them for the next twenty-five years, despite the public stature Conrad had attained by the middle of the next decade.[1]

In the 1940s, however, three major scholarly studies, one historical, the other two primarily critical, appeared. The first was John Dozier Gordan's majestic investigation of the sources of Conrad's early fiction (1940), which established Conrad's reliance on lived and historical experience. The next year brought Muriel Bradbrook's ambitious survey of Conrad's work, which argued his particular relevance in a world again at war, posited a career of three periods ('The Wonders of the Deep', 'The Hollow Men', and 'Recollections in Tranquility'), and traced common themes and different styles through these periods. While focussing chiefly on *Nostromo*, *The Secret Agent*, *Chance*, and *Victory*

---

[1] Curle, *Joseph Conrad: A Study* (1914), esp. pp. 61–3, 129, 188–93; Follett, *Joseph Conrad: A Short Study of His Intellectual and Emotional Attitude Toward His Work and of the Chief Characteristics of His Novels* (1915). For brief notices, see Gustav Morf, *The Polish Heritage of Joseph Conrad* (1930), who mentions 'The Secret Sharer' in his discussion of *Lord Jim* (p. 157); Hugh Walpole, *Joseph Conrad* (1916); V. Walpole, *Conrad's Method: Some Formal Aspects* (1930); and R. L. Mégroz, *Joseph Conrad's Mind and Method: A Study of Personality in Art* (1931), who associates, as John Masefield had earlier, 'A Smile of Fortune' with 'Heart of Darkness' (p. 127). The tales went utterly unmentioned in William Lyon Phelps's *The Advance of the English Novel* (1916), H. L. Mencken's *A Book of Prefaces* (1917), Percy Lubbock's *The Craft of Fiction* (1921), and Edward Crankshaw's *Joseph Conrad: Some Aspects of the Art of the Novel* (1936).

as representing Conrad's second and more ironic phase, Bradbrook found that the first and last stories of *'Twixt Land and Sea* exhibited the same sceptical and pessimistic vision as the novels and, like his other stories, brought the reader closer to Conrad the man than they did. 'Freya of the Seven Isles' is not only 'painful', but depicts 'helpless, fixed, unmitigated suffering'; the 'resentful, savage and pathetic Alice' in 'A Smile of Fortune' does not 'belong to the . . . world' of 'the captain and her papa'. On the other hand, 'The Secret Sharer' is more like the stories of Conrad's 'early days', to which his 'best stories' belong; it succeeds 'consummately' and is 'the perfected version' of the enlarged tale that became *Lord Jim*, though 'cooler, terser, yet with far more of pity and terror'.[1]

The third groundbreaking book of this decade was F. R. Leavis's classic *The Great Tradition* (1948), which confirmed Conrad as one of the masters of the English novel. Leavis's subsequent essay on 'The Secret Sharer', given as a lecture at the University of York as late as 1966 and published in 1967, belongs, intellectually, to that earlier phase and may be regarded as representative of it. In Leavis' view, what 'the great security of the sea' delivers is the shock of 'a headless body' resolving itself into a fugitive representing an 'unsupported individual defiance of code and law and precedent and all decision by the book'. The young untested Captain who hides this figure in his cabin has no guilt feelings: both men are possessed by a rational conviction strong enough to forgo codes and to defy legalism. What the tale rejects is 'sheltering convention and routine discipline'. This represents a critique of the romantic view of sea life indulged by the Captain before Leggatt's advent. It is the Captain who passes on to us the 'terrible immediacy' of the tempest during which Leggatt's so-called crime takes place. Archbold is narrowly correct but odious in locking up Leggatt. By virtue of their wrongness, failure, and paralysis during the emergency, Archbold and his crew hate Leggatt for the very 'rightness', 'decision', and 'adequacy' to which they owe their lives. The young Captain's own officers and crew identify with Archbold – hence the agonizing drama of the concealment. For Leavis 'creative action, collaborative though it must be, depends upon creative individuals and creative will'. Thus in spite of his *Conway* training, or because of his 'trained readiness', the

---

[1] Gordan, *Joseph Conrad: The Making of a Novelist* (1940); M. C. Bradbrook, *Joseph Conrad (Józef Teodor Konrad Nałęcz Korzeniowski): Poland's English Genius* (1941), esp. pp. 25, 31, 32, 36, 38.

young Captain reacts independently of its explicit ethos in protecting the fugitive and even endangering his ship to release his double.[1]

This reading, despite its moments of insistence and oversimplification, is more in tune with the elementary thrust of Conrad's inspiration than the abstract intellectualism of a good deal of the commentary that has followed it. But it may also be partly responsible for the tone of intransigent moralism that marks a surprising number of the critical essays that ensued. And in its exclusive emphasis on 'The Secret Sharer' it also anticipated one of the more regrettable features of the subsequent reception of 'Twixt Land and Sea: the relative critical neglect of 'A Smile of Fortune' and 'Freya of the Seven Isles' – tales which may not possess the glamorous intensity of 'The Secret Sharer' but which remain characteristically Conradian in their representation of lived experience within a fully realized social, economic, and political environment. As a result of the enormous prestige 'The Secret Sharer' attained, which has extended beyond academic circles to its adaptation as a Hollywood film starring James Mason (1952),[2] the three tales have not been discussed as parts of a rationally conceived collection, even in the two critical books on Conrad's shorter fiction that have so far appeared: Lawrence Graver's *Conrad's Short Fiction* (1969) and Daphna Erdinast-Vulcan's *The Strange Short Fiction of Joseph Conrad* (1999). Any attempt, therefore, to provide a summary account of the later reception of 'Twixt Land and Sea is obliged to take the tales separately.

A Smile of Fortune

ALTHOUGH Conrad agreed to reduce his frame narrative in order to meet the demands of the *London Magazine*, he was, as he told Pinker, 'disgusted at the silly job' (*Letters*, IV, 391). Yet he remained confident about the tale's quality. To Galsworthy, he described it as 'a good short serial' for which there would be 'a market' (*Letters*, IV, 362). Moreover, after its publication in 'Twixt Land and Sea, he was distressed by reviews that referred to Alice as 'a wild girl of the tropics' who inspired 'crude

---

[1] Leavis, *Anna Karenina and Other Essays* (1967), pp. 111–20.

[2] The early 1950s saw two productions of 'The Secret Sharer', this one distributed by RKO, and another in 1950 for television by the BBC; subsequent film productions included two more of 'The Secret Sharer' (Italian, French) in 1967, one of 'Freya of the Seven Isles' (Polish) in 1968, one of each of the stories in 1972 – of 'A Smile of Fortune' and 'Freya of the Seven Isles' for French–Italian–German television, of 'The Secret Sharer' for American schools – and another of 'The Secret Sharer' (French) in 1988. See Gene M. Moore, ed., *Conrad on Film* (1997), pp. 232–46.

animal passion' (the *Telegraph*) or who appeared to be an 'untamed animal of a woman' (the *Daily News*), pleading that he 'had tried to make her pathetic'.[1] Even if one reviewer (the maverick John Masefield) compared the tale to 'Heart of Darkness' and another described the three stories as 'each a masterpiece',[2] these references to Alice anticipated the mixed reception it would have from academic critics. Like 'Freya of the Seven Isles', 'A Smile of Fortune' has been so overshadowed by the glamour of 'The Secret Sharer' that it has had difficulty attracting the critical attention and thorough analysis it merits.

Many of the early studies, mesmerized by the Captain's dealings with Alice, disconnected this core episode not only from the rest of his experience of Mauritius – including his participation in the child's funeral, his encounter with the rich and nasty Ernest Jacobus, his introduction to some of the old colonial families, and his evocation of the island and its peoples – but also from his sea-voyages to and from the island, textually incomplete as these have been. Thomas Moser's 1957 book was the earliest, and remains the best-known, treatment of the thesis that after Conrad's breakdown, provoked by his two-year struggle with *Under Western Eyes* and brought on by the debacle of 'The Secret Sharer', he disastrously committed himself to the theme of sexual love. Yet Moser's verdict on the first such alleged failure – a tale which he reduced to the scenes between the Captain and Alice – was that 'Whatever Conrad's intention, he wrote in "A Smile of Fortune" a first-rate story of female sexuality and male impotence', though Moser's reasons for rating it so highly were not entirely clear. For Albert J. Guerard (1958), who also remained fixed on the scenes of moody dalliance in Jacobus' garden, the tale was much more ambivalent – to the point, indeed, of requiring him to invoke Conrad's failed proposal of marriage to Eugénie Renouf in order to support his hypothesis that the tale may 'represent a subtle form of revenge on life', since in the narrative it is the Captain who eventually repudiates Alice, and not the other way round. The story betrays Conrad's – and not the Captain's – 'clumsiness and evasion' in approaching the subject of sexual attraction. Its narrative picks up energy as soon as 'the slovenly and crouching Alice appears' and seizes the Captain's attention. However, for Guerard this attention 'could hardly be more voyeuristic'. When the Captain finally brings himself to make a sexual advance, he is prompted by her relief at being told

[1] *Daily Telegraph*, 16 October 1912, p. 16; Lynd, p. 8; Conrad to Galsworthy, 28 October 1912? (*Letters*, V, 121, 122).

[2] See above, p. lxxxvii.

that his visits to her have nothing to do with her father. Recalling the events that immediately follow, Guerard concludes: 'What the scene rather brilliantly dramatizes is a voyeuristic impotence and the . . . collapse of desire'.[1]

Osborn Andreas' discussion the next year (1959) dismissed the tale as offering little more than the story of 'a young captain's tendency to look with favor upon a boycotted family', which 'misleads him into biassed support of a man whose unsuitable daughter he nearly marries'.[2] The inadequacy of this view can stand as representing what is still a common response to it. Yet at about the same time the ever-alert Jocelyn Baines (1960) had a rather more positive response to 'A Smile of Fortune', a 'haunting' if not altogether successful story in which Alice might be part of a commercial transaction. Her father 'hopes to palm off Alice on the Captain, but he also wants to sell him a cargo of potatoes, and it is sometimes not quite clear whether he is using Alice as bait for the potatoes or the reverse'. The Captain's eventual acceptance of the unsavoury cargo is a sign of his own corruption: his uncandid behaviour towards Alice has deprived him of the will to resist her father's pressure. However, despite recognizing Conrad's psychological acuity, Baines concluded that it is doubtful whether Conrad realized 'how reprehensible he had made the conduct of the Captain appear'.[3]

Several years later Paul Kirschner (1966) regarded the tale as initiating Conrad's final phase, which (except for *The Shadow-Line*) he confined to 'the relationship between men and women'. Largely ignoring the maritime and Mauritian contexts, Kirschner too focussed on the Captain's relations with Alice. Her isolation and helplessness awaken in him not compassion but curiosity and covert desire. Her father behaves like a procurer, though it remains unclear whether he regards the potatoes as bait for the girl or the girl as bait for the potatoes. What is plain, however, is that the Captain shows little interest in her as a human being – which accounts for criticism's equivocal responses to the story. Kirschner was the first to have noted the extent of Conrad's dependence on Maupassant's 'Les Sœurs Rondoli' in the Alice episodes, and his analysis of this material is of exceptional value. He perceives a 'current of desolation' behind Maupassant's 'amoral cheerfulness',

[1] Moser, *Conrad: Achievement and Decline* (1957), pp. 52–3; Guerard, *Conrad The Novelist* (1958), pp. 52–4.

[2] Andreas, *Joseph Conrad: A Study in Nonconformity* (1959), pp. 134–44.

[3] Baines, *Joseph Conrad: A Critical Biography* (1960), pp. 374–5.

and he seeks to persuade us that Conrad did so, too. However, this view leads him to regard Conrad's story as an 'uneasy hybrid of personal experience and derivative experience',[1] though in making a case for Conrad's adaptation of material from Maupassant, he has also implicitly made one for an encounter of minds between the two writers.

By this time wider perspectives on the tale had begun to appear. As early as 1964 Jerome Zuckerman had sensed that the story deserved to be regarded as an organized whole. He recognized that it sought to juxtapose 'two themes in contrapuntal structure: a central love theme involving the protagonist–captain and Alice Jacobus, and a subordinate rule theme involving the protagonist-captain and his crew. The difficulty is', he argued, 'that the treatment of the rule theme seems sketchy and inadequately developed'. Pursuing an impressive insight based on the drastically abbreviated prologue available to him, he found that 'the rule situation implies in the last pages a counterpointed background emphasizing the protagonist's dual failure.'[2] This qualified perceptiveness he owed to his assumption that a full reading required the inclusion of all the tale's elements, not just its flawed idyll in a tropical garden. Yet, a few years on, Lawrence Graver (1969) was assuming that because the tale was written during Conrad's convalescence, it 'did not engage his full attention' – nor (he adds) did its two immediate successors, 'Prince Roman' (now regarded by many as a memorable and moving evocation of family piety) and 'The Partner' (an experimental study of the underside of Edwardian capitalism). Unsurprisingly, therefore, Graver thought that Conrad's alleged determination not to test the Captain's courage at sea (Conrad's *métier*) but to describe his sexual prowess and business skills on land made the tale 'fatally' self-divided and market-directed. The disreputable chandler uses his nubile daughter to trap the Captain into purchasing a cargo of rotting potatoes which realizes a poisoned profit on his return to Melbourne. Despite the Captain's alleged 'obtuseness' of observation, Graver found the comedy of the pre-Alice scenes successful. As for Alice, her 'mysteries' are 'exaggerated beyond credibility', and the Captain's indulgence of his 'secret vice' for her

[1] Kirschner, 'Conrad and Maupassant: Moral Solitude and "A Smile of Fortune"', *A Review of English Literature*, 7 (1966), 62–77, superseded by his *Conrad: The Psychologist as Artist* (1968), pp. 136–9.

[2] Zuckerman, '"A Smile of Fortune": Conrad's Interesting Failure', *Studies in Short Fiction*, 1 (1964), 99–102. Zuckerman cited the Dent collected (i.e., the first state of the Doubleday collected) text.

(a replication, apparently, of her father's debased passion for her circus-performer mother) remains unexplored. Conrad allows himself to be distracted from his satirical treatment of the Mauritians by his determination to create a marketable story. Since 'impotence, voyeurism, and the enervating power of sexual desire' were hardly fit for the *London Magazine,* he shied away from the dark undercurrents of the tale in order to remain with 'the more convivial aspects of realism and romance' – respectively, the potato deal and the 'stormy interlude with Alice'.[1]

Six years later, on the other hand, William Lafferty (1975) offered a well-sustained and suggestive interpretation built on the conflicting duties of a merchant-marine captain divided, as he has to be, between sailing his ship and selling his cargo. The voyage to Mauritius brings this tension to a head because the whole of Mauritian society is directly or indirectly driven by the profit motive. Using (some might think overusing) the story of the Biblical Jacob in his interpretation of the Jacobus brothers, Lafferty claimed that the Captain eventually resigns his commission from self-disgust at his obligatory collusion with commerce. But of course the story is more ambiguous than this implies. The relentlessly commercial ship-chandler Jacobus is also a romantic, who once pursued a *grande passion* to South Africa and beyond, who acknowledged the entirely uncommercial infant daughter it had brought him, and who did not flinch before the inflexible social outrage that her very existence in the island provoked.[2] Thus the Captain's infatuation with Alice is as much a product of her father's reckless romanticism as of his commercial cunning.

The early 1980s saw quite different views of the tale presented in books by well-known Conradian scholars. Daniel R. Schwarz (1982) presented the tale as a 'dramatic monologue in which the speaker's tormented conscience reveals a version of events different from the one he is telling'. He rightly worried about the Captain's malcontentment, not to say his cynicism, about the whole of his island experience, nourished as it is by an unholy alliance between romance and commerce – announced by the beauty of the approach to the island and revealed by the nastiness of life on it. However, while Schwarz was reaching the not entirely anticipated conclusion that the tale

---

[1] Graver, pp. 158–63. There is no evidence, of course, and some to the contrary, that Conrad had written the story with the *London Magazine* in mind. See pp. lxxv–lxxvi, 242.

[2] Lafferty, 'Conrad's "A Smile of Fortune": The Moral Threat of Commerce', *Conradiana,* 7 (1975), 63–74.

forces us to listen to 'the confessions of a disturbed young man who
has become obsessed with an even more disturbed young woman',[1]
Cedric Watts (1984) was abruptly hoisting the critical debate to a new
level. He regarded the tale as the intercalation of an overt narrative
and a covert plot. The first consists of 'a sea-captain's sexual infatuation . . . which leads to an unsavoury business transaction'. Within
this, however, simmers a second plot in which the Captain 'is gradually
decoyed into an ambush from which he extricates himself awkwardly
and feels sullied'. The tempter Jacobus, father of the girl who is used
as bait, is therefore a 'procurer' twice over – of sexual gratifications
and of commercial supplies. Additionally the tale offers two enigmas:
on the one hand, the contrast between a sea-captain obliged to bury
his newly born daughter and an old master-mariner grieving for the
loss of his ship's figurehead; and, on the other hand, a succession of
social, moral, and economic contrasts between the brothers Alfred
and Ernest Jacobus. Moreover, throughout its prevailingly naturalis-
tic narrative, the tale evokes 'glints and half-echoes of ancient myths'
(Sleeping Beauty, Cinderella, Pandarus, Calypso, Circe) distorted par-
odically. These create a blurred counterpoint of legends *not quite* transformed into the sordid reality of island life – and which could be said
to represent another kind of covert plot. Be that as it may, the following year, relinquishing 'Sleeping Beauty' *et al.*, Watts returned to
several of the more puzzling incidents, including the funeral, which
he then treated as interlinking one captain's grief at the loss of his
new-born child with another's prostration at the loss of his ship's figurehead, as complicating the distinction between right and wrong
feeling, and as a preparing for the much more elaborate ambiguities
of Alfred Jacobus' treatment of his daughter.[2] Although Watts ignored
the mutilated maritime frame-plot, and thus lost a significant further
ambiguity (sea-service as commercial service), the inclusiveness and
originality of his analysis, driven home by the clarity of his style, represented a significant contribution to the recovery of the tale's artistic
status.

Two substantial studies have revisited 'A Smile of Fortune' in the
last decade of the twentieth century. Yves Hervouet's re-examination
of the tale's dependence on Maupassant, in his phenomenal conspec-
tus of Conrad's indebtedness to French nineteenth-century literature,

---

[1] Schwarz, *Conrad: The Later Fiction* (1982), pp. 10–18.
[2] Watts, *The Deceptive Text: An Introduction to Covert Plots* (1984), pp. 125–32; 'The Narrative
Enigma of Conrad's "A Smile of Fortune"', *Conradiana*, 17 (1985), 131–6.

posthumously published (1990), has offered a further account of Conrad's debt to Maupassant's 'Les Soeurs Rondoli', to be sure, but also to Baudelaire and the French 'symbolistes'. The intensity and scale of Hervouet's research, however, may have slightly inhibited his account of the use Conrad made of these sources. In his view the Maupassant material shows up Conrad's puritanical voyeurism, which is a poor substitute for the sexual state-of-nature that, Maupassant roguishly implies, reigns over the happy populations of Southern France and Northern Italy.[1]

Finally, Daphna Erdinast-Vulcan's classy and ambitious chapter 'The Romantic Paradox' in her book on the shorter fiction (1999) shows that the tale has not remained immune to theoretically sophisticated readings. She takes Conrad's phrase 'the romantic feeling for reality' not to signify what it seems to mean (that 'romantic feeling' can enhance the perception of reality), but to signal an 'ideological tension . . . which lies at the core of Romanticism'. Thus Conrad's tale should not be regarded as a dramatization of experience, whether remembered or imagined, but as possessing a 'thematic core', which is 'the relation . . . of truth to fiction', and which assumes the form of an 'oscillation' between the affirmation that 'the word' has the power 'to create a world' and the recognition that this world is 'fictitious'. Out of this not altogether unfamiliar if paradoxical scenario, the magic plot of Shakespeare's *The Tempest* emerges as the sub-text of the tale, but inverted: the creepy Alfred Jacobus occupies the role of Prospero, the island's squalid business world fills the space of Prospero's magic isle, the 'Pearl of the Ocean' declines into a cash nexus unknown to or at least unrecognized in Shakespeare's sanitary play, and – to switch sources, or precedents – the fairy-tale Cinderella's slipper, far from winning the maiden a prince, triggers a rejection by a pusillanimous voyeur. Deeper analysis discloses that 'the idiom of romance and fairy tale' has been 'predicated on the self-proclaimed fictionality of the genre'. Thus all we are left with is the realization that reality may be 'a mere story that we cast ourselves into' and that 'the only liberty given to us is that of choosing between alternative texts'.[2] Whether or not this is Conrad's scenario, it is a bleak prospect indeed.

---

[1] Hervouet, *The French Face of Joseph Conrad* (1990), pp. 112–18. The knowing Maupassant published 'Les Soeurs Rondoli' in a raffish Parisian men's magazine.

[2] Erdinast-Vulcan, pp. 128–52; see her earlier '"A Smile of Fortune" and the Romantic Paradox', *The Conradian*, 15, no. 1 (1990), 1–11 (rpt *CA*, III, 266–73).

The Secret Sharer

THE CRITICAL attention lavished on 'The Secret Sharer' has been such that any attempt to deal chronologically with it would quickly become intolerable even to the most hardened reader of academic writing. It also means that coverage cannot hope to be complete. Indeed, wide-ranging as it is, the survey that follows does not cover the entire field in English and excludes articles, several very distinguished, written in French, German, Polish, and Italian. Even so, what remains is so extensive that in the interests of coherence and readability it must be loosely divided into what may be called categories of convenience.

NEW CRITICAL READINGS. The essays in this general category assume that the meaning of a text is determined less by cultural and biographical antecedents than by the formal organization of its material, whether moral, symbolic, thematic, or psychological. Robert W. Stallman's 1949 article is a classic of the kind. Quoting Conrad's warning to Arnold Bennett against mere documentation, Stallman raises two crucial questions. Why does the Captain risk his ship for *that* stranger? And why must he take his vessel so close to the land in order to release him? The answers are that Leggatt's self-possession and courage offer an inspiring challenge, and that the Captain needs to catch the land breezes in order to escape from the prevailing calm. For Stallman the two coincide: Leggatt presents the Captain with his utmost test as a man, which is also his initiation into professional command. Hence Stallman concludes, in a characteristically New-Critical move, that the 'situation' between the Captain and his secret sharer corresponds to that between the artist and his work – which of course effaces any possible contradiction between Conrad the master-mariner and Conrad the master-novelist.[1] Stallman's essay received support from

---

[1] Stallman, 'Conrad and "The Secret Sharer"', *Accent*, 9 (1949), 131–43 (rpt *CA*, III, 274–84). About ten years later, in a collection of essays, Stallman added a note resisting the view that Leggatt the fugitive is a 'failure' – an issue that had exercised and would continue to exercise criticism. He insisted that while Leggatt saves the *Sephora*, Archbold, his judge and prosecutor, is the embodiment of a pusillanimous and hollow authority. Deepening the psychological analysis, Stallman argued that the Captain's commitment is to 'the outer and conscious life of the ship and crew', whereas his other self, because guilty, must remain hidden, and has to be finally distanced. Command requires self-knowledge, especially of one's illegal self: Archbold is an instance of what the effects of a lack of such knowledge, both during and after the crisis, can be. See Robert W. Stallman, ed., *The Art of Joseph Conrad: A Critical Symposium* (1960), pp. 285–8.

Walter F. Wright (1949), who argued that the new Captain's feeling
of distance and even alienation from his men makes him specially
responsive to Leggatt's predicament; and that it is this very response,
ultimately expressed in the gift of his hat to Leggatt as he prepares to
disappear into Cambodia, that restores him to his ship. Thus the motif
of the good deed saving the doer, which is as old as the New Testament,
retains its potency even when it appears in a wholly secular context.[1]

In a brief common-sense account of the tale a few years later Douglas
Hewitt (1952) claimed that the presence of Leggatt on board is 'nightmarish', not because it makes the Captain aware of his own wrongness
but because 'the relation between them is . . . an objective correlative
of such knowledge'. It is only when 'strangeness' – the awareness of
doubling – has been expelled that 'normality is restored'. Neat as it is,
the simplicity of this diagnosis did not rise to the demands of Conrad's
narrative, though it might in part explain the success Hewitt's popular
book had. Like Hewitt, Carl Benson (1954) excised Archbold from the
narrative, concluding that the tale fails to realize the 'commonalities'
that are the point of *The Shadow-Line*, though it teaches us that in the
end the Captain has been brought 'a little nearer to a realization of
his communal duties than he was at the outset'.[2]

At the same time Marvin Mudrick (1954) was approaching the narrative in standard New-Critical terms 'as a made object discontinuous with but analogous to life and the world'. On that basis 'The
Secret Sharer' becomes an exception to what Mudrick is pleased to
call 'Conrad's bargain-basement fatalism' and his 'moral and meta-
physical . . . melodrama'. For Mudrick, Conrad's 'ghostly double' does
not 'anticipate psycho-analysis, but vulgarises it'. Similar judgemen-
talism marked Thomas Moser's otherwise distinguished and influential book (1957), which succinctly argued that despite its date
'The Secret Sharer' belongs not to Conrad's declining phase, but to
his 'early period'. The Captain allows evil to enter the ship in the
person of Leggatt. His subsequent actions proclaim his inadequacy,
and he loses the confidence of his men. 'Evil' is thus represented
by an officer who has straggled from the ranks. Leggatt, 'a patient,
unmoved convict', rightly looks the part; his slaying of the sailor, a

[1] Wright, *Romance and Tragedy in Joseph Conrad* (1949), pp. 48–50, 112–13.
[2] Hewitt, *Conrad: A Reassessment* (1952), pp. 70–79; Benson, 'Conrad's Two Stories of Initiation', *PMLA*, 69 (1954), 46–56.

deed which the Captain endorses, reveals that 'dark powers lurk within us all'.[1]

In 1962, Bruce Harkness edited a classroom text and critical compendium that gathered together some of the best interpretative and contextual research available at that date. It included an essay co-authored with Royal A. Gettmann which argued that the tale's psychological issue (the Captain's feeling of identity with the fugitive) had been well understood by criticism, but that the moral issue of the Captain's illegal sheltering of Leggatt had received at best cavalier treatment. The essay claimed, against Mudrick and others, that Leggatt's action requires subtle treatment in that although, without intending murder, he possesses a streak of violence, this entails a quality that makes the saving of the *Sephora* possible. The story's alleged principal source (the arrest and escape of the *Cutty Sark*'s mate following the killing of a sailor) is no such thing, for the story takes off where the 'source' ends. Conrad's is an inward problem of psychology and morality. If there *is* a psychology, it is one that only moral beings could possess; hence the Captain takes Leggatt in rather than arrests him. The essay makes a powerful case against easy moralism, noting as a counter-example that Heyst's helpless incapacity to confront violence in *Victory* is subtly complicit with the carnage that concludes that novel. In the same compendium, Daniel Curley's 'Legate of the Ideal' offered a judicious reading of the tale's sources in order to acknowledge that Conrad does not present Leggatt as 'a murderous ruffian', but uses him to expose the distinctions between the legal and moral aspects of a crime. Conrad brings Leggatt on board the new Captain's vessel in order to show that a master-mariner's legal responsibilities to his ship and its crew do not neatly overlap with his moral responsibilities for them. Thus an analysis that seeks to do justice to Conrad's nuanced intelligibility is able to argue that the tale ends in a balancing act which acknowledges the element of luck in both Leggatt's recovery of liberty and the Captain's achievement of authority – the two men being differentiated from Archbold, who champions moralistic legalism not out of conviction but from a self-deception born of too easy a career at sea.[2]

---

[1] Mudrick, 'Conrad and the Terms of Modern Criticism', *Hudson Review*, 7 (1954), 419–26; Moser, pp. 138–40.

[2] Royal A. Gettmann and Bruce Harkness, 'Morality and Psychology in "The Secret Sharer"', and Daniel Curley, 'Legate of the Ideal', in *Conrad's Secret Sharer and the Critics*, ed. Bruce Harkness (1962), pp. 125–32, 75–82.

That same year Charles G. Hofthiann (1962) proposed a brief, straightforward three-part analysis. The first part of the story establishes 'the subjective point of view' (the Captain's alleged 'land-consciousness' evoked by the impressionism of the opening description); the second part unfolds the 'objectification of self through identification with Leggatt' which leads to self-recognition; and the third enacts a test of 'the Captain's mastery of his ship and his self'. In this psycho-allegory Leggatt's services can be dispensed with once the Captain's 'self-knowledge' is achieved. His 'second-self' is an externalization of the point of view that permits the Captain to graduate from self-doubt to self-knowledge.[1] Similarly, Porter Williams, Jr (1964), while acknowledging that the Captain realizes Leggatt's emotional dependence on him must be broken for Leggatt's sake, promptly kept the vein of complacent moralizing alive and well. 'It was a matter of conscience', Williams claims, to give Leggatt 'a compelling demonstration of absolute understanding and sympathy by indulging an act of supreme daring', in order to convince the fugitive of 'the sincerity of [the Captain's] moral support' as he prepares to shed him. Leggatt has to be forced off the ship because the Captain requires the self-sufficiency needed to assert his authority over the crew. The nautical details provided by the tale 'record the exact moral significance of what the Captain thought he was doing': but this realization comes home to him after he has 'lost touch' with his responsibilities for running the ship. When, therefore, the crisis arrives, he does not know what the ship can do. However, both 'sharers' – the alleged murderer and the lucky navigator – are given a second chance: Conrad refuses to judge, creating 'an ambivalent realm' showing that he understands 'the precarious terms upon which success is won'[2] – an insight, perhaps, that could be as applicable to literary criticism as to the art of seafaring.

The see-saw continued to oscillate, however, as J. D. O'Hara (1965) held that Leggatt is the criminal and Archbold the 'moral center' of the tale. Conrad warns his readers throughout not to accept the narrator's point of view. The Captain's jettisoning of Leggatt is a foolishly romantic act of a piece with the equally romantic folly of taking him on board and keeping him under wraps below deck. In short, he proves himself quite incapable of learning from experience. Yet the same year

---

[1] Hofthiann, 'Point of View in "The Secret Sharer"', *College English*, 23 (1962), 651–4.

[2] Williams, 'The Matter of Conscience in Conrad's The Secret Sharer', *PMLA*, 79 (1964), 626–30.

J. L. Simmons (1965) claimed that any act performed at sea to keep a ship afloat is morally justified. In this perspective, Archbold represents 'land morality', Leggatt 'sea morality'. Archbold *rationalizes* his need to bring Leggatt under the law of the land by turning it into the law of the sea. For the Captain, on the other hand, the ideal is embodied in action. He must prove to himself that he can act without his secret sharer: that is, he must convince himself that his ideal self really belongs to him. He therefore commits himself to the 'morality of the sea' and, taking command, rectifies Archbold's failure by releasing Leggatt onto the land.[1]

Edward Said (1966) elegantly adopted a different kind of analysis to reach a similar conclusion the next year. Conrad ventures into the shadow-line between 'the psychological and the anagogic [i.e., mystical or revelatory] spheres' to create 'a convincing image of human kinship, modally altered to one expressed in terms of action and sympathy as opposed to action and thought': this 'sends the figure from the past back into the unknown, free from constricting troubles, and sends the present consciousness into the future, armed with reassured mastery'.[2] In still further dissent J. I. M. Stewart (1968) repudiated Albert J. Guerard's psychoanalytic reading (see pp. cvi–cvii) and held that Leggatt stands for the Captain's repressed personality, and he asserted that there is neither 'temptation ahead' nor 'identification with moral failure', but only 'an ordeal and a test'. Not only is the relationship between the two men much closer than the comparable relationship in their 'source' (that of Razumov and Haldin in *Under Western Eyes*), but the tale's outcome is also the reverse of the novel's in that Leggatt obtains his freedom and the Captain passes his test. By protecting Leggatt, the Captain defiantly sets personal loyalty above public duty: 'He has made . . . Antigone's choice'. Yet (and in this, one presumes, Conrad diverges from Sophocles) Conrad so 'insistently' expresses the Captain's sense of his stowaway as a *Doppelgänger* that (regretfully) Stewart finds it 'hard not to suppose' that this insistence is 'the reflection of some neurotic crisis of identity in the writer'.[3] In contrast, Paul Kirschner (1968) was at the same time persuasively treating psychology as the exploration of human motives in terms of

---

[1] O'Hara, 'Unlearned Lessons in "The Secret Sharer"', *College English*, 26 (1965), 444–50; Simmons, 'The Dual Morality in Conrad's "Secret Sharer"', *Studies in Short Fiction*, 2 (1965), 209–20.

[2] Edward W. Said, *Joseph Conrad and the Fiction of Autobiography* (1966), p. 132.

[3] Stewart, *Joseph Conrad* (1968), pp. 232–47.

self-knowledge. What the Captain notices about Leggatt is his self-possession as 'a complete human being whose sanity consists precisely in trusting his instinct'. When Leggatt eventually parts from the ship, the Captain insists that the fugitive, who bears 'no brand of the curse [of Cain] on his sane forehead to stay a slaying hand', is more at risk than Cain because less protected. Moreover, for all Conrad's psychodrama, the Captain retains an authority over the crew which his final manœuvre serves to drive home. Kirschner's culminating point is that a 'commander' must be emotionally independent of those he leads: thus the Captain brings the tale to a climax when he 'shows the courage of his sympathetic impulses – as opposed to the moral sclerosis of Captain Archbold'.[1]

The next year Lawrence Graver (1969) pointed out, against psychologizing critics like Stallman, that Leggatt cannot represent *both* the Captain's moral consciousness *and* the world that lies below his conscious life. Following a generous sampling of the available criticism, he posed the question of why the Captain has to 'shave the coast' and replied, reductively though not without reason, that the problem is generated by a 'fascinating and provocative story' whose details are often so vaguely portentous that readers are beguiled into hunting for a hidden symbolic consistency 'which the work does not possess'. Although Graver remains virtually the only one of an army of commentators who has seen that the tales of *'Twixt Land and Sea* were prompted by Captain Marris's visit to Conrad, he did nothing with this insight and adhered to the conviction, which he did not try to justify, that, while the tales seek to explore substantial themes, they 'are also full of conventional devices of bad magazine fiction'.[2] By contrast, Bruce Johnson (1971), who relied on common-sense psychology as well, found the story 'conservative, almost reactionary' in its affirmation of the 'power of renunciation within a mass of weakness'. He denounced Guerard (see pp. cvi–cvii) for regarding Leggatt as the Captain's 'lower self': 'Leggatt is not a symbol of the unconscious, but a man on precisely the same level as the young Captain'. For Conrad's sea-captains, there is something 'far worse than primitive impulse' – namely, 'a threat grounded in the difficulty of consciousness knowing what it is not'. However, the risk of smugness remains: 'knowledge of man's irrational nature never goes beyond a kind of self-congratulation that man is not absurd, that he is always at least

[1] Kirschner, *Conrad*, pp. 118–27. (See p. 118.)   [2] Graver, pp. 150–58.

possessed of instincts that can give meaning even to the life that has flirted with meaninglessness'.[1]

C. B. Cox, a few years onward (1974), was also given to the common-sense psychologism to which the New Criticism is prone. The Captain is 'anxious whether he has the ability to fulfil the new role, and so he fears he is a usurper': hence the Leggatt dimension of the story symbolizes the 'tension between subconscious guilt and a confident sense of responsibility'. However, by choosing to help the outlaw, 'the captain proves himself competent and resolute, and he eventually succeeds in getting rid of his scapegoat double'. According to Cox, this interpretation accounts for the exasperation with the psychoanalyzing Guerard that Jocelyn Baines felt in his pioneering biography (1960): 'there is no indication in the story, explicit or implicit, that the captain sees any of his dilemmas or difficulties in Leggatt or that he performs any self-examination'. Frederick R. Karl (1960) had also rendered this no-nonsense verdict: the Captain does not betray the outlaw; on the contrary he proves his manhood by arranging his escape; yet 'the story remains psychologically shallow'.[2]

However, in 1975 H. M. Daleski offered, despite some eccentricities, a more substantial reading. The Captain is a site of opposing qualities: he is self-possessed but capable of 'abandon', firm on ship and in accepting individual moral responsibility but 'morally lax', if not irresponsible, with respect to Leggatt's crime. This presents us with a paradox that is not easily domesticated by conventional morality. As a site of opposing qualities, he eludes easy definition. Unlike Leggatt, who keeps his head at sea but at the same time loses self-control, the Captain 'never loses his self-command' when bringing his ship round. On the other hand, Leggatt, who will kill if cornered, is little better than *The Secret Agent*'s demented Professor – as Leggatt implicitly recognizes by accepting the brand of Cain. Eventually, the Captain achieves command by shedding Leggatt and turning the ship away from land, that is, by 'a holding on that is simultaneously a letting go'. Although this neat conclusion did not quite open new interpretative possibilities, Daleski's essay was more provocative than Daniel R. Schwarz's later book chapter (1982), which adopted a form of *critique bavardage* to discover that 'The Secret Sharer' is 'a tale of initiation in which the Captain overcomes his insecurity'. In this view, Leggatt and the

---

[1] Johnson, *Conrad's Models of Mind* (1971), pp. 126–39.
[2] Cox, *Joseph Conrad: The Modern Imagination* (1974), pp. 137–50; Baines, p. 357; Karl, *A Reader's Guide to Joseph Conrad* (1960), p. 141.

Captain represent the split between 'mind and instinct'; the Captain's 'disbelief in the authenticity of the self' threatens his 'personality'; he is 'prejudiced by Leggatt against Archbold'; the (newly minted) 'myth of triumphant departure' is a conscience tranquillizer; Leggatt is 'flippant' about his resemblance to Cain, and so on. However, the Captain does to Leggatt what Conrad does to his work of art: 'he releases it back into the objective world' – that is, 'like the artist', the Captain 'withdraws into imagination at the expense of immediate participation in the community'.[1] In retrospect this essay could be viewed as having marked the exhaustion of the now old 'New Criticism'.

PSYCHOANALYTICAL AND ARCHETYPAL READINGS. The founding father of psychoanalytical readings of Conrad's fiction was, as already suggested, Albert J. Guerard, whose celebrated 'Introduction' to the Signet Classics edition of 'Heart of Darkness' and 'The Secret Sharer' (1950) became the source of post-Freudian and especially Jungian approaches. The premise was that the unconscious mind, which is by definition not directly available to consciousness, nevertheless exerts radical pressure on the psychic condition and hence the conduct of individuals. Guerard invoked Jung's claim that archetypal myth was interpretable as an introspective process requiring a risky 'descent' into the pre-conscious or even sub-conscious to effect a restorative return to 'the primitive sources of being'. All the major elements of 'The Secret Sharer' can be recruited into this programme: the 'night sea' signals the alter ego, the sleeping-suits the world of dream, and so on. Under this method, Leggatt becomes the Captain's unconsciously repressed 'primitive' self, which allows Guerard to read the tale as 'a psychological and symbolic story of self-exploration, self-recognition, and self-mastery'. Eight years later he returned to this method of interpretation (psychoanalysis as literary analysis) in *Conrad the Novelist* (1958). Still treating the tale as an enactment of the consequences of self-division and repression, generated by the sudden appearance of an outlaw figure who in provoking 'a crippling division in the narrator's personality . . . interferes with his seamanship', Guerard showed with considerably greater subtlety and justice how the Captain's division between his 'rational seaman-self' and his 'outlaw

---

[1] Daleski, '"The Secret Sharer": Questions of Command', *Critical Quarterly*, 17 (1975), 268–79, rpt with revisions in *Joseph Conrad: The Way of Dispossession* (1977), pp. 171–83 (rpt *CA*, III, 309–20); Schwarz, pp. 2–10.

self' is converted into a subtle narrative. The story, as such, is able to carry its Jungian freight by virtue of the rigid economy of its narrative and of the 'grave, quiet, brooding voice' of its narrator, which together are able to transform the *Cutty Sark*'s 1880 misadventures into a literary masterpiece charged with latent meanings.[1]

Guerard's talent for blending psychoanalysis and literary sensitivity would soon be set off by Robert A. Day's allegorizing (1963), which held that the initiation of the Captain is 'complemented by a symbolic presentation of the archetype of rebirth', where the Captain is the 'female element', the cramped and confined Leggatt is in a 'fetuslike' state, and his escape from the cabin is an 'agony of birth', with the Captain acting as mother. By contrast Joan E. Steiner's 1980 article revealed her to be one of the more accomplished of psychoanalytic critics. Focussing on the interacting psychologies of the Captain and Leggatt, she argued that 'doubling' is itself double, in that it simultaneously replicates and divides. Invoking E. T. A. Hoffmann, the German Romantic genius (a more plausible Conradian source than Jung) who combined the two, she showed that *both* are present in the Captain and in Leggatt and invited readers to regard 'The Secret Sharer' as exploring the psychological rather than the allegorical aspects of doubling. Steiner noted that elsewhere, notably in *The Mirror of the Sea*, Conrad requires of his mariners the dual virtues of 'a healthy sense of insecurity' and 'an absolute sense of self-confidence'. It is *this* doubling that the Captain of 'The Secret Sharer' needs to acquire and does acquire at the story's end. Leggatt, self-controlled and psychologically invulnerable, represents the integration which Archbold, at once muddled and defensive, shows is required. Leggatt demonstrates that the irrational or instinctive elements in human beings can be a source of strength. Both Leggatt and the Captain are cut off, one through experience, the other through inexperience: in the event, the manœuvre to help the fugitive helps the Captain, as both enter simultaneously into possession of their new lives.[2]

Given that, in their exuberant *jeu d'esprit*, Barbara Johnson and Marjorie Garber (1987) made no claim for the story's 'truth to life', offering their piece instead as an '*illustration* of an analytical

---

[1] Guerard, 'Introduction', in *Heart of Darkness & The Secret Sharer* (1950), pp. 7–15; Guerard, *Conrad The Novelist*, pp. 21–7.
[2] Day, 'The Rebirth of Leggatt', *Literature and Psychology*, 13 (1963), 74–81; Steiner, 'Conrad's "The Secret Sharer": Complexities of the Doubling Relationship', *Conradiana*, 12 (1980), 173–86.

extrapolation', it might be omitted here. Certainly it reads like a kind of sport in which the tale relates to the commentary rather as the apparatus relates to the gymnast. The five 'psychoanalytical routes' which the authors identify and which they explicitly distinguish from 'psychoanalytical readings' – namely, the 'pathology of the author', the 'pathology of the protagonist', the 'pathology of the text', the 'symptomology of the text', and the 'story' as 'an allegory of analysis' – generate a display of theoretical pyrotechnics that, we are again assured, casts no light whatsoever on 'Conrad's narrative'.[1] Is their piece, then, a parody of over-earnest psychoanalytical criticism, or an avant-garde demonstration that we should trust the tale even less than the teller? Whatever the answer, this performance seemed to have drawn a line under such readings of 'The Secret Sharer'.

But not quite. Two years later James F. White (1989) reinvoked the spirit of the Swiss 'discoverer' of the archetypes of the collective unconscious in order to discern in the textual depths of Conrad's tale a 'fertility theme' involving 'self-discovery' and 'initiation' and propagating a whole stream of symbolic actions from 'matchmaking', 'tryst', 'seduction', 'coupling', 'impregnation', 'gestation', and 'delivery' to 'childbirth'.[2] This sexy performance showed that 'implausibility' had become an endangered concept in some fin-de-siècle academic criticism.

ALLUSIVE READINGS. The text of 'The Secret Sharer' has turned out to be more allusively active than seemed – and to some still seems – possible. The first determined attempt to map this semantic no-man's-land was made by Louis H. Leiter (1960), who pursued 'echo structures' not only to illuminate character (for example, the Captain and Leggatt represent, respectively, our conscious and unconscious selves), but more generally to load every rift of Conrad's text with symbolic ore. The opening description of the flat coast anticipates or pre-echoes the arrival of the swimming Leggatt: the ' "half-submerged bamboo fences" for catching fish suggest the "ladder"' which the Captain ' "proceeded to get in"'; the 'mysterious system of ... fences' anticipates the Captain's astonishment at the 'immovableness of that ladder',

[1] Barbara Johnson and Marjorie Garber, 'Secret Sharing: Reading Conrad Psychoanalytically', *College English*, 49 (1987), 628–40.
[2] White, 'The Third Theme in "The Secret Sharer"', *Conradiana*, 46 (1989), 37–46.

and so on. Thus the second passage charges the first with 'meanings' unperceived at first, though these are linked together without reference to any criterion of overall plausibility. The implied assumption is that one thing resembles another because neither is like a third. The same approach operates in the identification and interpretation of 'parable' (the 'mystery' of the scorpion's appearance in the first mate's inkwell and Leggatt's sudden emergence out of the sea), of 'action' (the storm that threatens the *Sephora* and the 'Erebus' that looms over the Captain's vessel under Koh-Ring), and of 'archetype, myth, or Biblical story' (for example, Leggatt's hurricane and Jonah's storm). Leiter's view is that such parallels, however far-fetched, generate meaning by themselves, independently of narrative contexts.[1] Yet, perhaps because of its referential excesses, Leiter's *commentaire sans frontières* occasionally makes contact with the unfolding text; and in its hyper-activity it has prompted a number of responses.

Even eleven years later, for example, Paul Bidwell (1971) enlarged its allusive range to extend from Exodus 'waterside rushes' to 'promised land'. Then, Thomas R. Dilworth (1977) set out to scan the story's images for 'allusions, elusive evocations, and suggestions' previously overlooked, on the assumption that they would serve as analogues for the 'unconscious drama taking place in the young captain's psyche'. Prompted by the description of the looming mass of Koh-ring as 'the very gate of Erebus' (i.e., the entrance to the classical Hades), Dilworth found it inspired by Rodin's '*Porte de l'Enfer*' and proceeded to decode the tale's concluding moments in terms of his 'Dantesque' imagery, despite the facts that Mt Erebus was well known to sailors of the far southern latitudes as the most terrifying volcanic peak in the world and that (as he notes) Leggatt's escape is a *postponement* of the day of judgement. Likewise, despite the narrative's careful detailing of the circumstances bearing upon Leggatt's reflex strangulation of the rebellious sailor, Dilworth found it necessary to invoke Dante's use of '*legate*' in connection with fallen souls to explain Leggatt's act, thereby suggesting that a sane and perceptive reader can perhaps be driven slightly off kilter by the power and intensity of Conrad's tale. Another ten years on, Mark A. R. Facknitz (1987) revisited Leiter's study as well as Bidwell's attempt to fold in the book of Exodus, in order to interpret 'The Secret Sharer' as an allegory of divine and human law.

---

[1] Leiter, 'Echo Structures: Conrad's "The Secret Sharer"', *Twentieth Century Literature*, 5 (1960), 159–75 (rpt *CA*, III, 285–300).

He found the tale swarming with tropes and rituals understandable only as cryptic Old Testament allusions: many prove to be evident, several far-fetched, and some incredible. The range of Conradian and Biblical texts brought into play was impressive, but the failure to give priority to Conrad's narrative meant that his inquiry often lacked a verification trip-switch. Facknitz, however, ended with a reminder of Conrad's distaste for pseudo-science – which provides one way to steady critics' allusive zeal.[1]

In contrast, W. Eugene Davis (1995) has more recently examined British maritime law around 1880 in its bearing on the tale. Although there was no comprehensive code of the sea in Victorian England, it would appear that there existed a legal basis for the Captain's harbouring of Leggatt, and indeed for his rejections of any demands Archbold might make for the return of the fugitive. A master's prime duty was to the safety and order of his ship – which made Archbold's handling of Leggatt illegal on a number of counts. This well-researched report on a long-neglected topic concludes with a useful summary of the relevant laws.[2] The question remains, however, whether a Singapore or London trial of Leggatt, carrying as it would have done the weight of the combined 'evidence' of a defensive crew and of a hostile captain with a previously perfect record, would not have imposed a very long term of imprisonment on the alleged malefactor.

FORMALIST READINGS. Formal analysis of 'The Secret Sharer' came to maturity in 1977 with an article which Cedric Watts offered as an experiment in 'ethico-structuralism'. The tale awakens two simultaneous systems of expectation. The first is optimistic: it achieves a comic outcome, the *Sephora*'s captain confirms that Leggatt saved the ship, the Captain–narrator is virtuous and achieves command. The second is pessimistic: areas of apparent security are ambushes, the Captain–narrator is inexperienced, he alienates his men, he shelters a criminal, and he connives in the man's escape by risking his ship. Watts's case was strikingly put, though perhaps its predictive patterning was a trifle

---

[1] Bidwell, 'Leggatt and the Promised Land: A New Reading of the "Secret Sharer"', *Conradiana*, 3 (1971), 26–34; Dilworth, 'Conrad's Secret Sharer at the Gate of Hell', *Conradiana*, 9 (1977), 203–17; Facknitz, 'Cryptic Allusions and the Moral of the Story: The Case of Joseph Conrad's "The Secret Sharer"', *Journal of Narrative Technique*, 17 (1987), 115–30.
[2] Davis, 'The Structures of Justice in "The Secret Sharer"', *Conradiana*, 27 (1995), 64–73.

too rehearsed and diluted the tale's narrative intensity – a consideration which might have prompted his return to 'The Secret Sharer'
seven years later. In his 1984 book he read the tale as playing a super-
natural plot against a secular plot in order to generate an 'uncanny'
double. These two sequences predicting contradictory outcomes are
in very close balance. Hence, Watts pursues this dualism into every
aspect of the narrative: its diction (the classical Erebus against the Biblical Cain), its plot (Leggatt kills a man to save a ship, the Captain
risks his ship to save a man), its ideology (liberal values are forced
to accept illiberal values, and vice versa). 'If [the reader] sympathizes
with the ruthless Leggatt . . . he must be sympathetic to the humane
captain who shelters him. If he sympathizes with the humane captain,
he finds himself an accomplice of the captain's determination to help
Leggatt's evasion of justice.'[1] This confidently lucid and elegant essay
would prove to be as persuasive as formalism gets.

Pursuing a similar line of inquiry, Jakob Lothe (1989) soon offered
a highly focussed and controlled analysis of the tale on the presup-
position that its 'structure and narrative method perform a crucial
thematic function'. Symmetrical contrasts combine with the text's suspense principle to complicate the moral or ethical issues present in the
Captain's dual function as character and narrator. The narrator's 'test-
like experience' precipitated by Leggatt's arrival produces a process
of learning and maturation; the text's moral and thematic ambiguity, however, problematizes any inquiry into the terms and outcomes
of this process. Thus the narrator ends by being initiated into ideal
conduct rather than social responsibility: but the narrative method –
or, rather, the actual unfolding of the narrative – serves to destabilize
this idealism, just as the blend of technical virtuosity and psychological acumen relaxes the pressing moral dilemmas.[2] This essay offers
an exemplary demonstration of the rewards that await a formal analysis conducted on the assumption that the way in which a narrative is
written provides a means of getting at what it is saying.

Lothe's awareness of his reader may have given his essay a slight edge
over an intellectually sophisticated article by James Hansford (1990)
that appeared the next year. This remarkable piece, which defies
potted summary, provided a demonstration of the expressive possibilities of conceptual analysis. The argument is established through

---

[1] Watts, 'The Mirror-Tale: An Ethico-Structural Analysis of Conrad's "The Secret Sharer"',
  Critical Quarterly, 19 (1977), 25–37; Watts, *The Deceptive Text*, pp. 84–90.
[2] Lothe, *Conrad's Narrative Method* (1989), pp. 57–71.

the juxtaposition of two parallel narrative climaxes: the saving of the *Sephora* by the hoisting of a storm sail, which entails the loss of a man (the rebellious sailor), and the saving of the tyro Captain's ship from near-certain destruction by a floating white hat offering him a sea-mark, which allows him to achieve the confidence of command. The first of these two events generates Leggatt's concealment in the Captain's cabin, and the second climaxes in his equally secret liberation from it. Moreover, both events demonstrate that a 'closing' is also an 'opening'. The approach of Koh-ring ends Leggatt's confinement but also inaugurates his life as a fugitive, just as (more generally) the ending of the Captain's friendship with Leggatt is simultaneously his taking possession of his command: or (for Hansford's conceptual intensity saturates every moment of Conrad's story) the Captain's achievement of 'perfect communion' or 'one-ness' with his command is a consequence of his encounter with his other self – that is, of discovering, experiencing, and naturalizing his own duality. Although not all episodes are treated with equal success (for example, the discussion of the tale's opening panorama refuses to allow any detail the luxury of being itself), the essay's central critical concept, that of the threshold – where one is simultaneously inside and outside, leaving and entering, beginning and ending – allows Hansford to present doubling as an enactment of what it means to live in space–time, or singleness–community. Hansford recognizes that the difference in the Captain before he picks up Leggatt and after he releases him is the difference between the self-consciousness of the novice and the self-forgetfulness of the professional. However, it is in the time–space between this beginning and this end that the meaning of life under conditions of temporality and of plurality becomes visible. If the essay seems abstract, it is founded on the realities of Conrad's narrative as they are perceived from an unexpected perspective. Its special merit is that, whereas readings often tend to divide between commitment to the values of service *or* of communality, either damning or celebrating the tale's protagonist, Hansford's is able to attend to the ever-inconclusive interplay of singularity and plurality, and to the claims of a command equally dependent on self-reliance and camaraderie.[1]

Five years later, Mark Ellis Thomas (1995) would call into question the identification of the Captain and Leggatt as doubles. Leggatt, he

---

[1] Hansford, 'Closing, Enclosure and Passage in "The Secret Sharer"', *The Conradian*, 15, no. 1 (1990), 30–55 (rpt *CA*, III, 321–37).

would find, is a decoy serving to screen 'the latent and more significant doubling of the narrator and his earlier self'. Unfortunately,
this doubling is left unscrutinized by the narrative Conrad has left
us. The fact that the author–narrator was fifty-two when recalling his
life at thirty-two is not exposed to any textual-analytical pressure, presumably because the story 'frustrates the critic's attempts to center its
form'.[1]

SUSPICIOUS READINGS. Not every commentary on 'The Secret
Sharer' has been unreservedly enthusiastic. As already noted, Cedric
Watts, for example, took a detached view of the Captain's experience
of induction into his command. However, since the 1970s, a few other
readers have dissented from the chorus of approval the tale has enjoyed
from the time of its publication.[2]

   In 1979, for instance, David Eggenschwiler was arguing that Conrad
misuses the concept of the double to protect himself 'narcissistically'
against 'moral insight'. His line was that the story's obtrusively archetypal experiences are also psychological evasions. The Captain sees himself as a 'special and isolated' figure contemptuous of his crew 'in a
high drama'. Leggatt's appearance in the water is 'awash with gothic
symbolism' and invites a spurious transformation of himself into a
symbolic double, which generates a futile critical debate as to 'whether
Leggatt symbolizes the instinctual amoral self or a firm moral ideal'. All
Leggatt has to offer are the 'trite histrionics and Byronic posturings' to
which the infatuated narrator remains blind. But as Archbold shows
by sticking out his tongue, 'symbolic groupings obscure the black-
ened face of the strangled man', and Archbold remains 'still honest
and truly affected by what has happened to his ship'. The Captain's
reckless approach to the Cambodian coast is a 'bit of self-dramatized
showmanship'; if the narrator passes this test of nerves, it is because he
has invented it in order to demonstrate to himself 'that he is his ideal
self'. Indeed, the similarities between the tale's concluding scene and
the scene 'aboard the *Sephora* during the storm are so obvious that
one might overlook the differences' – to the comic discredit of the

---

[1] Thomas, 'Doubling and Difference in Conrad: "The Secret Sharer," *Lord Jim*, and *The Shadow
    Line*', *Conradiana*, 27 (1995), 222–34.
[2] See above, pp. cx–cxi; also Conrad to Galsworthy, 28 October 1912?, and to Garnett,
    5 November 1912 (*Letters*, v, 121–2, 128).

Captain. 'Throughout this essay', Eggenschwiler blandly concludes, 'I have been intentionally more polemical than tactful'.[1]

In a later essay of considerable subtlety driven by a strong sense of the moral problems posed by the tale, Steve Ressler (1984) raised suspicions in order to work through them. What brings narrative matters to a head is the Captain's unorthodox sheltering of Leggatt, in consequence of which his misconceptions and insecurities in authority are challenged, and Archbold's self-deceptions are exposed. For Ressler, 'the idea of acting for psychological and not moral reasons is critical to the story'. Fidelity to the double must, logically, become fidelity to the self: hence the Captain's achievement of authority and self-possession is dependent on Leggatt's escape. What the story's climax reveals is that for the Captain there needs to be an initiative beyond the rulebook. Thus the decision to release Leggatt duplicates the conditions faced by Leggatt in the tempest. For both officers, action – whether the saving of a ship or the saving of a man – is a matter of conscience that overrules regulation, whence we must deduce that law and duty do not always coincide. This means that for both men experience consists in an interweaving of innocence and guilt. Is there, perhaps, a higher justice than the legal? Whatever the answer (and there may be none), the fact remains that Leggatt's trouble allows the Captain to rise to his best self. Indeed, by achieving effectual leadership he becomes an 'unfallen Leggatt' – who, for his part, 'dies to the world', having quickened into life a redeemed image of himself. However, two years later, Michael Murphy (1986) returned to the charge – but with greater bluntness – in arguing that Leggatt's alleged determination to set the reefed foresail which saved the ship is rightly denigrated by Archbold in his attributing this deed to God, though neither Conrad nor his Captain–narrator seems to entertain any doubt that Leggatt's stay of execution (banishment into the wilderness, rather than delivery to the authorities) might be better deserved than the fratricidal Cain's identical fate.[2]

[1] Eggenschwiler, 'Narcissus in "The Secret Sharer": A Secondary Point of View', *Conradiana*, 11 (1979), 23–40. See also Gloria R. Dussinger, ' "The Secret Sharer": Conrad's Psychological Study', *Texas Studies in Language and Literature*, 10 (1969), 599–608, and Robert D. Wyatt, 'Joseph Conrad's "The Secret Sharer": Point of View and Mistaken Identities', *Conradiana*, 5 (1973), 12–26.

[2] Ressler, 'Conrad's "The Secret Sharer": Affirmation of Action', *Conradiana*, 16 (1984), 195–214; Murphy ' "The Secret Sharer": Conrad's Turn of the Winch', *Conradiana*, 18 (1986), 193–200.

A much more elaborate and uncompromising case for the prosecution has been mounted by Daphna Erdinast-Vulcan (1999). Those
who have thought that the 'strangeness' of 'The Secret Sharer' derived
from the psycho-drama of a sudden promotion to a position of absolute responsibility for a vessel and her crew are required to think again.
Similarly, we should question the assumption that Leggatt's adoption
by the Captain generates the need to keep up a private or secret life
in the midst of the obligations of duty and service. What we should
really take on board is less the narrative structure of the story considered as a whole than M. M. Bakhtin's famous distinction between
the 'self-created' and the 'other-created' subject – the first generating the 'discontinuous' experiencing self, the second asserting the
claims of the 'continuous' ethical self. Similarly the source of the tale
in *Under Western Eyes*, the tragic novel whose composition it interrupts,
should not be taken as representing a straightforward evolution from
self-entrapment (Razumov) to self-fulfilment (the Captain), or indeed
from the betrayal of a guilty 'other' (Haldin) to his protection and
escape (Leggatt). On the contrary, 'The Secret Sharer' dramatizes the
attempt to *objectify* the self by identifying it with 'the double'. Thus the
story has to be read as a 'symptom' generating a 'placebo effect of
self-enclosure' in the Captain's effort to turn himself into 'an other'.
In this view, what Erdinast-Vulcan terms the 'tensile relation' between
'aestheticised' or 'authored' selfhood (the Captain's with Leggatt) and
'the ethical "yet to be made" mode of consciousness' (the Captain without Leggatt) may represent 'the missing link in the postmodernist
critique of the transcendental subject'.[1]

As the 1990s closed, this essay did not stand alone in bringing to
bear upon Conrad's 1909 tale one of the several critical approaches
that have characterized academic criticism in the last decades of the
twentieth century. In 1997 Bedford Books published for the classroom
one of their 'Case Studies in Contemporary Criticism', edited by Daniel
R. Schwarz, which helped fill the niche formerly occupied by Bruce
Harkness's 1962 volume (see p. ci). It included a reprint of the received
text and original essays by some of America's leading academic critics,
who applied not only psychoanalytic criticism (Schwarz himself), but
also reader-response theory (James Phelan), new historicism (Michael
Levenson), gender criticism (Bonnie Kime Scott), and deconstruction
(J. Hillis Miller) in their discussions of the story. While these new essays

[1] Erdinast-Vulcan, pp. 30–50.

reaffirmed the ability of 'The Secret Sharer' to challenge academic critics by virtue of its enduring capacity to give back to new ways of reading as much as it receives from them, the publication of the volume itself showed that Conrad's tale had survived the canon reformation of those decades and indicated that it would continue to occupy a significant place in the classrooms and culture of the West in the next century.[1]

Freya of the Seven Isles

PINKER had difficulty placing the last of these three tales, which was turned down by several magazines on account of its 'overpowering gloom'.[2] In rejecting it for New York's *Century*, Edward Garnett provided the first recorded critical response: 'I do feel a certain weakness in the manipulation of the tragedy at the close', which he found 'too "willed" & led up to' (*Letters*, v, 128, n. 3). Although Conrad revised the text for publication in *'Twixt Land and Sea*,[3] his refusal to fake a 'sunny' ending seemed at first vindicated by early reviews that called it a 'wonderful pitiless story of revenge' and his 'greatest success'.[4] However, later critical response would often side with Garnett's judgement.

Osborn Andreas' discussion (1959) was probably the first such commentary on the tale – and certainly the first to highlight the fact that its male principals are free-lance entrepreneurs in a Dutch-controlled colonial possession. Although insisting that Conrad 'accentuates the identification of the opposing forces' by dividing them between a pair of isolated and innocent young lovers and the agents of 'the oppressive power of an absentee imperialist ruler over subject peoples', he delivered no more than a competent plot summary.[5]

Almost ten years later, negative views of the tale had become considerably more explicit. For example, in 1968 John A. Palmer observed, as a matter of course, that Freya's status as a fertility goddess 'interferes

---

[1] *Joseph Conrad: The Secret Sharer*, ed. Daniel R. Schwarz (1997), including Daniel R. Schwarz, '"The Secret Sharer" as an Act of Memory', pp. 95–111; James Phelan, 'Sharing Secrets', pp. 128–44; Michael Levenson, 'Secret History in "The Secret Sharer"', pp. 163–74; Bonnie Kime Scott, 'Intimacies Engendered in Conrad's "The Secret Sharer"', pp. 197–210; and J. Hillis Miller, 'Sharing Secrets', pp. 232–51. The 'authoritative text' reproduced was that of the '1924' (i.e., 1923) Doubleday subedition (on which, see pp. 285–8).

[2] Conrad to Pinker, [25? March 1911] (*Letters*, IV, 430–31). For more details, see p. 264.

[3] See 'The Texts', pp. 278–80, for Conrad's thorough revisions at this stage.

[4] Conrad to Garnett, 4 August 1911 (*Letters*, IV, 470). See above, pp. lxxxvi, lxxxvii.

[5] Andreas, *Joseph Conrad: A Study in Non-Conformity* (1959), pp. 145–50.

somewhat with Jasper's masculinity', and added that this gave 'the reader full license to speculate about Conrad's sexual powers'. The next year Lawrence Graver (1969) took a decidedly harder line, finding 'Freya of the Seven Isles' not only continuing the process of 'deterioration' revealed in 'A Smile of Fortune', but the most clumsily protracted of all Conrad's stories and a 'flamboyant melodrama'. At the start, old Nelson is the bumbling father of low comedy, his daughter 'a model of Scandinavian exuberance', Allen the 'conventionally impulsive lover', and his rival Heemskirk a 'sour and arrogant' brute. With the advent of the tragedy, Heemskirk is magnified into a 'Prometheus in the bonds of unholy desire', his victim Allen haunts the Macassar beachfront 'like a demented Empedocles', and the exuberant Freya turns into a helplessly consumptive Violetta. As for the narrative, it is a copy-book example of 'stylistic imprecision' and 'structural mismanagement'. Its conduct, divided between an authorial surrogate and an anonymous third-person story-teller who takes over half way through the narrative, is broken-backed. Despite Conrad's efforts to improve the tale for book publication, he only succeeded in increasing the 'clumsiness' of the initial version.[1]

Like these approaches, later ones have ignored the political and historical reality which informs the tale's narrative. Daniel R. Schwarz (1982), for instance, managed to produce, despite much commendably close reading, a dismissive account of a tale in which the heroine uses the power of her sexual glamour to manipulate the three men in her life – her 'paranoid' father, the 'infantile' Jasper, and the 'neurotic' Heemskirk – and treats a fourth (the narrator) as a Pandarus figure. In this view, Conrad vacillates between 'a comic perspective' and an 'expansive operatic perspective'.[2]

However, this current of disapprobation, and even distaste, did not go unchallenged. As early as 1968, Paul Kirschner's analysis had already shown what a more open-minded approach could discover. Freya imagines that she can be the mistress of her destiny, but control of her life is taken out of her hands by 'absurdity', a condition associated with the masculine figures that define her world: her father's selfish fear, her lover's febrile elation, and the ferocity of Heemskirk, whom she recklessly humiliates. Two minor figures also undermine her independence: the clowning maid Antonia and,

---

[1] Palmer, *Joseph Conrad's Fiction: A Study in Literary Growth* (1968), pp. 229–33; Graver, pp. 163–9.

[2] Schwarz, pp. 18–22.

indirectly, the kleptomaniac ship's mate, Schultz. Kirschner held that 'what makes Freya', the protagonist of the tale, 'more credible than most of Conrad's women is the mingling of her natural gift for senti-ment, diplomacy, and common-sense, with her equally natural desire for self-reliance, freedom, and a more direct assertion of power'.[1] Although brief, and inhibiting awareness of the tale's cultural and political dimensions, this analysis represented the first examination, and still one of the most perceptive discussions, of the interaction of the characters.

Two years earlier, Paul Wiley (1966) had acknowledged that the tale portrays more than merely private tragedies, but the historical context he invoked was not a specifically Indonesian conflict involv-ing Dutch and British colonial powers. Rather, he presented Conrad's later writing as 'rescue work' in a pre-world-war environment of disin-tegrating values symbolized by Jasper Allen's investment of his all in a brig freighted with obsolete chivalric ideals that Conrad, as agent or spokesman of history, 'iconoclastically' destroys. Yet not many years later Gloria Young (1975) would quarrel with Wiley in particular, and with the tradition of denigration in general, not over Wiley's historical claims, but with his assumption that the tale is a 'total disaster'. Find-ing support in Frederick P. W. McDowell's survey of criticism (1970), Young proposed a more generalized scenario in which Conrad's lovers believe in a world ordered by a decidedly un-Conradian 'divine pur-pose', but live in one governed by flux and chance. The tale's three main characters represent, as in a fable, 'attitudes towards life rather than a complexity of response'. While Jasper converts his exquisite *Bonito* into a 'house of dreams' for the reception of his 'divinity' Freya, and Freya as the 'Lady of the Isles' revels in powers that associate her with Nordic goddesses, they both neglect the threat posed by Heemskirk, embodiment of the evil and absurdity of the real world. This scenario, which Young evoked with considerable verbal elegance, expresses 'a vision of life too meaningless to be tragic and too tragic to be comic'.[2]

Recalling John A. Palmer's observation about 'Conrad's sexual powers', Monika M. Elbert (1994) has offered a gendered, rather than

---

[1] Kirschner, *Conrad*, pp. 139–43.
[2] Wiley, 'Conrad's Solitaries', in *Conrad: A Collection of Critical Essays*, ed. Marvin Mudrick (1966), pp. 63–73; Young, 'Chance and the Absurd in Conrad's "The End of the Tether" and "Freya of the Seven Isles"', *Conradiana*, 7 (1975), 253–61 (rpt *CA*, III, 338–46); McDowell, 'Joseph Conrad: Current Criticism and the "Achievement and Decline" Question', *Journal of Modern Literature*, 1 (1970–1), 261–72.

a feminist, reading that exonerates Conrad – whom she distinguishes from his narrators – of the charge of being 'a blatant sexist'. The fragmented masculinity of the tale's male figures is a consequence of the gender expectations they have of themselves, and it is this fragmentation that is the efficient cause of the tragedy. Indeed, the tale ends with a 'male sob' which betrays 'man's isolation and loss of power'. Moreover, this masculine disintegration means that the story's conclusion leaves both men and women bereft. Heemskirk disappears, Freya and Jasper die off, Schultz cuts his throat, and both the narrator and old Nelson can only wring their hands in the misery of fog-bound London.[1]

Finally, Daphna Erdinast-Vulcan (1999) has discussed the tale in terms of René Girard's distinction between 'romantic' and 'mimetic' desire, which she construes as a contrast between the autonomy of the self's capacity to generate its own desire, and the novelist's desire which (she claims) 'is always borrowed from a third party, acting as a mediator–rival from whom the second party imitates his desire'. Thus a man's desire for a woman is awakened and kept alive by that of a competitor. It follows that, although the cast of 'Freya of the Seven Isles' is a conventional one, its plot is transgressive – and indeed made all the more so by the omnipresence of 'mimetic desire'. Freya is vanquished by three men's absurdities – Jasper's, Heemskirk's, and (in terms of the erotic ballet choreographed by Conrad's plot) not old Nelson's but the narrator's – with whose help a structure of competitively symmetrical figures is established and sustained until it finally collapses into fragments. Thus Freya, who as a faithful daughter attempts to shield her father's political neurosis from exacerbation, postpones giving herself to her lover until she has driven him into substituting his precious brig for her body as the object of his desire. Thus, too, stimulated by Heemskirk's smouldering passion for her, she sadistically – indeed murderously – excites it by her defiant exhibitionism. And thus the narrator himself – present (the essay claims) on every occasion of Freya's and Jasper's trysts – maliciously recommends the unreliable Schultz to Jasper.[2] Whatever reservations one may entertain about it, this reading succeeds with characteristic brio in foregrounding for the first time the sexual psychology of a narrative that will become even

---

[1] Elbert, 'Freya of the Seven Isles and the Heart of Male Darkness', *Conradiana*, 26 (1994), 35–55.

[2] Erdinast-Vulcan, pp. 143–52. According to Conrad's narrative, Jasper has already and independently decided to appoint Schultz (p. 138) – but presumably the essay is concerned with the tale's hypothetical sub-text.

more interesting when, perhaps in the twenty-first century, the political psychology that permeates it is taken into account.

Conclusion

THE RECEPTION of *'Twixt Land and Sea* is marked by an extraordinary disjunction between the prestige of 'The Secret Sharer', which remains such that even dissenting readings become further proofs of its status as perhaps the most brilliant tale in the language, and the neglect in which 'A Smile of Fortune' and 'Freya of the Seven Isles' have languished as a result, at least in part, of that very brilliance. The brighter the sun, the darker the shadow.

But brief and impoverished as their critical reception has been, a deliberate effort should be made to remove them from the dazzling darkness to which their rival has consigned them, if only to decide how much lustre they actually possess. Elements of their critical history suggest that they more than stand up to being taken seriously. In general, readers of both tales should try harder to absorb them comprehensively, and to treat them as responsive to the world in which they were written. If they are indeed creative works, they will not only confirm what we know or want to know; they will also expose us to what we failed to see or understand. The recovery of the full prologue to 'A Smile of Fortune', which now balances its concluding episode so as to frame the central action, should make it possible to determine how far the ambiguous ethic of the merchant service, which opposes the voyage to the purpose of the voyage, and dissociates the solidarity of a common task from the individualism of the profit motive, should alter our understanding of events on an island that is at once the pearl and the sink of the ocean. Similarly, the discovery of the degree to which 'Freya of the Seven Isles' owes its existence to Captain C. M. Marris's visit to Conrad, with its news of ominous historical and geographical change, and its memories of youth spent in tropical seas recalled in uncomfortable and unrewarded middle age, should perhaps persuade us of the presence of an even more catastrophic menace than that of an approaching world war, though a much more silent and global one.

'TWIXT LAND AND SEA
TALES

Life is a tragic folly,
Let us mock at life and be jolly,
Or droop into melancholy:
Bring me a branch of holly:
Life is a tragic folly.
                              A. Symons

To

CAPTAIN C. M. MARRIS

AUTHOR'S NOTE

THE ONLY BOND between these three stories is so to speak geographical, for their scene, be it land, be it sea, is situated in the same region, which may be called the region of the Indian Ocean with its off-shoots and prolongations north of the equator, even as far as the Gulf of Siam. In point of time they belong to the period immediately after the publication of that novel with the awkward title *Under Western Eyes*, and, as far as the life of the writer is concerned, their appearance in a volume marks a definite change in the fortunes of his fiction. For there is no denying the fact that *Under Western Eyes* found no favour in the public eye whereas the novel called *Chance* which followed *'Twixt Land and Sea* was received on its first appearance by many more readers than any other of my books.

This volume of three tales was also well received both publicly and privately and from a publisher's point of view. This little success was a most timely tonic for my enfeebled bodily frame. For this may indeed be called the book of a man's convalescence, at least as to three fourths of it; because "The Secret Sharer," the middle story, was written much earlier than the other two.

For in truth the memories of *Under Western Eyes* are associated with the memory of a severe illness which seemed to wait like a tiger in the jungle on the turn of a path to jump on me the moment the last words of that novel were written. The memory of an illness is very much like the memory of a nightmare. On emerging from it in a much enfeebled state I was inspired to direct my tottering steps towards the Indian Ocean, a complete change of surroundings and atmosphere from the Lake of Geneva, as nobody would deny. Begun so languidly and with such a fumbling hand that the first twenty pages or more had to be thrown into the waste-paper basket, "A Smile of Fortune," the most purely Indian Ocean story of the three, has ended by becoming what the reader will see. I will only say for myself that I have been patted on the back for it by most unexpected persons, personally unknown to me, the chief of them of course being the editor of a popular illustrated magazine who published it serially in one mighty instalment. Who will dare say after this that the change of air had not been an immense success?

The origins of the middle story, "The Secret Sharer," are quite
5 other. It was written much earlier and was published first in *Harper's Magazine* during the early part, I think, of 1911. Or perhaps the latter part? My memory on that point is hazy. The basic fact of the tale I had in my possession for a good many years. It was in truth the common possession of the whole fleet of merchant ships trad-
10 ing to India, China and Australia: a great company the last years of which coincided with my first years on the wider seas. The fact itself happened on board a very distinguished member of it, *Cutty Sark* by name and belonging to Mr Willis, a notable ship-owner in his day, one of the kind (they are all underground now) who used
15 to see personally his ships start on their voyages to those distant shores where they showed worthily the honoured house-flag of their owner. I am glad I was not too late to get at least one glimpse of Mr Willis on a very wet and gloomy morning watching from the pier head of the New South Dock one of his clippers starting on a
20 China Voyage – an imposing figure of a man under the invariable white hat so well known in the Port of London, waiting till the head of his ship had swung down stream before giving her a dig-nified wave of a big gloved hand. For all I know it may have been the *Cutty Sark* herself though certainly not on that fatal voyage. I
25 do not know the date of the occurrence on which the scheme of "The Secret Sharer" is founded; it came to light and even got into newspapers about the middle eighties, though I had heard of it before, as it were privately, among the officers of the great wool fleet in which my first years in deep water were served. It came
30 to light under circumstances dramatic enough I think, but which have nothing to do with my story. In the more specially maritime part of my writings this bit of presentation may take its place as one of my two Calm-pieces. For, if there is to be any classifica-tion by subjects, I have done two Storm-pieces in *The Nigger of the*
35 *"Narcissus"* and in "Typhoon"; and two Calm-pieces: this one and *The Shadow Line*, a book which belongs to a later period.

Notwithstanding their autobiographical form the above two sto-ries are not the record of personal experience. Their quality, such as it is, depends on something larger if less precise: on the char-
40 acter, the vision, the sentiment of the first twenty independent

years of my life. And the same may be said of the "Freya of the
Seven Isles." I was considerably abused for writing that story, on
the ground of its cruelty, both in public prints and in private letters.
I remember one from a man in America who was quite furiously
angry. He told me with curses and imprecations that I had no   5
right to write such an abominable thing which, he said, had gratuitously and intolerably harrowed his feelings. It was a very interesting letter to read. Impressive too. I carried it for some days in my
pocket. Had I the right? The sincerity of the anger impressed me.
Had I the right? Had I really sinned as he said or was it only that   10
man's madness? Yet there was a method in his fury. . . . I composed
in my mind a violent reply, a reply of mild argument, a reply of
lofty detachment; but they never got on paper in the end and I
have forgotten their phrasing. The very letter of the angry man
has got lost somehow; and nothing remains now but the pages of   15
the story, which I cannot recall and would not recall if I could.

But I am glad to think that the two women in this book – Alice,
the sullen, passive victim of her fate, and the actively individual
Freya, so determined to be the mistress of her own destiny – must
have evoked some sympathies; because of all my volumes of short   20
stories this was the one for which there was the greatest immediate
demand.

J. C.

1920.

'TWIXT LAND AND SEA

A SMILE OF FORTUNE
HARBOUR STORY

A SMILE OF FORTUNE

THE SUN WAS no more than half an hour above the sea horizon; I had just gone below after spending the best part of the night on deck; but before I had time to arrange my aching legs comfortably on the couch a metallic, buzzing voice filled my cabin mysteriously with the glad tidings:

"I see the land now, sir."

It was the voice of Mr Charles Burns my chief-officer speaking down to me from the poop with his face buried in the cowl of the big ventilator.

"Whereabouts do you make it?" I cried jumping up briskly.

"Nearly right ahead. A little bit on the port bow."

My cheerful vociferation "Good landfall Mr Burns" was acknowledged by a hollow buzzing in the room as from a hoarse ghost "H'm yes" and a grim little laugh, not very pleasant.

It was not that Mr Burns was a malevolent person. I would not have kept him with me for more than a passage if that had been the case. And we had been together now for two years or more. A pretty good slice of life as life at sea goes. He might have been devoted to me; of that I am not certain to this day. Sentiment is all very well and I would not disparage its value. His great point however was his efficiency. It was worth any amount of mere devotion to duty and far above rubies in price.

Our first coming together had been rather unusual. When I joined the ship (in an eastern port) to take command, I did not find him on board. He was ashore with a bad fever in the hospital, a gloomy, little house in a gloomy, little, overgrown compound. Of course I went to see how he was getting on directly the cares of business permitted. Seeing an utter stranger by his bedside he knew that it could be no one else but the new captain; and the very first words he said to me, putting out a wasted feverish hand, were: "For God's sake don't leave me to die in this hole." Our good Consulate Doctor looked horror-struck at the mere idea of him being moved.

The request was clearly preposterous. But you should have heard the tone! It haunted me. His deep-seated conviction that he must die if I left him behind was irresistible. His despairing entreaties forced upon me the responsibility of saying: "Very well. I promise you that you shall go to sea in the ship." Thereupon he went off into a dead faint. Very encouraging! And the Consulate Doctor became extremely angry; he went so far as to write me a distinctly stiff official letter of remonstrance. But he was a good fellow and actually turned up himself to superintend the removal he disapproved of so strongly. He did it with grim, silent solicitude of a particularly relentless kind. He hardly would shake hands at parting.

Mr Burns turned out a confoundedly fractious invalid. In due course he revealed himself as the most fretful of convalescents. I didn't mind that so much. For many days the poor fellow was almost too weak to speak. He lay in my own deck-chair made fast to the rail, wrapped up in my own rugs, ghastly like one risen from the dead, looking on at the work of the ship and the conduct of the voyage, and visibly fretting himself with the inward criticism of all these proceedings in which he could take no part. The last worry he gave me was by insisting with mulish obstinacy on returning to duty before he was really fit for it. He came on deck one gloomy afternoon, winding a woolen comforter round his neck with shaking hands and looking so determined to look properly after the ship that I only bit my lip and turned my back on him. In fact short of putting my convalescent in irons (or some such violent act of authority) I don't see what I could have done. Yet to clap him in irons after six weeks of anxious nursing was an extreme too comical to be considered for a moment.

All this might have been the effect of his devotion; yet in the course of time I discovered that Mr Burns had acquired somehow a conviction that as a commander of a ship and as a man I had the disadvantage of being generally unlucky, the defect of being reckless, and the stupidity of being too good-natured.

How, why, wherefore this conviction – goodness only knows. It might have been the legacy of these fretful days of his convalescence. Anyway it was there. He knew better than to express it in so many words. And for my part after having disputed him inch by inch as it were to the Pale Death, I was not willing to throw him and his efficiency away. It would have been ridiculous and perhaps even weak to do so, I thought. Sometimes his idiosyncrasy even amused me.

Lingering for a moment in my cabin I could hear him moving about overhead. His irregular footsteps now slow, now hurried, stopping short sometimes to begin again abruptly, interpreted, reflected the nervous temperament of the man.

When I came on deck he put down the binoculars on the skylight and pointed forward with his extended arm, murmuring "There it is, sir."

After a while, not at once but after my eyes had become adjusted to the infinite brilliance of the morning, I made out the land we had been aiming at for so many days – a mere effect of faint blue shadow between the great, level glitter of the blue sea and the arch of the sky, luminous and blue.

It was a well known Island; known for centuries. The more enthusiastic of its inhabitants delighted in calling it in picturesque and hackneyed phrase: The Pearl of the Indian Ocean. A very good name. Let us call it The Pearl. There it was, indistinguishable from the darkling and mysterious vapours that arise sometimes on the clear-cut edge of the sea horizon, except that it did not change its place.

A mere bit of mist! But I had its engraved shape well fixed on my mind through long contemplations of the chart. It was a pear-shaped pearl of an island, distilling much sweetness upon the world.

It is but a fanciful manner of telling you that first-rate sugar-cane is cultivated there. All the Pearl's population lives by it and for it. Sugar is their daily bread; it is the food of their thoughts, the article of their faith, the aliment of their hopes, the sustenance of their charity. And I myself was coming to them in search of a cargo of sugar, in the hope of the crop having been good and of the freights being high.

That very circumstance spoiled for me the satisfaction natural to a shipmaster at the end of a passage. Matters of business are repugnant to a sailor generally. Sea life unfits one for the battle of commercial wits. To take a ship out to sea, to carry her safely across the sea, to bring her in from sea "all well," as the language of signals has it, is part of a trading operation, certainly, but the part most removed from the trading spirit. The whole inspiration of the call for the sea is altogether unworldly in that sense. A man who obeys it is obviously not born for the chaffering and the bargains of the market-place.

It was that very prospect of business which interfered with my enjoyment of my diaphanous landfall appearing before me like 5 the spirit of an island of dreams. I was anxious to do well by my owners, to do justice to the flattering latitude of my instructions, which were contained in one noble phrase: "we trust you to do the best you can for the ship" – and with only one limitation: "but you must not take her beyond the Cape." The Atlantic alone was 10 barred by these words, which left me yet two thirds of the globe for the display of my business talents. In comparison with the vastness of the stage, I beheld my abilities no bigger than a pin-head.

And as, trying to forget all these unsailorlike cares, I contemplated the delicate, mysterious vision risen from the sea, as if it 15 were a mere subtle emanation, the astral body of an Island, lo and behold, it faded and vanished before I had time to wink three times in succession. Mr Burns who had taken off his eyes to glance at something aloft on the main, exclaimed "Hallo!", peered using his hand as a shade, and at last turned to me with his absurd air 20 of making me responsible.

"Lost in the haze," I murmured entranced, amazed.

"The horizon seems clear as a bell," he grumbled reproachfully.

"Doesn't it! One would swear to it. That, Mr Burns, is one of the wonders of the sea. But I can tell you that there are very few people 25 who have had a sight of that Island at seventy miles off, like this."

"Much good it is to us" was his amiable remark.

It was not in him to be touched by the beauty of this rare phenomenon which is even mentioned in the sailing Directions in their own prosaic style. I was glad to have seen it. And I wondered 30 half seriously whether it was a good omen, whether what would happen to me on that island would be as luckily exceptional as this ethereal and striking vision so very few seamen bound on commercial errands had been privileged to behold.

The afternoon was well advanced before we sighted the island 35 again, this time in all the details of its abrupt stony coast, topped with the green folds of fertile uplands, down to the sombre rocks of its base, steeped in the white froth of a fast darkening sea. A motionless cloud, cutting clean across the slopes of the inland mountains, lay level like a low, dirty ceiling looking rusty in the 40 light of a red sunset. This grey-ribbed, mysterious and bare flank of the island reflecting the lurid gleams of dying light, the frowning cloud, the purple sea – nothing could have been more ill-omened, inhospitable and sinister.

It was too late in the day to even think of entering the harbour. No luck! The promising breeze of the morning had betrayed me; I would have to anchor outside for the night; with the grey wall of the coast on my left and the red sun sinking on my right hand I luffed close round point after point, pressing the ship to save a little daylight for my anchorage of which all I knew was that its holding ground was bad and the marks difficult to distinguish in the dusk.

From the black ravines, opening in the wall of rock higher than our mastheads, gusts of sudden wind fell into the sails causing the spars to creak, the canvas to strain, with an abrupt, loud humming in the rigging that sounded a menacing note. But I was not to be intimidated by these wild demonstrations.

The sun set. How uninhabited, and uninhabitable, that coast looked! Who could have guessed that within a few miles there was a nice little town, a harbour well known to ships! The only sign of human occupancy away to the southward was the cupola of a little screw-pile lighthouse; a dark speck looking no bigger than a floating basket in the distance. The departed sun seemed to have kindled a spark under that thing, a light which seemed about the size of a glowing cigar-end in all that empty, dusky loneliness of grey and purple shades swept by a chilly breeze.

With that glow alone to guide me I drove the ship straight at the wall-like shore. I shot her in so close to the cliffs as almost to frighten myself. She was an unconscionable time in losing her way. But the right moment came at last. I signed to Mr Burns who was watching me from forward, and in the dead silence of the ship, in the great stillness of coast, of the sea, of the whole world I heard in a strange detached way my own voice uttering quietly the words "Let go." And then the falling anchor seemed to take a load off my chest; some load of which I had not been aware till this moment of relief. I drew a deep breath.

An unpleasant and unrestful night followed. The clouds swirled down these porphyry crags with only occasional glimpses of the stars. The wind eddied round the ship and the solitary, feeble gleam of the tin-pot lighthouse astonished one by its steady pertinacity. You expected it to be blown out by the slightest puff and there it was, quite game, at the ship's elbow as it were and not even winking in the gusts.

In my wanderings between my cabin and the deck, for I could not sleep, I came upon Mr Burns who was restless too in this strange roadstead. An excellent chief-officer I tell you.

We listened to the wind making a great bullying noise among the naked spars, with interludes of sad moaning; and I remarked that it was lucky we had managed to fetch the anchorage in time. It was a nasty night to hang off a harbour under canvas.

But he was uncompromising in his fixed attitude.

"Luck you call it sir! – but what is it? A negative sort of luck at best. By rights we ought to have been snugly moored inside."

"We can't have always the best sort of luck. I am pleased enough with what I can get," I said making a show of philosophy.

I

BY HALF PAST seven in the morning, the ship being then inside the harbour at last, and moored within a long stone's throw from the quay, my stock of philosophy was nearly exhausted. I was dressing hurriedly in my cabin when the steward came tripping in with a morning suit over his arm.

Hungry, tired and depressed, with my head engaged inside a white shirt irritatingly stuck together by too much starch, I desired him peevishly to "heave round with that breakfast." I wanted to get ashore as soon as possible.

"Yes sir. Ready at eight sir. There's a gentleman from the shore waiting to speak to you sir."

This statement was curiously slurred over. I dragged the shirt violently over my head and emerged staring.

"So early!" I cried. "Who's he? What does he want?"

On coming in from the sea one has to pick up the conditions of an utterly unrelated existence. Every little event at first has the peculiar emphasis of novelty. I was greatly surprised by that early caller; but this was no reason for my steward to look so particularly foolish.

"Didn't you ask for the name," I inquired in a stern tone.

"His name's Jacobus I believe sir," he mumbled shamefacedly.

"Mr Jacobus!" I exclaimed loudly, more surprised than ever but with a total change of feeling. "Why couldn't you say so at once."

But the fellow had scuttled out of my room. Through the
momentarily opened door I had a glimpse of a tall, stout man
standing in the cuddy by the table on which the cloth was already
laid; a "harbour" table cloth, stainless and dazzlingly white. So far
good.   5

I shouted courteously, through the closed door, that I was dressing and would be with him in a moment. In return the assurance
that there was no hurry reached me in the visitor's deep, quiet
undertone. His time was my own. He dared say I would give him
a cup of coffee presently.   10

"I am afraid you will have a poor breakfast," I cried apologeti-
cally. "We have been sixty one days at sea, you know."

A quiet little laugh with a "That'll be all right Captain" was
his answer. All this, words, intonation, the glimpsed attitude of
the man in the cuddy, had an unexpected character, a something   15
friendly in it – propitiatory. And my surprise was not diminished
thereby. What did this call mean? Was it the sign of some dark
design against my commercial innocence.

Ah! These commercial interests – spoiling the finest life under
the sun. Why must the sea be used for trade – and for war as well.   20
Why kill and traffic on it, pursuing selfish aims of no very great
importance after all. It would have been so much nicer just to sail
about with here and there a port and a bit of land to stretch one's
legs on, buy a few books and get a change of cooking for a while.
But, living in a world more or less homicidal and desperately mer-   25
cantile, it was plainly my duty to make the best of its opportunities.

My owners' letter had left it to me, as I have said before, to
do the best for the ship within certain geographical limits. But it
contained also a postscript worded somewhat as follows: "without
meaning in the least to interfere with your liberty of action we are   30
writing by the outgoing mail to some of our business friends there
who may be of assistance to you. We desire you particularly to call
on Mr Jacobus, a prominent merchant and charterer. Should you
hit it off with him he may be able to put you in the way of profitable
employment for the ship."   35

Hit it off! Here was the prominent creature absolutely on board
asking for the favour of a cup of coffee; and life not being a fairy
tale, the improbability of the event almost shocked me. Had I
discovered an enchanted nook of the earth where wealthy merchants rush fasting on board ships before they are fairly moored?   40

Was this white magic or merely some black trick of trade? I came in the end (while making the bow of my tie) to suspect that perhaps I did not get the name right. I had been thinking of the prominent Mr Jacobus pretty frequently during the passage and my hearing 5 might have been deceived by some remote similarity of sound. . . . The steward might have said Jackson – or Antrobus.

But coming out of my stateroom with an interrogative "Mr Jacobus?" I was met by a quiet "Yes" uttered with a gentle smile. The "yes" was rather perfunctory. He did not seem to make much 10 of the fact that he was Mr Jacobus. I took stock of a big pale face, hair thin at the top, whiskers also thin, of faded nondescript colour, heavy eyelids. The thick, smooth lips in repose looked as if glued together. The smile was faint. A heavy tranquil man. I named my two officers who just then came down to breakfast – 15 but why Mr Burns' silent demeanour should suggest suppressed indignation I could not understand.

While we were taking our seats round the table some disconnected words of an altercation going on in the companion way reached my ear. A stranger apparently wanted to come down to 20 interview me and the steward was opposing him.

"You can't see him."

"Why can't I?"

"The Captain is at breakfast, I tell you. He'll be going ashore presently and you can speak to him on deck."

25 "That's not fair. You let . . ."

"I've had nothing to do with that."

"Oh yes, you have. Everybody ought to have the same chance. You let that fellow . . ."

The rest I lost. The person having been repulsed successfully, 30 the steward came down. I can't say he looked flushed: he was a mulatto; but he looked flustered. After putting the dishes on the table he remained by the sideboard with that lackadaisical air of indifference he used to assume when he had done something too clever by half and was afraid of getting into a scrape over it. The 35 contemptuous expression on Mr Burns' face as he looked from him to me was really extraordinary. I couldn't imagine what new bee had stung the mate now.

The captain being silent, no one else cared to speak, as is the way in ships. And I was saying nothing, simply because I had been made 40 dumb by the splendour of the entertainment. I had expected the

usual sea breakfast whereas I beheld spread before us a veritable
feast of shore provisions: eggs, sausages, butter which plainly did
not come from a Danish tin – Cutlets, and even a dish of potatoes.
It was three weeks since I had seen a real, live potato. I contemplated them with interest and Mr Jacobus disclosed himself as a   5
man of human, homely sympathies and something of a thought
reader.

"Try them Captain," he encouraged me in a friendly undertone.
"They are excellent."

"They look that," I admitted. "Grown on the island I suppose?"   10
"Oh no, imported. Those grown here would be much more
expensive."

I was grieved at the ineptitude of the conversation. Were these
the topics for a prominent and wealthy merchant to discuss. He
was clearly an unconventional individuality. I thought the sim-   15
plicity with which he made himself at home rather attractive. He
examined the dishes critically but benevolently. This reduced me
to despair. What is one to say to a man whose attention is occupied with the disinterested examination of the provender. One
can't turn the conversation abruptly upon the immortality of the   20
soul. To draw him on business would have been positively tactless,
almost indecent – and even worse: impolitic. What is one to talk
about to a man who comes on one suddenly after sixty one days at
sea, out of a totally unknown little town in an island one has never
seen before? What were (besides sugar) the interests of that crumb   25
of earth, its gossip, its topics of conversation? Mystery. And he himself appeared to me so mysterious in his homely quietness that all
I could do was to keep on the old track.

"Are the provisions generally dear here," I asked, fretting
inwardly at my inanity.   30

"I wouldn't say that," he answered placidly with that appearance
of saving his breath his restrained manner of speaking suggested.

He would not be more explicit, yet he did not evade the subject. Eyeing the table in a spirit of complete abstemiousness (he
wouldn't let me help him to any eatables) he went into details of   35
supply. The beef was for the most part imported from Madagascar;
mutton of course was rare and somewhat expensive; but good
goat's flesh . . .

"Are those goat's cutlets," I exclaimed hastily pointing at one of
the dishes.   40

Posed sentimentally by the sideboard the steward gave a start.
"Lor', no sir! It's real mutton!"

Mr Burns got through his breakfast impatiently, as if exasperated
by being made a party to some monstrous foolishness, muttered a
5   curt excuse and went on deck. Shortly afterwards the second mate
took his smooth red countenance out of the cabin. With the
appetite of a school-boy and after two months of sea-fare he appreciated the generous spread. But I did not. It smacked of extrava-
gance. All the same it was a remarkable feat to have produced it
10 so quickly and I congratulated the steward on his smartness in a
somewhat ominous tone. He gave me a deprecatory smile and, in
a way I didn't know what to make of, blinked his fine dark eyes in
the direction of the guest.

The latter asked under his breath for another cup of coffee,
15 and nibbled ascetically at a piece of very hard ship's biscuit. I
don't think he consumed a square inch in the end; but meantime he gave me, casually as it were, a complete account of the
sugar crop, of the local business houses, of the state of the freight
market. All that talk was interspersed with hints as to person-
20 alities, amounting to veiled warnings, but his pale, fleshy face
remained equable without a gleam, as if ignorant of his voice. As
you may imagine I opened my ears very wide. Every word was precious. My ideas as to the value of a business friendship were being
favourably modified. He gave me the names of all the disponible
25 ships together with their tonnage and the names of their commanders. From that, which was still commercial information, he
condescended to mere harbour gossip. The *Hilda* had unaccountably lost her figure-head in the Bay of Bengal, and her captain was
greatly affected by this. He and the ship had been getting on in
30 years together and the old gentleman imagined this strange event
to be a forerunner of his own early dissolution. The *Stella* had
experienced awful weather off the Cape – had her decks swept,
and the chief officer washed overboard; and only a few hours
before reaching port the little baby died. Poor Captain H— and
35 his wife were terribly cut up. If they had only been able to bring
it into port alive it could have been probably saved; but the wind
failed them for the last week or so, light breezes, and . . . the
baby was going to be buried this afternoon. He supposed I would
attend. . . .

40   "Do you think I ought to," I asked shrinkingly.

He thought so, decidedly. It would be greatly appreciated. All the captains in the harbour were going to attend. Poor Mrs H— was quite prostrated. Pretty hard on H— altogether.

"And you Captain – you are not married I suppose?"

"No. I am not married," I said. "Neither married nor even engaged."

Mentally I thanked my stars; and while he smiled in a musing, dreamy fashion I expressed my acknowledgements for his visit and for the interesting business information he had been good enough to impart to me. But I said nothing of my wonder thereat.

"Of course I would have made a point of calling on you in a day or two," I concluded.

He raised his eyelids distinctly at me and somehow managed to look rather more sleepy than before.

"In accordance with my owners' instructions," I explained. "You have had their letter of course."

By that time he had raised his eyebrows too but without any particular emotion. On the contrary he struck me then as absolutely imperturbable.

"Oh! You must be thinking of my brother."

It was for me then to say "Oh!" but I hope that no more than civil surprise appeared in my voice when I asked him to what then I owed the pleasure . . . . He was reaching for an inside pocket leisurely.

"My brother's a very different person. But I am well known in this part of the world. You've probably heard . . ."

I took the card he extended to me. A thick business card as I lived! Alfred Jacobus (the other was Ernest) dealer in every description of ship's stores! Provisions salt and fresh, oils, paints, rope, canvass etc., etc. Ships in harbour victualled by contract on moderate terms . . .

"I've never heard of you," I said brusquely.

His lowpitched assurance did not abandon him.

"You will be very well satisfied," he breathed out quietly.

But I was not placated. I had the sense of having been circumvented somehow. Yet I had deceived myself – if there was any deception. But the confounded cheek of inviting himself to breakfast was enough to deceive any one. And the thought struck me: Why! The fellow had provided all these eatables himself in the way of business. I said:

"You must have got up mighty early this morning."

He admitted with simplicity that he was on the quay before six o'clock waiting for my ship to come in. He gave me the impression that it would be impossible to get rid of him now.

5 "If you think we are going to live on that scale," I said looking at the table with an irritated eye "you are jolly well mistaken."

"You'll find it all right, Captain. I quite understand."

Nothing could disturb his equanimity. I felt dissatisfied, but I could not very well fly out at him. He had told me many useful 10 things – and besides he was the brother of that wealthy merchant. That seemed queer enough.

I rose and told him curtly that I must now go ashore. At once he offered me the use of his boat for all the time of my stay in port.

"I only make a nominal charge," he continued equably. "My 15 man remains all day at the landing steps. You have only to blow a whistle when you want the boat."

And standing aside at every doorway to let me go through first he carried me off in his custody after all. As we crossed the quarter deck two shabby individuals stepped forward and in mournful 20 silence offered me business cards which I took from them without a word under his heavy eye. It was a useless and gloomy ceremony. They were the touts of the other shipchandlers, and he placid at my back ignored their existence.

We parted on the quay after he had expressed quietly the hope of 25 seeing me often "at the store." He had a smoking room for captains there with newspapers and a box of "rather decent cigars." I left him very unceremoniously.

My consignees received me with the usual business heartiness, but their account of the state of the freight-market was by no 30 means so favourable as the talk of the wrong Jacobus had led me to expect. Naturally I became inclined now to put my trust in his version, rather. As I closed the door of the private office behind me I thought to myself: "H'm. A lot of lies. Commercial diplomacy. That's the sort of thing a man coming from sea has got to expect. 35 They would try to charter the ship under the market rate."

In the big outer room full of desks the chief clerk, a tall, lean, shaved person in immaculate white clothes and with a shiny closely cropped black head on which silvery gleams came and went, rose from his place and detained me affably. Anything they could do 40 for me? They would be most happy . . . . Was I likely to call again

in the afternoon? What? Going to a funeral . . . ? Oh yes – poor
Captain H— . . .

He pulled a long sympathetic face for a moment, then dismiss-
ing from this work-a-day world the baby, which had got ill in a
tempest and had died from too much calm at sea, he asked me
with a dental, shark-like smile (if sharks had false teeth) whether
I had made yet my little arrangements for the ship's stay in port.

"Yes, with Jacobus," I answered carelessly. "I understand he's
the brother of Mr Ernest Jacobus to whom I have an introduction
from my owners."

I was not sorry to let him know I was not altogether helpless
in the hands of his firm. He screwed his thin lips dubiously. . . .
"Why," I cried, "isn't he the brother . . . ?"

"Oh yes. . . . They haven't spoken together for eighteen years,"
he added impressively after a pause.

"Indeed! What's the quarrel about?"

"Oh nothing, nothing that one would care to mention," he
protested primly. "Only if I were you I wouldn't believe all he
says. Not *all*. Good morning Captain."

He went away mincingly to his desk. He amused me. He resembled an old maid, a commercial old maid, shocked by some impropriety. Was it a commercial impropriety? Commercial impropriety
is a serious matter for it aims at one's pocket. Or was he only a
purist in conduct who disapproved of Jacobus doing his own touting. It was certainly undignified. I wondered how the merchant
brother liked it. But then different countries, different customs.
In a community so isolated and so exclusively "trading" the social
standards have their own scale.

II

I WOULD HAVE gladly dispensed with the mournful opportunity of becoming acquainted by sight with all my fellow captains
at once. However I found my way to the cemetery. We made a
considerable group of bare-headed men in sombre garments. I
noticed that those of our company most approaching to the now
obsolete sea-dog type were the most moved – perhaps because they
had less "manner" than the new generation. The old sea-dog, away
from his natural element, was a simple and sentimental animal. I
noticed one, he was facing me across the grave, who was dropping

tears. They trickled down his weather-beaten face like drops of rain on an old rugged wall. I learned afterwards that he was looked upon as the terror of sailors, a hard man; that he had never had wife or chick of his own, and that engaged from his tenderest
5 years in deep-sea voyages he knew women and children merely by sight.

Perhaps he was dropping those tears over his own lost opportunities, from sheer envy of paternity and in a strange jealousy of a sorrow which he could never know. Man, and even the seaman, is
10 a capricious animal, the creature and the victim of lost opportunities. But he made me feel ashamed of my callousness. I had no tears. I listened with a horribly critical detachment to that service I had had to read myself, once or twice, over childlike men who had died at sea. The words of hope and defiance, the winged words
15 so inspiring in the free immensity of water and sky, seemed to fall wearily into that little grave. What was the use of asking Death where her sting was, before that small dark hole in the ground. And then my thoughts escaped me altogether – away into matters of life – and no very high matters at that – ships, freights, busi-
20 ness. In the instability of his emotions man resembles deplorably a monkey. I was disgusted with my thoughts – and I thought: Shall I be able to get a charter soon? Time's money. . . . Will that Jacobus really put good business in my way? . . . I must go and see him in a day or two.
25 Don't imagine that I pursued these thoughts with any precision. They pursued me rather: vague, shadowy, restless, shamefaced. Theirs was a callous, abominable, almost revolting pertinacity. And it was the presence of that pertinacious shipchandler which had started them. He stood mournfully amongst our little band of men
30 from the sea, and I was angry at his presence which, suggesting his brother the merchant, had caused me to become outrageous to myself. For indeed I had preserved some decency of feeling. It was only the mind which . . .

It was over at last. The poor father – a man of forty with black
35 bushy side-whiskers and a pathetic gash on his freshly shaved chin – thanked us all, swallowing his tears. But for some reason – either because I lingered at the gate of the cemetery, being somewhat hazy as to my way back, or because I was the youngest, or ascrib-ing my moodiness caused by remorse to some more worthy and
40 appropriate sentiment, or, simply because I was even more of a

stranger to him than the others – he singled me out. Keeping at my side he renewed his thanks which I listened to in a gloomy, conscience-stricken silence. Suddenly he slipped one hand under my arm and waved the other after a tall, stout figure walking away by itself down a side street in a flutter of thin, grey garments.   5

"That's a good fellow – a real good fellow" . . . he swallowed down a belated sob . . . "this Jacobus."

And he told me in a low voice that Jacobus was the first man to board his ship on arrival, and learning of their misfortune had taken charge of everything, volunteered to attend to all routine   10 business, carried off the ship's papers on shore, arranged for the funeral . . . .

"A good fellow. I was knocked over. I had been looking at my wife for ten days. And helpless. Just you think of that. The dear little chap died the very day we made the land. How I managed   15 to take the ship in – God alone knows! I couldn't see anything; I couldn't speak; I couldn't . . . . You've heard perhaps, that we lost our mate overboard on the passage. There was no one to do it for me. And the poor woman nearly crazy down below there all alone with the . . . . By the Lord! It isn't fair."   20

We walked in silence together. I did not know how to part from him. On the quay he let go my arm and struck fiercely his fist into the palm of his other hand.

"By God it isn't fair!" he cried again. "Don't you ever marry unless you can chuck the sea first. . . . It isn't fair."   25

I had no intention to "chuck the sea" and when he left me to go aboard his ship I felt convinced I would never marry. While I was waiting at the steps for Jacobus' boatman, who had gone off somewhere, the captain of the *Hilda* joined me, a slender silk umbrella in his hand and the sharp points of his archaic, gladstonian shirt   30 collar framing a small, clean-shaved, ruddy face. It was wonderfully fresh for his age, beautifully modelled and lit up by remarkably clear blue eyes. A lot of white hair, glossy like spun glass, curled upwards slightly under the brim of his valuable, ancient panama hat with a broad black ribbon. In the aspect of that vivacious,   35 neat, little old man there was something quaintly angelic and also boyish.

He accosted me, as though he had been in the habit of seeing me every day of his life from my earliest childhood, with a whimsical remark on the appearance of a stout negro woman who was sitting   40 upon a stool near the edge of the quay. Presently he observed amiably that I had a very pretty little barque.

I returned this civil speech by saying readily:

"Not so pretty as the *Hilda*."

5   At once the corners of his clear-cut sensitive mouth dropped dismally.

"O, dear! I can hardly bear to look at her now."

Did I know, he asked anxiously, that he had lost his figure-head? A woman in a blue tunic edged with gold, the face perhaps not
10   so very, very pretty but her bare white arms beautifully shaped and extended as if she were swimming. Did I? Who would have expected such a thing! . . . After twenty years, too. Nobody could have guessed from his tone that the woman was made of wood; his trembling voice, his agitated manner gave to his lamentations a
15   ludicrously scandalous flavour. . . . Disappeared at night – a clear fine night with just a slight swell – in the gulf of Bengal. Went off without a splash – no one in the ship could tell why, how, at what hour – after twenty years last October . . .

Did I ever hear . . .

20   I assured him sympathetically that I had never heard – and he became very doleful. This meant no good he was sure. There was something in it that looked like a warning. But when I remarked that surely another figure of a woman could be procured I found myself being soundly rated for my levity. The old boy flushed pink
25   under his clear tan as if I had proposed something improper. One could replace masts, I was told, or a lost rudder – any working part of a ship; but where was the use of sticking up a new figure-head? How could one care for it? What satisfaction? It was easy to see that I had never been shipmates with a figure-head for over twenty
30   years.

"A new figure-head!" he scolded in unquenchable indignation. "Why! I've been a widower now for eight and twenty years come next May and I would just as soon think of getting a new wife. You're as bad as that fellow Jacobus."

35   I was highly amused. "What has Jacobus done? Did he want you to marry again Captain?" I inquired in a deferential tone. But he was launched now and only grinned fiercely.

"Procure – indeed! He's the sort of chap to procure you anything you like for a price. I hadn't been moored here for an hour when
40   he got on board and at once offered to sell me a figure-head he

happens to have in his yard somewhere. He got Smith, my mate,
to talk to me about it. 'Mr Smith,' says I, 'don't you know me better
than that? Am I the sort that would pick up with another man's
cast-off figure-head?' . . . And after all these years too! The way
some of you young fellows talk . . ."   5

I affected great compunction and as I stepped into the boat I
said soberly:

"Then I see nothing for it but to fit in a neat fiddle head –
perhaps. You know, carved scroll work, nicely gilt."

He became very dejected after his outburst.   10

"Yes. Scroll work. May be. Jacobus hinted at that too. He's never
at a loss when there's any money to be extracted from a sailor man.
He would make me pay through the nose for that carving. A gilt
fiddle head did you say – eh? I dare say it would do for you. You
young fellows don't seem to have any feeling for what's proper."   15

He made a convulsive gesture with his right arm.

"Never mind. Nothing can make much difference. I would just
as soon let the old thing go about the world with a bare cut water,"
he cried sadly. Then as the boat got away from the steps he raised
his voice on the edge of the quay with comical animosity: 20

"I would! If only to spite that figure-head procuring bloodsucker. I am an old bird here and don't you forget it. Come and
see me on board some day!"

I spent my first evening in port quietly in my ship's cuddy; and
glad enough I was to think that the shore life, which strikes one   25
as so pettily complex, so discordant and so full of new faces on
first coming from sea, could be kept off for a few hours longer. I
was however fated to hear the Jacobus note once more before I
slept.

Mr Burns had gone ashore after the evening meal to have as he   30
said "a look round." As it was quite dark when he announced his
intention I didn't ask him what it was he expected to see. Some
time about midnight, while sitting with a book in the saloon, I
heard cautious movements in the lobby and hailed him by name.

Burns came in stick and hat in hand, incredibly vulgarised by   35
his smart shore togs, with a jaunty air and an odious twinkle in his
eye. Being asked to sit down he laid his hat and stick on the table,
and after we had talked of ship affairs for a little while:

"I've been hearing pretty tales on shore about that shipchandler
fellow who snatched the job from you so neatly, sir."   40

I remonstrated with my late patient for his manner of expressing himself. But he only tossed his head disdainfully. A pretty dodge indeed: boarding a strange ship with breakfast in two baskets for all hands and calmly inviting himself to the captain's table! Never
5 heard of anything so crafty and so impudent in his life.

I found myself defending Jacobus' unusual methods.

"He's the brother of one of the wealthiest merchants in the port." The mate's eyes fairly snapped green sparks.

"His grand brother hasn't spoken to him for eighteen or twenty
10 years," he declared triumphantly. "So there!"

"I know all about that," I interrupted loftily.

"Do you sir? H'm!"

His mind was still running on the ethics of commercial competition. "I don't like to see your good nature taken advantage of.
15 He's bribed that steward of ours with a five rupee note to let him come down – or ten for that matter. He don't care. He will shove that and more into the bill presently."

"Is that one of the tales you have heard ashore?" I asked.

He assured me that his own sense would tell him that much.
20 No; what he had heard on shore was that no respectable person in the whole town would come near Jacobus. He lived in a large old fashioned house in one of the quiet streets with a big garden. After telling me this Burns put on a mysterious air: "He keeps a girl shut up there who, they say . . ."
25 "I suppose you've heard all that gossip in some eminently respectable place," I snapped at him in my most sarcastic tone.

The shaft told because Mr Burns like many other disagreeable people was very sensitive himself. He remained as if thunderstruck, with his mouth open for some further communication, but I did
30 not give him the chance.

"And anyhow what the devil do I care?" I added retiring into my room.

And this was a natural thing to say. Yet somehow I was not indifferent. I admit it is absurd to be concerned with the morals of
35 one's shipchandler, if ever so well connected; but his personality had stamped itself upon my first day in harbour in the way you know.

After this initial exploit Jacobus showed himself anything but intrusive. He was out in a boat early every morning going round
40 the ships he served, and occasionally remaining on board one of them for breakfast with the captain.

As I discovered that this practice was generally accepted, I just nodded to him familiarly when one morning on coming out of my room I found him in the cabin. Glancing over the table I saw that his place was already laid. He stood, awaiting my appearance, very bulky and placid, holding a beautiful bunch of flowers in his thick podgy hand. He offered them to my notice with a faint, sleepy smile. From his own garden: had a very fine old garden: picked them himself that morning before going out to business: thought I would like . . . . He turned away.

"Steward, can you oblige me with some water in a large jar, please."

I assured him jocularly, as I took my place at the table, that he made me feel as if I were a pretty girl, and that he musn't be surprised if I blushed. But he was busy arranging his floral tribute at the sideboard.

"Stand it before the Captain's plate steward, if you please." He made this request in his usual undertone.

The offering was so pointed that I could do no less than to raise it to my nose; and as he sat down noiselessly he breathed out his opinion that a few flowers improved notably the appearance of a ship's saloon. He wondered why I did not have a shelf fitted all round the skylight for flowers in pots to take to sea with me. He had a skilled workman able to fit proper shelves in a day, and he could procure me two or three dozen good plants . . .

The tips of his thick round fingers rested composedly on the edge of the table on each side of his cup of coffee. His face remained immovable. Mr Burns was smiling maliciously to himself. I declared that I hadn't the slightest intention of turning my skylight into a conservatory only to keep the cabin table in a perpetual mess of mould and dead vegetable matter.

"Rear most beautiful flowers," he insisted with an upward glance. "It's no trouble really."

"Oh yes. It is. Lots of trouble," I contradicted. "And in the end some fool leaves the skylight open in a fresh breeze, a flick of salt water gets at them and the whole lot is dead in a week."

Mr Burns snorted a contemptuous approval. Jacobus gave up the subject passively. After a time he unglued his thick lips to ask me if I had seen his brother yet. I was very curt in my answer:

"No. Not yet."

"A very different person," he remarked dreamily and got up. His movements were particularly noiseless. "Well – thank you Captain.

If anything is not to your liking please mention it to your steward. I suppose you will be giving a dinner to the office-clerks presently?"

"What for?" I cried with some warmth. "If I were a steady trader to the port I could understand it. But a complete stranger! . . . I
5 may not turn up again here for years. I don't see why. I . . . . Do you mean to say it is customary?"

"It will be expected from a man like you," he breathed out placidly. "Eight of the principal clerks, the manager, that's nine, you three gentlemen, that's twelve. It needn't be very expensive.
10 If you tell your steward to give me a day's notice . . ."

"It will be expected of me! Why should it be expected of me? Is it because I look particularly soft – or what?"

His immobility struck me as dignified suddenly, his imperturbable quality as dangerous. "There's plenty of time to think
15 about that," I concluded weakly with a gesture that tried to wave him away. But before he departed he took time to mention regretfully that he had not yet had the pleasure of seeing me at his "store" to sample those cigars. He held a parcel of six thousand to dispose of, very cheap.

20 "I think it would be worth your while to secure some," he added with a fat melancholy smile and left the cabin.

Mr Burns struck his fist on the table excitedly.

"Did you ever see such impudence! He's made up his mind to get something out of you one way or another, sir."

25 At once feeling inclined to defend Jacobus, I observed philosophically that all this was business, I supposed. But my absurd mate muttering broken disjointed sentences, such as I cannot bear . . . mark my words . . . and so on, flung out of the cabin. If I hadn't nursed him through that deadly fever I wouldn't have
30 suffered such manners for a single day.

III

JACOBUS HAVING PUT me in mind of his wealthy brother, I concluded I would pay that business call at once. I had by this time heard a little more of him. He was a member of the Council
35 where he made himself objectionable to the authorities. He exercised a considerable influence on public opinion. A lot of people owed him money. He was an importer on a great scale of all sorts of goods. For instance the whole supply of bags for sugar was

practically in his hands. This last fact I did not learn till afterwards. The general impression conveyed to me was that of a local
personage. He was a bachelor and gave weekly card parties in his
house out of town which were attended by the best people in the
colony.   5

The greater, then, was my surprise to discover his office in shabby
surroundings, quite away from the business quarter, amongst a lot
of hovels. Guided by a black board with white lettering I climbed
a narrow wooden staircase and entered a room with a bare floor
of planks littered with bits of brown paper and wisps of packing-   10
straw. A great number of what looked like wine cases was piled up
against one of the walls. A lanky, inky, light-yellow mulatto youth,
miserably long-necked and generally recalling a sick chicken, got
off a three-legged stool behind a cheap deal desk and faced me as
if gone dumb with fright. I had some difficulty in persuading him   15
to take in my name, though I could not get from him the nature of
his objection. He did it at last with an almost agonised reluctance
which ceased to be mysterious to me when I heard him being
sworn at menacingly with savage, suppressed growls, then audibly
cuffed and finally kicked out without any concealment whatever;   20
because he came back flying head foremost through the door with
a stifled shriek.

To say I was startled would not express it. I remained still like a
man lost in a dream. Clapping both his hands to that part of his
frail anatomy which had received the shock the poor wretch said   25
to me simply:

"Will you go in please."

His lamentable self-possession was wonderful; but it did not
do away with the incredibility of the experience. A preposterous
notion that I had seen that boy somewhere before, a thing obvi-   30
ously impossible, was like a delicate finishing touch of weirdness
added to a scene fit to raise doubts as to one's sanity. I stared
anxiously about me like an awakened somnambulist.

"I say," I cried loudly. "There isn't a mistake – is there? This is
Mr Jacobus' office."   35

The boy only gazed at me with a pained expression – and somehow so familiar! A voice within growled offensively:

"Come in, come in, since you are there. . . . I didn't know."

I crossed the outer room as one approaches the den of some
unknown wild beast with intrepidity but in some excitement. Only,   40

no wild beast that ever lived would rouse one's indignation; the power to do that belongs to the odiousness of the human brute. And I was very indignant, which did not prevent me from being at once struck by the extraordinary resemblance of the two brothers.

5   This one was dark, instead of being fair like the other; but he was as big. He was without his coat and waistcoat; he doubtless had been snoozing in the rocking chair which stood in a corner furthest from the window. Above the great bulk of his crumpled white shirt, buttoned with three diamond studs, his round face 10 looked swarthy. It was moist; his brown moustache hung limp and ragged; he pushed a common, cane-bottomed chair towards me with his foot.

"Sit down."

I glanced at it casually, then, turning my indignant eyes full upon 15 him, I declared in precise and incisive tones that I had called in obedience to my owners' instructions.

"Oh yes. H'm! I didn't understand what that fool was saying. . . . But never mind! It will teach the scoundrel to disturb me at this time of the day," he added grinning at me with savage cynicism.

20   I looked at my watch. It was past three o'clock – quite the full swing of afternoon office-work in the port. He snarled imperiously:

"Sit down Captain."

I acknowledged the gracious invitation by saying deliberately:

"I can listen to all you may have to say without sitting down."

25   Emitting a loud vehement "Pshaw!" he glared for a moment very round-eyed and fierce. It was like a gigantic tom cat spitting at one suddenly.

"Look at him! What do you fancy yourself to be? What did you come here for? If you won't sit down and talk business you had 30 better go to the devil."

"I don't know him personally," I said. "But after this I wouldn't mind calling on him. It would be refreshing to meet a gentleman."

He followed me, growling behind my back.

"The impudence. I've a good mind to write to your owners what 35 I think of you."

I turned on him for a moment.

"As it happens I don't care. For my part I assure you I won't even take the trouble to mention you to them."

He stopped at the door of his office while I traversed the littered 40 anteroom. I think he was somewhat taken aback.

"I will break every bone in your body," he roared suddenly at the miserable mulatto lad, "if you ever dare to disturb me before half past three for anybody. D'ye hear? For anybody! . . . Let alone any damned skipper," he added in a lower growl.

The frail youngster swaying like a reed made a low moaning sound. I stopped short and addressed this sufferer with advice. It was prompted by the sight of a hammer (used for opening the wine-cases I suppose), which was lying on the floor.

"If I were you my boy I would have that thing up my sleeve when I went in next and at the first occasion I would . . ." What was there so familiar in that lad's yellow face? Entrenched and quaking behind the flimsy desk he never looked up. His heavy, lowered eyelids gave me suddenly the clue of the puzzle. He resembled – yes, these thick, glued lips – he resembled the brothers Jacobus. He resembled both, the wealthy merchant and the pushing shopkeeper (who resembled each other); he resembled them as much as a thin, light-yellow mulatto lad may resemble a big, stout, middle-aged white man. It was his exotic complexion and the slightness of his build which had put me off so completely. Now I saw in him unmistakably the Jacobus strain, weakened, attenuated, diluted as it were in a bucket of water – and I refrained from finishing my speech. I had intended to say "crack the brute's head for him." I still felt the conclusion to be sound. But it is no trifling responsibility to counsel parricide to any one, however deeply injured.

"Beggarly . . . cheeky . . . skippers."

I despised the emphatic growl at my back; only, being much vexed and upset, I regret to say that I slammed the door behind me in a most undignified manner.

It may not appear altogether absurd if I say that I brought out from that interview a kindlier view of the other Jacobus. It was with a feeling resembling partisanship that, a few days later, I called at his "store." That long, cavern-like place of business very dim at the back and stuffed full of all sorts of goods was entered from the street by a lofty archway. At the far end I saw my Jacobus exerting himself in his shirt sleeves amongst his assistants. The captain's room was a small, vaulted apartment with a stone floor and heavy iron bars in its windows, like a dungeon converted to hospitable purposes. A couple of cheerful bottles and several gleaming glasses made a brilliant cluster round a tall, cool, red earthenware pitcher on the centre-table which was littered with newspapers from all parts of the world. A well groomed stranger in a smart, grey check suit sitting with a leg flung over his knee put down one of these sheets briskly and nodded to me.

5 I guessed him to be a steamer captain. It was impossible to get to know these men. They came and went too quickly and their ships lay moored far out, at the very entrance of the harbour. Theirs was another life altogether. He yawned slightly.

"Dull hole isn't it?"

I understood this to allude to the town.

10 "Do you find it so?" I murmured.

"Don't you? But I'm off to-morrow – thank goodness."

He was a very gentlemanly person, good-natured and superior. I watched him draw the open box of cigars to his side of the table, take a big cigar-case out of his pocket and begin to fill it very

15 methodically. Presently on our eyes meeting, he winked like a common mortal and invited me to follow his example. "They are really decent smokes."

I shook my head. "I am not off to-morrow."

"What of that? Think I am abusing old Jacobus' hospitality?

20 Heavens! It goes into the bill of course. He spreads such little matters all over his account. He can take care of himself! Why it's business . . ."

I noted a shadow fall over his well-satisfied expression, a momentary hesitation in closing his cigar-case. But he ended by putting

25 it in his pocket jauntily. A placid voice uttered in the doorway:

"That's quite correct Captain."

The large, noiseless Jacobus advanced into the room. His quietness, in the circumstances, amounted to cordiality. He had put on his jacket before joining us and he sat down in the chair vacated

30 by the steamer-man, who nodded again to me and went out with a short, jarring laugh. A profound silence reigned. With his drowsy stare Jacobus seemed to be slumbering open-eyed. Yet, somehow, I was aware of being profoundly scrutinised by those heavy eyes. In the enormous cavern of the store somebody began to nail down a

35 case expertly: tap-tap . . . tap-tap-tap. Two other experts, one slow and nasal, the other shrill and snappy, started checking an invoice.

"A half-coil of three-inch manilla rope."

"Right!"

"Six assorted shackles."

40 "Right."

"Six tins assorted soups, three of paté, two asparagus, fourteen pounds tobacco – cabin."

"Right."

"It's for the captain who was here just now," breathed out the immovable Jacobus. "These steamer orders are very small. They pick up what they want as they go along. That man will be in Samarang in less than a fortnight. Very small orders indeed." The calling over of the items went on in the shop; an extraordinary jumble of varied articles, paint-brushes, Yorkshire Relish, etc., etc. . . . "Three sacks best potatoes" read out the nasal voice.

At this Jacobus blinked like a sleeping man roused by a shake, and displayed some animation. At his order shouted into the shop a smirking, half-caste clerk, with his ringlets much oiled and with a pen stuck behind his ear, brought in a sample of six potatoes which he paraded in a row on the table.

Being urged to look at their beauty I gave them a cold and hostile glance. Calmly, Jacobus proposed that I should order ten or fifteen tons – tons! I couldn't believe my ears. My crew could not have eaten such a lot in a year; and potatoes (excuse these practical remarks) are a highly perishable commodity. I thought he was joking – or else trying to find out whether I was an unutterable idiot. But his purpose was not so simple. I discovered that he meant me to buy them on my own account.

"I am proposing you a bit of business Captain. I wouldn't charge you a great price."

I told him that I did not go in for trade. I even added grimly that I knew only too well how that sort of spec. generally ended.

He sighed and clasped his hands on his stomach with exemplary resignation. I admired the placidity of his impudence. Then waking up somewhat:

"Won't you try a cigar Captain."

"No thanks. I don't smoke cigars."

"For once!" he exclaimed in a patient whisper. A melancholy silence ensued. You know how sometimes a person discloses a certain unsuspected depth and acuteness of thought; that is, in other words, utters something unexpected. It was unexpected enough to hear Jacobus say:

"The man who just went out was right enough. You might take one, Captain. Here everything is bound to be in the way of business."

I felt a little ashamed of myself. The remembrance of his horrid brother made him appear a quite decent sort of fellow. It was with some compunction that I said a few words to the effect that I could have no possible objection to his hospitality.

5   Before I was a minute older I saw where this admission was leading me. As if changing the subject Jacobus mentioned that his private house was about ten minutes' walk away. It had a beautiful, old walled garden. Something really remarkable. I ought to come round some day and have a look at it.

10   He seemed to be a lover of gardens. I too take extreme delight in them; but I did not mean my compunction to carry me as far as Jacobus' flower-beds, however beautiful and old. He added with a certain homeliness of tone:

"There's only my girl there."

15   It is difficult to set down everything in due order; so I must revert here to what happened a week or two before. The medical officer of the Port had come on board my ship to have a look at one of my crew who was ailing, and naturally enough he was asked to step into the cabin. A fellow-shipmaster of mine was there too; and in

20   the conversation, somehow or other, the name of Jacobus came to be mentioned. It was pronounced with no particular reverence by the other man, I believe. I don't remember now what I was going to say. The doctor, a pleasant, cultivated fellow with an assured manner, prevented me by striking in, in a sour vexed tone:

25   "Ah! You're talking about my respected papa-in-law."

Of course that sally silenced us at the time. But I remembered the episode, and at this juncture, pushed for something non-committal to say, I enquired with polite surprise:

"You have your married daughter living with you, Mr Jacobus?"

30   He moved his big hand from right to left quietly. No! That was another of his girls, he stated ponderously and under his breath as usual. She . . . . He seemed in a pause to be ransacking his mind for some kind of descriptive phrase. But my hopes were disappointed. He merely said:

35   "She's a very different sort of person."

"Indeed. . . . And by the way, Jacobus, I called on your brother the other day. It's no great compliment if I say that I found him a very different sort of person from you."

He had an air of profound reflection then remarked quaintly:

40   "He's a man of regular habits." He might have been alluding to

the habit of late siesta; but I mumbled something about "beastly habits anyhow" – and left the store abruptly.

IV

MY LITTLE PASSAGE with Jacobus the merchant became known generally. One or two of my acquaintances made distant 5 allusions to it. Maybe the mulatto boy had talked. I must confess that people appeared rather scandalized – but not with Jacobus' brutality. A man I knew remonstrated with me for my hastiness.

I gave him the whole story of my visit, not forgetting the tell-tale resemblance of the wretched mulatto boy to his tormentor. He 10 was not surprised. No doubt, no doubt. What of that? In a jovial tone he assured me that there must be many of that sort. The elder Jacobus had been a bachelor all his life. A highly respectable bachelor. But there never had been open scandal in that connection. His life had been quite regular. It could cause no offence to 15 anyone.

I said that I had been offended considerably. My interlocutor opened very wide eyes. Why? Because a mulatto lad got a few knocks? That was not a great affair, surely. I had no idea how insolent and untruthful these half-castes were. In truth he seemed 20 to think Mr Jacobus rather kind than otherwise to employ that youth at all; a sort of amiable weakness which could be forgiven.

This acquaintance of mine belonged to one of the old French families, descendants of the old colonists; all noble, all impoverished and living a narrow domestic life in dull, dignified decay. 25 The men as a rule occupy inferior posts in government offices or in business houses. The girls are almost always pretty, ignorant of the world, kind and agreeable and generally bilingual; they prattle innocently both in French and English. The emptiness of their existence passes belief. 30

I obtained my entry into a couple of such households because some years before, in Bombay, I had occasion to be of use to a pleasant, ineffectual young man who was rather stranded there, not knowing what to do with himself or even how to get home to his island again. It was a matter of two hundred rupees or 35 so, but when I turned up, the family made a point of showing their gratitude by admitting me to their intimacy. My knowledge of the French language made me specially acceptable. They had

meantime managed to marry the fellow to a woman nearly twice his age, comparatively well off; the only profession he was really fit for. But it was not all cakes and ale. The first time I called on the couple she spied a little spot of grease on the poor devil's pan-
5 taloons and made him a screaming scene of reproaches so full of sincere passion that I sat terrified as at a tragedy of Racine.

Of course there was never question of the money I had advanced him; but his sisters, Miss Angeli and Miss Mary, and the aunts of both families, who spoke quaint archaic French of pre-Revolution
10 period, and a host of distant relations adopted me for a friend outright in a manner which was almost embarrassing.

It was with the eldest brother (he was employed at a desk in my consignee's office) that I was having this talk about the merchant Jacobus. He regretted my attitude and nodded his head sagely. An
15 influential man. One never knew when one would need him. I expressed my immense preference for the shopkeeper of the two. At that my friend looked grave.

"What on earth are you pulling that long face about," I cried impatiently. "He asked me to see his garden and I have a good
20 mind to go some day."

"Don't do that," he said so earnestly that I burst into a fit of laughter; but he looked at me without a smile.

This was another matter altogether. At one time the public con-science of the island had been mightily troubled by my Jacobus.
25 The two brothers had been partners for years in great harmony, when a wandering circus came to the island and my Jacobus became suddenly infatuated with one of the lady-riders. What made it worse was that he was married. He had not even the grace to conceal his passion. It must have been strong indeed to carry
30 away such a large, placid creature. His behaviour was perfectly scandalous. He followed that woman to the Cape, and apparently travelled at the tail of that beastly circus to other parts of the world, in a most degrading position. The woman soon ceased to care for him, and treated him worse than a dog. Most extraordinary stories
35 of moral degradation were reaching the island at the time. He had not the strength of mind to shake himself free. . . .

The grotesque image of a fat, pushing shipchandler enslaved by an unholy love-spell, fascinated me; and I listened, rather open-mouthed, to the tale as old as the world, a tale which had been
40 the subject of legend, of moral fables, of poems, but which so

ludicrously failed to fit the personality. What a strange victim for
the gods!

Meantime his deserted wife had died. His daughter was taken
care of by his brother who married her as advantageously as was
possible in the circumstances.

"Oh! The Mrs Doctor," I exclaimed.

"You know that? Yes. A very able man. He wanted a lift in the
world and there was a good bit of money from her mother, besides
the expectations . . . . Of course they don't know him," he added.
"The doctor nods in the street I believe, but he avoids speaking to
him when they meet on board a ship, as must happen sometimes."

I remarked that this surely was an old story by now.

My friend assented. But it was Jacobus' own fault that it was
neither forgiven nor forgotten. He came back ultimately. But how?
Not in a spirit of contrition, in a way to propitiate his scandalised
fellow-citizens. He must needs drag along with him a child – a
girl . . .

"He spoke to me of a daughter who lives with him," I observed
very much interested.

"She's certainly the daughter of the circus-woman," said my
friend. "She may be his daughter too; I am willing to admit that
she is. In fact I have no doubt . . ."

But he did not see why she should have been brought into a
respectable community to perpetuate the memory of the scandal.
And that was not the worst. Presently something much more distressing happened. That abandoned woman turned up. Landed
from a mail-boat . . .

"What! Here? To claim the child perhaps," I suggested.

"Not it" – my friendly informant was very scornful. "Imagine
a painted, haggard, agitated, desperate hag. Been cast off in
Mozambique by somebody who paid her passage here. She had
been injured internally – by a kick from a horse; she hadn't a cent
on her when she got ashore; I don't think she even asked to see
the child. At any rate not till the last day of her life. Jacobus hired
for her a bungalow to die in. He got a couple of Sisters from the
hospital to nurse her through these few months. If he didn't marry
her *in extremis,* as the good sisters tried to bring about, it's because
she wouldn't even hear of it. As the nuns said: 'The woman died
impenitent.' It was reported that she ordered Jacobus out of the
room with her last breath. This may be the real reason why he

didn't go into mourning himself; he only put the child into black. While she was little she was to be seen sometimes about the streets attended by a negro woman, but since she became of age to put her hair up I don't think she has set foot outside that garden once.

5 She must be over eighteen now."

Thus my friend, with some added details: such as, that he didn't think the girl had spoken to three people of any position in the island; that an elderly female relative of the brothers Jacobus had been induced by extreme poverty to accept the position of gouver-

10 nante to the girl. As to Jacobus' business (which certainly annoyed his brother) it was a wise choice on his part. It brought him in contact only with strangers of passage; whereas any other would have given rise to all sorts of awkwardness with his social equals. The man was not wanting in a certain tact – only, he was naturally

15 shameless. For why did he want to keep that girl with him? It was most painful for everybody.

I thought suddenly (and with profound disgust) of the other Jacobus and I could not refrain from saying slily:

"I suppose if he employed her, say, as a scullion in his household

20 and occasionally pulled her hair or boxed her ears, the position would have been more regular – less shocking to the respectable class to which he belongs."

He was not so stupid as to miss my intention, and shrugged his shoulders impatiently.

25 "You don't understand. To begin with she's not a mulatto. And a scandal is a scandal. People should be given a chance to forget. I dare say it would have been better for her if she had been turned into a scullion or something of that kind. Of course he's trying to make money in every sort of petty way, but in such a business

30 there'll never be enough for anybody to come forward."

When my friend left me I had a conception of Jacobus and his daughter existing, a lonely pair of castaways on a desert island, the girl sheltering in the house as if it were a cavern in a cliff, and Jacobus going out to pick up a living for both on the beach – exactly

35 like two shipwrecked people, who always hope for some rescuer to bring them back at last into touch with the rest of mankind.

But Jacobus' bodily reality did not fit in with this romantic view. When he turned up on board in the usual course, he sipped the cup of coffee placidly, asked me if I was satisfied – and I

40 hardly listened to the harbour gossip he dropped slowly in his low,

voice-saving enunciation. I had then troubles of my own. My ship chartered, my thoughts dwelling on the success of a quick round voyage, I had been suddenly confronted by a shortage of bags. A catastrophe. The stock of one especial kind, called pock-ete, seemed to be totally exhausted. A consignment was shortly expected – it was afloat, on its way, but meantime, the loading of my ship dead stopped, I had enough to worry about. My consignees, who had received me with such heartiness on my arrival, now in the character of my charterers listened to my complaints with polite helplessness. Their manager, the old-maidish, thin man, who so prudishly didn't even like to speak about the impure Jacobus, gave me the correct commercial view of the position.

"My dear Captain," he was retracting his leathery cheeks into a condescending, shark-like smile, "we were not morally obliged to tell you of a possible shortage before you signed the charter-party. It was for you to guard against the contingency of a delay – strictly speaking. But of course we shouldn't have taken any advantage. This is no one's fault really. We ourselves have been taken unawares," he concluded primly, with an obvious lie.

This lecture I confess had made me thirsty. Suppressed rage generally produces that effect; and as I strolled on aimlessly I bethought myself of the tall earthen-ware pitcher in the captain's room of the Jacobus "store."

With no more than a nod to the men I found assembled there I poured down a deep, cool draught on my indignation, then another, and then becoming dejected I sat plunged in cheerless reflections. The others read, talked, smoked, bandied over my head some unsubtle chaff. But my abstraction was respected. And it was without a word to any one that I rose and went out, only to be quite unexpectedly accosted in the bustle of the store by Jacobus the outcast:

"Glad to see you Captain. What? Going away? You haven't been looking so well these last few days, I notice. Run down – eh?"

He was in his shirtsleeves – and his words were in the usual course of business, but they had a human note. It was commercial amenity, but I had been a stranger to amenity in that connection. I do verily believe (from the direction of his heavy glance towards a certain shelf) that he was going to suggest the purchase of Clarkson's Nerve Tonic which he kept in stock, when I said impulsively:

"I am rather in trouble with my loading."

Wide awake under his sleepy, broad mask with glued lips, he understood at once, had a movement of the head so appreciative that I relieved my exasperation by exclaiming:

"Surely there must be eleven hundred quarter bags to be found
5 in the Colony. It's only a matter of looking for them."

Again that slight movement of the big head, and in the noise and activity of the store that tranquil murmur:

"To be sure. But then people likely to have a reserve of quarter bags wouldn't want to sell. They'd need that size themselves."

10 "That's exactly what my consignees are telling me. Impossible to buy. Bosh! They don't want to. It suits them to have the ship hung up. But if I were to discover the lot they would have to . . . . Look here Jacobus! You are the man to have such a thing up your sleeve."

15 He protested with a ponderous swing of his big head. I stood before him helplessly, being looked at by those heavy eyes with a veiled expression as of a man after some soul-shaking crisis. Then suddenly:

"It's impossible to talk quietly here," he whispered. "I am very
20 busy. But if you could go and wait for me in my house. It's less than ten minutes' walk. . . . Oh yes. You don't know the way."

He called for his coat and offered to take me there himself. He would have to return to the store at once for an hour or so to finish his business, and then he would be at liberty to talk over with me
25 that matter of quarter bags. This programme was breathed out at me through slightly parted, still lips; his heavy, motionless glance rested upon me, placid for ever, the glance of a tired man – but I felt that it was searching too. I could not imagine what he was looking for in me and kept silent, wondering.

30 "I am asking you to wait for me in my house till I am at liberty to talk this matter over. You will?"

"Why! Of course," I cried.

"But I cannot promise . . ."

"I dare say not," I said. "I don't expect a promise."

35 "I mean I can't even promise to try the move I've in my mind. One must see first . . . . H'm."

"All right. I'll take my chance. I'll wait for you as long as you like. What else have I to do in this infernal hole of a port."

Before I had uttered my last word we had set off at a swing-
40 ing pace. We turned a couple of corners and entered a street

completely empty of traffic, of semi-rural aspect, paved with cobblestones nestling in grass tufts. The house came to the line of the
roadway; a single story on an elevated basement of rough stones,
so that our heads were below the level of the windows as we went
along. All the jalousies were tightly shut, like eyes, and the house   5
seemed fast asleep in the afternoon sunshine. The entrance was
at the side, in an alley even more grass-grown than the street: a
small door, simply on the latch.

With a word of apology as to showing me the way Jacobus preceded me up a dark passage and led me across the naked parquet   10
floor of what I supposed to be the dining room. It was lighted
by three glass doors which stood wide open onto a verandah
or rather loggia running its brick arches along the garden side
of the house. It was really a magnificent garden: smooth green
lawns and a gorgeous maze of flower-beds in the foreground, dis-   15
played around a basin of dark water framed in a marble rim, and
in the distance the massed foliage of varied trees concealing the
roofs of other houses. The town might have been miles away. It
was a brilliantly coloured solitude, drowsing in a warm, voluptuous
silence. Where the long, still shadows fell across the beds, and in   20
shady nooks, the massed colours of the flowers had an extraordinary magnificence of effect. I stood entranced. Jacobus grasped
me delicately above the elbow impelling me to a half-turn to the
left.

I had not noticed the girl before. She occupied a low, deep   25
wicker-work armchair, and I saw her in exact profile like a figure
in a tapestry, and as motionless. Jacobus released my arm.

"This is Alice," he announced tranquilly; and his subdued manner of speaking made it sound so much like a confidential communication that I fancied myself nodding understandingly and   30
whispering "I see, I see." Of course I did nothing of the kind.
Neither of us did anything; we stood side by side looking down at
the girl. For quite a time she did not stir, staring straight before
her as if watching the vision of some pageant passing through
the garden in the deep, rich glow of light and the splendour of   35
flowers.

Then coming to the end of her revery she looked round and
up.

If I had not at first noticed her, I am certain that she too had
been unaware of my presence till she actually perceived me by   40

her father's side. The quickened upward movement of the heavy eyelids, the widening of the languid glance passing into a fixed stare put that beyond doubt.

Under her amazement there was a hint of fear and then came a
5 flash as of anger. Jacobus after uttering my name fairly loud said: "Make yourself at home captain – I won't be gone long," and went away rapidly. Before I had time to make a bow I was left alone with the girl – who I remembered suddenly had not been seen by man or woman of that town since she had found it necessary
10 to put up her hair. It looked as though it had not been touched again since that distant time of first putting up; it was a mass of black lustrous locks, twisted anyhow high on her head, with long untidy wisps hanging down on each side of her clear sallow face; a mass so thick and strong and abundant that, nothing but to
15 look at, it gave you a sensation of heavy pressure on the top of your head and an impression of magnificently cynical untidiness. As she leaned forward, hugging herself with crossed legs, a dingy, amber-coloured, flounced wrapper of some thin stuff revealed the young, supple body drawn together tensely in the deep, low seat
20 as if crouching for a spring. I detected a slight quivering start or two which looked uncommonly like bounding away. They were followed by the most absolute immobility.

The absurd impulse to run out after Jacobus (for I had been startled too) once repressed, I took a chair, placed it not very
25 far from her, sat down deliberately, and began to talk about the garden, caring not what I said but using a gentle caressing intonation as one talks to soothe a startled wild animal. I could not even be certain that she understood me. She never raised her face or attempted to look my way. I kept on talking only to prevent her
30 from taking flight. She had another of these quivering, repressed, starts which made me catch my breath in apprehension. Ultimately I formed a notion that what prevented her perhaps from going off in one great, nervous leap, was the scantiness of her attire. The wicker armchair was the most substantial thing about her person.
35 What she had on under that dingy loose, amber wrapper must have been of the most flimsy and airy character. One could not help being aware of it. It was obvious. I felt it actually embarrassing at first, but that sort of embarrassment is got over easily by a mind not enslaved by narrow prejudices. I did not avert my gaze from Alice.
40 I went on talking with ingratiating softness, the recollection that

most likely she had never before been spoken to by a strange man adding to my assurance. I don't know why an emotional tenseness should have crept into the situation, but it did. And just as I was becoming aware of it a slight scream cut short my flow of urbane speech.

The scream did not proceed from the girl; it was emitted behind me and caused me to turn my head sharply. I understood at once that the apparition in the doorway was the elderly relation of Jacobus, the companion, the gouvernante. While she remained thunderstruck I got up and made her a low bow.

The ladies of Jacobus' household evidently spent their days in light attire. This stumpy old woman, with a face like a large, wrinkled lemon, beady eyes and a shock of iron grey hair, was dressed in a garment of some ashcoloured, silky, light stuff. It fell from her thick neck down to her toes with the simplicity of an unadorned nightgown. It made her appear truly cylindrical. She exclaimed:

"How did you get here!"

Before I could say a word she vanished; and presently I heard a confusion of shrill sounds and protestations in a distant part of the house. Obviously no one could tell her how I got there. In a moment with great outcries from two negro women following her, she waddled back to the doorway, infuriated.

"What do you want here?"

I turned to the girl. She was sitting straight up now, her hands posed on the arms of the chair. I appealed to her.

"Surely Miss Alice you will not let them drive me out into the street?"

Her magnificent black eyes, narrow, long in shape, swept over me with an undefinable expression; in a harsh, contemptuous voice she let fall in French a sort of explanation:

"C'est Papa."

I made another low bow to the old woman.

She turned her back on me in order to drive away her black henchwomen, and surveying my person in a peculiar manner, with one small eye nearly closed and her face all drawn up on that side as if with a twinge of toothache, she stepped out on the verandah, sat down in a rocking chair some distance away, and took up her knitting from a little table. Before she started at it she plunged one of the needles into the mop of her grey hair and stirred it vigorously.

Her elementary nightgown sort of frock clung to her ancient, stumpy and floating form. She wore white cotton stockings and flat, brown, velvet slippers. Her feet and ankles were obtrusively visible on the foot rest. She began to rock herself slightly while she
5 knitted. I had resumed my seat and kept quiet, for I mistrusted that old woman. What if she ordered me to depart. She seemed capable of any outrage. She had snorted once or twice; she was knitting violently. Suddenly she piped at the young girl in French a question which I translate colloquially:
10 "What's your father up to now?"

The young creature shrugged her shoulders so comprehensively that her whole body swayed within the loose wrapper; and in that unexpectedly harsh voice which yet had a seductive quality to the senses, like certain kinds of natural, rough wines one drinks with
15 pleasure:

"It's some captain. Leave me alone – will you!"

The rocking chair nodded quicker, the old woman's voice piped like a whistle:

"You and your father make a pair. He would stick at nothing –
20 that's well known. But I didn't expect this."

I thought it high time to air some of my own French. I remarked modestly but firmly that this was business. I had some matters to talk over with Mr Jacobus.

At once she piped out a derisive "Poor innocent!" Then with a
25 change of tone:

"The shop's for business. Why don't you go to the shop to talk with him?"

The furious speed of her fingers and knitting needles made one dizzy; and with squeaky indignation: "Sitting here staring at that
30 girl – is that what you call business?"

"No," I said suavely. "I call this pleasure – an unexpected pleasure. And unless Miss Alice objects . . ."

I half turned to her. She flung at me an angry and contemptuous "Don't care" and leaning her elbow on her knee took her chin in
35 her hand – a Jacobus chin undoubtedly. And those heavy eyelids, this black, irritated stare reminded me of Jacobus too – the wealthy merchant, the respected one. The design of her eyebrows also was the same, rigid and ill-omened. Yes! I traced in her a resemblance to both of them. It came to me as a sort of surprisingly remote
40 inference that both these Jacobuses were rather handsome men after all. I said:

"Oh! then I shall stare at you till you smile."

She favoured me again with an even more viciously scornful "Don't care."

The old woman broke in blunt and shrill:

"Hear his impudence. And you too! Don't care! Go at least and put some more clothes on. Sitting there like this before this sailor riff raff."

The sun was about to leave the Pearl of the Ocean for other seas, for other lands. The walled garden full of shadows blazed with colour as if the flowers were giving up the light absorbed during the day. The amazing old woman became very explicit. She suggested to the girl a corset and a petticoat with a cynical unreserve which humiliated me. Was I of no more account than a wooden dummy? The girl snapped out:

"Shan't."

It was not the naughty retort of a vulgar child; it had a note of desperation. Clearly my intrusion had somehow upset the balance of their established relations. The old woman knitted with furious accuracy, her eyes fastened down on her work.

"Oh you are the true child of your father. And *that* talks of entering a convent! Letting herself be stared at by a fellow."

"Leave off."

"Shameless thing."

"Old sorceress" the girl uttered distinctly, preserving her meditative pose, chin in hand, and a far away stare over the garden.

It was like the quarrel of the kettle and the pot. The old woman flew out of her chair, banged down her work and with a great play of thick limb, perfectly visible in that weird, clinging garment of hers, strode at the girl – who never stirred. I was experiencing a sort of trepidation when, as if awed by that unconscious attitude, the aged relative of Jacobus turned short upon me.

She was, I perceived, armed with a knitting needle; and as she raised her hand her intention seemed to be to throw it at me like a dart. But she only used it to scratch her head with, examining me the while at close range, one eye nearly shut and her face distorted by a whimsical, one-sided grimace.

"My dear man," she asked abruptly, "do you expect any good to come of this."

"I do hope so indeed Miss Jacobus." I tried to speak in the easy tone of an afternoon caller. "You see I am here after some bags."

"Bags! Look at that now! Didn't I hear you holding forth to that graceless wretch."

"You would like to see me in my grave," uttered the motionless girl hoarsely.

5   "Grave! What about me? Buried alive before I am dead for the sake of a thing blessed with such a pretty father," she cried; and turning to me: "You're one of these men he does business with. Well – why don't you leave us in peace my good fellow."

It was said in a tone – this "leave us in peace"! There was a sort of
10 ruffianly familiarity, a superiority, a scorn in it. I was to hear it more than once, for you would show an imperfect knowledge of human nature if you thought that this was my last visit to that house – where no respectable person had put foot for ever so many years. No, you would be very much mistaken if you imagined that this
15 reception had scared me away. First of all I was not going to run before a grotesque and ruffianly old woman.

And then you musn't forget these necessary bags. That first evening Jacobus made me stay to dinner; after, however, telling me loyally that he didn't know whether he could do anything at
20 all for me. He had been thinking it over. It was too difficult, he feared. . . . But he did not give it up in so many words.

We were only three at table; the girl by means of repeated "Won't," "Shan't" and "Don't care" having conveyed and affirmed her intention not to come to the table, not to have any dinner,
25 not to move from the verandah. The old relative hopped about in her flat slippers and piped indignantly, Jacobus towered over her and murmured placidly in his throat; I joined jocularly from a distance, throwing in a few words for which, under the cover of the night, I received secretly a most vicious poke in the ribs from
30 the old woman's elbow or perhaps her fist. I restrained a cry. And all the time the girl didn't even condescend to raise her head to look at any of us. All this may sound childish – and yet that stormy, petulant sullenness had an obscurely tragic flavour.

And so we sat down to food around the light of a good many
35 candles while she remained crouching out there, staring in the dark as if feeding her bad temper on the heavily scented air of the admirable garden.

Before leaving I said to Jacobus that I would come next day to hear if the bag affair had made any progress. He shook his head
40 slightly at that.

"I'll haunt your house daily till you pull it off. You'll be always finding me here."

His faint, melancholy smile did not part his thick lips.

"That will be all right Captain."

Then seeing me to the door, very tranquil, he murmured earnestly the recommendation "make yourself at home" and also the hospitable hint about there being always a "plate of soup." It was only on my way to the quay, down the ill-lighted streets, that I remembered I had been engaged to dine that very evening with the S— family. Though vexed at my forgetfulness (it would be rather awkward to explain) I couldn't help thinking that it had procured me a more amusing evening. And besides – business. The sacred business . . .

In a barefooted negro who overtook me at a run and bolted down the landing steps I recognised Jacobus' boatman, who must have been feeding in the kitchen. His usual "good night sah" as I went up my ship's ladder had a more cordial sound than on previous occasions.

He seemed to be a sort of henchman to the family, and when not down at the boat he was employed on odd jobs about the house, ran errands, and generally hung around the kitchen. Once he opened the street door to me with a large, white flash of a grin which lighted up the dark passage leading to the dining room. That room with its verandah was the only room I knew in the house. But I came to know it well.

V

FOR I KEPT my word to Jacobus. I haunted his home. He was perpetually finding me there of an afternoon when he popped in for a moment from the "store." The sound of my voice talking to his Alice greeted him on his doorstep; and when he returned for good in the evening ten to one he would hear it still going on in the verandah. I just nodded to him; he would sit down heavily and gently, and watch with a sort of approving anxiety my efforts to make his daughter smile.

I called her often Alice, right before him; sometimes I would address her as Miss "Don't Care"; and I exhausted myself in non-sensical chatter without succeeding once in taking her out of her peevish and tragic self. There were moments when I felt I must break out and start swearing at her till all was blue. And I fancied that had I done so Jacobus would not have moved a muscle. A sort of shady, intimate understanding seemed to have been established between us.

I must say that the girl treated her father exactly in the same way she treated me.

And how could it have been otherwise? She treated me as she treated her father. She had never received a visitor. She did not know how men behaved. I belonged to the low lot with whom her father did business at the port. I was of no account. So was her father. The only decent people in the world were the people of the island who would have nothing to do with him because of something wicked he had done. This was apparently the explanation Miss Jacobus had given her of the household's isolated position.

For she had to be told something! And I feel convinced that this version had been assented to by Jacobus. I must say the old woman was putting it forward with considerable gusto. It was on her lips the universal explanation, the universal allusion, the universal taunt.

One day Jacobus came in early and beckoning me into the dining room wiped his brow with a weary gesture and told me that he had managed to unearth a supply of quarter bags. "It's fourteen hundred your ship wanted, did you say Captain?"

"Yes! Yes!" I replied eagerly; but he remained calm. He looked more tired than I ever had seen him before.

"Well, Captain – you may go and tell your people that they can get that lot from my brother."

As I remained openmouthed at this he added his usual placid formula of assurance:

"You'll find it correct Captain."

"You spoke to your brother about it?" I was distinctly awed. "And for me? Because he must have known my ship's the only one hung up for bags. How on earth . . ."

He wiped his brow again. I noticed that he was dressed with unusual care, in clothes in which I had never seen him before. He avoided my eye.

"You've heard people talk of course. . . . That's true enough. He . . . I . . . We certainly . . . for several years . . ." His voice declined to a mere sleepy murmur. "You see, I had something to tell him of, something which . . ."

His murmur stopped. He was not going to tell me what this something was. And I didn't care. Anxious to carry the news to my charterers I ran back on the verandah to get my hat.

At the bustle I made, the girl turned her eyes slowly in my direction and even the old woman was checked in her knitting. I   5
stopped a moment to exclaim excitedly:

"Your father's a brick, Miss Don't Care. That's what he is."

She beheld my elation in scornful surprise. Jacobus with unwonted familiarity seized my arm as I flew through the dining room and breathed heavily at me a proposal about "a plate   10
of soup" that evening. I answered distractedly: "Eh? What? Oh! Thanks – Certainly, with pleasure," and tore myself away. Dine with him? Of course. The merest gratitude . . .

But some three hours afterwards in the dusky, silent street, paved with cobblestones, I became aware that it was not mere gratitude   15
which was guiding my steps towards the house with the old garden, where for years no guest other than myself had ever dined. Mere gratitude does not gnaw at one's interior economy in that particular way. Hunger might; but I was not feeling particularly hungry for Jacobus' food.   20

On that occasion too the girl refused to come to the table.

My exasperation grew. The old woman cast malicious glances at me. I said suddenly to Jacobus: "Here! Put some chicken and salad on that plate." He obeyed without raising his eyes. I carried it with a knife and fork and a serviette out on the verandah. The   25
garden was one mass of gloom, like a cemetery of flowers buried in the darkness, and she, in the chair, seemed to muse mournfully over the extinction of light and colour. Only whiffs of heavy scent passed like wandering, fragrant souls of that departed multitude of blossoms. I talked volubly, jocularly, persuasively, tenderly;   30
I talked in a subdued tone. To a listener it would have sounded like the murmur of a pleading lover. Whenever I paused expectantly there was only a deep silence. It was like offering food to a seated statue.

"I haven't been able to swallow a single morsel thinking of you   35
out here starving yourself in the dark. It's positively cruel to be so obstinate. You wound my feelings. Think of my sufferings."

"Don't care."

I felt as if I could have done her some violence – shaken her, beaten her may be. I said gently: 40

"Your absurd behaviour will prevent me coming here any more."

"What's that to me!"

"You like it."

"It's false," she snarled.

5   My hand fell on her shoulder; and if she had flinched I verily believe I would have shaken her. But there was no movement and this immobility disarmed my anger.

"You do. Or you wouldn't be found on the verandah every day. Why are you here then. There's plenty of rooms in the house. You 10 have your own room to stay in – if you did not want to see me. But you do. You know you do."

I felt a slight shudder under my hand and released my grip as if frightened by that sign of animation in her body. The scented air of the garden came to us in a warm wave like a voluptuous and 15 perfumed sigh.

"Go back to them," she whispered – almost pitifully.

As I re-entered the dining room I saw Jacobus cast down his eyes. I banged the plate on the table. At this demonstration of ill-humour he murmured something in an apologetic tone, and 20 I turned upon him viciously as if he were accountable to me for these "abominable eccentricities" I believe I called them.

"But I dare say Miss Jacobus here is responsible for most of this offensive manner," I added loftily.

She piped out at once in her brazen ruffianly manner:

25   "Eh? Why don't you leave us in peace my good fellow."

I was astonished that she should dare before Jacobus. Yet what could he have done to repress her? He needed her too much. He raised his heavy drowsy glance for an instant, then looked down again. She insisted with shrill finality:

30   "Haven't you done your business you two? Well, then . . ."

She had the true Jacobus impudence, that old woman. Her mop of iron-grey hair was parted on the side like a man's, raffishly, and she made as if to plunge her fork into it, as she used to do with the knitting needle, but refrained. Her little black eyes sparkled ven- 35 omously. I turned to my host at the head of the table – menacingly as it were.

"Well, and what do you say to that, Jacobus? Am I to take it that we have done with each other?"

I had to wait a little. The answer when it came was rather unex- 40 pected, and in quite another spirit than the question.

"I certainly think we might do some business yet with those potatoes of mine Captain. You will find, that . . ."

I cut him short:

"I've told you before that I don't trade."

His broad chest heaved without a sound in a noiseless sigh.   5

"Think it over Captain," he murmured, tenacious and tranquil; and I burst into a jarring laugh, remembering how he had stuck to the circus-rider woman – the depth of passion under the placid surface, which even cuts with a riding-whip (so the legend had it) could not ruffle into the semblance of a storm; something like the   10 passion of a fish would be if one could imagine such a thing as a passionate fish.

That evening I experienced more distinctly than ever the sense of moral discomfort which always attended me in that house lying under the ban of all "decent" people. I refused to stay on and   15 smoke after dinner; and when I put my hand into the thickly cushioned palm of Jacobus I said to myself that it would be for the last time under his roof. I pressed his bulky paw heartily nevertheless. Hadn't he got me out of a serious difficulty? To the few words of acknowledgement I was bound, and indeed quite willing, to   20 utter, he answered by stretching his closed lips in his melancholy, glued-together, smile:

"That will be all right, I hope Captain," he breathed out weightily.

"What do you mean?" I asked alarmed. "That your brother may   25 yet . . ."

"Oh no," he reassured me. "He's . . . he's a man of his word Captain."

My self-communion as I walked away from his door trying to believe that this was for the last time, was not satisfactory. I was   30 aware myself that I was not sincere in my reflections as to Jacobus' motives – and of course, the very next day I went back again.

How weak, irrational and absurd we are! How easily carried away whenever our awakened imagination brings us the irritating hint of a desire! I perceived that I cared for the girl in a particular way,   35 seduced by the moody expression of her face, by her obstinate silences, her rare, scornful words; by the perpetual pout of her closed lips, the black depths of her fixed gaze turned slowly upon me as if in contemptuous provocation, only to be averted next moment with an exasperating indifference.   40

Of course the news of my assiduity had spread all over the little town. I noticed a change in the manner of my acquaintances and even something different in the nods of the other captains when meeting them at the landing steps or in the offices where business
5 called me. The old-maidish head clerk treated me with distant punctiliousness and, as it were, gathered his skirts round him for fear of contamination. It seemed to me that the very niggers on the quays turned to look after me as I passed; and as to Jacobus' boatman his "good night sah!" when he put me on board was no
10 longer merely cordial – it had a familiarly confidential sound as though we had been partners in some villainy.

My friend S— the elder passed me on the other side of the street with a wave of the hand and an ironic smile. The younger brother, the one they had married to an elderly shrew, he, on the strength
15 of an older friendship and as if paying a debt of gratitude, took the liberty to utter a word of warning.

"You're doing yourself no good by your choice of friends my dear chap," he said with infantile gravity.

As I knew that the meeting of the brothers Jacobus was the
20 subject of excited comment in the whole of the sugary Pearl of the Ocean, I wanted to know why I was blamed.

"I have been the occasion of a move which may end in a reconciliation surely desirable from the point of view of the proprieties – don't you know."

25 "Of course if that girl were disposed of it would certainly facilitate . . ." he mused sagely, then, inconsequential creature, gave me a light tap on the lower part of my waistcoat: "You old sinner," he cried jovially, "much you care for proprieties. But you had better look out for yourself, you know, with a personage like Jacobus who
30 has no sort of reputation to lose."

He had recovered his gravity of a respectable citizen by that time and added regretfully:

"All the women of our family are perfectly scandalized."

But by that time I had given up visiting the S— family and the
35 D— family. The elder ladies pulled such faces when I showed myself and the multitude of the related young ladies received me with such a variety of looks – wondering, awed, mocking (except Miss Mary who spoke to me and looked at me with hushed, pained compassion as if I had been ill) – that I had no difficulty in giving
40 them all up. I would have given up the society of the whole town for

the sake of sitting near that girl, snarling and superb, and barely
clad in that flimsy, dingy, amber wrapper, open low on the throat.
She looked, with the wild wisps of hair hanging down her tense
face, as though she had just jumped out of bed in the panic of a
fire.

She sat leaning on her elbow, looking at nothing. Why did she
stay listening to my absurd chatter? And not only that; but why did
she powder her face in preparation for my arrival? It seemed to be
her idea of making a toilette, and in her untidy negligence a sign
of great effort towards personal adornment.

But I might have been mistaken. The powdering might have
been her daily practice and her presence in the verandah a sign of
an indifference so complete as to take no account of my existence.
Well it was all one to me.

I loved to watch her slow changes of pose, to look at her long
immobilities composed in the graceful lines of her body, to observe
the mysterious, narrow stare of her splendid black eyes, somewhat
long in shape, half closed, contemplating the void. She was like
a spell-bound creature with the forehead of a goddess crowned
by the dishevelled, magnificent hair of a gipsy tramp. Even her
indifference was seductive. I felt myself growing attached to her by
the bond of an irrealisable desire, for I kept my head – quite. And
I accepted the moral discomfort of Jacobus' sleepy watchfulness,
tranquil, and yet so expressive; as if there had been a tacit pact
between us two. I put up with the insolence of the old woman's
"Aren't you ever going to leave us in peace my good fellow"; with
her taunts, her brazen and sinister scolding. She was of the true
Jacobus stock, and no mistake.

Directly I got away from the girl I called myself many hard names.
What folly was this? I would ask myself. It was like being the slave
of some depraved habit. And I returned to her with my head clear,
my heart certainly free, not even moved by pity for that castaway
(she was as much of a castaway as any one ever wrecked on a
desert island) but as if beguiled by some extraordinary promise.
Nothing more unworthy could be imagined. The recollection of
that tremulous whisper when I gripped her shoulder with one
hand and held a plate of chicken in the other was enough to
make me break all my good resolutions.

Her insulting taciturnity was enough sometimes to make one
gnash one's teeth with rage. When she opened her mouth it was

only to be abominably rude in harsh tones to the associate of her reprobate father; and the full approval of her aged relative was conveyed to her by offensive chuckles. If not that, then her remarks always uttered in a tone of scathing contempt were of the
5 most appalling inanity.

And how could it have been otherwise? That plump, ruffianly Jacobus old maid in the tight grey frock, had never taught her any manners. Manners I suppose are not necessary for born cast-aways. No educational establishment could ever be induced to
10 accept her as a pupil – on account of the proprieties, I imag-ine. And Jacobus had not been able to send her away anywhere. How could he have done it? Who with? Where to? He, himself, was not enough of an adventurer to think of settling down any-where else. His passion had tossed him at the tail of a circus up
15 and down strange coasts, but, the storm over, he had drifted back shamelessly where, social outcast as he was, he remained still a Jacobus – one of the oldest families on the island, older than the French even. There must have been a Jacobus in at the death of the last Dodo. . . . The girl had learned nothing, she had never
20 listened to a general conversation, she knew nothing, had heard of nothing. She could read certainly – but all the reading matter that ever came in her way were the newspapers provided for the captain's room of the "store." Jacobus had the habit of bringing these sheets home now and then in a very stained and ragged
25 condition.

As her mind could not grasp the meaning of any matters treated there except police-court reports and accounts of crimes, she had formed for herself a notion of the civilised world as a scene of murders, abductions, burglaries, stabbing, affrays and every sort
30 of desperate violence. England and France, Paris and London (the only two towns of which she seemed to have heard) appeared to her sinks of abominations, reeking with blood, in contrast to her little island where petty larceny was about the standard of current misdeeds, with, now and then, some more pronounced crime –
35 and that only amongst the imported coolie labourers on sugar estates or the negroes of the town. But in Europe these things were being done daily by a wicked population of white men amongst whom, as that ruffianly, aristocratic, old Miss Jacobus pointed out, the wandering sailors, the associates of her precious papa, were
40 the lowest of the low.

It was impossible to give her a sense of proportion. I suppose she figured England to herself as about the size of the Pearl of the Ocean; in which case it would certainly have been reeking with gore and a mere wreck of burgled houses from end to end. One could not make her understand that these horrors on which she fed her imagination were lost in the mass of orderly life like a few drops of blood in the ocean. She directed upon me for a moment the uncomprehending glance of her narrowed eyes and then would turn her scornful, powdered face away without a word. She would not even take the trouble to shrug her shoulders.

At that time the batches of papers brought by the last mail reported a series of crimes in the East End of London; there was a sensational case of abduction in France and a fine display of armed robbery in Australia. One afternoon crossing the dining room I heard Miss Jacobus piping in the verandah with venomous animosity:

"I don't know what your precious papa is plotting with that fellow. But he's just the sort of man who's capable of carrying you off far away somewhere and then cutting your throat some day – for your money."

There was a good half of the length of the verandah between their chairs. I came out and sat down fiercely midway between them.

"Yes that's what we do with girls in Europe," I began in a grimly matter-of-fact tone. I think Miss Jacobus was disconcerted by my sudden appearance. I turned upon her with cold ferocity.

"As to objectionable old women they are first strangled quietly, then cut up into small pieces and thrown away, a bit here and a bit there. They vanish . . ."

I cannot go so far as to say I had terrified her. But she was troubled by my truculence, the more so because I had been always addressing her with a politeness she did not deserve. Her plump, knitting hands fell slowly on her knees. She said not a word while I fixed her with severe determination. Then as I turned away from her at last, she laid down her work gently and with noiseless movements retreated from the verandah. In fact – she vanished.

But I was not thinking of her. I was looking at the girl. It was what I was coming for daily; troubled, ashamed, eager; finding in my nearness to her a unique sensation which I indulged with dread, self contempt and deep pleasure, as if it were a secret vice bound to end in my undoing, like the habit of some drug or other which ruins and degrades its slave.

I looked her over, from the top of her dishevelled head, down the lovely line of the shoulder, following the curve of the hip, the draped form of the long limb, right down to the fine ankle below a torn, soiled flounce; and to the point of the shabby, high-heeled, blue slipper, dangling from her well-shaped foot which she moved slightly, with quick nervous jerks, as if impatient of my presence. And in the scent of the massed flowers I seemed to breathe her special and inexplicable charm, the heady perfume of the everlastingly irritated captive of the garden. I looked at her rounded chin, the Jacobus chin; at the full, red lips pouting in the powdered, sallow face; at the firm modelling of the cheek, the grains of white in the hairs of the straight, sombre eyebrows; at the long eyes, a narrow gleam of liquid white and intense motionless black, with their gaze so empty of thought and so absorbed in their fixity that she seemed to be staring at her own lonely image, in some far off mirror hidden from my sight amongst the trees.

And suddenly, without looking at me, with the appearance of a person speaking to herself, she asked in that voice slightly harsh yet mellow and always irritated:

"Why do you keep on coming here."

"Why do I keep on coming here," I repeated taken by surprise. I could not have told her. I could not even tell myself with sincerity why I was coming there. "What's the good of you asking a question like that?"

"Nothing is any good," she observed scornfully to the empty air, her chin propped on her hand, that hand never extended to any man, that no one had ever grasped – for I had only grasped her shoulder once – that generous, fine, somewhat masculine hand. I knew well the peculiarly efficient shape, broad at the base, tapering at the fingers, of that hand for which there was nothing in the world to lay hold of. I pretended to be playful.

"No! But do you really care to know."

She shrugged indolently her magnificent shoulders from which the dingy, thin wrapper was slipping a little.

"Oh . . . never mind . . . never mind."

There was something smouldering under those airs of lassitude. She exasperated me by the provocation of her nonchalance, by

something elusive and defiant in her very form which I wanted to
seize. I said roughly:

"Why? Don't you think I should tell you the truth."

Her eyes glided my way for a sidelong look, and she murmured
moving only her full, pouting lips:

"I think you would not dare."

"Do you imagine I am afraid of you? What on earth . . . . Well –
it's possible after all that I don't know exactly why I am coming
here. Let us say with Miss Jacobus that it is for no good. You do
seem to believe the outrageous things she says, if you do have a
row with her now and then."

She snapped out viciously:

"Who else am I to believe."

"I don't know," I had to own, seeing her suddenly very helpless
and condemned to moral solitude by the verdict of a respectable
community. "You might believe me, if you choose."

She made a slight movement and asked me at once, with an
effort as if making an experiment:

"What is the business between you and Papa?"

"Don't you know the nature of your father's business – come.
He sells provisions to ships."

She became rigid again in her crouching pose.

"Not that. What brings you here – to this house? . . ."

"And suppose it's you? . . . You would not call that business.
Would you? And now let us drop the subject. It's no use. My ship
will be ready for sea the day after to-morrow."

She murmured a distinctly scared "So soon" and getting up
quickly went to the little table and poured herself a glass of water.
She walked with rapid steps and with an indolent swaying of her
whole young figure above the hips. When she passed near me I felt
with tenfold force the charm of the peculiar, promising sensation
I had formed the habit to seek near her. I thought with sudden
dismay that this was the end of it; that after one more day I would
be no longer able to come into this verandah, sit on this chair and
taste perversely the flavour of contempt in her indolent poses,
drink in the provocation of her scornful looks and listen to the
curt insolent remarks uttered in that harsh and seductive voice.
As if my innermost nature had been altered by the action of some
moral poison, I felt an abject dread of going to sea.

I had to exercise a sudden self control, as one puts on a brake, to prevent myself jumping up to stride about, shout, gesticulate, make her a scene. What for? What about? I had no idea. It was just the relief of violence that I wanted; and I lolled back in my
5 chair trying to keep my lips formed in a smile, that half-indulgent, half-mocking smile which was my shield against the shafts of her contempt and the insulting sallies flung at me by the old woman.

She drank the water at a draught, with the avidity of raging thirst, and let herself fall on the nearest chair as if utterly over-
10 come. Her attitude, like certain tones of her voice, had in it some-thing masculine: the knees apart in the ample wrapper, the clasped hands hanging between them, her body leaning forward, with drooping head. I stared at the heavy black coil of twisted hair. It was enormous, crowning the bowed head with a crushing and
15 disdained glory. The escaped wisps hung straight down. And sud-denly I perceived that the girl was trembling from head to foot as though that glass of water had chilled her to the bone.

"What's the matter now," I said, startled, but in no very sympa-thetic mood.

20 She shook her bowed, overweighted head and cried in a stifled voice but with a rising inflexion:

"Go away! Go away! Go away!"

I got up then and approached her with a strange sort of anxiety. I looked down at her round, strong neck, then stooped low enough
25 to peep at her face. And I began to tremble a little myself.

"What on earth are you gone wild about Miss Don't Care?"

She flung herself backwards violently, her head going over the back of her chair. And now it was her smooth, full, palpitating throat that lay exposed to my bewildered stare. Her eyes were
30 nearly closed with only a horrible white gleam under the lids as if she were dead.

"What has come to you?" I asked in awe. "What are you terrifying yourself with?"

She pulled herself together, her eyes open frightfully wide now.
35 The tropical afternoon was lengthening the shadows on the hot, weary earth, the abode of obscure desires, of extravagant hopes, of unimaginable terrors.

"Never mind! Don't care." . . . Then after a gasp she spoke with such frightful rapidity that I could hardly make out the amazing
40 words:

"For if you were to shut me up in an empty place as smooth all round as the palm of my hand I could always strangle myself with my hair."

For a moment, doubting my ears, I let this inconceivable declaration sink into me. It is ever impossible to guess at the wild thoughts that pass through the heads of our fellow creatures. What monstrous imaginings of violence could have dwelt under the low forehead of that girl who had been taught to regard her father as "capable of anything" more in the light of a misfortune than that of disgrace; as evidently something to be resented and feared rather than to be ashamed of. She seemed indeed as unaware of shame as of anything else in the world; but in her ignorance, her resentment and fear took on a childish and violent shape.

Of course she spoke without knowing the value of words. What could she know of death, she who knew nothing of life. It was merely as the proof of her being beside herself with some odious apprehension, that this extraordinary speech had moved me, not to pity but to a fascinated, horrified wonder. I had no idea what notion she had of her danger. Some sort of abduction. It was quite possible with the talk of that atrocious old woman. Perhaps she thought she could be carried off bound hand and foot and even gagged. At that surmise I felt as if the door of a furnace had been opened in front of me.

"Upon my honour," I cried, "you shall end by going crazy if you listen to that abominable old aunt of yours . . ."

I studied her haggard expression, her trembling lips. Her cheeks even seemed sunk a little. But how I, the associate of her disreputable father, the "lowest of the low" from the criminal Europe, could manage to reassure her I had no conception. She was exasperating.

"Heavens and earth! What do you think I can do."

"I don't know." Her chin certainly trembled. And she was looking at me with extreme attention.

I made a step nearer to her chair.

"I shall do nothing. I promise you that. Will that do? Do you understand? I shall do nothing whatever, of any kind – and the day after to-morrow I shall be gone."

What else could I have said? She seemed to drink in my words with the thirsty avidity with which she had emptied the glass of water. She whispered tremulously, in that touching tone I had heard once before on her lips and which thrilled me again, with the same emotion:

"I would believe you. But what about Papa . . ."

"He be hanged!" My emotion betrayed itself by the brutality of my tone. "I've had enough of your papa. Are you so stupid as to imagine that I am frightened of him? He can't make me do anything."

All that sounded feeble to me in the face of her ignorance. But I must conclude that the "accent of sincerity" has, as some people say, a really irresistible power. The effect was far beyond my hopes – and even beyond my conception. To watch the change in the girl was like watching a miracle – the gradual but swift relaxation of her tense glance, of her stiffened muscles, of every fibre of her body. That black, fixed stare into which I had read a tragic meaning more than once, in which I had found a sombre seduction, was perfectly empty now, void of all consciousness whatever, and not even aware any longer of my presence; it had become a little sleepy in the Jacobus fashion.

But, man being a perverse animal, instead of rejoicing at my complete success I beheld it with astounded and indignant eyes. There was something cynical in that unconcealed alteration, the true Jacobus shamelessness. I felt as though I had been cheated in some rather complicated deal into which I had entered against my better judgement. Yes, cheated without any regard for, at least, the forms of decency.

With an easy, indolent, and, in its indolence, supple, feline movement, she rose from the chair, so provokingly ignoring me now, that for very rage I held my ground within less than a foot from her. Leisurely and tranquil, behaving right before me with the ease of a person alone in her room, she extended her beautiful arms with her hands clenched, her body swaying, her head thrown back a little – revelling contemptuously in a sense of relief, easing her limbs in freedom after all these days of crouching, motionless poses when she had been so furious and so afraid.

All this with supreme indifference, something incredible, offensive, exasperating, like ingratitude doubled with treachery.

I ought to have been flattered perhaps, but on the contrary my anger grew; her movement to pass by me as if I were a wooden post or a piece of furniture, that unconcerned movement, brought it to a head.

I won't say I did not know what I was doing, but, certainly, cool reflection had nothing to do with the circumstance that next moment both my arms were round her waist. It was an impulsive action as one snatches at something falling or escaping; and it had no hypocritical gentleness about it either. She had no time to make a sound and the first kiss I planted on her closed lips was vicious enough to have been a bite.

She did not resist, and of course I did not stop at one. She let me go on, not as if she were inanimate – I felt her there, close against me, young, full of vigour, of life, a strong desirable creature – but as if she did not care in the least, in the absolute assurance of her safety, what I did or left undone. Our faces brought close together in this storm of haphazard caresses, her big, black, wide open eyes looked into mine without the girl appearing either angry or pleased or moved in any way. In that steady gaze which seemed impersonally to watch my madness I could detect a slight surprise, perhaps – nothing more. I showered kisses upon her face and there did not seem to be any reason why this should not go on for ever.

That thought flashed through my head, and I was on the point of desisting, when, all at once, she began to struggle with a sudden violence which all but freed her instantly, which revived my exasperation with her, indeed a fierce desire never to let her go any more. I tightened my embrace in time, gasping out "No you don't!" as if she were my mortal enemy. On her part not a word was said. Putting her hands against my chest she pushed with all her might without succeeding to break the circle of my arms. Except that she was roused now, her eyes gave me no clue whatever. To meet her black stare was like looking into a deep well, and I was totally unprepared for her change of tactics. Instead of trying to tear my hands apart, she flung herself upon my breast and with a downward, undulating, serpentine motion, a quick sliding dive, she got away from me smoothly. It was all very swift; I saw her pick up the tail of her wrapper and run for the door at the end of the verandah not very gracefully. She appeared to be limping a little – and then she vanished; the door swung to behind her so noiselessly that I could not believe it was completely closed. I had a distinct suspicion of her black eye being at the crack to watch what I would do. I could not make up my mind whether to shake my fist in that direction or blow a kiss.

VI

EITHER WOULD HAVE been perfectly consistent with my feelings. I gazed at the door, hesitating, but in the end I did neither. The monition of some sixth sense – the sense of guilt may be, that
5 sense which always acts too late, alas! – warned me to look round; and at once I became aware that the conclusion of this tumultuous episode was likely to be a matter of lively anxiety. Jacobus was standing in the doorway of the dining room. How long he had been there it was impossible to guess; and remembering my strug-
10 gle with the girl I thought he must have been its mute witness from beginning to end. But this supposition seemed almost incredible. Perhaps that impenetrable girl had heard him come in and had got away in time.

He stepped on to the verandah in his usual manner, heavy-eyed,
15 with glued lips. I marvelled at the girl's resemblance to the man. Those long, Egyptian eyes, that low forehead of a stupid goddess, she had found in the sawdust of the circus; but all the rest of the face, the design and the modelling, the rounded chin, the very lips – all that was Jacobus, fined down, more finished, more
20 expressive.

His thick hand fell on and grasped with force the back of a light chair (there were several standing about) and I perceived the chance of a broken head at the end of all this – most likely. My mortification was extreme. The scandal would be horrible;
25 that was unavoidable. But how to act so as to satisfy myself I did not know. I stood on my guard and at any rate faced him. There was nothing else for it. Of one thing I was certain, that however brazen my attitude it could never equal the characteristic Jacobus impudence.

30 He gave me his melancholy, glued-together smile and sat down. I own I was relieved. The perspective of passing from kisses to blows had nothing particularly attractive in it. Perhaps – perhaps he had seen nothing? He behaved as usual, but he had never before found me alone on the verandah. If he had alluded to it,
35 if he had asked "Where's Alice" or something of the sort, I would have been able to judge of his intentions from his tone. He would give me no opportunity. The striking peculiarity was that he had never looked up at me yet. "He knows" I said to myself confidently. And my contempt for him relieved my disgust with myself.

"You are early home," I remarked.

"Things are very quiet; nothing doing at the store to day," he explained with a cast-down air.

"Oh well, you know, I am off," I said feeling that this perhaps was the best thing to do.

"Yes," he breathed out. "Day after to-morrow."

This was not what I had meant; but as he gazed persistently at the floor I followed the direction of his glance. In the absolute stillness of the house we stared at the high-heeled slipper the girl had lost in her flight. We stared. It lay overturned.

After what seemed a very long time to me, Jacobus hitched his chair forward, stooped with extended arm and picked it up. It looked a slender thing in his big, thick hands. It was not really a slipper, but a low shoe of blue glazed kid, rubbed and shabby. It had straps to go over the instep but the girl only thrust her feet in carelessly in her slovenly manner. Jacobus raised his eyes from the shoe to look at me.

"Sit down Captain," he said at last in his subdued tone.

As if the sight of that shoe had renewed the spell I gave up suddenly the idea of leaving the house there and then. It had become impossible. I sat down keeping my eyes on the fascinating object. Jacobus turned his daughter's shoe over and over in his cushioned paws as if studying the way the thing was made. He contemplated the thin sole for a time; then glancing inside with an absorbed air:

"I am glad I found you here Captain."

I answered this by some sort of grunt, watching him covertly. Then I added: "You won't have much more of me now."

He was still deep in the interior of that shoe on which my eyes too were resting.

"Have you thought any more of this deal in potatoes I spoke to you about the other day?"

"No I haven't," I answered curtly. He checked my movement to rise by an austere, commanding gesture of the hand holding that fatal shoe. I remained seated and glared at him. "You know I don't trade."

"You ought to Captain. You ought to."

I reflected. If I left that house now I would never see the girl again. And I felt I must see her once more, if only for an instant. It was a need, not to be reasoned with, not to be disregarded. No, I

did not want to go away. I wanted to stay for one more experience
of that strange, provoking sensation and of indefinite desire, the
habit of which made me – *me* of all people – dread the prospect of
going to sea.

5   "Mr Jacobus," I pronounced slowly. "Do you really think that
upon the whole and taking various matters into consideration – I
mean everything, do you understand? – it would be really a good
thing for me to trade – let us say, with you."

I waited for a while. He went on looking at the shoe which he
10   held now crushed in the middle, the worn point of the toe and
the high heel protruding on each side of his heavy fist.

"That will be all right," he said facing me squarely at last.

"Are you sure?"

"You'll find it quite correct Captain." He had uttered his habit-
15   ual phrases in his usual placid, breath-saving voice and stood my
hard, inquisitive stare sleepily without as much as a wink.

"Then let us trade," I said turning my shoulder to him. "I see
that you are bent on it."

I did not want an open scandal but I thought that outward
20   decency may be bought too dearly at times. I included Jacobus,
myself and the whole population of the island in the same contemptuous disgust as though we had been partners in an ignoble
transaction. And the remembered vision at sea, diaphanous and
blue, of the Pearl of the Ocean at sixty miles off, the unsubstan-
25   tial, clear marvel of it as if evoked by the art of a beautiful and
pure magic, turned into a thing of horrors too. Was this the fortune this vaporous and rare apparition had held for me in its hard
heart hidden within the shape as of fair dreams and mist. Was this
my luck!

30   "I think," Jacobus became suddenly audible after what seemed
the silence of a vile meditation, "that you might conveniently take
some thirty tons. That would be about the lot, Captain."

"Would it? The lot! I dare say it would be convenient, but I
haven't got enough money for that."

35   I had never seen him so animated.

"No!" he exclaimed with what I took for the accent of grim
menace. "That's a pity." He paused, then unrelenting: "How much
money have you got Captain," he inquired with awful directness.

It was my turn to face him squarely. I did so and mentioned
40   the amount I could dispose of. And I perceived that he was

disappointed. He thought it over, his calculating gaze lost in mine, for quite a long time before he came out in a thoughtful tone with the rapacious suggestion:

"You could draw some more from your charterers. That would be quite easy Captain." 5

"No I couldn't," I retorted brusquely. "I've drawn my salary up to date; and besides, the ship's accounts are closed."

I was growing furious. I pursued: "And I'll tell you what: if I could do it I wouldn't." Then throwing off all restraint I added: "You are a bit too much of a Jacobus, Mr Jacobus." 10

The tone alone was insulting enough but he remained tranquil, only a little puzzled, till something seemed to dawn upon him; but the unwonted light in his eyes died out instantly. As a Jacobus on his native heath what a mere skipper chose to say could not touch him, outcast as he was. As a shipchandler he could stand anything. 15 All I caught of his mumble was a vague "quite correct," than which nothing could have been more egregiously false at bottom – to my view at least. But I remembered, I had never forgotten, that I must see the girl. I did not mean to go. I meant to stay in the house till I had seen the girl once more. 20

"Look here!" I said finally. "I'll tell you what I'll do. I'll take as many of your confounded potatoes as my money will buy, on condition that you go off at once down to the wharf to see them loaded in the lighter and sent alongside the ship straight away. Take the invoice and a signed receipt with you. Here's the key of 25 my desk. Give it to Burns. He will pay you."

He got up from his chair before I had finished speaking but he refused to take the key. Burns would never do it. He wouldn't like to ask him even.

"Well then," I said eyeing him slightingly, "there's nothing for 30 it Mr Jacobus but you must wait on board till I come off to settle with you."

"That will be all right Captain. I will go at once."

He seemed at a loss what to do with the girl's shoe he was still holding in his fist. Finally, looking dully at me, he put it down on 35 the chair from which he had risen.

"And you Captain. Won't you come along too – just to see . . ."

"Don't bother about me. I'll take care of myself."

He remained perplexed for a moment, as if trying to understand; and then his weighty "Certainly, certainly Captain" 40 seemed to be the outcome of some sudden thought. His big chest heaved. Was it a sigh? As he went out to hurry off these potatoes he never looked back at me.

I waited till the noise of his footsteps had died out of the dining room, and I waited a little longer. Then turning towards the distant door I raised my voice along the verandah:

"Alice!"

Nothing answered me, not even a stir behind the door. Jacobus' house might have been made empty for me to make myself at home in. I did not call again. I had become aware of a great discouragement. I was mentally jaded, morally dejected. I turned to the garden again, sitting down with my elbows spread on the low balustrade, and took my head in my hands.

The evening closed upon me. The shadows lengthened, deepened, mingled together into a pool of twilight in which the flowerbeds glowed like coloured embers; whiffs of heavy scent came to me as if the dusk of this hemisphere were but the dimness of a temple and the garden an enormous censer swinging before the altar of the stars. The colours of the blossoms deepened, losing their glow one by one.

The girl, when I turned my head at a slight noise, appeared to me very tall and slender, advancing with a swaying limp, a floating and uneven motion which ended in the sinking of her shadowy form into the deep chair. And I don't know why or whence I received the impression that she had come too late. She ought to have appeared at my call. She ought to have . . . . It was as if a supreme opportunity had been missed.

I rose and took a seat close to her, nearly opposite her armchair. Her ever-discontented voice addressed me at once, contemptuously:

"You are still here."

I pitched mine low.

"You have come out at last."

"I came to look for my shoe – before they bring in the lights."

It was her harsh, enticing whisper, subdued, not very steady – but its low tremulousness gave me no thrill now. I could only make out the oval of her face, her uncovered throat, the long white gleam of her eyes. She was mysterious enough. Her hands were resting on the arms of the chair. But where was the mysterious and provoking

sensation which was like the perfume of her flower-like youth? I
said quietly:

"I have got your shoe here." She made no sound and I continued. "You had better give me your foot and I will put it on for
you."

She made no movement. I bent low down and groped for her
foot under the flounces of her wrapper. She did not withdraw
it and I put on the shoe, buttoning the instep strap. It was an
inanimate foot. I lowered it gently to the floor.

"If you buttoned the strap you would not be losing your shoe
Miss Don't Care," I said, trying to be playful without conviction.
I felt more like wailing over the lost illusion of vague desire, over
the sudden conviction that I would never find again near her the
strange, half-evil, half-tender sensation, which had given its acrid
flavour to so many days, which had made her appear tragic and
promising, pitiful and provoking. That was all over.

"Your father picked it up," I said, thinking she may just as well
be told of the fact.

"I am not afraid of Papa – by himself," she declared scornfully.

"Oh! It's only in conjunction with his disreputable associates,
strangers, the riff raff of Europe as your charming aunt or great
aunt says – men like me, for instance – that you . . ."

"I am not afraid of you," she snapped out.

"That's because you don't know that I am doing now business –
private business – with your father. Yes. I am in fact doing exactly
what he wants me to do. I've broken my promise to you. That's the
sort of man I am. And now – aren't you afraid? If you believe what
that dear, kind, truthful old lady says you ought to be."

It was with unexpected modulated softness that she affirmed:

"No. I am not afraid." She hesitated. . . . "Not now."

"Quite right. You needn't be. I shall not see you again before I go
to sea." I rose and stood near her chair. "But I shall often think of
you in this old garden, passing under the trees over there, walking
between these gorgeous flower-beds. You must love this garden . . ."

"I love nothing."

I heard in her sullen tone the faint echo of that resentfully tragic
note which I had found once so provoking. But it left me unmoved
except for a sudden and weary conviction of the emptiness in all
things under heaven.

"Good bye Alice," I said.

She did not answer, she did not move. To merely take her hand, shake it and go away seemed impossible, almost improper. I stooped without haste and pressed my lips to her smooth forehead. This was the moment when I realized clearly with a sort of terror my complete detachment from that unfortunate creature. And as I lingered in that cruel self-knowledge I felt the light touch of her arms falling languidly on my neck and received a hasty, awkward, haphazard kiss which missed my lips. No! She was not afraid; but I was no longer moved. Her arms slipped off my neck slowly, she made no sound, the deep wicker armchair creaked slightly; only the sense of my dignity prevented me fleeing headlong from that catastrophic revelation.

I traversed the dining room slowly. I thought: She's listening to my footsteps; she can't help it; she'll hear me open and shut that door. And I closed it as gently behind me as if I had been a thief retreating with his ill-gotten booty. During that stealthy act I experienced my last touch of emotion in that house, at the thought of the girl I had left sitting there in the obscurity, with her heavy hair and empty eyes as black as the night itself, staring into the walled garden, silent, warm, odorous with the perfume of imprisoned flowers, which, like herself, were lost to sight in a world buried in darkness.

The narrow, ill-lighted, rustic streets I knew so well on my way to the harbour were extremely quiet. I felt in my heart that the further one ventures, the better one understands how everything in our life is common, short and empty; that it is in seeking the unknown in our sensations that we discover how mediocre are our attempts and how soon defeated! Jacobus' boatman was waiting at the steps with an unusual air of readiness. He put me alongside my ship but did not give me his confidential "good evening sah," and, instead of shoving off at once, remained holding on to the ladder.

I was a thousand miles from commercial affairs when on the dark quarter deck Mr Burns positively rushed at me stammering with excitement. He had been pacing the deck distractedly for hours awaiting my arrival. Just before sunset a lighter loaded with potatoes had come alongside with that fat shipchandler himself sitting on the pile of sacks. He was now stuck immovable in the cabin. What was the meaning of it all. Surely I did not . . .

"Yes Mr Burns – I did," I cut him short. He was beginning to make gestures of despair when I stopped that too by giving him the key of my desk and desiring him in a tone which admitted of no argument to go below at once, pay Mr Jacobus' bill and send him out of the ship.

"I don't want to see him," I confessed frankly, climbing the poop ladder. I felt extremely tired. Dropping on the seat of the sky light I gave myself up to idle gazing at the lights about the quay, and at the black mass of the mountain on the south side of the harbour. I never heard Jacobus leave the ship with every single sovereign of my ready cash in his pocket. I never heard anything till, a long time afterwards, Mr Burns, unable to contain himself any longer, intruded upon me with his ridiculously angry lamentations at my weakness and good nature.

"Of course there's plenty of room in the after hatch. But they are sure to go rotten down there. Well! I never heard . . . . Seventeen tons! I suppose I must hoist in that lot first thing to-morrow morning."

"I suppose you must. Unless you drop them overboard. But I'm afraid you can't do that. I wouldn't mind myself, but it's forbidden to throw rubbish into the harbour, you know."

"That is the truest word you have said for many a day sir, Rubbish. That's just what I expect they are. Nearly eighty good gold sovereigns gone; a perfectly clean sweep of your drawer sir. Bless me if I understand!"

As it was impossible to throw the right light on this commercial transaction I left him to his lamentations and under the impression that I was a hopeless fool. Next day I did not go ashore. For one thing I had no money to go ashore with – no, not enough to buy a cigarette with. Jacobus had made a clean sweep. But that was not the only reason. The Pearl of the Ocean had in a few short hours grown odious to me. And I did not want to meet any one. My reputation had suffered. I knew I was the object of unkind and sarcastic comments.

The following morning at sunrise just as our stern-fasts had been let go and the tug plucked us out from between the buoys I saw Jacobus standing up in his boat. The nigger was pulling hard; several baskets of provisions for ships were stowed between the thwarts. The father of Alice was going his morning round. His countenance was tranquil and friendly. He raised his arm and

shouted something with great heartiness. But his voice was of the sort that doesn't carry any distance; all I could catch faintly, or rather guess at, were the words "next time" and "quite correct." And it was only of these last that I was certain. Raising my arm
5 perfunctorily for all response I turned away. I rather resented the familiarity of the thing. Hadn't I settled accounts finally with him, by means of that potato bargain.

This being a harbour story, it is not my purpose to speak of our passage. I was glad enough to be at sea, but not with the gladness
10 of old days. Formerly I had no memories to take away with me. I shared in the blessed forgetfulness of sailors, that forgetfulness natural and invincible which resembles innocence in so far that it prevents self-examination. Now however I remembered the girl. During the first few days I was for ever questioning myself as to
15 the nature of facts and sensations connected with her person and with my conduct.

And I must say also that Mr Burns' intolerable fussing with these potatoes was not calculated to make me forget the part which I had played. He looked upon it as a purely commercial transaction of a
20 particularly foolish kind, and his devotion – if it was devotion and not mere cussedness, as I came to regard it before long – inspired him with a zeal to minimize my loss as much as possible. Oh yes! He took care of those infamous potatoes with a vengeance, as the saying goes.
25 Everlastingly, there was a tackle over the after hatch and everlastingly the watch on deck were pulling up, spreading out, picking over, re-bagging and lowering down again some part of that lot of potatoes. My bargain with all its remotest associations mental and visual – the garden of flowers and scents, the girl with her provok-
30 ing contempt and her tragic loneliness of a hopeless castaway – was everlastingly dangled before my eyes for thousands of miles along the open sea. And as if by a satanic refinement of irony it was accompanied by a most awful smell. Whiffs from decaying potatoes pursued me on the poop; they mingled with my thoughts, with
35 my food, poisoned my very dreams. They made an atmosphere of corruption for the ship.

I remonstrated with Mr Burns about this excessive care. I would have been well content to batten the hatch down and let them perish under the deck.

That perhaps would have been unsafe. The horrid emanations might have flavoured the cargo of sugar. They seemed strong enough to taint the very ironwork. In addition Mr Burns made it a personal matter. He assured me he knew how to treat a cargo of potatoes at sea – had been in the trade as a boy, he said. He meant to make my loss as small as possible. What between his devotion – it must have been devotion – and his vanity, I positively dared not give him the order to throw my commercial venture overboard. I believe he would have refused point blank to obey my lawful command. An unprecedented and comical situation would have been created with which I did not feel equal to deal.

I welcomed the coming of bad weather as no sailor had ever done. In consequence when at last I hove the ship to, to pick up the pilot outside Port-Philip Heads, the after hatch had not been opened for more than a week and I might have believed that no such thing as a potato had ever been on board.

It was an abominable day, raw, blustering, with great squalls of wind and rain; the pilot, a cheery person, looked after the ship and chatted to me streaming from head to foot; and the heavier the lash of the downpour, the more pleased with himself and everything around him he seemed to be. He rubbed his wet hands with a satisfaction which to me who had stood that kind of thing for several days and nights seemed inconceivable in any non-aquatic creature.

"You seem to enjoy getting wet, Pilot," I remarked.

He had a bit of land round his house in the suburbs and it was of his garden he was thinking. At the sound of the word garden, unheard, unspoken for so many days, I had a vision of gorgeous colour, of sweet scents, of a girlish figure crouching in a chair. Yes. That was a distinct emotion breaking into the peace I had found in the sleepless anxieties of my responsibility during a week of dangerous bad weather. The Colony, the Pilot explained, had suffered from unparalleled drought. This was the first decent drop of water they had had for seven months. The root crops were lost. And, trying to be casual, but with visible interest he asked me if I had perchance any potatoes to spare.

Potatoes! I had managed to forget them. In a moment I felt plunged into corruption up to my neck. Mr Burns was making eyes at me behind the Pilot's back.

Finally he obtained a ton and paid ten pounds for it. This was twice the price of my bargain with Jacobus. The spirit of covetousness woke up in me. That night, in harbour, before I slept, the Custom-House galley came alongside. While his underlings were putting seals on the store-rooms the officer in charge took me aside confidentially: "I say Captain you don't happen to have any potatoes to sell?"

Clearly there was a potato famine in the land. I let him have a ton for twelve pounds and he went away joyfully. That night I dreamt of a pile of gold in the form of a grave in which a girl was buried, and woke up callous with greed. On calling at my ship-broker's office, that man after the usual business had been transacted pushed his spectacles up on his forehead:

"I was thinking Captain that coming from the Pearl of the Ocean you may have some potatoes to sell."

I said negligently: "Oh yes, I could spare you a ton. Fifteen pounds."

He exclaimed "I say!" but after studying my face for a while accepted my terms with a faint grimace. It seems that these people could not exist without potatoes. I could. I didn't want to see a potato as long as I lived; but the demon of lucre had taken possession of me. How the news got about I don't know, but returning on board rather late I found a small group of men of the coster type hanging about the waist while Mr Burns walked to and fro the quarter deck loftily, keeping a triumphant eye on them. They had come to buy potatoes.

"These chaps have been waiting here in the sun for hours," Burns whispered to me excitedly. "They have drunk the water cask dry. Don't you throw away your chances sir. You are too good-natured."

I selected a man with thick legs and a man with a cast in his eye to negotiate with, simply because they were easily distinguishable from the rest. "You have the money on you," I inquired before taking them down into the cabin.

"Yes sir," they answered in one voice, slapping their pockets. I liked their air of quiet determination. Long before the end of the day all the potatoes were sold at about three times the price I had paid for them. Mr Burns, feverish and exulting, congratulated himself on his skilful care of my commercial venture, but hinted plainly that I ought to have made more of it.

That night I did not sleep very well. I thought of Jacobus by fits and starts, between snatches of dreams concerned with castaways starving on a desert island covered with flowers. It was extremely unpleasant. In the morning, tired and unrefreshed, I sat down and wrote a long letter to my owners giving them a carefully thought-out scheme for the ship's employment in the East and about the China Seas for the next two years. I spent my day at that task and felt somewhat more at peace when it was done.

Their reply came in due course. They were greatly struck with my project; but considering that, notwithstanding the unfortunate difficulty with the bags (which they trusted I would know how to guard against in the future), the voyage showed a very fair profit, they thought it would be better to keep the ship in the sugar trade – at least for the present.

I turned over the page and read on.

"We have had a letter from our good friend Mr Jacobus. We are pleased to see how well you have hit it off with him; for, not to speak of his assistance in the unfortunate matter of the bags, he writes us that should you, by using all possible dispatch, manage to bring the ship back early in the season he would be able to give us a good rate of freight. We have no doubt that your best endeavours . . . etc. . . . etc. . . ."

I dropped the letter and sat motionless for a long time. Then I wrote my answer (it was a short one) and went ashore myself to post it. I wondered what dreams I would have that night – but as it turned out I did not sleep at all. At breakfast I informed Mr Burns that I had resigned my command.

He dropped his knife and fork and looked at me with indignation.

"You have sir! I thought you loved the ship."

"So I do Burns," I said. "But the fact is that the Indian Ocean and everything that is in it has lost its charm for me. I am going home as passenger by the Suez Canal."

"Everything that is in it," he repeated angrily. "I've never heard anybody talk like this. And to tell you the truth, sir, all the time we have been together I've never quite made you out. What's one ocean more than another? Charm, indeed!"

He was really devoted to me, I believe. But he cheered up when I told him that I had recommended him for my successor.

"Anyhow," he remarked, "let people say what they like, this Jacobus has served your turn. I must own that this potato business turned out wonderfully."

"Yes Mr Burns," I said. "Quite a smile of Fortune."

5 But I could not tell him that it was driving me out of a ship I had learned to love; and he must have wondered at my bitter and ironic tone. He had always looked on this affair as a purely commercial transaction.

"A wonderful piece of luck!" he said.

10   The End.

THE SECRET SHARER
AN EPISODE FROM THE COAST

THE SECRET SHARER

O N MY RIGHT HAND there were lines of fishing stakes resembling a mysterious system of half submerged bamboo fences, incomprehensible in its division of the domain of tropical fishes and crazy of aspect as if abandoned for ever by some nomad 5 tribe of brown fishermen now removed to the other end of the earth, for there was no sign of human habitation as far as the eye could reach. To my left a group of barren islets suggesting ruins of stone walls, towers and blockhouses had its foundations set in a blue sea that itself looked solid, so still and stable did it lie below my 10 feet. Even the track of light from the westering sun shone smoothly without that animated glitter which tells of an imperceptible ripple. And when I turned my head to take a parting glance at the tug which had just left us anchored outside the bar, I saw the straight line of the flat shore joined to the stable sea edge to edge with a 15 perfect and unmarked closeness in one levelled floor, half brown, half blue, under the enormous dome of the sky. Corresponding in their insignificance to the islets of the sea, two small clumps of trees, one on each side of the only fault in the impeccable joint, marked the mouth of the river Meinam we had just left on the first 20 preparatory stage of our homeward journey; and far back on the inland level a larger and loftier mass, the grove surrounding the great Paknam pagoda, was the only thing on which the eye could rest from the vain task of exploring the monotonous sweep of the horizon. Here and there gleams as of a few scattered pieces of 25 silver marked the windings of the great river; and on the nearest of them, just within the bar, the tug steaming right into the land became lost to my sight, hull and funnel and masts, as though the impassive earth had swallowed her up without an effort, without a tremor. My eye followed the light cloud of her smoke now 30 here, now there, above the plain according to the devious curves of the stream, but always fainter and farther away, till I lost it at last behind the mitre-shaped hill of the Great Pagoda. And then I was left alone with my ship anchored at the head of the Gulf of Siam.

She floated at the starting point of a long journey very still in
an immense stillness, the shadows of her spars flung far to the
eastward by the setting sun. At that moment I was alone on her
decks. There was not a sound in her – and around us nothing
5 moved, nothing lived, not a canoe on the water, not a bird in the
air, not a cloud in the sky. In this breathless pause at the threshold
of a long passage we seemed to be measuring our fitness for a long
and arduous enterprise, the appointed task of both our existences
to be carried on, day after day, far from all human eyes, with only
10 sky and sea for spectators and for judges.

There must have been some glare in the air to interfere with
one's sight, because it was only just before the sun left us that my
roaming eyes made out beyond the highest ridge of the principal
islet of the group something which did away with the solemnity of
15 perfect solitude. The tide of darkness flowed on swiftly and with
tropical suddenness a swarm of stars came out above the shadowy
earth, while I lingered yet, my hand resting lightly on my ship's
rail as if on the shoulder of a trusted friend. But with all that
multitude of celestial bodies staring down at one the comfort of
20 quiet communion with her was gone for good. And there were
also disturbing sounds by this time – voices, footsteps forward; the
steward flitted along the main deck, a busily ministering spirit; a
hand-bell tinkled urgently under the poop deck . . .

I found my two officers waiting for me near the supper table, in
25 the lighted cuddy. We sat down at once and as I helped the chief
mate I said:

"Were you aware that there is a ship anchored inside the islands.
I saw her mast-heads above the ridge as the sun went down."

He raised sharply his simple face overcharged by a terrible
30 growth of whisker and emitted his usual ejaculations "Bless my
soul sir! You don't say so."

My second mate was a round-cheeked, silent young man, grave
beyond his years I thought; but as our eyes happened to meet
I detected a slight quiver on his lips. I looked down at once. It
35 was not my part to encourage sneering on board my ship. It must
be said too that I knew very little of my officers. In consequence
of certain events of no particular significance, except to myself,
I had been appointed to the command only a fortnight before.
Neither did I know much of the hands forward. All these people
40 had been together for eighteen months or so and my position

was that of the only stranger on board. I mention this because it has some bearing on what is to follow. But what I felt most was my being a stranger to the ship; and if all the truth must be told I was somewhat of a stranger to myself. The youngest man on board (barring the second mate) and untried as yet by a position of the fullest responsibility, I was willing to take the adequacy of the others for granted. They had simply to be equal to their tasks; but I wondered how far I should turn out faithful to that ideal conception of one's own personality every man sets up for himself secretly.

Meantime the chief mate with an almost visible effect of collaboration on the part of his round eyes and frightful whiskers was trying to evolve a theory of the anchored ship. His dominant trait was to take all things into earnest consideration. He was of a painstaking turn of mind. As he used to say he "liked to account to himself for" practically everything that came in his way, down to a miserable scorpion he had found in his cabin a week before. The why and the wherefore of that scorpion – how it got on board and came to select his room rather than the pantry (which was a dark place and more what a scorpion would be partial to) and how on earth it managed to drown itself in the inkwell of his writing desk – had exercised him infinitely. The ship within the islands was much more easily accounted for; and just as we were about to rise from table he made his pronouncement. She was, he doubted not, a ship from home lately arrived. Probably she drew too much water to cross the bar except at the top of spring tides. Therefore she went into that natural harbour to wait for a few days in preference to remaining in an open roadstead.

"That's so," confirmed the second mate suddenly in his slightly hoarse voice. "She draws over twenty feet. She's the Liverpool ship *Sephora* with a cargo of coal. Hundred and twenty three days from Cardiff."

We looked at him in surprise.

"The tug boat skipper told me of her when he came on board for your letters sir," explained the young man. "He expects to take her up the river the day after tomorrow."

After thus overwhelming us with the extent of his information he slipped out of the cabin. The mate observed regretfully that he "could not account for that young fellow's whims." What prevented him telling us all about it at once, he wanted to know.

I detained him as he was making a move. For the last two days the crew had had plenty of hard work and the night before they had very little sleep. I felt painfully that I – a stranger – was doing something unusual when I directed him to let all hands turn in

5 without setting an anchor watch. I proposed to keep on deck myself till one o'clock or thereabouts. I would get the second mate to relieve me at that hour.

"He will turn out the cook and the steward at four," I concluded, "and then give you a call. Of course at the slightest sign of any sort

10 of wind we'll have the hands up and make a start at once."

He concealed his astonishment. "Very well sir." Outside the cuddy he put his head in the second mate's door to inform him of my unheard-of caprice to take a five hours' anchor watch on myself. I heard the other raise his voice incredulously: "What? The

15 Captain himself?" Then a few more murmurs, a door closed, then another. A few moments later I went on deck.

My strangeness which had made me sleepless had prompted that unconventional arrangement, as if I had expected in those solitary hours of the night to get on terms with the ship of which

20 I knew nothing, manned by men of whom I knew very little more. Fast alongside a wharf, littered like any ship in port with a tangle of unrelated things, invaded by shore people, I had hardly seen her yet properly. Now, as she lay cleared for sea, the stretch of her main deck seemed to me very fine under the stars. Very fine, very

25 roomy for her size and very inviting. I descended the poop and paced the waist, my mind picturing to myself the coming passage out through the Malay Archipelago, down the Indian Ocean and up the Atlantic. All its phases were familiar enough to me, every characteristic, all the alternatives which were likely to face me on

30 the high seas – everything! — except the novel responsibility of command. But I took heart from the reasonable thought that the ship was like other ships, the men like other men and that the sea was not likely to keep any special surprises expressly for my discomfiture.

35 Arrived at that comforting conclusion I bethought myself of a cigar and went below to get it. All was still down there. Everybody at the after end of the ship was sleeping profoundly. I came out on the quarter deck agreeably at ease in my sleeping suit on that warm breathless night, barefooted, a glowing cigar in my

40 teeth, and going forward I was met by the profound silence of the

fore-end of the ship. Only as I passed the door of the forecastle I heard a deep, quiet, trustful sigh of some sleeper inside. And suddenly I rejoiced in the great security of the sea as compared with the unrest of the land, in my choice of that untempted life presenting no disquieting problems, invested with an elementary moral beauty by the absolute straightforwardness of its appeal and by the singleness of its purpose.

The riding light in the forerigging burned with a clear, untroubled, as if symbolic flame, confident and bright in the mysterious shades of the night. Passing on my way aft along the other side of the ship I observed that the rope side-ladder, put over no doubt for the master of the tug when he came to fetch away our letters, had not been hauled in as it should have been. I became annoyed at this, for exactitude in small matters is the very soul of discipline. Then I reflected that I had myself peremptorily dismissed my officers from duty and by my own act had prevented the anchor watch being formally set and things properly attended to. I asked myself whether it was wise to have interfered with the established routine of duties even from the kindest of motives. My action might have made me appear eccentric. Goodness only knew how that absurdly whiskered mate would "account" for my conduct and what the whole ship thought of that informality of their new captain. I was vexed with myself.

Not from compunction certainly, but as it were mechanically I proceeded to get the ladder in myself. Now a side-ladder of that sort is a light affair and comes in easily, yet my vigourous tug which should have brought it flying inboard merely recoiled upon my body in a totally unexpected jerk. What the devil! . . . I was so astounded by the immovableness of that ladder that I remained stock still trying to account for it to myself like that imbecile mate of mine. In the end of course I put my head over the rail.

The side of the ship made an opaque belt of shadow on the darkling glassy shimmer of the sea. But I saw at once something elongated and pale floating very close to the ladder. Before I could form a guess a faint flash of phosphorescent light, which seemed to issue suddenly from the naked body of a man, flickered in the sleeping water with the elusive, silent play of summer lightning in a night sky. With a gasp I saw revealed to my stare a pair of feet, the long legs, a broad livid back right up to the neck immersed in a greenish cadaveric glow. One hand, awash, clutched the bottom rung of the ladder. He was complete but for the head. A headless corpse! The cigar dropped out of my gaping mouth with a tiny plop and a short hiss quite audible in the absolute stillness of all things under heaven. At that I suppose he raised up his face, a dimly

5 pale oval in the shadow of the ship's side. But even then I could only barely make out down there the shape of his black-haired head. However that much was enough, for the horrid frostbound sensation which had gripped me about the chest to pass off. The moment of vain exclamations was past too. I only climbed on the

10 spare spar and leaned over the rail as far as I could to bring my eyes nearer to that mystery floating alongside.

As he hung by the ladder like a resting swimmer the sea lightning played about his limbs at every stir; and he appeared in it ghastly, silvery, fishlike. He remained as mute as a fish too. He made no

15 motion to get out of the water either. It was inconceivable that he should not attempt to come on board and strangely troubling to suspect that perhaps he did not want to. And my first words were prompted by just that troubled incertitude.

"What's the matter?" I asked in my ordinary tone, speaking down

20 to the face upturned exactly under mine.

"Cramp," it answered, no louder. Then slightly anxious: "I say, no need to call any one."

"I was not going to," I said.

"Are you alone on deck?"

25 "Yes."

I had somehow the impression that he was on the point of letting go the ladder to swim away beyond my ken – mysterious as he came. But for the moment this being appearing as if he had risen from the bottom of the sea (it was certainly the nearest land to

30 the ship) wanted only to know the time. I told him. And he down there tentatively:

"I suppose your captain's turned in?"

"I am sure he isn't," I said.

He seemed to struggle with himself for I heard something like

35 the low bitter murmur of doubt: "What's the good." His next words came out with a hesitating effort.

"Look here my man. Could you call him out quietly."

I thought the time had come to declare myself.

"I am the captain."

I heard a "By Jove!" whispered at the level of the water. The phosphorescence flashed in the swirl of water all about his limbs; his other hand seized the ladder.

"My name's Leggatt."

The voice was calm and resolute. A good voice. The self posses- 5 sion of that man had somehow induced a corresponding state in myself. It was very quietly that I remarked:

"You must be a good swimmer."

"Yes. I've been in the water practically since nine o'clock. The question for me now is whether I am to let go this ladder and go 10 on swimming till I sink from exhaustion or – to come on board here."

I felt this was no mere formula of desperate speech but a real alternative in the view of a strong soul. I could tell by this that he was young; indeed it is only the young who are ever confronted by 15 such clear issues. But at the time it was pure intuition on my part. A mysterious communication was established already between us two – in the face of that silent, darkened tropical sea. I was young too, young enough to make no comment. The man in the water began suddenly to climb up the ladder, and I hastened away from 20 the rail to fetch some clothes.

Before entering the cabin I stood still listening in the lobby at the foot of the stairs. A faint snore came through the closed door of the chief mate's room. The second mate's door was on the hook but the darkness in there was absolutely soundless. He too was 25 young and could sleep like a stone. Remained the steward, but he was not likely to wake up before he was called. I got a sleeping suit out of my room and coming back on deck saw the man from the sea sitting on the main hatch glimmering white in the darkness, his elbows on his knees and his head in his hands. In a moment 30 he had concealed his damp body in a sleeping suit of the same grey-stripe pattern as the one I was wearing and followed me like my double on the poop. Together we moved right aft, barefooted, silent.

"What is it?" I asked in a deadened voice taking the lighted lamp 35 out of the binnacle, and raising it to his face.

"An ugly business."

He had rather regular features, a good mouth, light eyes under somewhat heavy dark eyebrows, a smooth, square forehead, no

growth on his cheeks, a small brown moustache, and a well-shaped round chin. His expression was concentrated, meditative under the inspecting light of the lamp I held up to his face; such as a man thinking hard in solitude might wear. My sleeping suit
5 was just right for his size. A well-knit young fellow of twenty five at most. He caught his lower lip with the edge of white, even teeth.

"Yes," I said replacing the lamp in the binnacle. The warm, heavy, tropical night closed upon his head again.
10 "There's a ship over there," he murmured.

"Yes. I know. The *Sephora*. Did you know of us?"

"Hadn't the slightest idea. I am the mate of her. . . ." He paused and corrected himself: "I should say I *was*."

"Aha! Something wrong?"
15 "Yes. Very wrong indeed. I've killed a man."

"What do you mean? Just now?"

"No, on the passage. Weeks ago. Thirty nine south. When I say a man . . ."

"Fit of temper," I suggested confidently.
20 The shadowy dark head, like mine, seemed to nod imperceptibly above the ghostly grey of my sleeping suit. It was, in the night, as though I had been faced by my own reflection in the depths of a sombre and immense mirror.

"A pretty thing to have to own up to for a *Conway* boy," mur-
25 mured my double distinctly.

"You're a *Conway* boy?"

"I am," he said as if startled. Then slowly . . . "Perhaps you too . . ."

It was so; but being a couple of years older I had left before he joined. After a quick interchange of dates a silence fell; and I
30 thought suddenly of my absurd mate with his terrific whiskers and the "bless my soul – you don't say so" type of intellect. My double gave me an inkling of his thoughts by saying:

"My father's a parson in Norfolk. You see me before a judge and jury on that charge. For myself I can't see the necessity. There are
35 fellows that an angel from heaven . . . And I am not that. He was one of these creatures that are just simmering all the time with a silly sort of wickedness. Miserable devils that have no business to live at all. He wouldn't do his duty and wouldn't let anybody else do theirs. But what's the good of talking! You know well enough
40 the sort of ill-conditioned snarling cur . . ."

He appealed to me as if our experiences had been as identical as our clothes. And I knew well enough the pestiferous danger of such a character where there are no means of legal repression. And I knew well enough also that my double there was no homicidal ruffian. I did not think of asking him for details when he told me 5
the story roughly in brusque, disconnected sentences. I needed no more. I saw it all going on as though I were myself inside that other sleeping suit.

"It was when setting a reefed foresail, at dusk. Reefed foresail – you understand the sort of weather – the only sail we had left to 10
keep her running, so you may guess what it had been like for days. Anxious sort of job that. He gave me some of his cursed insolence at the sheet. I tell you I was overdone with this terrific weather that seemed to have no end to it. Terrific I tell you – and a deep ship. I believe the fellow himself was half crazed with funk. That was no 15
time for gentlemanly reproof, so I turned round and felled him like an ox. He up and at me. We closed just as an awful sea made for the ship. All hands saw it and took to the rigging. I had him by the throat and went on shaking him like a rat, the men above us yelling 'Look out! look out!' Then a crash as if the sky had fallen. They 20
say that for ten minutes there was hardly anything to be seen of the ship – just the three masts and a bit of the forecastle head and of the poop all awash driving along wildly in a smother of foam. It was a miracle that they found us jammed together behind the forebits. Not a pretty miracle either. It's clear that I meant business 25
because I was holding him by the throat still. He was black in the face. It was too much for them; it seems they rushed us aft together gripped as we were screaming Murder! like a lot of lunatics and broke into the cuddy. And the ship running for her life touch and go all the time, any minute her last in a sea fit to turn your 30
hair grey only a-looking at it. I understand that the skipper too started raving like the rest of them. The man had been deprived of sleep for more than a week and to have this sprung on him at the height of a furious gale nearly drove him out of his mind. I wonder they didn't fling me overboard after getting the carcass of 35
their precious shipmate out of my fingers. They had rather a job to separate us I've been told. A sufficiently fierce story to make an old judge and a respectable jury sit up a bit. The first thing I heard when I came to myself was the maddening howling of that endless gale and on that the voice of the old man. He was hanging on to 40

my bunk, staring into my face out of his sou'wester. 'Mr Leggatt.
You have killed a man. You can act no longer as chief mate of this
ship.'"

His care to subdue his voice made it sound monotonous. He
5 rested a hand on the end of the skylight to steady himself with,
and all that time did not stir a limb as far as I could see. "Nice little
tale for a quiet tea party," he concluded in the same tone.

One of my hands too rested on the end of the skylight, neither
did I stir a limb as far as I knew. We stood less than a foot from
10 each other. It occurred to me that if old "Bless my soul – you don't
say so" were to put his head up the companion and catch sight
of us he would think he was seeing his captain double or imagine
himself come upon a scene of weird witchcraft: the strange captain
having a quiet confabulation by the wheel with his own grey ghost.
15 I became very much concerned to prevent anything of the sort.
I heard the other's soothing undertone: "My father's a parson in
Norfolk," it said. Evidently he had forgotten he had told me this
important fact before. Truly a nice little tale.

"You had better slip down into my stateroom now," I said moving
20 off stealthily. My double followed my movements; our bare feet
made no sound; I let him in, closed the door with care and after
giving a call to the second mate returned on deck to wait for my
relief.

"Not much sign of any wind yet," I remarked when he appeared.
25 "No sir. Not much," he assented sleepily in his hoarse voice with
just enough deference, no more, and barely suppressing a yawn.

"Well, that's all you have to look out for. You have got your
orders."

"Yes sir."

30 I paced a turn or two on the poop and saw him take up his
position, face forward with his elbow in the ratlines of the mizen
rigging, before I went below. The mate's faint snoring was still
going on peacefully. The cuddy lamp was burning over the table
on which stood a vase with flowers, a polite attention from the
35 ship's provision merchant – the last flowers we should see for the
next three months at the very least. Two bunches of bananas hung
from the beam symmetrically, one on each side of the rudder
casing. Everything was as before in the ship – except that two
of her captain's sleeping suits were simultaneously in use, one

motionless in the cuddy, the other keeping very still in the captain's stateroom.

It must be explained here that my cabin had the form of the capital letter L., the door being within the angle and opening into the short part of the letter. A couch was to the left, the bedplace to the right, my writing desk and the chronometers' table faced the door. But anyone opening it, unless he stepped right inside, had no view of what I call the long (or vertical) part of the letter. It contained some lockers surmounted by a bookcase and a few clothes, a thick jacket or two, caps, oilskin coat and such like hung on hooks. There was at the bottom of that part a door opening into my bathroom, which could be entered also directly from the saloon. But that way was never used.

The mysterious arrival had discovered the advantage of this particular shape. Entering my room, lighted strongly by a biggish bulkhead lamp swung on gimballs above my writing desk, I did not see him anywhere till he stepped out quietly from behind the coats hung in the recessed part. "I heard somebody moving about and went in there at once," he whispered.

I too spoke under my breath.

"Nobody is likely to come in here without knocking and getting permission."

He nodded. His face was thin and the sunburn faded as though he had been ill. And no wonder. He had been, I heard presently, kept under arrest in his cabin for something like six weeks. But there was nothing sickly in his eyes or in his expression. He was not a bit like me really; yet as we stood leaning over my bedplace, whispering side by side with our dark heads together and our backs to the door, anybody bold enough to open it stealthily would have been treated to the uncanny sight of a double captain busy talking in whispers with his other self.

"But all this doesn't tell me how you came to hang on to our side-ladder," I inquired, in the hardly audible murmurs we used, after he had told me something more of the proceedings on board once the bad weather was over.

"When we sighted Java Head I had had time to think all those matters out several times over. I had six weeks of doing nothing else and with only an hour or so every evening for a tramp on the quarter deck."

He whispered, his arms folded on the side of my bedplace, staring through the open port. And I could imagine perfectly the manner of this thinking out – a stubborn if not a steadfast operation – something of which I should have been perfectly incapable.

5   "I reckoned it would be dark before we closed with the land," he continued so low that I had to strain my hearing, near as we were to each other, shoulder touching shoulder almost. "So I asked to speak to the old man. He always looked damnably sick when he came to see me – as if he could not look me in the face. You know
10 that foresail saved the ship. She was too deep to have run long under bare poles. And it was I that managed to set it for him. Anyway he came. When I had him in my cabin (he stood by the door looking at me as if I had the halter round my neck already) I asked him right away to leave my cabin door unlocked at night
15 while the ship was going through Sunda Straits. There would be the Java coast within two or three miles, off Angier Point. I wanted nothing more. I've had a prize for swimming my second year in the *Conway*."

"I can believe it," I breathed out.

20 "God only knows why they locked me in every night. To see some of their faces you'd have thought they were afraid I'd go about at night strangling people. Am I a murdering brute? Do I look it? By Jove if I had been he wouldn't have trusted himself like that into my room. You'll say I might have chucked him aside and bolted
25 out there and then – it was dark already. Well no. And for the same reason I wouldn't think of trying to smash the door. There would have been a rush to stop me at the noise and I did not mean to get into a confounded scrimmage. Somebody else might have got killed – for I would not have broken out only to get chucked
30 back – and I did not want any more of that work. He refused, looking more sick than ever. He was afraid of the men, and also of that old second mate of his who had been sailing with him for years – a grey headed old humbug; and his steward too had been with him devil knows how long, seventeen years or more, a
35 dogmatic sort of loafer who hated me like poison, just because I was the chief mate. No chief mate ever made more than one voyage in the *Sephora* – you know. Those two old chaps ran the ship. Devil only knows what the skipper wasn't afraid of – all his nerve went to pieces altogether in that hellish spell of bad weather we
40 had – of what the law would do to him – of his wife perhaps. O! yes!

she's on board. Though I don't think she would have meddled.
She would have been only too glad to have me disappear out of
the ship in any way. The 'brand of Cain' business don't you see.
That's all right. I was ready enough to go off wandering on the face
of the earth – and that was price enough to pay for an Abel of that   5
sort. Anyhow he wouldn't. 'This thing must take its course. I represent the law here.' He was shaking like a leaf. 'So you won't?' –
'No!' – 'Then I hope you will be able to sleep on that,' I said, and
turned my back on him. 'I wonder that you can,' cries he, and
locks the door.   10

"Well, after that, I couldn't. Not very well. That was three weeks
ago. We have had a slow passage through the Java Sea; drifted about
Carimata for ten days. When we anchored here they thought I
suppose it was all right. The nearest land (and that's five miles) was
the ship's destination; the Consul would soon set about catching   15
me; and there would have been no object in bolting to these islets
there. I don't suppose there's a drop of water on them. I don't
know how it was but to-night that steward after bringing me my
supper went out to let me eat it and left the door unlocked. And I
ate it – all there was too. After I had finished I strolled out on the   20
quarter deck. I don't know that I meant to do anything. A breath
of fresh air was all I wanted I believe. Then a sudden temptation
came over me. I kicked off my slippers and was in the water before
I had made up my mind fairly. Somebody heard the splash and
they raised an awful hullabaloo! 'He's gone! Lower the boat! He's   25
committed suicide! No he's swimming!'

"Certainly I was swimming. It's not so easy for a swimmer like
me to commit suicide by drowning. I landed on the nearest islet
before the boat left the ship's side. I heard them pulling about in
the dark, hailing and so on, but after a bit they gave up. Everything   30
quieted down and the anchorage became as still as death. I sat
down on a stone and began to think. I felt certain they would start
searching for me at daylight. There was no place to hide on these
stony things – and if there had been what would have been the
good? But now I was clear of that ship I was not going back. So   35
after a while I took off all my clothes, tied them up in a bundle
with a stone inside and dropped them in the deep water on the
outer side of that islet. That was suicide enough for me. Let them
think what they liked but I didn't mean to drown myself. I meant
to swim till I sank – but that's not the same thing. I struck out   40

for another of these little islands and it was from that one that I first saw your riding light. Something to swim for. I went on easily and on the way I came upon a flat rock a foot or two above water. In the day time, I dare say, you might make it out with a glass from your poop. I scrambled up on it and rested myself for a bit. Then I made another start. That last spell must have been over a mile."

His whisper was getting fainter and fainter, and all the time he had stared straight out through the porthole in which there was not even a star to be seen. I had not interrupted him. There was something that made comment impossible in his narrative, or perhaps in himself; a sort of feeling, a quality, which I can't find a name for. And when he ceased all I found was a futile whisper: "So you swam for our light."

"Yes – straight for it. It was something to swim for. I couldn't see any stars low down because the coast was in the way, and I couldn't see the land either. The water was like glass. One might have been swimming in a confounded, thousand-feet deep cistern with no place for scrambling out anywhere; but what I didn't like was the notion of swimming round and round like a crazed bullock before I gave out; and as I didn't mean to go back . . . . No. Do you see me being hauled back stark naked off one of these little islands, by the scruff of the neck and fighting like a wild beast. Somebody would have got killed for certain, and I did not want any of that. So I went on. Then your ladder . . ."

"Why didn't you hail the ship," I asked a little louder.

He touched my shoulder lightly. Lazy footsteps came right over our heads and stopped. The second mate had crossed from the other side of the poop and might have been hanging over the rail for all we knew.

"He couldn't hear us talking – could he?" my double breathed into my very ear anxiously.

This anxiety was an answer, a sufficient answer, to the question I had put to him. An answer containing all the difficulty of that situation. I closed the porthole quietly, to make sure. A louder word might have been overheard.

"Who's that?" he whispered then.

"My second mate. But I don't know much more of the fellow than you do."

And I told him a little about myself. I had been appointed to take charge while I least expected anything of the sort, not quite a fortnight ago. I didn't know either the ship or the people. Hadn't had the time in port to look about me or size anybody up. And as to the crew all they knew was that I was appointed to take the ship 5 home. For the rest I was almost as much of a stranger on board as himself, I said. And at the moment I felt it most acutely. I felt that it would take very little to make me a sort of suspect person in the eyes of the ship's company.

He had turned about meantime and we, the two strangers in 10 the ship, faced each other in identical attitudes.

"Your ladder," he murmured after a silence. "Fancy finding a ladder hanging over at night in a ship anchored out here! I felt just then a very unpleasant faintness. After the life I've been leading for nine weeks, anybody would have got out of condition. I wasn't 15 capable of swimming round as far as your rudder-chains. And lo and behold there was a ladder to get hold of. After I gripped it I said to myself: What's the good? When I saw a man's head looking over I thought I would swim away presently and leave him shouting – in whatever language it was. I didn't mind being looked at. I – I 20 liked it. And then you speaking to me so quietly – as if you had expected me – made me hold on a little longer. It had been a confounded lonely time – I don't mean while swimming. I was glad to talk a little to somebody that didn't belong to the *Sephora*. As to asking for the captain that was a mere impulse. It could have 25 been no use with all the ship knowing about me and the other people pretty certain to be round here in the morning. I don't know – I wanted to be seen, to talk with somebody, before I went on. I don't know what I would have said – 'Fine night isn't it?' or something of the sort." 30

"Do you think they will be round here presently?" I asked, with some incredulity.

"Quite likely," he said faintly.

He looked extremely haggard all of a sudden. His head rolled on his shoulders. 35

"H'm. We shall see then. Meantime get into that bed," I whispered. "Want help – there."

It was a rather high bedplace with a set of drawers underneath. This amazing swimmer really needed the lift I gave him by seizing his leg. He tumbled in, rolled over on his back and flung one arm across his eyes. And then with his face nearly hidden he must have looked exactly as I used to look in that bed. I gazed upon my other self for a while before drawing carefully across the two green serge curtains which ran on a brass rod. I thought for a moment of pinning them together for greater safety, but I sat down on the couch and once there I felt unwilling to rise and hunt for a pin. I would do it in a moment. I was extremely tired in a peculiarly intimate way by the strain of stealthiness, by the effort of whispering and the general secrecy of this excitement. It was three o'clock by now and I had been on my feet since nine; but I was not sleepy; I could not have gone to sleep. I sat there, fagged out, looking at the curtains, trying to clear my mind of the confused sensation of being in two places at once and greatly bothered by an exasperating knocking in my head. It was a relief to discover suddenly that it was not in my head at all but on the outside of the door. Before I could collect myself the words "Come in" were out of my mouth and the steward entered with a tray bringing in my morning coffee. I had slept after all, and I was so frightened that I shouted "This way! I am here steward" as though he had been miles away. He put down the tray on the table next the couch and only then said very quietly: "I can see you are here sir." I felt him give me a keen look but I dared not meet his eyes just then. He must have wondered why I had drawn the curtains of my bed before going to sleep on the couch. He went out hooking the door open as usual.

I heard the crew washing decks above me. I knew I would have been told at once if there had been any wind. Calm, I thought, and I was doubly vexed. Indeed I felt dual more than ever. The steward reappeared suddenly in the doorway. I jumped out from the couch so quickly that he gave a start.

"What do you want here?"

"Close your port sir. They are washing decks."

"It is closed," I said reddening.

"Very well sir." But he did not move from the doorway and returned my stare in an extraordinary, equivocal manner for a time. Then his eyes wavered, all his expression changed and in a voice unusually gentle, almost coaxingly:

"May I come in to take the empty cup away sir."

"Of course." I turned my back on him while he popped in and out. Then I unhooked and closed the door and even pushed the bolt. This sort of thing could not go on very long. The cabin was as hot as an oven too. I took a peep at my double and discovered that he had not moved, his arm was still over his eyes; but his chest 5 heaved, his hair was wet, his chin glistened with perspiration. I reached over him and opened the port. "I must show myself on deck," I reflected.

Of course theoretically I could do what I liked with no one to say me nay within the whole circle of the horizon; but to lock my 10 cabin door and take the key away I did not dare. Directly I put my head out of the companion I saw the group of my two officers, the second mate barefooted, the chief mate in long india-rubber boots, near the break of the poop, and the steward half way down the poop ladder talking to them eagerly. He happened to catch 15 sight of me and dived, the second ran down on the main deck shouting some order or other and the chief mate came to meet me, touching his cap.

There was a sort of curiosity in his eye that I did not like. I don't know whether the steward had told them that I was "queer" only 20 or downright drunk, but I know the man meant to have a good look at me. I watched him coming with a smile which as he got into point-blank range took effect and froze his very whiskers. I did not give him time to open his lips.

"Square the yards by lifts and braces before the hands go to 25 breakfast."

It was the first particular order I had given on board that ship; and I stayed on deck to see it executed too. I had felt the need of asserting myself without loss of time. That sneering young cub got taken down a peg or two on that occasion and I also seized the 30 opportunity of having a good look at the face of every foremast man as they filed past me to go to the after braces. At breakfast time, eating nothing myself, I presided with such frigid dignity that the two mates were only too glad to escape from the cabin as soon as decency permitted; and all the time the dual working 35 of my mind distracted me almost to the point of insanity. I was constantly watching myself, my secret self, as dependent on my action as my open personality, sleeping in that bed, behind that door which faced me as I sat at the head of the table. It was very much like being mad, only it was worse because one was aware of it.

I had to shake him for a solid minute, but when, at last, he opened his eyes it was in the full possession of his senses, with an inquiring look. "All's well so far," I whispered. "Now you must vanish into the bathroom." He did so as noiseless as a ghost and I then rang for the steward and facing him boldly directed him to do my stateroom while I was having my bath – and be quick about it. As my tone admitted of no excuses he said "yes sir" and ran off to fetch his dust pan and brushes. I took a bath and did most of my dressing, splashing and whistling softly for the steward's edification, while the secret sharer of my life stood drawn up bolt upright in that little space, his face looking very sunken in daylight, his eyelids lowered under the stern, dark line of his eyebrows drawn together by a slight frown.

When I left him there to go back to my room the steward was finishing dusting. I sent for the mate and engaged him in some insignificant conversation. It was, as it were, trifling with the ter- rific character of his whiskers; but my object was to give him an opportunity for a good look at my cabin. And then I could at last shut with a clear conscience the door of my stateroom and get my double back into the recessed part. There was nothing else for it. He had to sit still on a small folding stool half smothered by the heavy coats hanging there. We listened to the steward going into the bathroom out of the saloon, filling the water-bottles there, scrubbing the bath, setting things to rights, whisk, bang, clatter . . . out again into the saloon . . . turn the key . . . click. Such was my scheme for keeping my second self invisible. Nothing better could be contrived under the circumstances. And then we sat; I at my writing desk ready to appear busy with some papers, he behind me out of sight of the door. It would not have been prudent to talk in day time; and I could not have stood the excitement of that queer sense of whispering to myself. Now and then glancing over my shoulder I saw him far back there sitting rigidly on the low stool, his bare feet close together, his arms folded, his head hanging on his breast – and perfectly still. Anybody would have taken him for me.

I was fascinated by it myself. Every moment I had to glance over my shoulder. I was looking at him when a voice outside the door said:

"Beg pardon sir!"

"Well!"

I kept my eyes on him, and so when the voice outside the door announced "There's a ship's boat coming our way sir" I saw him give a start – the first movement he had made for hours. But he did not raise his bowed head.

"All right. Get the ladder over."

I hesitated. Should I whisper something to him. But what? His immobility seemed to have been never disturbed. What could I tell him he did not know already? . . . Finally I went on deck.

The skipper of the *Sephora* had a thin red whisker all round his face and the sort of complexion that goes with hair of that colour; also the particular, rather smeary shade of blue in the eyes. He was not exactly a showy figure; his shoulders were high, his stature but middling – one leg slightly more bandy than the other. He shook hands looking vaguely around. A spiritless tenacity was his main characteristic I judged. I behaved with a politeness which seemed to disconcert him. Perhaps he was shy. He mumbled to one as if he were ashamed of what he was saying; gave his name (it was something like Archbold – but at this distance of years I hardly am sure), his ship's name – and a few other particulars of that sort in the manner of an unpenitent criminal making a reluctant and doleful confession. He had had terrible weather on the passage out – terrible – terrible. Wife aboard too.

By this time we were seated in the cabin and the steward brought in a tray with a bottle and glasses. Thanks! No. Never took liquor. Would have some water though. He drank two tumblerfuls. Terribly thirsty work. Ever since daylight had been exploring the islands round his ship.

"What was that for – fun?" I asked with an appearance of polite interest.

"No!" He sighed. "Painful duty."

As he persisted in his mumbling and I wanted my double to hear every word, I hit upon the notion of informing him that I regretted to say I was hard of hearing.

"Such a young man too!" He nodded keeping his smeary, blue, unintelligent eyes fastened upon me. "What was the cause of it – some disease?" he inquired without the least sympathy and as if he thought that if so I'd got no more than I deserved.

"Yes. Disease," I admitted in a cheerful tone which seemed to shock him. But my point was gained because he had to raise his voice to give me his tale. It is not worth while to record that version. It was just over two months since all this had happened and he had thought so much about it that he seemed completely muddled as to its bearings but still immensely impressed.

"What would you think of such a thing happening on board your own ship? I've had the *Sephora* for these fifteen years. I am a well known shipmaster."

He was, obviously, densely distressed – and perhaps I should have sympathised with him if I had been able to detach my mental vision from the unsuspected sharer of my cabin as though he were my second self. There he was on the other side of the bulkhead, four or five feet from us, no more, as we sat in the saloon. I looked politely at Captain Archbold (if that was his name) but it was the other I saw, in a grey sleeping suit seated on a low stool, his bare feet close together, his arms folded, and every word said between us falling into the ears of his dark head bowed on his chest.

"I have been at sea now, man and boy, for seven and thirty years and I've never heard of such a thing happening in any English ship. And that it should be my ship. Wife on board too."

I was hardly listening to him.

"Don't you think," I said, "that the heavy sea you have told me came aboard just then, might have killed the man. I have seen the sheer weight of a sea kill a man very neatly by simply breaking his neck."

"Good God!" he uttered impressively, fixing his smeary blue eyes on me. "The sea! No man killed by the sea ever looked like that."

He seemed positively scandalized at my suggestion. And as I gazed at him certainly not prepared for anything original on his part, he advanced his head close to mine and thrust his tongue out at me so suddenly that I couldn't help starting back.

After scoring over my calmness in this graphic way he nodded wisely. If I had seen the sight, he assured me, I would never forget it as long as I lived. The weather was too bad to give the corpse a proper sea burial. So next day at dawn they took it up on the poop, covering its face with a bit of bunting; he read a short prayer and then, just as it was in its oilskins and long boots, they launched it

amongst these mountainous seas that seemed ready every moment
to swallow up the ship herself and the terrified lives on board of
her.

"That reefed foresail saved you," I threw in.

"Under God – it did," he exclaimed fervently. "It's a special   5
mercy I firmly believe that it stood some of these hurricane
squalls."

"It was the setting of it . . ." I began.

"God's own hand in it," he interrupted me. "Nothing less could
have done it. I don't mind telling you that I hardly dared give the   10
order. It seemed impossible that we could touch anything without
losing it and then our last hope would have been gone."

The terror of that gale was on him yet. I let him go on for a bit,
then said casually – as if returning to a minor subject:

"You were very anxious to give up your mate to the shore people,   15
I believe?"

He was. To the law. His obscure tenacity on that point had in
it something incomprehensible and a little awful; something as
it were mystical quite apart from his anxiety that he should not
be suspected of countenancing any doings of that sort. Seven and   20
thirty virtuous years at sea of which over twenty of immaculate
command, and the last fifteen in the *Sephora*, seemed to have laid
him under some pitiless obligation.

"And you know," he went groping shamefacedly amongst his
feelings, "I did not engage that young fellow. His people had some   25
interest with my owners. I was in a way forced to take him on. He
looked very smart, very gentlemanly and all that. But do you know –
I never liked him somehow. I am a plain man. You see, he wasn't
exactly the sort of man for the chief mate of a ship like the *Sephora*."

I had become so connected in thoughts and impressions with   30
the secret sharer of my cabin that I felt as if I personally were being
given to understand that I too was not the sort of man that would
have done for the chief mate of a ship like the *Sephora*. I had no
doubt of it in my mind.

"Not at all the style of man you understand," he insisted super-   35
fluously looking hard at me.

I smiled urbanely. He seemed at a loss for a while.

"I suppose I must report a suicide."

"Beg pardon?"

"Sui-cide! That's what I'll have to write to my owners directly I get in."

"Unless you manage to recover him before tomorrow," I assented dispassionately. . . . "I mean alive."

5 He mumbled something which I really did not catch and I turned my ear to him in a puzzled manner. He fairly bawled:

"The land – I say the main land is at least seven miles off my anchorage."

"About that."

10 My lack of excitement, of curiosity, of surprise, of any sort of pronounced interest began to arouse his distrust. But except for the felicitous pretence of deafness I had not tried to pretend anything. I had felt simply incapable of playing the part of ignorance properly and therefore was afraid to try. It is also certain that he had
15 brought some ready-made suspicions with him, and that he viewed my politeness as a strange and unnatural phenomenon. And yet how else could I have received him? Not heartily! That was impossible for psychological reasons, which I need not state here. My only object was to keep off his inquiries. Surlily? Yes, but surliness
20 might have provoked a point-blank question. From its novelty to him and from its nature, a punctilious courtesy was the manner best calculated to restrain the man. But there was the danger of his breaking through my defence bluntly. I could not, I think, have met him by a direct lie also for psychological (not moral) reasons.
25 If he had only known how afraid I was of his putting my feeling of identity with the other to the test! But strangely enough (I thought of it only afterwards) I believe that he was not a little disconcerted by the reverse side of that weird situation, by something in me that reminded him of the man he was seeking – suggested a mysterious
30 similitude to the young fellow he had distrusted and disliked from the first.

However that might have been, the silence was not very prolonged. He took another oblique step:

"I reckon I had no more than a two mile pull to your ship. Not
35 a bit more."

"And quite enough too in this awful heat," I said.

Another pause full of mistrust followed. Necessity they say is mother of invention but fear too is not barren of ingenious suggestions. And I was afraid he would ask me point blank for news
40 of my other self.

"Nice little saloon isn't it," I remarked as if noticing for the first time the way his eyes roamed from one closed door to the other. "And very well fitted out too. Here for instance," I continued reaching over the back of my seat negligently and flinging the door open, "is my bathroom."

He made an eager movement but hardly gave it a glance. I got up, shut the door of the bathroom and invited him to have a look round as if I were very proud of my accommodation. He had to rise and be shown round but he went through the business without any raptures whatever.

"And now we'll have a look at my stateroom," I declared in a voice as loud as I dared to make it, crossing the cabin to the starboard side with purposely heavy steps.

He followed me in and gazed around. My intelligent double had vanished. I played my part:

"Very convenient – isn't it?"

"Very nice. Very comf . . . ." He didn't finish and went out brusquely as if to escape from some unrighteous wiles of mine. But it was not to be. I had been too frightened not to feel vengeful; I felt I had him on the run and I meant to keep him on the run. My polite insistence must have had something menacing in it, because he gave in suddenly. And I did not let him off a single item; mates' rooms, pantry, storerooms, the very sail-locker which was also under the poop – he had to look into them all. When at last I showed him out directly on the quarter deck he drew a long, spiritless sigh, and mumbled dismally that he must really be going back to his ship now. I desired my mate who had joined us to see to the captain's boat.

The man of whiskers gave a blast on the whistle which he used to wear hanging round his neck and yelled: "*Sephora*'s away!" My double down there in my cabin must have heard and certainly could not feel more relieved than I. Four fellows came running out from somewhere forward and went over the side, while my own men appearing on deck too lined the rail. I escorted my visitor to the gangway ceremoniously and nearly overdid it. He was a tenacious beast. On the very ladder he lingered and in that unique guiltily conscientious manner of sticking to the point:

"I say . . . you . . . you don't think that . . ."

I covered his voice loudly:

"Certainly not. . . . I am delighted. Goodbye."

I had an idea of what he meant to say and just saved myself by the privilege of defective hearing. He was too shaken generally to insist but my mate, close witness of that parting, looked mystified
5 and his face took on a thoughtful cast. As I did not want to appear as if I wished to avoid all communication with my officers, he had the opportunity to address me:

"Seems a very nice man. His boat's crew told our chaps a very extraordinary story if what I am told by the steward is true. I sup-
10 pose you had it from the captain, sir."

"Yes. I had a story from the captain."

"A very horrible affair – isn't it sir?"

"It is."

"Beats all these tales we hear about murders in Yankee ships."

15 "I don't think it beats them. I don't think it resembles them in the least."

"Bless my soul – you don't say so. But of course I've no acquaintance whatever with American ships, not I, so I couldn't go against your knowledge. It's horrible enough for me . . . . But the queerest
20 part is that those fellows seemed to have some idea the man was hidden aboard here. They had really. Did you ever hear of such a thing?"

"Preposterous – isn't it."

We were walking to and fro athwart the quarter deck. Not one
25 of the crew forward could be seen (the day was Sunday), and the mate pursued:

"There was some little dispute about it. Our chaps took offence. 'As if we would harbour a thing like that,' they said. 'Wouldn't you like to look for him in our coal hole.' Quite a tiff. But they made
30 it up in the end. I suppose he did drown himself. Don't you sir?"

"I don't suppose anything."

"You have no doubt in the matter sir."

"None whatever."

I left him suddenly. I felt I was producing a bad impression,
35 but with my double down there it was most trying to be on deck. And it was almost as trying to be below. Altogether a nerve-trying situation. But on the whole I felt less torn in two when I was with him. There was no one in the whole ship whom I dared to take into my confidence. Since the hands had got to know his story

it would have been impossible to pass him off for any one else, and an accidental discovery was to be dreaded now more than ever. . . .

The steward being engaged in laying the table for the dinner, we could talk only with our eyes when I first went down. Later in the afternoon we had a cautious try at whispering. The Sunday quietness of the ship was against us; the stillness of air and water around her was against us; the elements, the men were against us – everything was against us in our secret partnership. Time itself – for this could not go on for ever. The very trust in Providence was, I supposed, denied to his guilt. Shall I confess that this thought cast me down very much? And as to the chapter of accidents which counts for so much in the book of success I could only hope that it was closed. For what favourable accident could be expected?

"Did you hear everything," were my first words as soon as we took up our position side by side leaning over my bedplace.

He had. And the proof of it was his earnest whisper: "The man told you he hardly dared to give the order."

I understood the reference to be to that saving foresail: "Yes. He was afraid of its being lost in the setting."

"I assure you he never gave the order. He may think he did, but he never gave it. He stood there with me on the break of the poop, after the main topsail blew away, and whimpered about our last hope – positively whimpered about it and nothing else – and the night coming on. To hear your skipper go on like that in such weather was enough to drive any fellow out of his mind. It worked me up into a sort of desperation. I just took it into my own hands and went away from him – boiling, and . . . . But what's the use telling you? You know! Do you think that if I had not been pretty fierce with them I should have got the men to do anything? Not it. The boss'en perhaps? Perhaps! It wasn't a heavy sea – it was a sea gone mad. I suppose the end of the world will be something like that; and a man may have the heart to see it coming and be done with it – but to have to face it day after day . . . . I don't blame anybody. I was precious little better than the rest. Only I was an officer of that old coal-waggon anyhow . . ."

"I quite understand," I conveyed that sincere assurance into his ear. He was out of breath with whispering: I could hear him pant slightly. It was all very simple. The same strung-up force which had given some twenty four men, a chance at least for their lives had, in a sort of recoil, crushed out an unworthy mutinous existence.

But I had no leisure to weigh the merits of the matter – footsteps in the saloon, a heavy knock: "There's enough wind to get underway with sir" – here was the call of a new claim upon my thoughts and even upon my feelings.

"Turn the hands up," I cried through the door. "I'll be on deck directly."

I was going out to make the acquaintance of my ship. Before I left the cabin our eyes met – the eyes of the only two strangers on board. I pointed to the recessed part where the little campstool awaited him and laid my finger on my lips. He made a gesture – somewhat vague – a little mysterious, accompanied by a faint smile as if of regret.

This is not the place to enlarge upon the sensations of a man who feels for the first time a ship move under his feet to his own independent word. In my case they were not unalloyed. I was not wholly alone with my command; for there was that stranger in my cabin. Or rather I was not completely and wholly with her. Part of me was absent. That mental feeling of being in two places at once affected me physically as if the mood of secrecy had penetrated my very soul. Before an hour had elapsed since the ship had begun to move, having occasion to ask the mate (he stood by my side) to take a compass bearing of the Pagoda, I caught myself reaching up to his ear in whispers. I say I caught myself, but enough had escaped to startle the man. I can't describe it otherwise than by saying that he shied. A grave, preoccupied manner as though he were in possession of some perplexing intelligence did not leave him henceforth. A little later I moved away from the rail to look at the compass with such a stealthy gait that the helmsman noticed it – and I could not help noticing the roundness of his eyes. These are trifling instances though it's to no commander's advantage to be suspected of ludicrous eccentricities. But I was also more seriously affected. There are to a seaman certain words, gestures that should in given conditions come as naturally, as instinctively as the winking of a menaced eye. A certain order should spring on to his lips without thinking, a certain sign should get itself made, so to speak, without reflection. But all unconscious alertness had abandoned me. I had to make an effort of will to recall myself back (from that cabin) to the conditions of the moment. I felt that I was appearing an irresolute commander to those people who were watching me more or less critically.

And besides, there were the scares. On the second day out, for instance, coming off the deck in the afternoon (I had straw slippers on my bare feet) I stopped at the open pantry door and spoke to the steward. He was doing something there with his back to me. At the sound of my voice he nearly jumped out of his skin as the saying is and incidentally broke a cup.

"What on earth's the matter with you?" I asked astonished.

He was extremely confused. "Beg your pardon sir. I made sure you were in your cabin."

"You see I wasn't."

"No sir. I could have sworn I had heard you moving in there not a moment ago. It's most extraordinary. . . . Very sorry sir."

I passed on with an inward shudder. I was so identified with my secret double that I did not even mention the fact in those scanty, fearful whispers we exchanged. I supposed he had made some slight noise of some kind or other. It would have been miraculous if he hadn't at one time or another. And yet haggard as he appeared he looked always perfectly self controlled, more than calm – almost invulnerable.

On my suggestion he remained almost entirely in the bathroom, which upon the whole was the safest place. There could be really no shadow of an excuse for anyone ever wanting to go in there once the steward had done with it. It was a very tiny place. Sometimes he reclined on the floor, his legs bent, his head sustained on one elbow. At others I would find him on the campstool sitting in his grey sleeping suit and with his cropped dark head like a patient, unmoved convict. At night I would smuggle him into my bedplace and we would whisper together, with the regular footfalls of the officer of the watch passing and repassing over our heads. It was an infinitely miserable time. It was lucky that some tins of fine preserves were stowed in a locker in my stateroom; hard bread I could always get hold of; and so he lived on stewed chicken, pâté de foie-gras, asparagus, cooked oysters, sardines – on all sorts of abominable sham-delicacies out of tins. My early morning coffee he always drank; and it was all I dared do for him in that respect.

Every day there was the horrible manœuvring to go through so that my room and then the bathroom should be done in the usual way. I came to hate the sight of the steward, to abhor the voice of that harmless man. I felt that it was he who would bring on the disaster of discovery. It hung like a sword over our heads.

The fourth day out I think (we were then working down the east
5 side of the Gulf of Siam tack for tack in light winds and in perfectly smooth water) the fourth day I say of this miserable juggling with the unavoidable, as we sat at our evening meal, that man whose slightest movement I dreaded, after putting down the dishes, ran up on deck busily. This could not be dangerous. Presently he came
10 down again; and then it appeared that he had remembered a coat of mine which I had thrown over a rail to dry after having been wetted in a shower which had passed over the ship in the afternoon. Sitting stolidly at the head of the table I became terrified at the sight of the garment on his arm. Of course he made for my door.
15 There was no time to lose.

"Steward," I thundered. My nerves were so shaken that I could not govern my voice and conceal my agitation. This was the sort of thing that made my terrifically whiskered mate tap his forehead with his forefinger. I had detected him using that gesture while
20 talking on deck with a confidential air to the carpenter. It was too far to hear a word, but I had no doubt that this pantomime could only refer to the strange new captain.

"Yes sir." The pale-faced steward turned resignedly to me. It was this maddening course of being shouted at, checked with-
25 out rhyme or reason, arbitrarily chased out of my cabin, suddenly called into it, sent flying out of his pantry on incomprehensi- ble errands, that accounted for the growing wretchedness of his expression.

"Where are you going with that coat?"
30 "To your room sir."

"Is there another shower coming?"

"I'm sure I don't know sir. Shall I go up and see sir."

"No! never mind."

My object was attained as of course my other self in there could
35 hear everything that passed. During this interlude my two officers never raised their eyes off their respective plates; but the lip of that confounded cub, the second mate, quivered visibly.

I expected the steward to hook my coat on and come out at once. He was very slow about it; but I dominated my nervous-
40 ness sufficiently not to shout after him. Suddenly I became aware

(it could be heard plainly enough) that the fellow for some reason or other was opening the door of the bathroom. It was the end. The place was literally not big enough to swing a cat in. My voice died in my throat and I went stony all over. I expected to hear a yell of surprise and terror and made a movement but had 5
not the strength to get on my legs. Everything remained still. Had my second self taken the poor wretch by the throat. I don't know what I would have done next moment if I had not seen the steward come out of my room, close the door and then stand quietly by the sideboard. 10

"Saved," I thought. "But no! Lost. Gone. He was gone!"

I laid my knife and fork down and leaned back in my chair. My head swam. After awhile, when sufficiently recovered to speak in a steady voice, I instructed my mate to put the ship round at eight o'clock himself. 15

"I won't come on deck," I went on. "I think I'll turn in and unless the wind shifts I don't want to be disturbed before midnight. I feel a bit seedy."

"You did look middling bad a little while ago," the chief mate remarked without showing any great concern. 20

They both went out; and I stared at the steward clearing the table. There was nothing to be read on that wretched man's face. But why did he avoid my eyes? I asked myself. Then I thought I should like to hear the sound of his voice.

"Steward." 25

"Sir." Startled as usual.

"Where did you hang up that coat?"

"In the bathroom sir." The usual anxious tone. "It's not quite dry yet sir."

For some time longer I sat in the cuddy. Had my double vanished as he had come? But of his coming there was an explanation whereas his disappearance would be inexplicable. . . . I went slowly into my dark room, shut the door, lighted the lamp and for a time dared not turn round. When at last I did I saw him standing bolt upright in the narrow recessed part. It would not be true to say I 35
had a shock but an irresistible doubt of his bodily existence flitted through my mind: Can it be, I asked myself, that he is not visible to other eyes than mine? It was like being haunted. Motionless, with a grave face, he raised his hands slightly at me in a gesture which meant clearly "Heavens! What a narrow escape!" Narrow indeed. I 40

think I had come creeping quietly as near insanity as any man who has not actually gone over the border. That gesture restrained me, so to speak.

The mate with the terrific whiskers was now putting the ship on the other tack. In the moment of profound silence which follows upon the hands going to their stations I heard on the poop his raised voice "Hard a-lee" and the distant shout of the order repeated on the main deck. The sails, in that light breeze, made but a faint fluttering noise. It ceased. The ship was coming round slowly; I held my breath in the renewed stillness of expectation; one wouldn't have thought that there was a single living soul on her decks. A sudden brisk shout "Mainsail haul" broke the spell, and in the noisy cries and rush overhead of the men running away with the main brace we two down in my cabin came together in our usual position by the bedplace.

He did not wait for my question. "I heard him fumbling here and just managed to squat myself down in the bath," he whispered to me. "The fellow only opened the door and put his hand in to hang the coat up. All the same . . ."

"I never thought of that," I whispered back, even more appalled than before at the closeness of the shave, and marvelling at that something unyielding in his character which was carrying him through so finely. There was no agitation in his whisper. Whoever was being driven distracted it was not he. He was sane. And the proof of his sanity was continued when he took up the whispering again.

"It would never do for me to come to life again."

It was something that a ghost might have said. But what he was alluding to was his old captain's reluctant admission of the theory of suicide. It would obviously serve his turn – if I had understood at all the view which seemed to govern the unalterable purpose of his action.

"You must maroon me as soon as ever you can get amongst these islands off the Cambodie shore," he went on.

"Maroon you! We are not living in a boy's adventure tale," I protested. His scornful whispering took me up.

"We aren't indeed! There's nothing of a boy's tale in this. But there's nothing else for it. I want no more. You don't suppose I am afraid of what can be done to me? Prison or gallows or whatever

they may please. But you don't see me coming back to explain such
things to an old fellow in a wig and twelve respectable tradesmen.
Do you? What can they know whether I am guilty or not – or of
what I am guilty either. That's my affair. What does it say? 'Driven
off the face of the earth.' Very well. I am off the face of the earth 5
now. As I came at night so I shall go."

"Impossible!" I murmured. "You can't."

"Not. Not naked like a soul on the Day of Judgement. I shall
freeze on to this sleeping suit. The Last Day is not yet – and . . .
you have understood thoroughly. Didn't you?"   10

I felt suddenly ashamed of myself. I may say truly that I understood – and my hesitation in letting that man swim away from my
ship's side had been a mere sham sentiment, a sort of cowardice.

"It can't be done now till next night," I breathed out. "The ship
is on the offshore tack and the wind may fail us."   15

". . . As long as I know that you understand," he whispered. "But
of course you do. It's a great satisfaction to have got somebody to
understand. You seem to have been there on purpose." And in the
same whisper as if we two whenever we talked had to say things to
each other which were not fit for the world to hear he added: "It's 20
very wonderful."

We remained side by side talking on in our secret way – but
sometimes silent or just exchanging a whispered word or two at
long intervals. And as usual he stared through the port. A breath of
wind came now and again into our faces. The ship might have been 25
moored in dock so gently and on an even keel she slipped through
the water that did not murmur even at our passage, shadowy and
silent like a phantom sea.

At midnight I went on deck and to my mate's great surprise
put the ship round on the other tack. His terrible whiskers flitted 30
round me in silent criticism. I certainly should not have done it
if it had been only a question of getting out of that sleepy gulf as
quickly as possible. I believe he told the second mate who relieved
him that it was a great want of judgement. The other only yawned.
That intolerable cub shuffled about so sleepily and lolled against 35
the rails in such a slack, improper fashion that I came down on
him sharply.

"Aren't you properly awake yet?"

"Yes sir! I am awake."

"Well, then, be good enough to hold yourself as if you were. And keep a good lookout. If there's any current at all we'll be closing with some islands long before daylight."

The east side of the Gulf is fringed with islands, some solitary, others in groups. On the blue background of the high coast they seem to float on silvery patches of calm water, arid and grey, or dark green and rounded like clumps of evergreen bushes, with the larger ones a mile or two long showing the outlines of ridges, ribs of grey rock under the dank mantle of matted leafage. Unknown to trade, to travel, almost to geography, the manner of life they harbour is an unsolved secret. There must be villages – settlements of fishermen at least, on the largest of them and some communication with the world is probably kept up by native craft. But all that forenoon as we headed for them fanned along by the faintest of breezes, I saw no sign of man or canoe in the field of the telescope I kept on pointing at the scattered group.

At noon I gave no orders for a change of course and the mate's whiskers became much concerned and seemed to be offering themselves unduly to my notice. At last I said:

"I am going to stand right in. Quite in – as far as I can take her."

The stare of extreme surprise imparted an air of ferocity also to his eyes and he looked truly terrific for a moment.

"We're not doing well in the middle of the gulf," I continued casually. "I am going to look for the land breezes to-night."

"Bless my soul! Do you mean sir in the dark amongst the lot of all them islands and reefs and shoals?"

"Well – if there are any regular land breezes at all on this coast one must get close in-shore to find them – musn't one?"

"Bless my soul!" he exclaimed again under his breath. All that afternoon he wore a dreamy, contemplative appearance which in him was a mark of perplexity. After dinner I went into my stateroom as if I meant to take some rest. There we two bent our dark heads over a half unrolled chart lying on my bed.

"There," I said. "It's got to be Koh-ring. I've been looking at it ever since sunrise. It has got two hills and a low point. It must be inhabited. And on the coast opposite there is what looks like the mouth of a biggish river – with some town no doubt not far up. It's the best chance for you that I can see."

"Anything. Koh-ring let it be."

He looked thoughtfully at the chart as if surveying chances and distances from a lofty height – and following with his eyes his own figure wandering on the blank land of Cochin-china and then passing off that piece of paper clean out of sight into uncharted regions. And it was as if the ship had two captains to plan her 5 course for her. I had been so worried and restless running up and down that I had not had the patience to dress that day. I had remained in my sleeping suit with straw slippers and a soft floppy hat. The closeness of the heat in the Gulf had been most oppressive and the crew were used to see me wandering in that airy 10 attire.

"She will clear the south point as she heads now," I whispered into his ear. "Goodness only knows when, though – but certainly after dark. I'll edge her in to half a mile as far as I may be able to judge in the dark . . ." 15

"Be careful," he murmured warningly – and I realised suddenly that all my future, the only future for which I was fit, would perhaps go irretrievably to pieces in any mishap to my first command.

I could not stop a moment longer in the room. I motioned him to get out of sight and made my way on the poop. That unplayful 20 cub had the watch. I walked up and down for a while thinking things out, then beckoned him over.

"Send a couple of hands to open the two quarter-deck ports," I said mildly.

He actually had the impudence or else so forgot himself in his 25 wonder at such an incomprehensible order as to repeat:

"Open the quarter-deck ports! What for sir."

"The only reason you need concern yourself about is because I tell you to do so. Have them open wide and fastened properly."

He reddened and went off. But I believe he made some jeering 30 remark to the carpenter as to the sensible practice of ventilating a ship's quarter deck. I know he popped into the mate's cabin to impart the fact to him because the whiskers came on deck as it were by chance and stole glances at me from below – for signs of lunacy or drunkenness I suppose. 35

A little before supper feeling more restless than ever I rejoined for a moment my second self. And to find him sitting so quietly was surprising, like something against nature, inhuman.

I developed my plan in a hurried whisper.

"I shall stand in as close as I dare and then put her round. I shall presently find means to smuggle you out of here into the sail-locker which communicates with the lobby. But there is an opening, a sort of square for hauling the sails out, which gives straight on the
5 quarter deck and which is never closed in fine weather so as to give air to the sails. When the ship's way is deadened in stays and all the hands are aft at the main braces you shall have a clear road to slip out and over through the open quarter-deck port. I've had them both fastened up. Use a rope's end to lower yourself into the
10 water so as to avoid a splash – you know. It could be heard and cause some beastly complication."

He kept silent for a while, then whispered:

"I understand."

"I won't be there to see you go," I began with an effort. "The
15 rest . . . I only hope I have understood too."

"You have. From first to last" – and for the first time there seemed to be a faltering, something strained in his whisper. He caught hold of my arm but the ringing of the supper bell made me start. He didn't though; he only released his grip.

20 After supper I didn't come below again till well past eight o'clock. The faint steady breeze was loaded with dew; and the wet, darkened sails held all there was of propelling power in it. The night, clear and starry, sparkled darkly and the opaque, light-less patches shifting slowly amongst the low stars were the outlying
25 islets. On the port bow there was a big one more distant and shad-owily imposing by the great space of sky it eclipsed.

On opening the door I had a back-view of my very own self looking at a chart. He had come out of the recess and was standing near the table.

30 "Quite dark enough," I whispered.

He stepped back and leaned against my bed with a level, quiet glance. I sat on the couch. We had nothing to say to each other. Over our heads the officer of the watch moved here and there. Then I heard him move quickly. I knew what that meant. He was
35 making for the companion; and presently his voice was outside my door.

"We are drawing in pretty fast sir. Land looks rather close."

"Very well," I answered. "I am coming on deck directly."

I waited till he was gone out of the cuddy, then rose. My
40 double moved too; the time had come – to exchange our last

whispers – for neither of us was ever to hear each other's natural voice.

"Look here!" I opened a drawer and took out three sovereigns. "Take this anyhow. I've got six and I'd give you the lot only I must keep a little money to buy some fruit and vegetables for the crew from native boats as we go through Sunda Straits."

He shook his head.

"Take it," I urged him whispering desperately. "No one can tell what . . ."

He smiled and slapped meaningly the only pocket of the sleeping jacket. It was not safe certainly. But I produced a large, old silk handkerchief of mine and tying the three pieces of gold in a corner pressed it on him. He was touched I suppose because he took it at last and tied it quickly round his waist under the jacket, on his bare skin.

Our eyes met; several seconds elapsed before, our glances still mingled, I extended my hand and turned the lamp out. Then I passed through the cuddy leaving the door of my room wide open. "Steward."

He was still lingering in the pantry in the greatness of his zeal, giving a rub up to a plated cruet stand, the last thing before going to bed. Being careful not to wake up the mate whose room was opposite I spoke in an undertone.

He looked round anxiously. "Sir?"

"Can you get me a little hot water from the galley."

"I am afraid, sir, the galley fire's been out for some time now."

"Go and see."

He fled up the stairs.

"Now," I whispered loudly into the saloon – too loudly perhaps but I was afraid I couldn't make a sound. He was by my side in an instant – the double captain slipped past the stairs. A tiny dark passage . . . a sliding door. We were in the sail-locker scrambling on our knees over the sails. A sudden thought struck me. I saw myself wandering barefooted, bareheaded, the sun beating on my dark poll. I snatched off my floppy hat and tried hurriedly in the dark to ram it on my other self. He dodged and fended off silently. I wondered what he thought had come to me before he understood and suddenly desisted. Our hands met gropingly, lingered united in a steady, motionless clasp for a second . . . . No word was breathed by either of us when they separated.

I was standing quietly by the pantry door when the steward returned.

"Sorry sir. Kettle barely warm. Shall I light the spirit lamp?"

"Never mind."

5 I came out on deck slowly. It was now a matter of conscience to shave the land as close as possible – for now he must go overboard whenever the ship was put in stays. Must! There could be no going back for him. After a moment I walked over to leeward and my heart flew into my mouth at the nearness of the land on the bow.

10 Under any other circumstances I would not have held on a minute longer. The second mate had followed me down anxiously.

I looked on till I felt I could command my voice.

"She will weather," I said then in a quiet tone.

"Are you going to try that sir?" he stammered out incredulously.

15 I took no notice of him and raised my tone just enough to be heard by the helmsman.

"Keep her good full."

"Good full sir."

The wind fanned my cheek, the sails slept, the world was silent.

20 The strain of watching the dark loom of the land grow bigger and denser was too much. I had to shut my eyes. She must go closer. Must! The stillness was intolerable. Were we standing still?

When I opened my eyes the second view started my heart with a thump. The black southern hill of Koh-ring seemed to hang right

25 over the ship like a towering fragment of the everlasting night. On that enormous mass of blackness there was not a gleam to be seen, not a sound to be heard. It was gliding irresistibly towards us and yet seemed already within reach of the hand. I saw the vague figures of the watch grouped in the waist gazing in awed silence.

30 "Are you going on sir," inquired an unsteady voice at my elbow. I ignored it. I had to go on.

"Keep her full. Don't check her way. That won't do now," I said warningly.

"I can't see the sails very well," the helmsman answered me in

35 strange quavering tones.

Was she close enough? Already she was I won't say in the shadow of the land but in the very blackness of it, already swallowed up as it were, gone too close to be recalled, gone from me altogether.

"Give the mate a call," I said to the young man who stood at my

40 elbow as still as death. "And turn all hands up."

My tone had a borrowed loudness reverberated from the height of the land. Several voices cried out together: "We are all on deck sir."

Then stillness again with the great shadow gliding closer, towering higher without a light, without a sound. Such a hush had fallen on the ship that she might have been a bark of the dead floating in slowly under the very gate of Erebus.

"My God! Where are we!"

It was the mate moaning at my elbow. He was thunderstruck and as it were deprived of the moral support of his whiskers. He clapped his hands and absolutely cried out "Lost!"

"Be quiet," I said sternly.

He lowered his tone but I saw the shadowy gesture of his despair. "What are we doing here?"

"Looking for the land wind."

He made as if to tear his hair and addressed me recklessly:

"She will never get out. You have done it sir. I knew it'd end in something like this. She will never weather and you are too close now to stay. She'll drift ashore before she's round. Oh! my God!"

I caught his arm as he was raising it to batter his poor devoted head and shook it violently.

"She's ashore already," he wailed, trying to tear himself away.

"Is she? Keep good full there."

"Good full sir," cried the helmsman in a frightened, thin, child-like voice.

I hadn't let go the mate's arm and went on shaking it. "Ready about – do you hear. You go forward – shake – and stop there – shake – and hold your noise – shake – and see these head-sheets properly overhauled – shake – shake – shake."

And all the time I dared not look towards the land lest my heart should fail me. I released my grip at last and he ran forward as if fleeing for dear life.

I wondered what my double there in the sail-locker thought of this commotion. He was able to hear everything – and perhaps he was able to understand why, on my conscience, it had to be thus close – no less. My first order "Hard a-lee" re-echoed ominously under the towering shadow of Koh-ring as if I had shouted in a mountain gorge. And then I watched the land intently. In that smooth water and light wind it was impossible to feel the ship coming-to. No! I could not feel her. And my second self was making now ready to slip out and lower himself overboard. Perhaps he was gone already . . . ?

The great black mass brooding over our very mast-heads began to pivot away from the ship's side silently. And now I forgot the
5 secret stranger ready to depart and remembered only that I was a total stranger to the ship. I did not know her. Would she do it? How was she to be handled?

I swung the mainyard and waited helplessly. She was perhaps stopped, and her very fate hung in the balance with the black
10 mass of Koh-ring like the gate of the everlasting night towering over her taffrail. What would she do now? Had she way on her yet? I stepped to the side swiftly and on the shadowy water I could see nothing except a faint phosphorescent flash revealing a glassy smoothness of sleeping surface. It was impossible to tell – and I
15 had not learned yet the feel of my ship. Was she moving? What I needed was something easily seen, a piece of paper which I could throw overboard and watch. I had nothing on me. To run down for it I didn't dare. There was no time. All at once my strained, yearning stare distinguished a white object floating within a yard
20 of the ship's side. White on the black water. A phosphorescent flash passed under it. What was that thing? . . . I recognized my own floppy hat. It must have fallen off his head and he didn't bother. Now I had what I wanted – the saving mark for my eyes. But I hardly thought of my other self, now gone from the ship to
25 be hidden for ever from all friendly faces, to be a fugitive and a vagabond on the earth, with no brand of the curse on his sane forehead to stay the slaying hand – too proud to explain.

And I watched the hat – the expression of my sudden pity for his mere flesh. It had been meant to save his homeless head from the
30 dangers of the sun! And now – behold – it was saving the ship, by serving me for a mark to help out the ignorance of my strangeness. Ha! It was drifting forward warning me just in time that the ship had gathered sternway.

"Shift the helm," I said in a low voice to the seaman standing
35 still like a statue.

The man's eyes glistened wildly in the binnacle light as he jumped round to the other side and spun round the wheel.

I walked to the break of the poop. On the overshadowed deck all hands stood by the forebraces waiting for my order. The stars
40 ahead seemed to be gliding from right to left. And all was so still

in the world that I heard the quiet remark "She's round" passed
in a tone of intense relief between two seamen.

"Let go and haul."

The foreyards ran round with a great noise, amidst cheery cries.
And now the frightful whiskers made themselves heard giving var-   5
ious orders. Already the ship was drawing ahead. And I was alone
with her. Nothing, no one in the world should stand now between
us, throwing a shadow on the way of silent knowledge and mute
affection; the perfect communion of a seaman with his first command.   10

Walking to the taffrail I was in time to make out on the very edge
of a darkness thrown by a towering black mass like the very gateway
of Erebus, yes I was in time to catch an evanescent glimpse of my
white hat left behind to mark the spot where the secret sharer of
my cabin and of my thoughts as though he were my second self   15
had lowered himself into the water to take his punishment – a free
man, a proud swimmer striking out for a new destiny.

FREYA OF THE SEVEN ISLES
A STORY OF SHALLOW WATERS

FREYA OF THE SEVEN ISLES

I

ONE DAY – and that day was many years ago now – I received a long chatty letter from one of my old chums and fellow-wanderers in Eastern waters. He was still out there but settled down, and middle-aged, grown portly in figure and domestic in his habits; in short overtaken by that Fate common to all except to those who being specially beloved by the gods get knocked on the head early. The letter was of the reminiscent, "do you remember" kind – a wistful letter of backward glances. And amongst other things – "Surely you remember old Nelson," he wrote.

Remember old Nelson! Certainly. And, to begin with, his name was not Nelson. The Englishmen in the Archipelago called him Nelson because it was more convenient I suppose, and he never protested. It would have been mere pedantry. The true form of his name was Nielsen. He had come out East, long before the advent of telegraph cables, had served English firms, had married an English girl, had been one of us for years, trading and sailing in all directions through the Eastern Archipelago, across and around, transversely, diagonally, perpendicularly, in semicircles, and zig-zags and figures of eight. For years and years.

There was not a nook or cranny of these tropical waters that the enterprise of old Nelson (or Nielsen) had not penetrated in an eminently pacific way. His tracks if plotted out would have covered the map of the Archipelago like a cobweb – all of it, with the sole exception of the Philippines. He would never approach that part from a strange dread of Spaniards or, to be exact, of the Spanish authorities. What he imagined they could do to him it is impossible to say. Perhaps at some time in his life he had read some stories of the Inquisition.

But he was in general afraid of what he called "authorities"; not the English authorities which he trusted and respected, but the other two of that part of the world. He was not so horrified at

the Dutch as he was at the Spaniards but he was even more mistrustful of them. Very mistrustful indeed. The Dutch, in his view,
were capable of "playing any ugly trick on a man" who had the
misfortune to displease them. There were their laws and regula-
5   tions, but they had no notion of fair play in applying them. It was
really pitiable to see the anxious circumspection of his dealings
with some official or other and remember that this man had been
known to stroll up to a village of cannibals in New Guinea in a
quiet, fearless manner (and note that he was always fleshy all his
10 life and, if I may say so, an appetising morsel) on some matter of
barter that did not amount perhaps to fifty pounds in the end.

Remember old Nelson! Rather. Truly, none of us in my generation had known him in his active days. He was "retired" in our time.
He had bought or else leased part of a small island from the Sultan
15 of a little group called the Seven Isles, not far north from Banka.
It was I suppose a legitimate transaction, but I have no doubt that
had he been an Englishman the Dutch would have discovered a
reason to fire him out without ceremony. In this connection the
real form of his name stood him in good stead. In the character
20 of an unassuming Dane whose conduct was most correct, they let
him be. With all his money engaged in cultivation he was naturally
careful not to give even the shadow of offence, and it was mostly
for a prudential reason of that sort, that he did not look with a
favourable eye on Jasper Allen. But of that later. Yes! one remem-
25 bered well enough old Nelson's big hospitable bungalow erected
on a shelving point of land, his portly form, costumed generally
in a white shirt and trousers (he had a confirmed habit of taking
off his alpaca jacket on the slightest provocation), his round blue
eyes, his straggly, sandy-white moustache sticking out all ways like
30 the quills of the fretful porcupine, his propensity to sit down suddenly and fan himself with his hat. But there's no use concealing
the fact that what one remembered really was his daughter who at
that time came out to live with him – and be a sort of Lady of the
Isles.

35 Freya Nelson (or Nielsen) was the kind of girl one remembers.
The oval of her face was perfect; and within that fascinating frame
the most happy disposition of line and feature, with an admirable
complexion, gave an impression of health, strength and what I
might call unconscious self confidence – a most pleasant and, as
40 it were, whimsical determination. I will not compare her eyes to

violets because the real shade of their colour was peculiar, not so dark and more lustrous. They were of the wide open kind and looked at one frankly in every mood. I never did see the long dark eyelashes lowered – I dare say Jasper Allen did, being a privileged person – but I have no doubt that the expression must have been charming in a complex way. She could – Jasper told me once with a touchingly imbecile exultation – sit on her hair. I dare say, I dare say. It was not for me to behold these wonders; I was content to admire the neat and becoming way she used to do it up so as not to conceal the good shape of her head. And this wealth of hair was so glossy that when the screens of the west verandah were down making a pleasant twilight there, or in the shade of the grove of fruit trees near the house it seemed to give out a golden light of its own.

She dressed generally in a white frock with a skirt of walking length showing her neat, laced, brown boots. If there was any colour about her costume it was just a bit of blue perhaps. No exertion seemed to distress her. I have seen her land from the dinghy after a long pull in the sun (she rowed herself about a good deal) with no quickened breath and not a single hair out of its place. In the morning when she came out on the verandah for the first look westward, Sumatra way, over the sea, she seemed as fresh and sparkling as a dew drop. But a dew drop is evanescent and there was nothing evanescent about Freya. I remember her round, solid arms with the fine wrists and her broad, capable hands with tapered fingers.

I don't know whether she was actually born at sea; but I do know that up to twelve years of age she sailed about with her parents in various ships. After old Nelson lost his wife it became a matter of serious concern for him what to do with the girl. A kind lady in Singapore touched by his dumb grief and deplorable perplexity offered to take charge of his Freya. This arrangement lasted some six years during which old Nelson (or Nielsen) "retired" and established himself on his island; and then it was settled (the kind lady going away to Europe) that his daughter should join him.

As the first and most important preparation for that event the old fellow ordered from his Singapore agent a Steyn and Ebhart's "upright grand." I was then commanding a little steamer in the island trade and it fell to my lot to take it out to him – so I know something of Freya's "upright grand." We landed the enormous

packing case with difficulty on a flat piece of rock amongst some
bushes, nearly knocking the bottom out of one of my boats in
the course of that nautical operation. Then, all my crew assisting,
engineers and firemen included, by the exercise of much anx-
5   ious ingenuity and by means of rollers, levers, tackles and inclined
planes of soaped planks, toiling in the sun like ancient Egyptians
at the building of a Pyramid, we got it as far as the house and up
onto the edge of the west verandah – which was the actual drawing-
room of the bungalow. There, the case being ripped off cautiously,
10 the beautiful rosewood monster stood revealed at last. In reverent
excitement we coaxed it against the wall and drew the first free
breath of the day. It was certainly the heaviest movable object on
that islet since the creation of the world. The volume of sound it
gave out in that bungalow (which acted as a sounding board) was
15 really astonishing. It thundered sweetly right over the sea. Jasper
Allen told me that early of a morning on the deck of the *Bonito*
(his wonderfully fast and pretty brig) he could hear Freya playing
her scales quite distinctly. But the fellow always anchored foolishly
close to the point as I told him more than once. Of course these
20 seas are almost uniformly serene and the Seven Isles is a particularly calm and cloudless spot as a rule. But still, now and again, an
afternoon thunderstorm over Banka, or even one of these vicious
thick squalls, from the distant Sumatra coast, would make a sudden sally upon the group, enveloping it for a couple of hours in
25 whirlwinds and bluish-black murk of a particularly sinister aspect.
Then with the lowered rattan screens rattling desperately in the
wind and the bungalow shaking all over, Freya would sit down to
the piano and play fierce Wagner music in the flicker of blinding flashes with thunderbolts falling all round, enough to make
30 your hair stand on end; and Jasper would remain stock still on the
verandah, adoring the back-view of her supple, swaying figure, the
miraculous sheen of her fair head, the rapid hands on the keys,
the white nape of her neck – while the brig, down at the point
there, surged at her cables within a hundred yards of nasty, shiny,
35 black rock-heads. . . . Ugh!
     And this, if you please, for no reason but that, when he went on
board at night and laid his head on the pillow, he should feel that
he was as near as he could conveniently get to his Freya slumbering
in the bungalow. Did you ever! . . . And mind – this brig was the
40 home to be – their home – the floating paradise which he was

gradually fitting out like a yacht to sail his life blissfully away in, with Freya. Imbecile! But the fellow was always taking chances.

One day, I remember I watched with Freya on the verandah the brig approaching the point from the northward. I suppose Jasper made the girl out with his long glass. What does he do? Instead of standing on for another mile and a half along the shoals and then tacking for the anchorage in a proper and seamanlike manner, he spies a gap between two disgusting, old, jagged reefs, puts the helm down suddenly and shoots the brig through, with all her sails shaking and rattling, so that we could hear the racket on the verandah. I drew my breath through my teeth, I can tell you – and Freya swore. Yes! She clenched her capable fists and stamped with her pretty brown boot and said: "Damn!" Then looking at me with a little heightened colour – not much – she remarked: "I forgot you were there," and laughed. To be sure, to be sure. When Jasper was in sight she was not likely to remember that anybody else in the world was there. In my concern at this mad trick I couldn't help appealing to her sympathetic common sense.

"Isn't he a fool?" I said with feeling.

"Perfect idiot," she agreed warmly looking at me straight, with her wide open, earnest eyes and the dimple of a smile on her cheek.

"And that," I pointed out to her, "just to save twenty minutes or so in meeting you."

We heard the anchor go down and then she became very resolute and threatening.

"Wait a bit – I'll teach him."

She went into her own room and shut the door leaving me alone on the verandah with my instructions. Long before the brig's sails were furled Jasper came up three steps at a time, forgetting to say how d'ye do, and looking right and left eagerly.

"Where's Freya? Wasn't she here just now?"

When I explained to him that he was to be deprived of Miss Freya's presence for a whole hour "just to teach him," he said I had put her up to it, no doubt, and that he feared he would have yet to shoot me some day. She and I were getting too thick together. Then he flung himself into a chair and tried to talk to me about his trip. But the funny thing was that the fellow actually suffered! I could see it! His voice failed him and he sat there dumb, looking at the door with the face of a man in pain. Fact. . . . And the next,

still funnier, thing was that the girl calmly walked out of her room in less than ten minutes. And then I left. I mean to say that I went away to seek old Nelson (or Nielsen) on the back verandah, which was his own special nook in the distribution of that house, with the
5   kind purpose of engaging him in conversation lest he should start roaming about and intrude unwittingly where he was not wanted just then.

He knew that the brig had arrived though he did not know that Jasper was already with his daughter. I suppose he didn't think it
10 was possible in the time. A father naturally wouldn't. He suspected that Allen was sweet on his girl; the fowls of the air and the fishes of the sea, most of the traders in the Archipelago and all sorts and conditions of men in the town of Singapore were aware of it. But he was not capable of appreciating how far the girl was gone
15 on the fellow. He had an idea that Freya was too sensible to ever be gone on anybody – I mean to an unmanageable extent. No. It was not that which made him sit on the back verandah and worry himself in his unassuming manner during Jasper's visits. What he worried about were the Dutch "authorities." For it is a fact that
20 the Dutch looked askance at the doings of Jasper Allen owner and master of the brig *Bonito*. They considered him much too enterprising in his trading. I don't know that he ever did anything illegal; but it seems to me that his immense activity was repulsive to their stolid character and slow-going methods. Anyway in old
25 Nelson's opinion the captain of the *Bonito* was a smart sailor, and a nice young man but not a desirable acquaintance upon the whole. Somewhat compromising – you understand. On the other hand he did not like to tell Jasper in so many words to keep away. Poor old Nelson himself was a nice fellow. I believe he would have shrunk
30 from hurting the feelings even of a mop-headed cannibal – unless perhaps under very strong provocation. I mean the feelings – not the bodies. As against spears, knives, hatchets, clubs or arrows old Nelson had proved himself capable of taking his own part. In every other respect he had a timorous soul. So he sat on the back
35 verandah with a concerned expression and whenever the voices of his daughter and Jasper Allen reached him he would blow out his cheeks and let the air escape with a dismal sound like a much tried man.

Naturally I derided his fears which he, more or less, confided
40 to me. He had a certain regard for my judgement and a certain

respect, not for my moral qualities however, but for the good terms I was supposed to be on with the Dutch "authorities." I knew for a fact that his greatest bugbear the Governor of Banka (a charming, peppery, hearty, retired rear-admiral) had a distinct liking for him. This consoling assurance which I used always to put forward made old Nelson (or Nielsen) brighten up for a moment; but in the end he would shake his head doubtfully as much as to say that this was all very well but that there were depths in the Dutch official nature which no one but himself had ever fathomed. Perfectly ridiculous.

On this occasion I am speaking of, old Nelson was even fretty; for while I was trying to entertain him with a very funny and somewhat scandalous adventure which happened to a certain acquaintance of ours in Saïgon he exclaimed suddenly:

"What the devil he wants to turn up here for!"

Clearly he had not heard a word of the anecdote. And this annoyed me because the anecdote was really good. I stared at him.

"Come, come," I cried. "Don't you know what Jasper Allen is turning up here for."

This was the first open allusion I had ever made to the true state of affairs between Jasper and his daughter. He took it very calmly.

"Oh! Freya is a sensible girl," he murmured absently, his mind's eye obviously fixed on the authorities. No. Freya was no fool. He was not concerned about that. He didn't mind it in the least. The fellow was just company for her; he amused the girl; nothing more.

When the perspicacious old chap left off mumbling, all was still in the house. The other two were amusing themselves very quietly and no doubt very heartily. What more absorbing and less noisy amusement could they have found than to plan their future? Side by side on the verandah they must have been looking at the brig, the third party in that fascinating game. Without her there would have been no future. She was the fortune, and the home, and the great free world for them. Who was it who likened a ship to a prison? May I be ignominiously hanged at a yard-arm if that's true. The white sails of that craft were the white wings – pinions I believe would be the more poetical style – well, the white pinions of their soaring love. Soaring as regards Jasper. Freya, being a woman, kept a better hold of the mundane connections of this affair. But Jasper was elevated in the true sense of the word ever since that day when after they had been gazing at the brig in one of those decisive silences that alone establish a perfect communion between creatures gifted with speech he proposed that she should share the ownership of that treasure with him. Indeed he presented the brig to her altogether. But then his heart was in the brig since the day he bought her in Manilla from a certain middle-aged Peruvian in a sober suit of black broadcloth, enigmatic and sententious, who for all I know might have stolen her on the South American coast whence he said he had come over to the Philippines "for family reasons." This "for family reasons" was distinctly good. No true *caballero* would care to push on inquiries after such a statement.

Indeed, Jasper was quite the *caballero*. The brig herself was then all black and enigmatical – and very dirty; a tarnished gem of the sea – or rather a neglected work of art. For he must have been an artist, the obscure builder who had put her body together on lovely lines out of the hardest tropical timber fastened with the purest copper. Goodness only knows in what part of the world she was built. Jasper himself had not been able to ascertain much of her history from his sententious, saturnine Peruvian – if the fellow was a Peruvian and not the devil himself in disguise as Jasper jocularly pretended to believe. My opinion is that she was old enough to have been one of the last pirates, a slaver perhaps, or else an opium clipper of the early days, if not an opium smuggler. However that may be she was as sound as on the day she first took the water, sailed like a witch, steered like a little boat, and, like some fair women of adventurous life famous in history, seemed to have the secret of perpetual youth; so that there was nothing unnatural in Jasper Allen treating her like a lover. And that treatment restored the lustre of her beauty. He clothed her in many coats of the very best white paint so skillfully, carefully, artistically put on and kept clean by his badgered crew of picked Malays that no costly enamel such as jewellers use for their work could have looked better and felt smoother to the touch. A narrow gilt moulding defined her elegant sheer as she sat on the water, eclipsing easily the professional good looks of any pleasure-yacht that ever came to the East in those days. For myself I must say I prefer a moulding of deep crimson colour on a white hull. It gives a stronger relief besides being less expensive; and I told Jasper so. But no. Nothing less than the best gold leaf would do, because no decoration could be gorgeous enough for the future abode of his Freya.

His feelings for the brig and for the girl were as indissolubly united in his heart as you may fuse two precious metals together in one crucible. And the flame was pretty hot I can assure you. It induced in him a fierce inward restlessness both of activity and desire. Too fine in the face, with a lateral wave in his chestnut hair, spare, long-limbed, with an eager glint in his steely eyes and quick brusque movements he made me think sometimes of a flashing sword-blade perpetually leaping out of the scabbard. It was only when he was near the girl, when he had her there to look at, that this peculiarly tense attitude was replaced by a grave, devout watchfulness of her slightest movements and utterances. Her cool, resolute, capable, good-humoured self possession seemed to steady his heart. Was it the magic of her face, of her voice, of her glances which calmed him so? Yet these were the very things one must believe which had set his imagination ablaze – if love begins in imagination. But I am no man to discuss such mysteries; and it strikes me that we have neglected poor old Nelson inflating his cheeks in a state of worry on the back verandah.

I pointed out to him that after all Jasper was not a very frequent visitor. He and his brig worked hard all over the Archipelago. But all old Nelson said, and he said it uneasily, was:

"I hope Heemskirk won't turn up here while the brig's about."

Getting up a scare about Heemskirk now! Heemskirk! Really one hadn't the patience. . . .

II

FOR, PRAY, who was Heemskirk? You shall see at once how unreasonable was this dread of Heemskirk. . . . Certainly his nature was malevolent enough. That was obvious directly you heard him laugh. Nothing gives away more a man's secret disposition than the unguarded ring of his laugh. But, bless my soul, if we were to start at every evil guffaw like a hare at every sound we shouldn't be fit for anything but the solitude of a desert or the seclusion of a hermitage. And even there we should have to put up with the unavoidable company of the Devil.

However the Devil is a considerable personage, who had known better days and had moved high up in the hierarchy of Celestial Host; but in the hierarchy of mere earthly Dutchmen Heemskirk, whose early days could not have been very splendid, was merely a

naval officer forty years of age, of no particular connections or ability to boast of. He was commanding the *Neptun*, a little gunboat employed on dreary patrol duty up and down the Archipelago, to look after the traders. Not a very exalted position truly. I tell
5   you, just a common, middle-aged naval lieutenant of some twenty-five years' service and sure to be retired before long – that's all.

He never bothered his head very much as to what was going on in the Seven-Isles group, till he learned from some talk in Mintok
10 or Palembang, I suppose, that there was a pretty girl living there. Curiosity I presume caused him to go poking around that way, and then, after he had once seen Freya, he made a practice of calling at the group whenever he found himself within half a day's steaming from it.

15 I don't mean to say that Heemskirk was a typical Dutch naval officer. I have seen enough of them not to fall into that absurd mistake. He had a big, clean-shaven face: great flat, brown cheeks, with a thin hooked nose and a small, pursy mouth squeezed in between. There were a few silver threads in his black hair, and
20 his unpleasant eyes were nearly black too. He had a surly way of casting side-glances without moving his head, which was set low on a short, round neck. A thick, round trunk in a dark undress jacket with gold shoulder-straps was sustained by a straddly pair of thick, round legs, in white drill trousers. His round skull under a white
25 cap looked as if it were immensely thick too, but there were brains enough in it to discover and take advantage maliciously of poor old Nelson's nervousness before everything that was invested with the merest shred of authority.

Therefore Heemskirk would land on the point and perambu-
30 late silently every part of Nelson's plantation as if the whole place belonged to him, before he went to the house. On the verandah he would take the best chair, and would stay for tiffin or dinner, just simply stay on, without taking the trouble to invite himself by so much as a word.

35 He ought to have been kicked if only for his manner to Miss Freya. Had he been a naked savage armed with spears and poisoned arrows old Nelson (or Nielsen) would have gone for him with his bare fists. But these gold shoulder-straps – Dutch shoulder-straps at that – were enough to terrify the old fellow;

so he let the beggar treat him with heavy contempt, devour his daughter with his eyes and drink the best part of his little stock of wine.

I saw something of this and on one occasion I tried to pass a remark on the subject. It was pitiable to see the trouble in old Nelson's round eyes. At first he cried out that the lieutenant was a good friend of his; a very good fellow. I went on staring at him pretty hard so that at last he faltered and had to own that of course Heemskirk was not a very genial person outwardly, but all the same at bottom . . .

"I haven't yet met a genial Dutchman out here," I interrupted. "Geniality after all is not of much consequence, but don't you see . . ."

Nelson looked suddenly so frightened at what I was going to say that I hadn't the heart to go on. Of course I was going to tell him that the fellow was after his girl. That just describes it exactly. What Heemskirk might have expected or what he thought he could do I don't know. For all I can tell he might have imagined himself irresistible, or have taken Freya for what she was not, on account of her lively, assured, unconstrained manner. But there it is. He was after that girl. Nelson could see it well enough. Only he preferred to ignore it. He did not want to be told of it.

"All I want is to live in peace and quietness with the Dutch authorities," he mumbled shamefacedly.

He was incurable. I was sorry for him, and I really think Miss Freya was sorry for her father too. She restrained herself for his sake, and as everything she did, she did it simply, unaffectedly and even good humouredly. No small effort that, because in Heemskirk's attentions there was an insolent touch of scorn hard to put up with. Dutchmen of that sort are overbearing to their inferiors and that officer of the King looked upon old Nelson and Freya as quite beneath him in every way.

I can't say I felt sorry for Freya. She was not the sort of girl to take anything tragically. One could feel for her and sympathise with her difficulty but she seemed equal to any situation. It was rather admiration she extorted by her competent serenity. It was only when Jasper and Heemskirk were together at the bungalow, as it happened now and then, that she felt the strain, and even then it was not for everybody to see. My eyes alone could detect a faint shadow on the radiance of her personality. Once I could not help saying to her appreciatively:

"Upon my word you are wonderful."

She let it pass with a faint smile.

5   "The great thing is to prevent Jasper becoming unreasonable," she said; and I could see real concern lurking in the quiet depths of her frank eyes gazing straight at me. "You will help to keep him quiet – won't you."

"Of course we must keep him quiet," I declared, understanding
10   very well the nature of her anxiety. "He's such a lunatic too when he is roused."

"He is!" she assented in a soft tone; for it was our joke to speak of Jasper abusively. "But I have tamed him a bit. He's quite a good boy now."

15   "He would squash Heemskirk like a blackbeetle all the same," I remarked.

"Rather!" she murmured. "And that wouldn't do," she added quickly. "Imagine the state poor Papa would get into. Besides I mean to be mistress of the dear brig and sail about these seas, not
20   go off wandering ten thousand miles away from here."

"The sooner you are on board to look after the man and the brig, the better," I said seriously. "They need you to steady them both a bit. I don't think Jasper will ever get sobered down till he has carried you off from this island. You don't see him when he is
25   away from you as I do. He's in a state of perpetual elation which almost frightens me."

At this she smiled again and then looked serious. For it could not be unpleasant to her to be told of her power and she had some sense of her responsibility. She slipped away from me suddenly,
30   because Heemskirk, with old Nelson in attendance at his elbow, was coming up the steps of the verandah. Directly his head rose above the level of the floor his ill-natured black eyes shot glances here and there.

"Where's your girl Nielsen?" he asked in a tone as if every soul
35   in the world belonged to him. And then to me: "The goddess has flown – eh?"

Nelson's Cove (as we used to call it) was crowded with shipping that day. There was first my steamer, then the *Neptun*, gunboat, further out and the *Bonito*, brig, anchored as usual so close inshore that it looked as if with a little skill and judgement one could shy a hat from the verandah onto her scrupulously holystoned quarter deck. Her brasses flashed like gold, her white body-paint had a sheen like a satin robe. The rake of her varnished spars and the big yards squared to a hair gave her a sort of martial elegance. She was a beauty. No wonder that in the possession of a craft like that and the promise of a girl like Freya Jasper lived in a state of perpetual elation fit perhaps for the seventh heaven but not exactly safe in a world like ours.

I remarked politely to Heemskirk that with three guests in the house Miss Freya had no doubt domestic matters to attend to. I knew of course that she had gone to meet Jasper at a certain cleared spot on the banks of the only stream on Nelson's little island. The commander of the *Neptun* gave me a dubious black look and began to make himself at home, flinging his thick, cylindrical carcass into a rocking chair and unbuttoning his coat. Old Nelson sat down opposite him in a most unassuming manner, staring anxiously with his round eyes and fanning himself with his hat. I tried to make conversation to while the time away; not an easy task with a morose, enamoured Dutchman constantly looking from one door to another and answering one's advances either with a jeer or a grunt.

However the evening passed off all right. Luckily there is a degree of bliss too intense for elation. Jasper was quiet and concentrated silently in watching Freya. As we went on board our respective ships I offered to give his brig a tow out next morning. I did it on purpose to get him away at the earliest possible moment. So in the first cold light of the dawn we passed by the gunboat lying black and still without a sound in her at the mouth of the glassy cove. But with tropical swiftness the sun had climbed twice its diameter above the horizon before we had rounded the reef and got abreast of the point. On the biggest boulder there stood Freya, all in white and, in her helmet, like a feminine and martial statue, with a rosy face, as I could see very well with my glasses. She fluttered an expressive handkerchief and Jasper running up the main rigging of the white and warlike brig waved his hat in response. Shortly afterwards we parted, I to the northward and Jasper heading east with a light wind on the quarter, for Banjermassin and two other ports – I believe it was, that trip.

This peaceful occasion was the last on which I saw all these people assembled together; the charmingly fresh and resolute Freya,
the innocently round-eyed old Nelson, Jasper, keen, long-limbed,
lean-faced, admirably self-contained in his manner, because incon-
5   ceivably happy under the eyes of his Freya; all three tall, fair and
blue-eyed in varied shades, and amongst them the swarthy, arrogant, black-haired Dutchman, shorter nearly by a head, and so
much thicker than any of them that he seemed to be a creature
capable of inflating itself, a grotesque specimen of mankind from
10   some other planet.

The contrast struck me all at once as we all stood in the lighted
verandah after rising from the dinner table. I was fascinated by
it for the rest of the evening and I remember the impression of
something funny and ill-omened at the same time, in it, to this
15   day.

III

A FEW WEEKS later coming early one morning into Singapore
from a journey to the southward I saw the brig lying at anchor in
all her usual symmetry and splendour of aspect as though she had
20   been taken out of a glass case and put delicately into the water
that very moment.

She was well out in the roadstead but I steamed in and took
up my habitual berth close in front of the town. Before we had
finished breakfast a quartermaster came to tell me that Captain
25   Allen's boat was coming our way.

His smart gig dashed up alongside and in two bounds he was
up our accommodation ladder and shaking me by the hand with
his nervous grip, his eyes snapping inquisitively, for he supposed
I had called at the Seven-Isles group on my way. I reached into my
30   pocket for a nicely folded little note which he grabbed out of my
hand without ceremony and carried off on the bridge to read by
himself. After a decent interval I followed him up there and found
him pacing to and fro; for the nature of his emotions made him
restless even in his most thoughtful moments.

35   He shook his head at me triumphantly.

"Well my dear boy," he said, "I shall be counting the days now."

I understood what he meant. I knew that those young people had settled already on a runaway match without official

preliminaries. This was really a logical decision. Old Nelson (or Nielsen) would never have agreed to give up Freya peaceably to this compromising Jasper. Heavens! What would the Dutch "authorities" say to such a match! It sounds too ridiculous for words. But there's nothing in the world more selfishly hard than a timorous 5 man in a fright about his "little estate" as old Nelson used to call it in apologetic accents. A heart permeated by a particular sort of funk is proof against sense, feeling and ridicule. It's a flint.

Jasper would have made his request all the same and then taken his own way; but it was Freya who decided that nothing should 10 be said, on the ground that: "Papa would only worry himself to distraction." He was capable of making himself ill and then she wouldn't have the heart to leave him. Here you have the sanity of feminine outlook and the frankness of feminine reasoning. And for the rest Miss Freya could read "poor dear papa" in the way a 15 woman reads a man, like an open book. His daughter once gone, old Nelson would not worry himself. He would raise a great outcry and make no end of lamentable fuss – but that's not the same thing. The real agonies of indecision, the anguish of conflicting feelings would be spared to him. And as he was too unassuming to 20 rage he would after a period of lamentation devote himself to his "little estate" and to keeping on good terms with the authorities.

Time would do the rest. And Freya thought she could afford to wait, while ruling over her own home in the beautiful brig and over the man who loved her. This was the life for her who had 25 learned to walk on a ship's deck. She was a ship child, a sea-girl if ever there was one. And of course she loved Jasper and trusted him; but there was a shade of anxiety in her pride. It is very fine and romantic to possess for your very own a finely tempered and trusty sword-blade but whether it is the best weapon to counter 30 with the common cudgel-play of fate – that's another question.

She knew that she had the more substance of the two – you needn't try any cheap jokes; I am not talking of their weights. She was just a little anxious while he was away, and she had me who being a tried confidant took the liberty to whisper frequently 35 "the sooner the better." But there was a peculiar vein of obstinacy in Miss Freya and her reason for delay was characteristic. "Not before my twenty-first birthday; so that there shall be no mistake in people's minds as to me being old enough to know what I am doing."   40

Jasper's feelings were in such subjection that he never even remonstrated against the decree. She was just splendid, whatever she did or said, and there was an end of it for him. I believe that he was subtle enough to be even flattered at bottom – at times.

5 And then to console him he had the brig which seemed pervaded by the spirit of Freya, since whatever he did on board was always done under the supreme sanction of his love.

"Yes. I shall soon begin to count the days," he repeated. "Eleven months more. I'll have to crowd three trips into that."

10 "Mind you don't come to grief trying to do too much," I admonished him. But he dismissed my caution with a laugh and an elated gesture. Pooh! Nothing could happen to the brig, he cried, as if the flame of his heart could light up the dark nights of uncharted seas and the image of Freya serve for an unerring beacon amongst

15 hidden shoals; as if the winds had to wait on his future, the stars fight for it in their courses; as if the magic of his passion had the power to float a ship on a drop of dew or sail her through the eye of a needle – simply because it was her magnificent lot to be the servant of a love so full of grace as to make all the ways of the earth

20 safe, resplendent and easy.

"I suppose," I said after he had finished laughing at my innocent enough remark, "I suppose you will be off to-day."

That was what he meant to do. He had not gone at daylight only because he expected me to come in.

25 "And only fancy what has happened yesterday," he went on. "My mate left me suddenly. Had to. And as there's nobody to be found at a short notice I am going to take Schultz with me. The notorious Schultz! Why don't you jump out of your skin? I tell you I went and unearthed Schultz, late last evening after no end of trouble.

30 'I am your man Captain,' he says to me, in that wonderful voice of his, 'but I am sorry to confess I have practically no clothes to my back. I have had to sell all my wardrobe to get a little food from day to day.' What a voice that man has got! Talk about moving stones! But people seem to get used to it. I had never seen him before and

35 upon my word I felt suddenly tears rising to my eyes. Luckily it was dusk. He was sitting very quiet under a tree in a native compound, he was as thin as a lath, and when I peered down at him all he had on was an old cotton singlet and a pair of ragged pyjamas. I bought him six white suits and two pairs of canvas shoes. Can't

clear the ship without a mate. Must have somebody. I am going on
shore presently to sign him on and shall take him with me as I go
back on board to get under way. Now, I am a lunatic – am I not?
Mad of course. Come on! Lay it on thick. Let yourself go. I like to
see you get excited."   5

He so evidently expected me to scold that I took especial pleasure in exaggerating the calmness of my attitude.

"The worst that can be brought up against Schultz," I began
folding my arms and speaking dispassionately, "is an awkward habit
of stealing the stores of every ship he has ever been in. He will   10
do it. That's really all that's wrong. I don't credit absolutely that
story Captain Robinson tells of Schultz conspiring in Chantabun
with some ruffians in a Chinese junk to steal the anchor off the
starboard bow of the *Bohemian Girl*, schooner. Robinson's story
is too ingenious altogether. That other tale of the engineers of   15
the *Nan-shan* finding Schultz at midnight in the engine-room busy
hammering at the brass bearings to carry them off for sale on shore
seems to me more authentic. Apart from this little weakness let me
tell you that Schultz is a smarter sailor than many men who never
took a drop of drink in their lives, and perhaps no worse morally   20
than some men you and I know who have never stolen the value
of a penny. He may not be a desirable person to have on board
one's ship, but since you have no choice he may be made to do,
I believe. The important thing is to understand his psychology.
Don't give him any money till you have done with him. Not a cent   25
if he begs you ever so. For as sure as fate the moment you give him
any money he will begin to steal. Just remember that."

I enjoyed Jasper's incredulous surprise.

"The devil he will," he cried. "What on earth for. Aren't you
trying to pull my leg old boy."   30

"No. I am not. You must understand Schultz's psychology. He's
neither a loafer nor a cadger. He's not likely to wander about
looking for somebody to stand him drinks. But suppose he goes
on shore with five dollars or fifty for that matter in his pocket?
After the third or fourth glass he becomes fuddled and charitable.   35
He either drops his money all over the place or else distributes
the lot around; gives it to anyone who will take it. Then it occurs
to him that the night is young yet and that he may require a good
many more drinks for himself and his friends before morning. So

he starts off cheerfully for his ship. His legs never get affected, nor
his head either, in the usual way. He gets aboard and simply grabs
the first thing that seems to him suitable, the cabin lamp, a coil of
rope, a bag of biscuits, or a drum of oil and converts it into money
5   without thinking twice about it. This is the process and no other.
You've got only to look out that he doesn't get a start. That's all."

"Confound his psychology," muttered Jasper. "But a man with
a voice like his is fit to talk to the angels. Is he incurable do you
think?"

10   I said that I thought so. Nobody had prosecuted him yet but no
one would employ him any longer. His end would be, I feared, to
starve in some hole or other.

"Ah, well," reflected Jasper. "The *Bonito* isn't trading to any ports
of civilisation. That'll make it easier for him to keep straight."

15   That was true. The brig's business was on uncivilized coasts;
with obscure Rajahs dwelling in nearly unknown bays; with native
settlements up mysterious rivers opening their sombre forest-lined
estuaries amongst a welter of pale green reefs and dazzling sand-
banks, in lonely straits of calm blue water all aglitter with sunshine.

20   Alone, far from the beaten tracks, she glided all white round dark,
frowning headlands, stole out, silent like a ghost, from behind
points of land stretching out all black in the moonlight, or lay hove-
to, like a sleeping sea-bird, under the shadow of some nameless
mountain waiting for a signal. She would be glimpsed suddenly on

25   misty, squally days dashing disdainfully aside the short aggressive
waves of the Java Sea, or be seen far, far away, a tiny dazzling white
speck flying across the brooding purple masses of thunder-clouds
piled up on the horizon. Sometimes, on the rare mail-routes where
civilisation brushes against wild mystery, when the naïve passengers

30   crowding along the rail exclaimed pointing at her with interest:
"Oh! there's a yacht, look! Must be somebody's yacht," the Dutch
captain with a hostile glance would grunt contemptuously: "Yacht!
No. That's only English Jasper. A pedlar." . . .

"A good seaman you say," speculated Jasper, still in the matter

35   of the hopeless Schultz with the wonderfully touching voice.

"First rate. Ask any one. Quite worth having – only impossible,"
I declared.

"He shall have a chance to reform in the brig," said Jasper with a
laugh. "There will be no temptations either to drink or steal where

40   I am going to, this time."

I didn't press him for anything more definite on that point. In fact intimate as we were I had a pretty clear notion of the general run of his business.

But as we were going ashore in his gig he asked suddenly: "By the by! Do you know where Heemskirk is?"

I eyed him covertly and was reassured. He had asked this question not as lover but as a trader. I told him that I had heard in Palembang that the *Neptun* was on duty down about Flores and Sumbawa. Quite out of his way. He expressed his satisfaction.

"You know," he went on, "that fellow, when he gets on the Borneo coast, amuses himself by knocking down my beacons. I have had to put up a few to help me in and out of the rivers. Early this year a Celebes trader becalmed in a prau was watching him at it. He steamed the gunboat full tilt at two of them, one after another, smashing them to pieces, and then lowered a boat on purpose to pull out a third which I had a lot of trouble six months ago to stick up in the middle of a mudflat, for a tide mark. Did you ever hear of anything more provoking – eh?"

"I wouldn't quarrel with the beggar," I observed casually yet disliking that piece of news strongly. "It isn't worth while."

"I! quarrel!" cried Jasper. "I don't want to quarrel. I don't want to hurt a single hair of his ugly head. My dear fellow when I think of Freya's twenty-first birthday all the world's my friend, Heemskirk included. It's a nasty spiteful amusement all the same."

We parted rather hurriedly on the quay each of us having his own pressing business to attend to. I would have been very much cut up had I known that this hurried grasp of the hand with "So long old boy. Good luck to you" was the last of our partings.

On his return to the Straits I was away and he was gone again before I got back. He was trying to achieve three trips before Freya's twenty-first birthday. At Nelson's Cove I missed him again by only a couple of days. Freya and I talked of "that lunatic" and "perfect idiot" with great delight and infinite appreciation. She was very radiant, with a more pronounced gaiety, notwithstanding that she had just parted from Jasper. But this was to be their last separation.

"Do get aboard as soon as you can Miss Freya," I entreated.

She looked me straight in the face, her colour a little heightened and uttered with a sort of solemn ardour – if there was a little catch in her voice:

"The very next day."

Ah, yes! The very next after her twenty-first birthday. I was pleased at this hint of deep feeling. It was as if she had grown impatient at last of the self-imposed delay. I supposed that Jasper's
5 recent visit had told heavily.

"That's right," I said approvingly. "I shall be much easier in my mind when I know you have taken charge of that lunatic. Don't you lose a minute. He of course will be on time – unless heavens fall."

10 "Yes. Unless . . ." she repeated in a thoughtful whisper raising her eyes to the evening sky without a speck of cloud anywhere. Silent for a time we let our eyes wander over the waters below, looking mysteriously still in the twilight, as if trustfully composed for a long, long dream in the warm tropical night.
15 And the peace all round us seemed without limits and without end.

And then we began again to talk Jasper over in our usual strain. We agreed that he was too reckless in many ways. Luckily the brig was equal to the situation. Nothing apparently was too much for
20 her. A perfect darling of a ship said Miss Freya. She and her father had spent an afternoon on board. Jasper had given them some tea. Papa was grumpy. . . . I had a vision of old Nelson under the brig's snowy awnings nursing his unassuming vexation and fanning himself with his hat. A comedy father. . . . As a new instance of
25 Jasper's lunacy I was told that he was distressed at his inability to have solid silver handles fitted to all the cabin doors. "As if I would have let him," commented Miss Freya with amused indignation. Incidentally I learned also that Schultz, the nautical kleptomaniac with the pathetic voice, was still hanging on to his job, with Miss
30 Freya's approval. Jasper had confided to the lady of his heart his purpose of straightening out the fellow's psychology. Yes, indeed. All the world was his friend because it breathed the same air with Freya.

Somehow or other I brought Heemskirk's name into conver-
35 sation and to my great surprise startled Miss Freya. Her eyes expressed something like distress while she bit her lip as if to contain an explosion of laughter. Oh! Yes. Heemskirk was at the bungalow at the same time with Jasper, but he arrived the day after. He left the same day as the brig but a few hours later.

40 "What a nuisance he must have been to you two," I said feelingly.

Her eyes flashed at me with a sort of frightened merriment and suddenly she exploded into a clear burst of laughter. . . . Ha! Ha! . . . Ha!

I echoed it heartily but not with the same charming tone: "Ha! Ha! Ha! Isn't he grotesque! Ha! Ha! Ha! . . ." And the ludicrousness of old Nelson's inanely fierce round eyes in association with his conciliatory manner to the lieutenant, presenting itself to my mind, brought on another fit.

"He looks," I spluttered, "he looks – ha! ha! ha! amongst you three . . . like an unhappy blackbeetle. Ha! Ha! Ha!"

She gave out another ringing peal, ran off into her own room and slammed the door behind her leaving me profoundly astounded. I stopped laughing at once.

"What's the joke," asked old Nelson's voice half way down the steps.

He came up, sat down and blew out his cheeks looking inexpressibly fatuous. But I didn't want to laugh any more. And why on earth I asked myself have we been laughing in this uncontrollable fashion? I felt suddenly depressed. Oh yes. Freya had started it. The girl's overwrought, I thought. And really one couldn't wonder at it.

I had no answer to old Nelson's question but he was too aggrieved at Jasper's visit to think of anything else. He as good as asked me whether I wouldn't undertake to hint to Jasper that he was not wanted at the Seven-Isles group. I declared that it was not necessary. From certain circumstances which had come to my knowledge lately I had reason to think that he would not be much troubled by Jasper Allen in the future.

He emitted an earnest "Thank God!" which nearly set me laughing again; but he did not brighten up proportionately. It seems Heemskirk had taken special pains to make himself disagreeable. The lieutenant had frightened old Nelson very much by expressing a sinister wonder at the government permitting a white man to settle down in that part at all. "It is against our declared policy," he had remarked. He had also charged him with being in reality no better than an Englishman. He had even tried to pick a quarrel with him for not learning to speak Dutch.

"I told him I was too old to learn now," sighed out old Nelson (or Nielsen) dismally. "He said I ought to have learned Dutch long before. I had been making my living in Dutch dependencies. It was

disrespectful of me not to speak Dutch – he said. He was as savage
with me as if I had been a Chinaman."

It was plain he had been viciously badgered. He did not mention
how many bottles of his best claret he had offered up on the altar
5 of conciliation. It must have been a generous libation. But old
Nelson (or Nielsen) was really hospitable. He didn't mind that;
and I only regretted that this virtue should be lavished on the
lieutenant-commander of the *Neptun*. I longed to tell him that in
all probability he would be relieved from Heemskirk's visitations
10 also. I did not do so only from the fear (absurd I admit) of arousing
some sort of suspicion in his mind. As if with this guileless comedy
father such a thing were possible!

Strangely enough the last words on the subject of Heemskirk
were spoken by Freya – and in that very sense. The lieutenant was
15 turning up persistently in old Nelson's conversation at dinner. At
last I muttered a half-audible "Damn the lieutenant." I could see
that the girl was getting exasperated too.

"And he wasn't well at all – was he Freya?" old Nelson went on
moaning. "Perhaps it was that which made him so snappish, hey
20 Freya? He looked very bad when he left us so suddenly. His liver
must be in a bad state too."

"Oh he will end by getting over it – whatever it is," said Freya
impatiently. "And do leave off worrying about him, Papa. Very
likely you won't see much of him for a long time to come."

25 The look she gave me in exchange for my discreet smile had
no hidden mirth in it. Her eyes seemed hollowed, her face
gone wan in a couple of hours. We had been laughing too
much. Overwrought! Overwrought by the approach of the decisive
moment. After all, sincere, courageous and self-reliant as she was,
30 she must have felt both the passion and the compunction of her
resolve. The very strength of love which had carried her up to that
point must have put her under a great moral strain, in which there
might have been a little simple remorse too. For she was honest –
and there across the table sat poor old Nelson (or Nielsen) staring
35 at her round-eyed and so pathetically comic in his fierce aspect as
to touch the most lightsome heart.

He retired early to his room, to soothe himself for a night's rest
by perusing his account books. We two remained on the verandah
for another hour or so but we exchanged only languid phrases
40 on things without importance as though we had been emotionally

jaded by our long day's talk on the only momentous subject. And
yet there was something she might have told a friend. But she
didn't. We parted silently. She distrusted my masculine lack of
common sense perhaps. . . . O, Freya!

Going down the precipitous path to the landing stage I was 5
confronted in the shadows of boulders and bushes by a draped
feminine figure whose appearance startled me at first. It glided
into my way suddenly from behind a piece of rock. But in a moment
it occurred to me that it could be no one else but Freya's maid,
a half-caste Malacca Portuguese. One caught fleeting glimpses of 10
her olive face and dazzling white teeth about the house. I had
also observed her at times, from a distance, as she sat within call
under the shade of some fruit trees, brushing and plaiting her
long raven locks. It seemed to be the principal occupation of her
leisure hours. We had often exchanged nods and smiles – and a few 15
words too. She was a pretty creature. And once I had watched her
approvingly make funny and expressive grimaces behind Heemskirk's back.

I understood (from Jasper) that she was in the secret, like a
comedy camerista. She was to accompany Freya on her irregular 20
way to matrimony and "ever after" happiness. Why should she be
roaming by night near the cove – unless on some love affair of
her own? I asked myself. But there was nobody suitable within the
Seven-Isles group as far as I knew. It flashed upon me that it was
myself she had been lying in wait for. 25

She hesitated, muffled from head to foot, shadowy and bashful.
I advanced another pace – and how I felt is nobody's business.

"What is it?" I asked very low.

"Nobody knows I am here," she whispered.

"And nobody can see us," I whispered back. 30

The murmur of words "I've been so frightened" reached me.
Just then, forty feet above our heads, from the yet lighted verandah, unexpected and startling, Freya's voice rang out in a clear,
imperious call:

"Antonia!" 35

With a stifled exclamation the hesitating girl vanished out of
the path. A bush near by rustled – then silence. I waited, wondering. The lights on the verandah went out. I waited a while longer
then continued down the path to my boat wondering more than
ever. 40

I remember the occurrences of that visit especially, because this was the last time I saw the Nelson bungalow. On arriving on the Straits I found cable messages which made it necessary for me to throw up my employment at a moment's notice and go home at
5   once. I had a desperate scramble to catch the mail-boat which was due to leave next day; but I found time to write two short notes, one to Freya, the other to Jasper. Later on I wrote at length, this time to Allen alone. I got no answer. I hunted up then his brother, or rather half-brother, a solicitor in the city, a sallow, calm little
10 man who looked at me over his spectacles thoughtfully.

"We haven't heard for ages," he said.

Jasper was the only child of his father's second and late marriage, a transaction which had failed to commend itself to the first, grown-up, family.

15 "You haven't heard for ages," I repeated, with secret annoyance. "May I ask what 'for ages' means in this connection?"

"It means that I don't care whether I ever hear from him or not," retorted the little man of law turning nasty suddenly.

I could not blame Jasper for not wasting his time in correspon-
20 dence with such an outrageous relative. But why didn't he write to me – a decent sort of friend after all; enough of a friend to find for his silence the excuse of forgetfulness natural to a state of transcendental bliss. I waited indulgently, but nothing ever came. And the East seemed to drop out of my life without an echo like a
25 stone falling into a well of prodigious depth.

IV

I suppose praiseworthy motives are a sufficent justifica-
tion almost for anything. What could be more commendable in the abstract than a girl's determination that "poor papa" should
30 not be worried, and her anxiety that the man of her choice should be kept by any means from every occasion of doing something rash, something which might endanger the whole scheme of their happiness?

Nothing could be more tender and more prudent. We must
35 also remember the girl's self-reliant temperament and the general unwillingness of women, I mean women of sense, to make a fuss over matters of that sort.

As has been said already Heemskirk turned up the day after Jasper's arrival at Nelson's Cove. The sight of the brig lying right under the bungalow was very offensive to him. He did not fly ashore before his anchor touched the ground as Jasper used to do. On the contrary, he hung about his quarter deck mumbling 5 to himself; and when he ordered his boat to be manned it was in an angry voice. Freya's existence which lifted Jasper out of himself into a blissful elation was for Heemskirk a cause of secret torment, of hours of exasperated brooding.

While passing the brig he hailed her harshly and asked if the 10 master was on board. Schultz smart and neat in a spotless white suit leaned over the taffrail, finding the question somewhat amusing. He looked humourously down into Heemskirk's boat and answered in the most amiable modulations of his beautiful voice: "Captain Allen is up at the house sir." But his expression changed 15 suddenly at the savage growl "What the devil are you grinning at?" which acknowledged that information.

He watched Heemskirk land and, instead of going to the house, stride away by another path into the grounds.

The desire-tormented Dutchman found old Nelson (or Nielsen) 20 at his drying-sheds, very busy superintending the manipulation of his tobacco crop, which though small was of excellent quality, and enjoying himself thoroughly. But Heemskirk soon put a stop to this simple happiness. He sat down by the old chap and by the sort of talk which he knew was best calculated for the purpose 25 reduced him before long to a state of concealed and perspiring nervousness. It was a horrid talk of "authorities," and old Nelson tried to defend himself. If he dealt with English traders it was because he had to dispose of his produce somehow. He was as conciliatory as he knew how to be and this very thing seemed 30 to excite Heemskirk who had worked himself up into a heavily breathing state of passion.

"And the worst of them all is that Allen," he growled. "Your particular friend – eh? You have let in a lot of these Englishmen into this part. You ought to never have been allowed to settle here. 35 Never. What's he doing here now?"

Old Nelson (or Nielsen), becoming very agitated, declared that Jasper Allen was no particular friend of his. No friend at all – at all. He had bought three tons of rice from him to feed his work-people on. What sort of evidence of friendship was that? . . . Heemskirk burst out at last with the thought which had been gnawing at his vitals:

"Yes. Sell three tons of rice and flirt three days with that girl of

5 yours. I am speaking to you as a friend Nielsen. This won't do. You are only on sufferance here."

Old Nelson was taken aback at first, but recovered pretty quickly. Won't do! Certainly! Of course it wouldn't do! The last man in the world. But his girl didn't care for the fellow and was too sensible

10 to fall in love with any one. He was very earnest in impressing on Heemskirk his own feeling of absolute security. And the lieutenant casting doubting glances sideways was yet willing enough to believe him.

"Much you know about it," he grunted nevertheless.

15 "But I *do* know," insisted old Nelson with the greater desperation because he wanted to resist the doubts arising in his own mind. "My own daughter! In my own house, and I not to know! Come! It would be a good joke, Lieutenant."

"They seem to be carrying on considerably," remarked Heems-

20 kirk moodily. "I suppose they are together now," he added feeling a pang which changed what he meant for a mocking smile into a strange grimace.

The harrassed Nelson shook his hand at him. He was at bottom shocked at this insistence and was even beginning to feel annoyed

25 at the absurdity of it.

"Pooh! Pooh! I'll tell you what Lieutenant. You go to the house and have a drop of gin and bitters before dinner. Ask for Freya. I must see the last of this tobacco put away for the night, but I'll be along presently."

30 Heemskirk was not insensible to this suggestion. It answered to his secret longing which was not a longing for drink however. Old Nelson shouted solicitously after his broad back a recommendation to make himself comfortable and that there was a box of cheroots on the verandah.

35 It was the west verandah that old Nelson meant, the one which was the living room of the house and had split-rattan screens of the very finest quality. The east verandah, sacred to his own privacy, puffing out of cheeks and other signs of perplexed thinking, was fitted with stout blinds of sail cloth. The north verandah was not

40 a verandah at all really. It was more like a long balcony. It did not

communicate with the other two and could only be approached by a passage inside the house. Thus it had a privacy which made it a convenient place for a maiden's meditations without words, and also for the discourses, apparently without sense, which passing between a young man and a maid become pregnant with a diversity of transcendental meanings.

This north verandah was embowered with climbing plants. Freya, whose room opened out on it, had furnished it as a sort of boudoir for herself with a few cane chairs and a sofa of the same kind. On this sofa she and Jasper sat as close together as is possible in this imperfect world where neither can a body be in two places at once, nor yet two bodies can be in one place at the same time. They had been sitting together all the afternoon and I won't say that their talk had been without sense. Loving him, with a little judicious anxiety lest in his elation he should break his heart over some mishap, Freya naturally would talk to him soberly. He, nervous and brusque when away from her, appeared always as if overcome by her visibility, by the great wonder of being palpably loved. An old man's child, having lost his mother early, thrown out to sea out of the way while very young, he had not much experience of tenderness of any kind.

In this private, foliage-embowered verandah and at this late hour of the afternoon, he bent down a little and possessing himself of Freya's hands was kissing them one after another while she smiled and looked down at his head with the eyes of approving compassion. At that same moment Heemskirk was approaching the house from the north.

Antonia was on the watch on that side. But she did not keep a very good watch. The sun was setting; she knew that her young mistress and the captain of the *Bonito* were about to separate. She was walking to and fro in the dusky grove with a flower in her hair and singing softly to herself, when suddenly, within a foot of her, the lieutenant appeared from behind a tree. She bounded aside like a startled fawn but Heemskirk, with a lucid comprehension of what she was there for, pounced upon her and catching her arm clapped his other thick hand over her mouth.

"If you try to make a noise I'll wring your neck."

This ferocious figure of speech terrified the girl sufficiently. Heemskirk had seen plainly enough on the verandah Freya's golden head with another head very close to it. He dragged the unresisting maid with him by a circuitous way into the compound, where he dismissed her with a vicious push in the direction of the cluster of bamboo huts for the servants.

She was very much like the faithful camerista of Italian comedy, but in her terror she bolted away without a sound from that thick, short, black-eyed man with a cruel grip of fingers like a vice. Quaking all over at a distance, extremely scared and yet half inclined to laugh she saw him enter the house at the back.

The interior of the bungalow was divided by two passages crossing each other in the middle. At that point Heemskirk, by turning his head slightly to the left as he passed, secured the evidence of "carryings on" so irreconcilable with old Nelson's assurances that it made him stagger, with a rush of blood to his head. Two white figures distinct against the light stood in an unmistakeable attitude. Freya's arms were round Jasper's neck. Their faces were characteristically superimposed on each other, and Heemskirk went on, his throat choked with a sudden rising of curses, till on the west verandah he stumbled blindly against a chair and then dropped into another as though his legs had been swept from under him. He had indulged too long in the habit of appropriating Freya to himself in his thoughts: "Is that how you entertain your visitors you — " he thought, so outraged that he could not find a sufficiently degrading epithet.

Freya struggled a little and threw her head back. "Somebody has come in," she whispered. Jasper, holding her clasped closely to his breast, and looking down into her face, suggested casually: "Your father."

Freya tried to disengage herself but she had not the heart absolutely to push him away with her hands. "I believe it's Heemskirk," she breathed out at him.

He plunging into her eyes in a quiet rapture was provoked to a vague smile by the sound of the name. "The ass is always knocking down my beacons outside the rivers," he murmured. He attached no other meaning to Heemskirk's existence; but Freya was asking herself whether the lieutenant had seen them.

"Let me go kid," she ordered in a peremptory whisper. Jasper obeyed and stepping back at once continued his contemplation of her face under another angle. "I must go and see," she said to herself anxiously.

She instructed him hurriedly to wait a moment after she was gone and then to slip on to the back verandah and get a quiet smoke before he showed himself. "Don't stay late this evening," was her last recommendation before she left him.

Then Freya came out on the west verandah with her light, rapid step. While going through the doorway she managed to shake down the folds of the looped up curtain at the end of the passage so as to cover Jasper's retreat from the bower. Directly she appeared Heemskirk jumped up as if to fly at her. She paused and he made her an exaggerated low bow.

It irritated Freya. "Oh! It's you Mr Heemskirk. How do you do."

She spoke in her usual tone. Her face was not plainly visible to him in the dusk of the deep verandah. He dared not trust himself to speak, his rage at what he had seen was so great. And when she added with serenity: "Papa will be coming in before long," he called her horrid names silently, to himself, before he spoke with contorted lips.

"I have seen your father already. We had a talk in the sheds. He told me some very interesting things. Oh very. . . ."

Freya sat down. She thought: "He has seen us, for certain." She was not ashamed. What she was afraid of was some foolish or awkward complication. But she could not conceive how much her person had been appropriated by Heemskirk (in his thoughts). She tried to be conversational.

"You are coming now from Palembang I suppose?"

"Eh? What? Oh yes! I come from Palembang. Ha! ha! ha! You know what your father said? He said he was afraid you were having a very dull time of it here."

"And I suppose you are going to cruise in the Molluccas," continued Freya who wanted to impart some useful information to Jasper if possible. At the same time she was always glad to know that those two men were a few hundred miles apart when not under her eye.

Heemskirk growled angrily: "Yes. Molluccas," glaring in the direction of her shadowy figure. "Your father thinks that it's very quiet for you here. I tell you what Miss Freya. There isn't such a quiet spot on earth that a woman can't find an opportunity of making a fool of somebody."

Freya thought: "I musn't let him provoke me." Presently the Tamil boy who was Nelson's head-servant came in with the lights.

She addressed him at once with voluble directions where to put
the lamps, told him to bring the tray with the gin and bitters and
to send Antonia into the house.

"I will have to leave you to yourself Mr Heemskirk for a while,"
5   she said.

And she went to her room to put on another frock. She made
a quick change of it because she wished to be on the verandah
before her father and the lieutenant met again. She relied on
herself to regulate that evening's intercourse between these two.
10   But Antonia still scared and hysterical exhibited a bruise on her
arm which roused Freya's indignation.

"He jumped on me out of the bush like a tiger," said the girl
laughing nervously with frightened eyes.

"The brute," thought Freya. "He meant to spy on us, then."
15   She was enraged but the recollection of the thick Dutchman in
white trousers wide at the hips and narrow at the ankles, with his
shoulder-straps and black bullet head, glaring at her in the light
of the lamps was so repulsively comical that she could not help
a smiling grimace. Then she became anxious. The absurdities of
20   three men were forcing this anxiety upon her: Jasper's impetuosity,
her father's fears, Heemskirk's infatuation. She was very tender to
the first two and she made up her mind to display all her feminine
diplomacy. All this, she said to herself, will be over and done with
before very long now.

25   Heemskirk on the verandah lolling in a chair, his legs extended
and his white cap reposing on his stomach, was lashing himself
into a fury of an atrocious character, altogether incomprehensible
to a young girl. His chin was resting on his chest, his eyes gazed
stonily at his shoes. Freya examined him from behind the curtain.
30   He didn't stir. He was ridiculous. But this absolute stillness was
impressive. She stole back along the passage to the east verandah
where Jasper was sitting quietly in the dark, doing what he was told
like a good boy.

"Psst," she hissed. He was by her side in a moment.
35   "Yes. What is it?" he murmured.

"It's that beetle," she whispered uneasily. Under the impression
of Heemskirk's sinister immobility she had half a mind to let Jasper
know that they had been seen. But she was by no means certain
that Heemskirk would tell her father – and at any rate not that

evening. She concluded rapidly that the safest thing would be to get Jasper out of the way as soon as possible.

"What has he been doing?" asked Jasper in a calm undertone.

"Oh nothing! Nothing. He sits there looking cross. But you know how he's always worrying Papa." 5

"Your father's quite unreasonable," pronounced Jasper judicially.

"I don't know," she said in a doubtful tone. Something of old Nelson's dread of the authorities had rubbed off on the girl since she had to live with it day after day. "I don't know. Papa's afraid of 10 being reduced to beggary, as he says, in his old days. Look here, kid, you had better clear out to-morrow morning, first thing."

Jasper had hoped for another afternoon with Freya, an afternoon of quiet felicity with the girl by his side and his eyes on his brig, anticipating a blissful future. His silence was eloquent with 15 disappointment and Freya understood it very well. She too was disappointed. But it was her business to be sensible.

"We shan't have a moment to ourselves with that beetle creeping around the house," she argued in a low hurried voice. "So what's the good of your staying. And he won't go while the brig's here. 20 You know he won't."

"He ought to be reported for loitering," murmured Jasper with a vexed little laugh.

"Mind you get under way at daylight," recommended Freya under her breath. 25

He detained her after the manner of lovers. She expostulated without struggling because it was hard for her to repulse him. He whispered into her ear while he put his arms round her.

"Next time we two meet, next time I hold you like this, it shall be on board. You and I, in the brig – all the world, all the life. . . ." And 30 then he flashed out: "I wonder I can wait! I feel as if I must carry you off now, at once. I could run with you in my hands – down the path – without stumbling – without touching the earth. . . ."

She was still. She listened to the passion in his voice. She was saying to herself that if she were to whisper the faintest yes, if she 35 were but to sigh lightly her content, he would do it. He was capable of doing it – without touching the earth. She closed her eyes and smiled in the dark, abandoning herself in delightful giddiness, for an instant, to his encircling arms. But before he could be tempted to tighten his grip she was out of it, a foot away from him and in full possession of herself.

That was the steady Freya. She was touched by the deep sigh which floated up to her from the white figure of Jasper who did
5   not stir.

"You are a mad kid," she said tremulously. Then with a change of tone: "No one could carry me off. Not even you. I am not the sort of girl that gets carried off." His white form seemed to shrink a little before the force of that assertion and she relented. "Isn't it
10 enough for you to know that you have – that you have carried me away?" she added in a tender tone.

He murmured an endearing word and she continued. "I've promised you – I've said I would come – and I shall come of my own free will. You shall wait for me on board. I shall get up the
15 side – by myself, and walk up to you on the deck and say: 'Here I am, kid.' And then – and then I shall be carried off. But it will be no man who will carry me off – it will be the brig – your brig – our brig. . . . I love the beauty!"

She heard an inarticulate sound something like a moan wrung
20 out by pain or delight, and glided away. There was that other man on the other verandah, that dark surly Dutchman who could make trouble between Jasper and her father, bring about a quarrel, ugly words and perhaps a physical collision. What a horrible situation. But even putting aside that awful extremity she shrank from having
25 to live for some three months with a wretched, tormented, angry, distracted, absurd man. And when the day came, the day and the hour, what should she do if her father tried to detain her by main force – as was, after all, possible. Could she actually struggle with him hand to hand? But it was of lamentations and entreaties that
30 she was really afraid. Could she withstand them? What an odious, cruel, ridiculous position would that be.

"But it won't be. He'll say nothing," she thought as she came out quietly on the west verandah and seeing that Heemskirk did not move sat down on a chair near the doorway and kept her eyes
35 on him. The outraged lieutenant had not changed his attitude; only his cap had fallen off his stomach and was lying on the floor. His thick, black eyebrows were knitted by a frown, while he looked at her out of the corners of his eyes. And this sideways glance in conjunction with the hooked nose, the whole bulky, ungainly,
40 sprawling person struck Freya as so comically moody that, inwardly

discomposed as she was, she could not help smiling. She did her best to give that smile a conciliatory character. She did not want to provoke Heemskirk needlessly.

And the lieutenant perceiving that smile was mollified. It never entered his head that his outward appearance, a naval officer, in uniform, could appear ridiculous to that girl of no position – the daughter of old Nielsen. The recollection of her arms round Jasper's neck still irritated and excited him. "The hussy," he thought. "Smiling – eh? That's how you are amusing yourself. Fooling your father finely – aren't you. You have a taste for that sort of fun – have you? Well, we shall see." . . . He did not alter his position but on his pursed-up lips there also appeared a smile of surly and ill-omened amusement, while his eyes returned to the contemplation of his boots.

Freya felt hot with indignation. She sat radiantly fair in the lamp-light, her strong, well-shaped hands lying one on top of the other in her lap. . . . "Odious creature," she thought. Her face coloured with sudden anger. "You have scared my maid out of her senses," she said aloud. "What possessed you?"

He was thinking so deeply of her that the sound of her voice, pronouncing these unexpected words, startled him extremely. He jerked up his head and looked so bewildered that Freya insisted impatiently.

"I mean Antonia. You have bruised her arm. What did you do it for?"

"Do you want to quarrel with me," he asked thickly with a sort of amazement. He blinked like an owl. He was funny. Freya like all women had a keen sense of the ridiculous in outward appearance.

"Well no! I don't think I do." She could not help herself. She laughed outright a clear, nervous laugh in which Heemskirk joined suddenly with a harsh "Ha! ha! ha!"

Voices and footsteps were heard in the passage and Jasper with old Nelson came out. Old Nelson looked at his daughter approvingly, for he liked the lieutenant to be kept in good humour. And he also joined sympathetically in the laugh. "Now Lieutenant we shall have some dinner," he said rubbing his hands cheerily. Jasper had gone straight to the balustrade. The sky was full of stars, and in the blue, velvety night, the cove below had a denser blackness in which the riding lights of the brig and of the gunboat glimmered redly, like suspended sparks. "Next time this riding light glimmers

down there, I'll be waiting for her on the quarter deck to come
and say: 'Here I am,'" Jasper thought; and his heart seemed to
grow bigger in his chest, dilated by an oppressive happiness that
nearly wrung out a cry from him. There was no wind. Not a leaf
5   below him stirred and even the sea was but a still, uncomplaining
shadow. Far away on the unclouded sky the pale lightning, the
heat lightning of the tropics, played tremulously amongst the low
stars in short, faint, mysteriously consecutive flashes, like incomprehensible signals from some distant planet. . . .
10   The dinner passed off quietly. Freya sat facing her father, calm
but pale. Heemskirk affected to talk only to old Nelson. Jasper's
behaviour was exemplary. He kept his eyes under control, basking
in the sense of Freya's nearness as people bask in the sun without
looking up to heaven. And very soon after dinner was over, mindful
15   of his instructions, he declared that it was time for him to go on
board his ship.
Heemskirk did not look up. Ensconced in the rocking chair and
puffing at a cheroot he had the air of meditating surlily over some
odious outbreak. So at least it seemed to Freya. Old Nelson said at
20   once: "I'll stroll down with you." He had begun a professional conversation about the dangers of the New Guinea coast and wanted
to relate to Jasper some experience of his own "over there." Jasper
was such a good listener! Freya made as if to accompany them
but her father frowned, shook his head, and nodded significantly
25   towards the immovable Heemskirk blowing out smoke with half-
closed eyes and protruded lips. The lieutenant must not be left
alone. Take offence perhaps.
Freya obeyed these signs. "Perhaps it is better for me to stay," she
thought. Women are not generally prone to review their own con-
30   duct, still less to condemn it. The embarrassing masculine absurdities are in the main responsible for its ethics. But looking at Heemskirk Freya felt regret and even remorse. His thick bulk in repose
suggested the idea of repletion; but as a matter of fact he had eaten
very little. He had drunk a great deal however. The fleshy lobes
35   of his unpleasant big ears with deeply folded rims were crimson.
They quite flamed in the neighbourhood of the flat, sallow cheeks.
For a considerable time he did not raise his heavy, brown eyelids.
To be at the mercy of such a creature was humiliating; and Freya
who always ended by being frank with herself thought regretfully:
40   "If only I had been open with Papa from the first! But then what an

impossible life he would have led me!" . . . Yes. Men were absurd in many ways: loveably like Jasper, impracticably like her father, odiously like that grotesquely supine creature in the chair. Was it possible to talk him over? Perhaps it was not necessary? "Oh! I can't talk to him," she thought. And when Heemskirk, still without look-   5 ing at her, began resolutely to crush his half-smoked cheroot on the coffee tray she took alarm, glided towards the piano, opened it in tremendous haste and struck the keys almost before she sat down.

In an instant the verandah, the whole carpetless wooden bun-   10 galow raised on piles, became filled with an uproarious, confused resonance; but through it all she heard, she felt on the floor, the heavy prowling footsteps of the lieutenant moving to and fro at her back. He was not exactly drunk, but he was sufficiently primed to make the suggestions of his excited imagination seem perfectly   15 feasible and even clever; beautifully, unscrupulously clever. Freya aware that he had stopped just behind her went on playing without turning her head. She played with spirit, brilliantly, a fierce piece of music; but when his voice reached her she went cold all over. It was the voice not the words. The insolent familiarity of tone   20 dismayed her to such an extent that she could not understand at first what he was saying. His utterance was thick too.

"I suspected. Of course I suspected something of your little goings on. I am not a child. But from suspecting to seeing – seeing, you understand – there's an enormous difference. That sort of   25 thing. . . . Come! One isn't made of stone. And when a man has been worried by a girl as I have been worried by you Miss Freya – sleeping and waking, then of course. . . . But I am a man of the world. It must be dull for you here. . . . I say! Won't you leave off this confounded playing. . . ."   30

This last was the only sentence really which she made out. She shook her head negatively and in desperation put on the loud pedal; but she could not make the sound of the piano cover his raised voice.

"Only I am surprised that you should . . . . An English trading   35 skipper, a common fellow. Low, cheeky lot infesting these islands. I would make short work of such trash! . . . While you have here a good friend, a gentleman ready to worship at your feet – your pretty feet; an officer, a man of family. Strange isn't it? But what of that! You are fit for a prince."   40

Freya did not turn her head. Her face went stiff with horror and indignation. This adventure was altogether beyond her conception of what was possible. It was not in her character to jump up and run away. It seemed to her too that if she did move there was no saying what might happen. Presently her father would be back and then the other would have to leave off. It was best to ignore – to ignore. She went on playing loudly and correctly, as though she were alone, as if Heemskirk did not exist. That proceeding irritated him.

"Come! You may deceive your father," he bawled angrily, "but I am not to be made a fool of. Stop this infernal noise. . . . Freya. . . . Hey! you Scandinavian goddess of love do you hear? That's what you are – of love. . . . But the heathen gods are only devils in disguise and that's what you are too – a deep little devil. Stop it, I say, or I will lift you off that stool."

Standing behind her he devoured her with his eyes from the golden crown of her rigidly motionless head to the heels of her shoes, the line of her shapely shoulders, the curves of her fine figure swaying a little before the keyboard. She had on a light dress; the sleeves stopped short at the elbows in an edging of lace. A satin ribbon encircled her waist. In an access of irresistible, reckless hopefulness he clapped both his hands on that waist . . . and then the irritating music stopped at last. But quick as she was in springing away from the contact (the round music stool going over with a crash) Heemskirk's lips aiming at her neck landed a hungry smacking kiss just under her ear. A deep silence reigned for a time. And then he laughed rather feebly.

He was disconcerted somewhat by her white, still face, the big light violet eyes resting on him stonily. She had not uttered a sound. She faced him steadying herself on the corner of the piano with one extended hand. The other went on rubbing with mechanical persistency the place his lips had touched.

"What's the trouble?" he said offended. "Startled you? . . . Look here – don't let us have any of that nonsense. You don't mean to say a kiss frightens you so much as all that. I know better . . . and I don't mean to be left out in the cold."

He had been gazing into her face with such strained intentness that he could no longer see it distinctly. Everything round him was rather misty. He forgot the overturned stool, caught his foot against it and lurched forward slightly, saying in an ingratiating tone: "I am not bad fun really. You try a few kisses to begin with. . . ."

He said no more because his head received a terrific concussion accompanied by an explosive sound. Freya had swung her round strong arm with such force that the impact of her open palm on his flat cheek turned him half round. Uttering a faint, hoarse yell the lieutenant clapped both his hands to the left side of his face which had taken on suddenly a dusky, brick-red tinge. Freya, very erect, her violet eyes darkened, her palm still tingling from the blow, a sort of restrained determined smile showing a tiny gleam of her white teeth, heard her father's rapid, heavy tread on the path below the verandah. Her expression lost its pugnacity and became sincerely concerned. She was sorry for her father. She stooped quickly to pick up the music stool as if anxious to obliterate the traces. . . . But that was no good. She had resumed her attitude one hand resting lightly on the piano before old Nelson got up to the top of the stairs.

Poor father! How furious he will be; how upset! And afterwards what tremors! What unhappiness! Why had she not been open with him from the first? His round, innocent stare of amazement cut her to the quick. But he was not looking at her. His stare was directed to Heemskirk who with his back to him and with his hands still up to his face was hissing curses through his teeth and (she saw him in profile) glaring at her balefully with one black, evil eye.

"What's the matter?" asked old Nelson very much bewildered. She did not answer him. She thought of Jasper on the deck of the brig gazing up at the lighted bungalow and she felt frightened. It was a mercy that one of them at least was on board out of the way. She only wished he were a hundred miles off. And yet she was not certain that she did. Had Jasper been mysteriously moved that moment to re-appear on the verandah she would have thrown her consistency, her firmness, her self possession to the winds and flown into his arms.

"What is it? What is it?" insisted the unsuspecting Nelson, getting quite excited. "Only this minute you were playing a tune and . . ."

Freya unable to speak in her apprehension of what was coming (she was also fascinated by that black, evil, glaring eye) nodded slightly at the lieutenant as much as to say "Just look at him."

"Why yes," exclaimed old Nelson. "I see. What on earth. . . ."

Meantime he had cautiously approached Heemskirk who bursting into incoherent imprecations was stamping with both feet where he stood. The indignity of the blow, the rage of baffled purpose, the ridicule of the exposure and the impossibility of revenge maddened him to a point when he simply felt he must howl with fury. . . . "O! O! O!" he howled, stamping across the verandah as though he meant to drive his foot through the floor at every step.

"Why! Is his face hurt?" asked the astounded old Nelson. The truth dawned suddenly upon his innocent mind: "Dear me!" he cried enlightened. "Get some brandy, quick Freya. . . . You subject to it Lieutenant? Came on all at once? Fiendish – eh? I know, I know! Used to go crazy all of a sudden myself in the time. . . . And the little bottle of laudanum from the medicine chest too, Freya. Look sharp. . . . Don't you see he's got a toothache."

And indeed what other explanation could have presented itself to the guileless old Nelson, beholding this cheek nursed with both hands, these wild glances, these stampings, this distracted swaying of the body. It would have demanded a preternatural acuteness to hit upon the true cause. Freya had not moved. She watched Heemskirk's savagely inquiring, black stare directed stealthily upon herself. "Aha! You would like to be let off," she said to herself. She looked at him unflinchingly, thinking it out. The temptation of making an end of it all without further trouble was irresistible. She gave an almost imperceptible nod of assent and glided away. "Hurry up that brandy," old Nelson shouted as she disappeared in the passage.

Heemskirk relieved his deeper feelings by a sudden string of curses in Dutch and English which he sent after her. He raved to his heart's content flinging to and fro on the verandah and kicking chairs out of his way; while Nelson (or Nielsen) whose sympathy was profoundly stirred by these evidences of agonizing pain hovered round his dear (and dreaded) lieutenant, fussing like an old hen.

"Dear me! Dear me. Is it so bad? I know well what it is. I used to frighten my poor wife sometimes. Do you get it often like this, Lieutenant?"

Heemskirk shouldered him viciously out of his way with a short, insane laugh. But his staggering host took it in good part; a man beside himself with excruciating toothache is not responsible.

"Go into my room Lieutenant," he suggested urgently. "Throw yourself on my bed. We will get something to ease you in a minute."

He seized the poor sufferer by the arm and forced him gently onwards, to the very bed, on which Heemskirk in a renewed access of rage flung himself down with such force that he rebounded 5 from the mattress to the height of quite a foot. "Dear me!" exclaimed the scared Nelson, and incontinently ran off to hurry up the brandy and the laudanum, very angry that so little alacrity was shown in relieving the tortures of his precious guest. In the end he got these things himself. 10

Half an hour later he stood in the inner passage of the house surprised by faint spasmodic sounds of a mysterious nature between laughter and sobs. He frowned, then went straight towards his daughter's room and knocked at the door.

Freya, her glorious fair hair framing her white face and rippling 15 down a dark blue dressing gown, opened it partly.

The light in the room was dim. Antonia crouching in a corner rocked herself backwards and forwards uttering feeble moans. Old Nelson had not much experience in various kinds of feminine laughter but he was certain there had been laughter there. 20

"Very unfeeling, very unfeeling," he said with weighty displeasure. "What is there so amusing in a man being in pain? I should have thought a woman – a young girl . . ."

"He was so funny," murmured Freya whose eyes glistened strangely in the semi-obscurity of the passage. "And then you know 25 I don't like him," she added in an unsteady voice.

"Funny!" repeated old Nelson amazed at this evidence of callousness in one so young. "You don't like him? Do you mean to say that because you don't like him you . . . . Why! it's simply cruel. Don't you know it's about the worst sort of pain there is. Dogs have 30 been known to go mad with it."

"He certainly seemed to have gone mad," Freya said with an effort as if she were struggling with some hidden feeling. But her father was launched.

"And you know how he is. He notices everything. He is a fellow 35 to take offence for the least little thing – regular Dutchman; and I want to keep friendly with him. It's like this my girl: if that Rajah of ours were to do something silly – and you know he is a sulky rebellious beggar – and the authorities took into their heads that my influence over him wasn't good, you would find yourself without a roof over your head. . . ."

She cried "What nonsense Father" in a not very assured tone and discovered that he was angry, angry enough to achieve
5   irony – yes old Nelson (or Nielsen) – irony! Just a gleam of it.

"Oh, of course, if you have means of your own – a mansion, a plantation that I know nothing of. . . ." But he was not capable of sustained irony. "I tell you they would bundle me out of here," he whispered forcibly. "Without compensation of course. I know
10 these Dutch. And the lieutenant's just the fellow to start the trouble going. He has the ear of influential officials. I wouldn't offend him for anything – for anything – on no consideration whatever. . . . What did you say?"

It was only an inarticulate exclamation. If she ever had a half-
15 formed intention of telling him everything, she had given it up now. It was impossible, both out of regard for his dignity and for the peace of his poor mind.

"I don't care for him myself very much," old Nelson's subdued undertone confessed in a sigh. "He's easier now," he went on after
20 a silence. "I've given him up my bed for the night. I shall sleep on my verandah – in the hammock. No! I can't say I like him either. But from that to laugh at a man because he's driven crazy with pain is a long way. You've surprised me Freya. That side of his face is quite flushed."

25 Her shoulders shook convulsively under his hands which he laid on her paternally. His straggly, wiry moustache brushed her forehead in a good-night kiss. She closed the door and went away from it to the middle of the room before she allowed herself a tired out sort of laugh, without buoyancy.

30 "Flushed! A little flushed," she repeated to herself. "I hope so indeed! A little. . . ."

Her eyelashes were wet. Antonia in her corner moaned and giggled; and it was impossible to tell where the moans ended and the giggles began.

35 The mistress and the maid had been somewhat hysterical; for Freya on fleeing into her room had found Antonia there, and had told her everything. "I have avenged you my girl," she exclaimed. And then they had laughingly cried and cryingly laughed with admonitions "Ssh! Not so loud. Be quiet" on one part and inter-
40 ludes of "I am so frightened. . . . He's an evil man" on the other.

Antonia was very much afraid of Heemskirk. She was afraid of
him because of his personal appearance: because of his eyes and
his eyebrows and his mouth and his nose and his limbs. Nothing
could be more rational. And she thought him an evil man because
to her eyes he looked evil. No ground for an opinion could be   5
sounder. In the dimness of the room with only a night light burning
at the head of Freya's bed the camerista crept out of her corner
to crouch at the feet of her mistress, supplicating in whispers:

"There is the brig. Captain Allen. Let us run away at once! O!
Let us run away. I am so frightened. Let us! Let us!"   10

"I! – run away!" thought Freya to herself, without looking down
at the scared girl.

"Never."

Both the resolute mistress under the mosquito net and the
frightened maid lying curled up on a mat at the foot of the bed did   15
not sleep very well that night. The person that did not sleep at all
was Lieutenant Heemskirk. He lay on his back staring vindictively
in the darkness. Inflaming images and humiliating reflections succeeded each other in his mind, keeping up, augmenting, his anger.
A pretty tale this to get about. But it must not be allowed to get   20
about. The outrage had to be swallowed in silence. A pretty affair!
Fooled, led on and struck by the girl – and probably fooled by the
father too. But no. Nielsen was but another victim of that shameless hussy, that brazen minx, that sly, laughing, kissing, lying . . . .
"No! He did not deceive me on purpose," thought the tormented   25
lieutenant. "But I should like to pay him off all the same for being
such an imbecile." . . . Well! Some day perhaps. One thing he was
firmly resolved on: he had made up his mind to steal early out of
the house. He did not think he could face the girl without going
out of his mind with fury. "Fire and perdition. Ten thousand devils! 30
I shall choke here before the morning," he muttered to himself
lying rigid on his back on old Nelson's bed, his breast heaving for
air.

He arose at daylight and started cautiously to open the door.
Faint sounds in the passage alarmed him, and remaining con-   35
cealed he saw Freya coming out. This unexpected sight deprived
him of all power to move away from the crack of the door. It was
the narrowest crack possible but commanding the view of the end
of the verandah. Freya made for that end hastily to watch the brig
passing the point. She wore her dark dressing gown, her feet were   40

bare, because having fallen asleep towards the morning she ran out headlong in her fear of being too late. Heemskirk had never seen her looking like this – with her hair drawn back smoothly to the shape of her head and hanging in one heavy, fair tress down
5 her back and with that air of extreme youth, intensity and eagerness. And at first he was amazed and then he gnashed his teeth. He could not face her at all. He muttered a curse and kept still behind the door.

With a low, deep-breathed "Ah!" when she first saw the brig
10 already under way, Freya reached for Nelson's long glass reposing on brackets high up the wall. The wide sleeve of the dressing gown slipped back, uncovering her white arm as far as the shoulder. Heemskirk, gripping the door handle as if to crush it, felt like a man just risen to his feet from a drinking bout.

15 And Freya knew that he was watching her. She knew. She had seen the door move as she came out of the passage. She was aware of his eyes being on her, with scornful bitterness, with triumphant contempt. "You are there," she thought levelling the long glass. "Oh! Well! Look on then."

20 The green islets appeared like black shadows, the ashen sea was smooth as ice, the clear robe of the colourless dawn, in which even the brig appeared shadowy, had a hem of light in the east. Directly Freya had made out Jasper on deck with his own long glass directed to the bungalow she laid hers down and raised both her beautiful
25 white arms above her head. In that attitude of a supreme cry she stood still, glowing with the consciousness of Jasper's adoration going out to her figure held in the field of his glass away there, and warmed too by the feeling of evil passion, the burning covetous eyes of the other, fastened on her back. In the fervour of her love,
30 in the caprice of her mind, and with that mysterious knowledge of masculine nature women seem to be born to, she thought: "You are looking on – you will – you must! Then you shall see something."

She brought both her hands to her lips then flung them out
35 sending a kiss over the sea as if she wanted to throw her heart along with it on the deck of the brig. Her face was rosy, her eyes shone. Her repeated, passionate gesture seemed to fling kisses by the hundred again, and again, and again while the slowly ascending sun brought the glory of colour to the world, turning the islets

green, the sea blue, the brig below her white – dazzlingly white
in the spread of her wings – with the red ensign streaming like a
tiny flame from the peak. And each time she murmured with a
rising inflexion: "Take this – and this – and this . . ." till suddenly
her arms fell. She had seen the ensign dipped in response, and
next moment the point below hid the hull of the brig from her
view. Then she turned away from the balustrade and passing slowly
before the door of her father's room with her eyelids lowered and
an enigmatic expression on her face, she disappeared behind the
curtain.

But instead of going along the passage she remained concealed
and very still on the other side to watch what would happen. For
some time the broad, furnished verandah remained empty. Then
the door of old Nelson's room came open suddenly and Heemskirk staggered out. His hair was rumpled, his eyes bloodshot, his
unshaven face looked very dark. He gazed wildly about, saw his
cap on a table, snatched it up and made for the stairs quietly but
with a strange tottering gait, like the last effort of waning strength.

Shortly after his head had sunk below the level of the floor Freya
came out from behind the curtain with compressed, scheming lips
and no softness at all in her luminous eyes. He could not be allowed
to sneak off scot free. Never! Never! She was excited, she tingled
all over, she had tasted blood. He must be made to understand
that she had been aware of having been watched, he must know
that he had been seen slinking off shamefully. But to run to the
front-rail and shout after him would have been childish – crude –
undignified. And to shout – what? What word? What phrase? No!
it was impossible. Then how? . . . She frowned, discovered it,
dashed at the piano which had stood open all night and made the
rosewood monster growl savagely in an irritated bass. She struck
chords as if firing shots after that straddling, broad figure in ample
white trousers and a dark uniform jacket with gold shoulder-straps,
and then she pursued him with the same thing she had played
the evening before; a modern, fierce piece of love music which
had been tried more than once against the thunderstorms of the
group. She accentuated its rhythm with triumphant malice, so
absorbed in her purpose that she did not notice the presence
of her father who, wearing an old threadbare ulster of a check
pattern over his sleeping suit, had run out from the back verandah

to inquire the reason of this untimely performance. He stared at her.

"What on earth? . . . Freya!" . . . His voice was nearly drowned by the piano. "What's become of the lieutenant?" he shouted.

5 She looked up at him, as if her soul were lost in her music, with unseeing eyes.

"Gone."

"Wha-a-t! . . . Where?"

She shook her head slightly and went on playing louder than 10 before. Old Nelson's innocently anxious gaze starting from the open door of his room explored the whole place high and low, as if the lieutenant were something small which might have been crawling on the floor or clinging to a wall. But a shrill whistle coming somewhere from below pierced the ample volume of sound 15 rolling out of the piano in great vibrating waves. The lieutenant was down at the cove whistling for the boat to come and take him off to his ship. And he seemed to be in a terrific hurry too, for he whistled again almost directly, waited but a moment and then sent out a long, interminable, shrill call as distressful to hear 20 as though he had shrieked without drawing breath. Freya ceased playing suddenly.

"Going on board," said old Nelson perturbed by the event. "What could have made him clear out so early? Queer chap. Devilishly touchy too. I shouldn't wonder if it was your conduct last 25 night that hurt his feelings. I noticed you Freya. You as well as laughed in his face while he was suffering agonies from neuralgia. It isn't the way to get yourself liked. He's offended with you."

Freya's hands now reposed passive on the keys; she bowed her 30 fair head feeling a sudden inward discontent, a nervous lassitude as though she had passed through some exhausting crisis. Old Nelson (or Nielsen) looking aggrieved was revolving matters of policy in his bald head.

"I think it would be right for me to go on board just to inquire – 35 some time this morning," he declared fussily. "Why don't they bring me my morning tea? Do you hear, Freya? You have astonished me I must say. I didn't think a young girl could be so unfeeling. And the lieutenant thinks himself a friend of ours too! What? No? Well he calls himself a friend, and that's something to a person in 40 my position. Certainly! Oh! Yes. I must go on board."

"Must you?" murmured Freya listlessly; then added in her thought "poor man!"

V

IN RESPECT OF the next seven weeks all that is necessary to say is first that old Nelson (or Nielsen) failed in paying his politic 5 call. The *Neptun*, gunboat of H.M. the King of the Netherlands commanded by an outraged and infuriated lieutenant, left the cove at an unexpectedly early hour. When Freya's father came down to the shore (after seeing his precious crop of tobacco spread out properly in the sun) she was already steaming round the point. 10 Old Nelson regretted the circumstance for many days. "Now I don't know in what disposition the man went away," he lamented to his hard daughter. He was amazed at her hardness. He was almost frightened by her indifference.

Next it must be recorded that the same day, the gunboat *Neptun* 15 steering east passed the brig *Bonito* becalmed in sight of Carimata with her head to the eastward too. Her captain, Jasper Allen, giving himself up consciously to a tender, possessive reverie of his Freya, did not get out of his long chair on the poop to look at the *Neptun* which passed so close that the smoke belching out sud- 20 denly from her short black funnel rolled between the masts of the *Bonito*, obscuring for a moment the sunlit whiteness of her sails consecrated to the service of love. Jasper did not even turn his head for a glance. But Heemskirk, on the bridge, had gazed long and earnestly at the brig from the distance, gripping hard 25 the brass rail in front of him, till, the two ships closing, he lost all confidence in himself and retreating to the chart-room pulled the door to with a crash. There, his brows knitted, his mouth drawn on one side in sardonic meditation, he sat through many still hours – a sort of Prometheus in the bonds of unholy desire having his very 30 vitals torn by the beak and claws of humiliated passion.

That species of fowl is not to be shooed off as easily as a chicken. Fooled, cheated, deceived, led on, outraged, mocked at – beak and claws! A sinister bird. The lieutenant had no mind to become the talk of the Archipelago, as the naval officer who had had his face 35 slapped by a girl. Was it possible that she really loved that rascally trader? He tried not to think but, worse than thoughts, definite impressions, impressions of the senses, beset him in his retreat.

He saw her – a vision plain, close to, detailed, plastic, coloured, lighted up – he saw her hanging round the neck of that fellow. And he shut his eyes only to discover that this was no remedy. Then a piano began to play near by, very plainly – and he put his

5 fingers to his ears with no better effect. It was not to be borne. Not in solitude. He bolted out of the chart-room, and talked of indifferent things somewhat wildly with the officer of the watch on the bridge, to the mocking accompaniment of a ghostly piano.

The last thing to be recorded is that Lieutenant Heemskirk

10 instead of pursuing his course towards Ternate, where he was expected, went out of his way to call at Makassar where no one was looking for his arrival. Once there he gave certain explanations and laid a certain proposal before the governor or some other authority, and obtained the permission to do what he thought fit in

15 these matters. Thereupon the *Neptun* giving up Ternate altogether steamed north in view of the mountainous coast of Celebes and then crossing the broad straits took up her station on a low coast of virgin forests, inviolate and mute, in waters phosphorescent at night, deep blue in day time with gleaming green patches over

20 the submerged reefs. For days the *Neptun* could be seen moving smoothly up and down the sombre face of the shore, or hanging about with a watchful air near the silvery breaks of broad estuaries, under the great luminous sky never softened, never veiled and flooding the earth with the everlasting sunshine of the tropics; that

25 sunshine which in its unbroken splendour oppresses the soul with an inexpressible melancholy more intimate, more penetrating, more profound than the grey sadness of the northern mists.

* * *

The trading brig *Bonito* appeared gliding round a sombre forest-

30 clad point of land on the silvery estuary of a great river. The breath of air that gave her motion would not have fluttered the flame of a torch. She stole out into the open from behind a veil of unstir-ring leaves, mysteriously silent, ghostly white and solemnly stealthy in her imperceptible progress; and Jasper, his elbow in the main

35 rigging and his head leaning against his hand, thought of Freya. Everything in the world reminded him of her. The beauty of the loved woman exists in the beauties of nature. The swelling outlines of the hills, the curves of a coast, the free sinuosities of a river are less suave than the harmonious lines of her body and when she

moves gliding lightly, the grace of her progress suggests the power of occult forces which rule the fascinating aspects of the visible world.

Dependent on things as all men are, Jasper loved his vessel – the house of his dreams; he lent to her something of Freya's soul. 5 Her deck was the foothold of their love. The possession of his brig appeased his passion in a soothing certitude of happiness already conquered.

The full moon was some way up, perfect and serene, floating in air as calm and limpid as the glance of Freya's eyes. There was not 10 a sound in the brig. "Here she shall stand, by my side, on evenings like this," he thought with rapture.

And it was at that moment; in this peace, in this serenity, under the full, benign gaze of the moon propitious to lovers, on a sea without a wrinkle, under a sky without a cloud, as if all nature 15 had assumed its most clement mood in a spirit of mockery, that the gunboat *Neptun*, detaching herself from the dark coast under which she had been lying invisible, steamed out to intercept the trading brig *Bonito* standing out to sea.

Directly the gunboat had been made out emerging from her 20 ambush Schultz of the fascinating voice had given signs of a strange agitation. All that day, ever since leaving the Malay town up the river, he had shown a haggard face, going about his duties like a man with something weighing on his mind. Jasper had noticed it, but the mate turning away, as though he had not liked being 25 looked at, had muttered shamefacedly of a headache and a touch of fever. He must have had it very badly when dodging behind his captain he wondered aloud: "What can that fellow want with us?" . . . A naked man standing in a freezing blast and trying not to shiver could not have spoken with a more miserably uncertain 30 intonation. But it might have been fever. A cold fit.

"He wants to make himself disagreeable, simply," said Jasper with perfect good humour. "He has tried it on with me before. However we shall soon see."

And indeed before long the two vessels lay abreast within easy 35 hail. The brig, with her fine lines and her white sails, looked vaporous and sylph-like in the moonlight; the gunboat short, squat, with her stumpy, dark spars naked like dead trees, raised against the luminous sky of that resplendent night, threw a heavy shadow on the lane of water between the two ships. 40

Freya haunted them both like an ubiquitous spirit and as if she were the only woman in the world. Jasper remembered her earnest recommendation to be guarded and cautious in all his acts and words while he was away from her. In this quite unfore-
5 seen encounter he felt on his ear the very breath of these hurried admonitions customary to the last moment of their partings, heard the half-jesting final whisper of the "Mind, kid! I'd never forgive you" with a quick pressure on his arm, which he answered by a quiet, confident smile. Heemskirk was haunted in another fash-
10 ion. There were no whispers in it. It was more like visions. He saw that girl hanging round the neck of a low vagabond – *that* vagabond; the vagabond who had just answered his hail. He saw her stealing barefooted across a verandah with great clear, wide open, eager eyes, to look at a brig – *that* brig. If she had shrieked,
15 scolded, called names! . . . But she had simply triumphed over him. That was all. Led on (he firmly believed it), fooled, deceived, outraged, struck, mocked at. . . . Beak and claws! The two men so differently haunted by Freya of the Seven Isles were not equally matched.
20 In the intense stillness, as of sleep, which had fallen upon the two vessels, in a world that itself seemed but a delicate dream, a boat pulled by Javanese sailors crossing the dark lane of water came alongside the brig. The white warrant officer in her, perhaps the gunner, climbed aboard. He was a short man with a rotund
25 stomach and a wheezy voice. His immovable fat face looked lifeless in the moonlight and he walked with his thick arms hanging away from his body as though he had been stuffed. His cunning little eyes glittered like bits of mica. He conveyed to Jasper, in broken English, a request to come on board the *Neptun.*
30 Jasper had not expected anything so unusual. But after a short reflexion he decided to show neither annoyance, nor even sur-prise. The river from which he had come had been politically disturbed for a couple of years and he was aware that his visits there were looked upon with some suspicion. But he did not mind
35 much the displeasure of the authorities so terrifying to old Nelson. He prepared to leave the brig, and Schultz followed him to the rail as if to say something, but in the end stood by in silence. Jasper getting over the side noticed his ghastly face. The eyes of the man who had found salvation in the brig from the effects of

his peculiar psychology looked at him with a dumb, beseeching expression.

"What's the matter?" Jasper asked.

"I wonder how this will end," said he of the beautiful voice which had even fascinated the steady Freya herself. But where was its charming timbre now? These words had sounded like a raven's croak.

"You are ill," said Jasper positively.

"I wish I were dead," was the startling statement uttered by Schultz talking to himself in the extremity of some mysterious trouble. Jasper gave him a keen glance but this was not the time to investigate the morbid outbreak of a feverish man. He did not look as though he were actually delirious, and that for the moment must suffice. Schultz made a dart forward.

"That fellow means harm," he said desperately. "He means harm to you Captain Allen, I feel it – and I . . . ." He choked with inexplicable emotion.

"All right Schultz. I won't give him an opening," Jasper cut him short and swung himself into the boat.

On board the *Neptun* Heemskirk standing straddle-legs, in the flood of moonlight, his inky shadow falling right across the quarter deck, made no sign at his approach; but secretly he felt something like the heave of the sea in his chest at the sight of that man. Jasper waited before him in silence.

Brought face to face in direct personal contact they fell at once into the manner of their casual meetings in old Nelson's bungalow. They ignored each other's existence: Heemskirk moodily, Jasper with a perfectly colourless quietness.

"What's going on in that river you've just come out of?" asked the lieutenant straight away.

"I know nothing of the troubles if you mean that," Jasper answered. "I've landed there half a cargo of rice for which I got nothing in exchange and went away. There's no trade there now; but they would have been starving in another week if I hadn't turned up."

"Meddling. English meddling. And suppose the rascals don't deserve anything better than to starve – eh?"

"There are women and children there, you know," observed Jasper in his even tone.

"Oh yes. When an Englishman talks of women and children you may be sure there's something fishy about the business. Your doings will have to be investigated."

They spoke in turn as though they had been disembodied spirits,
5 mere voices in empty air; for they looked at each other as if there had been nothing there or, at most, with as much recognition as one gives to an inanimate object and no more. But now a silence fell. Heemskirk had thought all at once: "She will tell *him* all about it. She will tell him while she hangs round his neck laughing" – and
10 the sudden desire to annihilate Jasper on the spot almost deprived him of his senses by its vehemence. He lost the power of speech, of vision. For a moment he absolutely couldn't see Jasper. But he heard him inquiring as of the world at large:

"Am I then to conclude that the brig is detained?"
15 Heemskirk made a recovery in a flush of malignant satisfaction: "She is. I am going to take her to Makassar in tow."

"The courts will have to decide on the legality of this," said Jasper aware that the matter was becoming serious, but with assumed indifference.
20 "Oh yes. The courts. Certainly. And as to you I shall keep you on board here."

Jasper's dismay at being parted from his ship was betrayed by a stony immobility. It lasted but an instant. Then he turned away and hailed the brig. Mr Schultz answered: "Yes sir."
25 "Get ready to receive a towrope from the gunboat. We are going to be taken to Makassar."

"Good God! What's that for sir?" came an anxious cry faintly.

"Kindness, I suppose," Jasper, ironical, shouted with great deliberation. "We might have been – becalmed in here – for days. And
30 hospitality. I am invited to stay – on board here."

The answer to this information was a loud ejaculation of distress. Jasper thought anxiously: "Why! the fellow's nerve's gone to pieces," and with an awakened uneasiness of a new sort looked intently at the brig. The thought that he was parted from her (for
35 the first time since they came together) shook the apparently careless fortitude of his character to its very foundations – which were deep. All that time neither Heemskirk nor even his inky shadow had stirred in the least.

"I am going to send a boat's crew and an officer on board
40 your vessel," he announced to no one in particular. Jasper, tearing

himself away from the absorbed contemplation of the brig, turned round and without passion, almost without expression in his voice, entered his protest against the whole of these proceedings. What he was thinking of was the delay. He counted the days. Makassar was actually on his way; and to be towed there really saved time. On the other hand there would be some vexing formalities to go through. But the thing was too absurd. "The beetle's gone mad," he thought. "I'll be released at once. And if not, Mesman must enter into a bond for me. . . ." Mesman was a Dutch merchant with whom Jasper had had many dealings: a considerable person in Makassar.

"You protest. H'm," Heemskirk muttered and for a little longer remained motionless, his legs planted well apart and his head lowered as though he were studying his own comical, deeply split shadow. Then he made a sign to the rotund gunner who had kept at hand, motionless like a vilely stuffed specimen of a fat man with a lifeless face and glittering little eyes. The fellow approached and stood at attention.

"You will board that brig with a boat's crew."

"Ya, Mynherr."

"You will have one of your men to steer her all the time," went on Heemskirk giving his orders in English, apparently for Jasper's edification. "You hear?"

"Ya, Mynherr."

"You will remain on deck and in charge all the time."

"Ya, Mynherr."

Jasper felt as if, together with the command of the brig, his very heart were being taken out of his breast. Heemskirk asked with a change of tone:

"What weapons have you on board?"

At one time all the ships trading in the China seas had a license to carry a certain quantity of firearms for purposes of defence. Jasper answered:

"Eighteen rifles with their bayonets which were on board when I bought her four years ago. They have been declared."

"Where are they kept?"

"Fore-cabin. Mate has the key."

"You will take possession of them," said Heemskirk to the gunner.

"Ya, Mynherr."

"What is this for? What do you mean to imply!" cried out Jasper, then bit his lip. "It's monstrous," he muttered.

Heemskirk raised for a moment a heavy, as if suffering, glance. "You may go," he said to his gunner. The fat man saluted and 5 departed.

During the next thirty hours the steady towing was interrupted once. At a signal from the brig made by waving a flag on the forecastle the gunboat was stopped. The badly stuffed specimen of a warrant officer getting into his boat arrived on board the 10 *Neptun* and hurried straight into his commander's cabin, his excitement at something he had to communicate being betrayed by the wild blinking of his small eyes. These two were closeted together for some time, while Jasper at the taffrail tried to make out if anything out of the common had occurred on board the brig. 15 But nothing seemed to be amiss on board. However he kept a look out for the gunner and, though he had avoided speaking to anybody since he had finished with Heemskirk, he stopped that man when he came out on deck again to ask how his mate was.

20 "He was feeling not very well when I left," he explained.

The fat warrant officer, holding himself as though the effort of carrying his big stomach in front of him demanded a rigid carriage, understood with difficulty. Not a single of his features showed the slightest animation but his little eyes blinked rapidly at last.

25 "O, ya! The mate. Ya! Ya! He is very well. . . . But, mine Gott! he is one very funny man."

Jasper could get no explanation of that remark because the Dutchman got into the boat hurriedly and went back on board the brig. But he consoled himself with the thought that very soon 30 all this unpleasant and rather absurd experience would be over. The roadstead of Makassar was in sight already. Heemskirk passed by him going on the bridge. For the first time the lieutenant looked at Jasper with marked intention; and the strange roll of his eyes was so funny (it had been long agreed by Jasper and Freya that the 35 lieutenant was funny), so extatically gratified as though he were rolling a tasty morsel on his tongue – that Jasper could not help a broad smile. And then he turned to his brig again.

To see her, his cherished possession animated by something of his Freya's soul, the only foothold of two united lives on the wide 40 earth, the security of his passion, the companion of adventure,

the power to snatch the calm, adorable Freya to his breast and
carry her off to the end of the world; to see this beautiful thing
embodying worthily his pride and his love – to see her captive at
the end of a towrope was not indeed a pleasant experience. It had
something nightmarish in it as for instance the dream of a wild   5
sea-bird loaded with chains.

Yet what else could he want to look at? Her beauty sometimes
came to his heart with the force of a spell so that he would forget
where he was. And, besides, that sense of superiority which the
certitude of being loved gives to a young man, that illusion of   10
being set above the Fates by a tender look in a woman's eyes,
helped him, the first shock over, to go through these experiences
with an amused self confidence. For what evil could touch the
elect of Freya?

It was now afternoon, the sun being behind the two vessels as   15
they headed for the harbour. "The beetle's little joke shall soon be
over," thought Jasper without any great animosity. As a seaman well
acquainted with that part of the world a casual glance was enough
to tell him what was being done. "Hallo!" he thought. "He is going
in through Spermonde Passage. We shall be rounding Tamissa   20
reef presently." And again he returned to the contemplation of
his brig, that mainstay of his material and emotional existence
which would be soon in his hands again. On a sea, calm like a mill
pond, a heavy, smooth ripple undulated and streamed away from
her bows, for the powerful *Neptun* was towing at a great speed as if   25
for a wager. The Dutch gunner appeared on the forecastle of the
Bonito and with him a couple of men. They stood looking at the
coast – and Jasper lost himself in a loverlike trance.

The deep-toned blast of the gunboat's steam whistle made him
shudder by its unexpectedness. Slowly he looked about, swift as   30
lightning he leaped from where he stood, bounding forward along
the deck.

"You will be on Tamissa reef!" he yelled with all the strength of
his lungs.

High up on the bridge Heemskirk looked back over his shoul-   35
der heavily; two seamen were spinning the wheel round, and the
Neptun was already swinging rapidly away from the edge of the
pale water over the danger. Ha! Just in time. Jasper turned about
instantly to watch his brig; and even before he realized that (in
obedience it appears to Heemskirk's orders given beforehand to   40

the gunner) the towrope had been let go at the blast of the whistle, before he had time to cry out or to move a limb, he saw her cast adrift and shooting across the gunboat's stern with the impetus of her speed. He followed her fine, gliding form with eyes growing
5 big with incredulity, wild with horror. The cries on board of her came to him only as a dreadful and confused murmur through the loud thumping of blood in his ears – while she held on. She ran upright in a terrible display of her gift of speed, with an incomparable air of life and grace; she ran on till the smooth level of
10 water in front of her bows seemed to sink down suddenly as if sucked away; and with a strange, violent tremor of her mastheads she stopped, inclined her lofty spars a little – and lay still. She lay still on the reef while the *Neptun* fetching a wide circle continued at full speed up Spermonde Passage heading for the town.
15 She lay still, perfectly still, with something ill-omened and unnatural in her attitude. In an instant the subtle melancholy of things touched by decay had fallen on her in the sunshine; she was but a speck in the brilliant emptiness of space, already lonely, already desolate.
20   "Hold him," yelled a voice from the bridge.
   Jasper had started to run to his brig with a headlong impulse as a man dashes forward to pull away with his hands a living, breathing, loved creature from the brink of destruction. "Hold him! Stick to him," vociferated the lieutenant at the top of the bridge ladder
25 while Jasper struggled madly without a word, only his head emerging from the heaving crowd of the *Neptun*'s seamen who had flung themselves upon him obediently. "Gott fer dam! Hold. . . . I would not have that fellow drown himself for anything now."
   Jasper ceased struggling.
30   One by one they let go hold of him; they fell back gradually farther and farther, in attentive silence; leaving him standing unsupported in a widened, clear space as if to give him plenty of room to fall after the struggle. He did not even sway perceptibly. Half an hour later, when the *Neptun* anchored in front of the town, he
35 had not stirred yet, had moved neither head nor limb by as much as a hair's breadth. Directly the rumble of the gunboat's cable had ceased Heemskirk came down heavily from the bridge.
   "Call a sampan," he said in a gloomy tone as he passed the sentry at the gangway and then moved on slowly towards the spot where
40 Jasper the object of many awed glances stood, looking at the deck,

as if lost in a brown study. Heemskirk came up close and stared at him thoughtfully with his fingers over his lips. Here he was, the favoured vagabond, the only man to whom that infernal girl was likely to tell the story. But he would not find it funny. The story how Lieutenant Heemskirk . . . . No he would not laugh at it. He looked as though he would never laugh at anything in his life.

Suddenly Jasper looked up. His eyes without any other expression but bewilderment met those of Heemskirk, observant and sombre.

"Gone on the reef!" he said in a low astounded tone. "On – the – reef," he repeated still lower and as if attending inwardly to the birth of some awful and amazing sensation.

"On the very top of high-water, spring tides," Heemskirk struck in with a vindictive, exulting violence which flashed and expired. He paused as if weary, fixing upon Jasper his arrogant eyes over which secret disenchantment, the unavoidable shadow of all passion, seemed to pass like a saddening cloud. "On the very top," he repeated, rousing himself in fierce reaction to snatch his laced cap off his head with a horizontal, derisive flourish towards the gangway: "And now you may go ashore to the courts you damned Englishman," he said.

VI

THE AFFAIR OF the brig *Bonito* was bound to cause a sensation in Makassar, the prettiest and perhaps the cleanest-looking of all the towns in the Islands, which however knows few occasions for excitement. The "front," with its special population, was soon aware that something had happened. A steamer towing a sailing vessel had been observed far out to sea for some time and when the steamer came in alone leaving the other outside, attention was aroused. Why was that? Her masts only could be seen – with furled sails – remaining in the same place to the southward. And soon the rumour ran all along the crowded sea-shore street that there was a ship on Tamissa reef. That crowd interpreted the appearance correctly. Its cause was beyond their penetration: for who could associate a girl 900 miles away with the stranding of a ship on Tamissa reef, or look for the remote filiation of that event in the psychology of at least three people; even if one of them,

Lieutenant Heemskirk, was at that very moment passing amongst
them on his way to make his verbal report. No, the minds on the
"front" were not competent for that sort of investigation; but many
hands there, brown hands, yellow hands, white hands were raised
5   to shade the eyes gazing out to sea. The rumour spread quickly.
Chinese shopkeepers came to their doors, more than one white
merchant, even, rose from his desk to go to the window. After all a
ship on Tamissa was not an everyday occurrence. And presently the
rumour took a more definite shape. An English trader – detained
10   on suspicion at sea by the *Neptun* – Heemskirk was towing him in
to test a case and by some strange accident . . .

Later on the name came out. "The *Bonito*. . . . What! Impossible. . . . Yes, yes the *Bonito*. Look. You can see from here. Only two
masts. It's a brig. . . . Didn't think that man would ever let himself
15   be caught. . . . Heemskirk's pretty smart too. . . . They say she's
fitted out in her cabin like a gentleman's yacht. . . . That Allen is
a sort of gentleman too. An extravagant beggar."

A young man entered smartly Messrs: Mesman Brothers' office
on the "front," bubbling with some further information. "Oh yes.
20   That's the *Bonito* for certain. But you don't know the story I've
heard just now. The fellow must have been feeding that river with
firearms for the last year or two. Well, it seems he has grown so
reckless from long impunity that he has actually dared to sell the
very ship's rifles this time. It's a fact. The rifles are not on board.
25   What impudence! Only he didn't know that there was one of our
warships on the coast. But those Englishmen are so impudent that
perhaps he thought that nothing would be done to him for it. Our
courts do let off these fellows too often on some miserable excuse
or other. But at any rate there's an end of the famous *Bonito*. I have
30   just heard in the harbour office that she must have gone on at the
very top of high-water – and she is in ballast too. No human power,
they think, can move her from where she sits. I only hope it is so.
It would be fine to have the notorious *Bonito* stuck up there as a
warning to others."
35   Mr J. Mesman, a colonial-born Dutchman, a kind, paternal old
fellow with a clean-shaven, quiet, handsome face and a head of
fine, iron-grey hair curling a little on his collar, did not say a word
in defence of Jasper and the *Bonito*. He rose from his armchair
suddenly. His face was visibly troubled. It had so happened that
40   once, from a business talk of ways and means, island trade, money

matters and so on, Jasper had been led to open himself to him on
the subject of Freya; and the excellent man who had known old
Nelson years before and even remembered something of Freya
was much astonished and amused by the unfolding of the tale.
Well, well, well! Nelson! Yes – of course. A very honest sort of man. 5
There was a little child with very fair hair! Oh yes. He had a distinct recollection. And so she has grown into such a fine girl, so
very determined, so very. . . . And he laughed almost boisterously:
"Mind, when you have happily eloped with your future wife Captain Allen you must come along this way and we shall welcome her 10
here. . . . A little fair-headed child! I remember. I remember."

It was that inner knowledge which had brought trouble to his
face at the first news of the wreck. He took up his hat.

"Where are you going Mr Mesman?"

"I am going to look for Allen. I think he must be ashore. Does 15
anybody know?"

No one of those present knew. And Mr Mesman went out on
the "front" to make inquiries.

The other part of the town, the part near the church and the
Fort, got its information in another way. The first thing disclosed 20
to it was Jasper himself walking rapidly as though he were pursued.
And, as a matter of fact, a Chinaman, obviously a sampan man, was
following him at the same headlong pace. Suddenly while passing
the Oranje House Jasper swerved and went in or rather rushed
in, startling Gomez, the hotel-clerk, very much. But a Chinaman 25
beginning to make an unseemly noise at the door claimed the
immediate attention of Gomez. His grievance was that the white
man whom he brought on shore from the gunboat had not paid
him his boatfare. He had pursued him so far, asking for it all the
way. But the white man had taken no notice whatever of his just 30
claim. Gomez satisfied the coolie with a few coppers and then went
to look for Jasper whom he knew very well. He found him standing
stiffly by a little round table. At the other end of the verandah a
few men sitting there had stopped talking and were looking at him
in silence. Two billiard-players with cues in their hands had come 35
to the door of the billiard-room and stared too.

On Gomez coming up to him Jasper raised one hand to point
at his own throat. Gomez noted the somewhat soiled state of his
white clothes, then took one look at his face and fled away to order
the drink for which Jasper seemed to be asking. 40

Where he wanted to go – for what purpose – where he perhaps only imagined himself to be going, when a sudden impulse or the sight of a familiar place had made him turn into Oranje House – it is impossible to say. He was steadying himself lightly with the
5 tips of his fingers on the little table. There were on that verandah two men whom he knew well personally, but his gaze roaming incessantly as though he were looking for a way of escape passed and repassed over them without a sign of recognition. They on their side, looking at him, doubted the evidence of their own eyes.
10 It was not that his face was distorted. On the contrary; it was still; it was set. But its expression somehow was unrecognisable. Can that be Allen? they wondered, with awe.

In his head there was a wild chaos of clear thoughts. Perfectly clear. It was this clearness which was so terrible in conjunction
15 with the utter inability to lay hold of any single one of them all. He was saying to himself – or to them: "Steady, steady." A China boy appeared before him with a glass on a tray. He poured the drink down his throat and rushed out. His disappearance removed the spell of wonder from the beholders. One of the men jumped up
20 and moved quickly to that side of the verandah from which almost the whole of the roadstead could be seen. At the very moment when Jasper, issuing from the door of the Oranje House, was passing under him in the street below, he cried to the others excitedly.

"That was Allen right enough. But where is his brig?"
25 Jasper heard these words with extraordinary loudness. The heavens rang with them, as if calling him to account; for those were the very words Freya would have to use. It was an annihilating question; it struck his consciousness like a thunderbolt and brought a sudden night upon the chaos of his thoughts even as he walked. He
30 did not check his pace. He went on in the darkness for another three strides – and then fell.

The good Mesman had to push as far as the hospital before he found him. The doctor there talked of a slight heat-stroke. Nothing very much. Out in three days. . . . It must be admitted
35 that the doctor was right. In three days Jasper Allen came out of the hospital and became visible to the town – very visible indeed – and remained so for quite a long time; long enough to become almost one of the sights of the place; long enough to become disregarded at last; long enough for the tale of his haunting visibility to be
40 remembered in the Islands to this day.

The talk on the "front" and Jasper's appearance in the Oranje
House stand at the beginning of the famous *Bonito* case and give
a view of its two aspects – the practical and the psychological. The
case for the courts and the case for compassion; that last terribly
evident and yet obscure.   5

It has, you must understand, remained obscure even for that
friend of mine who wrote me the letter mentioned in the very
first lines of this narrative. He was one of those in Mr Mesman's
office and accompanied that gentleman in his search for Jasper.
His letter described to me the two aspects and some of the episodes   10
of the case. Heemskirk's attitude was that of deep thankfulness for
not having lost his own ship, and that was all. Haze over the land
was his explanation of having got so close to Tamissa reef. He saved
his ship; and for the rest he did not care. As to the fat gunner he
deposed simply that he thought at the time that he was acting for   15
the best by letting go the towrope, but admitted that he was greatly
confused by the suddenness of the emergency.

As a matter of fact he had acted on very precise instructions from
Heemskirk to whom through several years' service together in the
East he had become a sort of devoted henchman. What was most   20
amazing in the detention of the *Bonito* was his story how, proceeding to take possession of the firearms, as ordered, he discovered
that there were no firearms on board. All he found in the fore-
cabin was an empty rack for the proper number of eighteen rifles;
but of the rifles themselves never a single one – anywhere in the   25
ship. The mate of the brig, who looked rather ill and behaved excitedly as though he were perhaps a lunatic, wanted him to believe
that Captain Allen knew nothing of this; that it was he, the mate,
who had secretly sold these rifles in the dead of night to a certain
person up the river. In proof of this story he produced a bag of   30
silver dollars and pressed it on his, the gunner's, acceptance. Then
suddenly flinging it down on the deck he beat his own head with
both his fists and started heaping shocking curses upon his own
soul for an ungrateful wretch not fit to live.

All this the gunner reported at once to his commanding officer.   35

What Heemskirk intended by taking upon himself to detain the
Bonito it is difficult to say; except that he meant to bring some
trouble into the life of the man favoured by Freya. He had been
looking at Jasper with a desire to strike that man of kisses and
embraces to the earth. The question was how could he do it without   40

giving himself away? But the report of the gunner created a serious case enough. Yet Allen had friends – and who could tell whether he wouldn't somehow succeed in wriggling out of it. The idea of simply towing the brig so much compromised on to the reef came
5   to him while he was listening to the fat gunner in his cabin. There was but little risk of being disapproved now. And it should be made to appear an accident.

Going out on deck he had gloated upon his unconscious victim with such a sinister roll of his eyes, such a queerly pursed mouth
10 that Jasper could not help smiling. And the lieutenant had gone on the bridge saying to himself: "You wait! I shall spoil the taste of these sweet kisses for you. What tale you hear of Lieutenant Heemskirk in the future that name won't bring a smile on your lips, I swear. You are delivered into my hands."

15 And this possibility had come about without planning, one could almost say naturally, as if events had mysteriously shaped themselves to fit the purposes of a dark passion. The most astute scheming could not have served Heemskirk better. It was given to him to taste a transcendental, an incredible perfection of
20 vengeance: to strike a deadly blow into that hated man's heart and to watch him afterwards walking about with the dagger in his breast.

For that is what the state of Jasper amounted to. He moved, acted, weary-eyed, keen-faced, lank and restless with brusque
25 movements and fierce gestures; he talked incessantly in a frenzied and fatigued voice; but within himself he knew that nothing would ever give him back the brig, just as nothing can heal a pierced heart. His soul kept quiet in the stress of love by the unflinching Freya's influence was like a still but overwound string. The shock
30 had started it vibrating and the string had snapped. He had waited for two years in a perfectly intoxicated confidence for a day that now would never come to a man disarmed for life by the loss of the brig, and, it seemed to him, made unfit for love to which he had no foothold to offer.

35 Day after day he would traverse the length of the town, follow the coast, and, reaching the point of land opposite that part of the reef on which his brig lay stranded, look steadily across the water at her beloved form, once the home of an exulting hope and now, in her inclined desolated immobility towering above the lonely
40 sea horizon, a symbol of despair.

The crew had left her in due course in her own boats which directly they reached the town were sequestrated by the harbour authorities. The vessel too was sequestrated pending proceedings; but these same authorities did not take the trouble to set a guard on board. For indeed what could move her from there. Nothing unless a miracle; nothing unless Jasper's eyes fastened on her tensely for hours together as though he hoped, by the mere power of vision, to draw her to his breast.

All this story read in my friend's very chatty letter dismayed me not a little. But it was really appalling to read his relation of how Schultz the mate went about everywhere affirming with desperate pertinacity that it was he and he alone who had sold the rifles. "I stole them," he protested. Of course no one would believe him. My friend himself did not believe him; though he of course admired this self sacrifice. But a good many people thought that it was going too far to make oneself out a thief for the sake of a friend. Only it was such an obvious lie too that it did not matter perhaps.

I who, in view of Schultz's psychology, knew how true that must be, admit that I was appalled. So this was how a perfidious destiny took advantage of a generous impulse! And I felt as though I were an accomplice in this perfidy, since I did to a certain extent encourage Jasper. Yet I had warned him as well.

"The man seems to have gone crazy on this point," wrote my friend. "He went to Mesman with his story. He says that some rascally white man living amongst the natives up that river made him drunk with some gin one evening and then jeered at him for never having any money. Then he, protesting to us that he was an honest man and must be believed, described himself as being a thief whenever he took a drop too much, and told us that he went on board and passed the rifles one by one without the slightest compunction to a canoe which came alongside that night, receiving ten dollars a piece for them.

"Next day he was ill with shame and grief but had not the courage to confess his lapse to his benefactor. When the gunboat stopped the brig he felt ready to die with the apprehension of the consequences, and would have died happily, if he could have been able to bring the rifles back by the sacrifice of his life. He said nothing to Jasper hoping that the brig would be released presently. When it turned out otherwise and his captain was detained on board the gunboat, he was ready to commit suicide from despair; only he

thought it his duty to live in order to let the truth be known. 'I am an honest man! I am an honest man,' he repeated in a voice that brought tears to our eyes. 'You must believe me when I tell you that I am a thief – a vile, low, cunning, sneaking thief as soon as
5 I've had a glass or two. Take me somewhere where I may tell the truth on oath.'

"When we had at last convinced him that his story could be of no use to Jasper – for what Dutch court having once got hold of an English trader would accept such an explanation; and indeed
10 how, when, where could one hope to find proofs of such a tale – he made as if to tear his hair in handfuls; but calming down said 'Good bye then gentlemen' and went out of the room so crushed that he seemed hardly able to put one foot before the other. That very night he committed suicide by cutting his throat in the house of a
15 half-caste with whom he had been lodging since he came ashore from the wreck." That throat! I thought with a shudder, which could produce the tender, persuasive, manly but fascinating voice which had aroused Jasper's ready compassion and had secured Freya's sympathy! Who could have ever supposed such an end
20 in store for the impossible, gentle Schultz with his idiosyncrasy of naïve pilfering, so absurdly straightforward that, even in the people who had suffered from it, it aroused nothing more than a sort of amused exasperation. He was really impossible. His lot evidently should have been a half-starved, mysterious, but by no
25 means tragic, existence as a mild-eyed, inoffensive beachcomber on the fringe of native life. There are occasions when that irony of fate, which some people profess to discover in the working out of our lives, wears the aspect of crude and savage jesting. I shook my head over the manes of Schultz and went on with my friend's
30 letter. It told me how the brig on the reef, looted by the natives from the coast villages, acquired gradually the lamentable aspect, the grey ghostliness of a wreck; while Jasper fading daily into a mere shadow of a man strode brusquely all along the "front," with horribly lively eyes and a faint, fixed smile on his lips, to spend the
35 day on a lonely spit of sand looking eagerly at her, as though he had expected some shape on board to rise up and make some sort of sign to him over the decaying bulwarks. The Mesmans were taking care of him as far as it was possible. The "*Bonito* case" had been referred to Batavia where no doubt it would fade away in a fog of
40 official papers. . . . It was heartrending to read all this. . . . That

active and zealous officer, Lieutenant Heemskirk, his air of sullen, darkly pained self-importance not lightened by the approval of his action conveyed to him unofficially, had gone on to take up his station in the Molluccas. . . .

Then, at the end of the bulky, kindly meant, epistle, dealing with the Island news of half a year at least, my friend wrote: "A couple of months ago old Nelson turned up here – arriving by the mail-boat from Java. Came to see Mesman it seems. A rather mysterious visit and extraordinarily short, after coming all that way. He stayed just four days at the Oranje House with apparently nothing in particular to do, and then caught the south-going steamer for the Straits. I remember people saying at one time that Allen was rather sweet on old Nelson's daughter, the girl that was brought up by Mrs Harley and then went to live with him at the Seven-Isles group. Surely you remember old Nelson. . . ."

Remember old Nelson! Rather! The letter went on to inform me further that old Nelson, at least, remembered me, since some time after his flying visit to Makassar he had written to the Mesmans asking for my address in London!

That old Nelson (or Nielsen), the note of whose personality was a profound, echoless irresponsiveness to everything around him, should wish to write, or find anything to write about to any-body, was in itself a cause for no small wonder. And to me too of all people! I waited with uneasy impatience for whatever disclo-sure could come from that naturally benighted intelligence; but my impatience had time to wear itself out before my eyes beheld old Nelson's trembling, painfully formed, handwriting, senile and childish at the same time, on an envelope bearing a penny stamp and the postal mark of the Notting Hill office. I delayed opening it in order to pay the tribute of astonishment due to the event by flinging my hands above my head. So he had come home to England – to be definitely Nelson; or else was on his way home to Denmark where he would revert for ever to his original Nielsen! But old Nelson (or Nielsen) out of the tropics seemed unthink-able. And yet he was there. Asking me to call.

His address was at a boarding house in one of these Bayswater squares, once of leisure, which nowadays are reduced to earning their living. Somebody had recommended him there. I started to call on him on one of these January days in London, one of those winter days composed of the four devilish elements: cold, wet,

mud and grime, combined with a particular stickiness of atmosphere that clings like an unclean garment to one's very soul. Yet
on approaching his abode I saw, like a flicker far behind the soiled
veil of the four elements, the wearisome and splendid glitter of a
5 blue sea with the Seven Islets like minute specks swimming in my
eye, and the high red roof of the bungalow crowning the very
smallest of them all. This visual reminiscence was profoundly disturbing. I knocked at the door with a faltering hand.

    Old Nelson (or Nielsen) got up from the table at which he was
10 sitting with a shabby pocket-book full of papers before him. He
took off his spectacles before shaking hands. For a moment neither
of us said a word; then noticing me looking round, somewhat
expectantly, he murmured some words of which I caught only
"daughter" and "Hong-Kong," cast his eyes down and sighed.

15   His moustache sticking all ways out, as of yore, was quite white
now. His old cheeks were softly rounded, with some colour in
them; strangely enough that something childlike always noticeable
in the general contour of his physiognomy had become much
more marked. Like his handwriting he looked childish and senile.
20 He showed his age most in his unintelligently furrowed, anxious,
forehead and in his round, innocent eyes which appeared to me
weak, blinking and watery – or was it that they were full of tears? . . .

    To discover old Nelson fully informed upon any matter whatever
was a new experience. And after the first awkwardness had worn off
25 he talked freely with, now and then, a question to start him going
whenever he lapsed into silence; which he would do suddenly
clasping his hands on his waistcoat in an attitude which would
recall to me the east verandah of the bungalow where he used to
sit talking quietly and puffing out his cheeks in what seemed now
30 old, very old days. He talked in a reasonable, somewhat anxious
tone.

    "No, no. We did not know anything for weeks. Out of the way like
that, we couldn't – of course. No mail service to the Seven Isles. But
one day I ran over to Banka in my big sailing boat to see whether
35 there were any letters and saw a Dutch paper. But it looked only
like a bit of marine news: English brig *Bonito* gone ashore outside
Makassar roads. That was all. I took the paper home with me and
showed it to her. 'I will never forgive him,' she cries with her old
spirit. 'My dear,' I said, 'you are a sensible girl. The best man may
40 lose a ship. But what about your health?' I was beginning to be

frightened at her looks. She would not let me talk even of going
to Singapore before. But, really, such a sensible girl couldn't keep
on objecting for ever. 'Do what you like Papa,' she says. Rather
a job that. Had to catch a steamer at sea, but I got her over all
right. There, doctors of course. Fever. Anæmia. Put her to bed.   5
Two or three women very kind to her. Naturally in our papers the
whole story came out before long. She reads it to the end lying
on the couch, then hands the newspaper back to me, whispers
'Heemskirk' and goes off into a faint."

He blinked at me for quite a long time his eyes running full of   10
tears again.

"Next day," he began without any emotion in his voice, "she felt
stronger and we had a long talk. She told me everything."

Here old Nelson with his eyes cast down gave me the whole
story of the Heemskirk episode in Freya's words, then went on in   15
his rather jerky utterance and looking up innocently.

"'My dear,' I said, 'you have behaved in the main like a sensible
girl.' . . . . 'I have been horrid,' she cries, 'and he is breaking his
heart over there.' Well she was too sensible not to see she wasn't
in a state to travel. But I went. She told me to go. She was being   20
looked after very well. Anæmia. Getting better – they said."

He paused.

"You did see him," I murmured.

"Oh yes, I did see him," he started again talking in that reasonable voice as though he were arguing a point. "I did see him. I   25
came upon him. Eyes sunk an inch into his head, nothing but skin
on the bones of his face, a skeleton in dirty white clothes that's
what he looked like. How Freya . . . . But she never did. Not really.
He was sitting there the only live thing for miles along that coast,
on a drift-log washed up on the shore. They had clipped his hair   30
in the hospital and it had not grown again. He stared holding his
chin in his hand with nothing on the sea between him and the sky
but that wreck. When I came up to him he just moved his head a
bit. 'Is that you old man,' says he. . . . Like that.

"If you had seen him you would have understood at once how   35
impossible it was for Freya to have ever loved that man. Well.
Well. I don't say. She might have – something. She was lonely,
you know. But really to go away with him! Never. Madness. She
was too sensible! I began to reproach him gently. And by and by
he turns on me. 'Write to you! What about? Come to her! What   40

with? If I had been a man I would have carried her off – but she made a child – a happy child of me. Tell her that the day the only thing I had belonging to me in the world perished on this reef I discovered that I had no power over her. . . . Has she come here
5 with you?' he shouts, blazing at me suddenly with his hollow eyes. I shook my head. Come with me indeed. Anæmia.

"'Aha! You see? Go away then old man and leave me alone here with that ghost,' he says jerking his head at the wreck of his brig.

"Mad. It was getting dusk. I did not care to stop any longer all
10 by myself with that man in that lonely place. I was not going to tell him of Freya's illness. Anæmia. What was the good. Mad. And what sort of husband would he have made, anyhow, for a sensible girl, like Freya? Why! Even my little property I could not have left them. The Dutch authorities would never have allowed an Englishman
15 to settle there. It was not sold then. My man Mahmat, you know, was looking after it for me. Later on I let it go for a tenth of its value to a Dutch half-caste. But never mind. It was nothing to me then. Yes, I went away from him. I caught the return mail-boat. I told everything to Freya. 'He's mad,' I said, 'and my dear the only
20 thing he loved was his brig.'"

"'Perhaps,' she says to herself, looking straight away – her eyes were nearly as hollow as his – 'perhaps it is true. Yes! I would never allow him any power over me.'"

Old Nelson paused. I sat fascinated, and feeling a little cold in
25 that room with a blazing fire.

"So you see," he continued, "she never really cared for him. Much too sensible. I took her away to Hong-Kong. Change of climate they said. Oh! these doctors! My God! Winter time! There came ten days of cold mist and wind and rain. Pneumonia. . . . But
30 look here! We talked a lot together. Days and evenings. Who else had she? . . . She talked a lot to me – my own girl. Sometimes she would laugh a little. Look at me and laugh a little. . . ."

I shuddered. He looked up vaguely with a strange, childish, puzzled moodiness.

35 "She would say 'I did not really mean to be a bad daughter to you Papa.' And I would say 'Of course my dear. You could not have meant it.' She would lie quiet and then say 'I wonder.' And sometimes 'I've been really a coward' she would tell me. You know sick people they say things. And so she would say too 'I've been
40 conceited, headstrong, capricious. I sought my own gratification.

I was selfish or afraid. . . .' But sick people – you know they say anything. And once after lying silent almost all day she said: 'Yes, perhaps, when the day came I would not have gone. Perhaps! I don't know,' she cries. 'Draw the curtain Papa. Shut the sea out. It reproaches me with my folly.'" He gasped and paused.   5

"So you see," he went on in a murmur. "Very ill, very ill indeed. Pneumonia. Very sudden." He pointed his finger at the carpet while the thought of the poor girl vanquished in her struggle with three men's absurdities, and coming at last to doubt her own self, held me mute in a very anguish of pity.   10

"You see yourself," he began again in a downcast manner. "She could not have really . . . . She mentioned you by name several times. Good friend. Sensible man. So I wanted to tell you myself – let you know the truth. A fellow like that! How could it be? She was lonely. And perhaps for a while . . . . Mere nothing. There could   15
never have been a question of love for my Freya – such a sensible girl. . . ."

"Man!" I cried rising upon him wrathfully. "Don't you see that she died of it."

He got up too. "No! No!" he stammered as if angry. "The doctors.   20
Pneumonia. Low state. The inflammation of the . . . . They told me. Pneu . . ."

He did not finish the word. It ended in a sob. He flung his arms out in a gesture of despair, giving up his ghastly pretence with a low, heartrending cry: 25

"And I thought that she was so sensible!"

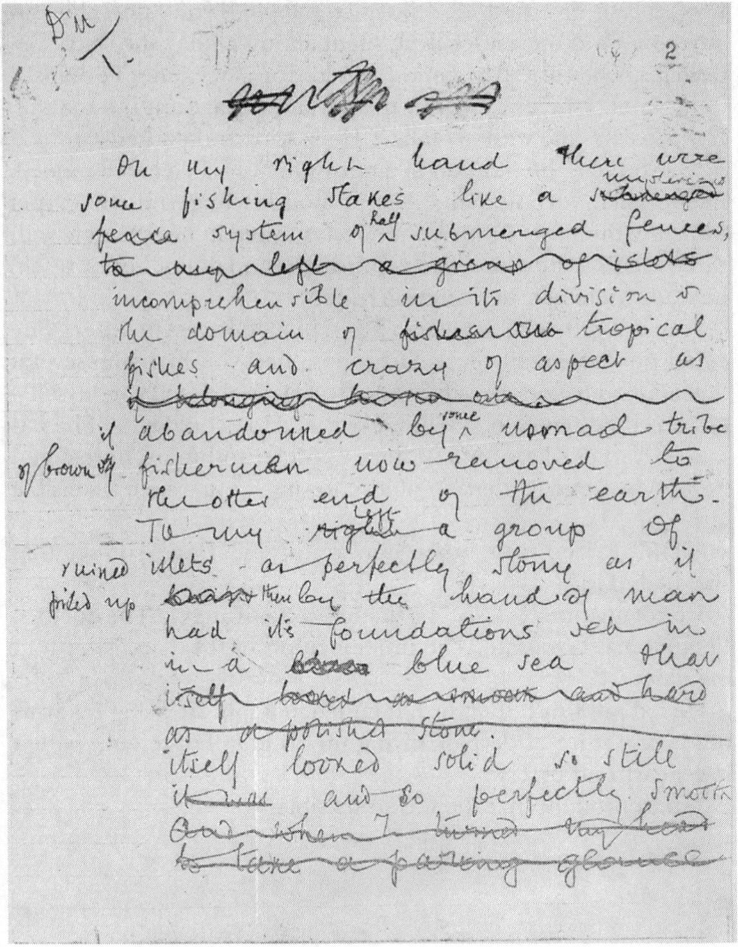
On my right hand there were
some fishing stakes like a mysterious [illegible]
fence system of half submerged fences,
[illegible]
incomprehensible in its division of
the domain of [illegible] tropical
fishes and crazy of aspect as
[illegible]
if abandoned by some nomad tribe
of brown fishermen now removed to
the other end of the earth.
To my left a group of
ruined islets as perfectly stony as if
piled up then by the hand of man
had its foundations set in
in a [illegible] blue sea that
[illegible]
itself looked solid so still
and so perfectly smooth
[illegible]

[1] Manuscript of 'The Secret Sharer', page 1.

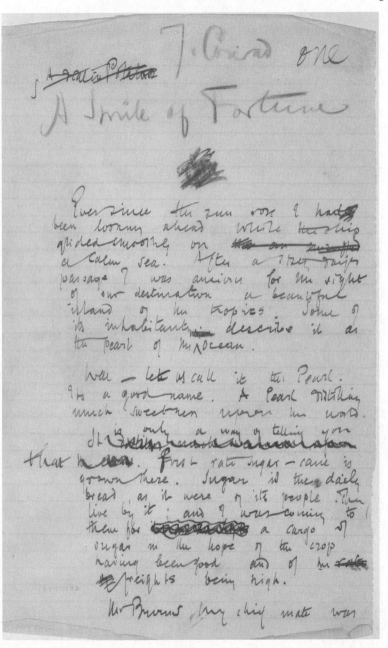

[2] Manuscript of 'A Smile of Fortune', page 1.

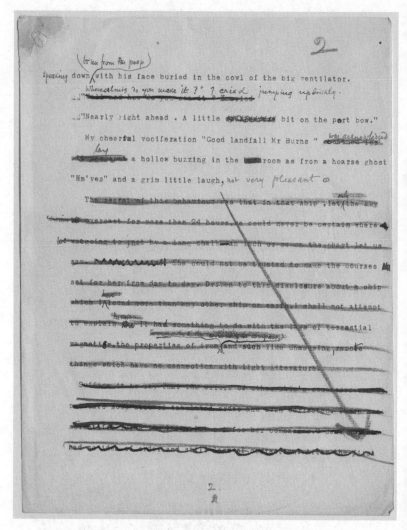

[3] First typescript of 'A Smile of Fortune', page 2.

THE SMILE OF FORTUNE

A Harbour Story.

By

J. Conrad.

The sun was no more than half-an-hour above the sea-
horizon; I had just gone below after spending the best part of
the night on deck; but before I had time to arrange my aching
legs comfortably on the couch a metallic, buzzing voice filled
my cabin mysteriously with the glad tidings:-

- "I see the land now, sir."

It was the voice of Mr. Charles Burns my chief-
officer speaking down to me from the poop with his face buried
in the cowl of the big ventilator.

"Whereabouts do you make it?" I cried jumping up
briskly.

"Nearly right ahead. A little bit on the port bow."

My cheerful vociferation "Good landfall, Mr Burns,"
was acknowledged by a hollow buzzing in the room as from a
hoarse ghost "Hm'yes" and a grim little laugh, not very pleasant.

[4] Second typescript of 'A Smile of Fortune', page 1.

"NICE LITTLE TALE FOR A QUIET TEA-PARTY," HE CONCLUDED

[5] Plate 1 for *Harper's* 'The Secret-Sharer'.

I SAW THE STEWARD TALKING TO THEM EAGERLY

[6] Plate 2 for *Harper's* 'The Secret-Sharer'.

THE STEWARD BROUGHT IN A TRAY AND GLASSES

[7] Plate 3 for *Harper's* 'The Secret-Sharer'.

ON THE VERY LADDER HE LINGERED

[8] Plate 4 for *Harper's* 'The Secret-Sharer'.

649

THE LONDON MAGAZINE COMPLETE NOVEL

FREYA OF THE SEVEN ISLES

By

JOSEPH CONRAD

Author of " The Nigger of the ' Narcissus,'" " Lord Jim," &c., &c.

TO CAPTAIN C. M. MARRIS, FORMERLY
MASTER AND OWNER OF THE *Araby
Maid*, ARCHIPELAGO TRADER, IN
MEMORY OF OLD DAYS.

JULY, 1912.

[9] Section title-page of *London Magazine*'s 'Freya of the Seven Isles'.

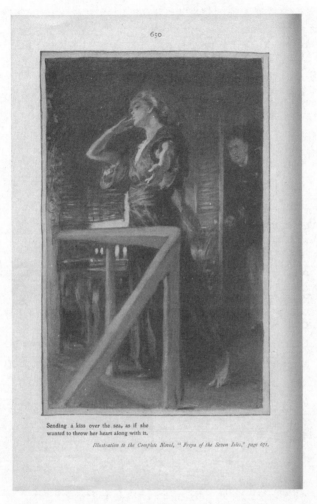

Sending a kiss over the sea, as if she
wanted to throw her heart along with it.

Illustration to the Complete Novel, " Freya of the Seven Isles," page 671.

[10] Illustration for *London Magazine*'s 'Freya of the Seven Isles'.

FREYA of the SEVEN ISLES

By
JOSEPH
CONRAD

ILLUSTRATED
BY
CLIFFORD
W. ASHLEY

FREYA NELSON (or Nielsen) was the kind of girl one remembers. The oval of her face was perfect; but within that fascinating frame the most happy disposition of line and feature, with an admirable complexion, gave an impression of health, strength and what I might call unconscious self-confidence—a most pleasant and, as it were, whimsical determination. I will not compare her eyes to violets because the real shade of their color was peculiar, not so dark but quite as deep. They were of the wide-open kind and looked at one frankly in every mood. I never did see the long, dark eyelashes lowered—I daresay Jasper Allen did, being a privileged person, but I have no doubt that the expression must have been charming in a complex way. She could—Jasper told me once with a touchingly imbecile exultation—sit on her hair. I daresay, It was not for me to behold these wonders; I was content to admire the neat and becoming way she used to do it up so as not to conceal the good shape of her head. And this wealth of hair was so glossy that when the screens of the west veranda were down, making a pleasant twilight there, or in the shade of the grove of fruit-trees near the house it seemed to give out a golden light of its own.

She dressed generally in a white frock with a skirt of walking length showing her neat, laced, brown boots. If there was any color about her costume it was just a bit of pale blue perhaps. No exertion seemed to distress her. I have seen her land from the dinghy after a long pull in the sun (she rowed herself about a good deal) with no quickened breath and not a single hair out of its place. In the morning when she came out on the veranda for the first look westward, Sumatra way, over the sea, she seemed as fresh and sparkling as a dew-drop. But a dew-drop is evanescent and there was nothing evanescent about Freya. I remember her round, solid arms with the fine wrists and her broad capable hands with tapering fingers.

I don't know whether she was actually born at sea; but I do know that up to twelve years of age she sailed about with her parents in various ships. After old Nelson lost his wife it became a matter of serious concern for him what to do with the girl. A kind lady in Singapore touched by his unassuming grief and deplorable perplexity, offered to take charge of Freya. This arrangement lasted some six years during which old Nelson "retired" and established himself on his island; and then it was settled (the kind lady going away to Europe for a long visit) that his daughter should join him.

As the first and most important preparation for that event the old fellow ordered from his Singapore agent a Steyn and Ebhart's "upright grand." I was then commanding a little steamer in the island trade and it fell to my lot to take it out to him. The volume of sound it gave out in that bungalow (which acted as a sounding board) was really astonishing. It thundered sweetly right over the sea. Jasper Allen told me that early of a morning on the deck of the *Bonito* (his wonderfully fast and pretty brig) he could hear Freya playing her scales quite distinctly. But the fellow always anchored foolishly close to the point, as I told him more than once. Of course these seas are almost uniformly serene and the Seven Isles is a particularly calm and cloudless spot as a rule. But still, now and again, the usual afternoon thunderstorm over Banka, or even one of those vicious, thick squalls from the distant Sumatra coast, would make a sudden sally upon the group, enveloping it for a couple of hours in whirlwinds and bluish-black murk of a particularly sinister. Then with the lowered rattan-screens desperately rattling in the wind and the bungalow shaking all over, Freya would sit down to the piano and play fierce Wagner music in the flicker of blinding flashes with thunder bolts falling all round, enough to make your hair stand on end; and Jasper would remain rock-still on the veranda, adoring the back-view of her supple, swaying figure, the miraculous sheen of her fair head, the rapid hands on the keys, the white nape of her neck—while the brig, down at the point there, surged at her cables within two hundred yards of nasty, shiny, black rock-heads ... Ugh!

And this, if you please, for no reason than that, when he went on board at night and had his head on the pillow, he should feel that he was as near as he could conveniently get to his Freya slumbering in the bungalow. Did you ever? And mind, this brig was the home to be—their home—the floating paradise that he was gradually fitting out like a yacht to sail his life blissfully away in, with Freya. Imbecile! But the fellow was always taking chances.

One day, I remember, I was standing with Freya on the veranda watching the brig approaching the point from the northward. I suppose Jasper made the girl out with his long glass. What does he do? Instead of standing on for another mile and a half along the shoals and then tacking for the anchorage in a proper and seamanlike manner, he spies a gap between two disgusting old jagged reefs, puts the helm down suddenly and shoots the brig through, with all the sails shaking and rattling, so that we could hear the racket on the veranda. I drew my breath through my teeth, I can tell you—and Freya swore. Yes! She clenched her capable fists and stamped with her pretty brown boot and said "damn!" Then looking at me with a little heightened color—not much—she remarked, "I forgot you were there," and laughed.

"Isn't he a fool?" I said with feeling.

"Perfect idiot," she agreed warmly, looking at me straight with her wide-open, earnest eyes and the dimple of a smile on her cheek.

"And that," I pointed out to her, "just to save twenty minutes or so in meeting you."

We heard the anchor go down and then she became very resolute and threatening.

"Wait a bit. I'll teach him."

She went into her room and shut the door, leaving me alone on the veranda with my instructions. Long before the brig's sails were furled Jasper came up three steps at a time, forgetting to say how d'ye do, and looking right and left eagerly.

"Where's Freya? Wasn't she here just now?"

When I explained to him that he was to be deprived of Miss Freya's presence for a whole hour, just to teach him, he said I had put her up to it no doubt, and that he feared he would have yet to shoot me some day. We two were getting too thick altogether. Then he flung himself onto a chair and tried to talk to me about his trip. But the funny thing was that the fellow actually suffered! I could see it! His voice failed him and he sat there dumb, looking at the door with the face of a man in pain. Fact! On my word. And the next still funnier thing was that the girl calmly walked out of her room in less than ten minutes. And then I left. I mean to say that I went away to seek old Nelson on the back veranda, which was more of his own special nook in the distribution of that house, with the kind purpose of engaging him in conversation lest he should start roaming about and intrude unwittingly where he was not wanted just then.

He knew that the brig had arrived though he did not know that Jasper was already in the house. I suppose he didn't think it was possible. A father naturally wouldn't. He couldn't ignore that Allen was sweet on his girl; the fowls of the air and the fishes in the sea, most of the traders in the Archipelago had all sorts and conditions of men in the town of Singapore were aware of it. But he was not capable of appreciating how far the girl was gone on the fellow. He had an idea that Freya was too sensible ever to be gone on anybody—I mean to an unmanageable extent. No. It was not that which made him sit on the back veranda and worry himself in his unassuming manner during Jasper's visits. What he worried about was the Dutch "authorities." For it is a fact that the Dutch looked askance at the doings of Jasper Allen, owner and master of the brig *Bonito*. They considered him much too enterprising in his trading. I don't know that he ever did anything illegal; but it seems to me that his immense activity was repulsive to their stolid character and slow going methods. Anyway in old Nelson's opinion the captain of the *Bonito* was a smart man, and a nice young man, but not a desirable acquaintance on the whole. Somewhat compromising—you understand.

On this occasion I am speaking of, old Nelson was even fretty; for while I was trying to entertain him with a very funny and somewhat scandalous adventure which happened to a certain acquaintance of ours in Saigon, he exclaimed suddenly:

"What the devil he wants to turn up here for!"

Clearly he had not heard a word of the anecdote. And this annoyed me because the anecdote was really good. I stared at him.

"Come, come," I cried, "don't you know what Jasper Allen is turning up here for?"

This was the first open allusion I had ever made to the true state of affairs between Jasper and his daughter. He took it very calmly.

"Oh! Freya is a sensible girl," he murmured absently, his mind's eye obviously fixed on the authorities. No, Freya was no fool. He was not concerned about that. He didn't mind it in the least. The fellow was just company for her; he amused the girl. That was all right.

When the perspicacious old chap left off mumbling, all was still in the house. The other two were amusing themselves very quietly and no doubt very heartily. What more absorbing and less noisy amusement could they have found than to plan their future? Side by side on the veranda they must have been looking at the brig, the third party in that fascinating game. Without her there would have been no future. She was the fortune and the home and the great free world for them. Who was it that likened a ship to a prison? May I be ignominiously hanged at a yard-arm if that's true. The white sails of that craft were the white wings—pinions I believe would be the more poetical style—well, the white pinions of their soaring love. Soaring as regards Jasper; Freya being a

20

[11] Section title-page of *Metropolitan Magazine*'s 'Freya of the Seven Isles'.

[12] Illustration for *Metropolitan Magazine*'s 'Freya of the Seven Isles'.

[13] Frontispiece of 'Twixt Land and Sea, Dent, 1918.

THE TEXTS
AN ESSAY

In the spring of 1912 Joseph Conrad and J. B. Pinker firmed up plans for a volume of his recent 'Between-land-and-sea-stories' to be published in both England and America. The book was part of a broader strategy to reduce Conrad's burdensome debts to his agent and would, along with *Chance*, help mend the breach with Pinker that one of its stories, along with *Under Western Eyes*, had helped create. The serialization of *Chance* was just concluding, and Conrad had just begun 'Dollars', a story that would become the novel *Victory*. Despite his engagement with a new tale and briefly with his second article on the *Titanic* affair, Conrad was taking several steps that would have major effects on his future as a professional author, while trying to capitalize on the shorter fiction he had produced from the time he had written *Under Western Eyes*.

The two editions of *'Twixt Land and Sea* that appeared by the end of the year contained three stories composed between late 1909 and early 1911: 'A Smile of Fortune' (written after he revised the typescript of *Under Western Eyes*), 'The Secret Sharer' (written as he was finishing the manuscript of that novel), and 'Freya of the Seven Isles' (written shortly before he resumed *Chance*). The publisher of the English edition was J. M. Dent, new to Conrad but eventually to become as important to his professional success at home as Doubleday (who would reissue the volume before publishing *Chance*) was about to become in America. The publisher of the American edition was George H. Doran (the anticipated publisher of *Chance* before Doubleday stepped in), who would soon sell the collection to Doubleday and much later merge with that firm.[1] The book of stories was a surprising success and heralded the turn in Conrad's professional fortunes that would be confirmed with the publication of *Chance* in book form a year later.

The collection had been in Conrad's vision and conversation since he had sent Pinker the first pages of 'A Smile of Fortune' in August

---

[1] On these matters and others involving the publication of the book editions, see the more detailed discussions below (pp. 280–84) and the 'Introduction', pp. lxxxiv–lxxxv, lxxxix.

1910. 'The Secret Sharer', written nine months earlier and then appearing in *Harper's Monthly Magazine*, was to be 'the first of that set', which was tentatively titled 'Tales of Experience'.[1] Unable to 'get on terms with' *Chance* after completing 'A Smile of Fortune' at the end of August, Conrad went on to finish 'Prince Roman' during September and early October and, towards the end of that month, to begin another story which he then put aside. This was probably 'The Partner', which he resumed in late November while shortening 'A Smile of Fortune' for the *London Magazine*. Early December saw the completion of that story, and after Christmas Conrad began 'Freya of the Seven Isles', which he concluded by the end of February 1911, while 'A Smile of Fortune' was appearing as that magazine's monthly feature.[2]

This 'Eastern seas tale ... quite suitable for serialising' was Conrad's last for some time, as *Chance* was to occupy him for the next year. A few days after finishing the novel in March 1912, Conrad was counting on it to bring £700, and on 'a vol of short stories' to be published that year to fetch another £200 towards reducing his debt to Pinker.[3] In early November 1911, they had discussed the collection of three stories as part of their publication plans for the next year. For a while the sticking point was 'Freya of the Seven Isles', which had just been accepted by the *London Magazine*, had yet to be placed in America, and might delay the book. At different times that month Conrad contemplated breaking off 'A Smile of Fortune' and 'Freya of the Seven Isles' and publishing them separately or in various combinations, often with 'The Partner' and sometimes also 'Prince Roman' filling the vacated space. In connection with these schemes he suggested Nelson, Blackwoods, and Macmillan as possible publishers.[4] When Dent came into sight early in December, the picture began to stabilize. Actual negotiations over the book apparently began in January, but its contents remained unsettled. For weeks Conrad was preoccupied with selling *Chance* in a shortened form to the *English Review*, and though by mid-May 'The Secret Sharer', 'A Smile of Fortune', and 'Freya of the Seven Isles'

[1] *Letters*, IV, 355. On the date of this letter, see p. 235, n. 3. This title appears in one of the typescripts of 'A Smile of Fortune' (see below, p. 227).

[2] Conrad's phrase appears in his 10 December letter to Pinker about completing *Chance* (*Letters*, IV, 395). His work on the stories is chronicled in his correspondence with Pinker, Galsworthy, and others (*Letters*, IV, 365–6, 370–71, 373, 379, 390, 393–5, 399, 407, 417–18). See also *Chronology*, pp. 79–81.

[3] Conrad to Pinker (*Letters*, IV, 417), to Galsworthy (*Letters*, V, 38). See *Chronology*, pp. 81–4. On the amount of that debt, see 'Introduction', p. xxxii.

[4] Conrad to Pinker and to John Quinn (*Letters*, IV, 498–500, 503–4, 506–8).

(recently serialized in New York's *Metropolitan Magazine*) were clearly to be included in the volume, he still thought 'The Partner' might be necessary to make a proper book.[1]

The title, too, remained unsettled, as Conrad was mooting 'Tales of Hearsay' as well as ''Twixt Land and Water . . . Tales' in June. Late that month, as 'Freya of the Seven Isles' was about to appear in the *London Magazine*, Pinker secured publication of the English edition with Dent for an advance equalling the £200 Conrad had earlier estimated and on a royalty of 25 per cent. Delighted with these terms, Conrad shortly thereafter sent off printer's copy for all four stories with a request to Pinker that 'The Partner' be withheld if possible because it did not 'match'. By the end of July the contents, title, epigraph, and dedication for the volume were settled.[2] Typesetting occurred in August and early September, Conrad passed the page proofs by the middle of that month, and the book was between boards by 7 October. On the 14th the English edition was published at 6 shillings.[3]

After publication in Dent's first English edition, which was followed on 3 December by Doran's American edition at $1.25 and in 1921 by Doubleday's and Heinemann's collected editions, the three stories' textual histories were essentially the same. Before, they were very different. Often they were complicated in various ways. Their several histories up to publication in the first English edition require separate discussion, which is best conducted in the order of their composition rather than of their eventual appearance in the collection.

THE SECRET SHARER

IN EARLY DECEMBER 1909, amidst the agony and frustration of producing the last few chapters of *Under Western Eyes*, Conrad paused to write a story set in the eastern seas. A diversion from a narrow point of view, the composition of the story was, in his literary life, a repetition of his earlier escape to the exotic world of the sea from a suffocating

[1] Conrad to Pinker, Galsworthy, Quinn, and Austin Harrison (*Letters*, IV, 519; *Letters*, V, 13, 30, 38, 44–6, 66–7).

[2] Conrad to Pinker, Stephen Reynolds, Galsworthy, Henry-D. Davray, and Quinn (*Letters*, V, 74–5, 80, 83–4, 87–90). The subtitles for the stories, reflected in the part-title pages of the book, were probably included with the revised printer's copy (the first two had been printed serially), but they might have been given to Dent with the book title, the epigraph, and the dedication, or with a contents page settling the stories' order in the collection.

[3] Conrad to Pinker (*Letters*, V, 105, 108, 113); *Chronology*, p. 86. See also *Bibliography*, A16a, 'Notes'; A16b, 'Notes'.

central Europe and from the domination of an avuncular benefactor (his agent) and of Russian influence (the novel). But it was also the first step in his departure from the 'political' tales that had engaged him for more than ten years, a return to the setting that had served him earlier and that would do so again in later stories and novels, and as such it launched the third phase of his literary career. Beginning his fifty-second year, looking both backward and forward, his work on *Under Western Eyes* suspended and himself suspended between two worlds, Conrad wrote 'The Secret Sharer' in a sort of becalmed state and with unusual fluidity and poise in the space of about ten days or two weeks.[1]

Only two documents remain to bear witness to this brief process, a manuscript (MS), the copy-text for the present edition, and a serial printing in *Harper's Monthly Magazine* (S), which along with the four book editions constitute the extant early texts. Two typescripts have, regrettably, perished: one (typed from the manuscript) in which Conrad made revisions that in effect continued and completed the act of composition, the other (typed from that revised typescript) which eventually became the printer's copy for *Harper's*, where many of Conrad's revisions have survived amidst a surprising array of changes introduced by its editor and printers. The extant documents and the relations of their texts are crucial to understanding Conrad's inscription and revision of a story in which, as he saw it, 'every word fits and there's not a single uncertain note'.[2]

Manuscript

THE MANUSCRIPT of some 16,400 words, now in the Berg Collection of the New York Public Library, Conrad wrote by his own account 'at great speed' in early December.[3] It consists of 126 pages inscribed in black ink on as many leaves of ruled cream-white paper, probably taken from one or more of the 'pads' that Conrad had received from Pinker in early August (*Letters*, IV, 269). Beginning on the first page of text, pagination in the upper left corner runs consecutively

---

[1] For the larger context, see the 'Introduction', pp. lxiv–lxviii, and for the number of days, p. lxv, n. 2. Ten days is Conrad's number for the time taken to write the manuscript, which might have required another day or so; two weeks represents the time he spent, give or take a day, writing the manuscript and revising the typescript, which amounted to the entire process of creation.

[2] Conrad to Edward Garnett, 5 November 1912 (*Letters*, V, 128).

[3] Conrad to Perceval Gibbon, 19 December [1909] (*Letters*, IV, 301–2).

throughout, except for a duplicated '116'; the first fourteen leaves also have 'DM' above the folio number, a confirmation of Conrad's statement to Pinker about the occasion of the tale's inception.[1] Holes in the upper left corner made by pins and then by sturdier fasteners indicate that the leaves were eventually kept together in several clutches (pages 1–20, 21–65, 66–109, 110–125).[2] A leaf of heavier stock containing an inked inscription 'The Secret-Sharer' has apparently been added, probably when Conrad sold the document to John Quinn two years later.[3] Page 1 contains what amounts to a head-title ('The Secret Sharer') in blue pencil, and in the top margins of pages 21 and 66 the letters 'SS' appear in the same medium.[4] Centred below the head-title is a roman numeral 'I.' also inscribed in blue pencil; between them is another 'I' both written and crossed out in ink. No such number, in either medium, precedes the normal paragraph break part way down page 62 that would become, when printed, the beginning of 'Part II'.

The general appearance of the document confirms the impression given in his letters that Conrad's composition proceeded with relative ease and at an unusually swift pace. Although words and passages are struck out and additions interlined or written in the left margin of nearly every page, these evidences of second thought seem minimal in both frequency and complexity when compared to the intricate tangle of text found in many of his manuscripts. Begun on either the 4th or more probably the 5th of December – that is, on a Saturday or a Sunday – the manuscript occupied the whole of the next week and the first few days of the following one.[5] By the 10th, Conrad felt confident

---

[1] 'The idea originated from a letter by Bashford of the *D. Mail* asking me for sketches or articles of 1200 words at £5 a piece' (*Letters*, IV, 297); also Conrad to Galsworthy, 22 December 1909 (*Letters*, IV, 304). See 'Introduction', p. lxvii. Bashford would re-enter the picture with a similar offer during the writing of 'A Smile of Fortune'; see p. 233, and 'The Texts' in *Notes on Life and Letters*, ed. J. H. Stape with Andrew Busza (2004), pp. 256–7.

[2] The pin holes suggest an initial grouping of leaves in smaller clutches (1–20, 21–29, 30–65, 66–99, 100–107, 108–115, 116a–123, 124–125) that were then combined in larger clutches held by fasteners. For further discussion of the significance of these clutches and of the 'SS' inscriptions (see below) associated with them, of the document's paper, and of its history, see Appendix A, 'Provenance of the Early Documents', and Appendix B, 'The Titles of the Tales'.

[3] See Conrad to Quinn, the New York collector of art and manuscripts, 11 December 1911 (*Letters*, IV, 521).

[4] For a facsimile of page 1, see Fig. 1. Throughout, citations of figures, plates, and maps refer to the illustrations on pp. 190–202 and at the end of this volume.

[5] See 'Introduction', pp. lxv–lxvi. See also Keith Carabine, '"The Secret Sharer": A Note on the Dates of its Composition', *Conradiana*, 19 (1987), 209–10; Carabine, p. 65; S. W. Reid and Robert W. Trogdon, '"The Secret Sharer": A Further Note on the Dates of its Composition',

enough to let both Pinker and John Galsworthy in on his secret and sufficiently advanced to send his agent 64, or perhaps 65, pages for typing.[1] Having completed the interview between the Captain and Leggatt (which became 'Part I') and begun that between the Captain and Archbold, he must have been at least several pages into what would amount to the slightly longer second half, for he promised to send Pinker 'the last 15 pp' later that day and no later than Monday the 13th.[2] On Tuesday the 14th, he reported to Galsworthy that he had indeed 'finished the short story' (*Letters*, IV, 296). That day or the next he sent Pinker the remainder of the manuscript, along with the first of several proposed titles, an underestimate of the tale's length and of the time taken to write it, and an elaborate though ill-fated justification of its very existence.[3]

Typescript Revisions

WHEN HE posted the first batch of manuscript to Pinker for typing, Conrad requested that the resulting typescript be sent back immediately, and he made another such request in the letter that went with the second and last batch, explaining his desire 'to close this episode at once and return wholly to the other work'.[4] The first batch of typescript should have been in his hands by the 12th or 13th, and he may have begun revising it by the time he 'dispatched the end of the story' – that is, by Wednesday the 15th.[5] The precise date on which he returned

---

· *Conradiana*, 39 (2007), 169–73. Different dates have traditionally been given: see Najder, p. 353; Karl, p. 675; *LL*, II, 5; Baines, p. 355; John Batchelor, *A Life of Joseph Conrad* (1994), p. 176.

[1] *Letters*, IV, 294. Page 66 contains one of the 'SS' notations in blue pencil, which seems to have been related to the processing of the manuscript by the typists. See Appendix B on the relations of these notations to the title.

[2] The next fifteen pages brought Conrad beyond the next episode, the interview with Archbold, and to the concluding actions, which proved to be about as long as those in the first sixty pages. To this extent the composition of 'The Secret Sharer' could be said to repeat the pattern, seen on a larger scale in nearly all the novels, of a prolonged conclusion and seriously underestimated length. But it does so only in little, as the conclusion was actually just a few days off.

[3] See *Letters*, IV, 297–9. This first proposed title was '*The Second Self*', which would soon modulate into '*The Secret Self*' and '*The other Self*' before he proposed '*The Secret Sharer*' (*Letters*, IV, 300). On the title, see Appendix B.

[4] That is, 'Razumov', still the working title for what would soon be called *Under Western Eyes*: *Letters*, IV, 297.

[5] *Letters*, IV, 294, 296. 'I have Sunday post' Conrad reminded Pinker when sending the first batch of manuscript.

the entire 'corrected type' for making the final typed printer's copy is a matter of conjecture, but it was almost certainly before Christmas and probably no later than the 19th, as subsequent developments indicate.[1] It was at this stage that Conrad proposed three further alternative titles, including at last '*The Secret Sharer*', though he suggested 'that may be too enigmatic'.[2]

In the week that he had the initial typescript which Pinker had promptly posted, Conrad made revisions throughout the story. Not surprisingly, they were more frequent at the beginning and end. Nearly the first ones he made developed more fully the idea of utter abandonment and isolation through the addition of what amounted to a word and a clause (81.5, 81.7–8).[3] Nearly the last one he made changed 'the sharer of my cabin' to 'the secret sharer of my cabin' (119.14). This alteration and others elsewhere[4] continued a trend begun midway in the manuscript itself, where he had started to grapple with the problem of how the Captain should refer to Leggatt, progressively moving away from almost exclusive dependence on the term 'double' to the use of the words 'secret', 'sharer', and 'self' in various phrases.[5]

Conrad's revisions in these days before Christmas were surprisingly numerous given the relative fluidity of the manuscript draft and the brevity of his work on the typescript. Some of them carried out a general decision to replace certain terms of the manuscript, such as the

---

[1] See *Letters*, IV, 300. The 17th, partly occupied by a visit from Galsworthy, is the earliest possible date for return of the typescript, which was not only 'corrected' in the usual sense but also much revised (see below); the 18th may be the latest for Conrad's effective work on the story, as that morning brought Pinker's letter of ultimatum regarding 'Razumov', which would absorb Conrad's attention from the 19th onward (see *Letters*, IV, 301–6) and leave him, for a time, 'unable to write a line'. The reference to William Rothenstein as 'a second self' in a letter of 17 December (*Letters*, IV, 300) and subsequent references to the story and to the novel during the developing dispute with Pinker show that the completed typescript was in Pinker's hands and the whole episode indeed closed in this limited sense, though not in the larger and more important one, by the 20th.

[2] *Letters*, IV, 300. The stroke beneath 'too' in Conrad's letter appears to be a rule dividing its paragraphs, rather than an underline, as the editors of the Cambridge *Letters* tentatively infer. On the question of the titles, see Appendix B.

[3] Citations of the page and line numbers of this edition refer throughout to its critical text and, where variation in the early texts occurs, particularly to the variants listed in the 'Apparatus'. Lower-case letters immediately following page–line numbers (e.g., 1.2a, 1.2b) distinguish entries that have readings in the same line. The variants of moment at present are those between the serial's text (S) and the manuscript's (MS). The destruction of both typescripts made the magazine central to the preservation and recovery of these revisions.

[4] See also 98.28, 101.31a, 102.38–40, 109.7, 115.33, 117.40–118.2.

[5] See 97.38b*n*. Cross-references to the 'Notes' in this volume take this form.

substitution of 'whiskers' for the chief mate's 'moustaches'.[1] Others dealt with problems he had experienced while making the first draft. For instance, he had first portrayed Leggatt as standing in the Captain's bathroom 'perfectly motionless' but, after redrafting, as 'drawn up very still' (98.12b); in revising the typescript Conrad finally described him as 'drawn up bolt upright', a phrase he had first hit upon two pages later while writing the manuscript and then exchanged for 'rigidly' while revising the typescript (see 98.34). By making the fishermen in the manuscript's first sentence 'brown' through a marginal addition, he had managed to suggest immediately the setting of his story and to begin to develop what became the image of a uniformly 'monotonous' (81.24) landscape, 'half brown, half blue' (81.16–17). Typescript revisions in the same paragraph solidified the image, as the 'grey and sombre flatness' of the shore was simplified to a 'flat shore' (81.15a) and the MS description of the ship as 'a white metallic cold bit inset between the warm brown stints and the unvaried blue' disappeared altogether.[2]

Many typescript revisions carried on alterations Conrad had made earlier in the manuscript, even when particular words rejected there reappeared in the text of the serial printing.[3] A number of additions made in the typescript amounted to elaborations and clarifications of MS phrasing, including the specification of the ship 'within the

---

[1] At 82.30, 83.12–13, 85.21, 88.30, 97.23, 98.19. This series of changes slackens off towards the end of the story, and some 'moustaches' became 'whiskers' only in E1. The change was nonetheless important to Conrad, as a subtle related one suggests (see 92.33n).

[2] See 81.21b in the 'Apparatus'. Besides introducing additional colours, this long phrase, which Conrad had laboured over in the manuscript, also shifted the description from the landscape to the ship and the perspective from the Captain's (as in the first two sentences) to one hovering above the sea; these disruptive effects were probably other reasons for its deletion. The importance of the landscape image to Conrad is evidenced in several ways, including his reinscription of 'blue sea' (81.10) in the manuscript.

[3] For instance, at 85.26 Conrad finally achieved the effect he was seeking in MS, where he had first written 'But the vicious tug I gave it simply', had then condensed that phrase by making it 'My vicious', and eventually compensated for the 'But' lost in the process by adding 'yet' in the typescript. A more complex instance is at 94.16–17: there 'and' for 'tho', and 'the land' for 'it' are words Conrad wrote in the manuscript; the first simply restores a word cancelled, but the second picks up a word replaced (by 'coast') two lines earlier and introduces it where another word ('that') had been cancelled. Less complex was the addition of 'or' (92.16), which amounted almost to a correction within what had been a marginal addition at the top of an MS page. Conrad had written the sentence after the fact, and the omission of 'or' was probably a simple oversight owing to his distraction while making the link between the addition and the main text clear. S's 'gave' (99.19b) fixed an incompletely executed revision partly occasioned by a line break in MS.

islands' (83.22c), a short sentence ('To the law.') giving Archbold's interpretation of the Captain's phrase 'to the shore people' (101.17), and a longer sentence explaining the Captain's 'fear' (102.38–40).[1] Similar additions that may have seemed almost gratuitous strengthened the narration in subtle ways, developing Leggatt's characteristic speech (89.31, 92.30), highlighting the Captain's isolation (112.32a, 116.34), giving a more emphatic tone to the conclusion (117.35–36, 119.7). A small group of substitutions and transpositions related to place and direction aboard ship and often involved further resolution of problems Conrad had encountered when writing the manuscript.[2] Verb tense, one of the banes of his writing life, continued to concern him. In passages already revised in the manuscript, he altered several verbs to the past perfect, usually without wholly consistent results, and made other adjustments of tense.[3] Occasionally such alterations in the typescript simply reversed changes he had made in the manuscript. A 'have' that he had got rid of when reworking the manuscript crept back into the text during his revision of the typescript (93.12) with the effect of re-emphasizing the Englishness of Leggatt's phraseology. This happened as well in an alteration of the manuscript's diction, which received attention throughout the typescript; at the end of the opening description, 'pealed', substituted for 'tinkled' in the manuscript, gave way to Conrad's first thought (82.23).

Other revisions in the typescript were less intimately connected with problems given attention in the manuscript. One cluster of changes focussed on the Captain's manner towards the 'skipper' of the *Sephora*. Phrasing that described his cheerfulness in responding to Captain Archbold's question about his presumed loss of hearing was carefully altered (100.1a–b), and a little later his 'scrupulous distant courtesy' became 'chilly, distant courtesy' (102.21b). Conrad added entire clauses, so that, for instance, Leggatt's 'I felled him' expanded to 'That was no time for gentlemanly reproof, so I turned round and felled him' (89.15–16). He also elaborated and clarified ideas, the MS phrase 'everything became quiet like death' evolving into 'everything

---

[1] See also the changes at 83.36, 88.5, 93.35, 97.13, 117.33–34; that at 97.13 repairs a cryptic form occasioned by a page break.

[2] See especially 85.10–11, 108.19n, 118.19–20. The addition of an entire phrase (98.16n) amounted to a gratuitous elaboration more than a clarification of the nautical dimensions of the act.

[3] See the additions at 83.22a, 83.22b, 84.2b, and 102.14–15; also the substitutions at 87.11a, at 101.22n (tense here shifts three times in MS), and at 111.10 (where 'have' was interlined in MS). Rarely is complete consistency of tense achieved in such revised passages.

quieted down and the anchorage was as still as death' (93.31a). He
made subtler alterations as well, sometimes to develop a point (98.35,
118.8–9), sometimes it would seem gratuitously (92.4, 107.27n).[1] The
latter, however, accorded with other revisions in the typescript, as well
as phrases in the manuscript, characterized by their use of distinctively British idioms (e.g., 84.10; 92.12, 92.17), often with the effect
of heightening the English flavour of the Captain's, and especially of
Leggatt's, speech.[2]

While revising the typescript's text Conrad presumably corrected
errors that he found there. But others he simply missed. Although
it is not always possible to distinguish errors produced by the typist and transmitted to the serial from those committed in the typesetting of *Harper's* itself, a number of departures from MS certainly
appear to be traceable to the typewriting process and the condition
of the manuscript's inscription. Some – 'men' for 'crew', 'afterward'
for 'afterwards', 'casual' for 'usual', 'head' for 'hand', 'Cambodje'[3]
for 'Cambodie' – were caught in later texts either by Conrad (84.2a,
109.28, 110.18) or by an editor (102.27, 110.34), where they were
either corrected or further modified. But more often such errors
escaped Conrad's notice in the typescript and his editors' in setting
copy or proof. Several were traceable to Conrad's interlineations in
the manuscript, which the typist either botched (89.21bn, 103.23n)
or simply skipped (90.12n, 93.2, 95.8, 99.22, 108.5, 116.21b).[4] Misconstructions of his inscription, like 'His' for 'This' and 'me' for 'one'
(94.33, 99.19a), and problems with his final -s and final -y (93.25,

---

[1] Other apparently gratuitous changes involved alterations (e.g., 99.21–22, 100.34) that
developed a fine point and that even a finicky editor (see below, pp. 217–21) would
have had no reason to make, including a cluster in the narrative preceding Archbold's
arrival, where the resulting phrasing was not always happy or idiomatic (e.g., 96.18b,
96.38, 97.4–5, 97.7, 97.15). The change of 'that' to 'this' at 100.34 resembles three similar substitutions that were truly indifferent. One of them avoided repetition (a recur-
ring reason for such alteration), but the other two seem to have occurred to Conrad in
the course of reviewing paragraphs while making more substantial changes (108.9; 99.26,
102.36).

[2] Conrad remarked on this feature of the story in a letter of 24 December 1912 to Edith
Wharton about translating it into French: 'And the thing (I need not point it out to you) is
so particularly English, in moral atmosphere, in feeling and even in detail – n'est-ce pas?'
(*Letters*, v, 152). See also his 28 October 1912 letter on Leggatt to Galsworthy (*Letters*, v,
121–2).

[3] Conrad's inscription of this name was particularly unsure, perhaps as a result of his own
attraction to the French form 'Cambodge', but MS has 'Cambodie', not S's 'Cambodje'. See
110.34n.

[4] See also 'thought' for 'thoughts' at 88.32, which also involved Conrad's final -s and was
corrected in the first English edition.

97.38a; 99.28–29, 100.21) were typical.[1] Others were more extraordinary, the most important perhaps being the corruption of 'my open personality' to 'my own personality'.[2] Whatever their precise nature, the difficulties of Conrad's inscription encouraged a levelling of his distinctive phrasing that tended to be invisible to his editors and at times eluded his own eye.

The typescript errors that he succeeded in correcting we can no longer identify, of course, because the evidence has disappeared along with the document itself. These corrections, as well as the revisions Conrad made there, proved to be his only ones before 1912, as he never saw the printer's copy made for Pinker from the revised typescript nor proofs of the serial text eventually typeset from that fair copy. The destruction of the fair copy after typesetting is hardly surprising. But the loss of the revised typescript indicates that in this case Pinker did not send it, along with the typescript copied from it, back to Conrad for final approval, and this breach of established practice suggests how seriously the relationship between author and agent had already deteriorated by the end of 1909. Conrad's alterations to the initial typescript must have been finished during the few days that followed his completion of the manuscript, around a presumably refreshing but brief visit from Galsworthy on the 17th, and before the full import of Pinker's ultimatum of the 18th regarding 'Razumov' began to be realized.[3]

Because neither the revised nor the fair typescript survives, the only evidence for concluding that Conrad did not see the second typescript is his preoccupation with other matters – namely, the ending of 'Razumov', which had to be written in the next few weeks – and the utter lack in his surviving letters of any mention of further work on 'The Secret Sharer'. Despite his reference to 'the vagaries of the infernal typists employed by the great P', Conrad probably felt constrained by his need to concentrate on the novel and by the story's precipitating role in his deteriorating relationship with Pinker to entrust his agent with preparation of printer's copy incorporating his corrections and

---

[1] See also S's 'the' for 'my' (81.8an), which is probably another such typist's misreading of the imprecise inscription in MS, though it could represent the *TS2* typist's confusion occasioned by Conrad's later interlineations (81.7–8, 81.8–9) in the first lost typescript (*TS1*). Jessie Conrad would make similar errors when typing 'A Smile of Fortune' nearly a year later (see pp. 239–40).

[2] See 97.38bn; see also 82.9a, 90.24, 98.29n, 107.1, 111.22n.

[3] See above, p. 209, n. 1.

revisions.[1] Although numerous, the revisions were not so extensive perhaps as to have absolutely required oversight of the new copy under
these sensitive circumstances. In these vexing days his agent's less
than enthusiastic reception of the story aggravated the situation and
severely affected Conrad's ability to get on with the novel,[2] though
Pinker appears to have responded quickly to Conrad's suggestion
regarding two American magazines that might be particularly open to
publishing it, Bliss Carman's *Gentleman's Journal*[3] and *Harper's Monthly
Magazine*.

Serialization

ABOUT *HARPER'S*, CONRAD wrote to Pinker in his December letter announcing the story's completion:

> I had lately a letter from Alden (Harper Mag) asking me for a contribution to
> their 60th anniversary N°. I had a curious little passage with Harper a month ago
> or more which ended in a cabled apology from them. (Too long to tell here –
> leave that till we meet). I think they'll want to be nice to me just at present. If you
> conclude to approach them let me know and I'll drop a note to Alden.[4]

Amidst a galling discussion of his progress on 'Razumov' as well as a
proposed volume of stories, Conrad reached an agreement with Pinker
that the story should be submitted to *Harper's*. By early January Conrad
had done as promised: 'I wrote to Alden re story saying that I asked
you to send it to him and that it was done as a contribution to the 60th
anniversary N° of their magazine – which is sufficiently true as I had

---

[1] Conrad to Gibbon, 19 December [1909] (*Letters*, IV, 301). His strategy regarding the title
suggests how delicate he felt the situation to be; see Appendix B.

[2] See *Letters*, IV, 302–6.

[3] Fairchild Publishing Company (New York) issued Carman's *Man's Book* monthly from
October 1908 to November 1910, sometimes as *Fairchild's Magazine* (November 1908–April
1909) or *The Gentleman's Journal* (May–December 1909). Carman, the Canadian-born poet,
was, it seems, sufficiently popular in North America and sufficiently known in literary circles
in Britain, where he had studied in the early 1880s, to attract submissions and warrant the
trust of the Fairchild company even when residing in Connecticut. His shaky venture and
the sturdy *Harper's* had been linked in Conrad's thinking since July: see *Letters*, IV, 254, 284,
298. See *The National Union Catalog: Pre-1956 Imprints, Volume 359* (1974), s.v. 'Man's book';
The National Cyclopædia of American Biography (1931), XXI, 429–30; *Who Was Who in America,
Volume I, 1897–1942* (1966), s.v. 'Carman'.

[4] *Letters*, IV, 298. The 'little passage', reported in bits and pieces to Pinker and Galsworthy
over the course of more than six months, concerned publishing *A Personal Record*: see *Letters*,
IV, 212, 216, 254, 278–9, 284, 292.

them rather in my eye.'[1] On 8 January *Harper's* wired Pinker accepting the story, for which they paid £100, but almost eight months passed before its publication.[2]

'The Secret-Sharer', as it was titled,[3] did not appear in *Harper's Monthly Magazine* until August and September of 1910 – two months after the anniversary number – where it followed instalments of William Dean Howells's reminiscences of Mark Twain (and poems as fillers) and preceded lavishly illustrated stories long since forgotten.[4] In the August number it began on the last leaf of one

---

[1] *Letters*, IV, 319. The exact chronology of events is difficult to determine, as it hinges on three undated letters from Conrad to Pinker, this one and two others (*Letters*, IV, 317, 318), that discuss the placing of the story and other on-going matters, including the progress on 'Razumov'. The Cambridge editors date these letters conjecturally as 6 ('Thursday'), 10 ('Monday'), and 12 ('Wednesday') January on the basis of several references and facts, most importantly the batch of *Under Western Eyes* manuscript enclosed with the middle ('Monday') letter, which presumably became Batch R of the typescript, dated 15 January. However, the evidence of negotiations with *Harper's* could be more persuasive for a week earlier: viz., 30 December 1909, 3 and 5 January 1910. By this dating Conrad wrote to the magazine's editor ten days before he accepted the story, with little lapse (except for Christmas Day and other such events) in the effort of agent and author to place the story; this dating better fits the letter from Sydney Brooks to the president of Harpers written 1 January, two days after Conrad's (see next note). The later dating, which is arguable on the premise that the last few batches of novel manuscript were typed and returned in a timely fashion, indicates that Conrad's third letter was written well after Pinker had sent the story to America and that Pinker kept Conrad in the dark as to its submission and acceptance throughout these weeks and as late as 12 January, four days after it had been accepted, and two after terms had been fixed. The later dates seem more probable not only on the evidence for the production of 'Razumov', but for a week's lapse in all activities (owing to illness) at the turn of the year, rather than over Christmas; their implications for the state of Conrad's and Pinker's relationship are somewhat sobering.

[2] Cable from *Harper's* to Pinker, 8 January 1910 (Berg); letter from *Harper's* to Pinker, 10 January 1910 (Berg); Colonel George Harvey to Sydney Brooks, 19 January 1910 (private collection), mentioning the sum of £100. Harvey's letter responded, sympathetically but negatively, to Brooks's of 1 January (private collection) proposing that Harpers make a long-term contract with Conrad; both shed light on Conrad's correspondence with Pinker about the volume of stories, in which Harpers figured significantly. Other stories accepted by *Harper's* ('An Anarchist', 'The Informer', 'The Partner') usually took several months to appear: Conrad had finished 'An Anarchist', for instance, by December 1905, and *Harper's* had accepted it and paid for it by March 1906, but it did not appear until August (*Letters*, III, 300, 369). Plans for the anniversary issue of *Harper's* in June might conceivably have delayed their publication of 'The Secret Sharer', but there is little evidence in that issue of special contents or other arrangements, except for the editor's piece on the event.

[3] On the source and form of the title, see Appendix B.

[4] Volume 121, no. 723, August 1910, pp. 349–59; no. 724, September 1910, pp. 530–41. For more on the contents of *Harper's* in these months, see S. W. Reid, 'American Markets, Serials and Conrad's Career', *The Conradian*, 28 (2003), 66–7, 89–96.

gathering,[1] occupied all the next, and ended at the top of the first leaf of another, whose recto was otherwise given over to a poem.[2] It was accompanied by two grey-tone illustrations printed on glossy paper: one of the Captain and Leggatt talking together over the sky-light before the helm, inserted in the centre fold of the central gathering, the other of the conversation between the steward and the two mates at the break of the poop, inserted between gatherings and thus just before the last part-page of the story.[3] The gathering containing the end of this first instalment and the poem that filled the rest of the page consisted entirely of glossy paper so as to accommodate engraved illustrations cut within columns of the text of Arthur E. McFarlane's 'Cut Off in Paris', a story that occupied the remainder of the gathering and ended in the next glossy gathering before regular text paper resumed.

In the September issue 'The Secret-Sharer' covered a full twelve pages, beginning on the back of the first leaf of a gathering of text stock and running half way through the next gathering of glossy stock, where it was followed immediately by George Harding's 'In Port', which enjoyed the special treatment given McFarlane's story the previous month. The first illustration for this second instalment, inserted so as to face the opening page of text, showed the two captains at the table in the cuddy being served by the steward. The second, depicting Archbold's departure, appeared on the first page of the next gathering and was followed by four full pages of text, bringing the tale to a conclusion at the very bottom of its last page; these text pages were printed on the glossy paper used for the last illustration and for the opening pages of the Harding story with their numerous engravings. The division of 'The Secret-Sharer' in *Harper's* was the result of the

---

[1] Each number of *Harper's* consisted of twenty four-leaf (eight-page) gatherings plus inserted plates containing illustrations, though some illustrations appeared on the same paper as text and were thus integral to the gatherings (see below). Although it was gathered in 4s, it may have been imposed and printed as an octavo. The shape and size of the leaves suggest this imposition, but the alternation of regular and glossy stock in various numbers suggests quarto imposition, unless layout and printing of a given number on the two kinds of paper was extremely complex and well plotted. Such material factors bore on the placement of the various kinds of matter – stories, poems, illustrations, editorial columns, and regular features – that made up each number of *Harper's* and ultimately determined the division of Conrad's story between two of them.

[2] Fannie Stearns Davis's 'Oh Strong Desires' in eight quatrains, printed complete as four irregular stanzas. This instalment of 'The Secret-Sharer' may have exceeded its estimated length by several lines.

[3] All four illustrations for Conrad's story were drawn by W. J. Aylward; the last was engraved by C. E. Hart. See Figs. 5–8.

magazine's production practices and layout, of the material exigencies of combining text and illustrations in other stories featured in the August and September issues, and not of presenting Conrad's in a form that reflected his own structuring of the tale.

Conrad's report of its publication, including its division, to John Galsworthy in an August 1910 letter is his first surviving word about it since January.[1] The intervening months had been eventful ones occupied with the 'completion' of the novel manuscript, the breach with Pinker, the prolonged illness in the wake of those events, the revision of the novel, the family's move from Aldington to Capel House, the four reviews for the *Daily Mail*, and the vexed writing of 'A Smile of Fortune'.[2] It is very unlikely that Conrad had seen proofs or had had any more to do with 'The Secret Sharer' before its appearance in *Harper's*.

In his correspondence with Pinker on this matter, Conrad had expressed his usual ambivalence about publishing in magazines, referring to his 'intense dislike for all these American humbugs in the publishing line'.[3] His letters to the distinguished editor of *Harper's*, of course, had a different tone. Henry Mills Alden, 'the greatest editor of his age', according to Poultney Bigelow, but now most remembered perhaps for censoring passages in Thomas Hardy's *Jude the Obscure* and a whole chapter of Henry James's translation of Alphonse Daudet's *Port Tarascon*,[4] had been the editor of *Harper's* since 1869, when he had inherited, according to one of his successors, a 'popular American magazine with . . . something approaching a national audience'.[5] The 'growing dignity, distinction, maturity, and range' of this 'general family magazine of good reading for everybody' during his tenure (which lasted until 1919) was in no small part owing to his editorial acumen. Under Alden, *Harper's* had continued to appeal to 'the solid and respectable citizenry from coast to coast' in America, where it had very wide circulation.[6] It had successfully competed with 'the younger *Century* and the still younger *Scribner's*' as well as with the 'somewhat more austere' *Atlantic Monthly* for fifty years, and lately with yet newer

---

[1] 5 August 1910 (*Letters*, IV, 354). Conrad's comment on the partition is quoted below.
[2] See above, pp. lxxi–lxxv or below, pp. 230–38.
[3] [22 December] 1909 (*Letters*, IV, 306); see also *Letters*, IV, 319.
[4] John Tebbel, *The American Magazine* (1969), p. 109.
[5] Frederick L. Allen, *"Harper's Magazine" 1850–1950* (1950), p. 14.
[6] *Harper's* had a more limited readership in Britain as well, where it was issued from Harpers' London office in Albemarle Street, but its primary audience was in America, where it was arguably the most influential magazine for decades.

rivals aimed at a mass market and featuring 'material less discreet, less literary, and more popular'. This success its editor had achieved by focussing on 'an upper class of refined tastes', rather than on 'the everyday interests of the rank-and-file'. During his tenure Alden, a man of 'sensitive and discriminating taste', had managed to maintain his large American audience of 'ladies and gentlemen of either means or intellectual interests, or preferably both' through an editorial policy characterized chiefly by 'fastidiousness and attention to propriety'.[1]

The policies at *Harper's*, if not Alden's own hand, revealed themselves in various ways in the text of Conrad's story. The most blatant of these was its division into two 'Parts' between the August and September numbers. This partition for physical fit and publishing convenience was immediately noticed by Conrad, who called it a 'Beastly shame' and remarked on other features of the August issue 'so inept that I feel sick to see myself there.'[2] *Harper's* fiction appeared in a two-column format, and typographical exigency apparently dictated more subtle changes. The manuscript phrase 'sort of man' (101.29), containing one of Conrad's most frequent locutions, became 'sort' in the penultimate line of the first column on the second page of text in the September number; as the last line, which concludes the paragraph, is nearly full, 'of man' would have caused the paragraph to spill over into the next column and to create a widow.[3] Towards the end of the story three successive instances of deleted words (112.2–3) appear to be traceable to a similar need to prevent a paragraph from running over a line and on to the next page – the one that was to follow the last illustration, which began the gathering on glossy paper.[4]

Actual editorial interventions were more frequent. The serial text eliminated an anglicism when Leggatt's 'Fancy finding' became

---

[1] Allen, pp. 14–17. This general view of Alden's editorship may need some qualification when it comes to special cases, for though he clearly believed Conrad's work, like that of James and Hardy, required some filtering for *Harper's* wide audience, he also clearly valued it; his commentary on *Lord Jim* in one of his monthly columns, for instance, concludes thus: 'in the best modern fiction … there are no rhetorical effects, no glosses of any sort; but there is the masque, the full imaginative investment, the play and indirection of thought following the fugitive and elusive truths of life' ('Editor's Study', November 1904, p. 972).

[2] Conrad to Galsworthy, 5 August 1910 (*Letters*, IV, 353).

[3] See p. 531 of the September number. It is likely, though less certain, that the identical deletion that followed in the next sentence resulted from the compositor's decision to remain consistent by cutting the phrase again (101.32).

[4] P. 538. This mechanical triumph of the compositor, which left a neat break for the illustration that intervened between text pages, would occasion difficulties during the printing of E1: see below, p. 221.

'Who'd have thought of finding' (95.12).[1] The Captain's 'say me nay' turned into the less quaint but also less easy 'say nay to me' (97.10), and in the first sentence his 'now removed', an idiom more appropriate in English speech than American, was diluted to 'now gone' (81.6b).[2] In this same opening sentence something approaching censorship occurred when the American editor, sensitive to racial connotations less acute in Britain – and actually misapprehended in this case – eliminated Conrad's deliberately added reference to 'brown' fishermen (81.6a).[3]

Similar but more subtle changes (100.24, 103.25n) ran counter to Conrad's tendency to develop, rather than diminish, distinctively English idioms in the speech of the Captain and Leggatt when revising the typescript. Leggatt's speech, particularly his account of the doings aboard the *Sephora*, received inordinate attention as small changes took the sharp edges off it, smoothing out his characteristic 'brusque, disconnected' (89.6) expressions, seen from the beginning (e.g., at 86.21–22, 87.37).[4] In S the *Sephora*'s captain no longer 'looked damnably sick'; he 'seemed very sick' (92.8). Leggatt's reference to hearing 'your skipper' became 'one's skipper' (105.26). He no longer followed his statement 'My father's a parson in Norfolk.' with a question beginning 'You see me'; he said quite properly 'Do you see me' (88.33n). These niceties and others[5] allow us to see *Harper's* fastidious editor plying his trade, making Leggatt a bit more polite, perhaps less bluff, and certainly more correct for his readers.

---

[1] Cf. Conrad's gratuitous addition in the next sentence (95.13–14) and his substitution to eliminate repetition just a little later (95.25n). Preliminary collations indicate that in 'An Anarchist' (*Harper's*, 1906) editorial alteration like that discussed here also occurred, though perhaps not to the same extent. When intermediate documents (e.g., a revised typescript) have gone missing, inferring the sources of variants is of course an exercise in informed analysis, whether bibliographical (as above) or textual (as here).

[2] Conrad uses the phrase 'say him nay' in 'The Censor of Plays' (1907), *Notes on Life and Letters*, 66.19. He does not normally rely on 'gone' to carry so much force. See 81.6bn for the particular unacceptability of his 'removed' in this context.

[3] On the associations of 'brown', especially in conjunction with 'removed', see 81.6an, 81.6bn.

[4] This tendency in the editorial changes contrasts with Conrad's revision, for instance, at 94.2, where the deletion of words that had survived revision of a passage in MS and that were then virtually repeated a little later (94.15) resulted in a fragment more characteristic of Leggatt's clipped speech.

[5] In two closely paralleled phrases, S substitutes 'so far as' for MS's 'as far as' (90.6, 90.9), but S's construction is virtually without precedent throughout Conrad's manuscripts and revised typescripts, where he habitually uses 'as far as' when followed by a pronoun and a verb, especially of knowing, seeing, or remembering. They are further instances of Alden's careful editing. See also the changes at 89.9, 89.18bn, 91.15, 91.25n, 91.35n, 98.8 and one (108.34–35n) involving tense (see below).

In a comparable case MS's natural phrasing of Leggatt's question 'What does it say?' became in S the more explicit 'What does the Bible say?' (111.4). Such literalism is one of the more distinguishing features of the serial's text. In *Harper's* the manuscript's colloquial 'keep her running' appeared as 'keep the ship running', and 'too much' as the almost redundant 'too much for me' (89.11, 116.21a). Whereas Conrad expanded on his own wording by making creative additions when revising the typescript, the editorial changes in S often had a literalistic character and reductive effect, so that the expression (again Leggatt's) 'as if the sky had fallen' became 'as if the sky had fallen on my head' (89.20n). Occasionally this narrowing of focus had an actually misguided and misleading result (see, e.g., 93.6n). In the first sentence the literalism of *Harper's* distinguished editor altered 'earth' to 'ocean' (a word Conrad eschews), eliminating what was arguably the manuscript's first evocation of the Cain motif (see 81.7n).

Some normalizations made by either the *Harper's* editor, proof-reader, or compositor were later restored to Conrad's manuscript form in the book editions. Conrad caught an alteration resulting in (if not motivated by) confusion, where the Captain's question to Leggatt 'Did you hear everything' became 'Did you hear anything' (105.16), but he overlooked S's substitution of 'against' for the British form 'amongst' (114.24a), which not only flattened but obscured his carefully wrought description. S's changes of sea idiom were occasionally corrected in the book texts, but sometimes were not (e.g., 103.30b, 107.32; 85.27n).[1]

A few editorial changes in S related to place and direction aboard ship. When some of Conrad's own alterations touched on these matters, they involved substitutions and transpositions and were often aimed at resolving problems he had had when writing the manuscript.[2] S's editorial interventions, by contrast, were either additions or deletions restricted to single words which attempted, often mistakenly, to clarify physical movements and the layout of the ship, itself sufficiently enigmatic in MS. Twice these deletions eliminated words that Conrad

---

[1] See 103.30bn on S's rationalization of an imprecise MS form involving nautical idiom, which might conceivably be attributed to the typist of *TS1*. Other normalizations in S (e.g., 85.40, 96.30b) could have been made by a compositor almost instinctively as well as by the editor deliberately.

[2] See above, p. 211, and n. 2.

had used in MS rather precisely to describe the Captain's movements at crucial junctures (see 103.25n, 116.11n).[1]

Editorial intervention in S's text extended to fine points of usage and idiom as well. In S four of Conrad's quirky 'these' forms were normalized to 'those' (88.36a, 93.33b, 101.1, 101.6). A distinctive 'that' got levelled to 'the'.[2] The editor adjusted two instances of muddled word order (85.39, 96.4), fiddled with tenses,[3] fussed with awkward articles and prepositions, and altered four of Conrad's characteristic 'afterwards' and 'towards' forms, though these last changes probably reflect American 'style' and one may represent a graphic error by the typist.[4]

First English Edition

MANY OF these serial alterations passed into the first English edition (E1) and the other book editions descended from it and thus became part of the received text. As his letters to Pinker in July and September 1912 indicate, Conrad used tear-sheets of *Harper's* to prepare printer's copy for E1.[5] The momentary panic in early September over the supposed loss of 'pp 537 & 538' of the copy sent to Dent's printer derived from the facts that an illustration occupied the first page of the glossy leaf containing these pages and that the previous page (p. 536) ended precisely with a full paragraph, carefully wrought by a compositor willing to make three cuts in the text.[6] *Harper's* division of the

[1] For other instances, see 84.38n, 103.23n, 108.32bn, 115.31n. See also Conrad's revisions at 115.18a and later at 91.13, as well as his two retrospective sketches (Figs. 18 and 19) and the present editors' conjectured 'Plan of the officers' quarters' (Fig. 20).

[2] See 'that cabin' (107.1). The substitution might be attributable to a typist faced with a poor inscription. It contrasts with two alterations of 'the' to 'that' which reflect Conrad's frequent troubles with this article (93.18, 94.34).

[3] As already argued, many of S's changes of tense probably reflect Conrad's revisions, especially to the past perfect, but three others (two in the narrative of Leggatt's account) go against his practices and represent normalizations by a precise editor of the nicest kind. See the alterations at 93.14 (which skews the tense contrary to a revision in MS), 94.9 (which reverses an addition in MS), and 108.34–35n.

[4] See the variants at 84.27, 118.13n, 118.27n; 82.22, 116.27, 117.30; 102.27. The second group of changes could possibly reflect compositorial house-styling rather than editorial.

[5] Both early in the month, though the precise dates are conjectural (*Letters*, v, 83, 105). For a genealogical chart, see Fig. 14 (p. 223).

[6] See above, p. 218. The clean paragraph break left E1's printers without any way of verifying the continuity of their copy. It is possible that the leaf with an engraving on its unpaginated recto but text on its verso had in fact been carelessly discarded, but in any case with the leaves separated from their binding, the break in pagination on the engraved illustration could have been sufficiently disorienting to cause concern about lost copy.

tale, its compositor's mechanically induced excisions (101.29, 112.2a, 112.2b, 112.3), its editor's three alterations in the first sentence (81.6an, 81.6bn, 81.7n), his additional Americanisms (e.g., 95.12, 97.10), his literalisms and glosses (e.g., 89.11, 111.4, 116.21a), his smoothing out of Leggatt's and the Captain's speech (e.g., 88.33n, 92.8, 100.24, 105.26), his normalizations (e.g., 88.36a, 93.33b), his righting of tenses (e.g., 93.14, 94.9, 108.34–35n), and his other niceties (e.g., 90.6, 98.8), as well as the typist's graphic errors (e.g., 93.25, 94.33, 110.34n), all got transmitted to E1 and thence to subsequent editions and to posterity.[1]

Although preparing copy for E1 in the wake of finishing *Chance*, writing a second article on the *Titanic*, and beginning *Victory*, Conrad managed to notice some of S's errors and to correct or further modify them in the week or so he spent on the work. He put right both subtle and more obvious graphic errors (84.2a, 88.32, 109.28) as well as typesetting or editorial mistakes, rationalizations, and normalizations (e.g., 98.26, 103.30b, 105.16, 107.32). He also sometimes spotted an outright error or fussy alteration in S and restored MS's sense if not its exact wording (e.g., 91.25n, 110.18).[2]

More frequent in E1's copy than such corrections were actual revisions. Although they were not nearly so numerous nor searching as those made in the initial typescript, a few of them revisited problems of the MS text that Conrad had dealt with during his first revision. Perhaps the most important was the excision of a joke that in S had continued to disrupt the atmosphere of physical calm and mental stillness, if not monotonous mood, he had laboured to create in the opening of the story preceding Leggatt's abrupt arrival (83.22b).[3] He further developed the concept of the secret sharer begun in the manuscript

---

[1] See also 103.23n, for a nice combination of typescript and serial error.

[2] He could not consult the manuscript because by this time it had been sold to John Quinn in New York (*Letters*, IV, 521). Had that not been the case, it probably would have made no difference. Jessie Conrad seems to have stored such documents in various places around the house, and Conrad rarely to have consulted them, as an analogous instance of revision in the typescript indicates. At 102.13 S adds 'utterly incapable' after MS's insufficient 'felt'; MS is heavily revised at this point, and its final phrasing is interlined above two words ('simply incapable') that Conrad mistakenly cancelled along with others. The change in S, which its wording suggests is Conrad's, attempted to repair the faulty revision process, but, unlike the correction at 102.11b for the same reason, it failed to recover both words. For a similar instance of unconsulted documents, see the discussion of the manuscript and typescripts of 'A Smile of Fortune' (p. 246) and esp. Appendix A.

[3] Cf. the deletion of a bit of sardonic humour (87.27), the change of 'undistinguished' to 'monotonous' (81.24), or the more gradual 'followed' for the 'caught' of MS and S (81.30).

The Secret Sharer

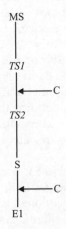

MS

TS1

C

TS2

S

C

E1

C→ Conrad's 'corrections'

Inferred (lost) documents (e.g., *TS1*)

[14] Genealogy of 'The Secret Sharer'.

and carried on in the typescript revisions (e.g., at 115.36), making S's 'secret occupant' (simply 'occupant' in MS) the 'secret sharer' in E1 (101.31a), and changing 'my other self' (in MS and S) to 'the secret sharer of my life' (98.12a). He elaborated and tweaked the description of the Captain's distanced demeanour towards Captain Archbold (99.17, 100.1b, 102.21b) and carried forward other revisions made for S or not completely implemented there.[1] Relatively few revisions for E1 occurred before Leggatt's appearance,[2] and, a perfunctory substitution of 'whiskers' aside, they virtually disappeared in the final escape scene except for two clusters, which both involved changes made in the typescript behind S (118.15–19, 118.39–119.1). His revisions

---

[1] See, for example, the variants at 93.31b, 108.19–20n; 103.29, 119.5.

[2] The most notable exceptions to this were the correction of MS's lapse 'river Mekong' to 'river Meinam' (81.20b) as well as the deletion (83.22b) and two substitutions associated with mood already noted.

for S having been heavy in the beginning and end of the tale, most of
Conrad's alterations for E1 concentrated in the middle of the story.
There he revised some nautical terms (92.31, 96.27, 97.27, 112.14n),
altered other diction to accord with wording already present (87.2b,
99.13, 106.6; cf. 86.13, 87.3, 99.37),[1] corrected errors resulting from
slips of the pen during revision of MS,[2] began new sentences where
breaks or pauses were appropriate to the narrative sense (93.30,
110.5), elaborated or clarified various minor points,[3] and made a tense
perfect (96.24). Only rarely did his alterations respond to an editorial
change found in S by compounding the problem instead of correcting
it (as at 85.18, 91.35n). Once he simply reversed a revision made for S
(118.39bn). Presumably he also altered the subtitle to fit it to the book
at this time.[4]

Very few errors occurred in E1's rapidly typeset text, and those that
did, in contrast to the changes in S, could have been made without
significant editorial intervention. The most egregious is traceable to
the typesetting process, a simple case of eyeskip that caused a sentence to be omitted (see 89.25n). The remainder mostly involved
fine points of expression that tended to be normalized and could be
attributed to indeliberate compositorial regularization or light supervision by proofreader or editor. E1's text smoothed out two arrest-
ing phrasings that must have seemed like obvious cases of idiomatic

---

[1] An interesting example is the alteration of 'recess-like part' to 'recessed part' (91.18). The
change in E1 brings the description into conformity with Conrad's other references to this
feature of the cabin (98.22, 106.12, 109.35) and with similar features of other ships throughout his canon. Although the MS form is perhaps odd enough to have been normalized by
editor or printer, the change anticipates these earlier phrasings of his that occur later in the
story and is apparently one of his several revisions of this famous account of the stateroom
(see 91.12, 91.13a, 91.13b, 91.14). This last is like a later change of 'that' to 'this' (96.10a),
which results in phrasing so unidiomatic as not to be attributable to a Dent's editor or
proofreader.

[2] At 111.16 Conrad first wrote 'As long as you understand' and then interlined 'know that you'
placing it after the 'you' instead of fully incorporating the revision; at 104.2a he began a new
paragraph with the idea of the 'privilege of defective hearing' and, cancelling that, rewrote
the opening with the first clause as an introduction to it. In both cases haste to incorporate
the new wording seems to have led to mis-writing and indeed to something approaching
nonsense, which in E1 Conrad finally put right.

[3] See, for instance, 89.19–20, 103.30a, 113.29b; 96.30a, 102.17, 102.19; 107.37.

[4] The alternative view is that he did so a few weeks later when settling the title for the book
with Dent (see p. 281), but it seems more likely that he made the change when actually
preparing the printer's copy of the stories themselves in early July. He made no revisions to
the rest of this tale or to the other two in Dent's proofs (see below, p. 283). On the story's
titles, see Appendix B.

lapse,[1] deleted words that may have seemed unnecessary if not awkward (83.34, 106.3n), and made a few other small improvements in diction (e.g., 86.7a, 89.15b). These alterations were passed on to the other book editions, which all derived ultimately from E1.[2]

A Smile of Fortune

BETWEEN THE MIDDLE of May and the end of August 1910, Conrad managed to compose, by false starts and major revisions, the long story called at various times 'A Deal in Potatoes', 'The Smile of Fortune', and 'A Smile of Fortune'. The composition process amounted to one of recovery from the breakdown over *Under Western Eyes* and was preceded by his revision of the typescript of that novel, punctuated by the family's move from Aldington to Capel House, and followed by his production of three other stories before he finally resumed *Chance*. The writing of the story was slower and more vexed than usual, and traces of the difficult process survive in the early documents, though presumably as many have perished as have come down to us. In addition to the four book editions and the serialization in the *London Magazine* (S), there remain a manuscript (MS), a complete typescript (TS1), and a partial typescript (TS2). The extant typescripts, which were preceded by at least one other typescript and followed by another now lost, contain a version of the beginning and the ending of the tale written later than that found in the manuscript and in all printed texts. The complete typescript, reconstructed from documents now held by two separate libraries, provides the copy-text for this edition.

Manuscripts and Typescripts

THE BERG COLLECTION of The New York Public Library and the Beinecke Rare Book and Manuscript Library at Yale University house all the early documents that have survived. Together they preserve the manuscript (in its entirety), the first extant typescript (once complete, but now divided between the institutions), and the second extant typescript (once partial, but now prefixed to the later pages of the first and kept as if they were one document). The present arrangement of the

---

[1] See 101.24n, 111.8an; both of E1's alterations level phrasing that may have functioned to characterize Leggatt or Archbold in distinctive ways.

[2] For more detail, see the discussion of the book editions below (pp. 280–88).

materials has its origins in their early histories, which can be reconstructed in part from their physical features, as well as from other evidence.

The manuscript in the Berg Collection consists of 140 pages written on as many leaves of foolscap paper in black ink. The paper stock seems to be uniform throughout and has the mark 'ENGLISH MADE BANK ROCK BROS L^{TD}'. The size was unusual for Conrad. Pagination begins with 'one' and continues from 2 through 140; the word 'one' is the only oddity in the sequence, and a 115 over 105 the only correction. The pagination occupies the upper right margin, except on pages 5–7 and 9–12, where it is centred. From page 13 onward the pagination and the text begin well down the page, leaving a generous margin of some six lines at the top, and even in the early leaves Conrad fails to fill the page. To the left in the top margin of the first page he has written a provisional title 'A deal in Potatoes' and later crossed it out in black ink. To the right and centred are 'J. Conrad' and then 'A Smile of Fortune' in blue pencil in the large hand he often used when marking documents for sale. The last page contains more than half a page of text followed by 'June–Aug^{st} | 1911' in ink in Conrad's hand, which was probably added when he sold the document to John Quinn in the summer of 1913.[1] The document is unusually free from the incidental inscriptions (instructions to typists, occasional doodles and jottings) often found in Conrad's manuscripts: the diagraphs 'æ' and 'Æ' at the top of page 9 are the only such marks in his hand, what is probably a librarian's number on page 23 the only such notation on an internal page. Words and phrases are struck out and additions interlined or written in the left margin on many pages, but these evidences of second thought are no more frequent than normal, and perhaps a little less so from the fourth or fifth section on, and that seems a bit surprising for a story that Conrad reported had been unusually difficult to write.

---

[1] Accompanying the document are Quinn's bookplate, laid in, and a shipping envelope that bears the address 'John Quinn Esqre | 31 Nassau Street | New York City | N.Y. | U.S.A.' in Conrad's hand; the same side of the envelope has British postage stamped 19 August 1913, Ham Street, and on its back are several stampings made by the New York post office with the date 28 August 1913 in various forms. The envelope also contains a stamped number, lower left, that looks like an accession record, large crosses in blue pencil on both sides, and other incidental inscriptions associated with its sale. The manuscript was not sent to Quinn until almost a year after the publication of 'Twixt Land and Sea; see Appendix A, 'Provenance of the Early Documents', pp. 461–3, for an overview of its history, and Fig. 2 for a facsimile of its first page.

The document now in Yale's Beinecke Library consists of thirty-eight leaves of typescript revised by Conrad in ink, together with three leaves of manuscript also in ink.[1] On the first page, which is holograph, is a head-title '*The Smile of Fortune.* | *A harbour story.* | by | J. Conrad.' in that ink, and above that he has written, in blue ink, 'Tales of Experience II', the first provisional title for what became *'Twixt Land and Sea.*[2] This first page of the document is on ruled quarto paper, a simulated 'laid' stock with a crown symbol and the mark 'FINE COMMERCIAL'. Two later manuscript pages on the same stock, finally numbered 29A and 29B, have been inserted between leaves of typescript. The typescript itself is on two kinds of paper, the first sixteen leaves also a 'laid' stock and bearing the mark 'EXCELSIOR | SUPERFINE | BRITISH MADE', the remaining leaves an unmarked wove. Three sequences of pagination occur.[3] Presumably the first (omitting the three manuscript pages) was that typewritten at the foot: 2 *3* 4–8 10–12 14–18 29–42 1–10; the page numbers are centred until the last ten leaves, which have the number against the left margin.[4] The second sequence, also centred at the foot but handwritten in ink, is based partly on the first and incorporates the three manuscript pages: 1 2 3 & 4 5 6 7 8 9 & *10 11 12* 13 & 14 *14 15 16* 9 18 19 10 22–32 32A 32B 33–42; the numbers 22–26 and 28–32 (over *32–36* and *38–42*) cancel the first typewritten digit and incorporate the second. Both '32A' and '32B' appear in the upper right corner, rather than at the foot. The third sequence, in blue pencil in the upper right corner, supersedes both and also incorporates the two inserted manuscript pages: 1–29 29A 29B 30–39; the numbers '34' and '35' have been written over '36' and '37'. In the bottom right corner of page 32 in the ink sequence (later, page 29 in blue pencil), Conrad has written 'to 32A.' in black pencil, presumably after writing the manuscript pages 32A and 32B, later renumbered 29A and 29B. Large cancellations in both ink and blue pencil, often accompanied by revisions in ink, occur on pages 2–8, 10, and 12–16.

---

[1] This document was item 158 in the catalogue of the 1925 Hodgson sale of material held by Jessie Conrad and by Richard Curle. It appears in the Keating catalogue, along with a facsimile of its first page (pp. 215–16). See Appendix A, for more detail, and Fig. 3.

[2] See *Letters*, IV, 355; see above, p. 204.

[3] Inferred numbers appear in italic. The chart in Appendix D, 'Pagination of the First Typescript Fragment', compares the three sequences of pagination; where pagination cannot be reasonably inferred, the symbol [] accounts for the presence of an unnumbered page (or a page number that cannot be recovered) in the sequence.

[4] The first digits of the sequence 29–42 are difficult to recover; but, as the renumbering in ink indicates, they do not appear to be the expected 19–32.

The first (holograph) page is a fair copy that contains only nine short lines of text and no alterations (apart from an interlined word) on its face, though it presumably reproduces a number of revisions, including substantial excisions, made in the heavily revised typescript leaves that it replaced.

The document in the Berg Collection is actually two different type-scripts which comprise 128 pages of text (including two holograph pages) together with a title page that bears the stamp of 'PAUL R. REYNOLDS | 70 Fifth Avenue | NEW YORK' top right and W. T. H. Howe's bookplate top centre.[1] The title, 'THE SMILE OF FORTUNE [broken rule] | A Harbour story [broken rule] | By | J. Conrad. [solid rule]', matches in its layout the head-title found on the first page of text, 'THE SMILE OF FORTUNE [broken rule] | A Harbour Story. [broken rule] | By | J. Conrad. [solid rule]', and comes from the same typewriter. This typewriter produced the first thirty-one pages of text, which the typist numbered with a full-stop in the upper right corner beginning on the second page. The last page in this group of leaves contains only eight lines and concludes with a part line so that the text carries on with the next page, the first of the other Berg typescript. These thirty-one pages have no revisions by Conrad, and indeed no handwritten marks whatsoever.

The remaining Berg pages come from a different typewriter (Jessie Conrad's), are on slightly shorter paper, contain revisions in ink and other marks made by Conrad, and constitute another typescript, itself composed of two groups of leaves, eventually numbered consecutively 40 through 130. The first and smaller group has two sequences of pagination. One is typewritten at the foot against the left margin and runs from 1 through 20. The inferred 9 is blotted with ink beyond recovery,[2] and a few other numbers have been struck through lightly in that ink. Meant to supersede this typewritten pagination, the second sequence, handwritten and centred at the foot, begins with 40 and continues through 59. Except for 52 and 55, these numbers are in the same ink and probably in Conrad's hand. They have in fact been written over an incomplete sequence made in pencil by a different

---

[1] This document, accompanied by a folded leaf of thick paper labelled 'Lot 159' in blunt blue pencil was item 159 in the catalogue of the 1925 Hodgson sale and later owned by William T. H. Howe, the Kentucky book collector and president of the American Book Company (Cincinnati, Ohio). See Appendix A for a discussion of its history and Fig. 4 for a facsimile of its first page.

[2] A '10' was perhaps typed, then cancelled in ink, and a '9' written over it all in pencil, but the inscriptions are highly conjectural.

hand (apparently that of Jessie Conrad) and clearly represented in the uncancelled 52 and 55.[1]

The final group of leaves, seventy-seven in number, carries on from page 60 to 130. Usually the pagination is centred at the bottom and typewritten, but the sequence is broken by duplicate numbers 62, 63, 98, and 116,[2] and it ends with an ink-written 130. An omitted 85 has been supplied in the hand that wrote the earlier 52 and 55; inferred *112* is missing altogether at the bottom of a page whose last line has been cancelled on the typewriter. Between pages 99 and 100 occur two holograph pages numbered 99A and 99B in Conrad's hand in ink in the upper right corner. The last page in this group, and in the document, contains the words 'The End.' centred towards the bottom and followed by 'J. Conrad' to the right, '30 Augst | 1910.' to the left, and 'about 29 000 words.' centred at the bottom above the page number, all written in ink.[3]

The typewritten pages at the Beinecke Library and the last two groups of typewritten pages at the Berg Collection once constituted a single document (TS1). The final numeration (in ink, then typewritten) of what is now physically the second Berg typescript[4] continues the final numeration (in blue pencil) of the Beinecke typescript. The text at the top of page 40 in the Berg typescript carries on both the typewritten and the revised texts from the complete line at the bottom of page 39 of the Beinecke typescript. The part line on the part page at the end of the first Berg typescript (page 31) derives from the revised text at the bottom of the last Beinecke leaf. The Beinecke leaves are almost certainly the pages '1 to 39' that Conrad sent to his agent Pinker in mid-August, what he then called the 'first half of story, ready for <u>clean</u> copy'.[5] The first Berg typescript, pages 1–31 (TS2), constitutes such a fair copy, and the broken rule in its head-title, repeated on

---

[1] The first few pages (40 through 44) and perhaps a few others are also numbered in pencil. The pencilled '42' might have originally been a '22'; the pen cancelling this number and the two previous ones laid ink inconsistently and made the sequence of inscriptions for these early numbers less clear than for the later.

[2] This last is inferential, as both 6s are missing (11 6, 11 6); similar mistyping occurs with 80, 92, and 11 7, where the typed '11' is followed by a handwritten 7 over an erasure.

[3] The total, precisely 27,725, was only slightly inflated.

[4] In the Berg document as presently constituted the physical relations of the pages differ from their temporal relations. Pages 40–130, which once belonged to the complete typescript (TS1), now follow leaves (pages 1–31) of the partial (TS2), though the latter were made after the former.

[5] *Letters*, IV, 355; the date is conjectural, but the second week of August seems very probable (see p. 235, n. 3 below).

its title-page, apparently represents the underlines that Conrad made when writing the title and subtitle on the first (holograph) page of the Beinecke document.

When Conrad sent pages '1 to 39' to Pinker, he claimed that the 'Great part of other half is already written', and certainly some and perhaps all of the second group of Berg pages – provisionally numbered 1–20 with the typewriter – had already been typed before the preceding '39' pages had been finally numbered in blue pencil.[1] How much more of the story Conrad actually had in this form by then is less clear. Although he had recently reported to John Galsworthy that some seventy pages were written and typed,[2] this statement begs several questions, for the manuscript is a provisional first draft, and between it and TS1 lay at least one lost document where Conrad largely revised the story and grappled particularly with its early sections. Any attempt to understand the peculiarly complex history of the story's composition must account for the array of both extant and lost documents, for Conrad's two separate references (on 13 July and 5 August) to having completed the same portion of it, and for the fact that he spent almost three months on it before he was ready to send Pinker the first '39' pages, which proved to be less than one-third when he delivered the remainder just a few weeks later. The only interpretation of the evidence which appears adequate is that Conrad's letters to Galsworthy of 13 July and 5 August refer to two different states of the prologue and opening episodes and that the version represented in the extant typescript made by Jessie Conrad came rather late in the creative process and only shortly before the first lot of pages went off to Pinker for final typing.

The principals in this complex process, besides Conrad, were his wife, his estranged agent, and his most reliable professional friend. Galsworthy had been a vital source of financial support during Conrad's illness in February and March, his preparation of *Under Western Eyes* for serialization in April and early May, and his initial work on 'A

---

[1] What with the substitution of the first page in holograph and the insertion of two other such pages numbered 29A and 29B, the number of leaves and of pages of text was actually forty-one, but for purposes of their relation to subsequent pages of TS1, to the pages of TS2 made from them, and to the course of the story's composition and transmission, it seems best to refer to them as thirty-nine pages.

[2] Conrad to Galsworthy, [13 July 1910] (*Letters*, IV, 346). The date seems assured by the reference to the completion of the 'second' review for the *Daily Mail* and to the column beginning on 'Sat next', i.e., 16 July, when Conrad's first review (eventually titled 'The Life Beyond') appeared. Letters to Graham and Thomas (*Letters*, IV, 348–9) support the date.

Smile of Fortune' in late May and June.[1] Conrad had been without Pinker's accustomed support, both financial and professional. He had been forced to rely on Robert Garnett for overseeing the typing of the printer's copy of the novel and mediating with the *English Review*, as well as for negotiating a new agreement with Pinker.[2] When he began his new story, Conrad was unable to count on Pinker's 'infernal typists' for the production of the initial typescript,[3] an arrangement that since the time of *Nostromo* had been central to his working methods, whereby unfinished and often heavily revised manuscript was in a few days returned with a typescript that he could then revise further in anticipation of at least one more typing.

This change as well as his lingering infirmity must have materially affected the way Conrad wrote 'A Smile of Fortune'. To his wife fell the task of producing the initial typescript of the story from his manuscript (*Letters*, IV, 346). The demands on her had been unusually heavy during the preceding months, and they would continue to be so right through the completion of the story. Amidst their early work on it, the Conrads were preparing to leave Aldington and take up residence at Capel House, and she assumed most of the responsibility for moving house as well. The relatively restrained revision exhibited in MS is probably due in part to Conrad's effort to minimize the difficulties he had normally dumped in the laps of the typists Pinker employed.[4] He seems to have approached this manuscript as a preliminary draft, anticipating typing by Jessie Conrad in batches of ten or twenty pages prior to his thorough reworking in that typescript. As might be expected, many (though not all) of the revised readings that do occur in MS

---

[1] See *Letters*, IV, 322, 329–30, 331, 335–6, 340–41; also 353, 355, 359.

[2] See 'Introduction', p. lxxii. Robert Singleton Garnett (1866–1932), elder brother of Edward, pursued his interests in book-collecting and Alexandre Dumas, the Elder, privately; as a senior partner in the law firm of Darley, Cumberland, for this brief period he represented Conrad's professional interests, as he sometimes did Ford's and D. H. Lawrence's.

[3] *Letters*, IV, 301. Karl (p. 683), summarizing Conrad's 17 May letter to Galsworthy (*Letters*, IV, 329), points out that Garnett was arranging with Pinker that Conrad would be paid £3 per 1,000 words only on actual delivery of 'manuscript' – that is, material which provided a sufficient basis for fair copy, marketing, and printing, which would usually have meant a typescript.

[4] It would be possible to account for this difference by postulating a previous lost and presumably rougher draft of which the extant document was a fair copy, along the lines pursued by the Keating cataloguer's speculation that the 39-page typescript preceded the manuscript (see above, p. 227, n. 1). But the conjecture is difficult to credit. See Appendix A.

appear in TS1, but they were likely transmitted through an intervening document, almost certainly a typescript, now lost (*TSo*).[1]

Composition, Typing, and Revision

FROM MID-MAY to early July, Conrad wrote, at first tentatively and
then with increasing command, the first half of the manuscript draft,
which Jessie Conrad made into a typescript now lost (*TSo*). In late July
and early August, he thoroughly revised these pages of that typescript,
rewriting the prologue entirely, and went on to revise the pages of
the new typescript (TS1) made to incorporate this round of revisions.
During the remainder of August he completed the manuscript draft
and revised both the pages of the lost typescript made from it and his
wife's retyping of them, which completed the extant TS1.

The month's work on 'A Smile of Fortune' that Conrad did from
18 May, when he apparently began it, till the move to Capel House
seems to have been limited to the prologue and perhaps the first one
or two episodes. On 23 May he wrote to Pinker – addressing him as
'Dear Sir' in their first contact since the break in January – that he
was 'under notice to quit' the Aldington house by 24 June.[2] Although
this proved to be a blessing, in that Conrad rightly despised the place
as a pigsty[3] and would find a much more suitable dwelling, it was for
the moment not calculated to settle his mind. For the next week or
two he worked at the story in short intervals, reporting to Galsworthy
a few days later that it went on 'halting a little' despite 'a sort of faint
relapse', and at the end of May that what he had up to then, given his
feeble condition and various interruptions, amounted to 'mere trial
run so to speak'. The early weeks of June were apparently not much

---

[1] For example, 'contained in one noble phrase' for 'resumed in one noble passage' (16.7);
'change of cooking' for 'change of food' (19.24); or 'His time was my own.' added in the
margin of MS, transmitted to TS1 in slightly altered form, and restored to MS form in the
prints (19.9). Amongst the revisions in MS that do not appear in the typewritten text of
TS1 are 'gale' (25.5), part of an interlined phrase further tweaked by Conrad in *TSo*; 'gash
on his freshly' (26.35b), also interlined in MS and possibly revised by Conrad in *TSo* but
more likely scrambled by Jessie Conrad when typing it; and 'waddled back' (47.22a) for his
cancelled 'returned', almost certainly replaced with 'toddled back' by her in *TSo*. On the
implications of these and similar revisions for the history of the manuscript, see Appendix
A; on Jessie Conrad's errors, see below, p. 239, and n. 2.

[2] *Letters*, IV, 334. This is at least the first surviving evidence of contact between them; it may
have been preceded by the letter to which Conrad refers there or by a telegram or a more
ephemeral scrap of paper.

[3] The word is not Conrad's but resembles his sentiment; see Karl, p. 682, Najder, p. 346 (also
p. 273 for an interesting coincidence).

better, and a month after beginning it he confessed he had not yet finished the story and was still 'in a sort of tottering state' and 'unable to keep up any sort of mental pace'.[1]

By 26 June the Conrads were settling into Capel House, which seems to have had an immediate effect on his work. It was at this time that Conrad, still 'intellectually giddy', received from Lindsay Bashford, the literary editor of the *Daily Mail*, an offer of a weekly book-review column that might also have helped him get into a more productive mode.[2] By 13 July he had completed two of those reviews and was reporting to Galsworthy that he had '70 pp of the short story written and typed', that '3 or 4' thousand more would finish the story, and that he was even working a little on *Chance* (*Letters*, IV, 346–7). Whatever we make of the reference to the novel, the second statement regarding the story was of course too optimistic, as it would grow to twice that length, and in view of his report that 'after an hour or so I grow confused' and he often had to stop writing, his first statement leaves some doubt about exactly what text he then had in hand.

Unless he was telling his friend and benefactor a fib, this statement indicates that by mid-July Conrad had reached the climactic action of the story, though only in draft form. The introduction of Alice with her massive, untidy hair (46.10) occurs precisely on page 70 of MS (page 69 of TS1), and by this point the entire story must have taken firm shape in his mind. Within a little more than two weeks of settling into Capel House, we must suppose, he had finished drafting much of the narrative up to the first episode in Jacobus' house. If he wrote this much in the unproductive weeks preceding the move and the more productive ones immediately following it, which included at least two or three days given over to the reviews for Bashford, he must have forged ahead with the manuscript draft without giving much attention to the initial typescript (*TSo*) that Jessie Conrad was making from it. Indeed, when recounting the results of Jacobus' second on-board visit, Conrad referred in the manuscript to Burns's 'serious illness'

---

[1] *Letters*, IV, 335, 340, 342. This episode Conrad remembered, though a bit inaccurately, as late as 1919, when composing the volume's 'Author's Note' (see 5.29–32).

[2] Conrad claimed he could produce the column in a day and a half, diverting little attention from his main work; the column gave him a regular income of five guineas a week to help reduce his enormous debt to Pinker. Although the arrangement lasted only a month, this apparently feasible task, along with the steady income and the new environment of Capel House, might well have contributed to Conrad's more effective work on his story. See Conrad to Galsworthy, [13 July 1910] (*Letters*, IV, 346), and 'The Texts' in *Notes on Life and Letters*, pp. 256–7.

(32.29a*n*); that phrase he would later replace in *TSo* with 'deadly fever' to make it conform to the typescript version of the prologue.[1] This remnant of the draft version of the prologue at the end of the second section of the MS confirms that Conrad had not begun to revise the initial typescript at this point, and it supports the view that he would not do so until he was half way through the fourth, in the second week of July. Such a scenario helps explain why it would be another three or four weeks before he would send any copy to Pinker, and then not enough to complete the second section.

Lacking the support of Pinker's typists and under extraordinary internal stress, Conrad had adopted a method for writing 'A Smile of Fortune' that was unusually complex even for him. During the end of June and early July, he completed and Jessie Conrad typed the rough draft of the prologue and the early episodes represented in MS. She presumably produced this typescript in batches as Conrad handed over manuscript pages with which he was finished. Having at least reached the Captain's first encounter with Alice in MS,[2] he apparently returned to revise the material he had up to this point in *TSo*. These pages he so thoroughly rewrote that he returned them for a second typing on much the same basis as he had MS, and Jessie Conrad produced TS1 on much the same basis as she had *TSo*, typing it in batches, changing paper and losing track of the pagination sequence between the prologue and the first section (hence typewritten '18' and '29',

---

[1] For the manuscript's version, which does not appear in this edition's critical text and is not reflected in the apparatus keyed to it, see Appendix F, 'The Serial Version of the Prologue and Ending'; subsequent citations of it contain a colon to distinguish it from the present edition's (and the typescript's) text. TS1's 'deadly fever' is a revision, made in *TSo*, in light of the typescript version of the prologue, which refers to Burns's 'bad fever' (13.26). TS1's phrase was perpetuated through all the published texts despite their use of the manuscript version's opening, which refers to Burns's 'desperate illness' (3:9). Conrad failed to remove this anomaly when shortening the story for S and later when preparing copy for E1 (see below). In the first episode he also changed another phrase in the typescripts to match the new version of the prologue but later restored it for the serial printing (19.28b*n*). For similar reasons apparently, he eventually restored in that episode the manuscript version of the Captain's meditations about conversing with Jacobus upon their first meeting (21.16–28), rejected at the end of the first section the typescripts' comment about business success and personal character (25.18–19) that led into the two holograph pages inserted in TS1 to conclude section I and open section II, and cut the passage about Jacobus' boatman (51.19–25) at the end of section IV that tied into the word that opened section V in the typescript version. On the occasion of these changes, see p. 244.

[2] It seems likely that he had got beyond it a bit and probably continued to draft this episode while revising *TSo*.

renumbered 18 and 19 in ink, 16 and 17 in blue pencil),[1] beginning
a new sequence of ten pages for the second section (typewritten 1–10,
pages 33–42 in ink, 30–39 in blue pencil), provisionally numbering
the next group, which contained the third section and the beginning
of the fourth, 1–20 (finally renumbered 40–59). This provisional numbering reflected Conrad's awareness, even when he had reached the
beginning of the climactic episodes in MS and *TSo*, that the material in
the earlier pages still required such revision that a single sequence of
pagination was premature.[2] It was only towards the middle of August[3]
that the prologue and first episodes, 'roughly 9000' words, were sufficiently settled to allow pages '1 to 39' to go off to Pinker for typing of
fair copy and to allow for the numbering of the next twenty (40–59)
based on that sequence,[4] which brought TS1 to within ten pages of
the introduction of Alice.

---

[1] The change of paper stock in TS1 occurs in the second page of what became the first section.
This does not quite coincide with the break in typewritten numeration (18 to 29) nor with
the shift from background narrative to the first episode. It suggests rather that the typing
of the first section resumed with the same paper, though after a break that caused the error
in numeration. The interruption might have had to do with Conrad's taking a day or so to
write a review for the *Daily Mail.*

[2] Indeed, the final pagination required two attempts, one in ink and then the one in blue
pencil; the one might have followed the other in relatively quick order, because Conrad's
alterations to the text in ink and blue pencil were concurrent, as the cancellations in both
ink and pencil and the revisions in ink show. The blue-pencil '34' and '35' over '36' and
'37' could suggest that these pages had been part of a different and longer sequence, but
nothing in the texts of the preceding and following pages indicates such revision in this
area, and it is more probable that Conrad made a simple numeration error at this point.

[3] Although dating Conrad's covering note to Pinker (*Letters*, IV, 355) is problematic, the
terms of the note agree so exactly with Conrad's report to Galsworthy on 15 August 1910
(*Letters*, IV, 359) that a date close to that seems very probable, as the Cambridge editors
suggest (see p. 355, n. 1). This note must certainly postdate that of the 5th, which in a sense
recapitulated old news (see p. 237). Conrad's statement regarding one more review yet to
be published in the *Daily Mail* would, then, refer to the lost one on hypnotism, which he
apparently did not know had been killed, as later complaints about non-payment indicate.
(See 'The Texts' in *Notes on Life and Letters*, p. 257.) The 'pp 1 to 39 roughly 9000, first half
of story, ready for clean copy' that Conrad sent Pinker give a *roughly* accurate estimate: the
end of section II (page 39 blue pencil) brought the total to 8,464, and page 39 contained
a bit of the beginning of section III. This was, however, to be roughly the first third of the
story, not the first half.

[4] As in the earlier pages (see n. 2), this final numbering apparently occurred in two stages, a
provisional and intermittent one in pencil (presumably by Jessie Conrad), and then Conrad's
own in ink. Even at this stage, there may have been some pages of revised TS1 replaced by
those now present in the document. The holograph fair copy of the first page is certainly one
such; the typescript pages it replaced must have been very heavily revised, to judge by the
next few pages, which contain major alterations and massive excisions (see the 'Apparatus')
and yet were retained.

At the end of August, looking back on his early work on the story, Conrad echoed what he had told Galsworthy at the end of May: 'June's work was mere fooling'. 'I was still too limp to grasp the subject', he continued, 'and most of the pages written then have been cancelled in type-script. It was strangely nerveless bosh' (*Letters*, IV, 362). The typescript version of the prologue, as preserved in TS1, quadrupled that in MS, so that some 600 words became almost 2,400, and four pages of manuscript became more than fifteen of typescript. Conrad added the nursing scene (13.18–14.30) and the elaborate descriptions of the island (15.10–15, 16.13–21, 16.34–17.25). The two lines at the bottom of page 3 of TS1 – the only ones surviving cancellation on this page – provided a join to the addition on the nursing scene. The five uncancelled lines at the top of page 10 provided a similar transition to the passage on the Captain's ambitions and talents that follows, which in turn introduced one of the Captain's added musings on the beauty of the island. Yet the nursing scene itself and the passages on the Captain's ambitions and musings were already present in TS1's typewritten text (TS1t) when Conrad revised it, though they are absent from the final MS version.[1] At least one document, likely destroyed once it had been superseded, must have contained this expanded version before the extant TS1 was created.[2]

In this typescript (*TSo*), made by Jessie Conrad from the manuscript, Conrad rewrote much of the beginning of the story. Some sentences in this typescript version altered those in MS only slightly (16.3–12, 17.36–18.9). Other sentences and paragraphs were wholly reordered (15.15–25, 15.26–30; 14.38–15.1, 16.22–33). Conrad expanded the account of the anchorage off the coast during a blustery night (17.26–35) and elaborated Burns's cynicism about the Captain's luck (13.13–15, 14.30–37, 16.26–33), besides adding the new passages already mentioned. This process of wholesale revision he carried forward in the

---

[1] Still more text associated with these additions was present as well in TS1t, though Conrad deleted it in the revisions he made in the document. For example, the two lines on page 3 that survived Conrad's revision were immediately preceded by a paragraph unprecedented in MS: 'That little laugh down the ventilator had that character – as much as to say A great piece of luck indeed! And in truth there was no special cause for jubilation in such a very ordinary landfall A navigator making for an island would naturally expect to see it right ahead. Yet everything is relative. And that little laugh of Mr Burns' meant also "It's a mercy we haven't had to grope for it all over the place!"' For more examples, see the 'Apparatus'.

[2] Indeed, the use made of the document probably effected its destruction. That there was yet another intermediate document in which Conrad revised and which Jessie Conrad retyped is of course possible, but postulating such a document is not necessary to explain the evidence, nor does it alter the main outlines of the story's textual history.

second – that is, the extant – typescript produced by his wife, revising words and phrases, cancelling large chunks of material, and interlining new material in place of typewritten, which he deleted in either ink or blue pencil. The substitution of TS1's holograph fair-copy page for its first two typed pages (now lost) is the most obvious sign of this continuing process. But it was to carry on through the whole of the prologue and into the first few sentences of the first episode (18.16 in section 1), and to varying degrees through the writing of the rest of the story.

Both the extent and nature of these revisions confirm Conrad's August statement that the MS prologue begun before the removal from Aldington was largely replaced by the typescript version produced after the Conrads had settled into Capel House. Despite the salvaging of some MS bits, the typescript version represents a new beginning that must be dated no earlier than mid-July. The revision and retyping of it and of the episodes that immediately followed it apparently took two or three weeks and consumed the latter part of July.[1]

By early August Conrad was pressing ahead with the rest of the story, without review deadlines for the *Daily Mail* to trouble him. His statement of 5 August to Galsworthy that he had '14 000 words of a long short-story ready' (*Letters*, IV, 354) expressed his relief regarding the portion of the story he had mentioned on 13 July, though by then in its rewritten and revised form. By this time Conrad apparently felt sufficiently secure about the story's shape to have the remainder of TS1 paginated as it was typed. Although Jessie Conrad would make errors, especially at the beginning of this sequence,[2] and Conrad would interpolate pages of holograph, major rewriting was behind him by the time the last half of TS1 was produced in the latter part of August. However, the writing of the rest of the story was by no means straightforward. Jessie Conrad still produced an intermediate *TSo*, presumably in batches as before, so that Conrad could make additions and other

---

[1] At a minimum the process must have occupied the last two weeks of July, from the 17th to the 31st; at the outside, which seems more likely, it ran from about 14 July (a Thursday) to 4 August (also a Thursday). In either case it presumably postdated the reviewing done for the *Daily Mail*, which may have been wound up by the 14th. Conrad's notice to Bashford giving up the column has not been located and the fact must be inferred from his early August letter to Pinker enclosing the first lot of typescript for the story (*Letters*, IV, 355), but the reviews that were published and the one that was killed all seem to have been written by mid-July. See 'The Texts' in *Notes on Life and Letters*, pp. 256–7.

[2] The duplicated 62, 63, 98 and 116; some of these interruptions of the pagination sequence were perhaps occasioned by rewriting and cancellation of typewritten pages now lost.

adjustments. Even in TS1, made from this typescript and incorporating his *TSo* revisions, he continued to revise extensively. By 17 August
he was writing to Pinker about resuming and publishing *Chance* after
finishing the story, but the drafting, rewriting, retyping, and revising
went on until the end of the month, when at the bottom of TS1's final
page he inscribed the date '30 Aug^st 1910' to mark the completion
of his first real piece of work since the breach with Pinker and the
breakdown over *Under Western Eyes*.[1]

The last lot of leaves went off to Pinker in the next day or two, and by
3 September Conrad was acknowledging receipt of payment from his
agent, having wired him the previous day seeking confirmation that the
document had arrived (*Letters*, IV, 365). Apparently Pinker received
only two lots in all, the first of '39' pages in the middle of the month,
and the remainder at the end.[2] By then he had presumably had the
first lot retyped and was awaiting copy for the 'other half . . . already
written' that Conrad had mentioned a few weeks earlier (*Letters*, IV,
355). From this new lot (actually, the last two-thirds of TS1) he had
a fair typescript made. This, together with either a further copy of
the 'clean copy' already in hand or a duplicate of it, constituted the
typescript (*TS3*) he would show round to the English magazines.[3] As
for American serialization, Conrad enquired at the end of November
about American copyright (*Letters*, IV, 392), and probably by then
Pinker had undertaken to market the story in New York. In the event,
and perhaps in a cautious attitude towards further financial outlays
involving Conrad, he attached the second lot of Conrad's own revised
typescript (TS1) to the thirty-one pages already in hand (TS2) and sent
that document to Paul R. Reynolds, his representative in America.[4]

---

[1] Conrad's letter to Galsworthy of Saturday, 27 August, suggests he was within reach of the
end and registers his determination to finish by the 29th. There is no reason to believe
he did not do so a day later than hoped. The letter of 2 September to Sanderson, which
mentions the finished story and that Jessie Conrad has been 'extremely busy', confirms
that the story was off (*Letters*, IV, 362, 364). Cf. *LL*, p. 114; *Chronology*, p. 79; Najder,
p. 366; Karl, p. 689; Batchelor, p. 191.

[2] This was in accord with the formal business relationship between the two then in force (see
p. 231, n. 3). Appendix A provides more detail on the handling of documents under this
arrangement.

[3] For a genealogical chart, see Fig. 15 (p. 247).

[4] See above, p. 228. The subsequent history of this document remains shadowy until its sale
in 1925, even during the crucial months of spring 1911 and summer 1912 (see below,
p. 246); for further details, see Appendix A.

The typescript pages that Conrad sent to Pinker and those later sent by him to Reynolds in New York contained graphic errors made by Jessie Conrad as well as corrections of them made by Conrad. These errors ranged from the simple substitution of 'the' for 'his', 'her', and 'my'[1] to the omission of entire phrases or sentences (28.8a, 71.24–25; 33.3–5). Many, like her 'ominously' and her omission of 'sinks of abomination' (34.21, 58.32b), were associated with interlineations or other revisions in MS. Eyeskip and line skip resulted in the loss or disruption of words, phrases, or sentences (23.35n, 28.8a, 49.33, 66.36, 75.37b; 20.14–15, 29.5), as did the occasional page break (39.8b, 57.7–8). Conrad had corrected a little more than half these errors by the time he had finished revising TS1, but some had to await correction in S. Either he, the typist of TS2, or S's editor corrected the handful of Jessie Conrad's simple literals. Conrad had equal success in spotting two of her three errors of memory when working in TS1 (37.6, 76.12a; 49.27) and her surprisingly frequent substitutions of 'said' for various interlocutory verbs (e.g., 22.40, 24.12a, 25.8, 25.17–18). Many of her omissions he also detected and restored there (e.g., 25.6, 26.17), but often those in the second half of the story, written and revised in the last few weeks of August, escaped his notice until he prepared the text of S (e.g., 46.31–32, 47.1, 68.37–38); indeed, one survived through the book editions (68.21a). These omissions of Jessie Conrad's resembled errors she committed elsewhere. She frequently erred where Conrad had revised (e.g., 33.32, 36.2b, 49.19) or where she found seemingly odd idioms or diction, which she normalized (e.g., 21.39a, 26.7a, 32.14–15b, 32.18, 33.15a, 70.2c), or other disconcerting wording, which she levelled (e.g., 22.6b, 22.8, 40.4, 47.19a, 52.8, 68.37, 76.11a, 76.23–24). In several cases, like the substitution of 'toddled' for 'waddled' and the omissions of the clause 'I showered kisses upon her face' and of the reference to 'thick' limbs, her changes concerned details in the episodes involving Alice and her aunt, about which she seems to have been particularly uncomfortable.[2]

More than a dozen other readings in TS1t look suspiciously like these sorts of errors but might represent revisions Conrad had made

---

[1] See, e.g., the variants at 28.8c, 31.19b, 31.26; 46.13, 62.28a, 71.7b; 24.3a, 44.37b, 72.18, 77.7b.

[2] See the changes at 47.22a (which survived through S), 65.17–18, and 49.28a; also those at 47.28b, 57.2b, 57.2c, 57.17, 57.29a, 60.3, 60.5c, 60.6b, 66.9–10, 70.22.

in *TSo* and then reversed in TS1r or later.[1] Likewise, his alterations of contractions in TS1r (23.26, 42.15–16, 44.9a) and presumably in S (42.1a) suggest that most of TS1t's changes of this kind, which both expand and collapse negatives for 'is', 'are', 'was', 'will', 'have', and 'did' in no apparent patterns, represent alterations he had made in *TSo*. However, the apostrophe that appears or disappears in TS1t's forms of possessives (usually for Burns, Jacobus, and his captain's room) is another matter; although some of these changes, often the result of ambiguity in MS, could represent Conrad's attempts to clarify as much as his wife's,[2] a few are clearly hers and are erroneous (e.g., 34.16b, 38.7b, 42.8c, 69.34, 73.4c). The alterations of tense found in TS1t are even more suspect. In those instances where some certainty is possible, Jessie Conrad tended to simplify complex constructions, usually moving towards the present and away from the perfect and the past perfect; at least four instances of this (26.13a, 27.9–10, 58.27–28, 67.7a) can be attributed confidently to her but none to Conrad, whereas no examples of complex pasts can be attributed solely to her initiative.[3] In this much vexed feature of Conrad's prose, she seems to have interfered more seriously with his expression than in other groups of changes that are problematic. Still, her outright errors in TS1t, which range from whole sentences and phrases to single words, amount to over 400 instances – understandable given the course of the story's composition, transmission, and revision, but alarming nonetheless.

Serialization

NOTHING CAME of Pinker's effort to place the story in America, and it was many weeks before he himself succeeded in finding an English magazine interested in taking it. During those weeks Conrad rested from his summer's labours, worried himself about Pinker's dealings with the *English Review* over *Under Western Eyes*, wrote 'Prince Roman', and attempted 'The Partner'. There is no evidence in the surviving letters for these weeks that he made revisions in the Pinker typescript

---

[1] Again, these are more frequent after page 69 of TS1: e.g., 26.15, 39.23a, 43.11a, 44.37–38, 46.24, 51.17, 68.38, 69.7a, 69.17, 70.29, 75.32, 76.14a, 76.28c.

[2] Cf., e.g., what appear to be his alterations at 20.35b, 32.15, 42.37b, and 74.17b as against those at 19.8a, 21.39b, 31.16a, 41.13a, and 67.22.

[3] An apparent exception is the change at 58.22, but this probably represents gravitation to consistency in the context of larger revision. The change at 68.33 is another instance of such consistency, which in this case muddles the main point.

(*TS3*), and under the circumstances such a step seems highly unlikely. Indeed he seems to have done nothing on 'A Smile of Fortune' until mid-November, when rather abruptly he was forced to respond to a proposal from the *London Magazine* to publish it in truncated form.

On 17 November, a Thursday, Conrad sent Pinker a 'copy', typewritten by Jessie Conrad, of what he called 'the 3 <u>material pars</u>:' of a letter written to W. C. Beaumont, the editor of the *London Magazine*, together with the postscript, in his own hand, for which he said there had been 'no room' in her typewritten copy. Shortly thereafter, Pinker received a letter from Hubert Filchew on behalf of Beaumont, dated the 19th, responding to Conrad's letter.[1] Filchew's letter probably arrived the day of its posting, if it was posted rather than delivered by hand,[2] as the reference to the next 'Monday' indicates. By then Conrad's letter of the 17th must also have reached Pinker. Both repeat much the same wording from Conrad's letter to Beaumont. The documents suggest that Conrad's letter to Pinker must have gone off almost simultaneously with his to Beaumont, and that there must have been previous correspondence between Pinker and Conrad on this subject which has now perished (along possibly with a note to Pinker enclosing the 'copy').

Earlier that week, presumably, Pinker had received a proposal from Beaumont stipulating what Filchew called 'some slight alterations to and deletions from the complete novel'. Pinker had communicated that fact to Conrad, and perhaps the fact that he had virtually agreed to these terms. Conrad responded directly to Beaumont, protesting rather heatedly that he would never alter a text 'to suit the tastes, opinion or criticism of any person whatever' and taking the high ground against allowing modifications of his works' 'inner texture' to be passed off as his own 'art of expression'. His copy to his agent did not mention his concluding statement, which was quoted by Filchew and was potentially most disturbing to Pinker: 'However, you don't think the story good enough – and there's an end of it'. Conrad's more temperate discussion of the story itself that followed his general proclamations of artistic integrity not only provided an explanation of his narrative strategies, but also mentioned alterations to the opening and closing

---

[1] See Appendix E, 'Correspondence with the *London Magazine*' for transcriptions of both letters, now held by the Bancroft Library, University of California, Berkeley.
[2] The offices of the *London Magazine* were but a few blocks from Pinker's, in the adjacent postal district.

that he might have been willing to consider had Beaumont been so good as to make 'suggestions of a practical kind'. The rhetorical strategies of this letter are not the central issue here; what is important is that Conrad, faced with a fait accompli, effectively managed to define the terms on which he would be willing to make changes as a concession to 'the conditions of serial-reading' – 'i.e., hurried reading, a danger to which a tale in a magazine is always exposed' – despite the fact that they 'would impoverish the composition'.

Whatever their inner springs, these concessions were conditioned by the facts that Pinker had already agreed in principle to some cuts and that Conrad was more desperate than ever for cash to reduce his debt to Pinker and to place his first work since *Under Western Eyes* in a way that would avoid alienating his agent any further. Unhappy with a magazine that he rated in a telegram to Pinker as 'third best', Conrad was nonetheless willing 'to tinker at it to fit it quite for that exalted destiny', as he told his closest professional friend.[1] In the event his alterations were those he had proposed in the letter to Beaumont, made all the more convenient by the fact that the supposedly new material already existed in the earlier, rejected version of the story present in the holograph manuscript written in May and early June and still in his possession.[2]

In his letter to Pinker, Filchew requested to have 'the MS back first thing on Monday' for further consideration, in effect prepared to accept the story more or less on Conrad's terms. Pinker may have followed this course and thus entered a further round of negotiations, or (in order to avoid possible rejection) he may simply have obtained Conrad's agreement to make the changes that he had mentioned in his letter of 17 November. In either case, the matter was apparently settled that Monday,[3] and Conrad presumably had the 'manuscript' in hand by the middle of the week and back to Pinker by the end as promised.

---

[1] Conrad to Pinker, [22 November 1910] (*Letters*, IV, 389); Conrad to Galsworthy, 22 November 1910 (*Letters*, IV, 390). The dating of the telegram is confirmed by the sequence of events described below. The *London Magazine* was one of several popular organs published by the Harmsworths' Amalgamated Press and not unjustly spurned by serious writers; see Appendix C, 'The *London Magazine*'.

[2] This document never went to Pinker of course and was apparently still in Capel House at the time; see Appendix A for more detail.

[3] The telegram to Pinker and the letter to Galsworthy both suggest that it had in effect been resolved by Tuesday, the 22nd (*Letters*, IV, 389–90). Conrad would have sent the typescript back to his agent on the 25th, the promised Friday, so Pinker was able to deliver the *London Magazine* copy the following Monday at the latest.

The typescript that was returned to Conrad from the *London Magazine* (apparently through Pinker) consisted of 113 pages (*Letters*, IV, 391). This lost complete typescript (*TS3*), which Pinker had made to serve as magazine copy, was apparently comparable in format to the 31-page fragment of the prologue and early episodes (TS2) now in the Berg Collection. Had the typing of this document been carried on, losing from one to one and a half pages for every ten pages of TS1 reproduced, the ninety pages of TS1 (from pages 40 to 130) would have become about eighty (from pages 32 to 112). The extant TS2 thus provides a fairly accurate representation of the early portion of the lost Pinker typescript that helps us reconstruct the means Conrad used to create the serial version, making large alterations to the beginning of the story and more isolated ones to the end.

Replacing one sentence 'at end of story on p 113' in the typescript version ('He had always looked on this affair as a purely commercial transaction.'), Conrad supplied Pinker a 'few lines of MS' ('And as I sat heavy-hearted at that parting, seeing all my plans destroyed, my modest future endangered – for this command was like a foot in the stirrup for a young man – he gave up completely for the first time his critical attitude.') which in turn expanded what he already had in the original holograph (see 78.6–8). The '$1\frac{1}{2}$ pp. of MS' that were 'inserted on page 112 of type. (A & B)' amounted to the 'half a page or so more at the end, giving a greater relief to our man's final feelings' that he had suggested to Beaumont. This addition (138:4–139:7)[1] was based on the rejected MS version but introduced some new readings, the most important of which emphasize the Captain's agony in posting the letter (138:4, 139:3), elaborate his ambivalent view of Jacobus (138:16), and develop the theme of fortune (138:12, 138:23) that in one way or another had already been compensated for still further in the typescript version.

The early pages of the lost Pinker typescript (*TS3*), virtually identical in length to those in the Berg Collection, had collapsed TS1's more than fifteen revised pages into nine. These nine pages 'of type', which contained the prologue, Conrad replaced with '5 pp of MS'. He apparently based these five pages of new manuscript on his original MS. The new manuscript contained much the same material as that in the extant holograph, some in slightly revised form (see, e.g., variants

---

[1] See Appendix F, 'The Serial Version of the Prologue and Ending' for this passage and for subsequent references to the serial version of the prologue and ending and the variants within them.

in the serial version at 1:5, 1:7, 1:10, 3:3, 3:8, 3:26), but it expanded the MS material with additional phrases at several points (2:1, 2:3–4, 2:20, 3:11, 4:4) helping to cause its four pages (of foolscap) to become five (probably of quarto). At one point the new manuscript reordered sentences of the old in the same way the typescript had.[1] By and large, however, the reworked manuscript text that Conrad resubmitted in November reversed the expansion of the MS version that he had made in late July when creating the typescript version (see above, pp. 236–7), and it did so very much in accord with his supposedly hypothetical statement to Beaumont regarding the prologue.

At this time presumably, Conrad took advantage of his access to *TS3* to make some additional revisions in it. Only a few of them – a phrase about his owners' instructions to the Captain, sentences about conversing with Jacobus when first meeting him, about professional versus personal life, about Jacobus' boatman, and some wording at the very end – were apparently related directly to the restored, serial version of the prologue.[2] Not surprisingly, there were a couple of other alterations at the very end. One (75.13–14) continued the process of revision already evidenced in the typescript, combining elements from MS and TS1, whereas another (77.33a) represented entirely new wording.

These kinds of revisions are present elsewhere in S's text, especially in the second half of the story (after page 69 of TS1). Those unprecedented in MS and TS1 involve small details and are the least frequent. Very few are not actually foreshadowed in some way (e.g., 39.14a, 39.26a, 46.29, 47.14b, 69.35b); many concern passages rewritten in *TSo* (e.g., 23.21b, 27.33a, 42.8b, 68.24, 73.37a, 73.38). The most frequent revisions found in S continue a process begun in *TSo* and carried on in TS1r. Sometimes these changes advance the process of revision further in the same direction either by adding to a word that first appears in TS1 (e.g., 20.12, 47.35) or by refining in some other way the revision made in the typescripts (e.g., 24.14b, 26.26, 41.4–5, 74.13–14).

---

[1] See 1:17–18 in Appendix F and 15.27–30 in the critical text.

[2] See the variants at 19.28b, 21.16–22, 21.26–28, 25.18–19, 51.19–25, 78.3. Burns's final but interrupted bit of scolding (78.3) seems to be part of the serial version of the ending (see 78.4b*n*). The other passages either occur strategically early in the opening episode or conclude later sections of the narrative. See 19.28b*n* and p. 234, n. 1. Two sentences on what compels the Captain's fascination with Alice (57.35, 63.40) are apparently part of Conrad's general revision of the tale (see 57.38, 63.40–64.1), as neither involves the larger questions that distinguish the typescript from the serial version.

More often Conrad reconsidered rather complex alterations he had made in the typescripts, usually at more than one stage. As in the first, transitional sentence in the initial section (18.16), he combined readings he had changed earlier (24.12a, 26.28) or reversed the direction of change and restored in part or in whole a reading of MS he had altered (47.19a, 69.7a; 27.14, 41.34–35). These compound revisions ranged from single words, like 'infuriated' (47.22b), to whole sentences, like 'I was highly amused' (28.35a). Rarely, Conrad simply changed his mind in a quite straightforward manner and reverted to the MS's word or phrase.[1] He gave some additional attention to features that had been a continuing concern in the typescripts: he fiddled with a few contractions (36.11a, 73.19b),[2] put right several possessives (19.27an, 23.15b, 32.32, 44.21, 52.14),[3] and altered some vexing tenses, often restoring an MS form in whole (26.13a, 27.9–10, 58.27–28) or in part (20.14–15), sometimes characteristically producing a superficially acceptable but actually inappropriate form (27.9–10, 27.17, 41.39, 42.4b). Nevertheless, during these few days he failed to correct various errors in the Pinker typescript that derived from TS1 and TS2.[4]

When it appeared with his recent alterations in the *London Magazine* for February 1911, Conrad's tale was accompanied by some fanfare. As the 'complete novel' in that number, it was given its own section title-page, and a full-page portrait of the author also preceded the text.[5] Furthermore, the first page of the editor's monthly 'Entre Nous' was devoted to a discussion of this department of the magazine, and more than a column devoted to 'Mr. Joseph Conrad' and his 'life, picturesque and wild, around the islands of the Malay Archipelago'

[1] Altogether there were very few such changes in the entire story, and most of them at the end: see 18.35, 31.34a, 67.9c, 67.10–11, in addition to the one already cited (78.4b). The first involves an alteration stimulated by what looks like Jessie Conrad's error; see also 23.35n.

[2] See also the expanded contraction at 1:13a in the serial version of the prologue where MS lacks the apostrophe; this could have been altered by either an editor or Conrad, who restored the MS form in E1.

[3] The last three are rather straightforward corrections and could be editorial.

[4] See, for instance, errors made by Jessie Conrad in the first episode at 18.33b, 19.21c, 20.38a, 21.11b, 21.39a, and so on.

[5] *The London Magazine*, 25, February 1911, pp. 801–36. On this section of the magazine, which helped motivate the editorial concern about the length of the story, see Appendix C; for the section title-page, used for both this story and 'Freya of the Seven Isles', see Fig. 11.

called the reader's attention to the fact that this 'literary genius' was amongst the authors whose works the magazine had been or would be publishing.[1]

Although predominant, Conrad's revisions were not the only new readings that eventually appeared in S. Some 'correcting' of the text took place. Predictably, an editor or perhaps a compositor normalized Conrad's 'these potatoes' to 'those potatoes' and smoothed out a few other odd idiomatic usages.[2] Word order was regularized (25.7a, 29.25), and a literal solution was imposed on a problem Conrad had been having with a metaphorical phrase (21.28b). Finally, an editor seems to have put right a few simple errors, not always with happy results (29.13, 48.34b, 50.34), altered colloquial phrasing (41.29a), and mistakenly levelled two possessives and a tense (35.35c*n*, 43.22; 22.9b).

First English Edition

MOST OF these changes in S reappeared in the text of Dent's first English edition (E1), along with numerous typists' errors that S had inherited from TS1 and TS2. Together these variants confirm the implication of Conrad's statements in the summer of 1912 that, in preparing copy for the printers of E1, he used serial tear-sheets. There, without referring to the documents that included the typescript version of the prologue and ending,[3] he corrected some of S's outright

---

[1] *London Magazine*, 25, February 1911, p. 837. The list of authors included, with almost equal self-congratulation, names now mostly forgotten. See Appendix C.

[2] See 70.2c, 74.17d; 44.27, 46.30b, 64.28–29*n*.

[3] Despite his earlier resolutions, Conrad apparently did not have effective control over the documents containing his second version of the prologue and the related changes in the ending, which dated from July–November 1910. (See Appendix A.) The nine cancelled pages of the Pinker typescript (*TS3*) that he claimed to have kept purposely for 're-insertion in' the book edition (*Letters*, IV, 392) seem to have perished and might have gone missing by June 1912. The composite typescript, with its fair copy of the opening pages (TS2), that Pinker had sent to Reynolds in New York may have still been there (see above, pp. 228, 238); Conrad's use of the original manuscript in 1911 for a possible French translation, his failure to sell the typescript to Quinn in 1912, and the later sale history of that document indicate that, had it already been returned to Pinker, it may still have been in his files and that, had he returned it to Conrad, it had been stowed away by his wife effectively beyond Conrad's reach. The heavily revised pages '1 to 39' of TS1, from which Pinker had TS2 made, had probably suffered a similar fate and in any case were so thoroughly altered as to be unusable without retyping in the week or so Conrad was revising the three stories for Dent, and was most concerned with the serial revisions of the most recent, which he was trying to recall because the *London Magazine* had failed to provide the duplicate revised proof of 'Freya of the Seven Isles' that he had requested (see below, pp. 275–6).

A Smile of Fortune

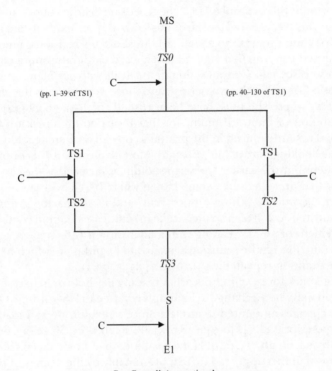

MS

TS0

(pp. 1–39 of TS1)   (pp. 40–130 of TS1)

C ──────▶

TS1   TS1

C ──────▶   ◀────── C

TS2   *TS2*

TS3

S

C ──────▶

E1

C→ Conrad's 'corrections'

Inferred (lost) documents (e.g., TS0)

[15] Genealogy of 'A Smile of Fortune'.

errors (e.g., 29.13), reversed its literalism (21.28b), and in the pro-logue further revised wording and phrasing already hastily revised for S (1:7, 1:10, 1:24b, 2:1, 2:4). As these changes suggest, his revisions for the book text in July 1912 repeated the patterns exhibited in the serial, and they were almost as numerous.[1]

---

[1] One exception to this statement is the almost complete absence in E1 of any continuing attention to contractions, possessives, or tenses. Conrad apparently restored one MS contraction in the prologue altered in S (1:13a). There is only one change of a tense, at 68.3, which by its indifference and superficial correctness is not prepossessing evidence of Conrad's agency. Along with S's change at 22.9b, it looks editorial.

The smallest group of revisions in E1 represented wording unprecedented in the earlier texts. The adjective 'dear' replaced a 'good' that had been in the text since MS, 'They' became 'These chaps', and the phrase 'his weather-beaten face' was added as an explicit detail for the first time (49.37a, 76.27, 26.1b). Most of E1's revisions, however, concerned wording that Conrad had altered earlier. In only a couple of these cases had Conrad's alterations dealt with problems created by Jessie Conrad in the typescripts, and those were towards the end of the story where she must have been rushed (67.8–9, 76.23–24). His substitution of the word 'dully' for 'hard' carried on a revision Conrad had first introduced in the printer's copy for S when he added the phrase 'looking hard at me' (69.35a). Most involved wording or phrasing altered in the earlier typescripts, often as far back as the lost one (*TSo*) that preceded the extant TS1, as when TS1t's 'without looking at him' became 'watching him covertly' and its 'menacing grimness' became 'the accent of grim menace'.[1] In some cases Conrad combined an element of an MS reading with a later variant (46.5, 72.36, 77.36, 78.3), and in a few he returned again to alter a phrase to which he had given attention repeatedly (31.10–11, 47.19a, 73.11).

This knack for recalling an earlier reading in whole or in part served Conrad well when a change in E1 simply reverted to MS wording. Often these changes amounted to a rejection of a revision he had made in the typescripts (22.14, 40.14a, 48.6, 51.18, 66.2b, 66.3, 66.22–23, 66.23, 67.8, 67.9a, 69.2b, 73.33b). Not a small number, however, concerned variants that first appeared in TS1t presumably by the agency of Jessie Conrad, particularly in the episodes involving Alice and her aunt (30.1, 47.22a, 48.1, 49.1, 68.37, 70.22, 76.11a, 76.23–24). The alterations in E1 are especially heavy from the beginning of the last section and suggest that Conrad realized this part of the story required more attention, having been brought to a conclusion rather quickly in late August 1910. Many of E1's alterations exhibit Conrad's extraordinary ability, so familiar in his earlier career, to spot problems and recall solutions in even the smallest and most subtle details. Still revising a story written two years earlier at one of the lowest points of his life, and since then succeeded by three other stories and the long-meditated *Chance*, he managed to recover words and phrases from MS in a way that suggests no diminution of this dimension of creative power.

---

[1] See the variants at 67.27b, 68.36–37; see also 27.9c, 40.39–40, 44.17a, 67.24a, 68.16a, 72.8–9, 72.17–18.

Although introducing numerous revisions and corrections, E1 generated relatively few new errors. Two regularizations occurred at the end of the first section (25.14, 25.27–28) and the beginning of the second (26.7b, 26.8). A phrase was omitted (55.35bn), diction improved (22.31, 33.36bn), and other wording given attention (31.6a, 52.32b, 56.10b, 68.31). E1's own changes along with Conrad's revisions were passed along to the subsequent editions of *'Twixt Land and Sea*, which all derive from it.[1]

FREYA OF THE SEVEN ISLES

THE LAST AND the longest of the tales he wrote after beginning *Under Western Eyes* and before resuming *Chance*, 'Freya of the Seven Isles' occupied Conrad for two months. Delaying the long-promised return to his deferred novel, he began the story shortly after Christmas 1910 and posted a complete and revised typescript to Pinker on 28 February 1911. The composition process, it seems, was neither as straightforward as that of 'The Secret Sharer' nor as complicated as that of 'A Smile of Fortune'. Surprisingly few letters remain from the time to chronicle this process, but some retrospective comments as well as two early documents help reconstruct it. Both the original manuscript (MS) and the typescript Conrad sent to Pinker (TS1) have been preserved. Although both copies of a fair typescript (*TS2*) prepared for serial publication have perished, texts printed from them survive in the American *Metropolitan Magazine* (SA) and the English *London Magazine* (SE), along with the still later texts in the four book editions of *'Twixt Land and Sea*. The immediate textual ancestor of the lost typescript text was the revised text of the extant typescript (TS1r), which provides the copy-text for this edition.

Conrad's letters help date the composition of 'Freya of the Seven Isles', but they provide little detail of the process and offer conflicting testimony about his progress. While indicating that he suffered a couple of bad weeks, though when is unknown, they represent a range of postures towards the story. The letters written between 26 December 1910 and 28 February 1911 give no hard evidence of the low period that he referred to in later letters. In a 12 January letter to Edward Garnett he said that the tale was nearly complete, whereas in fact it would

---

[1] For the textual history of the book editions and their relations to one another, see below, pp. 280–88.

take him nearly seven more weeks to finish it, and he then observed: 'I am in that state that I would hit Venus of Milo on the nose if anybody showed her to me. I am not trying to be funny I assure you: this state of mind is as near as damn it to cutting one's throat' (*Letters*, IV, 407). A month later, on 15 February, he was reversing this letter's view of the 'disgust my writing leaves behind' and instead commending the story to Warrington Dawson (who had a possible publisher for it in France) as 'quite good magazine stuff, quite Conradesque (in the easier style)'.[1] On that same day he wrote to John Galsworthy: 'I had a pretty bad time for a full 3 weeks – no two consecutive ideas, no six consecutive words to be found anywhere in the world' (*Letters*, IV, 414). By stressing how few productive days of writing he had actually enjoyed since beginning the tale and thus indicating that it had not consumed many days of actual writing, he prepared himself and others for criticism of his Conradesque but not Conradian story.

When corresponding with Pinker, however, he emphasized its market-value, making a point of the length of time taken to produce it as a way of convincing Pinker to pay him more than the usual short-story rate. In the letter sent with the typescript to Pinker, he said that 'It took me nearly three months to write' and commented that 'it would be but justice to make an advance at the rate of short story and a half'.[2] About six months later, he seems to have forgotten that he had stressed how long it took him to write the tale when, defending himself from what he perceived as Garnett's charge that the story represented earlier work, he underscored to Pinker that he was unable to write for a full two weeks after beginning it, as he had experienced one of his afflicted states. Amidst a continuing effort to rebuild their strained relationship, he wrote on 9 August: 'I can only hope that you think me incapable of sending you an old work accompanied by circumstantial lies as to the time it took me to write it – and so on – in order to get from you an increased advance, which you at once granted. This is the point which distresses me.'[3] Conrad may not have told Pinker or others 'lies' about the composition of the story, but he made it difficult to understand the process. Even if he did incorporate in his

---

[1] *Letters*, IV, 413. See also Dale B. J. Randall, ed., *Joseph Conrad and Warrington Dawson: The Record of a Friendship* (1968), p. 38.

[2] 28 February 1911 (*Letters*, IV, 417).

[3] *Letters*, IV, 470–71. On the question of this vexing misunderstanding, see Appendix G, 'The Garnett Controversy'. For the rehash of a paragraph present in the extant manuscript of the then unfinished 'The Rescuer' (which later would become *The Rescue*), see 'Introduction', pp. lix–lx.

new manuscript the description of a shipwreck from an earlier one, he started that manuscript from scratch and worked his way through it between late December 1910 and the end of February 1911.

Manuscript

THIS MANUSCRIPT survives in the Free Library of Philadelphia, which received it from Mrs Richard Gimbel, who acquired it indirectly from John Quinn. It exhibits variations in paper, different media, inconsistent foliation, and signs of discarded sheets, but this physical evidence represents what for Conrad was a usual process of ordinary stops, starts, missteps, and revision, rather than major interruptions of the composition or scavenging from separate versions of a story.

The document, which contains the complete narrative, was written on single sides of 223 leaves of wove, white, ruled paper, was divided into sections I through IV, and was paginated in two media, black ink and blue pencil. A new sequence of numbers written in black ink in the upper right corners begins each of the first three sections: section I, 1–15 16 & 17 18–26 27 28; section II, 1–2 3 3 4–46; sections III–IV, 1 2–50 51 & 52 53–109 111–145 146 146B 146 147–149. (Pagination in section I is written in words, not figures.) A single sequence is written in the lower right corners in blue pencil: 1–25 27–187 189–220 223 221 224–226. A title inscribed in black ink on the first leaf has been fitted in above the first section number. Several notations appear at the bottom of the last leaf in black ink: 'The End.', '28 Febr. 1911', and 'about 28000 words.'[1] The first seventy-four leaves have the watermark 'Fine Commercial' with a crown logo; the rest are of a lighter weight and without watermark. Leaves 162–173 and some subsequent leaves vary further in width and ruling. Holes in the upper left corners of the leaves indicate that the manuscript was originally secured with pins and that the sheets were not aligned squarely when the pins were inserted.[2] None of the variations and anomalies in pagination, paper stock, and physical grouping coincides with narrative blocks or

---

[1] The actual number of words is about 28,600; as often, Conrad's method of calculation resulted in inaccuracies, sometimes influenced by circumstances (see above pp. lxv–lxvi, lxx, and 229).

[2] Holes in both the upper left and lower right corner of the envelope in which the manuscript was once stored (see Appendix A, 'Provenance of the Early Documents') provide further evidence of the pins which once held the leaves of the manuscript together. The appearance of holes in opposite corners may mean that the manuscript was put into (and stored in) the envelope at least two different times.

indicates a major break in the composition or the splicing together of separate documents.

The blue-pencil notations in the manuscript likely originated at the same time as a note in that medium on the envelope used to package the document for sale to John Quinn.[1] The mistaken pagination sequence – '220', '223', '221' – appears on the leaves misnumbered '146', '146B', '146' in black ink during composition and is clearly based on that foliation, as are the numbers on the final leaves mistakenly posted to Quinn (see below). Blue pencil has been used to cancel two blocks of text. In section III, on page 145 (black-ink 71), eleven lines deleted in ink have been more definitely crossed out in pencil. In section IV, a block on page 212 (138) cancelled only in pencil follows one cancelled in ink at the bottom of page 211 (137); the marking in blue pencil represents an error of misunderstanding, since the passage in question is actually a reworking of that cancelled in ink on the previous page and is required for continuity of the narrative (it appears in all subsequent texts). In addition, a purple pencil or crayon appears on page 15 ('fifteen' in section I) as the medium used to excise another block that nonetheless appears in TS1 and subsequent texts.

The primary medium of the document is the black ink, in which the text of the tale is written entirely in Conrad's hand. A relatively straightforward manuscript (that is, for Conrad), its pages exhibit various degrees of rewriting but no signs of incorporating a separate act of composition. The inscriptions suggest two stages of revision. One occurred as Conrad drafted the story: he would begin a passage, then make a cancellation, and then continue writing, at times substituting all new words and at other times reusing some of the original words from the cancelled passage. For instance, in the last two lines on the first page he struck through the words 'and he never protested' and used this phrase to complete the sentence, which ended on the top of the next page (123.13–14). In a second stage, Conrad apparently read through successive pages, perhaps at the end of a day's writing, to make further changes after the initial phase of composition. These changes are interlined above or below the original inscriptions or inserted in the left-hand margin, and they are generally, though not always, in a finer or smaller script. In both stages he sometimes wrote on top of an original inscription, as when he used a heavy stroke to change the 'ing' of 'surging' to 'ed' (126.34; page 11) or wrote 'on' upon 'off'

[1] See Appendix A.

while altering 'without taking her eyes off him' to 'and kept her eyes on him' (154.35; page 105).

The text includes roman numerals specifying four sections, each beginning on a new leaf with the section number centred in the top margin.[1] The last leaf of each section also contains a marker such as 'End of section . . .' or words to that effect. Present also are just a few indicators for a typist. On one page (157), a note in black ink contains both a paragraph symbol and the instruction 'new line'. The fourth leaf from the end (page 221) contains an insertion encircled in the top margin and asterisked for placement mid-page – rare in this document, though not uncharacteristic of Conrad. Occasionally arrows, carets, balloons, or more frequently curving lines serve as guides through heavily rewritten passages.

In addition to the text of the story, the manuscript contains other authorial inscriptions in black ink. In the margins of two leaves (pages 84 and 138) are sketches of the floor plan of Nelson's bungalow in different layouts, reflecting changes in Conrad's sense of how the action unfolded within this setting.[2] Breaks in the sequences of pagination indicate difficulties experienced during composition. In section I page 'Sixteen and Seventeen' and the leaf lacking 'twenty-seven' immediately follow pages containing cancelled blocks, suggesting that rethinking was extensive enough to warrant discarding leaves. The second page '3' in section II has an additional inscription after the number that, although illegible, appears to acknowledge the duplication, which follows a long block cancelled on the previous page.

In the last two sections of the manuscript the absence of a leaf that should have been numbered '110' in black ink coincides with the cancellation of two lines at the bottom of page 109 which reappear in revised form at the top of page '111', indicating that Conrad either discarded a leaf or lost count of the pagination while revising during the initial drafting. At the end, page '146B' (blue-pencil '223') was originally numbered '145', and the following page, the second '146', was in blue pencil initially numbered '221'; an insertion made on the second '146' ('221') was likely transcribed from another leaf discarded

---

[1] The typescript divides the story into six sections based on these divisions. See below, p. 255.

[2] Differences between the two sketches on the manuscript show Conrad's visualization of the interior of the bungalow changing. While 'divided into four' (150.9) fits the floor plan depicted in the first drawing, it does not fit the second. Conrad's deletion of this phrase in E1 reflects his developing re-conceptualization. See Fig. 22.

during composition. The faulty pagination suggests Conrad's greater struggle towards the conclusion of composition, just after disposing of Jasper and when writing the last paragraphs on Freya, and serious enough to confuse even the pagination sequence in the blue pencil.

When concluding the tale, Conrad must have wholly rewritten the last two pages on new leaves but temporarily left the old ones in the document. Later, when preparing the document for John Quinn and using blue pencil to renumber the pages, Conrad apparently discarded the revised leaves rather than the originals.[1] The title, although written in black ink rather than blue pencil, and inscribed in a decorative manner and fitted into the upper margin above the first section number, must have been inserted, along with the words 'J. Conrad.', after the composition of the story and presumably at about the same time. It indicates the care Conrad took to make the manuscript's appearance acceptable for sale.[2]

Typescript

THE HOLOGRAPH manuscript that Conrad produced between December 1910 and February 1911 was typed by Jessie Conrad during these same months, and this typescript was posted to Pinker in complete and revised form on 28 February 1911.[3] Except for those

---

[1] The date Conrad inscribed on the final leaf of the manuscript agrees with the date (28 February) on which the typescript made from it was mailed to Pinker. This suggests two possibilities. Both the manuscript and the typescript might have been completed the same day, with Jessie Conrad producing typed copy as Conrad wrote; or he may have written the date on the manuscript in August when he prepared it for Quinn. Their practice of the previous summer, when she typed 'A Smile of Fortune' in batches, rather than strictly in tandem with Conrad's inscription (see above pp. 234–5), would not support the former scenario, whereas if Conrad discarded the two revised pages when readying the document for Quinn, he would have needed to add a new notation of the completion date on the last (but actually original) manuscript leaf.

[2] See Appendix A.

[3] Conrad to Pinker (*Letters*, IV, 417). The document was prepared by one typist with one typewriter. Like her typescript of 'A Smile of Fortune', it exhibits certain infelicities of technique, including frequent incorrect spacing of end punctuation and mis-spacing and mis-punctuation of items in series. These idiosyncrasies and the physical characteristics of the documents match in such a way that her responsibility for typing 'Freya of the Seven Isles' is patent. Her machine was sent out for repairs some time before late November 1910, but it was back in service by May 1911, when she was typing parts of *Chance*, and must have been returned by the end of the year. See Conrad to Pinker, [24 or 25? November 1910] (*Letters*, IV, 391) and Conrad to Galsworthy, [14 May 1911] (*Letters*, IV, 439). It was only a year later, when the composition of *Chance* was well advanced, that Conrad regained the full support of Pinker's typists: see Reid, p. 72.

in the last two rewritten manuscript pages (see above, p. 254), the
readings of MS were transmitted to the extant typescript (TS1) in such
a way that there clearly was no intervening manuscript or typescript.
The document contains the entire story typed double-spaced on one
side of 124 leaves of wove paper numbered consecutively, though not
uniformly, throughout. The first sixty leaves are buff-coloured and the
remainder white. An 'Imperial Parchment Note' watermark appears
on fols. 61–82, 97, 112, and 123, while fol. 83 is marked 'Inglewood';
the rest of the white leaves and all the buff-coloured appear to be
unmarked. Some leaves seem to have been fastened together at some
time.[1] The ink of the typed characters is now purple throughout.[2]
While exhibiting some physical inconsistencies, the document gives
no evidence of having been assembled from multiple sources.

The typescript contains Conrad's writing in black ink, blue pencil,
and lead (black) pencil. The first leaf has the title written in black
ink in a decorative style and script similar to that on the first page of
the manuscript. This similar treatment of the first page indicates his
preparation of the document for another party, in this case a prospective new publisher in France. Under the title appear a decorative line,
the author's name, and the first section number, also written in black
ink.[3]

Conrad has divided the typescript into six sections. Only sections I
and II are identical in the manuscript and typescript, and the latter
has two additional sections. Although Jessie Conrad did not type the
section numbers, she did leave extra white space where sections began
in the manuscript, and Conrad then wrote the section numbers in
black ink in these blank spaces. At the place where he divides the
manuscript's section II into II and III, Jessie Conrad had left a blank
line. Consequently section IV in the typescript starts where section
III in the manuscript did, and section V begins where the fourth
and last manuscript section had. Only where Conrad began section VI

---

[1] The upper left-hand corners of fols. 64–66 show a short tear, and a tear and pinholes are
present in fol. 69. An impression from an acorn fastener appears in the upper left-hand
corner of fol. 76.

[2] The inked impressions indicate that the ribbon was changed on fol. 53, but other physical evidence nevertheless shows that the document was produced as part of a continuous
effort.

[3] Conrad's misstep in first writing 'Islets' rather than 'Isles' in the title on the typescript probably reflects mis-recollection consequent on not being immediately engaged in composition;
it helps associate the title with the preparation of the document for France. See 186.5n and
Appendix A.

(page 103) does the typescript not have extra spacing. At this juncture in her transcription Jessie Conrad had made a mistake. When she had finished typing page 184 (111) of the manuscript, she had apparently turned over not only that page but the next as well and begun typing the words found at the top of manuscript page 186 (113), and she had then adjusted the wording (altering 'of that event' to 'events') to accommodate the discontinuity of the narrative (see 177.26c). At this point in the typescript a cancellation has been made in three media, lead pencil, black ink, and blue pencil, apparently in that order. First, Jessie Conrad seems to have taken a lead pencil and cancelled her mistyped passage. Then, when revising page 102 in black ink, Conrad indicated the end of section v at the paragraph break and inserted two lines in revised form at the top of page 103, where he also marked the beginning of section vi. Finally, he reaffirmed this adjustment in blue pencil, again cancelling the block beneath the end of the section notation already deleted in lead pencil. Since he had serialization of his story in mind, it is not surprising that he divided this long tale into two additional sections, but in doing so he took advantage of Jessie Conrad's mistake to make a new section division.

The leaves of the typescript are paginated 1–124 consecutively but inconsistently. Most numbers are centred at the bottom of the page and were typed in the same ribbon as the text. However, groups of pages were not numbered when typewritten; the numbers were added either in black ink (32–35, 44–46, 51–52, 97–99) or first in blue pencil that was then erased and replaced by black ink (47–50). Elsewhere a typewritten number has been corrected in black ink ('17' for '16', '116' for '117'), or by being typed over ('104'). The major variations in pagination probably reflect Jessie Conrad's typing of the document in batches, rather than the combining of separate documents, but the scant correspondence chronicling the composition process makes this inference unverifiable.

Although the last page has 'The End.' typed at the bottom, it also has 'The End' and '1911' inscribed in black ink, along with a calculation of the total number of words (28,290) and the number of pages (123).[1] Black ink has been used to cancel this page- and word-count, which were doubtlessly inscribed with Pinker and payment in mind. In addition, the last leaf contains an anomalous blotting of a phrase, now

---

[1] The '123' takes into account the few lines of typing present on the last page. The calculation of total words is based on 230 words per page. The actual word count is approximately 29,250 words.

unreadable, but possibly incorporated in the lost rewritten pages and now preserved in the printed texts (see 189.24).[1] Of all the black-ink revisions, only this one must postdate the sending of the document to Pinker for retyping.

Aside from the marks in black ink, a few others appear in the typescript. Blue pencil was used to add 'A' in the upper right-hand corner of the first page, 'B' on page 29, 'C' on page 56, 'D' on page 76. From 'B' on, these groupings do not correspond to section divisions in either the typescript or the manuscript. Nor do they correlate with the different means used to number the pages of the typescript, nor with the evidence that pages were pinned together. They, as well as the one short series of page numbers (47–50) and the reaffirmation of a cancellation (page 102) in blue pencil, almost certainly represent preparation of the document for sending to France after it had been retyped in London.[2]

Throughout the document Conrad revised the text Jessie Conrad typed (TS1t) and must have done so during the weeks he continued to work on completing his first draft in manuscript. Although the penstroke of his black-ink corrections and revisions varies in boldness, no physical or other evidence suggests that he inscribed them at another stage, except for the blotted phrase on the last page.

The alterations Conrad made to create the revised text of the typescript (TS1r) were almost equally divided among substitutions, additions, and deletions. Many were responses to Jessie Conrad's changes. She introduced a large number – about 340 in words and many more in forms. About 40 of her altered words were necessary corrections, but the others were neither correct nor apparently deliberate. Of her 300 substantive errors, Conrad let stand about 120. Misreading and mistyping were responsible for at least a third of her alterations, omissions of words being particularly prevalent. Articles were a notable casualty in this group (e.g., at 131.5a, 135.6, 179.24, 180.21, 180.40); they also suffered other kinds of change (124.30, 140.38, 157.36, 168.17b), and other parts of speech were altered to articles of her choosing (123.7a, 134.31a, 141.6, 173.19, 184.26b). Almost invariably these errors in articles escaped Conrad's notice, though he did fuss with articles at some other points (e.g., 124.3b, 124.8, 124.22, 129.34, 139.9, 177.24, 182.33). Among the deliberate and unnecessary changes that she

---

[1] See p. 254.

[2] For more on the history of the document, see Appendix A.

introduced, those of verb forms stand out, as in the change of 'lay' to 'lie' (140.22); he corrected or otherwise altered most of these errors. Her other changes of verbs were sometimes even more intrusive, as in the substitutions of 'came' for 'rose' (134.31b) and 'had' for 'got' (171.32).

Although making a number of corrections to apostrophes, she introduced errors of this kind as well, as when she changed 'years" to 'year's' (132.6a). In TS1r her alterations driven by idiom sometimes survived Conrad's correction (e.g., 147.35a, 169.33, 176.30, 180.32, 184.19, 186.29a). In other places, he reworded the passage, sidestepping the problem altogether (e.g., 127.37, 131.12–13, 131.33a). However, when she changed plurals or other words involving final -s, he was more apt to correct than to follow or to create a new reading (e.g., 128.24, 130.38a, 131.11, 172.17a, 188.29). Other kinds of changes are scattered throughout TS1t, from additions of words to alterations of adjectives, nouns, and prepositions, most of which cannot be defended on the grounds of correctness or idiom. As frequently as Conrad passed such errors he restored the MS reading. In the remaining instances, he created entirely new readings in TS1r.

Besides attempting to correct his typist's errors, Conrad fully engaged in altering the substance of his story, revising every page and paying most attention to individual words or short phrases. Among these 750 or so changes, approximately three-quarters were made independently of those Jessie Conrad had introduced. He often changed his mind about word choice: 'spears' replaced 'lances' (128.32), 'ablaze' replaced 'on fire' (131.15), and 'resolute' replaced 'firm' (163.14b). Substitutions brought greater precision or clarity, as when nouns replaced pronouns: 'it' became 'this simple happiness' in one instance (147.24), 'This north verandah' in another (149.7), and 'that smile' in a third (155.4). He often revised so that characters were named rather than represented by pronouns (e.g., 127.4, 131.21, 133.31b, 143.32, 164.2, 172.12b). Additions also aimed at greater precision and specificity: 'I am here' was tacked on to Antonia's 'Nobody knows' (145.29); 'of the door' was added after 'crack', 'unholy' before 'desire', and 'of a great river' after 'estuary' (163.37b, 167.30, 168.30c). He added a number of interlocutory phrases, some of which had the effect of informing the drama (e.g., 127.19, 133.11–13, 144.18–19, 162.19–20) or heightening the tone (e.g., 140.36–37, 147.33b, 150.39–40, 161.1a). Conrad sometimes made idiomatic changes, as when he substituted 'with' for 'to' in 'open to papa' (156.40a) and inserted a necessary 'of' in 'When an Englishman talks women and children' (172.1).

About one in six of his altered wordings restored a manuscript reading where there was a typist's error. He corrected 'brag' to 'brig' (147.10b) and 'appeared' to 'appeased' (169.7a). He rejected Jessie Conrad's change to the indefinite article in MS's 'quills of the fretful porcupine' (124.30) and her misjudgement in forming a plural for MS's 'some other authority' (168.14a). Sometimes he replaced one of her errors with a new reading. Where she omitted 'then' in 'He started then talking' (perhaps reacting to the awkwardness), he altered the sentence to 'Then he flung himself into a chair and tried to talk' (127.37). When she expanded the contraction in 'his face's hurt' (probably for a similar reason), he produced a question: 'Is his face hurt?' (160.8a). Some of his fussing with verb tense and mood may reflect uncertainty about idiom as well, if not refining of narrative strategy. Rethinking 'What more absorbing and less noisy amusement could they find than to plan their future?' he opted for the past perfect and changed 'find' to the smoother 'have found' (129.29). Another revision of this type, the change of 'when while they were gazing at the brig' to 'when after they had been gazing at the brig' (129.40), did more than smooth the language; it better reflected the narrative frame.[1]

In about ten places, Conrad substantially revised a sentence, usually refining characterization. Two changes (123.27, 124.17–18) developed Nelson's psychology – specifically his excessive, though not groundless, fear of political authorities.[2] A later revision made him more blamable for ignoring the threat that Heemskirk's interest posed to his daughter (133.21–22). A change in the narrator's commentary heightened the suggestion of Heemskirk's 'malevolent' nature, even as the narrator asserted Heemskirk's insignificance (131.35a), while in another case Heemskirk's nature was drawn more distinctly, and the recasting showed the extent to which his jealousy and hatred of Jasper clouded his senses and his judgement (172.11–12). Conrad also added a sexual edge to the narrator's awareness of Antonia that created a foil for Heemskirk's predatory interest in Freya (145.15–17).

In revising the typescript, Conrad seldom deleted words or phrases, but he did delete two whole sentences (152.33, 172.14) and thus

---

[1] Also see 130.36, 141.35, 149.14, 150.24, 160.21a, 172.4, 178.22, 183.40, 184.5, 184.35–36.
[2] On this question, see 'Introduction', p. lvii.

heightened the contrast between Jasper and Heemskirk. More often he added sentences.[1] Half of these additions were to dialogue. Most of the others affected the psychology of the characters. In about twenty instances he divided long sentences, most often into two and usually without other revision at that point.[2] The divisions often occurred at the point of a dash or connector word or, in some cases, of a typing error. In only a few instances did he combine sentences,[3] revising to a greater degree than when he divided them.

On nearly every page of the typescript Conrad changed punctuation and other forms. In large part he was responding to the hundreds of errors introduced by Jessie Conrad. But though he often restored his original forms or further revised at the site of her error, he let stand about 60 per cent of her unnecessary changes of this kind. These included punctuation at the ends of sentences, within clauses, and around interlocutory phrases. In two places she combined sentences, one of which he redivided.[4] She omitted commas in series (even after the first item) and before qualifiers, colons before and inverted commas around direct discourse, italics, dashes, and apostrophes in contractions. She levelled uppercase letters, altered word-division, and added punctuation here and there. She also made necessary corrections: supplied end punctuation, added opening and, more often, closing quotation marks, modified word-division, and altered apostrophes, commas, hyphens, and even ellipses. In these cases, Conrad almost invariably let her corrections stand. Far more often than responding to her alterations of this kind, he made other changes, adding new commas in series, between independent clauses, and with and around modifiers, parenthetical expressions, and other suspending constructions. He gave some attention to hyphens and punctuation in connection with direct discourse and altered a number of full-stops to exclamation points or question marks.

Having revised and corrected the typescript in both these large and minute ways, Conrad posted it directly to Pinker at the end of February 1911. In the letter transmitting it, he requested 'an advance at the rate of short story and a half – say sixty pounds' and declared:

---

[1] See 134.13–14, 140.5a, 140.13–14, 170.34–35, 182.5–6, 185.35, 186.19, 186.30–31, 187.21, 187.24–25, 187.27–28, 189.23b.

[2] See, e.g., 132.22a, 132.38a, 142.38–39, 158.30–31, 160.8c, 160.22, 168.36, 169.6.

[3] See 127.10, 150.26b, 160.6.

[4] Conrad kept TS1t's dots but otherwise corrected at 143.5; at 158.35 he let stand her change.

'I beg to say at once that no suggestion of alteration or curtailment will be entertained. Not a single word.' He also made another request: 'I beg you will kindly return me my corrected typed copy as soon as the clean one is made.'[1] Apparently Pinker returned TS1 to him, presumably within a week, but without sending a copy of the new typescript he had had produced in London (*TS2*). His agreement to both of Conrad's requests suggests a softening of his stance towards him, but one not sufficient to resume sending for further revision the 'clean' typescript produced by his typists.[2]

Soon after this, Conrad sent the typescript on to France, where Dawson had been trying to arrange for publication in a new magazine called *Progrès*, edited by Mme Adeline de Lano (Conrad's 'Mrs Demachy').[3] Before doing so, however, Conrad went through it again, this time with a lead pencil, and created fourteen additional readings in English and thirty-four translations of words and phrases into French.[4] Written in a finer script than those in English, the French translations end on page 35, but the last leaf of the typescript contains a pencilled notation in French indicating the word count. The translations are usually enclosed within round brackets and written in the space above the corresponding English term. In a number of instances something like a brace appears above the typed word or words to point to the French translation. Most of the translated terms concern sailing – boats, rank, nautical operations, and so on. Some are translations of idiomatic expressions, a couple are of descriptive terms, and one is of a geographical term.

---

[1] Conrad to Pinker, 28 February 1911 (*Letters*, IV, 417). Although Conrad took advantage of the unusual length of the story by requesting additional payment, the testiness of his declaration should probably be read against the backdrop of his experience with the *London Magazine* over the length of 'A Smile of Fortune' (see above, pp. lxxv–lxxvi, 241–3).

[2] Conrad acknowledged receipt of payment on 2 March (*Letters*, IV, 418). Pinker's treatment of 'Freya of the Seven Isles' compares favourably with the recent handling of 'A Smile of Fortune', and Conrad's letters to him in the next few weeks regarding 'Prince Roman' and 'The Partner' also give this impression. But it would be another year before full relations would be restored in the wake of the publication of both *Under Western Eyes* and *A Personal Record*, the steady and rapid composition of *Chance*, and the prospect of publishing what became *'Twixt Land and Sea*. For an overview, see Reid, pp. 71–2. See above, pp. 238, 240–41, and Appendix A on the Pinker typescripts for 'A Smile of Fortune'.

[3] See Appendix A.

[4] Appendix H, 'Marks in Pencil on the First Typescript', lists these pencilled notations. References to them cite the page and line of the typescript; this page–line citation contains a colon to distinguish it from citations of the text of the present edition and of variants keyed to it in the 'Apparatus'.

The French translations were almost certainly written by Conrad.[1] The notation for the word count on the last leaf looks like his handwriting, it appears next to the calculation which he had earlier recorded for Pinker and which was cancelled in black ink,[2] and its content exhibits his usual interest in this question. Although a reader on the Continent might have written some translations in an identical medium, stopping when it became apparent the work would not be published by Mme 'Demachy', Conrad probably began jotting down some French words and phrases before he posted the typescript, perhaps to show how the story could be translated, especially its nautical and technical language. That he had offered to the editor via Dawson to revise the translation which she would have to arrange indicates his general concern with the translation of his work. This concern had been exhibited a year earlier when he had taken the trouble to mark proofs of the French version of *The Nigger of the 'Narcissus'* while trying to bring his newest novel to an end. That earlier act, his offer to revise the translation made for Mme Demachy, and the documentary evidence itself all indicate that Conrad inscribed the French translations pencilled in the typescript.[3]

Indeed, this conclusion appears to be confirmed beyond reasonable doubt by one of the interlined French words, which is squeezed in above a pencilled alteration in English on page 19. The substance of the alteration in English (19:9) shows it was Conrad's hand that made it. Here in ink he had previously revised the MS's description of Heemskirk's clothing as a 'dark cloth uniform jacket' to a 'dark cloth undress jacket' (132.22c). In pencil, he cancelled 'cloth' and ruled again through the already cancelled 'uniform', so that the description became 'dark undress jacket'. Not only can Conrad be seen deliberating twice over this description in the typescript, but he would later make the same change on two separate occasions, when preparing the texts of the English magazine and first edition (see below, p. 279). The reappearance of this revision in two other texts manifests a level of interest in this detail that could only be the author's. The interlined French translation of this wording, which in itself would seem to be a

---

[1] Some doubt could be raised in one instance, the query placed after the translation of 'racket' to 'vacarme' (14:10), which seems odd for Conrad, whose French was generally good; but the significance of that mark is unclear, and in any case it cannot outweigh the other evidence.

[2] See above, p. 256; for a more general view of the various inscriptions in the document and their relationship, see Appendix A.

[3] Conrad to Dawson, 15 February 1911 (*Letters*, IV, 413); Conrad to Galsworthy, to Rothenstein, 15 November 1909 (*Letters*, IV, 288, 290).

fairly straightforward matter, reflects the same focus on this detail and must also be Conrad's.

Although Conrad marked the typescript in lead pencil with only thirteen other changes in English, these are dispersed throughout the typescript. Six of these readings are simple corrections of errors that Jessie Conrad and he had made (20:5, 31:19, 34:5, 43:11, 109:3, 114:15), whereas the other seven represent his reflexive response when reading through the typescript again, though they clear up things that might have been misread. All but one of the simple corrections predictably appear in the published texts.[1] On the other hand, one change of word order (62:16), driven by a concern for idiom, occurs only in the book editions (see the variant at 156.5a). Not present in these editions or the magazines is Conrad's cancellation of two words that confirm his earlier revisions (34:12 and 111:12; see the variants at 140.28 and 182.20b). In four other instances (12:6, 27:4, 115:14, 119:3), he expressed stylistic preferences that are evidenced elsewhere in his revising of 'Freya of the Seven Isles', though these particular readings are absent from all printed texts. These sporadic and ephemeral changes in pencil represent only casual tinkering, not the full engagement seen in the black-ink corrections and revisions made before the typescript was posted to Pinker, nor the kind of attention he typically gave a work when revising for publication. The lead-pencil alterations he made in English were not transmitted to the magazine and book texts through the Pinker typescript (*TS2*) and, even when independently duplicated there, remained outside the main textual tradition.

Serialization

WHILE CONRAD was still writing and revising the tale, he was already planning for serial publication.[2] In the event, placing the story with magazines took Pinker more time than either of them would have liked and occasioned some brief hard feelings between Conrad and Garnett.

---

[1] The single exception is 31:19 (139.12a). Conrad's pencilled correction of TS1t's 'Schultz's' for 'Schultz' is not found in SE; SA omits the entire passage at this point.

[2] To Dawson on 15 February 1911, Conrad observed: 'I am putting finishing touches to a story, (which I think I'll call *Freya of the Seven Isles*), length about 20 000 words (3 or four instalments)' (*Letters*, IV, 413). Dispatching the corrected typescript to Pinker two weeks later, Conrad described the tale as 'quite suitable for serialising'; a few days later, he noted, 'I reckoned 5 instalments at 36 each': Conrad to Pinker, 28 February 1911, 2 March 1911 (*Letters*, IV, 417, 419).

As usual, Conrad had ideas for placing his new story. Acknowledging receipt of payment for the typescript on 2 March 1911, he told Pinker that he had approached the editor of the *Pall Mall Magazine* about publishing 'Freya of the Seven Isles' and suggested that *Hampton's* might be an appropriate organ in America.[1] Over the course of the year, the tale was turned down by several magazines in both Britain and America. By the end of March Conrad knew that it had been rejected for American publication by either the *Century* or *Scribner's*.[2] The decision was made 'on the ground that: "its overpowering gloom makes it impossible for serialisation"', as he mentioned in July when, still stinging from this rejection, he wrote about his 'magazine-ish thing'[3] to Garnett, to whom Pinker had sent it in his new capacity as a reader for the *Century*. Conrad became even more irritated by Garnett's criticism of the ending of the story and incensed by his comment that he had read it years before.[4] By then Pinker was resorting to *Blackwood's*, which had been discussed earlier, but they also rejected it. Finally, in either late October or early November 1911, the tale was accepted by the *London Magazine*, which had already published 'A Smile of Fortune' in February and 'The Black Mate' in 1908.[5] In December 1911 Pinker sent Conrad the good news that an American magazine had been found as well.[6] He would learn later that it was the *Metropolitan Magazine* which had taken both 'Freya of the Seven Isles' and 'Prince Roman'.

In order to market the story in America and Britain, Pinker must have had prepared from Conrad's revised typescript (TS1r) a 'clean' typescript (*TS2*) in two copies (an original and a carbon), now lost

---

[1] Conrad also mentioned that publishing in *Pall Mall* would 'bar' *Harper's*, which had published 'The Secret Sharer' (*Letters*, IV, 418–19). Since *Harper's* published in both America and England, acceptance by *Pall Mall* would eliminate *Harper's* as a possible American outlet.

[2] Conrad's letters to Garnett on 18 and 29 July and 4 August (*Letters*, IV, 459–60, 464–5, 469–70) and to Pinker in March and on 1, 3, and 9 August (*Letters*, IV, 423, 430–31, 467–8, 468, 470–71) indicate that it was either the *Century* or *Scribner's* that had rejected the story in March, but do not make it possible to determine which. However, it appears that the story was sent to both for consideration.

[3] Conrad to Garnett, [29 July 1911] (*Letters*, IV, 464).

[4] Conrad to Garnett, [4 August 1911] (*Letters*, IV, 469–70). See 'Introduction', pp. lvii–lx, lxxxii, and Appendix G.

[5] *Letters to William Blackwood and David S. Meldrum*, p. 197. On 2 November, Conrad enquired again whether *Blackwood's* had made a decision, and knew the next day that the *London Magazine* had accepted the story: see Conrad to Pinker, 2 November 1911, and to Quinn, 3 November 1911 (*Letters*, IV, 498, 499).

[6] Conrad to Pinker, 8 December 1912 [1911] (*Letters*, IV, 521).

(*TS2a* and *TS2b*). Common errors in SA and SE show that the two magazine texts derive from the same text.[1] The presence of those errors in both SA and SE and the absence in Conrad's letters of any mention of the Pinker typescript indicate that he did not receive either copy, which indeed would have been unexpected at this point in their still strained working relationship. After sending TS1 to Pinker, Conrad was busy preparing 'The Partner' and 'Prince Roman' for serial publication, correcting proofs of *Under Western Eyes* for the *English Review* and the book editions, writing 'A Familiar Preface' for *A Personal Record*, and of course writing *Chance* for the *New York Herald*, a task, as he noted in his letters, from which he could not risk being diverted.[2] Soon after completing the manuscript of *Chance*, he had begun the short story ('Dollars') that would become *Victory*.[3]

The setting copy that the *Metropolitan Magazine* and the *London Magazine* received contained not only necessary corrections made by Pinker's typist, but typing errors occasioned by various physical conditions. TS1r's 'these' was frequently misread as 'those' because Jessie Conrad's typewriter made the letter 'e' appear closed and Conrad's usage was not always standard (e.g., 126.22, 132.38b, 185.36, 185.39). Often the typist of *TS2* seems to have had trouble reading Conrad's handwritten alterations; she mistook 'he is' for 'he's', the compressed 'I shall' for 'I'll', and the difficult but decipherable 'What' for 'When' (134.11, 138.8, 182.12b). The last instance was accompanied by an omission of 'tale' that made *TS2*'s new reading plausible.[4] Where TS1r has a lower-case 'h' typed over the upper-case, *TS2* produced 'He' and began a new sentence in error (187.24). On the next page a revision that runs into TS1's right margin (188.6b) caused her to overlook the beginning of a paragraph in the next line.

[1] For a genealogical chart, see Fig. 16. In addition to introducing errors, the Pinker typist may have made some of the acceptable corrections that appear in both SA and SE (e.g., 150.25, 176.36, 178.32a, 180.21, 181.19, 183.18b, 187.39b). Where SA omits the passage in question, the correction might have originated in either *TS2* or SE (e.g., 137.35, 160.21b, 163.20–21, 163.30b, 166.39a, 177.6, 177.35). Because the same corrections might have been made independently, they are less telling than the errors.

[2] See, e.g., Conrad to Pinker, [4? July 1911] (*Letters*, IV, 456). Between 24 August 1911 when he mailed the manuscript to Quinn and 19 May 1912 when he sent corrected proofs for the *London Magazine* to Pinker, his letters do not refer to working on 'Freya of the Seven Isles' (*Letters*, IV, 475, and V, 66).

[3] Conrad to Galsworthy, 27[?] March 1912; to Violet Hunt, 27 March 1912; to Pinker, [25 April 1912] (*Letters*, V, 39, 40, 56).

[4] See also 144.1 where either the Pinker typist mistranscribed 'disrespectful' as 'disgraceful' or the SA compositor made an error to produce its variant (SE omits the passage).

However, sometimes Pinker's typist simply missed a clearly typed word (157.8) or handwritten alteration (189.10, 189.12). Elsewhere, she misconstrued the situation and transcribed an uncancelled word instead of its replacement where Conrad had failed to strike through the typewritten word (182.20b).[1] In other cases, she substituted a similar word (173.3) or probably made a deliberate change: a missing 'too' looks like an effort to correct usage (185.23), while the insertion of 'to' in 'You have only to look out' and a correction of verb tense also appear intentional (140.6, 186.24).

Another group of readings common to SA and SE exhibit more complex behaviour on the part of Pinker's typist and the editors of the magazines, though they are nonetheless errors that she introduced. In some places, Conrad had interlined new words above others that, though marked for cancellation, yet remained legible (e.g., 132.30, 152.22, 152.28, 164.10a, 180.12a); the typist must have ignored these indicators, because the cancelled readings, rather than the interlined revisions, appear in both SE and SA. She also missed two simple insertions (185.26, 186.28b) and probably ignored two other revisions where a cancellation obscured the original readings (169.30, 175.26–27).[2] SA and SE sometimes responded differently to errors in TS2. When Pinker's typist retained the first of eight heavily cancelled words while incorporating the revised phrasing (see 133.28–30), SA further modified the wording while SE added a comma to accommodate TS2's awkward reading.[3] In another instance where TS2 had passed over TS1r's clear cancellation and revision, SE followed and SA corrected TS2's transcription of MS's grammatical error, which TS1t had reproduced (180.12a). Although SA and SE treated these TS2 errors differently, their shared errors show that they descended from a common ancestor, a typescript that Conrad did not correct, and they help explain his statement about 'the vagaries of the infernal typists employed by the great P'.[4]

When still writing and revising it, Conrad had thought of his long tale as one that would be serialized in instalments. In the end it was printed, with excisions, as a single magazine feature both in America

[1] At 140.28 the variant is part of a passage omitted in SA and SE, but a similar misjudgement seems to have been made here by the Pinker typist, as reflected in E1. Conversely, at 124.8 the typist appropriately wrote 'the a' as 'a'.

[2] Most pardonable is the omission at 186.28b, where the text is heavily revised.

[3] The SA and SE editors or compositors reacted differently to the survival of the awkward 'something' in this sentence, SA following the word with 'of' and SE adding a comma (133.29).

[4] Conrad to Gibbon, 19 December [1909] (Letters, IV, 301).

and in England. Although he had no hand in the alterations made for the *Metropolitan Magazine*, he did delete passages and make other changes for the *London Magazine*, as he had for their serialization of 'A Smile of Fortune' the year before, though this time without protest.[1] In neither magazine were the cuts driven by the location of advertisements, but in both they were often made at physically convenient places, such as the beginnings and ends of paragraphs. Not surprisingly, the editor of SA cut more than Conrad did for SE.[2]

American Serialization

ON 8 December 1911, not yet knowing what magazine had taken the tale, Conrad congratulated Pinker on the 'brilliant' arrangements he had made for American serialization of 'Freya of the Seven Isles', which appeared in the April 1912 number of the *Metropolitan Magazine*.[3] Although he wrote effusively to Pinker once a publisher had been found, the irritation in his August letter to Garnett had extended to the entire American magazine industry: 'As to faking a "sunny" ending to my story I would see all the American Magazines and all the american Editors damned in heaps before lifting my pen for that task. I have never been particularly anxious to rub shoulders with the piffle they print with touching consistency from year's end to year's end' (*Letters*, IV, 469).

Whatever basis Conrad had for this general condemnation, SA's treatment of 'Freya of the Seven Isles' betrayed its deliberate evolution from a mass-circulation magazine featuring, like many others in the 1890s, a '*naughty picture*' section to its self-proclaimed status as a '*fiction*' magazine publishing 'the best short-story writers of this country and England'.[4] In 1912 it published in a so-called 'tabloid' format, half the standard newspaper size and thus comparable to the *Saturday*

---

[1] See above, pp. lxxv–lxxvi, 241–4.

[2] TS1r's text amounts to approximately 29,250 words, SA's to 19,520, and SE's to 26,170.

[3] *Letters*, IV, 521. Conrad's enthusiasm may have been stirred by the $2,000 Pinker got for the story, rather than by the nature of the magazine. The price paid by the *London Magazine* had been disappointing: Conrad to Pinker, [4 November 1911] (*Letters*, IV, 499).

[4] Frank Luther Mott, *A History of American Magazines: 1885–1905*, vol. IV (1957), 47; 'Magazine Talk', *Metropolitan Magazine*, 31 January 1910, p. 556. The announcement, 'Metropolitan Story Writers for Next Year', that made this declaration in the January 1910 issue listed Conrad among contemporaries not readily recognized today, with the exception of O. Henry. *Munsey's Magazine*, a competitor, also regularly offered 'gorgeous' women, 'thinly clad if their station permitted'; see Richard Ohmann, *Selling Culture: Magazines, Markets, and Class at the Turn of the Century* (1996), p. 226.

Evening Post, with text printed in multiple columns and integrated to some extent with advertisements. It printed 'Freya of the Seven Isles' with a 'break-over', beginning it on ten pages, each in three columns and uninterrupted by advertising, and concluding it on four pages, each in four columns with text occupying half the page and advertisements the other half.[1] In all, it allocated one-third of the space given to the tale to illustrations and a title block that contained boilerplate decorations and displayed the illustrator's name as prominently as the author's. The illustrator was Clifford W. Ashley, an artist from Howard Pyle's school, who had sailing experience.[2] Four full pages were devoted to his work, with the third illustration printed across the top half of an opening. Featuring the 'characters' in pairs – Jasper and Freya, Freya and Heemskirk, Jasper and his ship – and then Jasper, drawn large, alone on the beach, the illustrations depicted the essential romantic relationships and conflicts but ignored Nelson. The slumped and solitary Jasper on the page preceding the break-over reflected Ashley's nautical interests, provided pathos equal to that which might have been evoked by an image of Freya on her deathbed, and accorded with the magazine's general approach to the story, which the managing editor summarized as 'holding the interest' of readers by providing fiction that was 'simple and direct, in which the element of suspense [was] fairly obvious and not too fine and psychological for them to grasp'.[3]

Having dispatched TS1 to Pinker, Conrad had no further role in the production of SA. When commending Pinker on making arrangements for American magazine publication in December 1911, he had enquired 'if I may hope to see proofs from there'. But his 22 October 1913 letter to Alfred A. Knopf indicates the response to that question was in effect negative: 'In the matter of the Metropolitan Magazine: They published Freya as a serial 2 years ago but never sent me a copy so I don't know at all how it was presented to the public'.[4] A 1916 letter

---

[1] *The Metropolitan Magazine*, 35, April 1912, pp. 20–29, 51–4. On 'break-overs' and 'jumps', see Kenneth E. Olson, *Typography and Mechanics of the Newspaper* (1930), pp. 247–8, 299; the editors referred to this technique as 'run-overs' ('Editorial Announcement: Beginning with the Thirty-Fifth Volume', *Metropolitan Magazine*, September 1911, p. 794).

[2] *The National Cyclopædia of American Biography* (1898–1984), vol. XXXVII (1951), 460–61. For examples, see Figs. 11 and 12.

[3] Carl Hovey to Knopf, 16 December 1913 (Berg). Knopf sent Hovey's letter to Conrad, who forwarded it to Pinker around 28 December 1913; see *Letters*, V, 322, and n. 2 for another excerpt from this letter.

[4] 8 December 1912 [1911] (*Letters*, IV, 521); *Letters*, V, 295. See also Conrad's later statement to Pinker 'I never get Am^can proofs as you know' (*Letters*, V, 538) and Hovey's 1 December 1917 letter to Robert MacAlarney indicating that the magazine rarely sent proofs to authors, whether in America or abroad (Berg).

from the magazine's president to Pinker also indicates that Conrad was not directly involved in the story's first printing and suggests the intrusiveness of the magazine's editorial staff: 'When we printed Freya two or three years ago we attempted to put the story into one issue and did very drastic cutting. I don't think the story was spoiled by the cutting, but the issue was spoiled by overloading it with too much of one author'.[1]

Although Conrad did not further revise the text for the magazine, SA introduced many changes. In spite of the editors' concern with its length, their cuts were not determined by the need to fit the story's text around advertisements. They shortened it about one-third by eliminating passages that did not advance its central action and by diminishing the narrator's presence, a step that in some instances shifted attention to the title character. A three-paragraph excision of the tale's opening changed the first line from 'One day – and that day was many years ago now – I received a long chatty letter from one of my old chums and fellow-wanderers in Eastern waters' to 'Freya Nelson (or Nielsen) was the kind of girl one remembers' (123.3–124.34). The change to the opening was carried over to the last section with the rewriting of a reference to 'the letter mentioned in the very first lines of this narrative' (181.7–8). At the end of section 11, deletion of the narrator's commentary on the last time he saw all the characters together altered the section's final image to Freya standing on a large boulder, 'like a feminine and martial statue', waving her handkerchief at Jasper and he his hat at her as his ship departed (135.37–136.15).

Such changes made the story even 'easier': Conrad had commended it to Dawson for this quality and as a '"no blush to the cheek of the young person" sort of thing. Perfectly safe. Eastern sea setting, but not too much setting' (*Letters*, IV, 413). SA further ensured that the story would be 'safe' by deleting a description that implied the *Bonito* had been used to abduct women into prostitution.[2] Like Ashley's illustrations, the editors' alterations of the text moved 'Freya of the Seven Isles' closer to the genre of popular romance that, at face value, its setting and subject matter suggested.

To accommodate its cuts, SA occasionally altered paragraphing and sometimes added phrases or reworded sentences. It also reversed

---

[1] H. J. Whigham, president of *Metropolitan Magazine*, to Pinker, 21 January 1916 (Berg).

[2] The passage describing the early history of the *Bonito* (130.11) never appeared in print: Conrad himself withheld it from the English serial and book editions (see below, pp. 272, 279).

two paragraphs to put the narrative's events in chronological order (179.37–180.5) and began a new paragraph to set up the story's newspaper account of the grounding of the *Bonito* as an excerpt. Some relative pronouns and small function words like prepositions were altered or added, and word order was varied. A more intrusive and deeper change was the abbreviation of Conrad's refrain 'Nelson (or Nielsen)' to the simple 'Nelson' (in most instances), which diminished a major theme.[1] Predictably, SA imposed house styling; word forms like 'onwards', 'towards' and 'amongst' as well as mere spellings were uniformly Americanized.

Absent from SA are the more than 100 new revisions that appear in SE. Notably present is 'cloth' in 'dark cloth undress jacket' (132.22c), which, given the opportunity, Conrad would have altered to the reading that appears in SE and E1 and that he had pencilled into TS1 before sending it to France (see pp. 262–3, 279). SA's numerous errors and its lack of fresh revisions confirms that he was not involved in the production of the magazine's text.[2] However, SA's text does provide useful evidence for identifying changes introduced in other texts, such as the errors made by Pinker's typist and the changes made in the *London Magazine*. Its general retention of TS1r's paragraphing shows, for instance, the extent to which the *London Magazine* was not similarly faithful.

English Serialization

BY 3 November 1911, Conrad knew that the *London Magazine* (SE) had accepted 'Freya of the Seven Isles'.[3] Although the story was actually placed in England a month earlier than in America, its London appearance in July 1912 followed its publication in New York by several months. Aware that the *London Magazine* did not enjoy the status of, for instance, *Blackwood's Edinburgh Magazine*, Conrad wrote disdainfully of it.[4] It was one of the numerous publications of the Harmsworths' Amalgamated Press, whose staff acted less as literary editors than as copy-readers and in most respects intruded little during production.[5]

---

[1] See 'Introduction', p. lvii, on the rivalry between the Dutch and the British and its historical dimensions.

[2] Other examples, among many that could be cited, include the change of person at 151.12b and 151.13a and the revisions to the description of Freya's eyes at 158.29a and 159.9a.

[3] Conrad to Quinn, 3 November 1911 (*Letters*, IV, 499).

[4] See Conrad to Pinker, [24 January 1908], [22 November 1910] (*Letters*, IV, 27, 389).

[5] For fuller discussion of these matters, see Appendix C, 'The London Magazine'.

As the *London Magazine*'s 'complete novel' for July 1912, 'Freya of the Seven Isles' was given a book-like presentation.[1] Set full measure and uninterrupted by advertising, it was introduced by a section title-page identical to that used for 'A Smile of Fortune', except for the title itself and a list of Conrad's well-known works that ended with '&c., &c.', giving the measure of his literary status through the extent of his authorship. A dedication to 'Captain C. M. Marris' on the page further amplified the book-like treatment.[2] Graphics included both decorative boilerplate and an original illustration, which departed from the maritime motif of the section title (see Figs. 9 and 10). The illustrator, Gilbert Holiday,[3] proffered a romanticized, glamorized portrait of Freya coiffed with stylish upswept hair, draped in a soft, clinging robe, and posed blowing kisses to Jasper. The single illustration's appearance as a frontispiece contributed to the book-like effect, and in this location did not interfere with the substantial revisions Conrad would make in proof. The text itself began after a standard decorative header, head-title, and notice that the story was 'Complete in this issue'. The last page completed the novel-like effect by printing 'The End' at the bottom.

For the most part, the *London Magazine* focussed on packaging its 'complete novel', rather than exerting deep editorial control of its text. Yet, though they left the wording largely untouched, the magazine's staff did make some changes. SE exhibits predictable formatting, as in labelling the sections 'chapters'.[4] The introduction of new paragraphing was the most prevalent kind of textual change, as when the narrative made a shift in time (e.g., 159.26) or where direct discourse began. In section VI, SE inserted quotation marks after its new paragraph opening (179.5), misinterpreting Conrad's complex narrative mode and necessitating a change from 'He' to 'I' and the closing of the quotation (179.6bn, 179.8). This group of changes reflected the somewhat greater editorial intrusion found in the latter part of the tale, as did the censoring of '"Gott for-dam!"' at the end

---

[1] *The London Magazine*, 28, July 1912, pp. 649–84. With illustrations by John Alan Maxwell, the story was reprinted in *The Golden Book Magazine*, August 1930, pp. 17–26; September 1930, pp. 105–13, 120, 124, 127–9; October 1930, pp. 84–92, 94, 105–9 (*Bibliography*, C220).

[2] On the text of this, and its eventual use in *'Twixt Land and Sea*, see Appendix I, 'The Epigraph and the Dedication'.

[3] Holiday was credited with illustrating another piece of fiction in the same number; he also worked for *The Strand*.

[4] See Appendix C for discussion of the 'Harmsworth touch'.

of section V (176.27n). Other house changes affected sentence structure, most often in order to join clauses or regularize grammar and idiom (131.35c–36a, 139.2, 182.12a, 183.23). In some cases a compositor may have omitted or altered words inadvertently (127.3a, 143.1, 152.35, 172.33b, 175.25) or deliberately, so as to avoid creating a new type line (136.26, 153.12).

In addition to such changes, SE contains approximately 130 revisions to wording and phrasing and 16 omissions of passages that range from 2 to 25 sentences in length, all of which appear to represent Conrad's work. These excisions tighten the narrative by reducing descriptive passages (e.g., 140.15–33, 155.35–156.9) and references to events that could be considered digressions, as when Freya and Nelson have tea on the *Bonito*, or the narrator visits Jasper's brother in London (142.18–27, 146.8–20). Conrad trimmed passages that developed the psychology of the principal characters (e.g., 128.39–129.9, 138.12–20, 143.34–144.2, 148.15–25, 154.23–31, 162.35–163.12, 163.13) and reduced information about secondary characters (e.g., 147.7–9). He was less concerned than SA's editor with restraining the presence of the narrator in the story, although he did in one instance reduce his editorializing (129.33–35). More often, rather than cutting indicators of the narrative frame, he reduced material concerning the principal characters inside the frame. Although none of the cuts in section I contributed to conventionalizing the story as romance fiction, Conrad exhibited greater sensitivity than SA's editor in ensuring that the story would be 'perfectly safe' by deleting three passages with charged elements, including the anecdote about a woman's apparent abduction (the most extreme element in the story), the narrator's attempt to 'entertain' Nelson with a 'very funny and somewhat scandalous adventure', and Antonia's late-night approach to the narrator (130.11, 129.10–27, 145.5–40). These three cuts kept the locus of tension in the central triangle, while dissipating the story's sexuality. By section VI, Conrad apparently felt that he had cut enough and made no more excisions, which could have altered the effect achieved in the denouement. Together with his changes to words and phrases, these excisions show him as much concerned with making his work 'suitable' for the *London Magazine* as with refining the art of his tale.

When preparing his third story for this magazine, Conrad made these and other adjustments specifically for its readers, and especially, it seems, to avoid improprieties and coarseness. In one instance, he softened the effect of Freya's reaction to Jasper's risky nautical manœuvres by inserting 'actually' between the words 'Freya swore', and in another he deleted '"you — "' to remove an invitation to fill in the blank with an epithet (127.12b, 150.21–22).[1] He altered wording, so that 'jokes' became 'jests', 'money' became 'cash', and 'bad' became 'seedy' (137.33, 140.4b, 144.20a). Elsewhere he tried out readings for more general artistic purposes, as in the substitution of topographical terms (126.19, 126.33, 126.35, 168.16),[2] or in various stylistic changes. He deleted superfluous words (127.39, 132.27, 133.38a, 138.27a, 150.7a, 150.10, 164.3, 188.15) and altered word choice (135.10a, 140.2a) and word order (135.24–25, 163.38). He strove for greater clarity and precision (138.37, 147.1, 164.21) and continued to struggle for the right word, as when he revisited the descriptions of Schultz's voice and Freya's eyes (138.30b, 158.29a).[3]

Whereas SE also contains acceptable corrections of TS1r's text that could have been made by either its compositors or Pinker's typist, as well as by the author,[4] the nature of these other changes, including the excisions, indicates that they were almost certainly Conrad's. Some of the alterations would have required more intimate understanding of the story than is evident in the formatting changes the magazine did make, and the operational structure of the Amalgamated Press suggests that the staff time required to achieve such understanding was not usually available. Conrad himself was convinced that the work would be 'mangled' if cut by anyone else,[5] and the manner in which 'A Smile of Fortune' was shortened for the *London Magazine*

---

[1] SA had deleted the latter phrase as well.

[2] The spellings of 'Mintok' and 'Chantabun' appear differently in SE, too (132.9c, 139.12b). On 16 January 1912 Conrad had written to Pinker regarding the manuscript text of *Chance* that formed the basis of serial publication: 'Writing quickly I stopped not to think but put in passages and effects on trial, as it were' (*Letters*, v, 5). Here he gently rebuked Pinker for sending on the raw copy without consulting with him, although his posture appears to have been disingenuous.

[3] See also 131.31b, 138.11–12, 163.40, 165.12.

[4] That is, in addition to those that SE has in common with SA (see above), which must generally be attributed to the typist; where SA omits a passage and SE contains a correction, the origin of its reading becomes unclear in proportion as the need for the change is obvious.

[5] A word he used to describe *Harper's* alterations to 'The Partner' (*Letters*, IV, 499). Conrad cut about one-third as much as the editors had excised for the *Metropolitan Magazine*. He deleted about 3,500 words, or about 12 per cent; SA had cut more than 10,000 words. Conrad's attitude on this matter was clear. Offering to make cuts to *The Secret Agent* for serial publication, he had said to Pinker in 1906: 'I can take out 2 to 3 thou. words if so desired – analysis. But no one else must mangle the thing' (*Letters*, III, 364). For more on the excisions that in fact occurred, see 'The Texts' in *The Secret Agent*, ed. Bruce Harkness and S. W. Reid with Nancy Birk (1990), pp. 251–3.

indicates that the editors would have left reducing this story to him. His alterations were apparently marked on proofs routed through Pinker. The *London Magazine* must have sent the proofs (i.e., galley slips) that Conrad corrected and returned on 19 May 1912 (*Letters*, v, 66). Having already made extensive revisions to TS1 before Pinker had it retyped, busy with other projects and preferring to work on typeset copy, he had waited for magazine proofs to make further revisions and corrections.[1] As Conrad marked these proofs, he did not have at hand either the manuscript or his own corrected and revised typescript.[2]

First English Edition

BY LATE June 1912, Pinker had settled plans for Dent's publication of the first book edition that would contain 'Freya of the Seven Isles'. Believing that it could come out as early as August,[3] Conrad, who had just finished his second article on the '*Titanic* affair' for the July number of the *English Review* against a firm deadline,[4] set to work preparing printer's copy for the book. Around 6 July, he sent Pinker the 'corrected text' of 'Freya of the Seven Isles' and of the other three stories (including 'The Partner') for Dent's edition of *'Twixt Land and Sea* (*Letters*, v, 83). For 'A Smile of Fortune' and 'The Secret Sharer' certainly, and probably for 'The Partner' (which was eventually held back), that copy consisted of revised tear sheets or proofs of the magazines in which the stories had been printed many months earlier.[5]

---

[1] For Conrad's commitments during these months, see the 'Chronology'; also pp. 204–5 and 265. The previous year, while asking Pinker to arrange for *Harper's* to send him galley slips of *Under Western Eyes*, Conrad had noted: 'one corrects better on the printed page – quicker too' (*Letters*, IV, 467–8). In July 1910 he had requested two sets of 'slips' for *Under Western Eyes* from the *English Review*, one of them to be used as the basis for the first English edition, and in January 1908 he had made a similar request in regard to the *London Magazine*: 'In reference to *Black Mate* please ask the Editor of London to send me proof as early as possible. That story is totaly unrevised as you know' (*Letters*, IV, 353, 31).

[2] For the location of the documents at this time, see Appendix A.

[3] Conrad to Galsworthy, 28 June 1912 (*Letters*, v, 80).

[4] 'Certain Aspects of the Admirable Inquiry into the Loss of the *Titanic*' occupied sixteen pages of the July number, which Conrad claimed was held back till his article was ready, the official inquiry having just concluded (*Letters*, v, 74–5, 80). See 'The Texts' in *Notes on Life and Letters*, pp. 298–9.

[5] In the case of 'The Secret Sharer' almost two years ago, of 'A Smile of Fortune' five months, of 'The Partner' four. See above, pp. 221–2, 246–7; on 'The Partner', for which the documents are peculiarly complex and early proofs rather than tear sheets were at one time in hand, see Emily Dalgarno, 'The Textual History of Conrad's "The Partner"', *The Library* v, 30 (1975), 41–4.

Freya of the Seven Isles

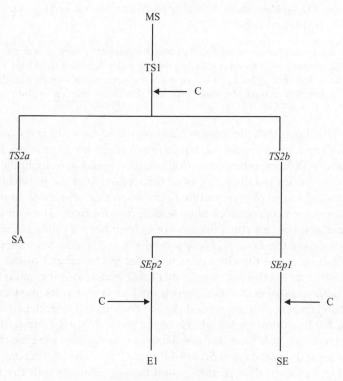

C→ Conrad's 'corrections'

Inferred (lost) documents (e.g., *TS2a*)

[16] Genealogy of 'Freya of the Seven Isles'.

For 'Freya of the Seven Isles' Conrad must have revised some form of the *London Magazine*.

The evidence, though scattered in bits, indicates that Conrad marked his revisions on a duplicate set of raw proofs (galley slips) of the *London Magazine* that still included the passages eventually cut from its published form (SE). No other document was in fact accessible. He had yet to see a copy of the *Metropolitan Magazine*, and he had never handled either copy of the Pinker typescript used to set up the magazines and undoubtedly discarded forthwith. Neither the manuscript nor the revised typescript was at hand, had he felt forced to consider the desperate option of re-creating typewritten copy for Dent's.[1] On 19 May, when returning to Pinker the marked set of proofs for SE, he had noted:

I am asking the Editor to send me a revise for myself, to keep. It will save me making the same corrections in the full text on galley slips; and then with a pair of scissors and some gum I can fit in the cut out parts without much trouble, to make a complete text for the book form. You don't want it in a great hurry – do you?[2]

The likelihood that the *London Magazine* would have obliged Conrad in this request is virtually nil, but its implications are instructive. Had revises of SE been returned to Conrad, they would have included his revisions but lacked the passages he had excised for serial publication. According to the plan he outlined, he was to take scissors to another document to prepare mocked-up setting copy for Dent. The only doc-ument available for this purpose would have been a duplicate set of galley slips of the *London Magazine* in which, as his request implies, he had not recorded the alterations made for SE. Whether Conrad had himself received this set directly or Pinker had held it for marketing the book to prospective publishers is unclear, but what seems virtually certain is that such a set, revised (i.e., re-revised) by Conrad, provided copy for E1. Although tear-sheets of the just-published *London Maga-zine* might possibly have been available in time for him to revise them for E1 – as they were for 'A Smile of Fortune' and 'The Secret Sharer' – E1's agreements, disagreements, and near-agreements with the revi-sions present in SE indicate that Conrad was forced to work on the raw set of galley slips to which he alluded in May.[3]

E1's readings indicate that it does in fact descend from the typeset-ting of the *London Magazine*, though not in its corrected and published

---

[1] See pp. 261, 265; see also Appendix A and, for the genealogical chart, Fig. 16 (p. 275).

[2] *Letters*, v, 66. As with 'A Smile of Fortune', Conrad received and returned proofs for the *London Magazine* via Pinker, but his phrasing suggests that his request, if there was one, was made directly to the *London Magazine*. It is possible that this statement was for Pinker's consumption, an indirect way of assuring him that the work on the story could be done on a deadline.

[3] Highly unlikely is that the *London Magazine*'s setting copy was returned to Pinker, who must have planned to market the book either with a set of raw SE proofs or without showing any copy of this tale to the prospective publisher. No less improbable is the other alternative, tear sheets of the published form, if that was actually issued the same week Conrad was preparing printer's copy of the entire book. The exact timing of these two events remains unclear, but they were essentially simultaneous, and in any case the tear sheets could not have provided the readings restored in E1 any more than revises.

form. Nearly all of the changes introduced by the compositors or other production staff, not to mention the changes made by the Pinker typist also found in SE, appear in E1. For the most part, E1 also contains SE's punctuation and the many changes it introduced in paragraphing. These include the new paragraph exhibiting SE's misinterpretation of Conrad's complex narrative mode and the interpolated inverted commas that came along with it (179.5, 179.6b*n*, 179.8). Where SE inserts a new paragraph associated with a narrative shift in time or perspective, E1 follows suit (e.g., 159.26), as it does in SE's censorship of '"Gott for-dam!"' (176.27*n*), its changes in sentence structure, and its regularization of grammar and idiom (131.35c–36a, 139.2, 182.12a, 183.23). Apparently inadvertent omissions and alterations attributable to SE's compositor (143.1, 172.33b, 175.25), as well as deliberate ones (136.26, 153.12), were transmitted to E1.

The readings in E1 make clear, however, that it was not set from revises of the *London Magazine*, and that instead Conrad marked a duplicate set of magazine proofs some time after he had made the changes that appear in SE. In about one-quarter of the more than 100 places where the *London Magazine* prints a revision Conrad had made in its proofs, E1 contains the rejected reading of TS1r. For instance, when revising for SE Conrad had noticed the problem with using 'glass' to describe the calmness of the sea just before the same word, signifying telescope, occurred, so he had changed the figure of speech to 'smooth as ice' (164.21); yet E1 retains TS1r's awkward repetition. Had Conrad been working with revises of SE, containing 'ice', he would not have restored the repetitive and potentially confusing TS1r reading. Moreover, on the first or second galley slip he had replaced 'There were' with 'They had' in the first clause of a compound sentence when revising for SE, but for E1 he retained TS1r's wording and inserted 'they had' in the second clause of the same sentence, with an arguably less effective result (124.4–5). A little later, where he had added 'loud laugh' after 'elated gesture' in SE, he inserted simply 'laugh' before that phrase in E1 (138.11–12). His preference for personal pronouns had exhibited itself in SE in his alteration of TS1r's 'that' to 'his', but here again E1 follows TS1r (133.30). In another instance, SE's change of 'clothed' to 'invested' had involved the deletion of 'that was', yet in recalling the substitution when revising for E1, he neglected to delete the superfluous wording (132.27).[1]

---

[1] Given Conrad's tendency to trim unneeded words, E1's reading looks more like an oversight than evidence that he restored or an editor added 'that was'.

The implications of E1's failures to reproduce SE's revisions of particular words and phrases find confirmation in its treatment of the passages Conrad excised for the magazine. In section IV Conrad had deleted for SE two sentences about Freya's horror and indignation, but E1 retained the first (found in TS1r) and took out only the second; when a sentence with the same wording – 'She could not utter a word' – reappeared in the text, he deleted it from E1 at that point (158.1–2, 159.21). But where SE had cut nine substantial sentences recounting Freya's fears about her father's likely behaviour (154.23–31), beginning with one he had added in TS1r, E1 lacks only that one and the next (154.23) and thus restores most of the passage found in TS1r. That he would have recalled seven such sentences verbatim, and indeed resisted the temptation to alter any details while rewriting them, is not credible. SE and E1 have so many similarities as well as differences in excisions of sentences and other passages, that the only viable conclusion is that E1 was not based on revises of SE, that it was Conrad himself who had made the cuts for SE, and that he repeated the process with variations when preparing copy for E1, even though Dent's did not require reductions for their book edition. E1's excisions must have been made by Conrad, who sometimes reproduced in whole and sometimes in part those he had made for the *London Magazine.*

Although Conrad often changed even the smallest detail in his work, if he had been using SE revises, he would not have restored TS1r readings in so many places where the SE reading was not tailored to the *London Magazine*'s audience and, in some cases, represented a less fulfilled artistic state. E1's restorations of TS1r's readings are so diverse in length and nature as to preclude the practical possibility that Conrad was working with any material but a duplicate raw proof of the original typesetting of the *London Magazine.* The minimal intervention of Dent's editor elsewhere in the text (see below) rules out intrusion by an external agent in these variations between the revisions found in SE and those found in E1.

During his preparation of copy for E1, Conrad recreated about half the revisions that he had made for SE. He must have done so from memory, even though duplicating changes in this way was not his preference.[1] The record of variants provides some clues as to how he was

---

[1] In a summer 1911 letter to Pinker regarding the publication of *Under Western Eyes*, Conrad asked for the *English Review* to use the corrected copy that he returned with his letter, noting that 'It will save me infinite trouble. I doubt too if I will be able to remember exactly the corrections I've just made' (*Letters*, IV, 436).

able to reproduce fifty-odd revisions made about seven weeks earlier. For example, a passage he had deliberated over a couple of times stood out for him: having already revised Heemskirk's 'strange tottering distressed gait' (the MS reading) to 'strange laborious gait' in TS1r, he recalled one of the two words from the manuscript, so that both SE and E1 read 'strange, tottering gait' (165.18a). Proximity was sometimes a further aid to recall, as in this same sentence he changed an article in both SE and E1 (165.18b*n*). Other changes he probably remembered because of their stylistic significance. On the opening page, he moved the word 'us', creating the construction 'those of us' (123.7c). He replicated 'dark undress jacket' (132.22c). He also changed a description of Freya's eyes (125.2), the actor in a sentence (151.12b–13a), and important nautical details – the unsafe distance from the shore at which Jasper dropped anchor in Nelson's Cove (126.34a) and the description of the *Bonito* before and after hitting the reef (176.2–3, 176.12, 176.13, 182.39). E1 matches SE in deleting the description of the woman's abduction on the *Bonito*, two editorial comments by the narrator, and the short sentence 'She had said nothing' (130.11, 141.22, 184.26a, 162.14b). Some changes reflected his characteristic eliminating of repetition and superfluous phrasing (e.g., 124.9, 179.4; 186.25a, 186.29a, 187.16); others simply illustrated his astounding ability to recall his own phrasing. But in about a dozen other places where SE has a revision, E1 contains yet another (e.g., 131.31b, 138.11–12, 158.29a, 159.9a, 165.12).

Conrad also created approximately 200 other new readings for E1 – twice as many as appear in SE – which, like the fifty-odd varied revisions for E1 and his decision not to reproduce many of SE's audience-driven changes, indicate a different treatment of the tale for the book edition. Additions were less frequent than deletions and usually enhanced clarity or specificity: 'pirates' provided another possibility for the history of the *Bonito*, a 'lateral' wave appeared in Jasper's hair, sounds from Freya's room that became 'mysterious' conveyed Nelson's inability to comprehend his daughter, which was also shown in an addition that had him assume her 'indifference' to Heemskirk's apparent pain (130.22, 131.5b, 161.12b, 167.14). Deletions tended to reduce wording that was superfluous, redundant, or vague. He eliminated the first qualifier in pairs such as 'pale blue', 'arduous nautical', 'gratuitously provoking', 'somewhat surly', 'already some', and 'heavy chains' (125.17c, 126.3, 141.18, 155.13, 169.9, 175.6). He reduced descriptive passages (168.20a, 168.34) and deleted bits depicting the characters' psychology, particularly Freya's in the long fourth section (e.g., 154.14, 154.23, 160.20–21).

Instead of adding or deleting words, Conrad frequently substituted them, stretching for the last time to find the right phrasing. Often new readings replaced already good ones. He altered 'side' to 'connections', 'brightness' to 'radiance', 'timbre' to 'tone', 'drawn together' to 'knitted', and 'meant in' to 'intended by' (129.38, 134.1, 143.4, 154.37, 181.36). More often, substitutions produced improvements: Freya was described as 'resolute' instead of 'fresh', Heemskirk's demeanour was 'surly' rather than 'ominous', clouds formed in 'purple' not 'black' masses (which allowed Conrad to reserve the latter adjective for descriptions of Heemskirk); Freya's gesture of flinging kisses to Jasper became 'passionate' rather than 'wide', Heemskirk was 'infuriated' rather than 'raging', and, giving testimony, Schultz 'protested' rather than 'affirmed' (131.11–12, 132.20, 140.27, 164.37, 167.7, 183.13). Conrad even reached back to the manuscript, as he did elsewhere (see above, p. 248), to change a description of Nelson from 'oppressed' to 'tried' (128.38). His changes to the treatment of characters and of the *Bonito* came at times in clusters, as in the description of Heemskirk in section 11, a passage Conrad had worked on earlier (132.19, 132.20, 132.22b), or the disquisition on Schultz in section 111 (139.14–15, 139.16, 139.18a–b, 139.31b, 139.37, 140.2b).

Although Conrad's revisions for E1 were numerous, changes attributable to the publishing process were few. In E1 'amongst' was regularized to 'among', and 'carryings on' to 'carrying on' (140.18, 150.12). E1 also introduced a few errors (e.g., 141.4, 145.32b) and some new paragraph openings. These changes, however, pale in the presence of the extensive and thorough revisions Conrad made within the week or so he prepared this long tale and two others for Dent's. The variants in subsequent editions are negligible and indicate that the changes he made at this time were his last for this story.

BOOK EDITIONS

HAVING RECEIVED SOME 3,500 copies of their first Conrad book by 7 October 1912 and duly deposited one with the British Museum by the 10th for copyright purposes, J. M. Dent and Sons officially published the first English edition of *'Twixt Land and Sea* (*Bibliography*,

A16a) on 14 October 1912 at a price of six shillings.[1] Based, as has been seen, on tear-sheets and proofs of magazine printings that had been revised by Conrad,[2] the book also included a title, an epigraph, and a dedication for which either Pinker or Conrad must have supplied copy. It seems more likely this material was supplied directly by Conrad and consisted of what came readily to hand – personal stationery with the title written out, the extant leaf of the epigraph that Arthur Symons had sent to him, and either a revised *London Magazine* proof sheet of 'Freya of the Seven Isles' or some form of manuscript.[3] Although he had forwarded marked copy for this and the other two tales to Pinker in early July, Conrad was in direct communication with Dent's and their printer, the Temple Press, about the book's title and epigraph a few weeks later and about copy for 'The Secret Sharer' and about proofs of the book in September.[4] Sometimes Pinker was simply by-passed in these later stages of production.

Conrad had earlier expressed interest in the physical design of the book and was not delighted with its 'spinach-coloured' cover, its measure, nor its 'fairly ugly' type and paper when he saw them, but he dismissed these matters as 'trifles' and was immensely pleased with Dent's marketing of the book and with its sales, which were robust enough to make up the £200 advance and yield royalties within a month.[5] The second printing, of 750 copies, in November was accompanied by his remark to Pinker about its 'very good reception', and the third, in January 1913, by gratitude for the 'cheering' news.[6] As late as

---

[1] *Letters*, v, 112; *Bibliography*, A16a, 'Notes'.

[2] See pp. 221–2, 246, 275–8.

[3] For more on the epigraph and dedication, including the variants in them, see Appendix I, 'The Epigraph and the Dedication'.

[4] *Letters*, v, 83, 87, 90, 105, 108. Probably the epigraph and the dedication were sent to Dent's along with the letter containing the title. Cf. Conrad to Pinker, [6 June 1912] (*Letters*, v, 74). Conrad must have turned the proofs around rather quickly, to judge by the fact that he had returned the lot a day before Pinker posted the last batch to New York for Doran's American edition. See below, pp. 282–3.

[5] *Letters*, v, 83, 108, 112, 221, 348. Dent's royalty was 25 per cent (*Letters*, v, 80). A colonial issue (i.e., an 'Australasian Edition') consisting of about 250 copies of the first printing bound in a light blue cover and making a more attractive book was issued in October as well, but Conrad may not have known of it and probably did not see it. Nor is it likely that an error in the first binding of the English issue came to his attention. Details of printing and issue are set out by Cagle and Trogdon in their *Bibliography*, A16a, 'Notes'. On the significance of the volume's success, which for Conrad was unprecedented, see Reid, pp. 71–6.

[6] *Letters*, v, 141, 165. Apparently Dent's waited till February 1913 to deposit their edition in the Bodleian Library and the National Library of Scotland, for which they used copies of the third impression (see *Bibliography*, A16a, 'Notes').

February of the next year, while deploring Methuen's handling of the well-received first edition of *Chance*, Conrad was moved to remark on Dent's success in selling nearly 5,000 copies of a book of stories in less than six months 'without lying advtis[t]' (*Letters*, V, 348).

In March 1914, Dent's reprinted their edition for issue in their 'Wayfarer's Library', the counterpart for modern authors of their 'Everyman's Library'; in this form it had a new title-page in colour to match a facing frontispiece showing Jacobus' introduction of his Alice to a captain who looks very much like Conrad.[1] Presumably printed from a duplicate set of plates, this subedition would have acquired a life of its own and was reprinted in 1918. Until they published their 'Uniform' collected edition of Conrad in 1923, Dent's kept their first Conrad book in print, issuing it in various bindings but without any variation in the text,[2] and as late as 1932 they were selling a 1920 printing as part of their 'Popular Edition of Modern Fiction'.

The American edition was still in preparation by the time Dent's English edition had reached a second impression in November 1912. George H. Doran, who also paid a £200 advance, had written to Pinker on 18 October explaining his reservations about publishing 'so important a book so late in the season' and assuring him that American copyright would meanwhile be secured, though he proposed to postpone issue till January or February of the next year.[3] Nonetheless, once the Vail Company in Ohio had completed printing at the end of November, Robert Rutter & Son of New York apparently bound the sheets almost immediately. Doran officially published their first American edition (*Bibliography*, A16b) at a price of $1.25 on 3 December 1912; the Library of Congress had received two depository copies to secure American copyright by the next day.[4]

Printer's copy for Doran's edition (A1) was proof sheets of the first English edition (E1) in an early and uncorrected state. As late as 7 October, Conrad reminded Pinker that A1 was to be typeset from E1, but Pinker had already posted three batches of 'first proofs' to New York a few weeks earlier – that is, by the time Conrad was returning Dent's proofs directly to them or to their printer, rather than through

---

[1] See Fig. 13, 'Frontispiece of '*Twixt Land and Sea*, Dent, 1918'.

[2] *Bibliography*, A16a, 'Notes'. Collation of four copies of the first printing in both its domestic and colonial issues and of a copy of the third shows type batter and slight distortions in the plates, together with the loss of one or two points here and there, but no evidence of alteration other than of the preliminaries to record reprinting.

[3] Doran to Pinker, 18 October 1912, 21 November 1912 (Berg). Doran's royalty was probably 20 per cent, which he offered for *Chance* on 19 January 1912 (Berg).

[4] U.S. Copyright Office; see *Bibliography*, A16b, 'Notes', for details.

him.[1] Dent's must have sent duplicate 'first proofs' to Pinker, and he in turn must have posted them, rather than revises, directly to Doran without waiting for corrections from Conrad. The proofs that Conrad returned to Dent's on 17 September contained no additional revisions. A1 reproduces not only all the errors Dent's agents introduced in E1, but also the revisions that Conrad made for it. Using uncorrected E1 proofs, Doran's printers committed about a dozen minor typesetting errors in wording, most of them look-alike literals (e.g., 'every' for 'very', 'ships" for 'ship's'), though a few bordered on normalization or Americanization.[2] In this respect Conrad was well served by Doran's first edition of his work.

The book also served him well in the marketplace. Like its English counterpart, the first American edition was a success, though less immediately. A more handsome book than Dent's, it appeared in a red cloth binding with Doran's usual imprint for this period, which included the line 'Hodder & Stoughton' above both 'New York' and 'George H. Doran Company'. Conrad must have seen copies, because in April 1913 he asked Pinker whether Doran was Hodder & Stoughton's partner in America.[3] Doran soon sold his rights in the book to F. N. Doubleday when Doubleday, Page acquired both it and *Chance* upon opening their campaign to promote Conrad. This larger strategy was the subject of Conrad's letter to Pinker in April 1913 when he asked about Hodder and Stoughton. In the middle of July he told John Quinn that Doubleday had acquired the book and in early August mentioned to both Pinker and Alfred A. Knopf that he had had a friendly letter from Doubleday himself. The legalities were concluded in September, and Conrad approved samples of Doubleday's new preliminaries, and perhaps of the binding, in October.[4]

[1] Conrad to Pinker, 17 September 1912, 7 October 1912 (*Letters*, v, 108, 112); P. B. Boyd to Pinker, 6 September 1912, and E. M. Boyd to Pinker, 24 September, 27 September 1912 (Berg). According to the last two letters, Pinker had posted proofs on the 11th and the 18th; he must have sent the first batch (of 48 pages) by the beginning of the month.

[2] See 51.9, 90.35a; 27.22b, 59.27, 92.13; see also 28.28b, 29.26a, 53.34, 71.30, 72.19a, 73.35b, 112.9, 173.13.

[3] Conrad to Pinker, [13 April 1913] (*Letters*, v, 215). Cagle and Trogdon point out that this imprint was Doran's common practice at the time and in fact reflected their business relationship (*Bibliography*, A16b, 'Notes'). Hodder and Stoughton held a minority interest in Doran's company (see *Letters*, v, 216, n. 2).

[4] *Letters*, v, 253, 268, 270; see *Bibliography*, A16b, 'Notes', for details of the sale and reprinting of the book. To what extent the young Knopf was responsible for Doubleday's decision to take up Conrad it is difficult to determine, but it seems clear that he was deeply involved in the promotional tactics the firm adopted for placing Conrad's name and work squarely before the American public. George H. Doran's selfless and heroic cooperation in this

By the end of the year Doubleday had the second printing of A1, with their imprint, ready for sale, just as they were preparing to publish *Chance*. Historic as the first of his works issued by the firm that would be Conrad's American publisher in the years that brought him commercial success, the book featured a ship device that would become a sort of hallmark, and it set the pattern for the series of reprints of Conrad's works that Doubleday would market during the next decade. The text of this impression was invariant from the first,[1] and it remained so in the 'Deep Sea' reprints that followed right through 1922, a year after Doubleday's sumptuous collected edition with a uniform typeface, layout, and binding had begun to appear.

The third group of volumes that Doubleday issued as part of their 'Sun-Dial edition' included *'Twixt Land and Sea* (1921), volume 'XII' of the series.[2] The first of the many forms that Doubleday's collected edition–typesetting would eventually take, the Sun-Dial issue was in active preparation from April 1919, when Conrad was assembling for Doubleday's first five volumes both the prefaces and the printer's copy for the works. By June he was planning the next group of five in order to take Doubleday through *Under Western Eyes*, but the 'Author's Note' for *Typhoon*, which would appear with *The Nigger of the 'Narcissus'* in the third volume, was giving him pause, though those for *A Personal Record* and *The Mirror of the Sea*, which would be combined in the eleventh, were ready by September, well before they were required. Doubleday had printer's copy and prefaces for the first ten volumes in hand by the end of 1919, except for the prefaces to *The Secret Agent*, which Conrad didn't manage till early the next March, and to *Under Western Eyes*. By this time Heinemann's collected edition was becoming separated from Doubleday's and was preoccupying both Conrad and Pinker.[3] Early April 1920 saw the most pressing elements of the new

---

programme, which required transfer of his rights in both *'Twixt Land and Sea* and *Chance* to Doubleday, is one of those unheralded acts that belies the cynical notion that publishers are interested only in 'business'.

[1] Collation of copies of Doran's first, Doubleday's second, and the 'Deep Sea' issues reveals plate batter but no variants other than those documenting different issue. On the ship device and Doubleday's format for the 'Deep Sea editions', see the remarks of Cagle and Trogdon in their *Bibliography*, A16b, 'Notes'; also Reid, pp. 74–5, 98.

[2] The 1921 date is given on the title-page. Official publication was apparently postponed till 1922 (see p. 285, n. 2 below). The printed sheets of Doubleday's first issue do not include volume numbers for the series, though labels affixed to the spines of the volumes have roman numerals. See *Bibliography*, AA1a(12).

[3] Conrad to Pinker, 3 April 1919, 30 April 1919, [4 June 1919], 14 August 1919, 10 December 1919, 10 February 1920, 12 February 1920, 26 February 1920; to Quinn, 10 April 1919; to Doubleday, 30 August 1919, 13 September 1919; to Wise, 30 September 1919 (*Letters*, VI, 401,

plan fairly settled. By the end of that month Conrad had written the 'Author's Note' for *'Twixt Land and Sea*, and by the end of the next was preparing to post it and printer's copy for the stories to New York.[1] It would be another year and a half, however, before the volume was published along with the other seven that completed Doubleday's initial series.[2]

The precise identity of the printer's copy for this volume is difficult to determine because so few variants exist between the texts of E1 and A1. By the rule of American efficiency, Doubleday should have simply used a copy of A1 in their possession. Conrad was, however, sending copy for various other volumes of the series to New York and seems to have followed this procedure with *'Twixt Land and Sea* – his secretary, L. M. Hallowes, having inspected the material before it went off.[3] Doubleday's new, collected edition (A2) does not follow any of the errors A1 introduced. Although the implausibility of most of them makes this negative evidence indecisive as a whole, the absence from A2 of a few A1 readings that would have recommended themselves to Doubleday's printers indicates that they in fact set up their text from a copy of E1, as Conrad's reference to the use of 'English Editions' for other volumes suggests.[4]

The text of A2 exhibits, however, more variant readings than A1's, though they also lack authority. A few are outright errors that level

---

411–12, 433–4, 464–6, 540–41; VII, 22–4, 25–6, 34–5; VI, 406–7, 479–80, 486–7, 499–500). See 'The Texts' in *The Secret Agent* for the history of its preface (pp. 311–22) and for a more careful and elaborate consideration of the complex history of the two collected editions and their eventual textual independence of one another (pp. 283–93). The preface to *Under Western Eyes* appears to have been ready by the end of April; see p. 305.

[1] Conrad to Eric Pinker, 8.4.20; Conrad to Pinker, [27 April 1920], 31 May 1920; Conrad to Wise, 20 May 1920 (*Letters*, VII, 73, 86–7, 102, 98). The sale of the typescript to Wise, though planned, was a sure sign Conrad had done with it by the middle of May.

[2] Production of *'Twixt Land and Sea* as well as of many other volumes in this third group probably occurred in the last half of 1921, as the date on the title-page suggests. But release seems to have been predicated on including *The Rescue* and *Notes on Life and Letters*, which Doubleday and Dent did not publish as separate editions until 1920 and 1921. Volumes 11 through 18 of the 'Sun-Dial edition' were officially deposited for copyright purposes on 11 February 1922. See *Bibliography*, AA1a, 'Notes', for details.

[3] ''Twixt Land and Sea and Within the Tides have been read through by Miss H who has discovered a few misprints and corrected them. Those volumes with their proper Prefaces will leave by this Wednesday's packet': Conrad to Pinker, 31 May 1920 (*Letters*, VII, 102).

[4] For example, A1's 'so prettily complex' for E1's 'so pettily complex' (29.26a), its 'I'm not afraid' for 'I am not afraid' (71.30), its 'halter around my neck' for 'halter round my neck' (92.13), and its 'dark mantle' for 'dank mantle' (112.9) are all readings that would ordinarily have been reproduced in A2 had they been present in Doubleday's copy. See Conrad to Pinker, 31 May 1920 (*Letters*, VII, 102).

Conrad's text and reflect serious misunderstanding: for instance, 'disposable' for the technical 'disponible', 'explaining' for 'exclaiming', 'flew' for 'fled', and 'may' for 'will'. Most of A2's other changes involve idiom and usage, the kinds of omission, addition, and substitution that Conrad's wording would have invited when being prepared for a collected edition aimed at a respectable though wide audience.[1] Even so, the number of such changes is modest for such a volume of stories, and it is doubtful that they represent the 'corrections' supposedly made by Miss Hallowes, and virtually certain that none of them originated with Conrad or had his particular sanction.

In England Heinemann issued their collected edition of 'Twixt Land and Sea (E2) more or less in tandem with Doubleday's American. By the end of summer 1920 they were producing their volumes independently of Doubleday. Conrad was to become more and more satisfied with this arrangement, as he had a voice in the design of the title-page and preliminaries of the series and was (at least prospectively) to have proofs of volumes submitted to him. But the actual typesetting of Heinemann's volumes was far in lag of Doubleday's, and there was a great flurry of work in the last months of 1920 simply to get the first group ready for release by January 1921. By early 1921 Conrad was busy with final preparations for *Notes on Life and Letters*, with signing sheets for the recently hatched *Notes on My Books*,[2] and with preparing to depart for Corsica. The actual production of E2 occurred in the last week of February while he was abroad working on his 'Napoleonic novel', and indeed more than a month after he had ceased giving any practical attention to the collected editions.[3] Moreover, no record of his providing Heinemann with printer's copy for 'Twixt Land and Sea is known to have survived. Presumably some form of E1, rather than A1, served, having probably been supplied by Pinker. As with A2, none of A1's variant readings found their way into E2, not even the most plausible ones.[4]

---

[1] See 22.24c, 44.3, 115.28, 116.13a; also 31.17a, 98.6–7, 109.8, 114.1–2, 114.7, 124.15a, 124.35b, 142.17, 175.16, 175.23. A few of these (e.g., 124.15a) are arguably simple errors.

[2] On this book, see pp. 306–8.

[3] Proofs of Heinemann's collected 'Twixt Land and Sea survive (HRHRC). Gatherings are generally stamped with a date on their first page, beginning with 21 February 1921 and ending with the 25th. The proofs exhibit the usual careful attention by the Heinemann editor–proofreader to details of typography and usage but no signs that Conrad marked or even examined them.

[4] See, for instance, A1's unique variants at 29.26a, 71.30, 92.13, 112.9.

Like other volumes in their series, Heinemann's collected edition of *'Twixt Land and Sea* generated a number of altered words amidst its carefully styled spelling, punctuation, and word-division. Less frequent than those in A2, E2's changes in wording by and large tended to conventionalize Conrad's prose and particularly to smooth out its rough spots. His typical 'these' twice became 'those', and editorial correction turned his 'furthest' and 'may' into 'farthest' and 'might'. As a result, some of Conrad's more carefully meditated revisions disappeared, while entirely new readings appeared for the first time.[1]

Because no further printings of the Heinemann collected edition were made after 780 copies had been wrought off for issue in 1921, some of these readings would have remained peculiar to E2 had they not become incorporated in the Doubleday edition. In 1923 Doubleday issued an entirely new complete set named the 'Concord Edition'. As in other volumes, they altered some wording for this printing of *'Twixt Land and Sea* by reference to a copy of the Heinemann collected edition, as well as points, line breaks, and other features. Ten words were brought into conformity with E2's text by means of conventional plate repair; half reflected normalization by E2's editor, while the others corrected A2's own errors.[2] The alterations appear to have been unsystematic and constrained by mechanical feasibility, with the result that but three-quarters of E2's variants got inserted, along with a few new readings that had no precedent there.[3] From these altered plates Doubleday printed the various issues of their collected edition that followed the Concord through the years, which together

[1] See 50.7b, 188.28b; 34.8; 71.17. An unhappy revision that E2 altered (98.12b) was offset by others that were perhaps less egregious and not always attributable to an editor: e.g., 52.5–6, 113.20, 113.29c, 176.34.

[2] E2's normalizations and other 'corrections' were incorporated at 50.7b, 71.17, 113.29c, 128.15, 188.28b; A2's genuine errors were corrected at 22.24c, 116.13a, 117.5, 124.15a, 168.5.

[3] The most interesting of these is the change in 'The Secret Sharer' of Doubleday's 'Cambodje shore' (A2a), which it derived from *Harper's* through E1 and ultimately from Pinker's typist, to 'Cambodge shore' (A2b); E2 had retained 'Cambodje' (110.34n). A2b's incredibly grammatical 'Whom' (58.12) is the only reading that all other texts also lack; 'than' for Conrad's 'as' is similar in motivation and in being unprecedented, but it occurs in the serial ending of 'A Smile of Fortune' and therefore has no counterpart in the typescript version presented here (see Appendix F, 'The Serial Version of the Prologue and Ending', 138:10b). In his attention to small matters like quotation marks, punctuation, and such details, Doubleday's plate alterer twice made 'Hong Kong' (A2a) into 'HongKong' (A2b) at the end of 'Freya of the Seven Isles'; this form seems to have been stimulated by the word's first, misleading appearance in E2 at a line break with a hyphen for the compound 'Hong-Kong' (as in the manuscript and typescript though in no other printed texts).

constitute a subedition (A2b) with its own distinct history and text.[1] This strangely mixed text of the stories has been the standard one in America since then.

Meanwhile, Dent's issued their 'Uniform Edition' as a counterpart to Doubleday's 'Concord' the same year. Instead of following the Heinemann collected edition, they acquired a set of Doubleday mats to print these volumes and, later, others.[2] The plates of *'Twixt Land and Sea* made from these mats reproduced the original state of Doubleday's typesetting, and they remained unaltered in subsequent years for Dent's various reprintings. They constitute another subedition (A2a) with its own history, virtually identical in text to the Sun-Dial printing but separate from the later Doubleday printings. Consequently, both the serious and the trivial errors introduced in America by Doubleday in 1921 found their way back to Britain, where they became part of the received text of the stories for the rest of the century and thus, in the case of the second one particularly, of the country's cultural heritage.

COPY-TEXTS

THE PRINTED EDITIONS of *'Twixt Land and Sea* that followed Dent's first English edition cannot provide a reasonable basis for editing any of the three stories. Their 'accidentals' – punctuation, spelling, capitalization, word-division – mainly derive from E1's and, when different, represent changes made in the publishing or printing houses without any authority. The situation is similar for E1 itself. All three of its texts derive from the English serial printings of the stories, and though Conrad may have altered the odd point or spelling while revising a magazine's wording, most of E1's changes in their forms reflect the preferences of the agents involved in making the book, whether a Dent editor (which seems least likely), a proofreader, or a compositor.

---

[1] In the dedication (in the volume's preliminary gathering), the Sun-Dial's correct 'Marris' appears as 'Harris' in some later issues (e.g., the 1924 'Canterbury' and 'Complete' and the 1925 'Kent'). This compositor's error suggests that the preliminaries were reset or that these plates at least were recast from mats that retained an error which had been corrected in proof before the Sun-Dial sheets were wrought off. No such variation from the Concord printing appears in the texts of the stories or of the 'Author's Note'.

[2] For instance, Gresham's 'Medallion' set (1925) and their own popular 'Collected' after the Second World War. Two alterations of case were made in the 'Author's Note' to make the Sun-Dial's 'the' part of the title of 'The Secret Sharer'; see below, p. 307.

For all three stories, then, the choice of copy-text comes down to a serial text or a manuscript or typescript.

A Smile of Fortune

FOR THE first tale in the collection, where a manuscript (MS), a complete typescript (TS1), and a partial 'clean' typescript (TS2) survive, the choice of copy-text is rather straightforward, though the different versions of the opening and closing pose a special problem. The text of 'A Smile of Fortune' that one would wish to reconstruct is generally present in the revised complete typescript (TS1r), where Conrad presumably gave its forms the most thorough attention. The text of MS is largely out of the question, not only because it is a draft typically lacking punctuation that Conrad planned to add in a later document, but also because its wording was often superseded during thorough revision in a lost typescript (*TSo*), the forms of which were mainly transmitted to TS1, where they were further subjected to Conrad's attention. The text of TS2, derived from the early pages of TS1r, offers no advantage over it, as it was not supervised by Conrad[1] and its differences in forms must represent those of one of Pinker's 'infernal typists' (*Letters*, IV, 301). The text of S, on the other hand, could preserve some accidentals presumably revised by Conrad during the few days he looked over the lost Pinker typescript (*TS3*) sent to him the week of 21 November 1910, when he made some revisions while substituting the shorter prologue and altering the ending. Unfortunately, it would be impossible to distinguish these presumed genuine revisions of forms, relatively few in number, from the changes imposed by the *London Magazine*, probably multitudinous and certainly made to bring the text into conformity with their own 'style'. Conrad's own revised text, that of TS1r, provides the best basis for constituting a critical text of most of this story.

A somewhat different question arises for the prologue and for the closing sentences that Conrad altered in connection with its two versions. The serial version, based on the once rejected and superseded MS version, is the one Conrad revised for E1 and in this sense represents his final text; the text of the pages Conrad sent, on or about 25 November, to replace the opening and closing pages of the Pinker

---

[1] At least not as such at the time of its production. If a duplicate of these pages constituted the early pages of the lost Pinker typescript (*TS3*), Conrad would have seen them when reverting to the shorter prologue for the *London Magazine* in late November 1910.

typescript would have to be reconstructed, to the very limited extent possible,[1] from S's text because Conrad revised the text in those lost pages, though basing it on his earlier MS draft. However, the serial version of the prologue is not the one Conrad wished to see printed when he was most deeply involved in its creation, nor indeed after he had made the cuts in order to get it published in the *London Magazine*. His objections to its editor's proposal and his artistic evaluation of the narrative strategies of the fuller typescript version were clearly articulated. His desire to reinstate this fuller version is clearly indicated in his act of retaining the cancelled pages of the Pinker typescript when returning copy in late November. His artistic preference for this later version is clearly evidenced in the thorough rewriting and revising he did in late July after reaching the Alice episodes and in his dismissive remarks about the earlier MS version in letters to Galsworthy both before and after he had scuttled it. His failure to restore the preferred version was apparently occasioned in part by the inaccessibility of the documents, one of them (TS2) perhaps still being in America, another (the much revised pages of TS1) perhaps still being in Pinker's files, or both having in effect gone missing along with the third (the nine retained pages of *TS3*) when coming into Jessie Conrad's hands.[2] The typescript version of the prologue and of the ending is the one Conrad submitted for publication and would have seen published had he been in a position to do so. We are now in that position. The text of this version represented in TS1r is for all practical purposes the one Conrad produced and provides a suitable basis for constituting a critical text. This choice, together with that for the rest of the text, has the additional, though not decisive, advantage of providing a uniform basis for a critical edition of the entire story.

The Secret Sharer

THE ONLY extant texts that directly reflect Conrad's composition and revision are those of the manuscript (MS), *Harper's Monthly Magazine* (S), and Dent's first English edition (E1), and the 'accidentals'

---

[1] The dense overlay of S's styling would of course limit such reconstruction drastically in the absence of any earlier document; the critical text produced would consequently differ in its accidentals texture from that found in the rest of the story, but this is a minor rather than decisive consideration in the choice of copy-text.

[2] See above, p. 246, n. 3, and Appendix A, 'Provenance of the Early Documents'.

of the last, as suggested above, must be dismissed from consideration. The alterations Conrad introduced in E1, by marking up tear sheets of *Harper's*, were fairly light compared to his work on the initial lost typescript behind the serial text, and they were presumably concerned mainly with wording rather than punctuation, spelling, capitalization, and word-division. Even had Conrad given these elements of S's text thorough attention, his revisions could not be disentangled from the styling imposed by Dent's compositors and other agents, whether proofreaders or editors, on that text, already styled for *Harper's*. E1 cannot provide a practical basis for recovering the forms of Conrad's story.

His work on these elements occupied only two weeks in December 1909, as he wrote the manuscript and revised the typescript made from it. As he almost certainly 'corrected'[1] some of its accidentals while working on the typescript, the text to be reconstructed for a critical edition is that of this lost revised typescript, which Conrad returned to Pinker around 19 December 1909, who then sent it to typists to create a fair copy that he could circulate to magazine editors. Candidates for copy-text are therefore the manuscript and serial texts.

The manuscript is not one of Conrad's typical early drafts, but a relatively finished document. Although it contains internal revisions, these evidences of second thought are minimal when compared to the intricate tangle of text that characterizes most of his manuscripts. It lacks some internal and terminal punctuation, as well as the revisions Conrad made in the lost typescript, and a few of its passages seem to have been deliberately left unsettled. It is, then, by no means a 'fair-copy manuscript' in the traditional or strictest sense. Nonetheless, most of its forms reflect the relative felicity with which Conrad wrote the story, and it therefore provides a sufficient basis for constituting a critical text.

On the other hand, the text of S predictably drew Conrad's indignation when he reported with some surprise to John Galsworthy the publication of the story in a form 'so inept that I feel sick to see myself there' (see *Letters*, IV, 354). Although this comment reflected Conrad's usual avowed view of 'all these American humbugs in the publishing line',[2] that view had some basis in his experience with commercial magazines that ordinarily altered and Americanized their

---

[1] Conrad to Pinker, [18 December 1909] (*Letters*, IV, 300).
[2] *Letters*, IV, 306. See pp. 217–21 for a fuller discussion.

texts to conform to the style of the organ in particular and the house in general. There is every reason to believe that *Harper's* text of Conrad's story, edited by an experienced and perhaps autocratic professional who enforced a policy characterized by 'fastidiousness and attention to propriety', received more than its share of American serial styling.

The text of MS is closer than S's to the text of the lost revised typescript in two ways. First, it lacks the changes that were introduced by the typists who made the second typescript for Pinker and that were thus present in the copy eventually sent to *Harper's*, which Conrad never saw. Second, it lacks the styling which was given that typescript's text first in the editor's office and then by the Harpers printing house.

Unfortunately, MS also lacks whatever revisions in accidentals Conrad made while working on the first typescript. Yet, some of these, and perhaps the most important, can be recovered from the text of S because they are part and parcel of the revisions in wording that Conrad made. The remainder cannot, without also inadvertently adopting transmissional changes, but these revisions are likely to have been relatively few, given the well-developed nature of MS's text. Indeed, the odds that any such variant represents a change introduced by the *Harper's* editor and printers are likely to exceed by far the possibility that it was an alteration made by Conrad in the course of revising the text of the initial typescript.

That revised typescript having perished, MS provides the best copytext for Conrad's story. Its text can be adjusted to reflect the revisions in wording and phrasing that appeared in both S and E1 without any appreciable disturbance to the general texture of accidentals that Conrad created when writing and revising it in 1909.

Freya of the Seven Isles

ONLY THREE extant texts could conceivably provide the basis for a modern critical edition, the manuscript (MS), the typescript as revised by Conrad (TS1r), and the first English serial (SE). Although Conrad had significant control over the substantives of SE, its immediate ancestor was a copy of the Pinker typescript (*TS2*) that presumably contained at least some alterations of its accidentals made by the typist and never approved by Conrad. This text was in turn subjected to styling by the staff of the *London Magazine*, who added commas, altered exclamation marks, treated hyphens in compounds freely, and introduced other changes. Whether 'correct' in the conventional sense or not, these changes did not represent Conrad's work. Although SE's text could preserve some accidentals that he presumably revised during the time he worked on the first proofs, it is now not feasible to disentangle these presumed genuine revisions of forms, relatively few in number, from the many changes imposed by the *London Magazine* to bring the text into conformity with their own 'style'. As copy-text SE simply will not do.

The choice, then, comes down to MS and TS1r. MS of course has the plain advantage of containing only forms that Conrad wrote. But its use as copy-text would require repeated emendation to the appropriate forms of TS1r. When revising the typescript, Conrad extensively altered passages containing punctuation as part of his continuing creative reconception of his work; in their thoroughly recast forms these passages are absent from MS. At the same time he revised other accidentals – that is, those that remained in a more stable context. In short, the accidentals of TS1r supersede those of MS. Unfortunately, the revised text of the typescript also includes some changes introduced by its typist, Jessie Conrad, that slipped past an author engaged with other matters. Although Conrad managed to correct many such errors, those that avoided correction, and were not themselves incorporated into some larger revision of a passage, represent readings that would normally be eschewed in a copy-text.

Nonetheless, on balance TS1r contains the forms of the new substantive readings Conrad created during revision of the typescript as well as the hundreds of other accidentals revised as the tale became a significantly different work both in substance and in form under his hand.[1] As the typist's errors it still contains can be corrected by reference to MS, the revised text of the typescript seems the best choice for copy-text.

EMENDATION

THE TEXTS OF this edition incorporate readings from authoritative texts other than the copy-texts when these can be identified as Conrad's revisions or as corrections of errors in the copy-text. The readings

[1] Strictly speaking, the text of TS1r is that of the typescript as revised in black ink and transmitted to Pinker: what his typist used to produce 'clean' copy for publication. In no instance do the pencilled changes introduced after the document was returned to Conrad constitute these accidentals. Pencilled alterations, which post-date TS1r and are not part of the copy-text, can be considered for emendation.

adopted from later texts represent revisions of wording Conrad made in a lost typescript (or proof)[1] that was the ancestor of a published magazine text or in the magazine tear-sheets (or proof) that provided copy for E1. Corrections, on the other hand, comprise both wording and 'accidentals' and may come from texts both earlier and later than the copy-text and even from unauthoritative texts. In each case the particular textual history and the nature and relations of the texts have been crucial in determining, to the extent possible, what readings need to be adopted.

A Smile of Fortune

THE COPY-TEXT for 'A Smile of Fortune', though a typescript carefully revised in Conrad's hand, requires some alteration to take account of his later revisions of wording as well as of unnoticed errors made by Jessie Conrad when typing both it (TS1) and the typescript from which it was copied (*TSo*). This edition adopts numerous readings that first appeared in S, most noticeably in the second half of the story, as reflecting revisions that Conrad made in the Pinker typescript (*TS3*) in November 1910. An addition at the very end (77.33a) is perhaps the most visible example of such revision, but others range across the story and involve further refinement of alterations made in TS1 or even as far back as the lost initial typescript.[2] Some are simple additions of words or phrases to passages added in the lost typescript (e.g., 20.12, 47.35), but often the revisions adopted here are more complex and combine readings that Conrad changed earlier or essentially restore an MS reading that he rejected in the typescripts.[3] These changes range from a word or two (e.g., 27.14) to whole sentences (e.g., 28.35a). Revised contractions, possessives, and tenses appear in the present text, sometimes reverting to an MS form or even producing an apparently acceptable but inappropriate construction that must be Conrad's.[4] Some corrections, like those of Jessie Conrad's simple

---

[1] As in the case of 'Freya of the Seven Isles' only. Please see the particular discussions below, and for the textual histories of each story the discussions above.

[2] See, e.g., the revisions at 24.14b, 26.26, 27.33a, 41.4–5, 42.8b, 68.24, 73.37a, 73.38, 74.13–14.

[3] As at 24.12a, 47.22b, 75.13–14; 26.28a, 28.35a, 41.34–35, 69.7a.

[4] See the variants at 36.11a, 73.19b; 19.27a*n*, 23.15b, 32.32, 44.21, 52.14; 26.13a, 27.9–10, 27.17, 41.39, 58.27–28. Some of these changes (e.g., 32.32, 44.21, 52.14) are rather straightforward and could be editorial.

literals, appear here as well, whether made by Conrad, one of Pinker's typists, or S's editor.

The readings adopted from E1 as representing Conrad's revisions in the magazine tear-sheets are almost as numerous as those drawn from S and often exhibit similar characteristics. Many concern wording already altered by Conrad either in the early typescripts or in the printer's copy for S.[1] Some again combine an element of an MS reading with a later variant (46.5, 72.36, 77.36) or carry on still further changes made repeatedly (31.10–11, 73.11). Others simply amount to a rejection of a revision Conrad had made in the typescripts.[2] In a few cases the present text includes a word or phrase of E1's text that represents a new departure from MS and subsequent texts (e.g., 26.1b, 49.37a, 76.27). These revisions in E1 occur throughout the story. So do E1's corrections of Jessie Conrad's typing errors that are accepted in the present text, though their frequency rises in the episodes involving Alice and her aunt, and particularly in the last section where, Conrad possibly remembered, she had been rushed.[3]

Besides adopting from these later texts many revisions and some corrections of the copy-text's substantives, this edition rejects various errors found in E1 and S. Excluded are a few instances of regularization, omission, and other variation in wording committed in E1.[4] More frequently the present text retains TS1r's readings despite S's normalizations of odd usage and word order,[5] its levellings of colloquial phrasing (41.29a) and possessives (35.35cn, 43.22), its mistaken corrections of simple errors (29.13, 48.34b, 50.34), and its literalisms (e.g., 21.28b). Finally, this edition restores MS wording that was altered by Jessie Conrad when producing the typescripts and was not recovered by Conrad when revising TS1, the lost Pinker typescript, or the tear-sheets of S for subsequent publication. These emendations repair her graphic errors in single words, phrases, and sentences, often involving interlineations and other revisions in MS as well as eyeskip, line skip, and page break;[6] her omissions (e.g., 25.6, 26.17, 33.4–5, 68.21a); and her normalizations of seemingly odd idioms, diction, and other

---

[1] See, e.g., the revisions at 27.9c, 40.39–40, 67.24a, 68.16a, 68.36–37, 72.8–9; 69.35a.

[2] As at 22.14, 40.14a, 51.18, 66.2b, 66.3, 66.22–23, 66.23, 67.9a, 69.2b.

[3] See, e.g., the variants at 30.1, 47.22a, 48.1, 48.6, 49.1, 67.8–9, 68.37, 70.22, 76.11a, 76.23–24.

[4] As at 25.14, 25.27–28, 26.7b, 26.8, 31.6a, 33.36bn, 55.35bn, 68.31; 22.31, 52.32b.

[5] See the variants at 25.7a, 29.25, 44.27, 46.30b, 64.28–29n, 70.2c, 74.17d.

[6] As at 23.35n, 28.8a, 28.8c, 31.19b, 31.26, 44.37b, 46.13, 49.27, 62.28a, 66.36, 71.7b, 71.24–25, 72.18, 77.7b. Those occasioned by line and page break are at 29.5 and 39.8b.

disconcerting wording, especially in the episodes involving Alice and her aunt.[1]

The unpublished prologue and the passages of the ending associated with it pose a special but relatively simple problem. No authoritative text other than the copy-text (TS1r) survives.[2] The text of TS2, derived directly from it, contains a number of changes made by the typist, a few of them corrections of simple errors present in TS1r. This edition adopts these few readings, but it otherwise presents a text of the words of the revised version as Conrad sent it to his agent in August 1910.[3]

The Secret Sharer

THE SELECTION and incorporation of variant readings from the texts of S and E1 is mostly a relatively straightforward matter once Conrad's revisions have been distinguished from the transmissional errors found in those texts. His revisions in the first typescript, now preserved in S, largely carried on the composition of MS. The text of the present edition includes the alterations that reflect Conrad's progressively developing use of the words 'secret' and 'self' in various phrases to refer to Leggatt (see 101.31a, 115.36) as well as the more numerous substitutions of 'whiskers' for the chief mate's 'moustaches' that appear in S (82.30, 83.12–13, 85.21, 88.30, 97.23, 98.19). It accepts the revisions in S's opening sentences that helped develop the images of a uniform landscape and monotonous mood (e.g., 81.15a, 81.16–17, 81.21b), the elaborations and clarifications of latent MS concepts throughout (83.22c, 88.17a, 94.17, 101.17, 102.38–40, 108.21–22, 117.26), and the additions that strengthened Leggatt's characteristic speech (89.31, 92.30), heightened the Captain's isolation (112.32a, 116.34), and made the tone of the conclusion more emphatic (117.35–36, 119.7) in S. Some of the serial's substitutions and transpositions

---

[1] See the changes at 21.39a, 32.18, 47.19a, 47.28b, 52.8, 60.5b, 66.15, 67.7b*n*, 71.24b.

[2] Technically TS1t is an authoritative text, but as its forms were superseded by Conrad's alterations, it is practically irrelevant to the editorial problem. It is possible to conjecture that Conrad revised the accidentals and perhaps even the wording of the nine pages of the Pinker typescript he withheld in the week of 21 November, which he had not previously seen, but given the circumstances, both present and past, it seems unlikely that he would have made any significant alterations, and in any case the point is impossible to prove or disprove and has no practical effect on the editorial choices that have to be made.

[3] Appendix F, 'The Serial Version of the Prologue and Ending', provides edited texts of the serial version of the prologue and ending, together with a collation of variants and emendations.

relating to place and direction aboard ship also helped resolve problems that arose in MS (85.10, 108.19–20n, 118.19–20) and should be
incorporated in a critical text.

Although less clearly associated with the writing of MS, other variants in S appear to reflect Conrad's revision of the lost typescript.
One change adopted here modified the Captain's manner towards
the 'skipper' of the *Sephora* (100.1), and another enhanced the English
flavour of his phraseology (84.10). Several alterations of verbs to the
past perfect and other adjustments of tense found in S appear in the
text of the present edition (83.22a, 84.2b, 93.12, 101.22n, 102.14–15,
104.38a, 107.18b, 111.10). Also adopted from S are various elaborations and clarifications of MS's text not obviously adumbrated there
(93.31a, 98.16n, 98.35, 118.8–9), a few additions to it (e.g., 89.15–16,
99.21–22, 100.34), and several apparently gratuitous or indifferent
changes (e.g., 92.4, 107.27n), including four alterations of 'that' to
'this' (82.6, 99.26, 102.36, 108.9).

Even when revising a copy of S for E1 two years later, Conrad often
continued the process of revision reflected in the serial text, though
the frequency of such changes diminished. This edition adopts E1's
substitutions of 'whiskers' for the chief mate's 'moustaches', all in the
latter part of the story, and new phrasing that involves 'secret' and
'self'.[1] It omits the spider joke that in S had continued to disrupt
the calm atmosphere of the story's opening (83.22b) as well as a similar example of sardonic humour (87.27), accepts E1's corrections
of errors resulting from slips of the pen during revision of MS (e.g.,
104.2a, 111.16), and adopts its alterations of nautical terms (92.31,
96.27, 97.27, 112.14n) as well as of other diction to mesh with existing wording (87.2b, 91.18, 96.10a, 99.13, 106.6). This edition includes
two new sentence breaks or pauses that appear in E1 (93.30, 110.5),
its elaborations and clarifications of some minor points (89.19–20,
103.30a, 113.29b; 96.30a, 102.17, 102.19; 107.37), and a change to
the perfect tense (96.24). It also accepts revisions that elaborated or
refined those made in S about the Captain's distanced demeanour
towards Archbold (99.17, 100.1b, 102.21b) and other details not fully
finished there (93.31b, 108.19–20n). Most of the readings adopted
from E1 occur in the middle of the story; the few elsewhere involve
important points that Conrad had not given sufficient attention when

---

[1] See the variants at 103.29, 108.18b, 110.4, 111.30, 112.18, 113.33, 117.10, 119.5; 98.12a,
101.31a.

revising the first typescript (81.20b, 81.24, 82.22, 118.15–19, 118.40b–119.1).

On the other hand, this edition rejects a surprisingly large number of variant readings that first appeared in S and a few from E1 as well. Where S varies from MS, E1 occasionally reverts to the readings of the manuscript, and this edition restores these MS readings, rejecting those of the serial as graphic errors of the typist (84.2a, 88.32, 109.28) or as mistakes or normalizations of the typesetting or editorial process (e.g., 98.26, 105.16, 107.32). In a few cases it restores MS readings where Conrad spotted an outright error or fussy alteration when working on the serial tear-sheets but E1 failed to correct it fully (85.18, 91.25n, 91.35n, 110.18). It also rejects some new readings of E1 itself, such as its omission of a sentence (see 89.25n), its refinement of a typescript revision about the killing aboard the *Sephora* (89.15b), its corrections of two odd phrasings (101.24n, 111.8an), and its trimming of words and other 'improvements' in diction (83.34, 86.7a, 106.3n).

More frequently, the present edition adopts the unpublished readings of MS where S and all texts derived from it print an alternative produced during the typing of one of the typescripts or the editing or typesetting of the serial. Rejected typist's errors traceable to MS inscriptions include those associated with interlineations (89.21bn, 90.12n, 93.2, 95.8, 99.22, 103.23n, 108.5, 116.21b), outright misreadings of Conrad's hand like 'His' for 'This' and 'me' for 'one' (94.33, 99.19a), mistaken final -s and final -y readings (93.25, 97.38a; 99.28–29, 100.21), and less direct misconstructions (81.8an, 82.9a, 90.24, 98.29n, 107.1, 111.22n), including 'my own personality' for 'my open personality' (97.38bn). Likewise, words deleted by a compositor to fit the text neatly within columns (101.29, 101.32) or pages (112.2–3) of the magazine appear in the text of this edition.

Still more numerous, and often more important, are the restorations of MS readings lost as a result of the careful supervision given Conrad's story by the fastidious editor of *Harper's*. The text of this edition includes Leggatt's 'Fancy finding', the Captain's 'say me nay', and other anglicisms of MS replaced by S's Americanisms (95.12, 97.10). It recovers Leggatt's 'brusque, disconnected' (89.6) expressions (e.g., 88.33n, 89.9, 89.18bn, 92.8, 105.26) as well as Conrad's supposedly muddled word order (85.39, 96.4), awkward articles and prepositions (84.27, 118.13, 118.27n), and his 'these' (88.36a, 93.33b, 101.1, 101.6), 'afterwards' (102.27), 'towards' (116.27, 117.30), and analogous forms.

It rejects the serial editor's literalisms and glosses (e.g., 87.28b, 89.11, 111.4, 116.21a), his additions and deletions related to place and direction aboard ship (see 103.25n, 116.11n), his normalizations (e.g., 85.40), his fiddling with tenses (e.g., 93.14, 108.34–35n), and his other niceties (e.g., 90.6, 98.8). It restores three words discarded by its editor in favour of others in S's first sentence, one reflecting Americanization, another censorship, the third an obtuse literalism with thematic consequences, all with deleterious effects (81.6an, 81.6bn, 81.7n). And it prints Conrad's story undivided, without the partitions given it by the magazine to fit its own format, and since then found in all published texts.

Freya of the Seven Isles

THE TEXT of this edition incorporates revisions found in texts subsequent to the copy-text (TS1r) as well as corrections found there and in MS, though the readings of SA, which has no authority, are uniformly ignored. Most of these adopted readings are drawn from E1 and comprise the 200 or so revisions Conrad made in the first week of July 1912. These ran the gamut from small additions and deletions to frequent substitutions, especially of adjectives and nouns, and excisions of sentences. Amongst these are the cluster of changes associated with the description of Heemskirk in section II (132.19, 132.20, 132.22b) and the extended discussion of Schultz in section III (139.14–15, 139.16, 139.18a–b, 139.31b, 139.37, 140.2b). Also included are the alterations Conrad made to deal with errors that had persisted through his assiduous work on the typescript, as when he provided an alternative solution to a typing error, which had eschewed a satisfactory revision in MS, and also made a further change that restored the sense of time originally conveyed in MS (160.34b, 160.35). In such instances E1's revisions must be accepted as of a piece, despite their accommodation of a typing error which can no longer be extricated from the larger context. It goes without saying, perhaps, that in other cases a variant reading in E1 that by its nature looks authorial sometimes finds confirmation in SE, which Conrad revised independently, but the decision on adoption still rests squarely on the nature of the reading, as E1 derived directly from an early form of SE.

The alterations found in SE raise another question. In revising for E1, Conrad was able to replicate about half the revisions that he had made for SE some seven weeks earlier, but the other fifty do not appear in E1. Many of these fifty may be dismissed as mere sops for serial readers, given Conrad's low estimate of the *London Magazine*; the passages he excised, for instance, may be retained without further ado. On the other hand, it is clear from his reported plan to use revises of SE when preparing copy for E1 that he valued some particular revisions and hoped not to lose them (see p. 276). Adopted here are a handful of readings that either accord with other revisions made for E1 or correct problems Conrad had earlier been trying to solve. SE's substitution of 'the day' for 'some time' (147.1) is of a piece with revisions made for E1 in the area and matches his earlier change of 'a day' to 'the day' in E1 (142.38), making the second reference to Heemskirk's arrival at the Seven Isles accord with the first. Likewise the substitution of 'ice' for 'glass' discussed above (p. 277) alleviated confusion that resulted from repetition of a term used in a completely different sense (164.21). Correction of a misplaced modifier in a passage Conrad had worked over in the manuscript and finally resolved in SE seems necessary as well (138.37), as do corrections of Heemskirk's uncharacteristic 'Nelson' rather than 'Nielsen' and of 'river' instead of 'rivers' (134.34, 150.33).[1]

The small group of changes in English that Conrad recorded in black pencil on the typescript are a special case.[2] Although associated with preparation of the document for possible French translation, these notations sometimes reflect an effort, however cursory, to clarify a few details left unresolved in the revised typescript. For instance, the changes first marked in pencil involving Heemskirk's uniform and word order appear as revisions in later texts (132.22c, 156.5a). But in other instances, Conrad confirmed, in pencil, revisions he had already made imperfectly in black ink, which were mishandled by Pinker's typist and thus not properly transmitted to subsequent texts. The present edition retains these two revisions despite their absence from later authoritative texts, while adopting six necessary pencilled corrections that appear in one or more of them, and rejecting all the merely tentative revisions Conrad made in this medium.[3]

[1] On this last see 'I have had to put up a few to help me in and out of the rivers' (141.11–12).
[2] See Appendix H, 'Marks in Pencil on the First Typescript', for a complete list.
[3] See Appendix H for Conrad's revisions at 129.8, 140.28, and 182.20 and the corrections made at 132.34, 139.12, 140.20, 145.22, 181.3, 184.11, which also appear in the appropriate apparatus. Rejected alterations occur at 12:6, 27:4, 115:14, 119:3.

Finally, the manuscript provides corrections of errors in the copy-text that are traceable to its typist, Jessie Conrad. In some cases Conrad failed to correct an error because he was distracted by other mistypings. For instance, the omission of 'his' escaped his notice while he was correcting the form 'Freda' (125.32a–b), and his effort to fix the misspelling 'concent' prevented him from detecting her botched transcription of 'content' (153.36).[1] In other cases he simply overlooked an outright typing error partly because her version amounted to more conventional English. MS's 'He has tried it on with me' (169.33), 'not a single of his features' (174.23a), and 'let go hold of him' (176.30) all got levelled by her and are here restored as emendations of TS1.

Indeed, throughout the tale possible readings of Conrad's – even if less conventional, idiomatic, or stylistically adept than those of another text traceable to transmission – appear in the text of this edition. Usually this policy has resulted in retention of the copy-text's reading in the face of other plausible alternatives. Less often it has required emendation of oversights, such as Conrad's failure to note every inconsistency in the rendering of Freya's name or in the hyphenation of 'Seven Isles' as an adjectival.

Accidentals

EMENDATION OF these three texts differs according to the nature of their various sources, but their accidentals have some problems in common. Those of the revised typescript (TS1r) that serves as copy-text for 'A Smile of Fortune' reflect two rounds of revision by Conrad, one on the face of the document itself, the other presumably in its ancestor (*TSo*), but mitigating factors make these accidentals less complete, less reliable, and more in need of emendation than they might otherwise have been. Conrad's alterations in both typescripts responded to the forms present in their typewritten texts (*TSot*, TS1t), and though some of these forms produced by the typist, Jessie Conrad, transmitted those inscribed by Conrad in her copy (MS, *TSor*), others clearly represent her own usage. The result, especially in the early pages of TS1r, where he was still struggling with conception and wording, is sometimes a mishmash of usages, satisfactory in many respects, but incomplete or inconsistent in others.

---

[1] Comparable instances of errors in wording or punctuation occur at 138.12, 154.38a–b, 176.27*n*, and 187.32.

Much less in need of emendation is the copy-text for 'The Secret Sharer', which provides a relatively finished text compared to those in Conrad's other manuscripts. Still, his habit of leaving details unsettled there in anticipation of later perfection in the typescripts surfaces in the odd word form and point. Variable spellings (e.g., of words with double consonants), capitalization (e.g., of 'sir'), and word-division (an almost impenetrable mystery) as well as deficient punctuation (e.g., commas missing in series, dashes used to terminate quotations, double and single quotation marks confused or omitted) would have demanded attention in his own day and require adjustment here.

Combining features of both these copy-texts, that for 'Freya of the Seven Isles' provides the most finished text of the three. The typescript made by Jessie Conrad transmitted many of the word forms and much of the punctuation from Conrad's manuscript, but it also contained some of her own. While revising it he gave conscientious attention to details he had earlier deferred as well as to forms she had altered. The accidentals of the text so produced were largely authorial and perhaps even more coherent than those of 'The Secret Sharer'. However, as in 'A Smile of Fortune' some of her errors inevitably escaped his notice, and still other problems remained unresolved that he must have expected to be put right during the course of publication.

Although some emendation of accidentals has therefore been necessary in each tale, this edition generally adopts the texture of pointing and of other forms found in the three copy-texts. It allows to stand Conrad's characteristically light punctuation and eschews alteration for the sake of mere consistency or of conformity either to today's usage or to what may be inferred, from professional typescripts and printed texts, to have been the prevailing standards of his own day.[1] It declines to insert the comma now expected in a sentence that joins two clauses, whether independent or dependent, and emends such passages only when the rhetorical context otherwise demands some adjustment; after a colon separating such clauses, it allows the copy-texts' upper-case and lower-case letters to stand. Likewise it usually does not add punctuation to set off parenthetical phrases and modifying clauses or to mark direct address, though it introduces emendations where Conrad provided one comma but failed to complete a pair and where inadvertent ambiguity would otherwise result. In both

---

[1] In these matters TS2 of 'A Smile of Fortune' and the *London Magazine*, where the forms usually represent the lowest common denominator of current usage, provide some particular information.

general rhetorical situations and specific contexts, the present edition tends to follow the punctuation of the copy-texts. Series, whether of adjectives or phrases, may end with or without a comma before 'and', as Conrad was apparently inconsistent in this matter. Quotations incorporated in larger statements may not be preceded by punctuation to separate them from introductory phrasing,[1] and indirect discourse is treated in a similarly flexible fashion. Questions, which in Conradian rhetoric often amount to half statements or exclamations, may be terminated by a full-stop, an exclamation mark, or a query.

Nonetheless, the rather rough texture of punctuation produced by Jessie Conrad in the typescripts of 'A Smile of Fortune' and 'Freya of the Seven Isles' and left standing by Conrad in the manuscript of 'The Secret Sharer', pending further revision, has required some adjustment in accord with what he would presumably have expected in the way of minimal correction from Pinker's professional typists and later from compositors. Even though this edition avoids mere regularization, certain recurrent lapses have called for emendation. The copy-texts occasionally lack necessary commas after the first of a series of phrases or adjectives with equivalent weight or function. Clauses that act as the ablative absolute, which Conrad tends to set off with commas, sometimes need them. The presentation of quotations often demands attention. This edition inserts commas around intermediate interlocutory phrases and supplies commas before them if punctuation is absent, though it retains other acceptable points. Unless such punctuation is present, it terminates introductory interlocutory phrases with a colon; in a few instances it removes the colon after the phrase 'as if' or in similar situations. Where quotations beginning at paragraph breaks are introduced by interlocutory phrasing, colons precede them, not only when a copy-text has that mark, but also when it lacks punctuation or has a full-stop. Unacceptable case and punctuation have been adjusted conservatively where quotations begin, and where they end, the full-stop and closing quotation marks have been retained or supplied (respectively) unless a copy-text has other acceptable points. The sequence of closing quotation marks (inverted commas) and punctuation has been regularized, without further report.

The forms of words generally appear here as they do in the several copy-texts, but a few have required particular attention. Ships' names are printed uniformly in italic (without further report), the word 'sir'

---

[1] Instances include the quotations at 87.1, 162.39–40, and 188.35.

in lower-case unless it is a title, and 'Captain' with the upper-case only when it is used as part of a proper name or as the equivalent of a proper name. Contractions and possessives follow Conrad's forms, though a necessary apostrophe has occasionally been added in accord with prevailing copy-text usage. Numbers below 100 have been written out. As for word-division, one of the continuously troublesome elements of Conrad's writing life, this edition adopts his prevailing forms for various compound nouns; unless the word is already closed in the copy-text, it supplies the hyphen in adjectivals, except in special cases (e.g., nautical terms like 'on shore') where Conrad's usage is virtually habitual.

The copy-texts employ dashes and dots for various purposes, some of them subtle and complex, and this edition reproduces these marks, although it makes some general adjustments in their forms and occasionally makes a particular emendation in accord with the prevailing usage of a copy-text. Successive dots represent suspensions of sentences, speeches, time, and action in the copy-texts, but their number and spacing in Conrad's manuscripts and especially in Jessie Conrad's typescripts vary widely and have been adjusted here, without further report. Dashes serve an even larger variety of purposes, not only performing the familiar parenthetical, appositional, and other syntactical functions, but also marking various kinds of pauses and breaks in speech and action, signalling logical shifts (as before an added idea or afterthought, the last clause of a compound sentence, a clarifying remark, or an appended question), and setting off direct address and even the odd interlocutory phrase. Conrad appears to have relied on these inscriptions to control rhythm and pace, sometimes in unorthodox ways, as well as to represent logical, temporal, and occasionally spatial relationships, and this edition generally reproduces them as simple one-em dashes without further report as to their position or length. Occasionally, however, they have required alteration in the context of the system prevailing in a copy-text. Reports of these emendations as well as of those to the other accidentals of the copy-texts, with the exceptions specified, appear in the apparatus.

THE 'AUTHOR'S NOTE'

THE PREFACE TO *'Twixt Land and Sea* was one of the group of essays Conrad wrote in the spring of 1920 for the collected editions. Having

managed at last to bring off that for *The Secret Agent*, which was wanted
for the second group of five volumes that Doubleday was producing,
Conrad turned to those required to finish out the series of eighteen
volumes.[1] The typescript of the 'Author's Note' for *'Twixt Land and
Sea*, which survives at Philadelphia's Free Library, he signed and dated
'April 1920' at the bottom of its last page, no doubt with sale to T. J. Wise
in mind. From the revised text of this document (TS1), the copy-text
for this edition, derived the texts in the collection of prefaces called
Notes on My Books (A1), in the Doubleday collected edition (A2), in the
Heinemann collected edition (E) and, finally, in the magazine article
titled 'Five Prefaces' that appeared in the *London Mercury* (S), which
together constitute the surviving early texts.

History and Documents

ACCORDING TO his letters Conrad wrote this preface during a time
when he could manage little else in the way of work. With his wife
again absent from home under medical care, he received a visit on
8 April from William Heinemann, who brought with him material illustrating the proposed design of his collected edition. Conrad approved,
and after that he seems to have gone forward with the next round of
prefaces, completing six of the eight then outstanding by the end of
May.[2] Whether he dictated the essay to Miss Hallowes or wrote out a
draft is unclear, though dictation seems more likely.[3] Besides exhibiting increasingly heavy revision of wording, especially in the paragraph on 'Freya of the Seven Isles', TS1 contains some alterations of

---

[1] See above, pp. 284–5, and 'The Texts' in *The Secret Agent*, pp. 311–12.

[2] See Conrad to Eric Pinker, 8 April; to Pinker, [27 April 1920], [3].5.20., 31st. May 1920; to
Wise, 20th. May 1920, 1 June 1920 (*Letters*, VII, 73, 86–7, 89, 102, 98, 103); also *Chronology*,
p. 111, which dates this preface as commencing 9 April. The prefaces to *A Personal Record*
and *The Mirror of the Sea* (volume 11 in the collected editions) had been written by the
previous September. That for *Notes on Life and Letters* (1921), which would complete the
series of prefaces on 9 October 1920, was not in the present count. Remaining to be done,
then, were those for *Under Western Eyes* (for the second group of volumes), *Chance* (the only
other novel needing immediate attention), *'Twixt Land and Sea*, *Within the Tides*, *Victory*, *The
Shadow-Line*, *The Arrow of Gold*, and *The Rescue*. Prefaces for the last two would be postponed
beyond May. By the end of April Conrad had posted two essays to New York, those for *'Twixt
Land and Sea* and *Within the Tides* not amongst them, and by mid-May had clearly finished
with these two and with those for *Chance* and *Under Western Eyes*. He appears to have tackled
the two novels and then the two collections of stories, though he might have taken each
volume more or less in order of planned appearance. He did not offer those for *Victory* and
The Shadow-Line to Wise until the very end of May.

[3] See Conrad to Pinker, 31 May 1920 (*Letters*, VII, 102); see also Karl, pp. 839–41.

punctuation. These changes are fewer than might have been expected in a 'dictated' typescript, and ordinarily their relative scarcity might be taken as evidence that the typewritten text was in fact copied from a manuscript draft. However, both the wording and forms of the revised text are on the whole considerably less finished than such texts often are. Consequently Conrad's alterations – or lack of them – do not clearly indicate whether the typescript was or was not originally dictated.

Indeed it seems apparent that Conrad did not give this preface repeated attention. One of many that had to be produced at the time, it must have been retyped by Miss Hallowes before a fair copy, or copies, went off to Doubleday, or perhaps to Pinker, and before Conrad sold the extant document to Wise. The number of copies she made and Conrad's lack of attention to the text of this second typescript (*TS2*) may be inferred not only from his casual remarks in letters of the time, but also from the subsequent textual history of the essay.[1] Although the variant readings in S and in A1, A2, and E are not sufficient to demonstrate conclusively anything about the history of the preface subsequent to its revision in TS1, it seems likely that Miss Hallowes produced more than one copy of *TS2*, that at least one such copy went to Pinker in addition to that going to Doubleday, and that Conrad revised none of them, and indeed made no revisions after he had made those present in TS1.

When Pinker sent J. C. Squire copy for the later prefaces that would appear in the March 1921 number of the *London Mercury*, he could not have relied on proofs from either collected edition to supply it.[2] Although he apparently did not see proofs for the typesetting of *Notes on My Books* that was published in early 1921,[3] it is barely conceivable that Pinker had available an extra set of printed sheets to send to Squire. However, in spring 1920, neither Conrad nor Pinker

---

[1] The letter to Pinker dated inferentially as [27 April 1920] seems to imply, as do others of the time, that Conrad was posting material directly to Doubleday. However, here and elsewhere, Conrad could be apprising Pinker of the status of material being handled routinely by his office. In any case Pinker seems to have had copy of some kind at hand to give to Heinemann and later to J. C. Squire.

[2] Proofs of the Heinemann volume of *The Secret Agent* were available and appear to have been used; see 'The Texts' in *The Secret Agent*, pp. 319–20. But proofs of *'Twixt Land and Sea* (not to mention the later volumes of *Chance, Victory*, and *The Shadow-Line*) were not pulled until late February. Doubleday, on the other hand, were busy publishing the first five volumes and preparing the next five, and had in any case proved unreliable in supplying proofs on deadline.

[3] Nor did Conrad for that matter. On the vexed history of this book, see *The Secret Agent*, p. 317.

expected the production of this book,[1] whereas they may have been anticipating the need to provide copy for Heinemann's increasingly independent collected edition, which they would fully realize only a few months later. Almost certainly S's copy for the 'Author's Note' of 'Twixt Land and Sea was not any of these prints, as two of its readings indicate.

The variants in wording that occur throughout the texts derived from TS1 are few, and because they amount to mere 'corrections' or improvements of Conrad's familiar stylistic 'lapses' that almost anyone, including the author, could have made, they are usually not decisive as a group or individually. Yet the two changes found in A1, A2, and E that look most likely to be traceable to him and therefore to have been present in *TS2* are in fact not present in S, which has the readings of TS1. Although these two variants – the substitution of 'people' for 'persons' just before the word 'personally', and the transposition of 'personally' with an infinitive not too much later (5.34, 6.15) – do not support the view that Conrad revised *TS2* at these points, they do indicate that S's copy was independent of the books, including A1, which S also fails to follow elsewhere (7.3). Pinker, then, must have had at least one copy of *TS2* at hand when it became necessary to send printer's copy for the *London Mercury* in early 1921.

He had probably been holding such a copy for about six months. As Heinemann's volume of 'Twixt Land and Sea was going to their printer about the same time, Pinker presumably had another copy of the same typescript made to supply one of the printers, more likely S's. Apparently E no more derived from one of the Doubleday printings than did S. In its case the evidence is largely external, the general independence of the Heinemann collected edition from Doubleday's by this time, but the absence from E of a plausible alteration found in A1 (7.3) lends some support to this view. On the other hand, the variant readings E shares with both A1 and A2[2] are so indifferent that they cannot support an argument for its derivation from either. Nor can

---

[1] Conrad to Pinker, [17 October 1920] (*Letters*, VII, 191); Conrad's words suggest that Pinker and Heinemann, who appears to have warmed progressively during the year to publishing the collected Conrad, hatched the idea shortly after Conrad had finished the prefaces for *The Arrow of Gold*, *The Rescue*, and *Notes on Life and Letters*, but Conrad's comment of early August regarding Jean-Aubry's interest in the prefaces could have planted the seed: Conrad to Heinemann, 4 August 1920 (*Letters*, VII, 156).

[2] In its later forms, the Doubleday edition eventually incorporated two of E's changes (5.19, 6.26), both concerned with making the 'Sun-Dial' printing's 'The' part of the title of 'The Secret Sharer'. By 1923 both the Doubleday plates and the Dent plates contained this change. See pp. 287–8 on the alteration of the Doubleday plates.

they show that one of Doubleday's typesettings derives directly from the other. Rather, A2's independence of A1 finds some confirmation in its failure to follow that same plausible change (7.3) and in one other change found in A1 (6.26). Doubleday seems to have used the same typescript for setting the preface to *'Twixt Land and Sea* and for the collection of prefaces printed in *Notes on My Books*.[1] The exact chronological relations of these two typesettings is undetermined, but the collection of prefaces was hastily assembled and produced at the end of 1920 and published early the next year, and this indicates its priority for the present 'Author's Note'.

It appears, then, that all four printed texts of the preface derived independently from the fair typescript Miss Hallowes made in the spring of 1920. It seems equally apparent that none of their new readings, even those they all share, reflects Conrad's revision. Most are the sorts of changes editors and printers were generally inclined to make in order to eliminate his unorthodox phrasing. The most obvious case is the one in the first sentence, the familiar confusion of 'those' and 'these'; this is so egregious that even Conrad might have altered it and would likely have been relieved to have it corrected. However, others contravene his habitual usage, or alter syntax deliberately left mushy, or interfere with constructions related to one of the basic thematic threads in the essay.[2] None of them represents the kind of thorough revision that is present in TS1 and is typical of his work.

Copy-text and Emendation

CONSEQUENTLY, CHOICE of copy-text is straightforward for this 'Author's Note'. The revised typescript (TS1) contains the only extant text that Conrad produced. The accidentals of the other texts are merely transmissional and must be dismissed. The authority of their substantive variants is equally suspect, though one or two represent necessary emendations. Because he revised it only once and in the course of doing so gave its forms only summary attention, the essay's

---

[1] Given the differences amongst the production schedules for the eighteen volumes, composite copy for this independent typesetting probably seemed the most practical strategy, and typescripts the most convenient option for the later volumes. A carbon-copy of Doubleday's typescript produced for the occasion is conceivable, and in so short a piece textual evidence of it would now likely be non-existent. On these matters, see 'The Texts' in *The Secret Agent*, pp. 317–19, and 'The Texts' in *Notes on Life and Letters*, p. 235.

[2] See 5.27, 6.40, 5.15, 7.3; the last probably is to be put down to A1's compositor and certainly cannot be attributed to Conrad.

punctuation requires some additional correction, such as Conrad apparently assumed it and the others he was producing at the time would receive during Doubleday's usual supervision of his work. However, the 'improvements' that have been part of the received texts of this brief but revealing piece can now be confidently ignored.

THE CAMBRIDGE TEXTS

THE CAMBRIDGE EDITION, then, presents to the modern reader deliberately eclectic texts of the 'Author's Note' for *Twixt Land and Sea* and of its three tales based on the original documents.[1]

The principal source of the text of the preface is the revised typescript, the only surviving text possessing authority. A few necessary corrections, which are present in the 1921 book editions, have been made to this text, but the 'improvements' found in the received texts have been rejected.

The texts of the tales, however, are less straightforward. The revised typescript of 'A Smile of Fortune', the manuscript of 'The Secret Sharer', and the revised typescript of 'Freya of the Seven Isles' provide the copy-texts for this edition and permit restoration of words and passages altered in the magazines and in the books that descended from them. This edition incorporates the revisions made by Conrad for the magazines, but not the excisions and divisions made by or for them. It restores the revised typescript version of the prologue and ending of the first tale which was suppressed for serialization in the *London Magazine,* prints the second tale without the partition introduced by *Harper's Monthly Magazine,* and retains the passages variously omitted from the two serial publications of the third. It reverses other changes made in the magazines that were passed to the first English edition, thence to the other editions of Conrad's lifetime, and thus to all subsequent printings. But it adopts from such later authoritative texts readings that represent alterations Conrad made either in a lost typescript from which a serial text derived, or in the magazine tearsheets or proofs that served as copy for the first English edition. And it

---

[1] The physical properties and typography of these documents, as distinguished from their texts, are not preserved here. Aside from typographical styling of display capitals and indentation, for example, new lineation has created new syllabication, but only the hyphens at the ends of certain lines (15.26, 29.21, 33.10, 35.17, 38.27, 40.38, 43.15, 60.6, 70.15, 76.29, 77.5, 123.4, 126.8, 130.5, 132.5, 140.18, 140.22, 156.25, 162.14, 181.23, 185.7) are intended to signify word-division in the critical text itself.

includes corrections both of wording and of accidentals which may be found in texts both earlier and later than the copy-texts. The result is three eclectic yet conservative texts which incorporate Conrad's revisions in the various magazines and the first editions, but which recover from his manuscripts and typescripts numerous and often significant unpublished words, phrases, and sentences that were obliterated by typists, compositors, and editors, by mistake, design, or chance, in texts that since then have enjoyed the trust of countless readers.

APPARATUS

EMENDATION AND VARIATION

This list records the present edition's emendations of substantive readings together with the variants in substantive readings amongst the texts collated. Each note provides the full history of the readings in these texts. The reading of the Cambridge text appears immediately after the page–line citation. It is followed by a bracket, then by a siglum (or sigla) identifying the text(s) in which it occurs, and then by the variant reading(s) of the remaining texts and their sigla. A substantive variant shared by more than one text appears here in the form (the 'accidentals') that it takes in the copy-text or, otherwise, in the earliest one recorded. A separate list (below) records emendations of accidentals.

Formal conventions and appurtenances of the documents – such as Conrad's signatures, serial bylines, editorial headings, and instalment statements – are ignored unless they bear upon variants otherwise being reported, as are differences in features of typography and styling (see the 'Preface', p. xvi). Excluded in the same way, and with the same proviso, are impossible word forms created by mere typographical errors as well as those involving unreadable or uncertain characters (usually typewritten text that has been blotted during revision). Also not reported as such are legitimate variants in word forms, including abbreviations. However, some of these (which generally occur in the preprinting texts) will be found in the list of Emendations of Accidentals. Variants in titles and subtitles are recorded in Appendix B ('The Titles of the Tales'), and those in the epigraph and the dedication in Appendix I ('The Epigraph and the Dedication').

Reports of major variation, usually in the preprinting or serial texts, employ two special symbols. First, the abbreviation OM appears when one or more texts lacks the entire passage in which occur those words that are the subject of the note. Second, when such a passage is present in a text, but in a version different from that in the other texts reported (owing, for instance, to general revision or recasting), the abbreviation VAR shows that the context for that reading is variant. In a few cases (e.g., 130.11) square brackets enclose words in TSt that vary from MS's within extensive passages that they otherwise share as against other texts; TSt's unique readings are represented in bold and a broken bracket (>) separates them from those of MS.

Emendations are recorded in entries headed by page–line citations in bold-face. Lower-case letters immediately follow page–line citations when lemmas occur in the same line. The paragraph symbol (¶) indicates the beginning of a new paragraph. Three unspaced dots (...) mean the note omits one or more words in a series, whereas spaced dots (. . .) are reserved for representing those that actually appear in the texts. An asterisk (*) represents an unreadable character in an early text (usually a typescript that has been revised); square brackets ([ ]) enclose such characters when they have been conjectured but not certainly established.

A vertical stroke (|) marks the break between lines. The en-rule appears between sigla when three or more texts in sequence agree in a given reading; when all subsequent texts agree, no siglum follows the en-rule (e.g., **TSr**–). The symbol **ED** identifies readings adopted for the first time in this edition – that is, not present in the texts collated. Editorial statements, which are enclosed in square brackets, appear in italic.

The list follows these conventions for both the 'Author's Note' and the tales themselves. However, it reports the readings of the partial second typescript of 'A Smile of Fortune' (TS2) in the prologue and the first two sections only (pp. 1–39); for that prologue (13.2–18.14) and a portion of the ending (77.25–8) the list reports the readings of the extant typescript(s) only. (See the discussion in 'The Texts', pp. 229–30; Appendix F provides critical texts of the serial version of these passages and reports the variant readings of the manuscript and the early printed texts.) Listed in sequence below their headings are the sigla used for the 'Author's Note' and for each of the stories, as well as the collated texts they represent. The sigla for the book editions of the tales are stated once because for all three they are uniform.

AUTHOR'S NOTE

TS	typescript with holograph revisions (Free Library, Philadelphia): copy-text
A1	first American edition: *Notes on My Books* (Doubleday, 1921, and Heinemann, 1921)
A2	second American edition: *'Twixt Land and Sea* (Doubleday collected), American (1921–) and British (1923–) issues
A2a	first state of **A2**, American Sun-Dial issue (1921)
A2b	second state of **A2**, all British issues (1923–); Concord and subsequent American issues (1923–)
E	English edition: *'Twixt Land and Sea* (Heinemann collected, 1921)
S	'Five Prefaces', *London Mercury*, March 1921

5.2	these] **A1**– those **TS1**	5.34	persons] **TS S** people **A1–E**
5.15	both publicly] **TS** publicly **A1**–	6.15	to see personally] **TS S** personally to see **A1–E**
5.19	three fourths] **A1**– three fourth's **TS**	**6.26**	The] **A1 E A2b S** the **TS A2a**
5.19	The] **E A2b S** the **TS–A2a**	6.40	the vision, the] **TS** vision and **A1**–
5.27	towards] **TS A1** toward **A2**–	7.3	in private] **TS A2**– private **A1**

'TWIXT LAND AND SEA

E1	first English edition (Dent, 1912)
A1	first American edition (Doran [later Doubleday], 1912)
A2	second American edition (Doubleday collected, 1921)
A2a	first state of **A2**, American Sun-Dial (1921) and all British issues (1923–)
A2b	second state of **A2**, Concord and subsequent American issues (1923–)
E2	second English edition (Heinemann collected, 1921)

A Smile of Fortune

MS   holograph manuscript (Berg)
TS1   typescript (Yale, Berg)
  TS1t   typewritten (unrevised) text of **TS** superseded by revision
  TS1r   revised text of **TS** (incorporating Conrad's alterations): copy-text
TS2   typescript, partial (Berg)
S   *London Magazine* (February 1911), pp. 801–36

13.1–8   A Smile of Fortune ¶ The ...
  speaking] **TS1r TS2** OM **TS1t**
13.9   down to ... poop] **TS1r TS2**
  down **TS1t**
13.11a   Whereabouts] **TS1r TS2** Well
  and how **TS1t**
13.11b   make] **TS1r TS2** see **TS1t**
13.11c   cried jumping up briskly]
  TS1r TS2 cried **TS1t**
13.13–14   was acknowledged by] **TS1r**
  TS2 obtained for all response **TS1t**
13.14   room] **TS1r TS2** bath room
  TS1t
13.15–16   laugh, not very pleasant. ¶
  It] **TS1r TS2** laugh. ¶ The secret of
this behavior was that in that ship,
let the sky be overcast for more than
24 hours, we could never be certain
where we going to; not by a long
chalk* an inch or so on the chart let
us say. Perfectly awful: She could
not be trusted to make the courses
set for her from day to day. Driven
to this disclosure about a ship which
I loved more than any other ship on
earth, I shall not attempt to explain
it. It has something to do with the
laws of terrestial magnetisam, the
properties of iron and such like
unamusing remote things which
have no connection with light
literature. ¶ Suffice it to say that the
errors of other ship's compasses can
be put into some sort of tabulated
order and even corrected. There
are scientific rules for that. But not
for her compasses. O dear no. She
had no idea of order and still less of
correction. After the first would get
so muddled that I couldn't achieve
the addition of two rows of six

figures without suspecting some
deadly mistake That was bad
enough but it was when the sky
remained clouded for more than
two days that I began to look really
careworn and Mr Burns began to
look sardonic with suppressed
irritation. I would catch him casting
searching glances in my direction.
It created a very trying atmosphere.
I don't know how to state it! It
seemed absurd to say but it was as
though the ship were a capricious
woman and he really had no
patience with my attitude. ¶ That
little laugh down the ventilator had
that character – as much as to say A
great piece of luck indeed! And in
truth there was no special cause for
jubilation in such a very ordinary
landfall A navigator making for an
island would naturally expect to see
it right ahead. Yet everything is
relative. And that little laugh of Mr
Burns' meant also "It's a mercy we
haven't had to grope for it all over
the place! It **TS1t**
13.16   Mr Burns] **TS1r TS2** he **TS1t**
13.17   kept] **TS1r TS2** had had **TS1t**
13.19–23   He might ... price.] **TS1r**
  TS2 ¶ He was of course perfectly
loyal. But that thank God is no
exceptional virtue at sea. His really
exceptional efficiency was a rarer
point. It was worth more than any
amount of devotion to duty could
be. I don't want to insinuate that
sentiment is a cheap thing. It may
be even priceless. But an ever-ready
efficiency has a solid value above
the price of rubies. And it may be

that he was devoted to me. It was impossible to say. **TS1t**

13.24   had been] **TS1r TS2** was **TS1t**

13.25   joined] **TS1r TS2** first joined **TS1t**

13.26   was ashore ... fever] **TS1r TS2** was **TS1t**

13.28   see how ... on] **TS1r TS2** see **TS1t**

13.30   knew ... but] **TS1r TS2** was certain that I was **TS1t**

13.31a   very] **TS1r TS2** very very **TS1t**

13.31b   said to me] **TS1r TS2** said **TS1t**

13.32a   were: "For ... don't] **TS1r TS2** "Don't **TS1t**

13.32b   to ... hole] **TS1r TS2** here **TS1t**

13.32c   Our good] **TS1r TS2** The **TS1t**

13.33–34   idea of ... moved] **TS1r TS2** idea **TS1t**

14.1   clearly preposterous] **TS1r TS2** preposterous **TS1t**

14.2   His deep-seated] **TS1r TS2** He repeated this request daily. Sometimes I found him delirious but he invariably managed to recall his wandering wits for that purpose. He did not whine. He asked for it as a supreme rervice a man might ask another for. The calmly dispairing **TS1t**

14.3   I left him] **TS1r TS2** left **TS1t**

14.3–4   His despairing entreaties] **TS1r TS2** In the end he **TS1t**

14.5   promise you] **TS1r TS2** promise **TS1t**

14.6   went ... faint] **TS1r TS2** swooned **TS1t**

14.7   became extremely] **TS1r TS2** was very **TS1t**

14.8a   stiff official] **TS1r** official **TS2**

14.8b   remonstrance] **TS1r TS2** remonstrance on the subject **TS1t**

14.11–13   relentless kind. He ... Burns] **TS1r TS2** rentless kind. ¶ After seeing the patient (who certainly looked more dead than

alive) stretched out in his bunk,he received my thanks without unbending and his last words before he left the ship were ¶ "Let me tell you once more that you have assumed this responsability recklessly." ¶ And he strod ashore over the gangway as angry as ever, but I was not offended because I quite understood my responsability. dibly. It was I who swore sometimes at my own folly, and preety frequently point blank at him. It was odious, but he was so intractable that he had to be bullied. Tha glances of hate from that sick man! Phew! But I had made up my mind to save him, and to this day I take some pride in my success. ¶ Later on he **TS1t**

14.13–14   out a ... as] **TS1r TS2** out **TS1t**

14.18   on at] **TS1r TS2** on **TS1t**

14.19–20   all these proceedings] **TS1r TS2** these things **TS1t**

14.21   by insisting ... returning] **TS1r TS2** insisting to return **TS1t**

14.22a   it.] **TS1r TS2** it. We were approaching a tempestuous region of the globe with the signs of the oncoming bad weather writ large all over the sky;violent mothon and high boarding seas would be our lot for many days. I did not think he was strong enough to take care of himself about the decks. I had visions of those wasted limbs being snapped like pipe stems. But he had his way in the end. **TS1t**

14.22b   came] **TS1r TS2** came out **TS1t**

14.24–25   determined to ... ship] **TS1r TS2** determined **TS1t**

14.25a   only bit] **TS1r TS2** bit **TS1t**

14.25b   In fact] **TS1r TS2** Indeed **TS1t**

14.26   my convalescent] **TS1r TS2** him **TS1t**

14.27a   don't] **TS1r TS2** didn't **TS1t**

14.27b   have ... clap] **TS1r TS2** do. But to put **TS1t**

14.29–30 considered ... ¶ All this]
TS1r TS2 thought of seriously. ¶
This TS1t

14.30a been the effect of] TS1r TS2
been TS1t

14.30b yet] TS1r TS2 yet being
taxingly displayed it caused for the
next few days, a distinct coolness
between my ex- | patient and myself.
And permanent too: for when that
had passed away there remained a
queer, subtle feeling between us, a
faint shade of antagonism. ¶ The
first six weeks of our common past
were never mentioned between us.
But TS1t

14.31 acquired] TS1r TS2 a aqquired
TS1t

14.33 unlucky,] TS1r TS2 unlucky
and TS1t

14.34 reckless, and ... good-natured]
TS1r TS2 reckless TS1t

14.36 might] TS1r TS2 might | might
TS1t

14.37 express it] TS1r TS2 express
TS1t

14.38–15.2 many ... me.] TS1r TS2
Mr Burns stayed on, since, as I have
said, he would not dismiss himself
and indulged his humour in such
outbursts as the sarcastic little laugh
down the ventilator, for instance.
TS1t

15.3 Lingering ... cabin] TS1r TS2
While dressing after my bath
TS1t

15.4 overhead. His] TS1r TS2 over- |
head; and these TS1t

15.5–6 interpreted, reflected] TS1r
TS2 seemed to interpret to reflect
TS1t

15.8–9 There it is, sir] TS1r TS2 here
it is TS1t

15.16 picturesque] TS1r TS2 poetical
TS1t

15.18 There it was,] TS1r TS2 And
here it was TS1t

15.20 its] TS1r TS2 it's TS1t

15.26 telling you] TS1r TS2 saying
TS1t

15.27 is cultivated] TS1r TS2 grows
TS1t

15.28 their] TS1r TS2 there TS1t

15.30 to them] TS1r TS2 along TS1t

15.33a That] TS1r TS2 And it that
TS1t

15.33b circumstance] TS1r TS2
circumstance which TS1t

15.34a end] TS1r TS2 ending TS1t

15.34b Matters] TS1r TS2 The cares
TS1t

15.35a Sea] TS1r TS2 His TS1t

15.35b one] TS1r TS2 him TS1t

15.36a commercial wits] TS1r TS2
wits TS1t

15.36b a] TS1r TS2 his TS1t

15.38 operation, certainly,] TS1r TS2
operation TS1t

15.40 unworldly] TS1r TS2 unworthy
TS1t

16.3a It] TS1r TS2 And it TS1t

16.3b prospect of business] TS1r TS2
prospect TS1t

16.4 landfall appearing before me]
TS1r TS2 landfall TS1t

16.5 I was anxious] TS1r TS2 ¶ And
to think that this poetical vision was
full of hard-headed people, brokers,
agents, merchants, characters ready
to do an innocent sailor out of a
sixpence per ton or to insert some
damring clause in the charter party
if one didn't look out. How
horrible! And yet how charming
and enticing at sixty miles off was
that rich and fertile island, this
Pearl of the Ocean lying in the lap
of hurricanes. ¶ This is the poetical
way of stating the geographical fact
that this island does indeed lie
within the curve of the cyclone
track as a fine mansion with cropt
grounds may unluckily stand within
the bend of a high road receiving
the dust and smell of madly
careering motor-cars. And this is a
disadvantage; for the dust and so to
speak the mere smell of the
hurricane careering over the indian
Ocean is enough to lift roofs off the

houses, lay low fields of sugar cane and fill the inexperienced hearts of strangers with dreadful misgivings is of the end of the world coming on; while the indabitants bar And I wanted **TS1t**

16.6   flattering latitude] **TS1r TS2** latitude **TS1t**

16.6–7   instructions, which] **TS1r TS2** instructions. They **TS1t**

16.7   noble ... do] **TS1r TS2** phrase: Do **TS1t**

16.8   you can for] **TS1r TS2** by **TS1t**

16.8–9   but you must not] **TS1r TS2** not to **TS1t**

16.9   Cape] **TS1r TS2** cape **TS1t**

16.10   barred by these words] **TS1r TS2** barred **TS1t**

16.13   trying ... these] **TS1r TS2** preoccupied with **TS1t**

16.14a   risen] **TS1r TS2** arisen **TS1t**

16.14b   as if] **TS1r TS2** as **TS1t**

16.15a   mere subtle] **TS1r TS2** mere **TS1t**

16.15b   an] **TS1r TS2** the **TS1t**

16.15c   lo] **TS1r TS2** to **TS1t**

16.16   to] **TS1r TS2** to think to **TS1t**

16.17   glance] **TS1r TS2** look **TS1t**

16.21   murmured entranced, amazed] **TS1r TS2** said **TS1t**

16.22   grumbled reproachfully] **TS1r TS2** grumbled **TS1t**

16.24a   you that] **TS1r TS2** you **TS1t**

16.24b   very few] **TS1r TS2** few **TS1t**

16.28–29   in their ... style.] **TS1r TS2** with prosaic comments. But **TS1t**

16.33   behold.] **TS1r TS2** behold. ¶ Meanwhile Mr Burns was inwardly chafing at something. I could feel it without looking at him. He spoke from the other side of the poop, bitterly, as if it were my fault. ¶ "This breeze is taking off, sir. Its taking off fast." ¶ I did not want to believe him. But it was true enough. Bad luck. **TS1t**

16.34   The ... advanced] **TS1r TS2** It was late in the afternoon **TS1t**

16.35a   this] **TS1r TS2** that **TS1t**

16.35b   coast,] **TS1r TS2** coast **TS1t**

16.36a   green folds] **TS1r TS2** green **TS1t**

16.36b   uplands] **TS1r TS2** lands **TS1t**

16.37   base,] **TS1r TS2** base **TS1t**

16.38a   cloud] **TS1r TS2** loud **TS1t**

16.38b   inland] **TS1r TS2** island **TS1t**

16.39   a ... ceiling] **TS1r TS2** the low ceiling of a dungeon **TS1t**

16.40   sunset] **TS1r TS2** sun **TS1t**

17.4   late in the day] **TS1r TS2** late **TS1t**

17.6a   would ... outside] **TS1r TS2** must anchor **TS1t**

17.6b   with] **TS1r TS2** and with **TS1t**

17.6–7   wall of the coast] **TS1r TS2** wall **TS1t**

17.7a   sinking on] **TS2** sink-: | on **TS1t** sink- | on **TS1r**

17.7b   right hand] **TS1r TS2** right **TS1t**

17.8–9   a ... for] **TS1r TS2** daylight to **TS1t**

17.10   in] **TS1t TS2** in | in **TS1r**

17.11   dusk.] **TS1r TS2** dusk. ¶ The prose of the Sailing Directors is not romantic, it is not picturesque but it is well fitted to instruct and to and to warn by its precision and earnestness. The warning in this particular was against the danger of being swept away by wind and tide before the anchor could bring the ship up. Some unlucky ships had been thus swept away into deep water with their anchors dangling from their hawes-pipes – a most disconcerting, abominable and humiliating adventure But I made up my mind that my ship was not going to be one of of these awful instances. ¶ I handleh her with judicious boldness. The sun had dipped as we opened the anchorage and instantly land, sea and sky assumed a gloomy inimical aspect. **TS1t**

17.12   of rock] **ED** or rock **TS1–**

17.13   sudden] **TS1r TS2** chilly **TS1t**

17.14   an abrupt] **TS1r TS2** a sudden **TS1t**

17.15   sounded] **TS1r TS2** had **TS1t**

17.16   wild] **TS1r TS2** hostile **TS1t**
17.17   The sun set. How] **TS1r TS2** How **TS1t**
17.18   Who] **TS1r TS2** Nobody **TS1t**
17.22   basket in the distance] **TS1r TS2** basket **TS1t**
17.23   that thing, a ... seemed] **TS1r TS2** that, something **TS1t**
17.24   loneliness] **TS1r TS2** immensity **TS1t**
17.25   shades swept ... breeze] **TS1r TS2** shades **TS1t**
17.27a   her in] **TS1r TS2** her **TS1t**
17.27b   close to the cliffs] **TS1r TS2** close **TS1t**
17.31   sea,] **TS1r TS2** sea **TS1t**
17.32a   uttering quietly] **TS1r TS2** uttering **TS1t**
17.32b   words] **TS1r TS2** words run **TS1t**
17.33   And then the] **TS1r TS2** followed by a heavy splash. The **TS1t**
17.34–35   chest; some ... relief.] **TS1r TS2** chest. **TS1t**
17.35   deep] **TS1r TS2** long **TS1t**
17.36–18.14   ¶ An ... philosophy.] **TS1r TS2** ¶ Heavens! What was this.? Instead of the dignified deliberate rumple of a properly controlled cable a fiercely accelerated racket of iron links affeced my scalp with the horrid sensation of many let beetles crawling under my cap. The chain flew out of the hawsepipe with one fiendish prolonged screech, as if some kind of submarine devil had seized the anchor in his mouth and were swiming away with it along the bottom. The windlass suddenly hidden from me by a fog of r rust was spitting sparks through it like an electric machine. My feet tingled with the tremor of the ship and the ghastly anticipation of the jerk in which all this had to end interfered seriously with my circulation so that my back became a mere piece of frozen flesh of the speaking trumpet because the fellow hung off on our quarter at a safe distance and, to revenge himself I suppose, kept on screec hing on his steam whistle in a ruffianly and derisive manner, so that we couldn't hear ourselves speak on board. ¶ As no claim for payment could conceivably be made for that performance I bore it with philosophic disdain. **TS1t**
18.1   ship's] **TS2** ships **TS1r** OM **TS1t**
18.15   I] **MS S–** OM **TS1 TS2**
18.16   By ... morning] **S–** In the morning **MS** However by half past seven **TS1t** However by half past seven in the morning **TS1r TS2**
18.16–17   then ... moored] **TS1–** moored inside the harbour **MS**
18.17a   long stone's] **TS1–** stone's **MS**
18.17b   from] **MS TS1r–** of **TS1t**
18.18–19   dressing hurriedly] **MS TS1r–** changing **TS1t**
18.19   cabin] **MS TS1r–** cabin to go on shore directly after breakfast **TS1t**
18.21   depressed, with] **TS1–** cross, **MS**
18.22a   irritatingly stuck] **TS1–** stuck **MS**
18.22b   by too much] **TS1–** with **MS**
18.23   "heave round with] **MS TS1r–** hurry up **TS1t**
18.23–24   I ... possible.] **TS1–** OM **MS**
18.24   as soon as possible] **TS1r–** quick **TS1t** OM **MS**
18.26a   speak to] **MS TS1r–** see **TS1t**
18.26b   you sir] **TS1–** you **MS**
18.27   curiously slurred] **TS1–** slurred **MS**
18.28a   violently over] **TS1–** over **MS**
18.28b   emerged] **TS1–** came up **MS**
18.29a   "So early!" I cried.] **MS E1–** "A gentleman! **TS1t** "Already!" I cried **TS1r–S**
18.29b   What] **MS TS1r–** hat **TS1t**
18.30a   in from] **TS1–** from **MS**
18.30b   the sea] **MS–TS2** sea **S–**
18.30c   pick up] **TS1–** visit **MS**
18.31   utterly unrelated] **TS1–** unrelated **MS**

18.32 novelty] **MS TS1r**– strangness **TS1t**

18.33a caller] **MS TS1r**– gentleman **TS1t**

18.33b this] **MS** there **TS1**–

18.33c to look] **MS TS1r**– looking **TS1t**

18.35 for the] **MS S**– his **TS1t** him his **TS1r TS2**

18.36a "His name's Jacobus] **TS1**– "Jacobus **MS**

18.36b believe sir] **TS1r** believe **MS TS1t TS2**–

18.36c mumbled] **TS1**– muttered **MS**

18.37 loudly, ... ever] **TS1r**– loudly **MS** loudly, not less surprised **TS1t**

18.38 you say] **TS1**– say **MS**

19.1a had scuttled] **TS1**– was scuttling **MS**

19.1b out of my room.] **S**– out of the room. **MS** out. **TS1 TS2**

19.3 table on which the] **TS1**– table. The **MS**

19.4 stainless and] **TS1**– clean, **MS**

19.6a shouted courteously] **MS TS1r**– raised my voice **TS1t**

19.6b that] **MS TS1r**– to say that **TS1t**

19.7 and] **TS1**– and that I **MS**

19.8a visitor's] **TS1**– visitors **MS**

19.8b quiet] **MS E1**– tranquil **TS1**–**S**

19.9a undertone.] **MS TS1r**– under | undertone. **TS1t**

19.9b my] **MS S**– all my **TS1 TS2**

19.9c dared] **MS TS1r**– bared **TS1t**

19.11 cried] **TS1**– shouted **MS**

19.12a have been] **MS E1**– are just in after **TS1**–**S**

19.12b sixty] **MS TS1r**– fifty **TS1t**

19.12c at] **MS S**– of **TS1 TS2**

19.12d sea, you know."] **TS1**– sea." **MS**

19.13a A quiet] **MS S**– An embarrassed **TS1 TS2**

19.13b with] **TS1**– and **MS**

19.14a words] **MS TS1 S**– word **TS2**

19.14b the] **TS1**– this **MS**

19.15 character, a] **MS TS1r**– modesty. It had **TS1t**

19.16a it] **MS TS1r**– it too **TS1t**

19.16b not] **TS1**– now **MS**

19.17a this call] **TS1r**– this **MS** it **TS1t**

19.17b it ... of] **TS1r**– it a sign of **MS** he nourishing **TS1t**

19.18a design] **MS S**– designs **TS1 TS2**

19.18b commercial] **TS1**– young **MS**

19.20 war as well.] **TS1**– war? **MS**

19.21a pursuing] **MS TS2**– pursing **TS1**

19.21b selfish aims] **TS1**– aims **MS**

19.21c very great] **MS** great **TS1**–

19.22a It would] **TS1**– Would it not **MS**

19.22b just to] **TS1**– to **MS**

19.23 port and ... land] **MS TS1r**– port **TS1t**

19.24a legs on] **MS TS1r**– legs **TS1t**

19.24b while] **TS1**– time **MS**

19.25–26 more ... mercantile] **TS1**– desperately homicidal and mercantile **MS**

19.26a was plainly] **TS1**– was **MS**

19.26b make the best] **TS1**– take every advantage **MS**

19.26c its opportunities] **MS TS1r**– its *************** **TS1t**

19.27a owners'] **S**– owners **MS** owner's **TS1 TS2**

19.27b it to me] **TS1**– to me **MS**

19.28a the best] **MS** my best **TS1**–

19.28b within ... limits] **TS1r TS2** in accordance with my own judgment **MS** certain limits geographical limits **TS1t** according to my own judgment **S**–

19.29a contained also] **MS S**– contained **TS1 TS2**

19.29b a postscript ... follows] **TS1**– the following passage **MS**

19.30 meaning ... least] **MS** in the least wishing **TS1 TS2** meaning **S**–

19.31a by ... of] **TS1**– to **MS**

19.31b business friends there] **MS TS1r**– friends **TS1t**

19.32a who ... to you] **TS1**– in the next mail **MS**

19.32b desire] **MS TS1r**– wish **TS1t**

19.32c you particularly] **TS1**– you **MS**

19.34 the] **MS TS1r**– tie **TS1t**

19.37a asking] **TS1**– and asking **MS**

19.37b of] **MS TS2**– ot **TS1**

19.37c   coffee; and life] **TS1**– coffee! Life **MS**

19.37d   fairy] **MS TS1r**– fair **TS1t**

19.38a   improbability] **TS1**– unprobability **MS**

19.38b   almost shocked me.] **MS TS1r**– shocked. **TS1t**

19.39a   discovered] **MS TS1r**– arrived into **TS1t**

19.39b   wealthy] **TS1r**– prominent **MS** weaithy **TS1t**

19.39c   merchants] **TS1**– merchant **MS**

19.40a   ships ... moored?] **TS1**– arriving ships? **MS**

19.40b   are] **TS1r**– were **TS1t** OM **MS**

20.1a   this white ... merely] **TS1**– this **MS**

20.1b   this] **TS1r**–, **MS** VAR it **TS1t**

20.1c   black trick] **MS S**– impure mystery **TS1t** impure trick **TS1r TS2**

20.1d   I came in] **TS1r**– In **MS** I could not even form a sane conjecture; I came in **TS1t**

20.2a   to] **TS1**– I began to **MS**

20.2b   perhaps I] **TS1**– I **MS**

20.3a   not] **MS TS1r**– not even **TS1t**

20.3b   thinking] **MS TS1r**– thin king **TS1t**

20.3–4   the prominent ... passage] **S**– Jabobus frequently of late **MS** Mr Jacobus pretty frequently during the passage **TS1 TS2**

20.4   hearing] **MS S**– pre-disposed brain **TS1 TS2**

20.5   deceived by ... sound. ...] **TS1**– deceived. **MS**

20.6a   The ... Antrobus.] **MS TS1r**– OM **TS1t**

20.6b   Jackson – or Antrobus] **MS** Antrobus – or maybe Jackson **TS1r**– OM **TS1t**

20.8   quiet] **MS TS1r**– low **TS1t**

20.11a   at] **MS** on **TS1**–

20.11b   faded] **MS** a faded **TS1**–

20.12–13a   The ... together.] **TS1**– OM **MS**

20.12   smooth lips] **S**– lips **TS1 TS2** OM **MS**

20.12–13b   looked ... together.] **TS1r**– had a melancholy expression. **TS1t** OM **MS**

20.13   The ... man.] **S**– The smile was faint, heavy, tranquil. **MS** A heavy tranquil man. **TS1t** The smile was sad. A heavy tranquil man. **TS1r TS2**

20.14–15   officers ... breakfast – but] **S**– officers who had just then come down to breakfast; but **MS** officers – but **TS1 TS2**

20.17   the] **MS TS1r**– tie **TS1t**

20.18–19   companion ... ear.] **TS1r**– companion way reached me from above. **MS** companion way. **TS1t**

20.19a   A] **MS TS1r**– Some **TS1t**

20.19b   apparently wanted] **TS1r**– was apparently trying **MS** wanted **TS1t**

20.19c   come] **TS1**– get **MS**

20.19d   down to interview me] **MS TS1r**– down **TS1t**

20.21   can't see him] **MS E1**– can't **TS1**–S

20.23a   Captain is] **TS1**– captain's **MS**

20.23b   breakfast, I tell you.] **MS TS1r**– breakfast. **TS1t**

20.23c   ashore] **MS** on shore **TS1**–

20.24   and] **TS1**– and then **MS**

20.25a   fair.] **MS TS1r**– ************ fair." **TS1t**

20.25b   You let ... "] **TS1r**– OM **MS TS1t**

20.26a   had nothing] **MS TS1r**– nothing **TS1t**

20.26b   that] **TS1**– it **MS**

20.27–28   Everybody ... fellow ..."] **TS1**– Everybody ... **MS**

20.29   sucessfully,] **MS TS1r**– sucessfully and **TS1t**

20.30   can't] **TS1**– won't **MS**

20.31a   mulatto; but he] **TS1**– mulatto. He **MS**

20.31b   the] **TS1**– the the **MS**

20.31c   dishes] **MS TS1r**– disher **TS1t**

20.32a   remained] **MS TS1r**– stood **TS1t**

20.32b   of] **MS TS1r**– of ***** **TS1t**

20.34   getting ... it] **TS1r**– the scrape he would get into **MS** getting into a scrape in consequence **TS1t**

20.35a   on] **MS** of **TS1–**

20.35b   Burns'] **TS1r–** Burn's **MS**
Burns **TS1t**

20.35–36   as ... extraordinary] **TS1–**
was really amazing **MS**

20.36a   couldn't] **TS1–** could not **MS**

20.36b   imagine] **TS1–** guess **MS**

20.36–37   new bee] **MS TS1r–** bee
TS1t

20.37   the mate] **MS TS1r–** him **TS1t**

20.38a   no one] **MS** nobody **TS1–**

20.38–39   cared ... ships.] **MS TS1r–**
spoke. **TS1t**

20.38b   speak, as] **MS S–** speak. Such
TS1r TS2 OM **TS1t**

20.39a   in] **E1–** of **MS TS1r–S** OM **TS1t**

20.39b   And I] **TS1t S–** I **MS TS1r TS2**

20.39c   simply because] **TS1–** for the
simple reason that **MS**

20.40a   the] **MS TS2–** the | the **TS1**

20.40b   entertainment] **TS1–** meal
MS

20.40–21.1   I had ... usual] **TS1–**
Instead of the expected **MS**

21.1a   whereas ... veritable] **TS1–** I saw
before me a **MS**

21.1b   us] **TS1 S–** me **TS2, MS VAR**

21.2–3   which ... from] **TS1–** not out
of **MS**

21.3   Danish tin – Cutlets, and] **MS**
TS1r– ******** tin – and **TS1t**

21.4a   live] **MS TS1r–** live *******
TS1t

21.4b   contemplated] **TS1–** gazed at
MS

21.5   disclosed] **MS TS1r–** hisclosed
TS1t

21.5–6   as ... human,] **TS1r–** a simple,
MS as a man of human and **TS1t**

21.6   something] **MS E1–** somewhat
TS1–S

21.10   "Grown on] **MS TS1r–** "From
TS1t

21.11a   Those grown here] **TS1–** The
natives **MS**

21.11b   much more] **MS** more **TS1–**

21.12a   grieved] **TS1–** uneasy **MS**

21.13b   conversation.] **MS TS1r–**
conversation. thus engaged **TS1t**

21.13c   these] **TS1r–** those **MS TS1t**

21.14a   and wealthy] **TS1–** wealthy **MS**

21.14b   merchant to discuss.] **MS**
TS1r– merchant? **TS1t**

21.14–15   He ... individuality.] **TS1**
TS2 OM **MS S–**

21.14c   He] **TS1r TS2** We **TS1t** OM **MS**
S–

21.15   I thought the] **TS1r–** The **MS**
There was something very attractive
in the **TS1t**

21.16   home rather attractive] **MS**
TS1r– home **TS1t**

21.16–22   attractive. He ... What] **TS1r**
TS2, TS1t VAR attractive; but what
MS S– [*see 21.16, 21.26d,*
21.26–27]

21.19–20   One ... upon] **TS1r TS2** It
would have been perhaps tactless to
raise the question of **TS1t** OM **MS S–**

21.20   the] **TS1t TS2** the the **TS1r** OM
MS S–

21.21–22   tactless, almost indecent –
and] **TS1r TS2** indecent – and **TS1t**
OM **MS S–**

21.22   to talk] **TS1–** to | to talk **MS**

21.23a   to a] **TS1–** with a **MS**

21.23b   on one] **MS TS1r–** upon you
TS1t

21.23–24   after ... sea] **TS1–** out of an
island one had never seen before
MS

21.23c   sixty one] **MS TS1r–** 51 **TS1t**
VAR **MS**

21.24–25   town in ... before?] **TS1–**
town. **MS**

21.24   an] **TS2–** a **TS1** OM **MS**

21.25   were (besides sugar)] **TS1–**
were **MS**

21.26a   earth] **MS TS1** the earth **TS2–**

21.26b   its] **TS1–** it's **MS**

21.26c   conversation] **MS TS1r–**
conversations **TS1t**

21.26d   Mystery.] **TS1 TS2** To draw
him on business at once would have
been indecent – and even worse
than indecent – impolitic. **MS** To
draw him on business at once would
have been almost indecent – or
even worse: impolitic. **S–** [*see*
21.16–22]

21.26–27   And ... that all] TS1 TS2 All
MS S– [see 21.16–22]

21.27   homely] TS1r TS2 homily TS1t
OM MS S–

21.28a   do] TS1 TS2 do at the
moment MS S–

21.28b   on ... track] TS1r TS2 on in the
old groove MS E1– on the opened
track TS1t on with the topic S

21.29–30   fretting inwardly ... inanity.]
TS1– fretfully. MS

21.33   evade] TS1– avoid MS

21.34a   Eyeing] MS S– Still eying TS1
TS2

21.34b   in a spirit] MS S– with an air
TS1 TS2

21.35a   wouldn't] TS1– would not MS

21.35b   him to] TS1– to MS

21.35c   any eatables] MS TS1r–
anything TS1t

21.39a   those] MS these TS1–

21.39b   goat's] TS1– goats MS

21.39–40   one of the dishes] TS1– the
dish MS

22.5a   curt] TS1– short MS

22.5b   second mate] TS1– second MS

22.6a   smooth] MS S– candid TS1 TS2

22.6b   red] MS TS1r– blue-eyed TS1t

22.6–7   With ... he] TS1– He had MS

22.7   two] TS1r– nearly two TS1t OM
MS

22.8   smacked of] MS S– was mere
TS1 TS2

22.9a   All the same] TS1–
Nevertheless MS

22.9–10   to ... and I] TS1r– in its way.
And I MS and I TS1t

22.9b   have produced] S– produce
TS1r TS2 OM MS TS1t

22.10   his smartness] TS1– it MS

22.11–13   gave ... guest] TS1– looked
deprecatory and smiled in the
direction of the guest in a way I did
not know what to make of MS

22.14   The latter] MS E1– That last
TS1–S

22.14–15   asked ... and nibbled] TS1–
nibbled MS

22.15   a piece of very] TS1– piece
about a square inch in area of MS

22.15–16   biscuit. I ... but] TS1–
bread. And MS

22.17   complete] TS1– full MS

22.18a   local] TS1– colony's MS

22.18b   houses, of the state] TS1–
prospects and MS

22.19a   All ... with] MS TS1r– And
there were TS1t

22.19b   that talk] TS1r– that MS OM
TS1t

22.19c   personalities,] MS TS1r–
personalities too TS1t

22.20a   veiled ... his] TS1r– warnings.
His MS veiled warnings. All the time
his TS1t

22.20b   fleshy face] TS1– face MS

22.21–22   equable without ... wide.]
TS1– equable. MS

22.22   word] TS1– word of his MS

22.23a   value] TS1– advantages MS

22.23b   a business] MS business TS1–

22.24a   favourably modified] MS S–
modified TS1 TS2

22.24–26   He ... commanders.] TS1–
OM MS

22.24b   me the] E1– the TS1–S OM
MS

22.24c   disponible] TS1–A1 E2 A2b
disposable A2a OM MS

22.25–26   commanders. From] TS1r–
commanders, and from TS1t OM MS

22.26a   From ... still] TS1– After this
MS

22.26b   commercial information,] MS
S– information, TS1 TS2

22.26–27   he condescended] MS
TS1r– condescended TS1t

22.27a   mere harbour] MS TS1r–
harbour TS1t

22.27b   gossip.] TS1– gossip. He gave
me the names of all the ships in
port their tonnage, the names of
their Captains. MS

22.27c   Hilda] MS TS1r– "Orama"
TS1t

22.27–28   had unaccountably lost] MS
S– lost TS1t had lost TS1r TS2

22.28a   Bengal, and her] MS TS1r–
Ben al. Her TS1t

22.28b   captain] TS1– master MS

22.29a   greatly] **S**– painfully **MS** very
much **TS1t** unreasonably **TS1r TS2**

22.29b   affected by this.] **MS TS1r**–
affected. **TS1t**

22.29–30   getting ... years] **MS S**–
growing old **TS1 TS2**

22.30a   together and the] **TS1**–
together. The **MS**

22.30b   imagined] **TS1**– was inclined
to consider **MS**

22.30c   this strange event] **S**– the
strange event **MS** this loss **TS1t** this
strange loss **TS1r TS2**

22.31   to ... forerunner] **TS1r**–**S** as an
omen **MS** to be a sign **TS1t** to be
the forerunner **E1**–

22.32   experienced awful] **TS1r**–
suffered from disastrous **MS** an
awful **TS1t**

22.32–33a   Cape – had ... chief
officer] **TS1**– Cape. Mate **MS**

22.32–33b   Cape – had ... the] **S**–
Cape – dec*s swept, **TS1t** Cape –
decks swept, **TS1r** Cape – decks
swep* **TS2** OM **MS**

22.33a   only a] **TS1**– a **MS**

22.33b   few hours] **MS TS1r**– day or
two **TS1t**

22.34   little baby] **MS** baby **TS1**–

22.35a   If] **TS1**– Had **MS**

22.35b   had ... able] **TS1r**– managed
MS had managed **TS1t**

22.36a   into ... it] **TS1**– in its life **MS**

22.36b   could] **TS1**– would **MS**

22.36c   been probably] **MS TS1r**–
been **TS1t**

22.37a   failed them] **TS1**– fell light
MS

22.37b   or ... and . . .] **TS1r**– of the
passage . . . and **MS**

22.37–38   the baby ... buried] **TS2**–
the baby was to be burried **MS** they
were going to bury it **TS1t** the baby
was going to buried **TS1r**

22.38a   this afternoon.] **TS1**– that
very afternoon . . . **MS**

22.38b   supposed] **TS1**– suppose **MS**

22.40   asked] **MS TS1r**– said **TS1t**

23.1   decidedly. It ... appreciated.]
TS1– decidedly. **MS**

23.2a   captains ... harbour] **S**–
shipmasters **MS** Captains **TS1 TS2**

23.2b   going to attend] **MS S**– coming
TS1 TS2

23.2c   Poor] **TS1**– My presence would
be appreciated. Poor **MS**

23.3   Pretty hard] **TS1**– Hard **MS**

23.4a   "And you Captain – you] **TS1**–
"You, Captain, I presume, **MS**

23.4b   married I suppose?"] **TS1**–
married?" **MS**

23.5–6   "No. ... engaged."] **TS1**– "Not
I. And not even engaged" I said **MS**

23.7   I thanked] **TS1**– thanked **MS**

23.7–8   smiled ... expressed] **TS1**– sat
musing I went to express **MS**

23.8–9   for ... information] **TS1**– of
the trouble **MS**

23.9   business information] **TS1r**–
information **TS1t** OM **MS**

23.9–10   been ... to me] **TS1r**– been
good enough to take **MS** given me
TS1t

23.11   "Of course I] **TS1**– "Naturally"
I concluded "I **MS**

23.12   two" I concluded.] **TS1r**– two".
MS TS1t

23.13a   his] **MS TS2**– the his **TS1**

23.13b   distinctly at] **TS1**– at **MS**

23.13–14   somehow ... rather] **TS1**–
looked **MS**

23.15a   accordance with] **TS1**–
pursuance of **MS**

23.15b   owners'] **S**– owner's **MS–TS2**

23.15c   instructions] **TS1**– desire **MS**

23.15d   explained] **MS S**– continued
TS1 TS2

23.15–16   "You ... course."] **TS1**–
Their letter has reached you
already. Surely." **MS**

23.16   have had] **TS1r**– had **TS1t** VAR
MS

23.17a   By that] **TS1**– This **MS**

23.17b   had raised] **TS1**– raised **MS**

23.17–18   without ... emotion] **TS1**–
unemotionally **MS**

23.18   On the contrary he] **TS1**– He
MS

23.19   imperturbable] **TS1**–
unperturbable **MS**

23.20　must be thinking] **MS TS1r**– are thinging **TS1t**

23.21a　It ... but I] **TS1**– I **MS**

23.21b　then ... "Oh!"] **S**– to be disconcerted **TS1 TS2** OM **MS**

23.21c　no more than] **TS1**– nothing but **MS**

23.22　to] **TS1**– "To **MS**

23.23　for an inside] **TS1**– inside his coat **MS**

23.25　well known] **TS1**– known too **MS**

23.26　You've probably] **TS1r**– You must have **MS** You probably **TS1t**

23.27a　the] **MS** a **TS1**–

23.27b　extended] **MS S**– was presenting **TS1 TS2**

23.27c　thick business] **S**– cheap business printed **MS** business **TS1 TS2**

23.28–29　in every description of] **TS1**– in **MS**

23.29–30　Provisions ... etc., etc.] **TS1**– OM **MS**

23.29　paints,] **MS TS2**– pants, **TS1** OM **MS**

23.30a　Ships] **MS TS1r**– Ship s **TS1t**

23.30b　victualled] **MS TS1r**– provisionned **TS1t**

23.30–31　by ... terms ...] **TS1**– on moderate terms by inclusive contract. – etc etc. **MS**

23.32　said brusquely] **MS S**– said rather brusquely **TS1r TS2** said **TS1t**

23.33　His ... him.] **TS1**– OM **MS**

23.34a　will] **MS–A2** well **E2**

23.34b　satisfied," he ... quietly.] **TS1**– satisfied". **MS**

23.35　But ... placated.] **ED** It was a conciliatory whisper. But I was not placated. **MS** I was angry. **TS1t** I was not mollified. **TS1r TS2** I was not placated. **S**–

23.35–37　I had ... deception.] **TS1**– OM **MS**

23.35–36　had ... circumvented] **S**– felt circumvented **TS1t** felt circumvented by him **TS1r TS2** OM **MS**

23.37　But the] **S**– The **MS–TS2**

23.37–38　breakfast was ... one.] **MS TS1r**– breakfast. **TS1t**

23.38–40　And ... business.] **TS1**– OM **MS**

24.2–3　was ... in] **TS1**– had waited for the ship to come in on the quay ever since six o'clock **MS**

24.3a　my] **S**– the **TS1 TS2**, **MS** VAR [see 24.2–3]

24.3b　He gave me] **TS1**– I received **MS**

24.4a　would be] **MS TS1r**– was **TS1t**

24.4b　him now.] **MS S**– him. **TS1 TS2**

24.5–6　we ... mistaken."] **TS1**– that I am going for expensive living you are jolly well mistaken." I said glancing at the table. **MS**

24.7　Captain. I quite understand."] **MS TS1r**– Captain." **TS1t**

24.8a　Nothing could disturb] **TS1**– He was not disturbed in **MS**

24.8b　dissatisfied,] **MS TS1r**– I had been circumvented; **TS1t**

24.8–9　I could ... him] **TS1**– there was nothing to fly out at him for **MS**

24.9　told] **TS1**– given **MS**

24.10　things – and ... merchant.] **TS1**– hints. And then there was his wealthy brother. **MS**

24.11　That ... enough.] **TS1r**– Queer enough – this connection. **MS** All this seemed queer. **TS1t**

24.12a　I rose ... him] **S**– I rose from table and told him **MS** So I said **TS1t** I told him **TS1r TS2**

24.12b　curtly that I] **TS1**– I **MS**

24.12c　must now] **MS TS1r**– had sow to **TS1t**

24.12d　ashore] **TS1**– on shore **MS**

24.12e　At once] **TS1**– Without delay **MS**

24.13a　offered me] **MS TS1** offered **TS2**–

24.13b　the use of his] **MS TS1r**– his **TS1t**

24.13c　boat for ... port.] **TS1**– boat. **MS**

24.14a　"I ... equably.] **TS1**– His charge was only nominal for all the ship's stay. **MS**

24.14b "My] **S**– His **MS** The **TS1t**
"The **TS1r TS2**

24.15a   remains all day] **TS1**– was **MS**

24.15b   landing steps.] **TS1r**– landing
steps all day. **MS** steps. **TS1t**

24.15c   You have] **TS1**– A captain had
MS

24.15d   a] **TS1**– his **MS**

24.16   whistle when ... boat."] **S**–
whistle . . . **MS** whistle." **TS1 TS2**

24.17   doorway to ... first] **TS1**–
doorway **MS**

24.18   his ... all] **MS S**– the end **TS1**
TS2

24.18–19   As ... individuals] **TS1**– Two
shabby individuals waiting on the
quarter deck **MS**

24.19–20   in mournful silence] **TS1**–
gloomily and uselessly **MS**

24.20–21   which ... word] **TS1**– of two
other shipchandlers, **MS**

24.21a   eye.] **TS1**– ignoring, eye. **MS**

24.21–23   It ... existence.] **TS1**– OM
MS

24.21b   ceremony.] **S**– rite. **TS1 TS2**
OM **MS**

24.22   he placid] **TS1t S**– he
triumphing placidly **TS1r TS2** OM
MS

24.24a   quay after] **TS1**– quay. I left
him I uncermoniously after **MS**

24.24b   expressed quietly] **TS1**–
expressed **MS**

24.25   often "at the store."] **TS1**–
soon at his "store". **MS**

24.25–26   smoking ... cigars."] **TS1r**–
Captain's room with "rather
decent" cigars and newspapers. **MS**
smoking room for Captains there
with newspapers and some samples
of "all sorts of cigars." **TS1t**

24.26–27   I ... unceremoniously.]
TS1– OM **MS**

24.28   with ... heartiness,] **MS TS1r**–
very heartily **TS1t**

24.28–29   heartiness, but their] **TS1**–
heartiness. Their **MS**

24.29–31   state ... expect] **TS1**–
freights was not very favourable
MS

24.31a   Naturally I] **TS1r**– I **MS** But I
TS1t

24.31b   became] **TS1r**– was **MS TS1t**

24.31c   inclined now] **TS1**– inclined
MS

24.31d   put] **MS TS1r**– but **TS1t**

24.31e   trust] **TS1**– trust preferably
MS

24.31–32   his version, rather] **TS1r**–
the information of the wrong
Jacobus **MS** him **TS1t**

24.32–33   office behind me] **TS1**–
office **MS**

24.33   A ... lies.] **MS TS1r**– They lie.
TS1t

24.34   That's ... expect.] **TS1**– OM
MS

24.35   They ... rate."] **MS TS1r**– OM
TS1t

24.36   big outer room] **TS1**– general
office **MS**

24.36–37   a ... shiny] **TS1**– rose from
his place. He was lean clean shaved,
immaculately clad in a white suit of
clothes. Silvery gleams pasted on his
MS

24.37   shiny closely] **TS1r**– close **MS**
closely **TS1t**

24.38–39   head on ... and] **TS1**–
head. He **MS**

24.40   me? They] **MS** me, they **TS1**–

25.3   face ... moment, then] **TS1**–
face; then **MS**

25.4   baby] **TS1**– little baby **MS**

25.5   tempest] **TS1**– gale **MS**

25.6   dental, ... teeth)] **MS TS1r**–
shark-like smile **TS1t**

25.7a   made ... little] **TS1r TS2**
completed all my little **MS** made my
TS1t yet made my little **S**–

25.7b   arrangements ... port] **TS1r**–
arrangements – **MS** arrangements
for the ship **TS1t**

25.8   answered] **MS TS1r**– said **TS1t**

25.9   Ernest Jacobus] **MS TS1r**–
Jacobus **TS1t**

25.9–10   an ... owners."] **TS1**– a letter
of introduction." **MS**

25.11–12   was not altogether ... of]
TS1– did not depend solely on **MS**

25.13 "Why," I ... brother ... ?"] **S–**
"Why!" I cried. "Isn't he the
brother.? **MS** "Why? Is'nt he?" **TS1t**
"Why? Is'nt he the brother. .? **TS1r
TS2**

25.14   together] **MS–S** to each other
E1–

25.15 added impressively] **MS S–** aid
slowly **TS1t** added slowly **TS1r TS2**

25.16 "Indeed! ... about?"] **MS S–**
"What's wrong? **TS1t** "Indeed!
What's the quarrel?" **TS1r TS2**

25.17   "Oh ... one] **TS1–** "Nothing.
Nothing one **MS**

25.17–18   care ... primly.] **MS TS1r–**
mention." he said primly. **TS1t**

25.18–19   "Only ... *all.*] **TS1r TS2** "His
business is quite large. Best
provision merchant here. No doubt
of that. But there is such a thing as
personal character too – isn't there.
MS "Only I would'nt believe all he
says. Not all. **TS1t** "He's got quite a
large business. The best
ship-chandler here, without a
doubt. Business is all very well, but
there is such a thing as personal
character, too, isn't there? **S–**

25.20–28   He went ... scale.] **MS
TS1r–** OM **TS1t**

25.20   desk. He amused me.] **TS1r–**
desk. **MS** OM **TS1t**

25.21a   maid, a] **TS1r–** maid – it
amused me – a **MS** OM **TS1t**

25.21b   some] **TS1r–** some
commercial **MS** OM **TS1t**

25.21–23   impropriety. Was ...
pocket.] **TS1r–** impropriety. **MS** OM
TS1t

25.24   who disapproved of] **TS1r–**
shocked by **MS** OM **TS1t**

25.26   then] **TS1r–** us sailors say
philosophically: **MS** OM **TS1t**

25.26–27   customs. In ... "trading"]
TS1r– customs, and in very isolated
communities **MS** OM **TS1t**

25.27–28   the social standards]
TS1r–S social values **MS** social
standards **E1–** OM **TS1t**

25.29 II] **MS S–** OM **TS1 TS2**

25.30–26.3   I ... hard] **MS TS1r–** OM
TS1t

25.31a   acquainted by sight] **TS1r–**
acquainted **MS** OM **TS1t**

25.31b   fellow captains] **TS1r–**
fellow-ship-masters **MS** OM **TS1t**

25.32–33   made ... group] **TS1r–**
grouped ourselves, a considerable
knot **MS** OM **TS1t**

25.34   of] **TS1r–** in **MS** OM **TS1t**

25.35   moved – perhaps because
they] **TS1r–** moved They **MS** OM
TS1t

25.36–37   sea-dog, away ... element]
TS1r– sea dog **MS** OM **TS1t**

25.37–38   I ... facing] **TS1r–** One –
facing **MS** OM **TS1t**

25.38   grave, who] **TS1r–** grave – **MS**
OM **TS1t**

26.1a tears] **MS E1–** tears down his
weather-beaten stolid face **TS1r**
tears down his weather-beaten face
TS2 S OM **TS1t** [*see 26.1b*]

26.1–2   They ... wall.] **TS1r–** OM **MS**
OM **TS1t**

26.1b down ... face] **E1–** down
TS1r–S OM **MS** OM **TS1t**

26.2–3   was ... as the] **TS1r–** was a **MS**
OM **TS1t**

26.3   sailors, a] **TS1r–** sailors and that
this **MS** OM **TS1t**

26.3–4   man; that ... engaged] **TS1r–**
man engaged **MS** wife or chick of
his own, and that engaged **TS1t**

26.4   tenderest] **TS1–** earliest **MS**

26.5   he knew] **TS1–** knew **MS**

26.7a those] **MS S–** these **TS1 TS2**

26.7–8   over ... in] **TS1–** from **MS**

26.7b   own lost] **TS1–S** lost **E1–** OM
MS

26.8   a strange] **MS–S** strange **E1–**

26.9   he ... know] **MS TS1r–** could
never be his **TS1t**

26.10   a ... victim] **TS1r–** a victim **MS** a
capricious animal, the very creature
TS1t

26.11   But ... callousness. I] **TS1–** But
I **MS**

26.12a   a horribly] **MS TS1r** an
absurdly **TS1t** horribly **TS2–**

26.12b   that] **MS TS1r**– the words of the **TS1t**

26.13a   had had to read] **MS S**– had read **TS1t** had to read **TS1r TS2**

26.13b   myself, once or twice] **E1**– myself **MS** myself more than once **TS1–S**

26.14–16   The ... grave.] **TS1**– OM **MS**

26.14   defiance, the winged words] **TS1r**– defiance **TS1t** OM **MS**

26.15   fall] **TS1r**– droop **TS1t** OM **MS**

26.16a   that] **TS1 TS2** the **S**– OM **MS**

26.16b   use of asking] **TS1**– good to ask **MS**

26.16c   Death] **TS1**– death **MS**

26.17   hole in the ground.] **MS TS1r**– hole. **TS1t**

26.18a   And then my] **TS1**– My **MS**

26.18b   altogether – away into] **TS1**– altogether at times – into **MS**

26.19a   life – and no] **TS1**– life: and two **MS**

26.19b   matters at that – ships] **TS1**– matters: ships **MS**

26.20   instability] **TS1**– mobility **MS**

26.21a   I was] **TS1**– And **MS**

26.21b   my thoughts – and] **TS1r**– my thoughts **MS** myself. **TS1t**

26.21–22   I thought: Shall ... soon?] **TS1**– I was asking myself: Will that Jacobus put realy good business in my way: . . **MS**

26.22   be ... get] **TS1r**– get **TS1t** VAR **MS**

26.22–23   Time's ... way? . . .] **TS1**– OM **MS**

26.23   put ... way? . . .] **TS1r**– do business? **TS1t** OM **MS** [*see 26.21–22*]

26.23–24   go ... two] **TS1**– delay going to see him **MS**

26.25–26   Don't ... shamefaced.] **TS1**– Those thoughts – vague, shadowy, remorseful pursued me. **MS**

26.26   restless, shamefaced] **S**– restless, at the back of my head **TS1t** restless, dodging shamefaced at the back of my head **TS1r TS2** VAR **MS**

26.27a   Theirs] **TS1r**– I **MS** It **TS1t**

26.27b   a callous, ... And] **TS1**– ashamed of this callousness and **MS**

26.28a   the presence of that] **MS S**– that **TS1 TS2**

26.28b   pertinacious shipchandler] **TS1**– ship-chandler **MS**

26.28c   which] **MS S**– who **TS1 TS2**

26.29a   started them] **TS1**– called them out **MS**

26.29b   stood mournfully] **TS1r**– stood **MS** was there **TS1t**

26.29–30   amongst ... suggesting] **TS1**– among us, suggesting by his presence **MS**

26.31   had ... outrageous] **TS1**– and making me odious **MS**

26.32   indeed ... preserved] **TS1**– I have **MS**

26.32–33   It was only] **TS1**– It's **MS**

26.33   mind which. . . .] **MS TS1r**– mind. **TS1t**

26.34a   It ... last.] **TS1**– Over at last! **MS**

26.34b   poor father] **TS1**– father **MS**

26.35a   side-whiskers] **MS TS1r**– whiskers **TS1t**

26.35b   gash ... freshly] **MS S**– fresh gash on his **TS1 TS2**

26.36–37   But ... cemetery] **TS1r**– For some reason he singled me out and as I hesitated at the gate of the cemetery **MS** But for some reason, either because I seemed to linger **TS1t**

26.37–27.1   being ... out] **TS1**– slipped his hand under my arm **MS**

26.37–38   being ... back] **TS1r**– not being certain of my way **TS1t** OM **MS**

26.39   some more] **TS1r**– some more to some more **TS1t** OM **MS**

27.1–3   Keeping ... silence] **TS1**– Conscience-stricken I did not resist **MS**

27.1–2   at my] **TS1r**– my **TS1t** VAR **MS**

27.2   listened to] **TS1r**– received **TS1t** VAR **MS**

27.3–4   Suddenly ... away] **TS1**– Waving his disengaged hand at a bulky figure going off **MS**

27.4   waved] **S–** waving **TS1 TS2, MS**
VAR

27.5a   by ... street] **MS** down a street
TS1t hurriedly down a street **TS1r**
TS2 by itself down a street **S–**

27.5b   grey] **MS S–** ample **TS1**
TS2

27.6–7   swallowed down] **TS1r–**
swallowed **MS** kept down **TS1t**

27.8a   me in ... voice] **TS1–** me **MS**

27.8b   that Jacobus was] **S–** that
Jacobus, **MS** how Jacobus was **TS1**
TS2

27.9a   to] **TS1–** on **MS**

27.9b   ship on arrival] **MS TS1r–** ship
TS1t

27.9c   and learning of] **E1–** hearing of
MS and discovering **TS1–S**

27.9–10   had taken] **MS S–** took **TS1**
TS2

27.10–11   everything, ... arranged]
TS1r– everything – arranged **MS**
everything, carried off the ship's
papers on shore, arranged **TS1t**

27.13   been looking] **MS TS1t S–** to
look **TS1r TS2**

27.14   And ... that.] **S–** Helpless. **MS**
Just you think of that. **TS1r TS2** OM
TS1t

27.14–15a   The ... land.] **TS1–** OM **MS**

27.14–15b   dear little] **TS1r–** little
TS1t OM **MS**

27.15a   the very day] **TS1r–** as **TS1t**
OM **MS**

27.15b   the land] **TS1r–** lands **TS1t**
OM **MS**

27.15c   How] **MS S–** However **TS1t**
TS2 How ever **TS1r**

27.15–16   managed to take] **MS**
TS1r– took **TS1t**

27.16–18   I couldn't see ... our] **TS1r–**
We had lost our **MS** I couldn't see
anything I couldn't speak – and you
know I lost my **TS1t**

27.17   You've ... we] **S–** and, you've
heard perhaps, we had **TS1r TS2**
VAR **MS TS1t**

27.18   overboard ... no] **S–** overboard.
No **MS** overboard on the passage so
there was no **TS1t** overboard on the

passage, so that there was no **TS1r**
TS2

27.19a   the] **TS1–** the | the **MS**

27.19b   crazy] **TS1–** crazy | crazy **MS**

27.19–20   all alone with the] **TS1r–** all
alone with **MS** with the **TS1t**

27.21a   We ... together. I] **TS1–** I **MS**

27.21b   part from] **TS1r–** part with
MS leave **TS1t**

27.22a   On] **TS1–** In silence we
walked to **MS**

27.22b   quay] **MS–E1 A2 E2** way **A1**

27.22c   he] **TS1–** where he **MS**

27.22–23   arm and ... hand] **TS1–**
arm **MS**

27.24   fair!" he ..."Don't] **MS TS1r–**
fair! Don't **TS1t**

27.25a   sea first] **MS TS1r–** sea **TS1t**

27.25b   It isn't fair."] **TS1–** OM **MS**

27.26–27   me to ... ship] **TS1–** me
MS

27.27   convinced] **MS** convinced that
TS1–

27.27–28   While ... Jacobus'] **TS1–**
The Jacobus **MS**

27.28a   who had] **TS1–** had **MS**

27.28b   off] **TS1–** of **MS**

27.28–29   somewhere,] **TS1–**
somewhere. I stood at the steps and
MS

27.29a   *Hilda* joined me] **TS1r–** *Hilda*
MS "Hilda" came down **TS1t**

27.29b   slender silk] **TS1r–** slender
MS slendersilk slender silk **TS1t**

27.30   his ... shirt] **TS1r–** a
Gladstonian **MS** his archaoo shirt
TS1t

27.31a   a small] **TS1r–** his small **MS**
his **TS1t**

27.31b   ruddy] **MS S–** delicate **TS1**
TS2

27.31c   face] **TS1–** face – joined me
MS [*see 27.29a*]

27.31–33   It ... eyes.] **TS1–** OM **MS**

27.33a   clear] **S–** candid **TS1 TS2** OM
MS

27.33b   glossy like] **TS1–** like **MS**

27.34a   upwards slightly] **S–** slightly
MS–TS2

27.34b   brim] **MS TS1r–** rim **TS1t**

27.34c valuable, ancient] **S**– valuable old **MS** white **TS1t** ancient **TS1r TS2**

27.35 broad black] **TS1**– black **MS**

27.35–36 that ... old] **TS1r**– that vivacious old neat **MS** the neat little old **TS1t**

27.36 quaintly ... also] **MS TS1r**– angelic and **TS1t**

27.38–39 accosted ... with a] **TS1**– addressed me with perfect familiarity with **MS**

27.40 the ... stout] **TS1**– a fat **MS**

27.40–28.1 who ... upon] **TS1r**– sitting on **MS** who sat upon **TS1t**

28.1 Presently] **TS1**– Then **MS**

28.1–2 observed ... barque] **TS1**– complimented me on my "pretty little barque" **MS**

28.2 barque.] **MS TS1r**– barque. ¶ "Not as pretty as the Hilda" **TS1t**

28.3a returned ... speech] **TS1**– made a return **MS**

28.3b saying readily] **TS1r**– saying **MS TS1t**

28.5–6 At ... dismally.] **TS1**– OM **MS**

28.5a once] **S**– this **TS1 TS2** OM **MS**

28.5b sensitive mouth] **S**– moutd **TS1t** innocent mouth **TS1r TS2** OM **MS**

28.7a "O, dear!] **MS TS1r**– "Oh! **TS1t**

28.7b her now."] **TS1**– her." The corners of his mouth dropped. **MS**

28.8a I ... that he] **MS TS1r**– I. now he **TS1t**

28.8b anxiously] **MS S**– at once **TS1r TS2** OM **TS1t**

28.8c his figure-head] **MS** the figure-head **TS1t** the figure-head of his ship **TS1r**–

28.9a tunic ... gold] **TS1**– tunic, gold girdle **MS**

28.9b edged] **TS1r**– ed. ed **TS1t** OM **MS**

28.9–10 the ... very] **TS1r**– not perhaps **MS** the face not so very **TS1t**

28.10 her ... arms] **TS1r**– her bare arms most **MS** the white arms **TS1t**

28.11a extended] **TS1r**– gracefuly extended **MS** disposed **TS1t**

28.11b as ... were] **TS1**– in the act of **MS**

28.11–12 Did ... thing! ...] **TS1r**– Did I? ... Went off. **MS** OM **TS1t**

28.12 After ... too.] **MS TS1r**– OM **TS1t**

28.13 tone] **TS1r**– talk **MS** tale **TS1t**

28.13–15 wood; his ... flavour. ...] **TS1**– wood. His lamentations had a somewhat scandalous aspect ... **MS**

28.14a gave to] **MS TS1r**– gave **TS1t** VAR **MS**

28.14b his lamentations] **S**–, **MS** VAR it **TS1t** the tale **TS1r TS2**

28.15 scandalous] **E1**–, **MS** VAR scandalous and pathetic **TS1–S**

28.15–16 night – a ... Bengal] **TS1**– night – clear fine night **MS**

28.16 gulf] **TS1–A2** Gulf **E2** OM **MS**

28.17a no one in the ship] **TS1r**– no one **MS** nobody **TS1t**

28.17b tell why, how,] **S**– tell why, when, **MS** guess **TS1 TS2**

28.19 Did I ever hear ...] **MS S**– "Did you ever hear ....." **TS1 TS2**

28.20a him] **MS TS2**– his **TS1**

28.20b sympathetically that] **TS1**– that **MS**

28.21a This ... good] **TS1r**– Bad that **MS** It meant no good **TS1t**

28.21b he was sure] **S**– he felt **TS1r TS2** OM **MS TS1t**

28.22a in it that] **MS** there **TS1t** there which **TS1r TS2** in it which **S**–

28.22b looked ... warning] **MS S**– he couldn't understand **TS1t** was inexplicable **TS1r TS2**

28.22c remarked] **MS S**– suggested **TS1 TS2**

28.23a surely another] **TS1r**– another **MS TS1t**

28.23b figure of a woman] **MS TS1r**– fi. ure **TS1t**

28.23c procured] **TS1**– placed there **MS**

28.24–25 The ... proposed] **TS1**– He resented it like **MS**

28.25a proposed] **S**– suggested **TS1**
TS2 VAR **MS**

28.25b something] **MS TS1t E1**–
something highly **TS1r–S**

28.25c improper] **MS TS1r**–
indecent **TS1t**

28.25–27 One ... a ship] **TS1**– Masts,
a rudder, any working part of a ship
one could replace **MS**

28.26 masts, I was told] **S**– masts **TS1**
TS2 VAR **MS**

28.27a but ... up] **TS1r**– but who
would think of sticking up **MS** But
was the sense of having **TS1t**

28.27b use] **S**– sense **TS1r TS2**, **TS1t**
VAR VAR **MS**

28.28a How ... satisfaction?] **ED** Who
would care for it? What satisfaction
... No. **MS** How could one care for
it. **TS1t** What satisfaction? How
could one care for it? **TS1r**–

28.28b was] **MS–E1 A2 E2** was as **A1**

28.28c easy to see] **MS TS1r**– clear
TS1t

28.28–29 see that] **TS1**– say **MS**

28.29a never been] **TS1**– never **MS**

28.29b shipmates] **MS TS1r**– ship- |
master **TS1t**

28.29c over twenty] **MS TS1r**– twenty
TS1t

28.31a "A ... in] **E1**– He scolded with
MS "Another figure head" he
exclaimed in **TS1t** "Another
figure head!" he scolded in
TS1r–S

28.31b indignation] **TS1**– vigour
MS

28.32a I've] **TS1**– I have **MS**

28.32–33 now ... May] **TS1**– 24 years,
MS

28.32b eight and twenty] **S**– two and
thirty **TS1 TS2** VAR **MS**

28.33 as] **TS1**– a **MS**

28.35a I ... amused] **MS S**– He quite
confounded me **TS1t** It was as good
as a play **TS1r TS2**

28.35b Jacobus done?] **MS E1**– he
done. **TS1t** Jacobus done now.
TS1r–S

28.36 inquired in ... tone] **MS S**–
inquired **TS1t** inquired
deferentially **TS1r TS2**

28.36–37 But he ... only] **TS1**– He
MS

28.37 launched] **TS1r**– launched out
TS1t OM **MS**

28.38 sort of chap] **MS TS1r**– chap
TS1t

28.38–39 anything you like] **TS1**–
things **MS**

28.39–29.1 I ... have] **TS1**– He
happens to have a figure-head **MS**

28.39 for an] **S**– an **TS1 TS2** OM **MS**

28.40a he got ... once] **TS1r**– he **TS1t**
OM **MS**

28.40b offered] **S**– wanted **TS1 TS2**
OM **MS**

29.1 He got Smith] **MS TS1r**– Got
TS1t

29.2a me] **MS TS1t S**– me first **TS1r**
TS2

29.2b 'Mr Smith,' says I] **TS1**– Says I
"Mr Smith" **MS**

29.3a that? Am ... pick] **TS1**– to think
I would take **MS**

29.3b the] **TS1r**– of the **TS1t** OM **MS**

29.3c with another] **TS1 S**– another
TS2 OM **MS**

29.4 And after] **TS1**– After **MS**

29.5 you young fellows] **MS TS1r**–
you **TS1t**

29.6 great compunction] **TS1r**–
compunction **MS TS1t**

29.7–9 said ... gilt."] **TS1**– ventured
to suggest a fiddle-head as a remedy
Carved and gilt scrollwork. **MS**

29.10 became] **MS S**– looked **TS1**
TS2

29.11 Scroll work.] **TS1r**– OM **MS**
TS1t

29.12 a sailor man] **TS1r**– us sailors
MS somebody **TS1t**

29.13 me] **MS–TS2 E1**– us **S**

29.13–14 A ... say – eh?] **TS1r**– Gilt –
eh? **MS** A filt fiddle-head – eh? **TS1t**

29.14a I ... you.] **TS1r**– I daresay. **MS**
You think so? **TS1t**

29.14b You] **MS TS1r**– But you **TS1t**

29.15a fellows] **MS S–** fellows nowadays **TS1 TS2**

29.15b seem to have] **TS1–** have **MS**

29.15c feeling ... proper] **TS1r–** feelings for what's proper **MS** feelings **TS1t**

29.16 made ... arm] **TS1–** moved his right arm convulsively **MS**

29.17–18 I ... let] **S–** Let **MS** For the few days that are left me I would as soon let **TS1t** For the few days that are left me yet I would as soon let **TS1r TS2**

29.18a the old thing] **MS TS1r–** her **TS1t**

29.18b about the world] **TS1r–** about **MS TS1t**

29.19 cried] **MS TS1r–** said **TS1t**

29.19–20a Then ... animosity:] **TS1–** He raised his voice after the boat with comical fury. **MS**

29.19–20b raised ... of] **TS1r–** cried after me from **TS1t** VAR **MS**

29.22–23 I ... day!"] **MS TS1r–** Oh, he's a wonder, but I am an old bird." **TS1t**

29.23 on ... day!"] **TS1r–** some day on board my ship" **MS** OM **TS1t**

29.24a spent ... evening] **MS TS2–** spent the end of my first day **TS1t** spent the my first evening **TS1r**

29.24b quietly ... cuddy;] **TS1r–** quietly; **MS** quietly on board **TS1t**

29.25 I was] **MS–TS2** was I **S–**

29.26a pettily] **MS TS1r–E1 A2 E2** *rettily **TS1t** prettily **A1**

29.26b so discordant and so] **MS** discordant and **TS1t** discordant and so **TS1r–**

29.27 few hours longer] **TS1r–** little while longer **MS** few hours **TS1t**

29.27–28 I was ... to] **TS1–** It was however written that I should **MS**

29.30–31 meal to ..."a look] **TS1–** meal. He wanted, he said, to have a "look **MS**

29.31 quite dark] **MS TS1r–** dark **TS1t**

29.32 what it was] **MS TS1r–** what **TS1t**

29.33 midnight, while ... saloon] **S–** midnight while sitting in the cuddy with a book **MS** midnight **TS1t** midnight, as I sat with a book in the saloon, **TS1r TS2**

29.33–34 I heard] **MS S–** hearing **TS1 TS2**

29.34 and hailed] **MS S–** I haile **TS1t** I hailed **TS1r TS2**

29.35a Burns] **MS TS1r–** He **TS1t**

29.35b in ... in hand] **MS TS1r–** into the cabin **TS1t**

29.35c incredibly] **MS E1–** looking incredibly **TS1–S**

29.37 laid] **TS1–** put **MS**

29.39a I've] **TS1–** I have **MS**

29.39b pretty ... shore] **S–** a few tales **MS** a little on shore **TS1 TS2**

29.39c about] **MS TS1r–** of **TS1t**

29.40 you so neatly] **MS TS1r–** you **TS1t**

30.1 his] **MS E1–** that **TS1–S**

30.3a boarding a strange] **S–** boarding a **MS** board the **TS1t** board a strange **TS1r TS2**

30.3b breakfast in two baskets] **TS1r–** breakfast **MS TS1t**

30.4 calmly inviting] **TS1r–** inviting **MS TS1t**

30.5a of anything] **MS S–** anything **TS1 TS2**

30.5b so impudent] **TS1–** impudent **MS**

30.6 Jacobus' unusual methods] **TS1r–** Jacobus' business methods **MS** that Jacobus **TS1t**

30.8a port."] **MS TS1r–** place. **TS1t**

30.8b The mate's] **MS TS1r–** His **TS1t**

30.9 eighteen or twenty] **TS1–** eighteen **MS**

30.10 years," he ... there!"] **MS TS1r–** years. **TS1t**

30.11 all ... loftily] **TS1r–** all about it" **MS** that" I confessed loftily **TS1t**

30.13 of commercial] **MS TS1r–** commercial **TS1t**

30.14 to ... nature] **TS1r–** to see you **MS** your good nature **TS1t**

30.15–16   with ... matter] **TS1r**– to let him go down with a five or ten rupee note **MS** with a five rupee note – or ten for that matter **TS1t**

30.16–17   He don't ... more] **MS TS1r**– All that will be shoved **TS1t**

30.18a   one of the tales] **MS S**– the tale **TS1 TS2**

30.18b   you have] **TS1**– you've **MS**

30.19a   would] **MS** could **TS1**–

30.19b   that much] **MS TS1r**– that **TS1t**

30.20a   he] **TS1**– he | he **MS**

30.20b   heard on shore] **MS TS1r**– heard **TS1t**

30.20–21   person in ... town] **MS TS1r**– person **TS1t**

30.21a   lived in] **MS TS1r**– had **TS1t**

30.21b   large] **S**– good sized **MS** rather fine **TS1 TS2**

30.22a   old fashioned] **TS1**– old **MS**

30.22b   one ... streets] **TS1**– a back street, **MS**

30.22c   big] **TS1**– large **MS**

30.23a   After ... this] **S**– Thereupon **MS** After telling me all this **TS1 TS2**

30.23b   Burns ..."He keeps] **MS S**– he added mysteriously "He has **TS1 TS2**

30.24a   shut up there] **MS S**– there **TS1 TS2**

30.24b   who, they say ..."] **MS TS1r**– who sees no one. **TS1t**

30.25   that] **MS** this **TS1**–

30.26a   snapped ... tone] **MS TS1r**– suggested in a sarcastic manner **TS1t**

30.26b   my] **MS** a **TS1r**–, **TS1t VAR**

30.27   The] **MS TS1r**– This **TS1t**

30.27–28   told ... himself.] **TS1**– told. Mr Burns was sensitive. **MS**

30.28   remained as if thunderstruck] **MS TS1r**– remained **TS1t**

30.29   communication] **TS1**– gossip **MS**

30.29–30   but ... chance] **MS S**– as if thunder struck **TS1t** but I cut him short **TS1r TS2**

30.31   devil] **MS** deuce **TS1**–

30.32   room] **MS TS2**– cabin **TS1t** own room **TS1r**

30.33   this] **MS TS1r**– that **TS1t**

30.33–34   indifferent] **TS1**– so indifferent. **MS**

30.34a   it ... concerned] **TS1**– the absurdity of concerning oneself **MS**

30.34b   morals] **MS E1**– individuality **TS1–S**

30.35a   if ever so] **MS S**– however **TS1 TS2**

30.35b   connected; but his personality] **MS S**– connected. That personality however **TS1t** connected. His personality however **TS1r TS2**

30.38a   After] **MS S**– But after **TS1 TS2**

30.38b   Jacobus] **MS S**– he **TS1 TS2**

30.38c   showed himself] **TS1**– was **MS**

30.38d   anything but] **MS TS1r**– not especially **TS1t**

30.39a   a] **TS1**– his **MS**

30.39b   early every morning] **TS1**– early **MS**

30.40   one] **TS1**– one or another **MS**

30.41a   for] **MS TS1 S**– for a **TS2**

30.41b   breakfast with the captain] **TS1**– breakfast **MS**

31.1   discovered] **TS1**– found **MS**

31.3   room] **MS TS1r**– stateroom **TS1t**

31.3–4   Glancing ... that his] **TS1**– His **MS**

31.4   stood, awaiting my appearance] **TS1**– stood **MS**

31.5a   beautiful bunch] **MS S**– bunch **TS1 TS2**

31.5b   flowers] **MS TS1r**– flower **TS1t**

31.6a   podgy hand] **TS1–S** paw **MS** hand **E1**–

31.6b   notice] **TS1**– notice me **MS**

31.7   garden: had ... garden:] **TS1**– garden: **MS**

31.8   himself that morning] **MS TS1r**– himself **TS1t**

31.9   He turned away.] **MS TS1r**– OM **TS1t**

31.10–11   oblige ... please."] **E1**– oblige me with a jug of water please?" **MS** bring me a big tumbler

with a little water in it." **TS1t** oblige
me with a long drink tumbler with a
little water in it." **TS1r TS2** oblige
me with some water in, large
tumbler, please." **S**

31.12a   assured him jocularly] **MS**
TS1r– told him **TS1t**

31.12b   place ... table] **TS1**– seat
MS

31.13   musn't] **TS1** must not **MS**
mustn't **TS2**–

31.14a   I blushed] **TS1**– he saw me
blushing **MS**

31.14b   But ... his] **TS1**– He was
arranging the **MS**

31.15   the sideboard] **TS1**– sideboard
MS

31.16a   Captain's plate] **TS1**– captains
MS

31.16b   steward, if you please."] **MS**
steward. **TS1t** steward, please".
TS1r–

31.16–17   He ... request] **MS TS1r**– he
directed **TS1t**

31.17a   this] **MS TS1r–A1 E2** his **A2**
OM **TS1t**

31.17b   his usual undertone.] **MS TS1**
S– [**TS2**, *which ends with* 'his', *not*
reported from here on]

31.18   to raise] **TS1**– raise **MS**

31.19a   nose; and ... noiselessly] **TS1**–
nose. After a time **MS**

31.19b   his] **MS** the **TS1**–

31.20a   a few flowers] **TS1**– flowers
MS

31.20b   improved notably] **MS TS1r**–
greatly improved **TS1t**

31.21a   ship's saloon] **MS TS1r**– cabin
TS1t

31.21b   wondered ... not] **TS1**–
suggested I should **MS**

31.21–22   all round] **TS1**– in **MS**

31.22   to sea with me] **MS** with me to
sea **TS1**–

31.23a   able] **TS1**– he could send on
board **MS**

31.23b   proper] **MS** up **TS1**–

31.23c   shelves in a day] **TS1**– shelves
MS

31.24   procure] **TS1**– procure for **MS**

31.25a   The ... fingers] **S**– His hands
MS His thick round fingers **TS1t**
The tips of thick round fingers
TS1r

31.25b   rested composedly] **MS S**–
rested **TS1**

31.25–26   on ... table on] **TS1**– on **MS**

31.26   his] **MS S**– the **TS1**

31.28a   declared] **MS S**– said hurriedly
TS1

31.28b   that I] **TS1**– I **MS**

31.28c   hadn't] **TS1**– had not **MS**

31.28–29   turning ... keep the] **TS1**–
keeping my **MS**

31.31a   Rear most] **MS TS1r**– Most
TS1t

31.31b   insisted] **MS S**– murmured
TS1

31.33a   yes. It is.] **TS1r** yes it is. **MS S**–
no. **TS1t**

31.33b   in the end] **MS TS1r**– then
TS1t

31.34a   some fool] **MS S**– somebody
TS1

31.34b   fresh breeze] **TS1**– breeze **MS**

31.35a   water] **MS S**– spray **TS1**

31.35b   at them] **TS1**– them **MS**

31.36   a contemptuous] **TS1**–
contemptuous **MS**

31.37   passively. After ... ask] **TS1r**–
and asked **MS** passively. He sat
silent breathing equably like a
slumbering man. After a time he
unglued his thick lips to ask **TS1t**

31.38   was ... answer] **TS1**– answered
curtly **MS**

31.41   thank you] **TS1**– thanks **MS**

32.1   is not] **TS1**– isn't **MS**

32.2a   suppose] **TS1**– conclude **MS**

32.2b   office-clerks presently?"] **MS**
E1– office." **TS1t** office-clerks" **TS1r**
S

32.3–4   warmth. "If ... stranger! ...]
TS1– warmth. I am a complete
stranger in the port. **MS**

32.5a   up again] **TS1**– up **MS**

32.5b   years. I ... why.] **TS1**– years. **MS**

32.5c   why. I] **E1**– why? **MS–S**

32.7   will] **MS S**– may **TS1**

32.8   "Eight ... nine,] **TS1**– "With **MS**

32.9a   that's twelve] **TS1–** it will be twelve covers **MS**

32.9b   needn't] **TS1t S–** need not **MS** won't **TS1r**

32.11a   "It ... me!] **TS1–** OM **MS**

32.11b   will] **S–** may **TS1** OM **MS**

32.11–12   me? Is it because] **TS1–** me?" I cried. "Do **MS**

32.14–15a   "There's ... with] **TS1–** I made **MS**

32.14–15b   think ... concluded] **S–** consider that question," I said **TS1t** think about it" I said **TS1r** VAR **MS**

32.15   that] **TS1–** which **MS**

32.16   But ... departed he] **TS1r–** He went – but before he departed he **MS** But he **TS1t**

32.18   held] **MS** had **TS1–**

32.19   of, very cheap] **TS1–** of cheap **MS**

32.20   would be] **TS1–** be **MS**

32.21   smile and] **E1–** smile – and **MS** smile just before he **TS1 S**

32.25   At ... inclined] **TS1–** Feeling inclined I don't know why **MS**

32.26   all this was] **TS1r–** this was all **MS** this was **TS1t**

32.29a   deadly fever] **TS1–** serious illness **MS**

32.29b   have] **TS1–** have | have **MS**

32.30   for a single] **MS TS1r–** a **TS1t**

32.31   III] **MS S–** OM **TS1**

32.32   Jacobus] **MS TS1t S–** Jacobus' **TS1r**

32.33   that ... once] **MS S–** my call **TS1t** my business call **TS1r**

32.33–34   this time] **MS** that time **TS1r–** the **TS1t**

32.34a   of him] **TS1–** about him **MS**

32.34b   a member of] **TS1–** on **MS**

32.35a   made ... to] **TS1–** annoyed **MS**

32.35b   authorities] **MS S–** governor **TS1t** Governor **TS1r**

32.35–36a   He ... opinion.] **TS1–** OM **MS**

32.35–36b   exercised] **TS1r–** had **TS1t** OM **MS**

32.36a   influence on public opinion.] **TS1r–** influence. **TS1t** OM **MS**

32.36b   A lot] **MS** Lots **TS1–**

32.37–38   He ... goods.] **TS1–** OM **MS**

32.38a   goods] **S–** wares **TS1** OM **MS**

32.38b   For instance the] **TS1–** The **MS**

32.38c   sugar] **MS S–** the colony **TS1**

33.1–2   last ... afterwards] **TS1–** I only learned later – much later **MS**

33.2a   conveyed to me] **TS1–** I obtained of him **MS**

33.2b   to me] **TS1r–** by the public talk **TS1t** VAR **MS**

33.3–5   personage. He ... colony.] **TS1r–, MS** VAR OM **TS1t**

33.3a   personage. He ... gave] **TS1r–** personage – a bachelor, hospitable, giving **MS** OM **TS1t**

33.3b   weekly card] **MS S–** card **TS1r** OM **TS1t**

33.4   which ... by] **TS1r–** and receiving **MS** OM **TS1t**

33.4–5   people in the colony.] **MS S–** people. **TS1r** OM **TS1t**

33.7   quite away] **TS1–** far **MS**

33.7–8   amongst ... hovels] **TS1r–** amongst a lot hovels **MS** of the town **TS1t**

33.8   Guided] **TS1–** Directed **MS**

33.10   bits of brown] **TS1–** brown **MS**

33.10–11   wisps of packing-straw.] **TS1–** straw. **MS**

33.11a   great ... cases] **TS1r–** stack of wine case (apparently) **MS** lot of white wood cases **TS1t**

33.11b   was] **MS TS1r** were **TS1t S–**

33.12   one of the walls] **TS1–** a wall **MS**

33.12–13   inky, light-yellow ... and] **TS1–** inky miserably thin necked light yellow mulatto youth, **MS**

33.13   miserably] **TS1r–, MS** VAR miserable **TS1t**

33.14a   three-legged stool ... desk] **TS1–** stool **MS**

33.14b   behind a cheap] **TS1r–** before an inkstained **TS1t** OM **MS**

33.15a   gone dumb] **MS S–** dumb **TS1**

33.15–17   I ... objection.] **MS TS1r–** OM **TS1t**

33.15b   some] **MS S–** great **TS1r** OM **TS1t**

33.15c difficulty in] **TS1r**– difficulty of **MS** OM **TS1t**

33.17a did it at last] **MS TS1r**– took in my name **TS1t**

33.17b at last] **TS1r**– last **MS** VAR **TS1t**

33.17c almost agonised] **TS1**– *agonised* **MS**

33.18 mysterious to me] **MS TS1r**– mysterious **TS1t**

33.19 suppressed growls] **S**– low growls **MS TS1r** growls **TS1t**

33.20a finally] **MS E1**– at last **TS1 S**

33.20b kicked out] **MS S**– kicked **TS1**

33.21a because] **TS1**– for **MS**

33.21b back] **MS TS1t S**– back to me **TS1r**

33.21c foremost ... door] **TS1**– foremost **MS**

33.23 remained still] **S**– was **MS** remained still with astonishment **TS1**

33.24a lost in] **MS S**– in **TS1**

33.24b that] **TS1**– the **MS**

33.28 lamentable self-possession] **MS TS1r**– self-possession **TS1t**

33.29a of] **TS1**– of | of **MS**

33.29b experience.] **MS E1**– experience. On the contary – it augmented the feeling of unreality which had stolen over me. **TS1t** experience. On the contary – it augmented the feeling of unreality. **TS1r S**

33.30 that boy] **MS** this boy **TS1**–

33.31 touch of weirdness] **MS TS1r**– touch **TS1t**

33.32 fit ... as to] **MS TS1r**– apt to make one doubt **TS1t**

33.33 about me] **TS1**– all about **MS**

33.36–37a The ... familiar!] **TS1**– OM **MS**

33.36a The boy only gazed] **TS1r**– He didn't answer. He gazed **TS1t** OM **MS**

33.36b only gazed] **TS1r S** gazed **E1**–, **TS1t** VAR OM **MS**

33.36–37b with ... somehow] **TS1r**– openmouth[ed] – and somedow **TS1t** OM **MS**

33.39 room] **TS1**– room with intrepidity **MS**

33.40a unknown wild ... excitement] **TS1**– wild beast **MS**

33.40b beast ₍ ₎] **TS1** beast; **S**– VAR **MS**

33.40c but in] **S**– and **TS1** OM **MS**

33.40d Only] **MS S**– Yet **TS1**

34.1 would] **MS S**– could **TS1**

34.1–2 the ... belongs to] **MS TS1r**– that can be only called out by **TS1t**

34.3–4 being ... by] **TS1**– perceiving **MS**

34.4 brothers.] **MS TS1r**– brothers to each other. **TS1t**

34.5–6 dark, instead ... big] **S**– dark unlike the other but he was as big **MS** as big as the other **TS1**

34.6 and] **MS TS1r**– and his **MS**

34.6–7 he ... been] **MS** and had been clearly **TS1t** he had been doubtless **TS1r**–

34.7 which stood in a] **TS1**– in the **MS**

34.8 furthest] **MS**–**A2** farthest **E2**

34.8–9 crumpled white] **MS E1**– white **TS1 S**

34.9a three diamond] **MS S**– diamond **TS1**

34.9b round] **MS S**– big **TS1**

34.10a swarthy. It ... his] **TS1r**– swarthy, and moist with the **MS** swar[h]hy. It was moist and his **TS1t**

34.10b brown] **MS S**– black **TS1**

34.10c hung] **TS1**– hanging **MS**

34.11–12 towards ... foot] **S**– with his foot **MS TS1t** with his foot, towards me **TS1r**

34.14 I] **MS TS1r**– I only **TS1t**

34.15a him] **MS S**– his face **TS1**

34.15b I declared] **TS1**– declared **MS**

34.15c called] **MS S**– called on him **TS1t** called on him only **TS1r**

34.16a obedience to] **TS1**– pursuance of **MS**

34.16b owners'] **MS TS1r**– owner's **TS1t**

34.17a Oh yes.] **MS TS1** Oh! Yes. **S**–

34.17b H'm!] **MS TS1r**– Ah! **TS1t**

34.17–18 saying. . . . But never mind!]
TS1r– saying. MS saying . . . . . never
mind. TS1t

34.18 the scoundrel] TS1– him MS

34.19 time of ... cynicism.] TS1–
time ... MS

34.20 watch.] TS1– watch at once.
MS

34.20–21 It ... port.] TS1– Three
o'clock. MS

34.21 imperiously] TS1r–
ungraciously MS ominously TS1t

34.23a I ... deliberately:] TS1– OM
MS

34.23b I acknowledged] TS1r– I did
not acknowledge TS1t OM MS

34.23c gracious invitation by] TS1r–
invitation otherwise than be TS1t
OM MS

34.24a all] TS1– anything MS

34.24b down."] TS1– down" I said
deliberaty in answer to the gracious
invitation MS

34.25a loud] MS loud and TS1–

34.25b for a moment] TS1– at me
MS

34.26–27a and fierce. It ... suddenly.]
TS1– a fierce like a gigantic tom-cat.
MS

34.26–27b spitting at one suddenly]
TS1r– spitting TS1t OM MS

34.28 him! What ... be?] TS1– *him.*
MS

34.31 I said. "But] TS1– But MS

34.33 He ... back.] TS1r– I went out;
he growled at my back. MS He
followed me growling behind TS1t

34.34 The ... mind to] TS1– See his
impudence. I'll MS

34.37 I ... I won't] TS1– I won't MS

34.39–40 door of ... anteroom.] TS1–
door. MS

34.40a think] TS1– think that MS

34.40b somewhat taken aback] MS S–
disconcerted somewhat TS1

35.1a I will] TS1– I'll MS

35.1b roared suddenly] S– roared MS
TS1

35.2 mulatto lad] S– mulatto MS
youth TS1t yellow youth TS1r

35.2–4 ever dare ... growl] TS1– dare
disturb me any damned skipper
again" MS

35.5a The] MS TS1r– The attenuated
TS1t

35.5b frail ... made] S– frail reed-like
youngster made MS attenuated frail
yellow youngster answered by TS1t
frail yellow youngster produced
TS1r

35.6a short and] MS E1– without
looking back and TS1t short and,
without looking back, TS1r S

35.6b this sufferer] TS1r– that
sufferer MS Jacobus' victim TS1t

35.6–8 It ... floor.] TS1– There was a
hammer on the floor – for opening
wine cases I suppose. MS

35.9–10 when ... at] TS1– the next
time and on MS

35.10 in next] TS1r– in TS1t VAR MS

35.11 Entrenched and quaking]
TS1r– Quakingly entrenched MS
He stood entrenched and quaking
TS1t

35.12a he never looked] MS TS1r–
not daring to look TS1t

35.12b His] MS TS1r– Those TS1t

35.12c lowered] MS S– dropped TS1

35.13a me suddenly] TS1– me MS

35.13b these] MS TS1 those S–

35.14 glued lips] TS1– lips MS

35.14–16 He resembled ... other); he]
S– He MS He resembled both, the
wealthy merchant and the pushing
shopkeeper (who resembled each
other), and that last even more
than the first; which made him
more sympathetic. He TS1

35.16 them] TS1– them both MS

35.17 a big, stout,] S– stout MS two
big, stout, TS1

35.18a man] S– men MS TS1

35.18b his] MS the TS1–

35.18c complexion] MS S– colourin.
g TS1

35.18–19 and ... build which] TS1–
which MS

35.19a his build] TS1r– the form
TS1t OM MS

35.19b   off so completely. Now] **TS1**–
off; but now **MS**

35.19c   saw] **MS S**– perceived **TS1**

35.20   unmistakably ... weakened,]
TS1– the weakened strain **MS**

35.20–21   diluted ... water – and]
TS1– diluted in a bucket of water as
it were – and **MS**

35.21   refrained from finishing] **MS**
S– did not finish **TS1t** failed to
finish **TS1r**

35.22a   had intended] **MS S**– was
going **TS1**

35.22b   the brute's] **ED** the brutes **MS**
his **TS1** this brute's **S**–

35.22–23   I still felt the] **TS1**– The
MS

35.23a   still felt] **TS1r**– felt **TS1t** OM
MS

35.23b   the conclusion] **S**–, **MS VAR**
this conclusion **TS1**

35.23c   to ... is] **TS1**– was sound, but
it's **MS**

35.26a   growl ... back; only,] **TS1**–
growl. Only **MS**

35.26b   only,] **S**–, **MS VAR** but **TS1t** yet
TS1r

35.26c   much] **TS1**– very much **MS**

35.27–28   regret ... me] **TS1**–
slammed the outer door – I am
sorry to say, **MS**

35.29   not ... brought] **MS TS1r**–
appear absurd to you*but I b*ought
TS1t

35.30   that interview] **TS1**– this visit
MS

35.31   a ... later, I] **TS1**– I **MS**

35.32a   his] **TS1**– the **MS**

35.32b   That long, cavern-like] **TS1r**–
That **MS** It was a long cavern-like
TS1t

35.32c   place of business] **MS S**– place
TS1

35.32–33   very ... and] **TS1r**– OM **MS**
TS1t

35.33a   stuffed ... goods] **TS1**– OM **MS**

35.33b   was] **MS TS1r**– and **TS1t**

35.33–34   entered from the street] **S**–
entered **MS TS1**

35.34   far] **MS TS1r**– far off dim **TS1t**

35.34–35   my ... himself] **MS TS1r**–
him very busy **TS1t**

35.35a   amongst] **ED** amongs **MS**
among **TS1**–

35.35b   assistants] **TS1**– assistance
MS

35.35c   captain's] **TS1** captains **MS**
captains' **S**–

35.36   a small] **TS1r**– small **MS** a
square **TS1t**

35.36–37   with ... windows, like] **TS1**–
like **MS**

35.38a   cheerful bottles] **TS1**– bottles
MS

35.38b   several] **TS1**– many **MS**

35.39a   made ... cluster] **TS1**–
clustered **MS**

35.39b   red earthenware] **MS S**–
earthenware **TS1**

35.40–36.1a   which ... world] **TS1**–
covered with a litter of newspapers
MS

35.40   which was littered] **S**– littered
TS1 OM **MS**

35.40–36.1b   all ... world] **S**– Europe
TS1 OM **MS**

36.2a   sitting with a leg] **MS** a leg **TS1t**
one leg **TS1r** sitting with one leg **S**–

36.2b   flung ... put] **S**– thrown over his
knee put **MS** over the knee flung
TS1t flung over the knee put **TS1r**

36.3   sheets briskly] **MS TS1r**– sheets
TS1t

36.4–5   get to know these] **TS1**–
chum with those **MS**

36.5–6   came ... harbour] **TS1**–
merely flitted through **MS**

36.6–7   Theirs was another] **TS1**–
Another **MS**

36.8   hole isn't] **TS1**– hole? Isn't **MS**

36.9   I ... town.] **TS1**– OM **MS**

36.10   so?" I murmured.] **TS1**– so?"
MS

36.11a   I'm] **S**– I am **MS TS1**

36.11b   to-morrow – thank
goodness."] **TS1r**– to-morrow". **MS**
TS1t

36.12   good-natured] **MS TS1r**–
bored **TS1t**

36.13a   I ... draw] **TS1**– He drew **MS**

36.13b the open] **TS1r**– the **MS** an
open **TS1t**

36.13–14 to ... pocket] **TS1**– towards
him **MS**

36.14a take ... out] **S**– take out a big
cigar-case **TS1t** take out a big
cigar-case out **TS1r** OM **MS**

36.14b begin] **TS1**– began **MS**

36.14c it very] **TS1**– his case **MS**

36.15a Presently on] **MS TS1r**– But
happening to look up **TS1t**

36.15b meeting] **MS TS1r**– met and
TS1t

36.15–16 a common] **TS1**– common
MS

36.16 invited] **MS S**– exhorted **TS1**

36.16–17 "They ... smokes."] **TS1**–
OM **MS**

36.17 decent smokes] **S**– quite g*odk
TS1t quite good **TS1r** OM **MS**

36.18a I shook my] **TS1r**– my **TS1t**
OM **MS**

36.18b to-morrow."] **TS1**–
to-morrow" I said **MS**

36.20–21a It ... account.] **TS1**– OM **MS**

36.20 He spreads] **TS1r**– He'll
spread **TS1t** OM **MS**

36.20–21b such little matters] **E1**– it
TS1t those little matters **TS1r S** OM
MS

36.21–22 Why it's business ..."] **TS1**–
It's business – sheer business". **MS**

36.23 fall] **TS1**– come **MS**

36.23–24 well-satisfied ... his] **TS1**–
face – a check in his occupation
with the **MS**

36.24–25 putting ... pocket] **TS1**–
pocketing it **MS**

36.27 noiseless Jacobus] **TS1**–
Jacobus **MS**

36.27–28 room. His ... cordiality.]
TS1– room now in his jacket,
noiseless and cordial. **MS**

36.28 in] **S**– under **TS1** VAR **MS**

36.28–29 He ... he sat] **TS1**– He sat
MS

36.30a nodded ... went] **TS1r**– went
MS TS1t

36.30b nodded again] **S**– nodded
TS1r OM **MS TS1t**

36.31a short, jarring] **MS TS1r**–
jarring short **TS1t**

36.31b laugh. A ... reigned.] **TS1**–
laugh. **MS**

36.31c his] **TS1**– a **MS**

36.32a seemed ... slumbering] **TS1**–
slumbered **MS**

36.32b open-eyed. Yet, somehow,]
TS1r– open eyed; but **MS**
open-eyed and yet somehow **TS1t**

36.33a I ... being] **S**– I felt I was **MS** I
felt myself being **TS1**

36.33b profoundly scrutinised] **TS1**–
scrutinised **MS**

36.34 enormous cavern] **TS1**– cavern
MS

36.34–35 somebody ... case] **TS1**– a
case was being nailed **MS**

36.35 slow] **TS1**– shrill **MS**

36.36a nasal] **TS1**– snappy **MS**

36.36b shrill ... started] **TS1r**– slow
and nasal began **MS** shrill and
happy started **TS1t**

36.37 A ... rope."] **TS1**– Coil manilla
rope. **MS**

36.39–40 shackles." "Right."] **MS**
TS1r– shackles." **TS1t**

37.1a Six tins] **TS1**– Six **MS**

37.1b three of paté, two] **TS1**– two
patés, thre **MS**

37.2 pounds] **MS S**– pound **TS1**

37.4a It's] **MS S**– Its **TS1**

37.4b captain] **TS1**– man **MS**

37.4–5 the immovable Jacobus] **TS1**–
Jacobus **MS**

37.5 Jacobus] **MS TS1r**– Jacobus
without waking up as it were **TS1t**

37.5–6 These ... along.] **TS1**– He has
given a small order. **MS**

37.6 That man will] **TS1r**– He'll **MS**
What man will **TS1t**

37.7a less ... fortnight] **S**– ten days
MS less than ten days **TS1**

37.7b orders] **TS1**– order **MS**

37.8a The calling over of] **MS TS1r**–
The calling ouer **TS1t**

37.8b on] **MS TS1r**– on outside, **TS1t**

37.8–9 an ... articles, paint-brushes,]
TS1– paintbrushes, **MS**

37.10a sacks] **MS** sacks of **TS1**–

37.10b read out] **MS TS1r–** cried
TS1t

37.11–12 At ... animation.] **TS1–**
Jacobus stirred – woke up. **MS**

37.13a smirking, half-caste] **S–** half
caste **MS** smirking mulatto **TS1**

37.13b clerk] **TS1–** assistant **MS**

37.14a stuck behind] **TS1–** behind
MS

37.14b brought in] **TS1–** paraded in
a row **MS**

37.14–15 potatoes which ... row]
TS1– potatoes **MS**

37.16a Being urged] **TS1–** Urged
MS

37.16b cold and] **TS1–** low **MS**

37.17a Calmly] **TS1–** The calm **MS**

37.17b ten or fifteen] **TS1–** fifteen
MS

37.18–20 ears. My ... commodity.]
TS1– ears. **MS**

37.21 trying ... an] **TS1–** taking me
for a **MS**

37.24–25 I wouldn't ... price] **TS1–**
My prices are moderate **MS**

37.26 him that] **E1–** him **MS** him
loftily that **TS1 S**

37.26–27 I even ... knew only] **TS1–** I
knew **MS**

37.27 generally ended] **MS TS1r–**
ended **TS1t**

37.29 I ... his] **TS1–** His was an
admirable **MS**

37.30 waking up somewhat] **TS1–**
suddenly **MS**

37.34 sometimes] **E1–** at times **MS** it
happens sometimes that **TS1 S**

37.35a unsuspected depth] **TS1–**
depth **MS**

37.35b thought; that is, in] **TS1–**
thought. In **MS**

37.36 utters] **TS1–** says **MS**

37.38 went out] **TS1–** went **MS**

37.39 one, Captain. Here] **MS TS1r–**
one here **TS1t**

38.1 remembrance] **TS1–** contrast
MS

38.2a appear] **TS1–** a | appear **MS**

38.2b a quite] **MS** quite a **TS1–**

38.2c sort of fellow] **TS1–** fellow **MS**

38.3–4 could ... possible] **TS1–** had
no **MS**

38.5 this admission was] **MS TS1r–**
these words were **TS1t**

38.6 As ... Jacobus] **TS1r–** Jacobus
suddenly **MS** He did not seem to
have heard them at all; but as if
changing the subject he **TS1t**

38.7a about ten] **TS1–** only a few **MS**

38.7b minutes'] **MS TS1r–** minutes
TS1t

38.7c a beautiful] **TS1–** an **MS**

38.8a really remarkable] **TS1–** out of
the common **MS**

38.8b to] **MS TS1r–** really **TS1t**

38.8–9 come round] **MS TS1r–** come
TS1t

38.9 have a look at] **MS TS1r–** see
TS1t

38.10 seemed] **TS1–** appeared **MS**

38.10–11 too ... in] **TS1–** also love **MS**

38.12a Jacobus' flower-beds] **TS1–**
that enclosed wonder of a garden
MS

38.12–13 He ... tone:] **TS1–** OM **MS**

38.12b added] **TS1r–** added after
tranquily **TS1t** OM **MS**

38.14 my girl there."] **TS1r–** my girl
there" added Jacobus in a homely
tone. **MS** a girl there." **TS1t**

38.15 down everything] **MS**
everything down **TS1–**

38.15–16 order; so ... happened]
TS1– order. Let me revert to **MS**

38.16 before] **TS1–** back **MS**

38.16–17 medical ... at] **TS1–** port
doctor came to attend **MS**

38.18a crew] **TS1–** men **MS**

38.18b and naturally enough he]
TS1r– and of course **MS** Naturally
enough he **TS1t**

38.18–19 to step into] **TS1–** into **MS**

38.19 there too; and] **MS TS1r–**
there; and it came about that **TS1t**

38.20–23 the conversation, ... say.]
TS1– conversation Jacobus' name
was pronounced by the other man I
believe. **MS**

38.23–24 a ... striking in, in] **TS1–**
struck in with **MS**

38.24a striking in,] **S**– saying **TS1** VAR **MS**

38.24b vexed tone:] **TS1 S** expression. **MS** tone: **E1**–

38.25 Ah! You're] **TS1**– Oh! You are **MS**

38.26–28 Of ... say,] **TS1**– I remembered the saying then – it had silenced us at the time – and **MS**

38.29 living] **TS1**– residing **MS**

38.30a hand] **MS S**– head **TS1**

38.30b That] **TS1**– It **MS**

38.31–32 girls, he ... usual.] **TS1**– girls. **MS**

38.32 in ... ransacking] **TS1**– to stop in order to ransack **MS**

38.33 phrase] **TS1**– expression **MS**

38.34 He merely said] **TS1** All he could do was to produce his stereotyped definition **MS** He merely produced his stereotyped definition **S**–

38.36a way,] **MS** bye **TS1**–

38.36b called on] **S**– went to see **MS** have called on **TS1**

38.37 found him] **MS TS1r**– found **TS1t**

38.38 sort of person] **TS1**– person **MS**

39.3 IV] **MS S**– OM **TS1**

39.4 became] **MS TS1r**– seemed to be **TS1t**

39.5–6 One ... it.] **TS1**– My acquaintances ventured on allusions. **MS**

39.6a Maybe] **MS** Perhaps **TS1**–

39.6b talked] **MS TS1r**– spoken **TS1t**

39.6–7 I ... but not] **TS1**– People appeared somewhat scandalised but **MS**

39.6c confess] **S**– say **TS1** VAR **MS**

39.7 scandalized – but] **S**– scandalized than otherwise – but **TS1** VAR **MS**

39.8a remonstrated] **MS S**– even remonstrated **TS1**

39.8b me for my hastiness] **MS TS1r**– me **TS1t**

39.9–11 I ... surprised.] **TS1**– Put in possession of the details he showed no surprise. A mulatto boy? **MS**

39.11a that] **TS1**– it **MS**

39.11b jovial] **TS1**– jocular **MS**

39.12 sort] **TS1**– sort – girls too very likely **MS**

39.14a But there] **S**– There **MS TS1**

39.14b never had] **MS** had never **TS1**–

39.14c open scandal] **MS S**– a scandal **TS1**

39.14–15 scandal in that connection] **S**– scandal **MS** scandal in it of any sort **TS1t** scandal of any sort **TS1r**

39.15a His ... been] **TS1r**– Everything **MS** It had been **TS1t**

39.15b It could cause no] **TS1r**– No **MS** It caused no **TS1t**

39.17 that I ... considerably] **TS1r**– I had been considerably offended **MS** that it had offended me considerably **TS1t**

39.17–18 My interlocutor opened] **TS1**– He made **MS**

39.18a eyes] **TS1**– eyes at that **MS**

39.18b a mulatto ... few] **TS1**– of a cuffs and **MS**

39.19 knocks? That ... surely.] **TS1**– knocks? **MS**

39.20a insolent] **TS1**– lazy **MS**

39.20b truth] **MS** fact **TS1**–

39.21–22 otherwise to ... forgiven] **TS1**– otherwise **MS**

39.23a This ... mine] **MS S**– My interlocutor **TS1**

39.23b belonged to] **TS1**– belonged **MS**

39.24a families,] **TS1**– families – older than Dutch; **MS**

39.24b descendants] **MS S**– remaining **TS1**

39.24–25 the old ... dignified] **TS1**– early colonists, noble, poor, dignified in their **MS**

39.25 dull, dignified] **S**– dignified **TS1** VAR **MS**

39.26a as a rule occupy] **S**– occupy **MS TS1**

39.26b inferior posts] **TS1**– posts **MS**

39.26–27   government ... houses]
    TS1– business or gov^t offices **MS**
39.27   girls] **TS1**– girl **MS**
39.27–29   are ... both] **TS1**– generally
    pretty and bilingual sit at home and
    chatter **MS**
39.30   passes belief] **MS TS1r**– is
    appalling **TS1t**
39.31–32   I ... because some] **TS1**–
    Some **MS**
39.31   a couple] **S**– one **TS1** OM **MS**
39.32a   before] **TS1**– before being **MS**
39.32b   had] **TS1**– had met and had
    MS
39.33a   pleasant, ... was] **S**– pleasant
    ineffectual young man, **MS** young
    man sailor who was **TS1t** young
    man who was **TS1r**
39.33b   there] **TS1**– there and **MS**
39.34a   knowing ... even] **TS1**–
    knowing **MS**
39.34b   home] **TS1**– back **MS**
39.35   two] **MS S**– a **TS1**
39.35–36   rupees or so] **TS1**– rupees
    MS
39.36   the family ... showing] **TS1**– his
    people showed **MS**
39.37–38   intimacy. My ...
    acceptable.] **TS1**– intimacy. **MS**
39.38–40.1   They ... marry] **TS1**–
    Meantime they had married **MS**
40.1a   fellow] **MS S**– young man **TS1**
40.1b   nearly twice] **MS S**– twice **TS1**
40.2a   comparatively] **TS1**– and
    rather **MS**
40.2–3a   off; the ... for.] **TS1**– off. **MS**
40.2b   profession] **TS1r**– occupation
    TS1t OM **MS**
40.2–3b   really fit] **TS1r**– fit **TS1t** OM
    MS
40.3   all cakes] **TS1**– cakes **MS**
40.3–4   called ... couple] **S**– called **MS**
    called on them **TS1**
40.4   devil's] **MS S**– fellow's **TS1**
40.5   a] **TS1**– a a **MS**
40.5–6   reproaches ... at] **TS1**–
    passionate reproaches terrible like
    an bit from **MS**
40.7–8   Of ... him; but] **TS1**– Anyway
    his aunts, **MS**

40.8a   sisters] **TS1**– sister **MS**
40.8b   Angeli] **MS** Angele **TS1**–
40.8–10   the aunts ... relations] **TS1**–
    even a lot of unrelated young ladies
    friends **MS**
40.9   archaic] **MS TS1r**– armchair
    TS1t
40.10–11   a friend ... embarrassing]
    TS1– one of themselves **MS**
40.11   was almost embarrassing]
    TS1r– almost embarrassed me **TS1t**
    VAR **MS**
40.12a   the] **TS1r**– his **MS TS1t**
40.12b   was employed at] **TS1**– had
    MS
40.13   having ... about] **TS1**– talking
    of Jacobus **MS**
40.13–14   merchant Jacobus] **TS1**–
    merchant **MS**
40.14a   attitude] **MS E1**– hastiness
    TS1 S
40.14b   nodded] **TS1**– waggled **MS**
40.14c   head sagely] **TS1**– head **MS**
40.14–15   An influential] **TS1**–
    Influential **MS**
40.15   One ... him.] **TS1**– Might want
    him some day . . . **MS**
40.16   immense preference] **TS1**–
    preference **MS**
40.17a   At that my] **TS1**– My **MS**
40.17b   my friend] **MS TS1r**– he **TS1t**
40.18–19   cried impatiently] **TS1**–
    cried **MS**
40.19–20   He ... go] **TS1**– I have a
    mind to go and see his garden **MS**
40.21   that," he ... that] **TS1**– that." **MS**
40.21–22   fit of laughter] **TS1**– laugh
    MS
40.23a   This was another] **S**– Another
    MS That was another **TS1**
40.23b   altogether] **TS1**– this – quite
    MS
40.23c   At one time the] **TS1**– The
    MS
40.23–24   conscience of the island]
    TS1– conscience **MS**
40.24   mightily troubled] **TS1r**–
    mightily troubled at one time **MS**
    troubled **TS1t**
40.25   brothers] **TS1**– brother **MS**

40.25–26 had ... when] **TS1r**– were excellent friends – in business together Then **MS** had been partners for years when **TS1t**

40.26 to the island] **TS1**– along **MS**

40.27 suddenly infatuated with] **TS1**– infatuated by **MS**

40.27–28 lady-riders. What ... was] **TS1**– lady-riders – notwithstanding **MS**

40.28a He] **TS1**– Well, he **MS**

40.28b even the] **TS1**– the **MS**

40.29 indeed to] **TS1**– to **MS**

40.30–31 His ... scandalous] **TS1**– Behaviour scandalous – awful **MS**

40.31 He followed that] **TS1**– Followed the **MS**

40.31–32 Cape, and ... travelled] **TS1**– Cape; dragged **MS**

40.32 circus to ... world] **TS1**– circus **MS**

40.33a a most] **TS1**– the most **MS**

40.33–34 position. The ... dog.] **TS1**– position; treated worse than a dog. Woman never cared for him. **MS**

40.33b soon ceased to] **TS1r**– did not **TS1t** VAR **MS**

40.35a degradation were reaching] **TS1**– turpitude reached **MS**

40.35b island at the time] **MS** island **TS1t** island at that time **TS1r**–

40.36a not the strength] **TS1**– no strength **MS**

40.36b shake himself free. ...] **TS1**– free himself. **MS**

40.37–39 The ... to the] **TS1**– I listened to this **MS**

40.37 fat] **S**– common fat **TS1** OM **MS**

40.39–40 a tale ... subject] **E1**– the subject **MS** which had been the subject **TS1 S**

40.40 legend, ... poems] **TS1**– poems, of legends of moral fables **MS**

41.1 for] **TS1**– of **MS**

41.4 his brother] **TS1**– the other Jacobus **MS**

41.4–5 her ... circumstances] **S**– as well as the circumstances permitted **MS** her as advantageously as was possible **TS1**

41.6–7 "Oh! The ... A] **TS1**– to the doctor – a **MS**

41.7 very able man. He] **TS1**– clever young fellow who **MS**

41.8a world and ... money] **TS1**– world. There was some money **MS**

41.8b money from her mother] **S**– money **TS1** coming in to her **MS**

41.9–11 Of ... sometimes."] **TS1**– Of course the doctor avoided Jacobus as much as he could. **MS**

41.10 nods] **TS1r**– nods to him **TS1t** OM **MS**

41.11 must happen] **S**– it must happen **TS1r** it happens **TS1t** OM **MS**

41.12 I remarked ... was] **TS1r**– "Surely" I said, "this is **MS** I remarked that this must be **TS1t**

41.13a Jacobus'] **TS1**– Jacobus **MS**

41.13b that] **TS1**– if **MS**

41.14 neither] **TS1**– not **MS**

41.14–16 He ... fellow-citizens.] **TS1**– How did he come back. In a spirit of contrition toward his fellow citizen. Not a bit of it. **MS**

41.16 along] **TS1**– along a child **MS**

41.16–20 a girl ... ¶ "He ... certainly] **TS1**– girl – certainly **MS**

41.18 a daughter] **TS1r**– the daughter **TS1t** OM **MS**

41.20–21 circus-woman," said ... be] **TS1**– circus woman. Very likely **MS**

41.21–22 too; I ... is] **TS1**– too **MS**

41.22 doubt ...] **TS1**– doubt – there's a resemblance I am told. **MS**

41.23–24 brought ... perpetuate] **TS1**– flouted in the face of the community. It was only perpetuating **MS**

41.23 into] **TS1r**– into the midst of **TS1t** VAR **MS**

41.25–26 And that was not the worst. Presently something much more distressing happened. That] **TS1**– And what was more the **MS**

41.26 up.] **TS1**– up too. Later. **MS**

41.26–27 Landed from a] **TS1**– In a Zanzibar **MS**

41.28a What! Here? To] **TS1**– To **MS**

41.28b   child ... suggested] **TS1**– child
– was it? I cried **MS**

41.29a   it] **TS1** she **S**–, **MS** VAR [*see 41.29b*]

41.29b   it" – my ... "Imagine! **TS1**–
she. Imagine **MS**

41.30–31   in Mozambique by] **TS1r**–
by **MS** in Mozambique by | by **TS1t**

41.31–32   She ... injured internally –]
TS1– Injured **MS**

41.32a   internally] **TS1r**– somehow
TS1t OM **MS**

41.32b   horse; she hadn't] **TS1**–
horse, not **MS**

41.33   her when ... ashore;] **TS1**–
her . . . **MS**

41.34   child. At ... life.] **TS1r**– child.
MS child till the last day of her life.
TS1t

41.34–35   Jacobus ... bungalow] **S**–
Jacobus hired a bungalow for her
MS It was in a bungalow Jacobus
had hired for her **TS1**

41.35–39   He ... impenitent.'] **TS1**–
OM **MS**

41.38   the nuns ... woman] **TS1r**– it
was said she had **TS1t** OM **MS**

41.39   It ... Jacobus] **S**– She ordered
him **MS** A man had let out that the
woman had ordered Jacobus **TS1t** It
was even reported that she had
ordered Jacobus **TS1r**

41.40a   This ... why] **TS1**– So **MS**

41.40b   This] **TS1r**– This is **TS1t** OM
MS

42.1a   didn't go] **MS S**– refrained
from going **TS1**

42.1b   himself; he] **S**– for her himself
MS himself; but he **TS1**

42.1c   only put] **MS S**– put **TS1**

42.2a   was to be] **TS1r**– was **MS** would
be **TS1t**

42.2b   seen sometimes] **TS1**– seen **MS**

42.3   she became ... to] **TS1**– she **MS**

42.4a   her hair up] **MS TS1r**– up her
hair **TS1t**

42.4b   I ... has] **S**– she hadn't **MS** I
don't think she **TS1**

42.6   friend, with ... that he] **TS1**–
friend. He **MS**

42.7a   spoken] **TS1**– ever spoken
once **MS**

42.7b   any position] **TS1**– position
MS

42.8–9   island; that ... position] **TS1**–
island. An old poor relation of
Jacobus acted as **MS**

42.8a   island; that] **MS TS1r**– island.
That **TS1t** VAR **MS**

42.8b   an elderly] **S**– a distant **TS1**
VAR **MS**

42.8c   brothers] **TS1r**– brother's **TS1t**
VAR **MS**

42.8d   had] **TS1r**– has **TS1t** VAR **MS**

42.9–10   of gouvernante] **TS1r**– a sort
of gouvernante **MS** of a sort of
gouvernante **TS1t**

42.10a   the girl] **TS1**– her **MS**

42.10b   business] **TS1**– business of
provision merchant **MS**

42.10c   certainly annoyed] **TS1**–
annoyed **MS**

42.11–13   part. It ... equals.] **TS1**–
part. **MS**

42.13–14   The ... tact – only, he] **TS1**–
Only the man **MS**

42.15   For why] **TS1**– Why **MS**

42.15–16   It was most] **TS1r**– Most **MS**
It's most **TS1t**

42.18   could ... from saying] **TS1**– said
MS

42.19   employed her, say,] **S**–
employed **MS** had kept her **TS1**

42.19–20   in ... occasionally] **TS1**–
and **MS**

42.20–22   ears, the ... belongs] **TS1**–
ears from time to time it would
regularise the position in the eyes
of respectability **MS**

42.23   was] **TS1**– did **MS**

42.25–26   You ... forget.] **TS1**– A
scandal is a scandal. **MS**

42.27–28   had ... into] **TS1**– were **MS**

42.28–30   Of ... anybody] **TS1**– Who,
do you think, will have the face **MS**

42.31a   When ... me] **TS1**– And he
left me. Alone **MS**

42.31b   my friend] **S**– he **TS1**, **MS** VAR

42.31c   conception] **S**– momentary
conception **MS** distinct vision **TS1**

42.32 existing, a ... castaways] **S–**
existing alone **MS** living as lonely as
a pair of castaways **TS1**

42.33a the girl] **MS S–** she **TS1**

42.33b if it ... cliff] **S–** in a cavern **MS**
if in a safe cavern **TS1**

42.34 going ... beach] **TS1–** scouring
the beach to pick up a living for
both **MS**

42.34–35 exactly ... for] **S–** and
everlastingly hoping like all
castaways for **MS** exactly like two
shipwrecked people on a desert
island have always the hope of some
ship being sighted of **TS1t** exactly
like two shipwrecked people on a
desert island, who always hope for
TS1r

42.36 back at ... of] **TS1–** back to
MS

42.37a But] **TS1–** Only **MS**

42.37b Jacobus'] **TS1r–** Jacobus **MS**
the man's **TS1t**

42.37c in with] **TS1–** with **MS**

42.37d view.] **MS TS1r–** view. I forgot
it promptly. **TS1t**

42.38 When he] **TS1r–** He **MS** The
once or twice he **TS1t**

42.38–39 in the ... satisfied – and]
TS1– regularly but **MS**

42.40–43.1 the harbour ...
enunciation] **TS1–** his placid
harbour gossip **MS**

43.1a had then] **S–** had **MS TS1**

43.1b own] **TS1–** own then **MS**

43.1–7 My ... about.] **TS1–** My
loading was stopped for want of
bags of a certain size. **MS**

43.4–5 pockete] **TS1r** pockets **TS1t**
S– OM **MS**

43.7 consignees] **TS1–** consignee **MS**

43.8 who ... now in] **TS1–** so hearty at
first, now as **MS**

43.9a charterers] **MS TS1r–** charters
TS1t

43.9b listened to] **TS1–** received **MS**

43.9c with] **MS S–** with a manner of
TS1

43.10 Their manager, the] **TS1–** The
MS

43.11a prudishly] **MS TS1r–**
promptly **TS1t**

43.11b didn't] **TS1–** did not **MS**

43.11c the impure Jacobus] **MS S–**
Jacobus **TS1**

43.13–14 was ... a condescending]
TS1– condescended a **MS**

43.15–16 before ... charter-party]
TS1– of Bags **MS**

43.16 for ... delay] **TS1–** your look
out **MS**

43.17 of ... any] **TS1–** we had no idea
of taking **MS**

43.17–18 advantage. This ... really.]
TS1– advantage. **MS**

43.18a is] **S–** is however **TS1** OM **MS**

43.18b ourselves] **TS1–** too **MS**

43.19 unawares," he ... obvious] **TS1–**
unawares." ¶ Which was a **MS**

43.20 lecture I confess] **TS1–** lecture
MS

43.20–21 thirsty. Suppressed ...
effect] **TS1–** thirsty – common
effect of suppressed rage **MS**

43.21 as I] **MS TS1r–** I **TS1t**

43.21–22 strolled on aimlessly I
bethought myself of the tall
earthen-ware pitcher] **TS1–** went
along I remembered the drinks
MS

43.22 captain's] **MS TS1** captains' **S–**

43.23 Jacobus "store] **TS1r–** 'Store
MS TS1t

43.24a no more than] **TS1–** merely
MS

43.24b found assembled] **TS1–**
found **MS**

43.25 down] **TS1–** myself **MS**

43.25–26 deep, ... I] **TS1–** glass of
water – then another – and **MS**

43.27 The] **TS1–** The | the **MS**

43.27–28 read, ... chaff] **TS1–** made
the usual noise of such a gathering
MS

43.28 chaff. But ... respected.] **TS1–**
chaff. **MS**

43.29–32 out, only ... away? You]
TS1r– out. In the bustle of the store
I was accosted by the outcast
Jacobus. ¶ "You **MS**

43.30   store] **MS TS1r**– bulky store
TS1t

43.33   these ... notice] **TS1**– I notice
for the last few days, Captain **MS**

43.34–35   He ... note.] **TS1**– OM **MS**

43.35–36   amenity, but ... amenity]
TS1– but friendly; and I have been
unused to kindness **MS**

43.36–38   do ... that] **TS1**– really
believe **MS**

43.38a   suggest] **S**– propose me **MS**
TS1

43.38b   of] **TS1**– of a bottle of **MS**

43.39a   Tonic] **TS1**– tonic **MS**

43.39b   kept] **TS1**– had **MS**

44.1   broad mask ... lips] **TS1**– mask
MS

44.2   at] **TS1**– at at **MS**

44.3   exclaiming] **MS**–**A1 E2**
explaining **A2**

44.4   eleven hundred] **TS1**– 1000 **MS**

44.4–5   to be found in] **TS1**– in **MS**

44.5   only a] **TS1**– a **MS**

44.6–8   Again ... sure.] **TS1**– "To be
sure! To be sure". His voice came
quietly through the noise of the
store. **MS**

44.8   then people] **TS1r**– people **MS**
those **TS1t**

44.8–9   of ... want] **TS1**– wouldn't
wish **MS**

44.9a   They'd] **TS1r**– They would **MS**
They **TS1t**

44.9b   that size] **TS1**– it **MS**

44.10–11   me. Impossible to buy.]
TS1– me! **MS**

44.11–12   want to. It ... up.] **TS1**–
care. to buy. **MS**

44.12   But ... discover] **TS1**– Only if
found **MS**

44.15–16   I ... with] **TS1**– His eyes
fixed on me had **MS**

44.16   heavy eyes] **E1**– eyes **TS1 S**, **MS**
VAR

44.17a   of a man] **E1**– if **MS** of a man
resting **TS1 S**

44.17b   some soul-shaking] **TS1**– a
mental **MS**

44.17–18   crisis. Then suddenly:]
TS1– crisis **MS**

44.19–20   quietly here," ... busy.]
TS1– here" he whispered. **MS**

44.20a   and ... in] **TS1**– to **MS**

44.20b   It's] **TS1**– Its **MS**

44.21   minutes'] **S**– minutes **MS TS1**

44.22   coat and ... himself] **TS1**– coat
MS

44.23a   have to] **TS1**– take me there
and **MS**

44.23b   store at once] **TS1**– store **MS**

44.23–24   or ... liberty to] **TS1**– to
conclude some business. Then we
could **MS**

44.24   over with me] **TS1**– over **MS**

44.25   quarter] **TS1**– the **MS**

44.25–29   This ... wondering.] **TS1**–
¶ His eyes rested on me searchingly
I couldn't imagine why. I looked at
him in silence **MS**

44.26   lips; his] **TS1r**– lips and a **TS1t**
VAR **MS**

44.27   for] **TS1** as **S**– VAR **MS**

44.29   for in me] **S**– for **TS1** VAR **MS**

44.30–31   "I ... will?"] **TS1**– "Will you
wait at my home?" **MS**

44.32   course," I cried.] **TS1**– course".
MS

44.34a   not," I said. "I] **TS1**– not. I **MS**

44.34b   expect] **TS1**– ask for **MS**

44.35a   the move] **MS TS1r**– what
TS1t

44.35b   I've] **TS1**– I have **MS**

44.37a   I'll] **TS1**– I will **MS**

44.37b   my] **MS** the **TS1**–

44.37–38   I'll ... like.] **MS TS1r**– Wait!
TS1t

44.37c   wait for you] **TS1r**– wait **MS**
OM **TS1t**

44.38   What ... port.] **TS1**– OM **MS**

44.39a   word] **MS** words **TS1**–

44.39b   had set] **TS1**– set **MS**

44.39–40   swinging ... and] **TS1**–
brisk pace, and very soon **MS**

45.1a   completely ... paved with] **TS1**–
paved **MS**

45.1b   traffic] **S**– people **TS1** OM **MS**

45.2   grass tufts] **TS1**– grass, and of a
rustic aspect **MS**

45.3a   roadway] **MS S**– street **TS1**

45.3b   a single] **TS1**– single **MS**

45.3c on ... stones] **TS1r–** elevated on a basement **MS** on an elevated rough wall **TS1t**

45.4 level ... windows] **TS1–** window sills **MS**

45.5 along] **TS1–** past **MS**

45.5–6 All ... asleep] **TS1–** It slumbered with shut jalousies **MS**

45.7a at the side] **TS1–** round the corner **MS**

45.7b an alley ... street] **TS1–** a grass-grown alley **MS**

45.9a With ... of] **TS1–** Jacobus muttered an **MS**

45.9b apology] **TS1–** apologies **MS**

45.9c me the way] **TS1–** the way **MS**

45.9–10 Jacobus preceded] **TS1–** and led **MS**

45.10a and ... naked] **TS1–** across a **MS**

45.10b parquet] **TS1–** parqueted **MS**

45.11 what ... the] **TS1–** the **MS**

45.11–12 It ... which] **TS1–** Three glass doors lighted it. They **MS**

45.12 open onto a] **TS1–** open. Outside there was **MS**

45.13a running its] **TS1–** of **MS**

45.13b along] **TS1–** the full extent of **MS**

45.13–14 garden side ... house] **TS1–** garden-side **MS**

45.14 really ... garden] **TS1–** magnificent **MS**

45.14–15 smooth ... maze] **TS1r–** smooth lawns, a maze **MS** lawns and a maze **TS1t**

45.15–16 displayed around] **TS1–** round **MS**

45.16a a basin] **TS1–** a | a basin **MS**

45.16b framed in] **TS1–** with **MS**

45.16c marble] **MS TS1t S–** white marble **TS1r**

45.16–17 rim, and in] **S–** rim. In **MS** rim; in **TS1**

45.17a massed] **TS1–** varied **MS**

45.17b varied] **TS1–** big **MS**

45.17–18 trees concealing ... houses.] **TS1–** trees. No roofs were visible. **MS**

45.18–19 It ... drowsing] **TS1–** And all this drowsed **MS**

45.19a drowsing] **TS1r–** gorgeous and drowsy **TS1t** VAR **MS**

45.19b a warm, voluptuous] **S–** a voluptuous **MS** the profound **TS1**

45.20a Where ... and in] **TS1–** In **MS**

45.20b and in] **TS1r–** in **TS1t, MS** VAR [see 45.20a]

45.21a massed colours] **TS1–** colours **MS**

45.21–22 had ... effect] **TS1–** blazed magnificently **MS**

45.21b had] **S–** glowed with **TS1** VAR **MS**

45.22 entranced] **E1–** admiring **MS** as if entranced **TS1 S**

45.22–23 grasped ... impelling me] **TS1–** impelled me gently **MS**

45.25 occupied] **MS TS1r–** sat in **TS1t**

45.25–26 deep wicker-work] **TS1–** wicker-work **MS**

45.26 saw her] **MS TS1r–** saw **TS1t**

45.27 arm] **TS1–** shoulder **MS**

45.28 tranquilly; and his] **TS1–** tranquilly. His **MS**

45.29–30 so ... communication] **TS1–** like a confidence – so **MS**

45.30 fancied ... and] **TS1–** nearly nodded understandingly **MS**

45.32–33 Neither ... she] **TS1–** For a long time the girl **MS**

45.33 girl] **E1–, MS** VAR seated girl **TS1 S**

45.34a vision] **TS1–** passage **MS**

45.34b some] **MS TS1r–** a **TS1t**

45.34–35 pageant passing ... garden] **TS1–** pageant **MS**

45.35 rich glow] **MS TS1r–** glow **TS1t**

45.37 coming to] **TS1–** at **MS**

45.39–40 If ... unaware] **TS1–** I am certain she had not been aware **MS**

45.40– presence till ... side] **TS1–**
46.1 presence **MS**

46.1 quickened upward movement] **TS1–** widening **MS**

46.1–3 heavy ... stare] **TS1–** stare **MS**

46.2a eyelids] **TS1r–** eyelids widening **TS1t** OM **MS**

46.2b   glance] **TS1r**– glances **TS1t** OM **MS**

46.2–3   fixed stare] **TS1r**– stare **TS1t**, **MS** VAR

46.3–5   doubt. ¶ Under ... anger.] **TS1**– doubt. **MS**

46.5a   name fairly loud] **TS1**– name **MS**

46.5b   said] **MS E1**– told me **TS1 S**

46.6   be gone] **TS1**– be **MS**

46.7a   away] **TS1**– off **MS**

46.7b   Before I ... I] **TS1**– I **MS**

46.7c   time] **TS1r**– the time **TS1t** OM **MS**

46.8   who I remembered suddenly] **TS1**– who **MS**

46.9a   man] **MS** any man **TS1**–

46.9b   that] **TS1**– the **MS**

46.9c   since she] **TS1**– she **MS**

46.10   It] **MS S**– I saw that it **TS1**

46.11   again since ... up; it] **TS1**– since. It **MS**

46.12–13a   high ... down] **TS1**– on the top of her head. Untidy wisps hung **MS**

46.12–13b   long untidy] **TS1r**– wavy **TS1t** VAR **MS**

46.13   her] **MS** the **TS1**–

46.13–15   face; a ... a] **TS1**– face. The mass gave one the **MS**

46.15–16   heavy ... impression] **TS1**– weight and **MS**

46.17a   As she] **TS1** She **MS S**–

46.17b   hugging herself with] **TS1**– with **MS**

46.17–19   legs, a ... body] **TS1**– legs, **MS**

46.20   I ... slight] **MS S**– She had even a **TS1t** She gave even a **TS1r**

46.21–22   away. They ... by] **TS1r**– away. Followed **MS** away followed by **TS1t**

46.23–24   (for ... repressed] **TS1**– once repressed | once repressed (I was startled too) **MS**

46.24   placed it] **TS1r**– and placing it **MS** standing there **TS1t**

46.25   her, sat ... and] **TS1**– her **MS**

46.26a   not] **MS S**– not for **TS1**

46.26b   a gentle caressing] **TS1**– an gentle **MS**

46.27–30   I ... flight.] **TS1**– OM **MS**

46.28   or] **TS1r** or even **TS1t** nor **S**– OM **MS**

46.29   my way] **S**– up **TS1** OM **MS**

46.30a   taking flight] **TS1r**– bounding away **TS1t** OM **MS**

46.30b   these] **MS TS1** those **S**–

46.31   in] **MS** with **TS1**–

46.31–32   Ultimately I] **MS S**– I **TS1**

46.32a   formed a notion] **TS1r**– arrived at the conclusion **MS** formed at notion **TS1t**

46.32b   her perhaps from] **S**– from **MS** her from **TS1**

46.32–33   going ... leap] **TS1**– taking a flight **MS**

46.34   thing ... person] **MS S**– part of her covering **TS1**

46.35a   on] **TS1**– on her **MS**

46.35b   that] **TS1**– a **MS**

46.35c   amber] **S**– amber coloured **MS** thin **TS1**

46.35–36   must ... character] **TS1**– she wore, was hardly worth speaking of **MS**

46.36   airy] **S**– scanty **TS1** VAR **MS**

46.36–37   One ... felt it] **TS1**– It was **MS**

46.38a   embarrassment] **TS1**– shyness **MS**

46.38b   is] **MS TS1r**– may be **TS1t**

46.39–40a   I ... softness, the] **TS1**– The **MS**

46.39–40b   Alice. I ... talking] **E1**– Alice, and all the time I talked on **TS1** Alice, and all the time I went on talking **S** OM **MS**

46.40   softness] **S**– urbanity **TS1** OM **MS**

47.1   never before] **MS S**– never **TS1**

47.2   adding] **TS1**– added **MS**

47.3a   should have] **MS TS1r**– had **TS1t**

47.3b   but it did. And] **MS S**– and **TS1**

47.4   cut short] **MS S**– cut **TS1**

47.4–5   flow ... speech] **S**– fine speeches **MS** flow of words **TS1**

47.6a   The scream] **MS S**– It **TS1**

47.6b   was emitted] **MS TS1r**– was
TS1t

47.7   turn my head] **TS1**– turn **MS**

47.7–8   understood ... that] **TS1**–
guessed **MS**

47.8a   was] **TS1**– to be **MS**

47.8b   elderly] **S**– poor **MS** destitute
TS1

47.8–9   relation ... companion,]
TS1r– relation – **MS** relation, the
companion, **TS1t**

47.9   she] **MS TS1r**– she still **TS1t**

47.10   her a low] **MS S**– a solemn **TS1t**
her a solemn low **TS1r**

47.11a   Jacobus'] **TS1**– Mr Jacobus'
MS

47.11b   spent] **MS E1**– passed **TS1 S**

47.12–13   a large, ... eyes] **TS1**– an old
lemon **MS**

47.14a   garment] **TS1**– single
garment **MS**

47.14b   some ... light] **S**– ashcoloured
silky **MS** some ashcoloured, silky,
TS1

47.15a   thick neck down] **TS1**– neck
right **MS**

47.15b   her] **TS1**– hear **MS**

47.15c   toes ... of] **TS1**– to feet like
MS

47.16   It made her appear] **TS1**– he
appeared in it **MS**

47.18a   say a word] **TS1**– open my
mouth **MS**

47.18b   presently] **TS1**– very soon **MS**

47.19a   sounds and protestations] **MS**
voices **TS1** questions and
protestations **S** protestations **E1**–

47.19b   in] **MS TS1r**– an **TS1t**

47.20a   Obviously no] **MS TS1r**– no
TS1t

47.20b   got] **TS1**– came **MS**

47.20c   there] **MS TS1r**– into the
house **TS1t**

47.20–21   In a moment with] **TS1**–
With **MS**

47.21a   from] **TS1**– on the part of **MS**

47.21b   women following her] **TS1**–
women **MS**

47.22a   waddled] **MS E1**– toddled **TS1**
S

47.22b   the doorway, infuriated] **S**–
us – infuriated **MS** the doorway **TS1**

47.24–25   She ... chair.] **TS1**– OM **MS**

47.25a   posed on] **TS1r**– on **TS1t** OM
MS

47.25b   I ... her.] **MS TS1r**– OM **TS1t**

47.26   into] **MS E1**– on **TS1t** of **TS1r S**

47.27   street?"] **MS E1**– house." **TS1 S**

47.28a   Her] **MS S**– She had **TS1**

47.28b   narrow, long in shape,] **MS**
which **TS1** narrowed, long in shape,
S–

47.29a   undefinable] **MS** indefinable
TS1–

47.29b   expression;] **MS** expression,
then **TS1**–

47.29c   contemptuous] **TS1**– scornful
MS

47.30a   let fall] **MS S**– said **TS1**

47.30b   French a ... explanation:] **S**–
French. **MS TS1**

47.33   in order to drive] **TS1**– drove
MS

47.34a   and] **MS** then **TS1**–

47.34b   person] **TS1**– face **MS**

47.34–36   a peculiar ... she] **TS1**– her
one-eyed fashion **MS**

47.35   one small eye] **S**– one **TS1t** one
eye **TS1r** VAR **MS**

47.36   verandah,] **TS1**– verandah.
She **MS**

47.37   away] **TS1**– off **MS**

47.37–38   her ... table] **TS1r**– her
knitting **MS** some knitting work
from a little table **TS1t**

47.39   the mop ... hair] **TS1**– her grey
mop **MS**

48.1   clung to] **MS E1**– defined **TS1 S**

48.1–2   ancient, stumpy] **MS TS1r**–
ancient, **TS1t**

48.2   cotton stockings] **TS1**–
stockings **MS**

48.3–4   slippers. Her ... visible] **TS1**–
slippers, propping her feet **MS**

48.4   foot rest. She ... rock] **S**– foot
rest obtrusively. She knitted,
rocking **MS** foot-rest as she rocked
TS1

48.4–5   slightly while she knitted]
TS1– slightly **MS**

48.5 I ... for I] **TS1**– I **MS**

48.6 to depart.] **MS E1**– out of the house? **TS1 S**

48.7–8 She ... she] **TS1**– She **MS**

48.8–9 girl in ... colloquially] **TS1**– girl a question in French **MS**

48.10 your] **MS S**– you **TS1**

48.11 comprehensively] **TS1**– violently **MS**

48.12a her ... wrapper] **TS1**– the chair creaked **MS**

48.12b that] **TS1**– her **MS**

48.13 unexpectedly] **MS TS1r**– unexpected **TS1t**

48.13–14 which ... certain] **TS1**– like some **MS**

48.14a senses,] **E1**– senses, you know, **TS1 S** OM **MS**

48.14b natural, rough] **TS1**– rough natural **MS**

48.16 alone – will you!"] **TS1**– alone." **MS**

48.17–18 The ... whistle:] **MS TS1r**– OM **TS1t**

48.17a rocking chair nodded] **MS** chair rocked **TS1r**– OM **TS1t**

48.17b woman's] **MS** thin **TS1r**– OM **TS1t**

48.17c piped] **MS** was **TS1r**– OM **TS1t**

48.19–20 "You ... nothing – that's] **TS1**– "A pair of you! He's up to anything. That's **MS**

48.20 didn't] **TS1**– did not **MS**

48.21 thought ... time] **TS1**– judged opportune **MS**

48.21–23 some ... Jacobus.] **TS1**– my french in a modest remark that I was there on business. **MS**

48.24–27 Then ... him?"] **TS1**– Go to the shop for business. **MS**

48.26–27 the shop ... him] **S**– wait for him there **TS1** VAR **MS**

48.28a The furious] **TS1**– To look at the **MS**

48.28b fingers ... needles] **TS1**– knitting **MS**

48.30 girl – is ... call] **TS1**– girl! . . You call that **MS**

48.31a suavely] **MS S**– urbanely **TS1**

48.31b I ... unexpected] **E1**– I call that **MS** That's pleasure – an unexpected **TS1 S**

48.33 angry] **MS TS1r**– irritated **TS1t**

48.34a leaning] **TS1**– took **MS**

48.34–35 elbow ... undoubtedly] **TS1**– Jacobus chin in her hand **MS**

48.34b knee] **TS1** knees **S**– OM **MS**

48.35 And those] **TS1**– Her **MS**

48.36a this] **TS1**– the **MS**

48.36b irritated] **MS TS1r**– ****** **TS1t**

48.36–37 the wealthy merchant, the] **TS1**– the **MS**

48.37–39 The ... them.] **TS1**– She reminded me of both. **MS**

48.39 sort ... remote] **TS1r** surprising **MS** sort of surprise by remote **TS1t** sort of surprising remote **S**–

48.40 both ... rather] **TS1**– they were **MS**

48.40–41 men after all] **TS1**– men **MS**

49.1 stare] **MS E1**– look hard **TS1 S**

49.2 again ... even] **TS1**– with a still **MS**

49.4 broke ... shrill:] **TS1r**– interfered shrilly **MS** broke in blunt and shrill. ¶ "Go and put on your corsets and a petticoat at least." ¶ "Wont." **TS1t**

49.5 "Hear his impudence.] **TS1**– "The impudence! **MS**

49.6 this sailor] **TS1**– that **MS**

49.8a The sun] **MS TS1r**– This from an unselfish point of view seemed to me sound advice. The sun **TS1t**

49.8–9 leave the ... lands] **TS1**– depart **MS**

49.8b Pearl of the Ocean] **MS TS1r**– pearl of the ocean **TS1t**

49.9 walled garden full of shadows] **TS1**– shadows of the walled garden **MS**

49.9–10 blazed ... if] **TS1**– blazed with **MS**

49.10 flowers] **MS TS1r**– flowers themselves **TS1t**

49.10–11 were giving ... day] **TS1**– giving up their colours at the fall of the dusk **MS**

49.11–12 The amazing old woman became very explicit. She suggested to the girl] **TS1**– The amazing old woman suggested cynically **MS**

49.12a suggested ... girl] **TS1r**– mentioned **TS1t** VAR **MS**

49.12b a cynical] **TS1**– an **MS**

49.13a humiliated ... account] **MS S**– made me feel of less account to these women **TS1**

49.13b humiliated] **S**– angered **MS** VAR **TS1**

49.13c than] **MS TS1r**– that **TS1t**

49.14–15 The ... out: ¶ "Shan't."] **TS1**– ¶ "Shan't" the girl snapped out **MS**

49.16 naughty retort] **TS1**– naughtiness **MS**

49.16–18 child; it ... relations.] **TS1**– child tho'. **MS**

49.18–19 with furious accuracy] **TS1**– rapid and furious **MS**

49.19 fastened down on] **TS1r**– fastened on **MS** down on **TS1t**

49.20 "Oh ... father. And] **TS1**– "And **MS**

49.21 by a] **TS1**– quasi naked by that **MS**

49.22 off] **TS1**– off – you **MS**

49.24 sorceress"] **MS TS1r**– witch" **TS1t**

49.24–25 distinctly, preserving ... pose,] **TS1**– distinctly, **MS**

49.25a in] **MS TS1r**– an **TS1t**

49.25b and] **TS1**– and with **MS**

49.25c stare ... garden] **TS1**– look **MS**

49.26 woman] **TS1**– woman with a visible play of thick limb in the weird thin garment **MS**

49.27 her] **MS** the **TS1**–

49.27–29 chair, banged ... stirred.] **TS1**– chair. **MS**

49.28a thick limb] **TS1r**–, **MS** VAR limb **TS1t** [see 49.26]

49.28b that] **TS1r**– the **TS1t** OM **MS**

49.29–30 I ... when] **TS1**– But **MS**

49.30–33 that ... me] **TS1**– the girl's immobility she turned on me, a knitting needle in hand poised **MS**

49.33 be to throw it] **TS1r**– throw **TS1t** VAR **MS**

49.34a used ... scratch] **TS1**– scratched **MS**

49.34b with] **TS1**– with it **MS**

49.35a the ... close] **TS1**– with a whimsical grimace, a short **MS**

49.35b shut] **MS E1**– closed **TS1 S**

49.35–36 and ... grimace] **TS1**– OM **MS**

49.37a dear] **E1**– good **MS–S**

49.37b man," she ... "do] **TS1**– man. Do **MS**

49.39a "I do ... indeed] **TS1**– "Indeed I hope so **MS**

49.39b tried to speak in] **TS1**– tried **MS**

49.40 "You see I] **TS1**– "I **MS**

50.1a Didn't I hear] **TS1**– Weren't **MS**

50.1b forth] **TS1**– out **MS**

50.5a "Grave! What] **TS1**– "What **MS**

50.5b me? Buried] **TS1r**– me, buried **MS TS1t**

50.5c alive before ... for] **TS1**– alive **MS**

50.6–7 cried; and ... me:] **TS1**– cried. She turned to me. **MS**

50.6 and] **TS1r**– the **TS1t** VAR **MS**

50.7a "You're] **TS1**– "You are **MS**

50.7b these] **MS–A1 A2a** those **E2 A2b**

50.8a Well – why don't] **MS TS1r**– Well **TS1t**

50.8b good fellow] **MS TS1r**– boy **TS1t**

50.9 It ... peace"!] **TS1**– What a tone! **MS**

50.9–10 sort of ruffianly] **TS1**– ruffianly **MS**

50.10 a superiority, a scorn] **TS1**– a scorn **MS**

50.10–13 more ... years.] **TS1**– frequently. **MS**

50.14a No, you] **TS1**– You **MS**

50.14b very ... this] **TS1**– mistaken to think that her **MS**

50.14c this] **TS1r**– her **MS** my **TS1t**

50.15a had ... away] **MS TS1r**– would turn me off **TS1t**

50.15b was not] **TS1**– wasn't **MS**

50.16 grotesque and ruffianly] **TS1**– ruffianly **MS**

50.16–17 woman. ¶ And ... bags.] **TS1**– woman and then – business. The sacred business. **MS**

50.18 made me stay to] **MS TS1r**– kept me to **TS1t**

50.19 didn't] **TS1**– did not **MS**

50.19–20 know ... me] **TS1r**– see his way much **MS** know that he could do anything for me **TS1t**

50.20–21 He ... feared. . . .] **TS1**– OM **MS**

50.21 did not] **TS1**– didn't **MS**

50.22 We ... table; the] **TS1**– The **MS**

50.23a "Won't," ... care"] **TS1**– Shants, Won't's and Don't care's **MS**

50.23b conveyed and affirmed] **TS1**– conveyed **MS**

50.24a come ... table] **TS1**– leave the verandah and **MS**

50.24b not to have] **TS1r**–, **MS** VAR nor to have **TS1t**

50.25 not ... verandah] **E1**– we were only three at table **MS** to stay in the verandah **TS1t** and to stay in the verandah **TS1r S**

50.25–26 about in ... slippers] **MS TS1r**– about **TS1t**

50.30–32 I ... us.] **TS1**– OM **MS**

50.31 condescend to raise] **TS1r**– raise **TS1t** OM **MS**

50.32a sound] **TS1**– appear **MS**

50.32b and yet] **TS1**– but **MS**

50.32–33 that ... had] **ED** her petulant stormy sullenness had **MS** in that stony petulance stare was **TS1t** that stony, petulant sullenness had **TS1r**–

50.34–35 And ... while she] **TS1**– She **MS**

50.34 to] **ED** to to **TS1** to the **S**– OM **MS**

50.35 staring in] **S**– in **MS** staring into **TS1**

50.36a dark] **S**–, **MS** VAR dark garden **TS1**

50.36b feeding ... on the] **S**– to feed her temper on the **MS** feeding her

excitement of **TS1t** feeding her bad temper of **TS1r**

50.36c heavily scented] **TS1**– scented **MS**

50.36–37 air of ... garden] **MS S**– air **TS1**

50.38a come next day] **TS1**– return **MS**

50.38b to] **MS TS1r**– and to **TS1t**

50.40 slightly at that] **TS1**– slightly **MS**

51.1a house daily] **TS1**– daily house **MS**

51.1b till] **MS TS1t S**– till till **TS1r**

51.1c You'll] **TS1**– You shall **MS**

51.3a His ... smile] **TS1r**– His smile **MS** He had his faint melancholy smile which **TS1t**

51.3b thick lips] **TS1**– lips **MS**

51.4 That will] **TS1**– That'll **MS**

51.6a earnestly the] **TS1r**– the earnest **MS** earnestly a **TS1t**

51.6b recommendation] **MS TS1r**– recommendation to **TS1t**

51.7a the ... about] **S**– hinted at **MS** something fainter about **TS1**

51.7b a "plate] **MS** "a plate **TS1**–

51.7–8 It was only on] **TS1r**– On **MS** It was only when making **TS1t**

51.8–9 down ... remembered] **TS1**– I remembered that **MS**

51.9–10 that ... family] **TS1**– with the **S** — family that evening **MS**

51.9 very] **TS1**–**E1 A2 E2** every **A1** OM **MS**

51.10 at my forgetfulness] **MS** with my forgetfulness **TS1r**– with myself **TS1t**

51.11a awkward] **TS1**– difficult **MS**

51.11b it] **MS TS1r**– this **TS1t**

51.12a procured me a] **TS1r**– procured for me a **MS** been much **TS1t**

51.12b amusing evening] **MS TS1r**– amusing **TS1t**

51.12–13 And ... sacred business . . .] **TS1**– OM **MS**

51.14 overtook] **TS1**– passed **MS**

51.15 landing steps] **TS1**– steps **MS**

51.15–16 boatman, who ... kitchen]
TS1– boatman **MS**

51.17 my] **TS1**– the **MS**

51.18 occasions] **MS E1**– evenings
TS1 S

51.19–25 He ... well.] **TS1** OM **MS S–**

51.26 V] **MS S**– OM **TS1**

51.27a For I] **TS1** I **MS S–**

51.27b haunted] **TS1**– was
perpetually haunting **MS**

51.27–29 home. He ... "store."] **TS1**–
home. **MS**

51.30 Alice] **TS1**– daughter **MS**

51.30–34 his doorstep; and ... smile.]
TS1– the doorstep. **MS**

51.33 my] **TS1**r– by **TS1**t OM **MS**

51.35 often ... before] **TS1**– Alice –
right in front of **MS**

51.35–36 would address] **TS1**–
addressed **MS**

51.38 There ... when] **TS1**–
Sometimes **MS**

51.38–52.1 I must ... swearing] **TS1**–
tempted to swear **MS**

52.1 was blue] **MS TS1**r– blue **TS1**t

52.1–2 fancied ... so] **TS1**– had done
so I fancy **MS**

52.2 not ... muscle] **TS1**– have
remained unmoved **MS**

52.3 shady, intimate] **TS1**r– shady **MS**
horrible **TS1**t

52.5 that the] **MS** the **TS1**–

52.5–6 in the same way] **TS1–A2** as
MS in the same way as **E2**

52.7–8 otherwise? She ... father.]
TS1– otherwise? **MS**

52.8 received] **MS** seen **TS1**–

52.9–10 the low ... port] **TS1**– a low
lot **MS**

52.10 account. So] **TS1**– account,
and so (the old woman hinted)
MS

52.11 people of] **TS1**– people in **MS**

52.12 do with] **TS1**– say to **MS**

52.12–13 something wicked] **MS S**–
something **TS1**

52.13–17 This ... gusto.] **TS1**– OM **MS**

52.13–14 apparently ... her] **S**– the
explanation she had been given
TS1 OM **MS**

52.14 household's] **S**– households'
TS1 OM **MS**

52.15 For she] **S**– She **TS1** OM **MS**

52.15–16 something! And ... Jacobus.]
S– something and in due course I
gathered that she was told that by
Jacobus' own instructions. **TS1** OM
MS

52.17 was ... forward] **S**– carried them
out **TS1** OM **MS**

52.18–19 explanation, ... taunt] **TS1**–
taunt and universal explanation of
their solitude **MS**

52.20a One] **TS1**– But one **MS**

52.20b early and beckoning] **TS1**–
earlier than usual. Beckoning **MS**

52.21a wiped] **TS1**– he wiped **MS**

52.21b brow with ... gesture] **MS S**–
brow **TS1**

52.21–22 told ... bags] **TS1**– asked
MS

52.23 hundred] **TS1**– hundred bags
MS

52.24a replied] **MS S**– cried **TS1**

52.24b eagerly; but he] **TS1**– eagerly.
He **MS**

52.24c calm. He looked] **MS TS1**r–
calm though looking **TS1**t

52.25 ever had] **MS** had ever **TS1**–

52.26 go and tell] **TS1**– tell **MS**

52.28a As ... this] **TS1**– And seeing
my extreme wonder **MS**

52.28b added] **MS S**– added with **TS1**

52.28c usual placid] **TS1**– placid **MS**

52.31 "You] **TS1**– I was awe-struck.
"You **MS**

52.31–32 it?" ... for me?] **TS1**– me?
MS

52.32a Because] **TS1**– For **MS**

52.32b known] **MS–S** known that **E1**–

52.32c ship's] **TS1**– ship is **MS**

52.34–35 I ... before.] **TS1**– He had
his best clothes on. **MS**

52.35 him] **TS1**r– him wearing **TS1**t
VAR **MS**

52.38–39 certainly ... for ...
murmur.] **TS1**– certainly . . **MS**

52.39 You see] **TS1**– However **MS**

52.40 him ... which ..."] **TS1**– him –
of and so – " **MS**

53.1   stopped. He ... this] **TS1**–
stopped and I was not to know what
that **MS**

53.2   And I didn't] **TS1**– But neither
did I **MS**

53.2–3   Anxious ... on] **TS1**– I ran
into **MS**

53.4   At] **MS TS1r**– In **TS1t**

53.5   old ... in] **TS1**– horrid old Miss
Jacobus stopped **MS**

53.5–6   I stopped a moment] **TS1**– I
MS

53.6   to exclaim] **S**– cried **MS** to cry
TS1

53.8   in scornful surprise] **TS1**– with
contempt **MS**

53.8–9   with unwonted familiarity]
TS1– unwontedly familiar **MS**

53.10a   breathed] **TS1**– muttered
MS

53.10b   at ... proposal] **TS1**– in my ear
something **MS**

53.11   What?] **MS E1**– What? Yes. **TS1**
S

53.11–12   Oh! Thanks – Certainly]
TS1– Certainly **MS**

53.16a   was guiding] **MS TS1r**–
guided **TS1t**

53.16b   towards] **TS1**– to **MS**

53.18–19   Mere ... way.] **TS1**– OM **MS**

53.18a   one's] **TS1r**– ones **TS1t** OM
MS

53.18b   interior economy] **TS1r**–
interior **TS1t** OM **MS**

53.19a   might; but] **TS1**– was it? But
MS

53.19b   was not] **TS1**– wasn't **MS**

53.19c   not feeling] **TS1**– not **MS**

53.20   Jacobus'] **TS1**– his **MS**

53.21   On ... too the] **TS1**– The **MS**

53.21–22   table. ... The] **TS1**– table,
the **MS**

53.23   said suddenly] **TS1**– said **MS**

53.23–24   chicken and salad] **TS1**–
chicken **MS**

53.24–25   plate." He ... it] **TS1**– plate"
– and I carried the plate **MS**

53.25   with ... verandah] **TS1**– on to
the verandah, with a knife and fork
and a serviette **MS**

53.25–27   The garden ... chair,] **TS1**–
The girl in the dark **MS**

53.26   buried] **TS1r**– busied **TS1t** OM
MS

53.28   colour. Only] **TS1**– colour; **MS**

53.28–29   heavy scent] **TS1**– scent **MS**

53.29   wandering,] **MS TS1r**– the
TS1t

53.30–31   talked ... I talked] **TS1**–
talked to her **MS**

53.31   To ... like] **TS1r**– It sounded
tender love **MS** and suddenly it
sounded to me like **TS1t**

53.32–33   lover. Whenever ... silence.]
TS1– lover. **MS**

53.34–36   statue. ¶ "I ... dark.] **TS1**–
statue. **MS**

53.34   statue] **MS**–**E1 A2 E2** statute **A1**

53.37   obstinate. You ... sufferings.]
MS obstinate. **TS1t** obstinate. Think
of my sufferings. **TS1r**–

53.39   as ... done] **TS1**– tempted to
do **MS**

53.39–40   violence – shaken ... be.]
TS1– violence. Shake her. Beat her
– maybe. **MS**

53.40   said gently:] **MS** said. **TS1**–

54.4   false," she snarled.] **TS1r**–
false." she said. **MS** false" **TS1t**

54.5–6   I verily believe] **TS1**– the least
bit I think **MS**

54.6–7   there ... this] **TS1**– that **MS**

54.8a   You ... day.] **TS1**– OM **MS**

54.8b   You do.] **TS1r**– You . **TS1t** OM
MS

54.9a   then.] **TS1**– then" I said. **MS**

54.9b   There's ... house.] **TS1**– OM **MS**

54.9c   There's] **TS1 S** There are **E1**–
OM **MS**

54.9d   of rooms] **TS1t S**– rooms **TS1r**
OM **MS**

54.10a   own room] **TS1**– room **MS**

54.10b   did not] **TS1**– didn't **MS**

54.10–15   But ... sigh.] **TS1**– The
scented air of the garden came to
us like a voluptuous and perfumed
sigh. I felt a slight shudder under
my hand let go. **MS**

54.14–15   a voluptuous ... sigh] **TS1r**–,
MS VAR somebody sighing **TS1t**

54.16a   "Go back] **TS1**– Leave me –
go **MS**

54.16b   whispered – almost pitifully.]
MS TS1r– whispered. **TS1t**

54.17   As ... his] **TS1**– I did so.
Jacobus dropped his heavy **MS**

54.18–19   table. At ... ill-humour]
TS1– table and **MS**

54.19   tone, and] **TS1**– tone. **MS**

54.20   upon] **MS** on **TS1**–

54.20–21   as ... these] **TS1**– making
him accountable for the **MS**

54.21   I believe ... them.] **TS1**– of his
daughter (I think I called them).
MS

54.22a   "But ... say Miss] **TS1**– "Miss
MS

54.22b   here is responsible] **TS1**–
here **MS**

54.23–24   loftily. She ... manner:]
TS1– loftily. **MS**

54.25a   Why don't you leave] **MS**
TS1r– Leave **TS1t**

54.25b   in peace] **TS1**– alone **MS**

54.25c   fellow."] **TS1**– fellow she
piped out brazenly. **MS**

54.26–27   I ... much.] **TS1**– OM **MS**

54.27   done to repress her?] **TS1r**–
done? **TS1t** OM **MS**

54.27–28   He raised] **TS1**– Jacobus
raised **MS**

54.28a   his] **MS** a **TS1**–

54.28b   for ... then] **TS1**– and **MS**

54.30   two? Well, then] **TS1r**– two.
MS too – well then **TS1t**

54.31a   She] **TS1**– That old maid **MS**

54.31b   the] **MS TS1r**– a **TS1t**

54.31c   impudence, that old woman.]
TS1– impudence. **MS**

54.31–34   Her ... refrained.] **TS1**– OM
MS

54.32   side like a man's] **TS1r**– side
TS1t OM **MS**

54.34   little black] **TS1**– black **MS**

54.35   host at ... table] **TS1**– host **MS**

54.37   "Well, and what] **TS1**– "What
MS

54.37–38   say ... have] **TS1**– say? Are
we **MS**

54.38a   have] S– are **TS1, MS VAR**

54.38b   each other?"] **TS1**– other
Jacobus?" **MS**

54.39–40a   I ... question.] **TS1**– His
answer for which I had to wait a
little came in quite another spirit.
MS

54.39   little. The] **TS1r**– little, and
the **TS1t VAR MS**

54.39–40b   unexpected, and in quite
another spirit than the question.]
TS1r– unexpected. **TS1t VAR MS**

55.1   some business yet] **TS1**–
business **MS**

55.5   a noiseless] **TS1**– noiseless **MS**

55.6   murmured] **TS1**– muttered **MS**

55.8a   circus-rider] **TS1**– circus **MS**

55.8b   the placid] **MS** that placid **TS1**–

55.9   which] **MS TS1r**– with **TS1t**

55.10a   not] **MS** never **TS1**–

55.10b   the semblance of a] **TS1**– a
MS

55.11–12   thing as ... fish.] **MS TS1r**–
thing. **TS1t**

55.13–15   I ... people.] **TS1**– OM **MS**

55.13   the sense] **TS1r**– that sense
TS1t OM **MS**

55.15–17   on ... Jacobus] **TS1**– and
smoke. And **MS**

55.17–18   it ... roof] **TS1**– this must be
my last dinner in that house lying
under the ban of all "decent"
people **MS**

55.17a   it] **E1**– this **TS1 S, MS VAR**

55.17b   would be for] **TS1r**– was for
for **TS1t VAR MS**

55.18   his roof] **E1**– that roof **TS1 S**
VAR MS

55.19   Hadn't ... difficulty?] **TS1**– He
had helped me notably. **MS**

55.20a   acknowledgement] **TS1**–
thanks which **MS**

55.20b   quite willing] **TS1**– willing **MS**

55.21   closed lips] **TS1**– lips **MS**

55.23–24   Captain," he ... weightily]
TS1– Captain" **MS**

55.25a   asked] **TS1**– cried **MS**

55.25b   may] **MS** might **TS1**–

55.27   He's] **MS** He **TS1**–

55.29   My self-communion] **TS1**– I
was discontended with myself **MS**

55.29–30a   door trying ... was] **TS1**–
door **MS**

55.29–30b   trying to believe] **MS**
TS1r– saying to myself **TS1t** OM **MS**

55.30   time, was not satisfactory.]
TS1– time. **MS**

55.30–32   I was ... motives – and]
TS1– And **MS**

55.31   Jacobus'] **TS1r**– his **TS1t** OM
MS

55.33–35   are! How ... desire!] **TS1**–
are – easily carried away by our
awakened imagination bringing the
first hint of desire. **MS**

55.35a   a desire] **TS1r**– desire **TS1t**,
MS VAR

55.35b   I perceived that I] **TS1 S** I **MS**
E1–

55.35c   particular] **TS1**– peculiar **MS**

55.36–37   moody ... perpetual] **TS1**–
perpetual scornful **MS**

55.37   by the] **TS1r**– the **TS1t** OM **MS**

55.38   fixed gaze] **TS1**– gaze **MS**

55.39a   me ... only] **TS1**– me – only
MS

55.39b   next] **TS1**– the next **MS**

55.40   an exasperating] **TS1**–
exasperating **MS**

56.1   Of course] **TS1**– Naturally **MS**

56.1–2   little town] **TS1**– town **MS**

56.3   even something] **TS1**–
something **MS**

56.3–4   when ... in the] **TS1**– at the
landing steps and when meeting in
MS

56.4   business] **TS1**– my business **MS**

56.5–6   treated ... gathered] **TS1**–
gathered as it were **MS**

56.6   as] **TS1r**–, **MS VAR** at **TS1t**

56.9   when ... board was] **TS1**– was **MS**

56.10a   it had] **MS S**– it was now of
TS1

56.10b   familiarly] **TS1 S** familiar **MS**
E1–

56.10c   sound] **MS S**– nature **TS1**

56.12a   My ... elder] **MS S**– As to my
friend S – the elder, he **TS1**

56.12b   passed me] **TS1**– passed **MS**

56.17a   "You're] **TS1**– "You are **MS**

56.17b   friends] **TS1**– friend **MS**

56.19   brothers Jacobus] **TS1**–
brothers **MS**

56.22   "I have] **TS1**– "I've **MS**

56.22–23   reconciliation] **MS S**–
reconciliation which is **TS1**

56.23   the proprieties] **MS S**–
proprietie | proprieties **TS1t**
proprieties **TS1r**

56.25   disposed of] **MS S**– removed
TS1

56.26   creature,] **MS TS1r**– creature,
he **TS1t**

56.27   lower ... waistcoat] **MS TS1r**–
stomach **TS1t**

56.28a   cried jovially] **TS1**– cried **MS**

56.28b   proprieties] **MS S**– that **TS1**

56.29a   yourself, ... with] **TS1**–
yourself. With **MS**

56.29b   personage] **TS1r**– man **MS**
creature **TS1t**

56.30   has ... lose] **S**– has no
reputation to lose **MS** would stick at
nothing **TS1t** no sort of reputation
to lose **TS1r**

56.31   citizen] **MS S**– man **TS1**

56.33a   family] **MS TS1r**– families
TS1t

56.33b   perfectly] **MS TS1r**– very **TS1t**

56.36   the related] **MS** related **TS1**–

56.38a   Mary] **MS S**– Mary's **TS1**

56.38b   spoke ... at me] **TS1**– looked
at me and spoke to me **MS**

56.38c   with] **MS S**– in a sort of **TS1**

56.39   if] **MS** though **TS1**–

57.1   snarling] **MS TS1r**–
bad-tempered **TS1t**

57.2a   clad] **TS1**– clothed **MS**

57.2b   flimsy] **MS E1**– ever lasting
TS1t old flimsy **TS1r S**

57.2c   low on] **MS** at **TS1t** low at **TS1r**–

57.2–3   throat. She looked] **MS TS1r**–
throat and looking **TS1t**

57.4–5   a fire] **MS TS1r**– an alarm of
fire **TS1t**

57.6a   She ... nothing.] **TS1**– OM **MS**

57.6b   sat] **TS1r**– sat there **TS1t** OM
MS

57.6c   did] **TS1**– would **MS**

57.6d   she] **MS TS1r**– he **TS1t**

57.7a   stay listening] **TS1**– listen **MS**

57.7b   And ... but] **TS1**– And **MS**
57.7–8   did ... face] **MS S**– her face with powder **TS1**
57.8   arrival? It] **MS S**– arrival – which **TS1**
57.9   of making] **TS1**– of **MS**
57.9–10   in ... sign of] **TS1**– a **MS**
57.10   towards] **MS S**– for **TS1**
57.11   The powdering] **TS1**– It **MS**
57.12   and her ... verandah] **TS1**– or **MS**
57.13   an indifference so ... existence.] **TS1**– indifference. **MS**
57.16–17   to observe the] **TS1r**– the **MS** with a **TS1t**
57.17   splendid] **MS TS1r**– still **TS1t**
57.17–18   somewhat long in shape] **TS1r**– long in shape **MS** a little long **TS1t**
57.18–19   was ... creature] **MS TS1r**– seemed then a creature under a spell **TS1t**
57.20a   dishevelled, magnificent] **TS1**– magnificent **MS**
57.20b   Even her] **TS1**– Her very **MS**
57.21   felt myself growing] **TS1r**– felt **MS** felt myself **TS1t**
57.22a   bond of] **TS1**– bond **MS**
57.22b   And] **MS S**– And yet **TS1**
57.23   accepted] **MS** put up with **TS1**–
57.24   a tacit pact] **MS TS1r**– an understanding **TS1t**
57.25   woman's] **TS1r**– woman **MS** **TS1t**
57.27   her brazen] **MS** with her brazen **TS1**–
57.28   and no mistake] **MS S**– that one **TS1**
57.29a   girl] **MS S**– house **TS1**
57.29b   many] **MS E1**– by many **TS1 S**
57.30   this? I ... myself.] **S**– this? **MS** that – I asked myself? **TS1t** that – I would ask myself? **TS1r**
57.32   free, ... by] **TS1**– free from **MS**
57.33   of a castaway] **TS1**– that **MS**
57.35   imagined.] **MS S**– imagined. It was not even an honest, straightforward fascination of the senses. **TS1**
57.36   her shoulder] **TS1**– her **MS**

57.37   in] **MS** with **TS1**–
57.38   resolutions.] **MS TS1r**– resolutions. ¶ All I reaped was only a rich crop of exasperation. **TS1t**
57.39   was enough sometimes] **TS1r**– was enough **MS** sometimes was enough **TS1t**
57.40   gnash] **MS TS1r**– grind **TS1t**
57.40–58.4   opened her ... always] **TS1**– spoke her remarks **MS**
58.1   harsh] **TS1r**– hoarse **TS1t** OM **MS**
58.2   father; and] **TS1r**– father with **TS1t** OM **MS**
58.3a   was ... by] **TS1r**– conveyed **TS1t** OM **MS**
58.3b   by] **S**– by a series of **TS1** OM **MS**
58.4   a tone] **MS** the tone **TS1**–
58.6a   And how] **MS** How **TS1**–
58.6b   have been] **MS TS1r**– be **TS1t**
58.7   maid in ... frock,] **TS1**– maid **MS**
58.10   the proprieties] **MS S**– proprieties **TS1**
58.12a   Who] **MS–A2a** $E2 Whom **A2b**
58.12b   He, himself,] **MS TS1r**– And he **TS1t**
58.13a   think] **MS TS1r**– thing **TS1t**
58.13b   settling down] **TS1**– settling **MS**
58.17   families on the island] **TS1**– families **MS**
58.18   French even] **TS1**– French **MS**
58.19   The girl] **MS TS1r**– She **TS1t**
58.20   had] **MS** she had **TS1**–
58.21   certainly – but] **TS1**– and that's all. But **MS**
58.22   ever came] **TS1r**– came **MS** had ever come **TS1t**
58.23a   captain's] **MS TS1** captains' **S**–
58.23b   bringing] **MS** taking **TS1**–
58.24   very ... ragged] **TS1r**– very ragged and stained **MS** stained and ragged **TS1t**
58.27–28   had formed] **MS S**– formed **TS1**
58.28a   a notion] **MS TS1r**– the notion **TS1t**
58.28b   a scene] **TS1**– scene **MS**

58.32a   her] **TS1**– her in contrast with her peaceful little island **MS**

58.32b   sinks of abominations, reeking] **MS TS1r**– reeking **TS1t**

58.32c   abominations] **MS** abomination **TS1r**– OM **TS1t**

58.32–40   blood, in ... low.] **TS1**– blood. **MS**

58.33   was] **TS1r**– as **TS1t** OM **MS**

58.33–34   current misdeeds] **TS1r**– misdeeds **TS1t** OM **MS**

58.35–36   coolie ... estates] **TS1r**– coolie – labourers **TS1t** OM **MS**

58.36   these] **TS1r**– there **TS1t** OM **MS**

58.38   as that] **TS1r**– that **TS1t** OM **MS**

59.1–4   I ... end.] **TS1**– OM **MS**

59.2a   figured] **TS1r**– imagined **TS1t** OM **MS**

59.2b   herself as] **TS1r**– be **TS1t** OM **MS**

59.4   gore] **S**– blood **TS1** OM **MS**

59.5–6   these horrors ... imagination] **MS TS1r**– these****s **TS1t**

59.7–8   directed ... moment] **TS1r**– fixed on me **MS** turned upon me for a moment **TS1t**

59.8   the uncomprehending] **MS TS1r**– an uncomprehending **TS1t**

59.9   scornful, powdered face] **TS1**– face **MS**

59.10   to shrug] **TS1**– shrug **MS**

59.11–14   At ... Australia.] **TS1**– OM **MS**

59.11a   At that time] **TS1r**– Just then **TS1t** OM **MS**

59.11b   mail] **S**– nail **TS1** OM **MS**

59.12   End] **S**– end **TS1** OM **MS**

59.14   One afternoon] **TS1**– I called one afternoon and while **MS**

59.15–16   in ... animosity] **TS1**– venomously in the verandah **MS**

59.17   precious papa] **MS TS1r**– papa **TS1t**

59.18   who's ... carrying] **TS1r**– to carry **MS** capable of carrying **TS1t**

59.19   cutting] **TS1**– cut **MS**

59.19–20   some day – for your money] **TS1r**– for your money **MS** someday **TS1t**

59.21   a ... verandah] **TS1r**– almost half the length of the verandah **MS** a good half the length of the verandah **TS1t**

59.24a   with girls in] **E1**– with young girls in **MS** in **TS1 S**

59.24b   a grimly] **S**– a grim **MS** a **TS1**

59.25   think] **TS1**– think that **MS**

59.25–26   by ... appearance] **MS S**– at being overheard **TS1t** at my appearance **TS1r**

59.26a   upon] **MS S**– to **TS1**

59.26b   her] **MS S**– her suddenly **TS1**

59.27   objectionable] **MS**–**E1 A2 E2** the objectionable **A1**

59.31–32a   truculence, the ... deserve.] **TS1**– truculence. **MS**

59.31–32b   had ... addressing] **TS1r**– have always addressed **TS1t** OM **MS**

59.33   fell] **TS1**– sank **MS**

59.34   severe determination] **TS1**– a severe glance **MS**

59.38–39   my ... her] **MS TS1r**– that **TS1t**

60.1   undoing, like the] **TS1**– undoing. A **MS**

60.3   her over] **MS TS1r**– at her **TS1t**

60.4   lovely line] **MS TS1r**– line **TS1t**

60.5a   right down] **TS1r**– down **MS TS1t**

60.5b   the] **MS** her **TS1**–

60.5c   ankle] **MS TS1r**– ankle showing **TS1t**

60.6a   to] **MS** as far as **TS1**–

60.6b   shabby] **MS TS1r**– absurd **TS1t**

60.7   well-shaped foot] **TS1**– foot **MS**

60.8   quick nervous] **TS1**– nervous **MS**

60.10a   her ... perfume] **TS1**– the heady parfume, the special charm **MS**

60.10b   heady] **TS1r**–, **MS VAR** heavy **TS1t**

60.10c   perfume] **TS1r**–, **MS VAR** perfumes **TS1t**

60.11   of the everlastingly] **MS TS1r**– everlasting **TS1t**

60.14a   the hairs of the] **MS TS1r**– the **TS1t**

60.14b eyebrows;] **MS S**– eyebrows, **TS1t** eyebrow; **TS1r**

60.15 narrow] **MS** narrowed **TS1**–

60.15–16 motionless black] **TS1r**– black **MS** motionless **TS1t**

60.16–17 gaze ... at] **TS1**– empty thoughtless gaze apparently fixed on **MS**

60.17 their] **S**– its **TS1** VAR **MS**

60.18 hidden ... sight] **MS TS1r**– away there **TS1t**

60.19 without] **TS1**– not **MS**

60.24 her. I ... with] **TS1**– her – nor yet myself in all **MS**

60.27–28 to ... hand, that] **TS1**– chin in hand – that **MS**

60.30 somewhat] **MS S**– yet somewhat **TS1**

60.30–32 hand. I ... hand] **TS1**– hand, I knew so well and **MS**

60.31 the] **TS1r**– its **TS1t** VAR **MS**

60.32 fingers, of ... for] **TS1r**– fingers – for **TS1t** VAR **MS**

60.32–33 in ... of] **TS1**– to lay hold of in the world **MS**

60.34–61.2 "No! ... roughly:] **TS1**– OM **MS**

61.3 should] **MS TS1r**– would **TS1t**

61.7 What on earth . . . .] **TS1**– OM **MS**

61.8a it's] **MS TS1r**– its **TS1t**

61.8b possible after all] **TS1**– possible, **MS**

61.8c know exactly] **TS1**– know **MS**

61.8–9 why ... here] **MS TS1r**– why **TS1t**

61.9–10 do seem] **MS** seem **TS1**–

61.10–11 have ... her] **TS1**– quarrel **MS**

61.13 Who else] **TS1r**– Who **MS TS1t**

61.16 choose] **MS TS1** chose **S**–

61.17–18 once, with ... experiment:] **TS1**– once – experimentaly **MS**

61.20 the ... father's] **TS1**– his **MS**

61.23a brings] **TS1**– bring **MS**

61.23b house] **MS S**– house – to sit for hours **TS1**

61.24 And ... you? . . .] **MS S**– It's no business. **TS1**

61.24–25 You ... you?] **S**– There is no business in it whatever. **TS1** OM **MS**

61.25–26 subject. It's ... sea] **S**– subject. My ship will be ready for sea **MS** subject because I am going away **TS1t** subject because you see I am going away **TS1r**

61.27 and getting] **TS1**– got **MS**

61.28a quickly] **MS E1**– with an undulating motion **TS1 S**

61.28b the little] **MS S**– a little **TS1**

61.29 swaying of] **TS1**– of **MS**

61.30 hips. When ... me] **TS1r**– hips and **MS** hips as she passed near me **TS1t**

61.31 with ... peculiar, promising] **TS1**– tenfold the peculiar charm of the promising **MS**

61.33a that this ... it; that] **TS1**– that **MS**

61.33b more day] **MS TS1r**– day **TS1t**

61.34 to come ... chair] **TS1**– to **MS**

61.34–62.15 and taste ... glory. The escaped] **MS TS1r**– OM **TS1t**

61.34–35 and taste] **TS1r**– taste the **MS** OM **TS1t**

61.35–37 contempt ... that] **TS1r**– her contempt, to hear her **MS** OM **TS1t**

61.37 remarks] **S**– remarks remarks **TS1r** OM **MS** OM **TS1t**

61.38 my innermost nature] **TS1r**– my my innermost **MS** OM **TS1t**

61.38–39 of some moral] **TS1r**– some subtle **MS** OM **TS1t**

61.39 an] **MS S**– and **TS1r** OM **TS1t**

62.2 stride ... gesticulate] **TS1r**– gesticulate, shout **MS** OM **TS1t**

62.3 for? What ... idea.] **TS1r**– for – I had no notion. **MS** OM **TS1t**

62.3–4 It ... wanted; and] **E1**– I just wanted the relief of violence. And **MS** It was just violence that I wanted; and **TS1r S** OM **TS1t**

62.5–6 smile, that ... smile] **TS1r**– mocking smile **MS** OM **TS1t**

62.7 flung ... by] **S**– of **MS** slung at me by **TS1r** OM **TS1t**

62.8 drank the water] **MS S**– drank **TS1r** OM **TS1t**

62.9 let ... on] **TS1r**– dropped into **MS** OM **TS1t**

62.9–15   as if … The escaped] **TS1r**–
the knees apart, her body leaning
forward, with drooping head. **MS**
OM TS1t

62.15   wisps … down.] **TS1**– **OM MS**

62.16   the girl] **TS1**– she **MS**

62.17a   though] **TS1**– if **MS**

62.17b   water] **MS** iced water **TS1**–

62.18a   said, startled, but] **TS1**– asked
MS

62.18b   no] **TS1**– no no **MS**

62.18–19   sympathetic] **TS1**– gentle
MS

62.19   mood] **MS TS1r**– tone **TS1t**

62.20–21   cried in … a] **TS1**– cried
with **MS**

62.23   with a … of] **TS1**– with **MS**

62.24   looked … enough] **TS1**–
stooped low **MS**

62.25a   And I] **TS1**– I **MS**

62.25b   a little myself] **TS1**– myself
MS

62.27   backwards violently] **TS1**–
backwards **MS**

62.28a   of her] **MS** of the **TS1**–

62.28–29   chair. And … exposed]
TS1– chair, exposing her white,
papitating throat **MS**

62.28b   her smooth] **TS1r**– smooth
TS1t OM MS

62.29–30   were nearly … only] **TS1**–
nearly closed had **MS**

62.30–31   under … were] **TS1**– as of
the **MS**

62.32–33   awe. "What … with?"] **TS1**–
awe. **MS**

62.36   weary earth] **TS1r**– earth **MS**
cary earth **TS1t**

62.36–37   of extravagant hopes, of]
TS1– and **MS**

62.37   terrors] **MS E1**– fears **TS1 S**

62.38   Then … spoke] **TS1**– She
gasped and went on **MS**

62.39a   frightful rapidity] **MS TS1r**–
rapidity **TS1t**

62.39b   make out the] **TS1r**– follow
her **MS** follow the sense of her **TS1t**

63.1a   an empty] **TS1r**– a **MS TS1t**

63.1b   smooth] **MS TS1r**– small **TS1t**

63.3   my] **TS1**– my own **MS**

63.4–5   doubting … me.] **TS1**– I
doubted my ears. **MS**

63.6   thoughts] **MS E1**– thoughts,
hopes, fears, **TS1 S**

63.7–11   imaginings … of.] **TS1**–
dwelt in her low forehead! **MS**

63.10a   disgrace] **TS1** a disgrace **S**–
OM MS

63.10b   disgrace; as evidently] **TS1r**–
disgrace evidently **TS1t OM MS**

63.11–12   She … in her] **TS1**– Her **MS**

63.12a   anything] **S**– everything **TS1**
OM MS

63.12b   the world] **S**– this world **TS1**
OM MS

63.12–13   her resentment] **S**– her fear
MS resentment **TS1**

63.13a   fear] **TS1**– anger **MS**

63.13b   took on] **TS1** took **MS S**–

63.13c   a childish] **MS TS1r**– childish
TS1t

63.13d   shape] **MS TS1r**– shapes **TS1t**

63.14   Of … words.] **TS1**– **OM MS**

63.15–18   It … wonder.] **TS1**– She was
beside herself with the fear of
danger. **MS**

63.15–16   was merely as] **TS1r**– was
TS1t VAR MS

63.18   fascinated] **MS TS1r**– s****
fascinated **TS1t**

63.18–19   I … danger.] **TS1**– What?
MS

63.19–20   abduction. It … woman.]
TS1– abduction. **MS**

63.21   thought] **TS1**– thought that
MS

63.22a   At that surmise I] **MS TS1r**– I
TS1t

63.22b   the door] **TS1**– a door **MS**

63.24   shall] **MS–A1** will **A2 E2**

63.25   old aunt] **MS TS1r**– aunt **TS1t**

63.26–27   expression, her … little.]
TS1– expression. **MS**

63.27   But how] **TS1**– How **MS**

63.28–29   the criminal] **TS1**–
criminal **MS**

63.29a   could manage to] **TS1r**–
could **MS TS1t**

63.29b   conception] **MS TS1r**– idea
TS1t

63.30 She was exasperating.] **TS1**– OM **MS**

63.32a chin] **MS S**– teeth **TS1**

63.32b certainly trembled] **S**– quivered **MS** certainly chattered **TS1**

63.35–36 you that. Will ... kind – and] **TS1**– you. Nothing whatever. And **MS**

63.37 shall] **MS S**– will **TS1**

63.38 What ... drink] **TS1**– She drank **MS**

63.39a thirsty] **TS1**– same **MS**

63.39b had ... of] **TS1**– drank the **MS**

63.40 water.] **MS S**– water. I was certainly sincere. **TS1**

63.40–64.1 that ... and] **TS1r**– the tone **MS** that tone I heard once and **TS1t**

64.1–2 again, ... emotion] **TS1r**– with the well known emotion **MS** again **TS1t**

64.5 so stupid as] **MS TS1r**– stupid enough **TS1t**

64.6 that ... frightened] **TS1**– I am afraid **MS**

64.8 feeble to me] **TS1**– feeble **MS**

64.9a has] **MS TS1r**– is **TS1t**

64.9b some people] **TS1**– people **MS**

64.10 a ... power] **MS TS1r**– eally irresistible **TS1t**

64.10–11 The ... conception.] **TS1**– OM **MS**

64.11 the change] **TS1**– the | the change **MS**

64.12–13 but ... muscles,] **TS1**– relaxation **MS**

64.13 stiffened muscles] **TS1r**– muscles **TS1t** OM **MS**

64.14a That] **TS1**– The **MS**

64.14b into] **TS1**– in **MS**

64.14c read] **TS1**– seen **MS**

64.15a more ... found] **TS1**– and felt **MS**

64.15b than] **S**– that **TS1** VAR **MS**

64.16a perfectly empty] **TS1**– empty **MS**

64.16b consciousness ... not] **TS1**– consciousness – not **MS**

64.17a aware any longer] **TS1**– aware **MS**

64.17b had become] **TS1**– was **MS**

64.18 fashion.] **MS S**– fashion, nothing more. **TS1**

64.20 complete success] **TS1**– success **MS**

64.20–22 it ... as though] **TS1**– the change with indignant eyes – as if **MS**

64.22 been] **TS1**– been cynically **MS**

64.23–24 deal ... without any] **TS1**– bargain, without **MS**

64.24 for, at least,] **TS1**– for **MS**

64.26–29 With ... her.] **TS1**– OM **MS**

64.26 and] **TS1r**– and and **TS1t** OM **MS**

64.27 me] **TS1r**– my presence **TS1t** OM **MS**

64.28 from] **TS1** of **S**– OM **MS**

64.29 right before] **TS1**– within a foot of **MS**

64.30a her room] **MS** a room **TS1**–

64.30b extended] **MS E1**– extended widely **TS1 S**

64.31 with ... clenched, her] **TS1**– her **MS**

64.32 a little – revelling contemptuously] **TS1r**– easing her limbs **MS** a little – * **TS1t**

64.32–33 relief, ... freedom] **TS1**– perfect security **MS**

64.33–34 motionless ... been] **TS1**– when she was **MS**

64.35a All this with] **TS1**– Her **MS**

64.35b something incredible,] **TS1** was **MS** incredible, **S**–

64.36 treachery.] **TS1**– treachery – incredible – offensive – cynical with the true Jacobus inpudence. **MS**

64.37 perhaps, but ... contrary] **TS1**– perhaps. But **MS**

64.38a grew; her] **TS1r**– grew. Her **MS** grew and her **TS1t**

64.38b wooden post] **TS1**– post **MS**

64.39a or a] **MS TS1r**– a **TS1t**

64.39b that unconcerned movement, brought] **TS1**– brought **MS**

65.1 did not] **TS1**– didn't **MS**

65.5   about it either] **MS TS1r**– about **TS1t**

65.6a   her] **MS TS1r**– those **TS1t**

65.6b   closed lips] **TS1**– lips **MS**

65.8   one. She] **MS TS1r**– one; and she **TS1t**

65.10a   me, young,] **MS TS1r**– me **TS1t**

65.10b   vigour, of life,] **TS1**– vigour, **MS**

65.10c   a strong] **MS TS1r**– strong **TS1t**

65.11   least, ... her] **TS1**– assurance of perfect **MS**

65.12–13   Our ... wide open] **TS1**– Her **MS**

65.14   into mine] **MS S**– at me **TS1**

65.15a   way.] **MS S**– way. Yes. **TS1t** way. Yes this! **TS1r**

65.15b   In] **MS TS1r**– There could be read in **TS1t**

65.15c   steady] **TS1**– steady impersonal **MS**

65.15d   gaze] **MS E1**– stare **TS1** glare **S**

65.15–16   which ... madness I] **TS1**– I **MS**

65.16a   madness I could detect] **MS TS1r**– madness **TS1t**

65.16b   a slight] **TS1**– slight **MS**

65.17–18   I ... and there] **MS TS1r**– There **TS1t**

65.17   upon] **TS1r**– on **MS** OM **TS1t**

65.18   to be any] **TS1**– any **MS**

65.20   flashed] **TS1**– passed **MS**

65.22–23   which revived ... indeed] **S**– reviving my exasperation with her, **MS** At this my exasperation revived **TS1**

65.23–24   a ... more] **MS TS1r**– OM **TS1t**

65.23   never] **TS1r**– not **MS** OM **TS1t**

65.25   not] **TS1**– not | not **MS**

65.26   Putting ... pushed] **TS1**– She pushed against my chest **MS**

65.28   was roused] **MS** seemed thoroughly awake **TS1**–

65.29   well, and] **MS TS1r**– well. **TS1t**

65.30   totally unprepared] **MS TS1r**– unprepared **TS1t**

65.30–31   Instead ... apart, she] **MS TS1r**– She **TS1t**

65.32a   a downward, undulating,] **TS1**– a **MS**

65.32b   serpentine motion] **MS TS1r**– motion **TS1t**

65.32c   a quick sliding] **MS E1**– a sort of quick **TS1t** a sort of quick sliding **TS1r S**

65.34   for] **TS1**– towards **MS**

65.34–35   at ... verandah] **TS1**– of her room **MS**

65.35–36   be limping ... vanished] **TS1**– limp – and vanished **MS**

65.36a   swung to] **MS** swung **TS1**–

65.36b   behind] **TS1**– behin **MS**

65.37   completely closed] **TS1r**– completely shut **MS** closed **TS1t**

65.38   suspicion] **MS S**– notion **TS1**

65.38–39   being ... what] **TS1**– watching at the crack what **MS**

66.1   VI] **MS S**– OM **TS1**

66.2a   Either] **MS E1**– Either action **TS1 S**

66.2b   been] **MS E1**– made a **TS1 S**

66.2–3   with my feelings] **MS E1**– conclusion to the scene **TS1 S**

66.3   neither.] **MS E1**– neither of these things. **TS1 S**

66.4   monition] **MS TS1r**– nomition **TS1t**

66.5–6   round; and at] **TS1**– round. At **MS**

66.6   conclusion] **TS1**– end **MS**

66.8–9   doorway ... and] **TS1**– door-way – and **MS**

66.9–10   my struggle with the girl] **MS TS1r**– the struggle **TS1t**

66.10–11   witness from ... end.] **MS TS1r**– witness. **TS1t**

66.12   Perhaps ... and had] **TS1**– The girl had **MS**

66.13   time] **TS1**– time – surely **MS**

66.14   manner, heavy-eyed,] **TS1**– manner – heavy eyed, **MS**

66.15   the] **MS** this **TS1**–

66.15–16   man. Those] **MS S**– man, those **TS1**

66.18   the design ... modelling, the] **TS1**– the **MS**

66.19   lips – all that was] **TS1**– lips –
         was **MS**

66.21a   on and] **TS1**– on **MS**

66.21b   grasped with force] **MS TS1r**–
         grasped **TS1t**

66.22   chair ... and] **TS1**– chair – and
         MS

66.22–23   perceived the chance of]
         MS E1– thought there would be
         TS1 S

66.23   most likely] **MS E1**– for certain
         TS1 S

66.24–25   The ... unavoidable.] **TS1**–
         The inavoidable scandal! Horrible!
         MS

66.25a   to act so as to] **TS1**– to **MS**

66.25b   myself] **MS S**– at least myself
         TS1

66.26   I stood ... rate] **TS1**– I **MS**

66.30   glued-together] **MS** glued
         TS1–

66.31a   I own I] **TS1**– I **MS**

66.31b   perspective] **MS TS1r**–
         prospective **TS1t**

66.32   attractive] **MS S**– inspiring
         TS1

66.32–34   it. Perhaps – ... verandah.]
         TS1– it. **MS**

66.34–35a   alluded ... sort,] **TS1**–
         asked wheres Alice? **MS**

66.34–35b   it, if he had] **TS1r**– it,
         TS1t OM **MS**

66.36   of ... from his] **MS** from the
         TS1–

66.37a   The ... that he] **TS1**– He
         MS

66.37b   peculiarity] **TS1r**– thing **TS1t**
         OM **MS**

67.1   home,"] **MS E1**– home to day"
         TS1 S

67.2   store to day,"] **E1**– store"
         MS–S

67.4   know, I] **TS1**– know. I **MS**

67.4–5   said feeling ... do.] **TS1**– said.
         MS

67.7a   had meant] **MS TS1r**– meant
         TS1t

67.7b   gazed persistently at] **MS** stared
         persistently on **TS1 S** gazed
         persistently on **E1**–

67.8   glance. In] **MS E1**– glance; and
         then in **TS1 S**

67.8–9   absolute stillness] **E1**– stillness
         MS solute silence **TS1t** absolute
         silence **TS1r S**

67.9a   we stared] **MS E1**– there were
         two of us to stare **TS1 S**

67.9b   the] **MS TS1r**– an **TS1t**

67.9c   high-heeled] **MS S**– overturned
         high-heeled **TS1**

67.10–11   We ... me] **MS S**– During
         the minute of silence which elapsed
         TS1

67.11   Jacobus] **MS E1**– he **TS1 S**

67.13–14   really a slipper] **TS1**– a
         slipper really **MS**

67.14–16   It had ... manner.] **TS1**– OM
         MS

67.15   only] **E1**– used to **TS1 S** OM
         MS

67.15–16   in carelessly in] **TS1** in,
         after **S**– OM **MS**

67.16   her] **TS1r**– a **TS1t** OM **MS**

67.16–17   eyes from the shoe] **TS1**–
         eyes **MS**

67.19   that] **TS1**– the **MS**

67.21–22   impossible. I ... object.]
         TS1– impossible. **MS**

67.22   daughter's] **TS1**– daughter
         MS

67.22–23   over and ... paws]
         TS1– in his cushioned paws over
         and over **MS**

67.23–24   way ... time; then]
         TS1– make of the thing – then
         MS

67.24a   time] **E1**– long time **TS1 S** OM
         MS

67.24b   glancing] **MS E1**– peering
         TS1 S

67.24–25   inside with ... air] **TS1**–
         inside **MS**

67.27a   this] **TS1**– him **MS**

67.27b   grunt, watching him covertly.]
         E1– grunt. **MS** grunt, without
         looking at him. **TS1 S**

67.28   Then I added "You] **TS1**– ¶
         "You **MS**

67.29–30   eyes too] **MS TS1r**– eyes
         TS1t

67.33   haven't," I answered curtly.]
TS1– haven't." MS

67.34a   rise] MS TS1r– raise TS1t
67.34b   austere] MS TS1r– austerely
TS1t
67.34c   of] MS TS1r– with TS1t
67.34d   hand] MS TS1r– very hand
TS1t

67.35a   fatal shoe] TS1– shoe MS
67.35b   glared at him] MS TS1r–
muttered TS1t

67.37   to Captain. You ought to."] MS
TS1r– to. TS1t

67.38–39   If ... instant.] TS1– I must
see her again. I wanted to stay for
one more experience of the
provoking sensation, of indefinite
desire – the habit of which made
me – *me* of all people dread the
prospect of going to sea. MS

67.40–68.4   reasoned with, ... sea.]
TS1– resisted . . . MS

68.2   provoking sensation and of]
TS1r– sensation of exasperation
and TS1t VAR MS

68.3   made] TS1 S, MS VAR had made
E1–

68.5a   pronounced] TS1– answered
MS
68.5b   think that] TS1– think MS

68.6   the] MS TS1r– he TS1t
68.6–7   consideration – I ... it] TS1–
consideration – that it MS

68.7–8   really a good thing] MS good
TS1t a good thing TS1r–

68.8   trade – let us say,] TS1– trade
MS

68.10–11   middle, the ... fist.] TS1–
middle. MS

68.13   "Are you sure?"] TS1– "Sure?
MS

68.14–15   He had ... and] TS1– He
MS

68.14   had uttered] TS1r– uttered
TS1t OM MS

68.16a   inquisitive stare] E1– stare MS
direct stare TS1 S

68.16b   sleepily ... much as] E1–
without MS sleepily but without as
much as TS1 S

68.17   trade," I said turning] TS1–
trade." I turned MS

68.17–18   him. "I see that] MS him "if
TS1t him. "I see TS1r–

68.18   bent] MS TS1r– so bent
TS1t

68.19   did not want an] TS1– desired
no MS

68.20a   dearly at times] TS1– dearly
MS

68.20b   included] MS E1– viewed TS1
S

68.21a   myself and] MS myself,
TS1–

68.21b   in] MS E1– with TS1 S
68.21c   the same] TS1– a feeling of
MS

68.22   as ... ignoble] TS1r– for the
whole ignoble MS as partners in a
monstrous TS1t

68.23–26   And ... too.] TS1– Was this
my luck? MS

68.23   vision at sea] TS1r– vision TS1t
VAR MS [*see 68.27b*]

68.24   sixty] S–E2, MS VAR seventy
TS1 [*see 68.27b*]

68.24–25   unsubstantial, clear marvel]
E1– unsubstantial shape TS1t
unsubstantial and clear marvel
TS1r S OM MS

68.25a   of it ... of a] TS1r– of TS1t OM
MS

68.25b   art] S– arts TS1r OM MS
TS1t

68.27a   this vaporous] TS1– the
vaporous MS

68.27b   and rare apparition] TS1–
apparition of the island at sixty
miles off – a vision as of fair
diaphanous dreams MS

68.28a   heart hidden ... mist.] TS1–
heart? MS

68.28b   hidden within] TS1r– within
TS1t OM MS

68.28–29   Was this my luck!] TS1– A
thing of horror! MS

68.30–31   after what ... of] TS1– after
MS

68.31   a vile] MS–S vile E1–
68.33   be] MS S– have been TS1

68.34 haven't got] **TS1**– haven't **MS**

68.36–37 with ... menace] **E1**– menacingly grim, as it were **MS** with what I took for menacing grimness **TS1 S**

68.37 unrelenting] **MS E1**– relentless **TS1 S**

68.37–38 much money] **MS S**– much **TS1**

68.38 directness] **MS S**– simplicity **TS1**

68.40–69.1 And ... over,] **TS1**– He was disappointed, **MS**

69.2a for ... before] **TS1**– till **MS**

69.2b thoughtful tone] **MS E1**– meditative accent **TS1 S**

69.4a draw some] **TS1r**– easily draw **MS** get some **TS1t**

69.4–5 charterers. That ... Captain] **TS1**– charterers Captain **MS**

69.4b charterers] **MS TS1r**– charteress **TS1t**

69.6 couldn't," ... "I've] **TS1**– couldn't – and if I could I wouldn't do it. Moreover I've **MS**

69.7a and ... are] **MS S**– my account with them is **TS1**

69.7b and besides,] **S**– and **MS** OM **TS1**

69.8–9 growing ... throwing] **TS1**– very brusque. I was growing furious. Throwing **MS**

69.10a "You] **MS S**– "Your **TS1**

69.10b a bit too] **TS1**– too **MS**

69.11 enough but he] **TS1**– enough. He **MS**

69.11–12 tranquil, only ... puzzled,] **TS1**– tranquil, **MS**

69.12 upon] **TS1**– on | on **MS**

69.13 in ... instantly] **TS1r**– died out his eyes instantly **MS** in his eyes died out **TS1t**

69.13–15 As ... anything.] **TS1**– OM **MS**

69.14 chose to] **S**– could **TS1** OM **MS**

69.16 was a vague] **S**– was a **MS** were the words **TS1t** were a vague **TS1r**

69.16–18 than ... least] **TS1**– a grossly false statement at bottom **MS**

69.17 have been] **TS1r**– be **TS1t** OM **MS**

69.18–19 But I ... go. I] **TS1**– But I **MS**

69.19–20 in ... more.] **MS TS1r**– on. **TS1t**

69.20 the girl once more] **MS** her **TS1r** her once more **S**– OM **TS1t**

69.21a said finally] **MS TS1r**– said **TS1t**

69.21b I'll] **TS1**– I will **MS**

69.22a many] **MS TS1r**– much **TS1t**

69.22b confounded potatoes] **TS1r**– potatoes **MS TS1t**

69.22–24 buy, on ... away.] **TS1**– buy. But you must load them at once and go on board yourself with the lighter. **MS**

69.23 down to the wharf to] **TS1r**– to **TS1t** OM **MS**

69.24 alongside the ship] **TS1r**– alongside **TS1t** OM **MS**

69.25 invoice and ... receipt] **TS1**– invoice **MS**

69.27 had finished] **TS1**– finished **MS**

69.29 him even.] **TS1**– him. **MS**

69.30a "Well then,"] **TS1**– "Well" **MS**

69.30b nothing] **MS TS1r**– nothin. **TS1t**

69.31a it Mr Jacobus] **TS1**– it **MS**

69.31b wait on board] **TS1**– even wait there **MS**

69.31c off] **TS1**– on board **MS**

69.33 Captain. I ... once.] **TS1**– Captain. **MS**

69.34 girl's] **MS TS1r**– girls **TS1t**

69.34–35 he ... fist] **TS1r**– in his hand **MS** he held still in his fist **TS1t**

69.35a looking ... he] **E1**– he **MS TS1** looking hard at me, he **S**

69.35b down] **MS S**– down hurriedly **TS1**

69.35c on] **TS1**– in **MS**

69.36　he] **TS1**– he | he **MS**

69.37　come ... see] **TS1r**– come to
see that **MS** co[]e along to see **TS1t**

69.38　bother about me] **TS1**– bother
MS

69.40a　understand; and then his] **S**–
understand. Then his **MS**
understand. His **TS1**

69.40b　weighty] **MS S**– grave **TS1**

69.40c　certainly Captain] **TS1**–
Captain! Certainly! **MS**

70.1a　some] **S**– a **MS** another
TS1

70.1b　thought] **MS S**– enlightenment
TS1

70.1–2　His ... sigh?] **TS1**– Did he
sigh? **MS**

70.2a　As he] **TS1**– He **MS**

70.2b　hurry off] **MS TS1r**– look after
TS1t

70.2c　these] **MS TS1r** those **TS1t S**–

70.3a　he never looked] **TS1**– without
looking **MS**

70.3b　back at me] **MS TS1r**– back
TS1t

70.4　waited till the] **TS1**– waited. The
MS

70.4–5　had died ... longer] **TS1**– died
out **MS**

70.5　Then turning towards] **TS1**– I
turned to **MS**

70.6–7　I raised ... verandah: ¶
"Alice!"] **TS1**– and raising my
voice: – ¶ "Alice" I called along the
verandah. **MS**

70.8　Nothing ... door.] **TS1**– No
answer! **MS**

70.10a　did not call again] **TS1**–
called no more **MS**

70.10–11　I had ... dejected.] **TS1**– OM
MS

70.10b　I had become] **S**– My head
was clear, my heart free I became
TS1t My head was clear, my heart
free but I became **TS1r** OM **MS**

70.11　dejected.] **MS S**– dejected. And
TS1

70.11–12　turned ... with] **TS1**– OM
MS

70.12　my elbows spread] **TS1r**–
spread my elbows **MS** my elbow
resting **TS1t**

70.12–13　low balustrade] **TS1**–
balustrade **MS**

70.13　and took my] **MS S**–
my **TS1**

70.14–16　The evening ... embers;
whiffs] **TS1**– Whiffs **MS**

70.16　embers;] **TS1r**– embers and
TS1t OM **MS**

70.17a　the] **MS TS1t S**– the
illimitable **TS1r**

70.17–18　dusk ... garden] **TS1**–
garden had been **MS**

70.17b　dusk ... hemisphere] **TS1r**–
dusk **TS1t** OM **MS**

70.18–19　swinging ... of the] **TS1**– in
the temple of **MS**

70.19a　altar] **MS TS1r**– alter **TS1t** OM
MS

70.19b　colours of the blossoms] **TS1**–
colours **MS**

70.20　one by one] **TS1**– of coloured
embers – growing cold **MS**

70.21–22　when ... slender,
advancing] **TS1**– tall and slender (a
slight noise had made me turn my
head) advanced **MS**

70.22　swaying] **E1–E2**, **MS** VAR slight
swaying **TS1 S**

70.22–23　a floating ... motion] **TS1**–
an uneven and floating motion. a
swaying limp **MS**

70.23　shadowy] **MS TS1r**– va.ue
TS1t

70.24a　into] **TS1**– in **MS**

70.24b　deep] **MS** deep low **TS1**–

70.24c　chair.] **S**– armchair. **MS** chair,
her accustomed seat. **TS1**

70.24d　don't] **TS1**– did not **MS**

70.24e　whence] **MS TS1r**– hence
TS1t

70.26　call. She ought to have] **E1**–
call. **MS** call. She ought to **TS1 S**

70.27　opportunity] **MS TS1r**–
moment **TS1t**

70.28–29a　I ... armchair.] **TS1**– OM
MS

70.28   I] **S**– But I **TS1** OM **MS**

70.28–29   opposite her armchair.]
TS1r– opposite. **TS1t** OM **MS**

70.29   ever-discontented] **MS TS1r**–
everlastingly discontented **TS1t**

70.29–30   me at once,
contemptuously] **TS1**– me **MS**

70.32   pitched mine] **TS1**– spoke
MS

70.34   shoe – before ... lights] **TS1**–
shoe **MS**

70.35–36   not ... gave] **TS1**– giving
MS

70.36a   its low] **TS1r**– low **TS1t** OM
MS

70.36b   could only make out] **TS1**–
saw **MS**

70.37–38   face, her ... eyes.] **TS1**–
face. **MS**

70.38   eyes. She ... enough.] **TS1**–
eyes. **MS**

70.39   the mysterious] **TS1**– her
mysterious **MS**

70.39–71.1   and ... which was] **TS1**–
attraction **MS**

71.3–4   here." She ... and I] **TS1**–
here. I **MS**

71.5   you] **TS1**– you if you give me
your foot **MS**

71.6   low down and groped] **TS1**– low,
groping **MS**

71.7a   foot under] **TS1**– foot; under
MS

71.7b   of her] **MS** of the **TS1**–

71.7–8   wrapper. She ... strap.] **TS1**–
wrapper she did not withdraw it.
MS

71.8   strap] **TS1r**– straps **TS1t** OM
MS

71.8–9   an inanimate foot. I] **TS1**–
inanimate. I put the shoe on and
MS

71.11   said, trying ... conviction.] **TS1**–
said. **MS**

71.12   more like] **TS1**– like **MS**

71.12–14   of vague ... strange,] **TS1**–
of the **MS**

71.14–15   which ... to] **TS1**– the acrid
fascination of **MS**

71.14a   which] **TS1r**– that **TS1t** OM
MS

71.14b   acrid] **MS TS1r**– acid **TS1t**

71.15–16   which ... promising,] **TS1**–
tragic **MS**

71.16   That] **TS1**– It **MS**

71.17–18   thinking ... fact] **TS1**– by
way of warning **MS**

71.17   may] **MS–A1 A2a** might **E2 A2b**

71.19   himself," she declared
scornfully.] **TS1**– himself. **MS**

71.20   It's] **TS1**– Its **MS**

71.20–21   with his ... strangers,] **TS1**–
with **MS**

71.21–22   aunt or great aunt] **TS1**–
aunt **MS**

71.22   men ... you] **TS1**– his associates
that you are afraid **MS**

71.24a   "That's] **TS1**– "Thats **MS**

71.24b   doing now] **MS** now doing
TS1–

71.24–25   business – private business]
MS business **TS1**–

71.25–26   Yes. I ... do.] **TS1**– That's
the sort of man I am. **MS**

71.26   I've broken] **TS1**– I broke
MS

71.26–27   you. That's ... am.] **TS1**–
you. **MS**

71.27   And now] **TS1**– Now **MS**

71.27–28   afraid? If ... be."] **TS1**–
afraid? **MS**

71.29–30   It ... affirmed: ¶ "No. I am
not afraid."] **TS1**– ¶ "No! **MS**

71.30   I am] **TS1–E1 A2 E2** I'm **A1** OM
MS

71.31   You needn't be.] **TS1**– Why
should you be? **MS**

71.31–33   again before ... you] **TS1**–
again. I am off to sea – and you shall
remain **MS**

71.33a   old garden] **TS1**– garden **MS**

71.33b   the trees over there] **TS1**–
these trees **MS**

71.34a   these gorgeous] **TS1**– these
MS

71.34b   flower-beds.] **TS1**–
flower-beds. And I shall remember
you . . . **MS**

71.36a   I ... faint] **TS1**– It was the
    sullen **MS**
71.36b   resentfully] **TS1**– resentful
    and **MS**
71.37   provoking] **TS1**– promising **MS**
71.38   in] **MS** of **TS1**–
72.2   not answer, she did not] **TS1**–
    not **MS**
72.2–3   move. To ... improper.] **TS1**–
    move. **MS**
72.4–5   forehead. This ... clearly]
    TS1– forehead, feeling **MS**
72.5   realized clearly] **TS1r**–
    realized **TS1t** OM **MS**
72.6–7   And ... in] **TS1**– In the
    moment of **MS**
72.7–8   touch ... on] **TS1**– fall of her
    arms on **MS**
72.8–9   a hasty, awkward, haphazard]
    E1– haphazard a hasty, unskilfull
    MS a hasty, unskillful, haphazard
    TS1 S
72.9–10   No! She ... moved.] **TS1**–
    But I was no longer moved by the
    girl without fear. **MS**
72.10–14   slowly, ... revelation. ¶ I
    traversed] **TS1**– languidly. The
    wicker-chair creaked. It was a
    catastrophic revelation. ¶ Nothing
    but the sense of my dignity
    prevented me from running off
    headlong. I crossed **MS**
72.12a   the sense] **TS1t**, **MS** VAR a
    sense **TS1r**–
72.12b   my dignity] **TS1r**–**E2**, **MS** VAR
    dignity **TS1t**
72.14–16   I thought: ... been] **TS1**– At
    the moment of closing the door
    with the care of **MS**
72.16   had been] **TS1r**– were **TS1t** OM
    MS
72.17–18   During ... I] **E1**– I **MS** It was
    in that stealthy act that I **TS1 S**
72.18   experienced my] **MS** found the
    TS1t experienced the **TS1r**–
72.19a   the girl] **TS1**–**E1 A2 E2** that
    girl **MS** a girl **A1**
72.19b   I had ... obscurity] **TS1**–
    staring into the garden warm,

odorous with the perfume of
    imprisoned flowers **MS**
72.20–22   eyes ... were] **TS1**– black
    eyes **MS**
72.22   which] **E1**– that **TS1 S** OM **MS**
72.24   The ... well] **TS1**– In the
    ill-lighted streets **MS**
72.25a   the harbour] **MS S**– he
    harbour **TS1**
72.25b   were extremely quiet. I]
    TS1r– I **MS** were extremely quiet
    and I **TS1t**
72.25–27   that ... empty; that] **TS1**–
    that **MS**
72.27   seeking] **TS1**– seeking for **MS**
72.29–30   boatman ... readiness. He]
    TS1– boatman **MS**
72.31a   my ship] **MS** the ship **TS1**–
72.31b   confidential] **TS1**– usual **MS**
72.31c   evening] **TS1**– night **MS**
72.31d   sah] **MS S**– sir **TS1**
72.32a   instead ... once, remained]
    TS1– remained **MS**
72.32b   on to] **MS** by **TS1**–
72.34–35   I was ... dark] **TS1**– On the
    MS
72.35   positively rushed] **TS1**– rushed
    MS
72.36–37   pacing ... arrival] **TS1r**–
    awaiting my return distractedly **MS**
    pacing the deck feverishly for hours
    TS1t
72.36   distractedly] **E1**–**E2**, **MS** VAR
    feverishly **TS1r S**, **TS1t** VAR
72.37a   Just ... a lighter] **TS1**– A
    lighter had come alongside **MS**
72.37b   loaded with] **MS S**– full of
    TS1
72.38a   had come alongside] **TS1**–
    and **MS**
72.38b   shipchandler himself] **TS1**–
    shipchandler **MS**
72.39   stuck immovable] **TS1**– stuck
    MS
72.40a   it all] **TS1**– it **MS**
72.40b   did not] **TS1**– didn't **MS**
73.1–2   He ... make] **TS1**– And I
    stopped his **MS**
73.2   when ... too by] **TS1**– by **MS**

73.2–3   him the] **TS1**– him the | him the **MS**

73.3–6   and desiring ... ship. ¶ "I] **TS1**– with appropriate instructions ¶ "Send him out of the ship. I **MS**

73.4a   below] **TS1r**– in **TS1t** OM **MS**

73.4b   once,] **TS1r E1**– once and **TS1t** once to **S** OM **MS**

73.4c   Mr Jacobus'] **TS1r–A2** Mr Jacobus **TS1t** Jacobus's **E2** OM **MS**

73.4d   send] **S–E2**, **MS** VAR see **TS1**

73.6   him," I ... climbing] **TS1**– him." I confessed frankly. ¶ I climbed **MS**

73.7a   felt] **TS1**– was **MS**

73.7b   tired. Dropping] **TS1r**– tired and **MS** tired and dropping **TS1t**

73.8–9   gave ... side] **TS1**– gazed idly at the light **MS**

73.8   and at] **TS1r**– except **TS1t** OM **MS**

73.11   ready cash] **E1**– cash **MS** own money **TS1** money **S**

73.11–13   a long ... intruded upon] **TS1**– Burns intruded on **MS**

73.15–17   Of ... Seventeen tons!] **TS1**– Seventeen tons! Well I never heard ... **MS**

73.16   Seventeen] **MS TS1r**– fifteen **TS1t**

73.17a   hoist] **TS1**– take **MS**

73.17b   in that lot] **MS TS1r**– all that in **TS1t**

73.17–18   to-morrow morning.] **TS1**– in the morning? **MS**

73.19–20   Unless ... that.] **TS1**– OM **MS**

73.19a   them] **TS1r**– the lot **TS1t** OM **MS**

73.19b   I'm] **S**– I am **TS1** OM **MS**

73.20a   myself] **TS1**– dropping it overboard **MS**

73.20b   it's] **TS1**– it is **MS**

73.22   "That is the] **TS1**– "Rubbish! The **MS**

73.22–23   many ... are] **TS1**– years sir **MS**

73.23   Nearly eighty] **TS1**– Eighty **MS**

73.24a   gone; a perfectly] **TS1**– gone in one **MS**

73.24b   sweep of your drawer sir.] **TS1**– sweep. **MS**

73.25   understand] **TS1**– can understand **MS**

73.26–28   As ... a hopeless] **TS1**– I am afraid he thought me a **MS**

73.26a   As] **TS1r**– And **TS1t** OM **MS**

73.26b   throw the right light] **TS1r**– light **TS1t** OM **MS**

73.29   no money ... enough] **TS1**– not enough money **MS**

73.30a   cigarette with] **MS** cigarette **TS1**–

73.30b   sweep] **TS1**– sweep of my drawer **MS**

73.30–32   But ... me.] **TS1**– OM **MS**

73.32a   And] **TS1**– And besides **MS**

73.32b   any one] **TS1**– anybody **MS**

73.33a   knew I was] **TS1**– had been **MS**

73.33b   and] **MS E1**– or **TS1 S**

73.34   comments] **TS1**– remarks **MS**

73.35–74.7   The ... bargain.] **TS1**– OM **MS**

73.35a   The following] **E1**– Next **TS1 S** OM **MS**

73.35b   stern-fasts] **TS1–E1 A2 E2** stern-facts **A1** OM **MS**

73.36   the] **TS1r**– a **TS1t** OM **MS**

73.37a   standing up in] **S**– in **TS1** OM **MS**

73.37b   pulling hard] **TS1r**– pulling **TS1t** OM **MS**

73.38   for ships were stowed] **S**– stood **TS1t** for ships stood **TS1r** OM **MS**

74.1   great heartiness] **S**– some emphasis **TS1t** great emphasis **TS1r** OM **MS**

74.5   the] **TS1r**– this **TS1t** OM **MS**

74.6   him,] **S**– him with all the censorious world **TS1t** him, with all the censorious and virtuous world, **TS1r** OM **MS**

74.7   that potato] **S**– an ignoble **TS1** OM **MS**

74.8–9   it ... passage] **TS1**– I will only say I was glad when we unmoored and went to sea **MS**

74.8   our] **TS1r**– the **TS1t** VAR **MS**

74.9   glad enough] **TS1**– glad **MS**

74.10–11   I had ... me. I] **TS1**– I **MS**

74.11–12   that ... far] **TS1**– which is so far like innocence **MS**

74.12   resembles] **TS1r**– in some respects resembles **TS1t** VAR **MS**

74.13   however I remembered] **TS1**– I had to remember **MS**

74.13–14   girl. During ... days] **S**– girl and **MS** girl a good deal – and **TS1**

74.14–15   I was ... sensations] **TS1**– question my feelings and my conduct **MS**

74.15–16   person and ... conduct.] **TS1**– person. **MS**

74.17a   And I must say also] **TS1**– I must also say **MS**

74.17b   Burns'] **TS1r**– Burns **MS** **TS1t**

74.17c   intolerable fussing] **TS1r**– fussing **MS** **TS1t**

74.17d   these] **TS1** the **MS** those **S**–

74.18–24   was ... goes] **TS1**– did not help me to forget **MS**

74.23–24   potatoes ... goes] **E1**– potatoes, as the saying goes, with a vengeance **TS1 S** OM **MS**

74.25–26   and everlastingly] **TS1**– and **MS**

74.26a   the watch on deck] **MS S**– a knot of hands **TS1**

74.26b   were] **TS1**– were everlastingly **MS**

74.26–27   spreading ... down] **TS1**– picking over, lowering **MS**

74.27   again some part] **MS S**– part **TS1**

74.28a   potatoes.] **TS1r**– potatoes. He wanted to minimize my loss as much as possible. **MS**

74.28b   My bargain with all] **TS1**– His devotion – if it was devotion and not mere cussedness – kept the bargain before my eyes with **MS**

74.28–29   associations ... visual – the] **TS1**– associations – the **MS**

74.29–30   with ... tragic] **TS1**– contemptuous and tragic in her **MS**

74.30–31   hopeless castaway – was] **TS1r**– hopeless – was **TS1t** VAR **MS**

74.30–32   castaway – was ... sea.] **TS1r–E2, TS1t** VAR castaway. **MS**

74.32   as if] **TS1**– as **MS**

74.33–37   smell. Whiffs ... care.] **TS1**– smell of decaying potatoes. **MS**

74.37   care.] **S**– care for these potatoes. **TS1** OM **MS**

74.38–39   well content ... deck] **TS1**– content to throw my commercial venture overboard **MS**

74.38   the hatch] **S**– them **TS1** VAR **MS**

74.39   perish under the deck.] **S**– perish. **TS1** VAR **MS**

75.1–6   That ... possible.] **TS1**– OM **MS**

75.6   What between his] **TS1**– But Mr Burns' **MS**

75.7   devotion – and] **TS1**– that – and also **MS**

75.7–8   I ... overboard] **TS1**– stood in the way **MS**

75.8–9   I ... obey] **TS1**– He would in his zeal, have perhaps refused to carry out **MS**

75.9–10   command. An ... comical] **TS1**– order of destruction – and a comically unprecedented **MS**

75.10–11   been created] **TS1**– ensued **MS**

75.12   I welcomed ... of] **TS1**– But **MS**

75.12–13   as ... done.] **TS1**– came on. **MS**

75.13   done. In consequence when] **MS** done, when **TS1t** done. When **TS1r**–

75.13–14   the ship ... the pilot] **S**– to for a pilot **MS** the ship to, for the pilot-schooner **TS1**

75.14a   outside] **TS1–E1 A2 E2** outside the **MS** outside of **A1**

75.14b Heads] **MS TS1r–** heads **TS1t**

75.14–15 not been opened] **S–** been battened **MS** been battened down **TS1**

75.16 been on board] **TS1–** existed **MS**

75.17–18 an ... rain] **TS1–** a blustering raw day of rain squalls **MS**

75.18–21 looked ... hands] **TS1–** streaming from head to foot chatted to me rubbing his wet hands under the lashing downpour **MS**

75.22–24 which ... creature] **TS1–** that seemed very unnatural to me **MS**

75.25–32 remarked. ¶ He ... weather.] **TS1–** said bitterly. I had had nearly ten days of it. **MS**

75.27 word garden,] **TS1r–** word **TS1t** OM **MS**

75.32 Colony, the Pilot explained,] **MS TS1r–** Colony, **TS1t**

75.34a they had had for seven] **TS1–** for **MS**

75.34b lost.] **TS1–** lost. It was of his garden that he was thinking. **MS**

75.36 to spare] **TS1–** for sale **MS**

75.37a managed to forget] **TS1–** forgotten **MS**

75.37b In a moment I] **MS TS1r–** I **TS1t**

75.37–38 felt ... neck.] **TS1–** had a vision of gorgeous colour – of a girlish figure lonely in a chair. Emotion broke into me I felt corrupted. **MS**

75.39 Pilot's] **TS1–** pilots **MS**

76.1a Finally he obtained] **TS1–** I sold him **MS**

76.1b and paid] **TS1–** for **MS**

76.1–2 for it. This ... Jacobus. The spirit] **TS1–** and the spirit **MS**

76.3–4 before I slept, the Custom-House] **TS1–** the Customs **MS**

76.4–6 While ... confidentially:] **TS1–** The officer in charge took me

aside away from his underlings. **MS**

76.6 I ... to] **TS1–** Do you **MS**

76.7–8 sell?" ¶ Clearly ... land] **TS1–** sell Captain?" he asked confidentially **MS**

76.10 pile ... buried] **TS1–** girl buried in a heap of gold **MS**

76.11a callous] **MS E1–** feverish **TS1 S**

76.11b at my ship-broker's office] **TS1–** on my shipbroker **MS**

76.12a the usual business] **TS1r–** business **MS** his usual business **TS1t**

76.12b had been transacted pushed] **MS TS1r–** pushed **TS1t**

76.14a thinking] **MS TS1r–** thing **TS1t**

76.14b the Pearl of the Ocean] **TS1–** that trip **MS**

76.15 may] **TS1–** must **MS**

76.16 I said negligently: "Oh] **TS1–** "Oh **MS**

76.18 face for a while] **TS1–** face **MS**

76.21–22 lived; but ... me.] **TS1–** lived. **MS**

76.22 How ... returning] **TS1–** When I went **MS**

76.23a board rather late] **TS1r–** board **MS TS1t**

76.23b a small] **TS1–** Mr Burns on the quarter deck keeping a triumphant eye on a **MS**

76.23–24 the coster type] **E1–** the corter type. **MS** various types **TS1 S**

76.24–25 hanging ... them] **TS1–** OM **MS**

76.25 a triumphant eye] **TS1r–E2, MS VAR** his triumphant eyes **TS1t** [*see 76.23b*]

76.27 These chaps] **E1–** They **MS–S**

76.27–28 waiting ... excitedly] **TS1–** here since this morning **MS**

76.28a me excitedly.] **S–** me. **TS1** OM **MS**

76.28b have] **MS E1–** have nearly **TS1 S**

76.28c drunk] **MS S–** drank **TS1**

76.29   dry. Don't ... sir.] **TS1–** dry"
Mr Burns informed me excitedly.
MS

76.29–30   You are too
good-natured."] **TS1–** "Don't
you be too good natured Sir"
MS

76.31–32   eye to negotiate with,]
TS1– eye **MS**

76.33a   rest] **TS1–** others **MS**

76.33b   inquired] **TS1–** asked **MS**

76.36   Long] **TS1–** All the potatoes
were sold **MS**

76.37a   day all ... sold] **TS1–** day
MS

76.37b   about three times] **TS1–**
triple **MS**

76.37–38   I ... them] **TS1–** of my
purchase **MS**

76.38–39   congratulated ... care]
TS1– at the success **MS**

76.39   commercial venture] **TS1–**
venture **MS**

76.39–40   but hinted plainly] **TS1–**
complained **MS**

76.40   ought ... it] **TS1–** had not
made the most of my opportunities
MS

77.1–2   Jacobus by ... starts] **TS1–**
Jacobus **MS**

77.2a   dreams] **TS1–** dream **MS**

77.2b   concerned with] **TS1–** about
MS

77.3   on ... flowers] **TS1–** of flowery
but desert islands **MS**

77.3–4   extremely unpleasant] **TS1t**
S– unrefreshing **MS** extremely
pleasant **TS1r**

77.4   In ... and] **TS1–** In I **MS**

77.5   carefully] **MS TS1r–** careful
TS1t

77.5–6   thought-out scheme] **TS1–**
drawn plan **MS**

77.6   about the] **TS1–** in **MS**

77.7a   the] **MS TS1t S–** the | the
TS1r

77.7b   my day] **MS** the day **TS1–**

77.7c   that task and] **TS1–** this and
when it was done I **MS**

77.8   when it was done] **TS1–** with
myself **MS**

77.9–10   greatly ... project] **TS1–**
impressed **MS**

77.10–14   notwithstanding ... least]
TS1– the voyage showed a fair
profit they thought it better to keep
the ship in the sugar trade **MS**

77.16a   had a letter] **TS1–** heard **MS**

77.16b   Jacobus. We] **TS1–** Jacobus
and **MS**

77.17   to see how well] **TS1–** that **MS**

77.17–18   for, ... of] **TS1–** so well as to
obtain **MS**

77.18–19   he writes us] **TS1–** (against
which we trust you will guard
yourself in the future). He says **MS**

77.19–20   you, by ... manage to] **TS1–**
you **MS**

77.20   early ... would] **TS1–** with
dispatch he will **MS**

77.20–21   be able to give] **TS1r–** be
able to offer **MS** promise **TS1t**

77.21–22   doubt that ... endeavours]
TS1– doubt **MS**

77.24   answer (it was a short one)]
TS1– answer **MS**

77.24–25   myself to post it] **TS1–** to
post it myself at the dock gate **MS**
[*See Appendix F*]

77.25a   dreams ... night] **TS1–** my
dreams would be **MS**

77.25b   as it] **MS TS1r–** it **TS1t**

77.26a   out] **TS1–** out that night **MS**

77.26b   did not] **TS1–** didn't **MS**

77.28   looked at me] **TS1–** said **MS**

77.30   I thought you] **TS1–** Didn't
you say that **MS**

77.31a   Burns," I said. "But] **TS1–**
Burns. But **MS**

77.31b   the fact ... the] **TS1–** the **MS**

77.31c   Ocean] **TS1–** ocean **MS**

77.32a   that is] **TS1–** that's **MS**

77.32b   its] **MS S–** it's **TS1**

77.33a   home as passenger] **S–** home
MS TS1

77.33b   Suez Canal] **TS1–** Canal **MS**

77.34   Everything that is in] **TS1–**
Everything – in **MS**

77.34–35   "I've ... this.] **TS1**– "What
sort of talk is it? What's one ocean
more than another? **MS**

77.35   And to] **TS1**– To **MS**

77.36a   I've never quite] **TS1**– I
haven't **MS**

77.36b   made you out.] **MS E1**–
understood you. **TS1 S**

77.36–37   What's ... another?] **TS1**–
OM **MS**

77.38a   He] **TS1**– I believe he **MS**

77.38b   me, I believe.] **TS1**– me.
MS

77.39–40   I had ... successor] **TS1**– he
would probably succeed me in the
command **MS**

78.1–2   remarked, "let ... that] **TS1**–
remarked **MS**

78.2   own] **TS1 S** admit **E1**– OM
MS

78.3   turned out wonderfully."] **TS1**
has paid well. If only you had ..."
MS turned out wonderfully well. Of
course, if you ..." **S** has paid

extremely well. Of course, if only
you had — " **E1**–

78.4a   said] **TS1** interrupted him **MS**
interrupted **S**–

78.4b   Fortune] **TS1** fortune **MS**
S–

78.5a   could] **MS TS1r**– did **TS1t**

78.5b   was driving] **MS TS1r**– had
driven **TS1t**

78.5c   a] **MS** the **TS1**–

78.6–8   love; and ... transaction.] **TS1**
love, and endangering my modest
future. And as I sat mute and
heavy-hearted he gave up
completely for the first time his
critical attitude. **MS** love. And as I
sat heavy-hearted at that parting,
seeing all my plans destroyed, my
modest future endangered – for
this command was like a foot in the
stirrup for a young man – he gave
up completely for the first time his
critical attitude. **S**–

78.10   The End.]**TS1r** OM **MS TS1t S**–

The Secret Sharer

MS   holograph manuscript (Berg): copy-text
S   *Harper's Monthly Magazine* (August, September 1910), 349–59, 530–41

81.2a   On] **MS** Part I. | On **S** I | On
E1–

81.2b   lines of] **S**– some **MS**

81.3   resembling] **S**– like **MS**

81.3–4   bamboo fences] **S**– fences **MS**

81.5   abandoned for ever] **S**–
abandoned **MS**

81.6a   brown fishermen] **MS**
fishermen **S**–

81.6b   removed] **MS** gone **S**–

81.7   earth] **MS** ocean **S**–

81.7–8   for there ... reach] **S**– OM **MS**

81.8a   my] **MS** the **S**–

81.8b   barren] **S**– ruined **MS**

81.8–9   suggesting ... blockhouses] **S**–
as perfectly stony as if piled up
there by the hand of man **MS**

81.9   in] **S**– in | in **MS**

81.10   stable] **S**– so perfectly smooth
MS

81.15a   flat shore] **S**– shore its grey
and sombre flatness **MS**

81.15b   stable] **S**– blue of the **MS**

81.16   in] **S**– as it were **MS**

81.16–17   floor, half ... blue,] **S**– floor
MS

81.17a   under] **E1**– for **MS S**

81.17b   Corresponding] **S**– Above this
level, corresponding **MS**

81.18a   sea,] **S**– sea, rose **MS**

81.18b   small clumps] **S**– clumps **MS**

81.19   of the] **S**– of a | the **MS**

81.20a   marked] **S**– of that floor,
which was **MS**

81.20b   Meinam] **E1**– Mekong **MS S**

81.21a   our] **S**– the **MS**

81.21b journey; and far] **S–** journey, a white metallic cold bit inset between the warm brown stints and the unvaried blue. Further **MS**

81.24 monotonous] **E1–** undistinguished **MS S**

81.26 on] **S–** through **MS**

81.27a steaming] **S–** steamed **MS**

81.27b land] **S–** land and at once **MS**

81.29 an effort] **S–** a gulp **MS**

81.30 My eye followed] **E1–** But presently my eye caught **MS S**

81.31 the plain] **S–** the | the plain **MS**

81.33 Great Pagoda] **MS** great pagoda **S–**

82.3a eastward] **S–** East **MS**

82.3b At ... alone] **S–** I was the only man **MS**

82.4–5 us ... water,] **S–** there was no man, no canoe afloat nothing moving, **MS**

82.6 this ... at] **S–** that moment of our united lives on **MS**

82.7a to be] **S–** in a loving accord of self-communion to be absorbed in **MS**

82.7b fitness for] **S–** strength and testing our hearts before entering on **MS**

82.9a on, day after day,] **MS** out, **S–**

82.9b eyes,] **E1–** eye, and **MS** eye, **S**

82.10 spectators] **S–** witnesses **MS**

82.11–12 air to ... sight] **S–** air **MS**

82.14 the solemnity] **S–** that sense **MS**

82.15 tide ... and] **S–** swift twilight obliterated everything and then **MS**

82.16 came out] **S–** appeared **MS**

82.17 ship's] **S–** ships **MS**

82.18 But] **S–** But the sense of quiet communion was gone for good **MS**

82.19–20 one the ... good.] **S–** one. **MS**

82.21 disturbing sounds] **S–** sounds **MS**

82.22 spirit;] **E1–** spirit; shortly afterwards **MS** spirit; shortly afterward **S**

82.23 tinkled] **S–** pealed **MS**

82.28 ridge as ... down] **S–** ridge **MS**

82.30 growth of whisker] **S–** pair of moustaches **MS**

82.33 years] **S–** years as **MS**

83.12–13 whiskers ... evolve] **S–** moustaches had evolved **MS**

83.15a mind. As] **S–** mind and, as **MS**

83.15b he "liked] **S–** "liked **MS**

83.16 himself for"] **ED** himself for – **MS** himself" for **S–**

83.20 partial] **S–** used **MS**

83.22a had exercised] **S–** exercised **MS**

83.22b infinitely.] **E1–** infinitely. We had scorpion at every meal and the second mate's lip had been kept on the quiver all the time. **MS** infinitely. We had been having scorpion at every meal, and the second mate's lip had been kept on the quiver all the time. **S–**

83.22c ship within the islands] **S–** ship **MS**

83.24 he] **S–** the mate **MS**

83.27 into] **S–** in **MS**

83.30–31 Liverpool ship *Sephora*] **S–** "Sephora" **MS**

83.32 Cardiff] **S–** home **MS**

83.34 me of her] **MS S** me **E1–**

83.36 the river the day] **S–** the day **MS**

84.2a crew] **MS E1–** men **S**

84.2b had had] **S–** had **MS**

84.4 all] **S–** all the **MS**

84.6 I] **S–** Then I **MS**

84.7 me at that hour] **S–** me **MS**

84.10 have] **S–** get **MS**

84.13a unheard-of caprice] **S–** singular whim **MS**

84.13b hours'] **S–** hour **MS**

84.14 What? The] **S–** the **MS**

84.17a My] **S–** It was my **MS**

84.17b sleepless] **S–** sleepless and **MS**

84.22 shore] **MS** unrelated shore **S–**

84.27 out through] **MS** through **S–**

84.30 seas – ... novel] **S–** seas. Everything but the **MS**

84.31 took heart from] **E1–** comforted myself with **MS S**

84.36 went] **S–** ran **MS**

84.38 out] **MS** out again **S–**

85.4 in my choice of] **S–** of **MS**

85.5   an] **S**– a sort of **MS**
85.9   confident ... in] **S**– confidently facing **MS**
85.9–10   mysterious shades] **E1**– impenetrable mysteriousness **MS S**
85.10   on ... aft] **S**– back **MS**
85.11   ship] **S**– ship on my way aft **MS**
85.12   the tug] **S**– tug **MS**
85.14   annoyed] **S**– very annoyed **MS**
85.18   to have interfered] **MS** to interfere **S** ever to interfere **E1**–
85.20   My action] **E1**– It **MS S**
85.21   whiskered] **S**– moustachioed **MS**
85.23   new] **E1**– strange **MS S**
85.26   easily, yet my vigourous] **S**– easily. My vicious **MS**
85.27   inboard] **MS** on board **S**–
85.32a   The] **S**– Just there the **MS**
85.32b   an ... of] **S**– a more opaque **MS**
85.33a   sea] **S**– in the water sea **MS**
85.33b   something] **E1**– something fishlike **MS S**
85.38   night] **S**– quiet **MS**
85.39   back ... immersed] **MS** back immersed right up to the neck **S**–
85.40   cadaveric] **MS** cadaverous **S**–
86.1–2   head. A headless corpse!] **E1**– head. **MS S**
86.7a   that much] **MS S** it **E1**–
86.7b   horrid] **S**– sort of **MS**
86.8a   which] **S**– that **MS**
86.8b   pass off] **S**– go off at last **MS**
86.10   leaned] **S**– hung **MS**
86.15   motion] **E1**– attempt **MS S**
86.16   attempt] **S**– want **MS**
86.17   want to] **S**– to **MS**
86.18   incertitude] **S**– certitude **MS**
86.28   But] **E1**– This impression remained though **MS S**
86.35   doubt] **E1**– a doubtful man **MS S**
86.37   him out] **E1**– him **MS S**
87.2a   water] **MS** the water **S**–
87.2b   his limbs] **E1**– him **MS S**
87.6   induced] **S**– produced **MS**
87.7a   quietly] **E1**– seriously **MS S**
87.7b   remarked] **S**– said **MS**
87.8   must be] **S**– are **MS**

87.10–11   and ... swimming] **S**– to swim straight out to sea **MS**
87.11a   sink] **S**– sank **MS**
87.11b   exhaustion] **S**– sheer exhaustion **MS**
87.14   could tell by] **MS** should have gathered from **S**–
87.19   make no comment] **S**– keep silent **MS**
87.21   rail to ... clothes] **S**– rail **MS**
87.23   stairs.] **E1**– stairs. Everybody slept. **MS S**
87.27   called] **E1**– called and wander out of his berth to have a look at the weather **MS S**
87.28a   back] **E1**– out **MS S**
87.28b   man] **MS** naked man **S**–
87.30–31   In ... body] **S**– He was clothed in a moment **MS**
87.32a   grey-stripe] **E1**– grey **MS S**
87.32b   was wearing] **S**– had on **MS**
88.5   his size] **S**– him **MS**
88.10   over there] **S**– there **MS**
88.13   I *was*] **S**– *I was* **MS**
88.14   wrong] **S**– very wrong **MS**
88.17a   No, on the passage.] **S**– No. **MS**
88.17b   south] **S**– south somewhere **MS**
88.22a   in] **S**– in | in **MS**
88.22b   a] **S**– some **MS**
88.30   whiskers] **S**– moustachios **MS**
88.32   thoughts] **MS E1**– thought **S**
88.33   You] **MS** Do you **S**–
88.34   can't ... necessity] **S**– can stand it **MS**
88.36a   these] **MS** those **S**–
88.36b   creatures] **S**– fellows **MS**
89.5a   think of asking] **S**– ask **MS**
89.5b   when] **MS** and **S**–
89.9   was when] **MS** happened while we were **S**–
89.10   sort of weather] **S**– weather **MS**
89.11   her] **MS** the ship **S**–
89.15a   fellow himself] **S**– fellow **MS**
89.15–16   That ... and] **S**– I **MS**
89.15b   That] **S** It **E1**– ᴏᴍ **MS**
89.18a   it] **MS** it coming **S**–
89.18b   rigging. I] **MS** rigging, but I **S**–

89.19–20 yelling 'Look ... out!'] **E1–** yelling. **MS S**

89.20 fallen] **MS** fallen on my head **S–**

89.21a ten] **MS** over ten **S–**

89.21b there ... anything] **MS** hardly anything was **S–**

89.23 along wildly] **MS S** along **E1–**

89.25 forebits. Not ... either.] **MS S** forebits. **E1–**

89.26 still] **MS** still when they picked us up **S–**

89.30 your] **S–** you **MS**

89.31 only a-looking] **S–** looking **MS**

89.32a started raving] **S–** raved **MS**

89.32b The ... deprived] **S–** He had not a wink **MS**

89.33–34 to have ... mind] **S–** it nearly did for him **MS**

89.37a to separate us] **S–** with that **MS**

89.37b A sufficiently] **S–** I tell you its a pretty **MS**

90.6 as far] **MS** so far **S–**

90.9 as far] **MS** so far **S–**

90.12 his captain double] **MS** double **S–**

90.13 strange captain] **S–** Captain **MS**

90.16 other's] **S–** others **MS**

90.20 my movements] **S–** me blindly **MS**

90.22 to wait for] **MS** for **S–**

90.24 appeared] **MS** approached **S–**

90.34 vase with] **E1–** bunch of **MS S**

90.35a ship's] **MS–E1 A2 E2** ships' **A1**

90.35b last] **E1–** very last bunch of **MS S**

91.10 a thick] **S–** thick **MS**

91.12 which] **E1–** which last **MS S**

91.13a that way] **E1–** that door **MS S**

91.13b never used] **E1–** kept always locked **MS S**

91.14 this] **E1–** that **MS S**

91.15 biggish] **MS** big **S–**

91.18 recessed] **E1–** recess-like **MS S**

91.25 something like six] **MS** nearly nine **S** nearly seven **E1–**

91.35 once] **ED** after **MS** the *Sephora* after **S** the *Sephora* once **E1–**

91.36 Head] **S–** head **MS**

92.4 should] **S–** would **MS**

92.5 reckoned] **S–** could see **MS**

92.6a I had] **S–** had **MS**

92.6b near] **S–** close **MS**

92.8 looked damnably] **MS** seemed very **S–**

92.10 was ... to] **S–** could not **MS**

92.13 round] **MS–E1 A2 E2** around **A1**

92.16 or three] **S–** three **MS**

92.23 trusted himself] **S–** come **MS**

92.30 that work] **S–** that **MS**

92.31 men] **E1–** hands **MS S**

92.33 grey headed] **S–** grey whiskered **MS**

92.35 loafer] **S–** man **MS**

92.38 skipper] **S–** old man **MS**

93.2 disappear out] **MS** out **S–**

93.6 wouldn't] **MS** wouldn't listen to me **S–**

93.12 have had] **S–** had **MS**

93.14 was] **MS** is **S–**

93.15 ship's] **S–** ships **MS**

93.18 that] **S–** the **MS**

93.25 boat] **MS** boats **S–**

93.30 up. Everything] **E1–** up and everything **MS S**

93.31a quieted ... still as] **S–** became quiet like **MS**

93.31b became] **E1–**, **MS VAR** was **S**

93.32 felt] **E1–** became **MS S**

93.33a searching] **S–** looking **MS**

93.33b these] **MS** those **S–**

93.35 clear of that ship] **S–** clear **MS**

94.2 Something] **S–** That was something **MS**

94.2–3 I ... and on] **S–** On **MS**

94.5a poop] **S–** deck **MS**

94.5b rested myself] **S–** rested **MS**

94.9 had stared] **MS** stared **S–**

94.16a down because the] **S–** down. That **MS**

94.16b and] **S–** tho' **MS**

94.17 the land] **S–** it **MS**

94.23 fighting] **S–** lighting **MS**

94.24 got] **S–** been **MS**

94.31 my] **MS** My **S–**

94.33 This] **MS** His **S–**

94.34 that] **S–** the **MS**

94.38 My] **S–** The **MS**

95.8 sort of suspect] **MS** suspect **S–**

95.8–9 the eyes ... company] S– their eyes MS

95.12 Fancy] MS Who'd have thought of S–

95.13–14 felt just then] S– felt MS

95.16 as your] S– to the MS

95.18 a] S– a | a MS

95.21 speaking to] S– addressing MS

95.25 mere impulse] S– sudden fancy MS

96.1a on] E1– flat on MS S

96.1b one] E1– his MS S

96.2 with his] S– his MS

96.4 carefully across] MS across carefully S–

96.9–10 by the effort of] S– and MS

96.10a this] E1– that MS S

96.10b It] S– And it MS

96.18a entered] S– came in MS

96.18b tray bringing in] S– tray – MS

96.23 I dared] S– dared MS

96.24 had drawn] E1– drew MS S

96.27 crew] E1– hands MS S

96.30a reappeared] E1– appeared MS S

96.30b out] MS up S–

96.38 coaxingly] S– coaxing MS

97.4–5 double and ... he] S– double. He MS

97.7 over him] S– over MS

97.10 say me nay] MS say nay to me S–

97.13 chief mate] S– chief MS

97.15 them eagerly] S– them MS

97.23 whiskers] S– moustaches MS

97.27 particular] E1– general MS S

97.38a action] MS actions S–

97.38b open] MS own S–

98.6–7 I then] MS–A1 E2 then I A2

98.7 do] MS tidy up S–

98.8 and ... it.] MS "and ... it." S–

98.11 steward's] S– stewards MS

98.12a the ... life] E1– my other self MS S

98.12b up bolt upright] S–A2 up very still MS bolt upright E2

98.16 there to ... room] S– there MS

98.18 conversation] S– conversion MS

98.19 whiskers] S– moustaches MS

98.23 still] S– there MS

98.26 setting] MS E1– settling S

98.27 Such was my] E1– That completed the MS S

98.28 my second self] S– him MS

98.29 then] MS there S–

98.34 rigidly] S– bolt upright MS

98.35 close together] S– together MS

99.11 The] MS Part II. | The S II | The E1–

99.13 smeary] E1– intense MS S

99.15–16 the other] S– other MS

99.17 behaved with a] E1– received him with an icy punctilious MS S

99.19a one] MS me S–

99.19b gave] S– declined MS

99.21 ship's] S– ships MS

99.21–22 other particulars] S– particulars MS

99.22 an unpenitent] MS a S–

99.26 this] S– that MS

99.28–29 Terribly] MS Terrible S–

99.37 He] MS he S–

99.38–39a "What ... disease?"] MS S What ... disease? E1–

99.38–39b cause of it – some] S– cause – a MS

99.39 inquired ... and] S– asked with an air MS

99.40 that ... got] S– I got there MS

100.1a admitted] S– admitted cheerfully MS

100.1b cheerful tone] E1– sort of impenitent manner MS cheerfully polite tone S

100.10 obviously, densely] MS densely S–

100.21 any] MS an S–

100.24 you have told me] MS which, you told me, S–

100.31–32 certainly not ... part] S– not expecting anything of the sort MS

100.34 this graphic] S– that MS

100.39 long boots] S– boots MS

101.1 these] MS those S–

101.5a exclaimed] S– assented MS

101.5b It's] MS It was by S–

101.6 these] MS those S–

101.8 it] MS that sail which S–

101.9 hand in it] S– mercy MS

101.11a   we] S– it **MS**

101.11b   touch anything] S– be touched **MS**

101.17   was. To the law.] S– was. **MS**

101.18–19   something as ... mystical] S– something **MS**

101.20   countenancing ... sort.] **MS** "countenancing ... sort." S–

101.22   have laid] S– lay **MS**

101.24   went] **MS S** went on, **E1**–

101.26   on.] S– on. Our senior partner spoke to me himself. **MS**

101.28   somehow. I ... man.] S– somehow. **MS**

101.29   sort of man] **MS** sort S–

101.30   thoughts] S– thought **MS**

101.31a   the secret sharer] **E1**– occupant **MS** the secret occupant S

101.31b   if I personally] S– if **MS**

101.32   sort of man] **MS** sort S–

101.33   of a ship like] S– of **MS**

101.35   man you] **ED** man" You **MS** man. You S–

102.1   owners] S– owners about it **MS**

102.3   manage to recover] S– can get hold of **MS**

102.4   dispassionately.... "I mean alive."] S– dispassionately **MS**

102.11a   distrust] S– suspicion **MS**

102.11b   except for] S– except **MS**

102.12   pretend] **E1**– pretend to **MS S**

102.13   felt simply incapable] **ED** felt **MS** felt utterly incapable S–

102.14–15   had brought] S– brought **MS**

102.16a   politeness] **E1**– cold politeness **MS S**

102.16b   and] S– an **MS**

102.17   Not heartily!] **E1**– Heartily? **MS S**

102.19   Surlily? Yes, but surliness] **E1**– Surliness **MS S**

102.21a   nature] S– very nature **MS**

102.21b   a punctilious] **ED** a scrupulous distant **MS** a chilly, distant S punctilious **E1**–

102.25   his] S– him **MS**

102.25–26   feeling ... other] S– duality **MS**

102.27   afterwards] **MS A2 E2** afterward S–A1

102.29–30   suggested ... to] S– a sort of subtle identity with **MS**

102.33   He] **E1**– Then he **MS S**

102.36   this] S– that **MS**

102.38–40   suggestions. And ... self.] S– suggestions. **MS**

103.1   saloon] **E1**– cabin **MS S**

103.17   didn't finish and went] S– went **MS**

103.18   some ... mine] S– me right away **MS**

103.22   And I] S– I **MS**

103.23   mates' rooms] **ED** mate's rooms **MS** mate's room S–

103.25   out directly] **MS** out S–

103.29   The ... whiskers] **E1**– He **MS** The man of mustaches S

103.29–30   he used] S– used **MS**

103.30a   neck and yelled:] **E1**– neck. **MS S**

103.30b   *Sephora*s] **MS E1 A1** *Sephora*'s S **A2 E2**

104.1   I am delighted] **E1**– Quite the contrary **MS S**

104.2a   an] **E1**– no **MS S**

104.2b   and ... by] **E1**– but it was **MS S**

104.3   defective] **E1**– the defective **MS** S

104.14   murders in Yankee] S– Yankee **MS**

104.21   hidden aboard] **E1**– aboard **MS S**

104.24   Not] **ED** No **MS**–

104.38a   dared] S– dare **MS**

104.38b   to take] **MS** take S–

105.2   now more] S– more **MS**

105.4   the dinner] **MS** dinner S–

105.11   supposed] **MS** suppose S–

105.13–14   could ... it was] S– only wished to believe it **MS**

105.16   everything] **MS E1**– anything S

105.21   its] **MS** it S–

105.24–25   our last hope] S– it **MS**

105.26   your] **MS** one's S–

105.34a   that; and a] S– that. A **MS**

105.34b   coming] **MS** coming once S–

106.2 some twenty four] MS twenty-four S–

106.3 crushed out] MS S crushed E1–

106.4 weigh ... matter] S– meditate on these things MS

106.5 heavy knock] S– knock at the door MS

106.6 here] E1– there MS S

106.19 my] S– my own MS

106.27 startle] E1– be caught by MS S

106.28–29 though he were] S– of a man MS

106.31 stealthy] S– slealthy MS

106.32 roundness] MS unusual roundness S–

107.1 that cabin] MS the cabin S–

107.4 besides,] S– besides that MS

107.7 me] S– the door MS

107.18a supposed] ED suppose MS–

107.18b had made] S– did make MS

107.23–24 bathroom, which ... whole] S– bathroom. It MS

107.24a safest] S– safer MS

107.24b could be] S– was MS

107.27 reclined] S– lay MS

107.29a and with his] E1– and MS S

107.29b head] MS hair S–

107.30 smuggle him into] S– have him in MS

107.32 of] MS E1– on S

107.34 stateroom] S– room MS

107.37 My] E1– The MS S

107.38 respect] E1– way MS S

107.39–40 so that] S– to let MS

107.40 should be] S– be MS

108.5 and in] MS and S–

108.5–6 perfectly smooth] MS smooth S–

108.7 meal] S– dinner MS

108.9 This] S– That MS

108.10 again; and ... that] S– again. It seems MS

108.18a that] S– which MS

108.18b whiskered] E1– mustachioed MS S

108.19 detected him using] E1– a sight of him once down on the main deck use MS caught a sight of him using S

108.20 talking on deck] S– talking MS

108.21–22 this ... captain] S– it referred to me MS

108.32a I go] S– go MS

108.32b up] MS up again S–

108.34–35 could hear] MS would have heard S–

108.36–37 the lip of that] S– that MS

108.37 mate, quivered visibly] S– mate's lip quivered MS

109.5 movement] S– movement to get up MS

109.6a strength to ... legs] S– strength MS

109.6b Everything remained] S– All MS

109.7 my ... wretch] S– he taken him MS

109.8 would] MS–A1 E2 could A2

109.16 in] S– it MS

109.28 usual] MS E1– casual S

109.30 my double] S– he MS

109.36 existence] S– presence MS

109.39 a grave] S– a | a grave MS

110.4 whiskers] E1– moustaches MS S

110.5 tack. In] E1– tack; and in MS S

110.18 hand] MS head S arm E1–

110.34 Cambodie] MS Cambodje S–A1 A2a E2 Cambodge A2b

111.4 it] MS the Bible S–

111.8a Not.] MS S Can't? E1–

111.8b shall] E1– will MS S

111.10 understood] S– understand MS

111.13a ship's] S– ships MS

111.13b had] S– has MS

111.16 I] E1– you MS S

111.22 talking on] MS talking S–

111.30 whiskers] E1– moustaches MS S

112.2a good lookout] MS lookout S–

112.2b current at all] MS current S–

112.3 long before] MS before S–

112.4a Gulf] MS gulf S–

112.4b islands] S– island MS

112.9 dank] MS–E1 A2 E2 dark A1

112.14 forenoon] E1– day MS S

112.18 whiskers] E1– moustaches MS S

112.21 ferocity also] S– ferocity MS

112.23–24   gulf," I continued casually.] S– gulf. **MS**

112.32a   we two] S– we **MS**

112.32b   dark heads] S– heads **MS**

112.39   let it] S– it shall **MS**

113.9   Gulf] **MS** gulf S–

113.18   any mishap to] S– the wreck of **MS**

113.20   on] **MS–A2** on to **E2**

113.25   so forgot] S– forgot **MS**

113.26a   at] S– and **MS**

113.26b   incomprehensible order] S– incomprehensible **MS**

113.27   What for] S– What's the reason **MS**

113.29a   tell] **E1–** told **MS S**

113.29b   to do so] **E1–** so **MS S**

113.29c   open] **MS–A1 A2a** opened **E2 A2b**

113.30   he made] **ED** made **MS–**

113.33   whiskers] **E1–** moustaches **MS S**

114.1–2   shall presently] **MS–A1 E2** will presently **A2**

114.6   ship's] S– ships **MS**

114.7   shall] **S–A1 E2** will **MS A2**

114.8   over] **MS** get overboard S–

114.9–11   up. Use ... complication.] S– up. **MS**

114.19   his grip] S– my arm **MS**

114.24a   amongst] **MS** against S–

114.24b   outlying] **MS** drifting S–

115.1   other's] S– others **MS**

115.5   vegetables for the crew] S– vegetables **MS**

115.14   at last] S– last **MS**

115.16   before] **MS** till S–

115.18a   passed ... cuddy] S– came out into the cabin **MS**

115.18b   wide open] S– open **MS**

115.26   fire's been] S– fire is **MS**

115.28   fled] **MS–A1 E2** flew **A2**

115.29   too] S– to **MS**

115.31   stairs. A] **MS** stairs – through a **S E1 A2 E2** stairs – through the **A1**

115.33   myself] S– him **MS**

115.34   my] S– his **MS**

115.36   my other self] S– him **MS**

115.37   wondered] **ED** wonder **MS–**

115.38   lingered] S– remained **MS**

116.11   me down] **MS** me S–

116.13a   will] **MS–A1 E2 A2b** may **A2a**

116.13b   said then] S– said **MS**

116.16   the] S– a **MS**

116.20   loom of the land] S– loom **MS**

116.20–21   grow bigger and denser] S– grow **MS**

116.21a   much] **MS** much for me S–

116.21b   to shut] **MS** shut S–

116.21c   eyes. She] **MS** eyes – because the ship S–

116.22a   Must!] **MS** She must! S–

116.22b   was] S– grew **MS**

116.24a   black southern] S– southern **MS**

116.24b   Koh-ring] S– Koh-rong **MS**

116.27   towards] **MS A2** toward S–**A1 E2**

116.28–29   vague figures] S– figures **MS**

116.29   the watch] S– men **MS**

116.30   inquired] S– said **MS**

116.34   answered me] S– answered **MS**

116.36   Already she] S– She **MS**

116.40   turn ... up] S– call all hands **MS**

117.1–2   from the height of] S– from **MS**

117.5   a light] **MS–A1 E2 A2b** light **A2a**

117.10   whiskers] **E1–** moustaches **MS S**

117.18–19   close now] S– close **MS**

117.19   stay. She'll ... round.] S– stay. **MS**

117.21   it] S– him **MS**

117.22   wailed, trying ... away.] S– wailed **MS**

117.23–25   there." ¶ "Good ... voice.] S– there." **MS**

117.26   the mate's] S– his **MS**

117.28–29   noise – shake – ... overhauled] S– noise **MS**

117.30   towards] **MS A2** toward S–**A1 E2**

117.31   I released] S– He escaped from **MS**

117.31–32   he ... dear] S– seemed to run forward for his **MS**

117.33–34   thought of this commotion] S– thought **MS**

117.35 why, ... it] **S–** too. It **MS**
117.35–36 thus close – no less] **S–** close **MS**
117.36 Hard a-lee] **S–** Hard-n-lee **MS**
117.37a towering] **S–** great **MS**
117.37b shadow of Koh-ring] **S–** shadow **MS**
117.38 And ... intently] **S–** I waited **MS**
117.39 the ship] **S–** her **MS**
117.40–118.2 coming-to. No! ... already ... ?] **S–** coming-to. **MS**
118.3 brooding] **S–** that seemed to brood **MS**
118.4 pivot] **S–** swing **MS**
118.6 total stranger] **S–** stranger **MS**
118.8–9 perhaps stopped] **S–** stopped **MS**
118.10 mass of Koh-ring] **S–** mass **MS**
118.13 a glassy] **MS** the glassy **S–**
118.14 sleeping] **MS S** the sleeping **E1–**
118.15a learned yet] **S–** learned **MS**
118.15b ship. Was she moving?] **S–** ship. **MS**
118.15–16 I needed] **E1–** was wanted **MS S**
118.18–19 strained, yearning stare] **E1–** eyes **MS** forced, yearning stare **S**
118.19 distinguished] **S–** perceived **MS**
118.19–20 within a yard of] **S–** close to **MS**
118.20–21 White ... it.] **S–** I had what I wanted. **MS**
118.21a What] **S–** But what **MS**
118.21b I recognized my] **S–** My **MS**
118.23 bother. Now ... eyes.] **S–** bother. **MS**

118.24 my other] **S–** him my second **MS**
118.25a hidden for ever] **S–** hidden **MS**
118.25b friendly faces] **S–** faces **MS**
118.26a the] **S–** the the **MS**
118.26b brand] **S–** mark **MS**
118.26–27 curse on ... forehead] **S–** curse **MS**
118.27 the slaying] **MS** a slaying **S–**
118.29 had been meant] **S–** was **MS**
118.30 sun! And now – behold –] **S–** sun – but now **MS**
118.32–33 was ... had gathered] **S–** drifted forward! She had **MS**
118.34–35 voice to ... statue] **S–** voice **MS**
118.36 wildly] **S–** cheerily **MS**
118.37 jumped ... spun round] **S–** spun **MS**
118.39a the forebraces] **S–** forebraces **MS**
118.39b The] **MS E1–** All the **S**
118.40a seemed ... left] **S–** glided to the left **MS**
118.40b still] **E1–** quiet **MS S**
119.1 quiet remark] **E1–** remark **MS S**
119.5 whiskers made themselves] **E1–** moustaches were being **MS S**
119.7 one in the world] **S–** one **MS**
119.8 throwing a shadow on] **S–** blocking **MS**
119.13 catch] **S–** have **MS**
119.14 secret sharer] **E1–** sharer **MS** secret-sharer **S**
119.16–17 water to ... man,] **S–** water – **MS**

Freya of the Seven Isles

MS holograph manuscript (Philadelphia)
TS1 typescript (Berg)
TS1t typewritten (unrevised) text of **TS1** superseded by revision
TS1r revised text of **TS1** (incorporating Conrad's alterations): copy-text
SA *Metropolitan Magazine* (April 1912), 20–29, 51–54
SE *London Magazine* (July 1912), 649–84

123.2   I] **MS TS1 E1**– Chapter I. **SE** OM **SA**

123.3–124.34   One ... Isles.] **MS TS1 SE**– OM **SA**

123.6   middle-aged,] **MS** middle aged; I imagined him **TS1 SE**– OM **SA**

123.7a   that] **MS** the **TS1 SE**– OM **SA**

123.7b   Fate] **MS TS1** fate **SE**– OM **SA**

123.7c   all] **SE**– us all **MS TS1** OM **SA**

123.7d   except to] **TS1r SE**– except **MS TS1t** OM **SA**

123.8   those] **MS TS1t SE**– those of us **TS1r** OM **SA**

123.8–9   get ... early] **TS1r SE**– die young **MS TS1t** OM **SA**

123.11   Surely] **TS1r SE**– do **MS TS1t** OM **SA**

123.15–16   form of his name] **TS1r SE**– form **MS TS1t** OM **SA**

123.17   advent of telegraph] **TS1r SE**– era of telegraph **MS** telegraph **TS1t** OM **SA**

123.19   Eastern Archipelago] **TS1r SE**– Archipelago **MS TS1t** OM **SA**

123.21   eight] **MS TS1 SE E2** eights **E1–A2** OM **SA**

123.21–22   For ... years. ¶ There] **TS1r SE**– ¶ There **MS TS1t** OM **SA**

123.22   not a] **MS** no **TS1 SE**– OM **SA**

123.23   an] **TS1r SE**– his **MS TS1t** OM **SA**

123.24   tracks] **MS TS1r SE**– tracts **TS1t** OM **SA**

123.25   cobweb] **TS1r SE**– tangled skein of thread **MS TS1t** OM **SA**

123.27   of the] **MS TS1r SE**– the **TS1t** OM **SA**

123.28a   he ... him] **TS1r SE**– was the reason of that deep seated horror **MS TS1t** OM **SA**

123.28b   impossible] **TS1r SE**– difficult **MS TS1t** OM **SA**

123.29a   some] **MS TS1 E1**– some remote **SE** OM **SA**

123.29b   time in his life] **TS1r E1**– time **MS TS1t** time of his life **SE** OM **SA**

123.29c   some stories of] **TS1r SE**– something about **MS TS1t** OM **SA**

123.31   afraid] **TS1r SE**– singularly afraid **MS TS1t** OM **SA**

124.1   even more] **TS1r SE**– excessively **MS TS1t** OM **SA**

124.2   The Dutch] **TS1r SE**– They were **MS TS1t** OM **SA**

124.3a   were capable] **TS1r SE**– capable **MS TS1t** OM **SA**

124.3b   any] **TS1r SE**– an **MS TS1t** OM **SA**

124.4   There were] **MS TS1 E1**– They had **SE** OM **SA**

124.5   but ... of] **E1**– and no **MS TS1t** but no notion of **TS1r SE** OM **SA**

124.6   anxious] **TS1r SE**– anxiously civil **MS TS1t** OM **SA**

124.8   a] **SE**– the most **MS TS1t** the a **TS1r** OM **SA**

124.9   fearless] **SE**– and unassuming **MS TS1t** unassuming **TS1r** OM **SA**

124.11   amount] **MS TS1r SE**– amount to ftif **TS1t** OM **SA**

124.12   Truly] **E1**– Of course **MS TS1 SE** OM **SA**

124.14a   or else] **TS1r SE**– or **MS TS1t** OM **SA**

124.14b   Sultan] **TS1r SE**– Chief or Sultan **MS TS1t** OM **SA**

124.15a   called] **MS TS1 SE–A1 E2 A2b** call **A2a** OM **SA**

124.15b   Seven] **MS TS1r SE**– seven **TS1t** OM **SA**

124.15c   far north] **TS1r SE**– far **MS TS1t** OM **SA**

124.17–18   discovered a reason] **TS1r SE**– found some excellent excuse **MS TS1t** OM **SA**

124.18   out without ceremony] **TS1r SE**– out **MS TS1t** OM **SA**

124.18–19   In ... of] **TS1r SE**– There **MS TS1t** OM **SA**

124.19   name] **TS1r SE**– name Nielsen **MS TS1t** OM **SA**

124.20   unassuming] **E1**– unassuming unnattached **MS** unassuming unattathed **TS1t** unattached **TS1r SE** OM **SA**

124.22a   the shadow] **MS TS1 E1**– a shadow **SE** OM **SA**

124.22b offence] **TS1r SE–** an offence **MS TS1t** OM **SA**

124.23a a prudential reason] **TS1r** prudential reasons **MS TS1t SE–** OM **SA**

124.23b of that sort] **TS1r SE–** I believe **MS TS1t** OM **SA**

124.23c did] **MS TS1r SE–** did | did **TS1t** OM **SA**

124.25 old Nelson's] **TS1r SE–** his **MS TS1t** OM **SA**

124.29 out all ways] **TS1r SE–** out **MS TS1t** OM **SA**

124.30 the fretful] **MS TS1r SE–** a fretful **TS1t** OM **SA**

124.33a came out to live] **TS1r SE–** came to live **MS** was **TS1t** OM **SA**

124.33b be] **TS1r SE–** became **MS TS1t** OM **SA**

124.35a Freya] **TS1r–** Frida **MS** Freda **TS1t**

124.35b girl] **MS–A1 E2** a girl **A2**

124.36 of] **MS TS1r–** of of **TS1t**

124.40 determination] **TS1r–** serenity **MS TS1t**

125.1 their colour] **TS1r–** colour **MS TS1t**

125.2 and more lustrous] **SE–** but still deep **MS TS1t** but quite as deep **TS1r SA**

125.5a I have] **TS1r–** have **MS TS1t**

125.5b that the] **TS1r–** the **MS TS1t**

125.17a her costume] **TS1r–** her **MS TS1t**

125.17b was] **MS–SA E1–** would be **SE**

125.17c blue] **E1–** pale blue **MS–SE**

125.18 land from] **TS1r–** come out of **MS TS1t**

125.19 long pull ... sun] **TS1r–** good mile pull **MS TS1t**

125.24 Freya] **MS TS1r–** Freda **TS1t**

125.25 round] **MS TS1r–** sound **TS1t**

125.26 tapered] **MS** tapering **TS1–**

125.30 for] **TS1r–** to **MS** t* **TS1t**

125.31 dumb] **E1–** unassuming **MS–SE**

125.32a of his] **MS** of **TS1–**

125.32b Freya] **TS1r–** Frida **MS** Freda **TS1t**

125.33 Nelson (or Nielsen)] **MS TS1 SE–** Nelson **SA**

125.35 Europe] **MS TS1 SE–** Europe for a long visit **SA**

125.37–38 from ... Ebhart's] **TS1r–** an **MS TS1t**

125.39–126.13 him – so ... world.] **MS TS1 SE–** him. **SA**

125.40 Freya's] **TS1r SE–** Frida's **MS** Freda's **TS1t** OM **SA**

125.40–126.1 the ... case] **TS1r SE–** it **MS TS1t** OM **SA**

126.3 nautical] **E1–** arduous nautical **MS TS1 SE** OM **SA**

126.4a engineers and firemen] **TS1r SE–** firemen **MS TS1t** OM **SA**

126.4b much] **TS1r SE–** most **MS TS1t** OM **SA**

126.6a planks] **TS1r SE–** planks and **MS TS1t** OM **SA**

126.6b toiling in the sun] **TS1r–** toiling **MS TS1t** OM **SA**

126.8–9 drawing-room] **MS TS1r–** rawing room **TS1t** OM **SA**

126.12 object] **TS1r SE–** object that ever was **MS TS1t** OM **SA**

126.17 Freya] **MS TS1r–** Freda **TS1t**

126.19 point] **MS–SA E1–** shore **SE**

126.21 an] **E1–** the usual **MS–SE**

126.22 these] **MS TS1 E1–A2** those **SA SE E2**

126.25a whirlwinds] **MS TS1r–** a whirlwinds **TS1t**

126.25b aspect] **E1–** hue **MS–SE**

126.26–27 rattling ... wind] **SE–** desperately rattling **MS TS1t** desperately rattling in the wind **TS1r SA**

126.27 Freya] **TS1r–** Frida **MS** Freda **TS1t**

126.28 flicker] **TS1r–** midst **MS TS1t**

126.30 remain stock still] **TS1r–** sit **MS TS1t**

126.31 verandah] **TS1r–** verandah too **MS TS1t**

126.32 rapid] **TS1r–** masterful rapid **MS TS1t**

126.33 at the point] **MS–SA E1–** in the cove **SE**

126.34a a] **SE–** two **MS–SA**

126.34b   nasty] **MS–E1 A2 E2** the nasty **A1**

126.35   rock-heads] **MS–SA E1–** rocks **SE**

126.36a   this] **TS1r–** all this **MS TS1t**

126.36b   but] **MS TS1 SE–** than **SA**

126.38   Freya] **TS1r–** Frida **MS** Freda **TS1t**

126.40   which] **E1–** that **MS–SE**

127.2   Freya] **TS1r–** Frida **MS** Freda **TS1t**

127.3a   remember I watched] **E1–** was standing **MS TS1t** remember I was standing **TS1r SA** remember I was **SE**

127.3b   Freya] **TS1r–** Frida **MS** Freda **TS1t**

127.3c   verandah] **E1–** verandah watching **MS–SE**

127.3–4   the brig] **TS1r–** him **MS TS1t**

127.4   Jasper] **TS1r–** he **MS TS1t**

127.5   the girl] **TS1r–** her **MS TS1t**

127.8a   gap] **TS1r–** break **MS TS1t**

127.8b   reefs] **TS1r–** ledges **MS TS1t**

127.9–10   all her sails] **SE–** the sails all **MS TS1t** all the sails **TS1r SA**

127.10   rattling, so that we] **TS1r–** rattling. We **MS TS1t**

127.12a   Freya] **TS1r–** Frida **MS** Freda **TS1t**

127.12b   swore] **MS–SA E1–** actually swore **SE**

127.14   remarked] **TS1r–** said **MS TS1t**

127.15   there," and laughed.] **TS1r–** there." **MS TS1t**

127.15–18   To ... sense.] **MS TS1 SE–** OM **SA**

127.16   anybody else] **TS1r SE–** anybody **MS TS1t** OM **SA**

127.17   concern at ... trick] **TS1r SE–** concern **MS TS1t** OM **SA**

127.18   sympathetic common sense] **TS1r SE–** sound judgment **MS TS1t** OM **SA**

127.19   fool?" I ... feeling.] **TS1r–** fool?" **MS TS1t**

127.20   agreed warmly] **TS1r–** assented **MS TS1t**

127.25   then] **TS1–** the **MS**

127.28   her own] **SE–** her **MS–SA**

127.35–36   have yet] **TS1r–** have **MS TS1t**

127.36a   some day] **TS1r–** before long **MS TS1t**

127.36b   She and I] **E1–** We two **MS–SE**

127.36c   together] **MS TS1 SE–** altogether **SA**

127.37   Then ... talk] **TS1r–** He started then talking **MS** He started talking **TS1t**

127.39   failed him] **MS–SA E1–** failed **SE**

127.40a   pain] **TS1r–** despair **MS TS1t**

127.40b   And] **E1–** On my word . . . And **MS–SE**

128.3   Nelson (or Nielsen)] **MS TS1 SE–** Nelson **SA**

128.4   his] **SE–** more of his **MS–SA**

128.9a   with his daughter] **SE–** in the house **MS–SA**

128.9b   think] **MS TS1r–** thing **TS1t**

128.10a   possible in the time] **E1–** possible **MS–SE**

128.10b   suspected] **E1–** couldn't ignore **MS–SE**

128.11–12   fishes of] **MS TS1 SE–** fishes in **SA**

128.12   most of] **TS1r–** all **MS TS1t**

128.14   gone] **MS TS1r–** one **TS1t**

128.15   to ever] **MS TS1 SE–A1 A2a** ever to **SA E2 A2b**

128.18   during] **MS TS1r–** owing to **TS1t**

128.22   ever did] **TS1r–** did **MS TS1t**

128.24   character] **MS TS1r–** characters **TS1t**

128.25   sailor] **E1–** young man **MS** man **TS1–SE**

128.27–38   On ... man.] **MS TS1 SE–** OM **SA** [*see 128.39–129.9*]

128.29   himself was] **SE–** was really **MS TS1** OM **SA**

128.31   very] **TS1r SE–** a very **MS TS1t** OM **SA**

128.32   spears] **TS1r SE–** lances **MS TS1t** OM **SA**

128.33–34   In ... respect] **TS1r SE–** Otherwise **MS TS1t** OM **SA**

128.34a he] **E1**– it must be admitted that he **MS TS1 SE** om **SA**

128.34b had] **TS1r SE**– was **MS TS1t** om **SA**

128.38 tried] **MS TS1t E1**– oppressed **TS1r SE** om **SA**

128.39–129.9 Naturally ... ridiculous.] **MS TS1 E1**– om **SA SE** [*see 128.27–38, 129.10–27*]

129.1 not for] **MS TS1r E1**– for **TS1t** om **SA SE**

129.2 was supposed to be] **TS1r E1**– was **MS TS1t** om **SA SE**

129.4 retired rear-admiral] **TS1r E1**– old naval officer **MS TS1t** om **SA SE**

129.10–27 On ... house.] **MS–SA E1**– om **SE** [*see 128.39–129.9*]

129.25 girl; nothing more] **E1**– girl. *That* was all right **MS–SA** om **SE**

129.29 have found] **TS1r**– find **MS TS1t**

129.30 at] **TS1**– a **MS**

129.33–35 Who ... true.] **MS–SA E1**– om **SE**

129.33 who] **MS** that **TS1 SA E1**– om **SE**

129.34 a] **TS1r SA E1**– the **MS TS1t** om **SE**

129.36 I believe] **MS TS1r**– beleive **TS1t**

129.38 connections] **E1**– side **MS–SE**

129.40a that] **MS** the **TS1**–

129.40b after] **TS1r**– while **MS TS1t**

129.40c had been] **TS1r**– were **MS TS1t**

130.1a that ... a] **TS1r**– when **MS TS1t**

130.2 between ... speech] **TS1r**– is established **MS TS1t**

130.5 since ... he] **TS1r**– ever since he **MS TS1t**

130.5–6 middle-aged] **TS1r**– thick short, elderly **MS TS1t**

130.8–9 over to the Philippines] **E1**– over **MS–SE**

130.9–11 This ... statement.] **MS TS1 SE**– om **SA** [*see 130.11, 130.12–23*]

130.11 statement.] **SA**– statement. Jasper used to tell us the whole story of his queer pertractations. He was given possession of his purchase at dusk the peruvian's [peruvian's > **Peruvian's**] people going hurriedly ashore all together in a boat carrying off a woman who appeared amongst them at the last moment from some recess where Jasper had never even suspected her presence. By her voice he judged her to be a young creature in a deuse [deuse > **duce**] of a temper, because while that ruffianly gang were helping her over the side she kept on scolding them with astonishing volubility. The black coated enigmatic Peruvian remained the last of on deck and turning to Jasper declared that [declared that > **declared**] he was glad to leave the vessel in the hands of a gentleman. **MS TS1t** statement. Jasper used to tell us the whole story of his queer pertractations which ended in him being given possession of his purchase at dusk, the Peruvian's people going hurriedly ashore all together in a boat, carrying off a woman who appeared amongst them at the last moment from some recess down below where Jasper had never even suspected her presence. By her voice he judged her to be a young creature with a temper of her own, because while that ruffianly gang were helping her over the side she kept on scolding them with astonishing volubility. The black-coated, enigmatic, Peruvian remained the last on deck and turning to Jasper declared he was glad to leave the vessel in the hands of a gentleman. **TS1r** [*see 130.9–11, 130.12–23*]

130.12–23 Indeed, ... smuggler.] **MS TS1 SE–A2 E2** om **SA** [*see 130.9–11, 130.11*]

130.12 the] **MS SE**– the the **TS1** om **SA**

130.14 must have been] **TS1r SE**– was **MS TS1t** om **SA**

130.18–19   much ... history] **TS1r SE–**
that fact **MS TS1t** OM **SA**

130.22   pirates, a slaver] **E1–** slavers
MS TS1 SE OM **SA**

130.23–24   However ... be she] **MS
TS1 SE–** The brig herself **SA**

130.24   the day] **MS TS1r–** that day
TS1t

130.25   sailed ... witch, steered] **MS
TS1r–** steered **TS1t**

130.26a   women] **MS TS1r–** woman
TS1t

130.26b   famous in] **E1–** not unknown
to **MS–SE**

130.29   clothed] **E1–** arrayed **MS–SE**

130.33   moulding] **TS1r–** moulding
along her side **MS TS1t**

130.35   pleasure-yacht] **TS1r–** yacht
MS TS1t

130.36–40   For ... Freya.] **MS TS1 SE–**
OM **SA**

130.36   must ... prefer] **TS1r SE–**
would have preferred **MS TS1t** OM
SA

130.37   white] **TS1r SE–** ship's white
MS ship white **TS1t** OM **SA**

130.38a   besides] **MS TS1r SE–** beside
TS1t OM **SA**

130.38b   less expensive] **TS1r SE–**
cheaper **MS TS1t** OM **SA**

130.39   no decoration] **TS1r SE–**
nothing **MS TS1t** OM **SA**

131.1   as indissolubly] **TS1r–**
somehow **MS TS1t**

131.2   fuse] **TS1r–** melt **MS TS1t**

131.4   induced ... inward] **TS1r–**
seemed to consume him with a sort
of fiery **MS TS1t**

131.5a   the face] **MS** face **TS1–**

131.5b   lateral wave] **E1–** wave
MS–SE

131.6a   glint] **TS1r–** snap **MS TS1t**

131.6b   quick] **E1–** his quick **MS–SE**

131.10a   this] **MS TS1r–** his **TS1t**

131.10b   peculiarly ... by] **TS1r–**
peculiar tenseness of personality
seemed to relax in **MS** peculiar
tenseness of per**nality seemed to
relax in **TS1t**

131.10c   grave] **E1–** gravely **MS–SE**

131.10d   devout] **TS1r–** beatific **MS**
beautiful **TS1t**

131.11   movements] **MS TS1r–**
movement **TS1t**

131.11–12   resolute] **E1–** fresh **MS–SE**

131.12–13   seemed ... heart] **TS1r–**
soothed him somehow **MS** soothed
him somewhat **TS1t**

131.13a   the magic of her] **TS1r–** her
MS TS1t

131.13b   of her voice, of] **TS1r SE–**
her voice **MS TS1t** of her voice, or
of **SA**

131.13–14   glances ... so] **E1–** glances
MS–SE

131.15   ablaze] **TS1r–** on fire **MS TS1t**

131.16   to discuss] **TS1r–** for **MS TS1t**

131.19–20   a ... visitor] **TS1r–** *always*
coming here **MS TS1t**

131.21   old Nelson] **TS1r–** he **MS TS1t**

131.25   II] **MS TS1 E1–** Chapter II. **SE**
OM **SA**

131.26–38   You ... merely] **MS TS1
SE–** Merely **SA**

131.26–27   unreasonable was] **SE**
unreasonable **MS TS1 E1** OM **SA**

131.29   more ... disposition] **TS1r SE–**
a man's heart more **MS TS1t** OM **SA**

131.31a   start at] **TS1r SE–** quail
before **MS TS1t** OM **SA**

131.31b   evil] **E1–** malevolent **MS TS1**
ill-natured **SE** OM **SA**

131.32   a desert] **MS TS1 SE E1 A2 E2**
the desert, **A1** OM **SA**

131.33a   hermitage. And even there]
TS1r SE– hermitage where anyhow
MS hermitage where anyway **TS1t**
OM **SA**

131.33b   should] **MS TS1r SE–** would
TS1t OM **SA**

131.34   Devil] **MS TS1r** devil **TS1t SE–**
OM **SA**

131.35a   However ... who] **TS1r SE–**
So you see there's not much use in
quailing And, besides, there is
reason in things. The Devil **MS TS1t**
OM **SA**

131.35b   Devil] **MS TS1** devil **SE–**
OM **SA**

131.35c   had] **MS TS1** has **SE–** OM **SA**

131.36a   days ... moved] **TS1r** days **MS TS1t** days and has moved **SE**– OM **SA**

131.36b   Celestial] **E1**– the Celestial **MS TS1 SE** OM **SA**

131.37   Dutchmen] **TS1r SE**– multitudes **MS TS1t** OM **SA**

132.2   little] **SE**– little black **MS TS1** OM **SA**

132.5   naval lieutenant] **MS** lieutanant **TS1**–

132.6a   years'] **MS TS1r**– year's **TS1t**

132.6b   before long] **E1**– very soon **MS**–**SE**

132.9a   in] **MS TS1r**– in all **TS1t**

132.9b   learned] **TS1r**– must have learned **MS TS1t**

132.9c   Mintok] **MS TS1r SA E1**– Minton **TS1t** Muntok **SE**

132.10a   Palembang, I suppose,] **TS1r**– Palembang **MS TS1t**

132.10b   pretty girl] **TS1r**– girl **MS TS1t**

132.13   half a day's] **MS TS1 SE**– a day's **SA**

132.16   that absurd] **SE**– such a **MS** that **TS1t SA**

132.17a   clean-shaven] **TS1r**– clean shaven **MS TS1t**

132.17b   brown] **TS1r**– browned **MS TS1t**

132.19   his] **E1**– his coarse **MS**–**SE**

132.20   a surly] **E1**– an ominous **MS**–**SE**

132.22a   neck. A thick, round] **TS1r**– neck above a thick **MS TS1t**

132.22b   in] **E1**– clothed in **MS**–**SE**

132.22c   undress] **SE**– cloth uniform **MS TS1t** cloth undress **TS1r SA**

132.23a   gold shoulder-straps] **TS1r**– shoulder straps **MS TS1t**

132.23b   was sustained] **TS1r**– sustained **MS TS1t**

132.24   drill trousers] **TS1r**– trousers **MS TS1t**

132.24–28   His ... authority.] **MS TS1 SE**– OM **SA**

132.25   cap] **TS1r E1**– uniform cap **MS TS1t** peaked cap **SE** OM **SA**

132.27–28   nervousness ... authority.] **TS1r SE**– absurd nervousness. **MS** nervousness. ¶ousness.h **TS1t** OM **SA**

132.27   that was invested with] **E1**– that was clothed in **TS1r** invested with **SE** OM **MS TS1t SA**

132.29   Therefore Heemskirk] **TS1r** He **MS TS1t** Heemskirk **SA**–

132.30   Nelson's] **TS1r** the **MS TS1t SA**–

132.33   trouble] **SE**– trouble even **MS**–**SA**

132.33–34   himself by ... word] **SA**– himself by so much as ** a word **TS1r** himself **MS TS1t**

132.36   Had he] **TS1r**– If he had **MS TS1t**

132.37   Nelson (or Nielsen)] **MS TS1 SE**– Nelson **SA**

132.38a   fists. But] **TS1r**– fists, but he was terrified by **MS TS1t**

132.38b   these] **MS TS1 E1**– those **SA SE**

132.39   that – were ... fellow] **TS1r**– that – **MS TS1t**

133.1   treat] **TS1r**– who treated **MS TS1t**

133.4–25   I saw ... incurable.] **MS TS1 SE**– OM **SA**

133.8   had to own] **TS1r SE**– added muttering **MS TS1t** OM **SA**

133.9   Heemskirk] **TS1r SE**– he **MS TS1t** OM **SA**

133.11   yet met] **SE**– met yet **MS TS1** OM **SA**

133.11–13   here," I ... see ...”] **TS1r SE**– here – not of that type anyhow, so that's of not much consequence but ... **MS TS1t** OM **SA**

133.14   what] **TS1r SE**– what he thought **MS TS1t** OM **SA**

133.16   his] **TS1r SE**– the **MS TS1t** OM **SA**

133.17   Heemskirk] **TS1r SE**– he **MS TS1t** OM **SA**

133.19   irresistible, or] **TS1r SE**– irresistible and **MS TS1t** OM **SA**

133.21a   girl. Nelson] **TS1r SE**– girl and Nelson **MS TS1t** OM **SA**

133.21–22   enough. Only ... not] TS1r
SE– enough but didn't MS TS1t OM
SA

133.21b   Only] E1– But MS TS1 SE
OM SA

133.22   it.] TS1r SE– it. And so I
refrained. MS TS1t OM SA

133.26   restrained] E1– contained
MS–SE

133.27a   as] MS–A1 like A2 E2

133.27b   everything she did] MS TS1
SE– she did everything SA

133.28–30   in Heemskirk's ... with]
TS1r– Heemskirke's attentions were
odious to her. There was something
slightly insolent in the fellow's
manner to her MS TS1t

133.29   was] TS1r E1– VAR MS TS1t
was something, SE was something
of SA

133.30   that] MS–SA E1– his SE

133.31a   looked] MS TS1r– booked
TS1t

133.31b   old ... Freya] TS1r– them MS
TS1t

133.33   felt] TS1r– was MS TS1t

133.34   and sympathise] TS1r–
sympthise MS TS1t

133.35a   her difficulty] TS1r– her MS
TS1t

133.35b   equal] TS1r– too equal MS
TS1t

133.35c   situation] TS1r– situation for
one to be sorry MS TS1t

133.38a   it happened] MS–SA E1–
happened SE

133.38b   and] MS SA– an TS1

133.39   alone could detect] TS1r–
discerned something like MS
discovered something like TS1t

134.1   radiance] E1– brightness
MS–SE

134.4   it] E1– that MS–SE

134.6   and] MS TS1r– And | And TS1t

134.7   will] SE– must MS–SA

134.9a   must keep him quiet,] TS1r–
must MS TS1t

134.9b   declared] E1– said MS–SE

134.10   very well] TS1r– well MS
TS1t

134.10–11   too when ... roused] TS1r–
too MS TS1t

134.11   he is] TS1r he's SA– OM MS
TS1t

134.12   in a soft tone] TS1r– softly MS
TS1t

134.13–14   "But ... now."] TS1r– OM
MS TS1t

134.15–16a   "He ... remarked.] MS
TS1r– OM TS1t

134.15–16b   blackbeetle all ...
remarked] TS1r– blackbeetle" I
pursued with absolute conviction
MS OM TS1t

134.20   ten thousand] TS1r– ten MS
TS1t

134.22   said] TS1r– uttered MS TS1t

134.28   some] TS1r– the full MS TS1t

134.31a   his] MS TS1r– the TS1t

134.31b   rose] MS came TS1–

134.34   Nielsen] SE Nelson MS–SA
E1–

134.37–135.9   Nelson's ... ours.] MS
TS1 SE– OM SA

134.38a   was first] E1– was MS TS1 SE
OM SA

134.38b   then the] E1– the MS TS1
SE OM SA

134.38c   *Neptun*, gunboat,] MS TS1
SE *Neptun* gunboat E1– OM SA

134.39   further] MS TS1 SE–A2
farther E2 OM SA

135.2   her] TS1 SE– her her MS OM
SA

135.4   rake] E1– loftiness MS TS1 SE
OM SA

135.6   the possession] MS possession
TS1 SE– OM SA

135.10a   remarked] MS–SA E1–
pointed out SE

135.10b   three] E1– three more or less
unexpected MS–SE

135.11   domestic] TS1r– many MS
TS1t

135.12   at] TS1r– in MS TS1t

135.14   a] TS1r– only a MS TS1t

135.18   tried] TS1r– devoted myself
MS TS1t

135.20   Dutchman] TS1r– animal MS
TS1t

135.24–25 concentrated ... watching]
TS1r SA E1– indeed silent MS TS1t
silently concentrated in watching SE

135.26 his] E1– the MS–SE

135.31a had rounded] TS1r–
rounded MS TS1t

135.31b reef] TS1r– reefs MS reefr
TS1t

135.33 all ... martial] E1– white like a
feminine and, with her helmet, a
martial MS–SA white, like a
feminine and, with her helmet, a
martial SE

135.37–136.15 Shortly ... day.] MS
TS1 SE– OM SA

136.3 Nelson] E1– Nelson (or
Nielsen) MS TS1 SE OM SA

136.5 happy] E1– happy in his heart
MS TS1 SE OM SA

136.6–7 varied ... arrogant,] TS1r
SE– their own shades and in their
midst the swarthy-faced overbearing
MS TS1t OM SA

136.8 thicker] MS TS1r SE– thinker
TS1t OM SA

136.9 mankind] TS1r SE– man-like
population MS manlike ***utation
TS1t OM SA

136.10 planet] TS1r SE– globe MS
world TS1t OM SA

136.11 we all] MS we TS1 SE– OM SA

136.14a something] TS1r SE– a
something MS TS1t OM SA

136.14b time, in it,] MS TS1 E1–
time SE OM SA

136.16 III] TS1r SA E1– Chapter III.
SE OM MS TS1t

136.20 delicately ... water] TS1r– into
the water delicately MS TS1t

136.22–23 She ... town.] MS TS1 SE–
OM SA

136.26 up alongside] MS–SA
alongside, SE–

136.28 his] MS TS1 SE– a SA

136.29 Seven-Isles] TS1r– Seven MS
TS1t

136.30 of] TS1– o MS

136.31 on] MS–SA E1– on to SE

136.33 his emotions] MS TS1r–
emotions TS1t

136.35 me triumphantly] E1– me
MS–SE

136.36 Well, ... now.] TS1r– No. Not
yet. Not this time. MS TS1t

136.38 without] E1– without any
MS–SE

137.1–2 Old ... Nielsen)] MS TS1
SE– It is certain old Nelson SA

137.2 Freya peaceably] TS1r– Freya
MS TS1t

137.5 selfishly hard] MS–SA E1–
selfish SE

137.12–138.7 He ... love.] MS TS1
SE– OM SA

137.15 way] MS TS1r SE– was TS1t
OM SA

137.16 gone] MS TS1r SE– gave TS1t
OM SA

137.20a feelings] TS1r SE– feeling
MS TS1t OM SA

137.20b be ... him] E1– not be his MS
TS1 SE OM SA

137.22 on good terms] TS1r SE– well
MS TS1t OM SA

137.23 Freya thought she] TS1r SE–
she MS TS1t OM SA

137.24 beautiful brig] TS1r SE– brig
MS TS1t OM SA

137.30 counter] E1– meet MS TS1 SE
OM SA

137.33 jokes] MS TS1 E1– jests SE
OM SA

137.35 confidant] SE– confident MS
TS1 OM SA

137.36a peculiar] TS1r SE–
masculine MS TS1t OM SA

137.36b vein of obstinacy] SE– vein
MS TS1 OM SA

137.38a twenty-first] MS TS1r SE–
twenty; first TS1t OM SA

137.38b shall] TS1r SE– should MS
could TS1t OM SA

138.1 never] MS had never TS1 SE–
OM SA

138.4a at] MS TS1r SE– pat TS1t OM
SA

138.4b bottom – at times] TS1r SE–
bottom MS TS1t OM SA

138.5 to console him] TS1r SE–
meantime MS TS1t OM SA

138.6   on] **MS TS1r SE**– or **TS1t** OM
SA

138.8   I shall] **TS1r** I'll **MS TS1t SA**–

138.11   But] **MS SA**– But But **TS1**

138.11–12   laugh ... gesture] **E1**– wide
elated gesture **MS–SA** wide, elated
gesture and a loud laugh **SE**

138.12–20   Pooh! ... easy.] **MS–SA E1**–
OM **SE**

138.12   Nothing] **MS** Nothing
nothing **TS1 SA E1**– OM **SE**

138.13   uncharted] **MS TS1 E1**–
unchartered **SA** OM **SE**

138.14   amongst] **MS TS1 E1**– among
SA OM **SE**

138.16   as if] **TS1r SA E1**– and **MS
TS1t** OM **SE**

138.23   That] **TS1r**– Yes. That **MS**
Yes That **TS1t**

138.25   has happened] **MS–SA E1**–
happened **SE**

138.26   as there's] **MS TS1r**– there's
TS1t

138.27a   a short] **MS–SA E1**– short **SE**

138.27b   notice] **TS1r**– notice so **MS
TS1t**

138.27c   going to] **MS TS1r**– to **TS1t**

138.28–139.5   I tell ... excited."] **MS
TS1 SE**– OM **SA**

138.30a   says to me,] **TS1r** says **MS
TS1t SE**– OM **SA**

138.30b   wonderful] **E1**– nice **MS TS1**
heavenly **SE** OM **SA**

138.31   confess] **E1**– say **MS TS1 SE**
OM **SA**

138.37   he was as] **SE** as **MS TS1 E1**–
OM **SA**

139.2   shall] **MS TS1** I shall **SE**– OM
SA

139.4   Come on] **E1**– Come **MS TS1
SE** OM **SA**

139.9   an] **TS1r SA E1**– the **MS TS1t**
his **SE**

139.11–18   I ... authentic.] **MS TS1
SE**– OM **SA**

139.12a   Schultz] **MS E1**– Schultz's
TS1 SE OM **SA**

139.12b   Chantabun] **MS TS1r E1**–
Chantaban **TS1t** Chentabun **SE** OM
SA

139.14   Robinson's] **E1**– The **MS TS1
SE** OM **SA**

139.15   That] **E1**– But that **MS TS1 SE**
OM **SA**

139.16   Schultz] **E1**– him **MS TS1 SE**
OM **SA**

139.18a   seems ... more] **E1**– – that's
perfectly **MS TS1r SE** – that'
perfectly **TS1t** OM **SA**

139.18b   this little weakness] **E1**– that
weakness **MS** that **TS1t** that little
weakness **TS1r–SE**

139.19   many men] **MS** many **TS1**–

139.23a   you] **TS1**– you must **MS**

139.23b   no ... to] **TS1r**– him he will
MS TS1t

139.25   any] **TS1r**– any of his **MS TS1t**

139.31a   I am] **MS** I'm **TS1**–

139.31b   must] **E1**– don't **MS–SE**

139.34   or] **TS1**– of **MS**

139.37   around; gives it] **E1**– around
MS–SE

139.39   his friends before morning]
SE– his friends **TS1 SA** friends **MS**

140.2a   usual] **MS–SA E1**– ordinary
SE

140.2b   gets aboard and simply] **E1**–
simply **MS–SE**

140.4a   biscuits, or] **MS** biscuits, **TS1**–

140.4b   money] **MS–SA E1**– cash **SE**

140.5a   it. This ... other.] **TS1r**– it. **MS
TS1t**

140.5b   This is] **E1**– That's **TS1r–SE**
OM **MS TS1t**

140.6   You've got only to] **MS** You
have only **TS1** You have only to **SA**–

140.11   any longer] **TS1r**– either **MS
TS1t**

140.11–14   His ... straight."] **MS TS1
SE**– OM **SA** [*see 140.15–33,
140.34–37*]

140.13–14   ports ... straight.] **TS1r
SE**– shiining ports. **MS** shu | ports.
TS1t OM **SA**

140.15–33   That ... pedlar." ...] **MS
TS1 E1**– OM **SA SE** [*see 140.11–14,
140.34–37*]

140.15   coasts] **E1**– coasts where
Jasper had friends of strange aspect
MS TS1 OM **SA SE**

140.16   nearly] **MS TS1r E1**– near- |
TS1t OM **SA SE**

140.18   amongst] **MS TS1** among **E1**–
OM **SA SE**

140.19a   aglitter] **TS1 E1**– a glitter
MS OM **SA SE**

140.19b   sunshine] **E1**– pitiless
sunshine **MS TS1** OM **SA SE**

140.20   tracks] **MS E1**– tracts **TS1** OM
SA SE

140.22   lay] **MS TS1r E1**– lie **TS1t** OM
SA SE

140.22–23   hove-to,] **E1**– hove-to still
MS TS1 OM **SA SE**

140.27   purple] **E1**– black **MS TS1** OM
SA SE

140.27–28   thunder-clouds ...
horizon] **E1**– a thunder-cloud **MS
TS1t** a thunder-cloud piled up on
the horizon **TS1r** OM **SA SE**

140.28   mail-routes] **TS1r** mail tracks
MS TS1t E1– OM **SA SE**

140.29   wild mystery,] **TS1r E1**–
mystery **MS TS1t** OM **SA SE**

140.29–30   naïve passengers
crowding] **TS1r E1**– passengers **MS
TS1t** OM **SA SE**

140.31   there's a yacht, ... yacht] **MS**
Here's a yacht **TS1 E1**– OM **SA SE**

140.32a   captain] **MS E1**– Captain
TS1t Captain of the mailboat **TS1r**
OM **SA SE**

140.32b   hostile] **E1**– casual cold **MS
TS1** OM **SA SE**

140.34–37   "A ... declared.] **MS TS1
SE**– OM **SA** [*see 140.11–14,
140.15–33*]

140.34–35   say," speculated ... voice.]
MS TS1 E1– say?" **SE** OM **SA**

140.34   speculated Jasper] **TS1r** he
continued **MS TS1t** ejaculated
Jasper **E1**– OM **SA SE**

140.35   wonderfully] **MS TS1r E1**–
wonderful **TS1t** OM **SA SE**

140.36–37   impossible," I declared]
TS1r SE– impossible **MS TS1t** OM
SA

140.38   a] **MS** his **TS1**–

140.40   going to] **MS TS1 SE**– going
SA

141.1–2   In fact] **TS1r**– Indeed **MS
TS1t**

141.4   were] **MS–SE E2** are **E1–A2**

141.5   by! Do] **MS TS1** way, do **SA**–

141.6   this] **MS** the **TS1**–

141.7   lover] **MS** a lover **TS1**–

141.16a   which I had] **TS1r**– I took
MS TS1t

141.16b   trouble six months ago]
TS1r– trouble **MS TS1t**

141.18   provoking] **E1**– gratuitously
provoking **MS–SE**

141.22a   hurt] **MS TS1r**– hunt **TS1t**

141.22b   head.] **SE**– head. I tell you
the world's good enough for me.
It's jolly good anyhow. **MS–SA**

141.29–30   he ... back. He was] **E1**– he
was gone again before my return,
MS TS1t he was gone again before I
got back, **TS1r** before I got back he
was gone again **SA** he was gone
again before I got back, **SE**

141.31   Nelson's] **TS1**– Nelson **MS**

141.32–142.17   Freya ... strain.] **MS
TS1 SE**– OM **SA** [*see 142.18–27,
142.28–143.30*]

141.32   Freya and I] **TS1r SE**– We **MS
TS1t** OM **SA**

141.35   to be their] **TS1r SE**– their
MS TS1t OM **SA**

141.39   uttered with] **MS** with **TS1 SE**–
OM **SA**

142.1   next] **MS** next day **TS1 SE**– OM
SA

142.4   the] **E1**– that **MS TS1 SE** OM **SA**

142.8   heavens] **E1**– the heavens **MS
TS1 SE** OM **SA**

142.12a   Silent] **TS1r SE**– Falling
silent **MS TS1t** OM **SA**

142.12b   for a time we] **MS–SA E1**– we
SE

142.12c   eyes] **MS TS1r SE**– eves **TS1t**
OM **SA**

142.15   peace] **MS TS1r SE**– place
TS1t OM **SA**

142.17   began again] **MS TS1 SE–A1
E2** began **A2** OM **SA**

142.18–27   We ... indignation.] **MS
TS1 E1**– OM **SA SE** [*see
141.32–142.17, 142.28–143.30*]

142.21   an] **TS1 E1**– an an **MS** OM **SA SE**

142.26   doors] **MS TS1r E1**– windows **TS1t** OM **SA SE**

142.28–143.30   Incidentally ... proportionately.] **MS TS1 SE**– OM **SA** [*see 141.32–142.17, 142.18–27*]

142.32   because] **E1**– on the ground as it were, that **MS TS1r SE** on the as it were, that **TS1t** OM **SA**

142.34–35   conversation] **E1**– the conversation **MS TS1 SE** OM **SA**

142.37   Heemskirk] **TS1r SE**– He **MS TS1t** OM **SA**

142.38   the day] **E1**– a day **MS TS1 SE** OM **SA**

142.38–39   after. He ... later.] **TS1r SE**– after and left more than twenty-four hours before the brig. **MS TS1t** OM **SA**

142.40   been to you two,] **TS1r SE**– been **MS TS1t** OM **SA**

143.1   me with] **MS TS1** me **SE**– OM **SA**

143.4   tone:] **E1**– timbre **MS TS1 SE** OM **SA**

143.5   Isn't] **MS** . . . Isn't **TS1r SE**– . . . and isn't **TS1t** OM **SA**

143.16–17   inexpressibly] **MS TS1r SE**– as inexpressibly **TS1t** OM **SA**

143.17   why] **MS** what **TS1 SE**– OM **SA**

143.18a   earth I asked myself] **TS1r SE**– earth **MS TS1t** OM **SA**

143.18b   we] **MS TS1r SE**– you **TS1t** OM **SA**

143.19   Freya] **E1**– She **MS TS1 SE** OM **SA**

143.22   to old Nelson's question] **TS1r SE**– for old Nelson **MS TS1t** OM **SA**

143.24   Jasper] **TS1r SE**– him **MS TS1t** OM **SA**

143.25   Seven-Isles] **SE**– Seven **MS TS1** OM **SA**

143.30   seems] **MS** seemed **TS1 SE**– seemed that **SA**

143.31   Heemskirk] **MS TS1 SE**– Heemskirk, who had been there at the same time, **SA**

143.32   old Nelson] **TS1r**– him **MS TS1t**

143.33   a white man] **TS1r**– him **MS TS1t**

143.34–144.2   "It ... Chinaman."] **MS–SA E1**– OM **SE**

143.38   to learn now,] **TS1r SA E1**– now to learn **MS** to learn **TS1t** OM **SE**

143.38–39   Nelson (or Nielsen)] **MS TS1 E1**– Nelson **SA** OM **SE**

143.39a   said] **MS TS1 E1**– said that **SA** OM **SE**

143.39b   learned Dutch] **TS1r SA E1**– learned **MS TS1t** OM **SE**

144.1   disrespectful] **MS TS1** disgraceful **SA E1**– OM **SE**

144.2   me] **MS TS1 E1**– me about it **SA** OM **SE**

144.4   altar] **MS TS1r**– alter **TS1t**

144.5–14   It ... sense.] **MS TS1 SE**– OM **SA**

144.7   that] **MS TS1r SE**– all **TS1t** OM **SA**

144.13   on] **E1**– of **MS TS1 SE** OM **SA**

144.16a   I muttered] **MS TS1r**– muttered **TS1t**

144.16b   see] **TS1r**– see too **MS TS1t**

144.18–19   Freya?" old ... moaning.] **TS1r**– Freya? **MS TS1t**

144.20a   bad] **MS–SA E1**– seedy **SE**

144.20b   us so suddenly] **TS1r**– us **MS TS1t**

144.20–21   His ... too.] **TS1r**– Liver touched – Eh? **MS TS1t**

144.22   it – Whatever it is,] **MS** it **TS1**–

144.24a   won't] **TS1r**– wont **MS TS1t**

144.24b   long time to come] **TS1r**– time **MS TS1t**

144.25–34   The ... and there] **MS TS1 SE**– There **SA**

144.34   Nelson (or Nielsen)] **MS TS1 SE**– Nelson **SA**

144.37–145.4   He ... Freya!] **MS TS1 SE**– OM **SA** [*see 145.5–40, 146.1*]

145.3   distrusted] **MS TS1r SE**– distressed **TS1t** OM **SA**

145.5–40   Going ... ever.] **MS TS1 E1**– OM **SA SE** [*see 144.37–145.4, 146.1*]

145.8   a] **MS E1**– a a **TS1** OM **SA SE**

145.15–17 We ... make] **TS1r E1–** But
except a nod and a smile I had
never any communication with her.
Oh! I forgot. I saw her once make a
very **MS TS1t** OM **SA SE**

145.17 grimaces] **TS1r E1–** grimace
MS TS1t OM **SA SE**

145.22 cove] **MS E1–** c**e cove **TS1**
OM **SA SE**

145.24 Seven-Isles] **TS1 E1–** Seven
Islets **MS** OM **SA SE**

145.27 pace – and ... business] **TS1r**
E1– pace **MS TS1t** OM **SA SE**

145.29 knows I am here] **TS1r E1–**
knows **MS TS1t** OM **SA SE**

145.31 words] **E1–** the words **MS TS1**
OM **SA SE**

145.32a Just then] **E1–** But at that
moment **MS TS1** OM **SA SE**

145.32b heads] **MS TS1 E2** head
E1–A2 OM **SA SE**

145.34 imperious] **E1–** imperious,
anxious **MS TS1** OM **SA SE**

146.1 I ... because this] **MS TS1 SE–**
This **SA** [*see 144.37, 145.5–40*]

146.2 on] **MS** at **TS1–**

146.3a messages] **E1–** messages
awaiting me **MS–SE**

146.3b necessary for me] **TS1r–**
necessary **MS TS1t**

146.8a I got] **MS TS1r–** got **TS1t**

146.8–20 I hunted ... relative.]
MS–SA E1– OM **SE**

146.8b hunted up then] **MS TS1 E1–**
then hunted up **SA** OM **SE**

146.10–11 thoughtfully. ¶ "We ...
said.] **MS TS1** thoughtfully. **SA E1–**
OM **SE**

146.12a father's] **TS1 SA E1–** father
MS OM **SE**

146.12b second and late] **MS** second
TS1 SA E1– OM **SE**

146.13 commend] **MS TS1r SA E1–**
command **TS1t** OM **SE**

146.20a relative] **TS1r SA E1–** sort of
relation **MS TS1t** OM **SE**

146.20b But why] **MS–SA E1–** Why
SE

146.25a well] **MS TS1r–** deep well
TS1t

146.25b depth.] **MS TS1 SE–** depth.
Of what follows I heard in part from
Freya; the rest from sources to be
named later. **SA**

146.26 IV] **TS1r SA E1–** III. **MS**
Chapter IV. **SE** OM **TS1t**

146.28 almost for] **MS TS1 SE–** for
almost **SA**

146.31 any] **E1–** all **MS–SE**

147.1–2 the ... Cove] **MS TS1 SE–** at
Nelson's Cove during Jasper's last
visit there **SA**

147.1 the day] **SE** some time **MS TS1**
E1– VAR **SA**

147.3 bungalow] **E1–** bungalow as it
were **MS–SE**

147.3–7 He ... voice.] **MS TS1 SE–** OM
SA [*see 147.7–9, 147.18–19*]

147.7–9 Freya's ... brooding.] **MS TS1**
E1– OM **SA SE** [*see 147.3–7,
147.10–11, 147.11–17, 147.18–19*]

147.8 blissful elation] **E1–** sort of
transport **MS TS1** OM **SA SE**

147.8–9 torment, of ... brooding]
TS1r E1– exasperation **MS TS1t** OM
SA SE

147.10–11 While ... board.] **MS–SA**
E1– OM **SE** [*see 147.7–9,
147.11–17, 147.18–19*]

147.10a While ... brig he] **MS TS1**
E1– He **SA** OM **SE**

147.10b brig] **MS TS1r E1–** brag
TS1t OM **SA SE**

147.11–17 Schultz ... information.]
MS–SA E1– OM **SE** [*see 147.7–9,
147.10–11, 147.18–19*]

147.13 Heemskirk's] **TS1r SA E1–** the
MS TS1t OM **SE**

147.14 modulations] **E1–** modulation
MS–SA OM **SE**

147.16–17 at?" which ... information.]
MS TS1 E1– at?" **SA** OM **SE**

147.18–19 He ... grounds.] **MS TS1**
E1– OM **SA SE** [*see 147.3–7,
147.7–9, 147.10–11, 147.11–17,
147.20–148.14, 148.15–25,
148.26–34*]

147.19 stride away] **TS1r E1–** strike
out **MS** strode out **TS1t** OM **SA**
SE

147.20–148.14   The ... nevertheless.]
MS TS1 SE– OM SA [*see 147.18–19,*
148.15–25, 148.26–34]

147.24   this simple happiness] TS1r
SE– it MS TS1t OM SA

147.26   concealed and perspiring]
TS1r SE– perspiring MS TS1t OM SA

147.31   to excite] TS1 SE– excite MS
OM SA

147.33a   them all] TS1r SE– them MS
TS1t OM SA

147.33b   Allen," he growled.] TS1r
SE– Allen. MS TS1t OM SA

147.35a   to never] MS never to TS1
SE– OM SA

147.35b   have] MS SE– have | have
TS1 OM SA

147.35c   settle here] TS1r SE– settle
MS TS1t OM SA

147.37   declared] TS1r SE– moved
and declared MS raved and
declared TS1t OM SA

148.2   which] MS that TS1 SE– OM SA

148.8   it wouldn't] MS TS1r SE– it
wouldn't it wouldn't TS1t OM SA

148.9–10   was ... fall] E1– had no
notion of falling MS TS1 SE OM
SA

148.11   feeling] E1– sense MS TS1 SE
OM SA

148.12   willing enough] MS willing
TS1 SE– OM SA

148.14   grunted nevertheless] TS1r
SE– growled MS TS1t OM SA

148.15–25   "But ... of it.] MS TS1 E1–
OM SA SE [*see 147.18–19,*
147.20–148.14, 148.26–34]

148.16   because] MS TS1r E1–
became because TS1t OM SA SE

148.19   on] MS E1– or TS1 OM SA SE

148.26–34   "Pooh! Pooh! ...
verandah.] MS TS1 SE– OM SA [*see*
147.18–19, 147.20–148.14,
148.15–25]

148.27   Ask for] E1– Ask MS TS1 SE
OM SA

148.31   longing which ... however]
TS1r SE– longing MS TS1t OM SA

148.35a   It ... one which] MS TS1 SE–
The west verandah SA

148.35b   west verandah] TS1– West
Verandah MS

148.37a   east] SA– East MS TS1

148.37b   his] MS TS1 SE– Nelson's SA

148.37c   own privacy] TS1r– privacy
MS TS1t

148.39   verandah] MS TS1r–
verandah was not a verandah TS1t

149.3   meditations] MS TS1r–
meditations. meditations TS1t

149.4   sense] TS1r– much sense MS
TS1t

149.6   meanings] TS1r– meaning MS
TS1t

149.7   This north verandah] TS1r– It
MS TS1t

149.8   furnished it as] TS1r– made of
it MS TS1t

149.9a   boudoir for herself] TS1r–
boudoir MS TS1t

149.9b   chairs] TS1– chair MS

149.12a   nor] MS TS1r– not TS1t

149.12b   can be] MS TS1 SE– be SA

149.12–13   place at ... time] TS1r–
place MS TS1t

149.14   had been] TS1r– was MS
TS1t

149.15   elation] MS TS1r– elatory
TS1t

149.28   Antonia] MS TS1 SE– Freya's
maid, Antonia, a half-caste Malacca
Portuguese, SA

149.34   comprehension] TS1r–
apprehension MS TS1t

149.37   wring] MS twist TS1–

150.4–5   She ... but in] MS TS1 SE–
In SA

150.5   in her terror she] TS1r– she
MS TS1t

150.7a   over at a distance] MS–SA E1–
over SE

150.7b   and yet] MS and TS1–

150.9   divided] E1– divided into four
MS–SE

150.10   At that point Heemskirk]
MS–SA E1– Heemskirk SE

150.11–13   secured ... head. Two] MS
TS1 SE– saw two SA

150.12   carryings] MS TS1 SE
carrying E1– OM SA

150.13 head] **MS TS1r SE**– head as
he went on **TS1t** OM **SA**

150.14 stood in] **MS TS1 SE**– in **SA**

150.15 faces were] **TS1**– faces was **MS**

150.21–22 visitors you —] **MS TS1**
E1– visitors? **SA SE**

150.22 so outraged that ... epithet]
TS1r– outraged **MS TS1t**

150.23 epithet] **MS–SA E1**– epithet
for the girl **SE**

150.24 Freya] **TS1r SA E1**– Freya had
MS TS1t Meantime Freya **SE**

150.25 holding] **SA**– held **MS TS1t**
helding **TS1r**

150.26a to ... and looking] **TS1r**– and
looked **MS TS1t**

150.26b face,] **E1**– face as though he
had heard no warning. But he **MS**
TS1t face as though he had heard
no warning, **TS1r–SE**

150.26c casually] **E1**– indifferently
MS–SE

150.33 rivers] **SE** river **MS–SA E1**–

150.39–40 see," she ... anxiously.]
TS1r– see." **MS TS1t**

151.1–2 moment after ... gone] **TS1r**–
moment **MS TS1t**

151.2 to slip] **TS1r**– slip out **MS** slip
TS1t

151.3 himself] **MS–SA E1**– himself in
front **SE**

151.6 While] **MS TS1r**– When **TS1t**

151.7a curtain] **MS** curtains **TS1**–

151.7b at] **SA E1**– on **MS TS1 SE**

151.12a She spoke in] **MS–SA E1**– It
was **SE**

151.12b Her] **SE**– His **MS–SA**

151.13a him] **SE**– her **MS–SA**

151.13b verandah.] **E1**– verandah. He
made another very low bow. **MS–SE**

151.14 speak] **MS–SA E1**– speak yet
SE

151.16–17 with contorted lips] **TS1r**–
explosively **MS TS1t**

151.18–19 "I ... very. ...."] **MS TS1**
SE– OM **SA**

151.22 But] **TS1r**– And **MS TS1t**

151.24 tried to be conversational]
TS1r– said conversationally **MS** was
conversational **TS1t**

151.35 thinks that] **MS** thinks **TS1**–

151.37 can't] **SE**– wouldn't **MS–SA**

151.39 Presently] **E1**– Just at that
moment **MS–SE**

151.40a Tamil] **MS SA**– Tamie Tamie
TS1t Tamie Tamil **TS1r**

151.40b Nelson's] **TS1r**– the **MS TS1t**

152.1 to] **TS1**– to to **MS**

152.8 met again] **MS TS1 SE**– met
SA

152.9 evening's] **TS1**– evenings **MS**

152.10a scared and] **TS1r**– a littlel
showed **MS TS1t**

152.10b exhibited] **TS1r**– showed **MS**
TS1t

152.11a which] **TS1**– with **MS**

152.11b roused] **MS TS1 SE**–
aroused **SA**

152.12 jumped on me] **TS1r**–
jumped **MS TS1t**

152.15–19 enraged but ... grimace.]
MS–SA E1– enraged. **SE**

152.22 display all her] **E1**– deal with
the last with **MS TS1t SA SE**
circumvent the last with **TS1r**

152.23 said to] **MS–SA E1**–
comforted **SE**

152.28 young girl] **TS1r** girl like
Freya **MS TS1t SA**–

152.32–33 doing ... told like] **TS1r**–
like **MS TS1t**

152.33 boy.] **TS1r**– boy. He too was
motionless in old Nelson's chair.
MS TS1t

152.35 it?" he murmured.] **MS–SA**
E1– it?" **SE**

152.37 Heemskirk's] **TS1**–
Heemskirk **MS**

153.3–5 "What ... Papa."] **MS TS1 SE**–
OM **SA** [*see 153.6–11, 153.11–17*]

153.5 Papa] **MS** papa **TS1 SE**– OM **SA**

153.6–11 "Your ... days.] **MS TS1 E1**–
OM **SA SE** [*see 153.3–5, 153.11–17*]

153.11–17 Look ... sensible.] **MS TS1**
SE– OM **SA** [*see 153.3–5, 153.6–11*]

153.12 to-morrow morning] **MS TS1**
to-morrow **SE**– OM **SA**

153.19 around] **MS–SA** round **SE**–

153.20 good of your staying] **TS1r**–
good **MS TS1t**

153.22–25 "He ... breath.] **MS–SA E1–** OM **SE**

153.22 reported for loitering] **TS1r SA E1–** reported **MS TS1t** OM **SE**

153.28 he ... her] **TS1r–** pressing her to his breast **MS TS1t**

153.32a now, at once] **TS1r–** now **MS TS1t**

153.32b I could] **MS TS1 SE–** Could **SA**

153.36 content] **MS** concent **TS1t** consent **TS1r–**

153.38 delightful] **MS** a delightful **TS1–**

153.39 arms] **ED** arm **MS–**

154.1 grip] **MS** grasp **TS1–**

154.4 floated] **MS TS1 SE–** fleeted **SA**

154.7 could] **MS–SA E1–** can **SE**

154.10 have –] **E1–** have – | yes – **MS–SE**

154.11 added ... tone] **E1–** asked **MS** cried **TS1t** cried in a low tone **TS1r–SE**

154.14 will.] **E1–** will. On the day. By myself. **MS–SE**

154.20–23 There ... collision.] **MS TS1 SE–** OM **SA** [*see 154.23, 154.23–31, 154.32–155.35, 155.35–156.9*]

154.22–23 bring ... words] **TS1r SE–** an explanation **MS TS1t** OM **SA**

154.23 collision.] **SE–** collision. Of course Jasper would be careful but she had no idea how far her father would go. **MS TS1t** collision. Men were so absurd Of course Jasper would be careful, but she had no idea how far her father would go. **TS1r** OM **SA**

154.23–31 What ... that be.] **MS TS1 E1–** OM **SA SE** [*see 154.20–23, 154.23, 154.32–155.35, 155.35–156.9*]

154.25–26 angry, distracted, absurd] **TS1r E1–** angry, helpless distracted **MS** distracted **TS1t** OM **SA SE**

154.32–155.35 "But ... laugh.] **MS TS1 SE–** OM **SA** [*see 154.20–23, 154.23, 154.23–31, 155.35–156.9*]

154.33a quietly] **MS** quick ly **TS1** quickly **SE–** OM **SA**

154.33b west verandah] **TS1 SE–** West Verandah **MS** OM **SA**

154.35 outraged] **MS TS1t SE–** tormented **TS1r** OM **SA**

154.37 knitted] **E1–** drawn together **MS TS1 SE** OM **SA**

154.38a this] **MS** their **TS1 SE–** OM **SA**

154.38b sideways] **MS TS1r SE–** sideway **TS1t** OM **SA**

155.1 discomposed] **TS1r SE–** perturbed **MS TS1t** OM **SA**

155.2 conciliatory] **TS1 SE–** conciliatory | conciliatory **MS** OM **SA**

155.4 that smile] **TS1r SE–** it **MS TS1t** OM **SA**

155.10 You have] **E1–** Have **MS TS1 SE** OM **SA**

155.12 pursed-up] **TS1r SE–** thin **MS TS1t** OM **SA**

155.13 surly] **E1–** somewhat surly **MS TS1 SE** OM **SA**

155.15 felt] **TS1r SE–** was **MS TS1t** OM **SA**

155.33 Old Nelson] **E1–** That last **MS TS1 SE** OM **SA**

155.35–156.9 "Now ... planet. ....] **MS TS1 E1–** OM **SA SE** [*see 154.20–23, 154.23, 154.23–31, 154.32–155.35*]

155.36 some dinner] **MS TS1r E1–** dinner **TS1t** OM **SA SE**

155.40 redly,] **E1–** reddish **MS TS1** OM **SA SE**

156.2 Jasper] **TS1r E1–** he **MS TS1t** OM **SA SE**

156.4 him] **E1–** him to trouble the quiet night which he faced **MS TS1** OM **SA SE**

156.5 but a] **E1–** a **MS TS1t** a but **TS1r** OM **SA SE**

156.6 Far] **E1–** Only far **MS TS1** OM **SA SE**

156.10–11 Freya ... Nelson.] **MS–SA E1–** OM **SE**

156.11 Nelson.] **E1–** Nelson. He even got into some argument with him during which he addressed him as "my poor friend" in a superior pitying tone, while the corner of his mouth nearest to Freya twitched persistently, with a sardonic effect. Of Jasper as usual he took not the slightest notice. **MS TS1t** Nelson. He even drew him into some argument during which he addressed him as "my poor friend" in a markedly pitying tone, while the corner of his mouth nearest to Freya twitched persistently with sardonic amusement. Of Jasper as usual he took not the slightest notice. **TS1r SA** OM **SE**

156.12 kept] **MS TS1r**– keep **TS1t**

156.15 time for him] **MS TS1r**– time **TS1t**

156.16 board his ship] **TS1r**– board **MS TS1t**

156.17 Heemskirk ... up. Ensconced] **MS–SA E1**– Heemskirk, ensconced **SE**

156.18a at] **MS SA**– at | at **TS1**

156.18b he had] **MS–SA E1**– had **SE**

156.20 "I'll] **TS1**– I'll will **MS**

156.23 such a] **TS1r**– a **MS TS1t**

156.25 towards] **MS TS1 SE**– toward **SA**

156.27 alone. Take offence perhaps.] **TS1r**– alone. **MS TS1t**

156.32–37 His ... eyelids.] **MS–SA E1**– OM **SE**

156.32a His] **E1**– From his **MS–SA** OM **SE**

156.32b repose] **E1**– repose he **MS–SA** OM **SE**

156.40a with] **MS TS1r**– to **TS1t**

156.40b Papa] papa **MS**–

157.1–2 absurd in many ways] **TS1r**– absurd **MS TS1t**

157.4 necessary?] **E1**– necessary? But fixing her eyes on him she became suspicious of that supineness. **MS–SE**

157.5 when] **TS1r**– when suddenly **MS TS1t**

157.6a at] **E1**– up at **MS–SE**

157.6b began resolutely] **TS1r**– began **MS TS1t**

157.7a took alarm, glided] **TS1r**– glided **MS TS1t**

157.7b towards] **MS TS1 SE**– toward **SA**

157.7c opened] **TS1r**– swiftly opened **MS TS1t**

157.8 almost before] **MS TS1** before **SA**–

157.17a aware] **TS1r**– became aware **MS TS1t**

157.17b her] **TS1r**– her and she **MS TS1t**

157.20 tone] **MS–SA E1**– his tone **SE**

157.22 thick too] **TS1r**– thick **MS TS1t**

157.23 something of your] **TS1r**– your **MS TS1t**

157.25 sort] **MS TS1r**– sore **TS1t**

157.30 confounded playing] **TS1r**– playing **MS TS1t**

157.32 head negatively] **TS1r**– head **MS TS1t**

157.36 these islands] **TS1r**– the islands **MS** this island **TS1t**

157.37 such trash!] **E1**– them. Trash! **MS–SE**

158.1 turn] **TS1**– dare turn **MS**

158.1–2 Her ... indignation.] **E1**– Her face went stiff with horror and indignation. She could not utter a word. **MS–SA** OM **SE**

158.3 possible. It] **MS–SA E1**– possible, but it **SE**

158.5 Presently] **MS TS1t E1**– Presently, she thought, **TS1r–SE**

158.7 ignore. She] **E1**– ignore ... and she **MS TS1t** ignore. ... And she **TS1r–SE**

158.12 love do] **MS** love stop **TS1t** love! Stop! Do **TS1r**–

158.23 the irritating] **E1**– the **MS TS1t** that irritating **TS1r–SE**

158.24 the contact] **TS1r**– that contact **MS TS1t**

158.26a just under] **TS1r**– under **MS TS1t**

158.26b A deep] **MS TS1r**– deep **TS1t**

158.28 big] **TS1r**– stony **MS TS1t**

158.29a   light violet] **E1**– grey **MS–SA**
dark **SE**

158.29b   resting ... stonily] **TS1r**–
without expression **MS TS1t**

158.30a   him] **TS1r**– him now **MS
TS1t**

158.30b   on] **E1**– with one hand on
MS–SE

158.30–31   piano with ... hand. The]
E1– piano while the **MS TS1t** piano.
The **TS1r–SE**

158.31a   other] **MS–SA E1**– other
hand **SE**

158.31b   went ... with] **TS1r**– rubbed
with a **MS TS1t**

158.32a   the] **E1**– at the **MS–SE**

158.32b   his ... touched] **TS1r**– he
had kissed **MS TS1t**

158.35   better . . . and I] **MS** better. . . .
I **TS1**–

158.36   out] **MS SA**– out | out **TS1**

158.39   He] **MS TS1r**– He | He **TS1t**

159.2a   I am] **MS** I'm **TS1**–

159.2b   try a ... with. . . ."] **TS1r**–
try . . ." **MS TS1t**

159.3   He ... his] **TS1r**– His **MS TS1t**

159.7   the lieutenant] **TS1r**– he **MS
TS1t**

159.9a   violet eyes] **E1**– grey eyes
MS–SA eyes **SE**

159.9b   darkened] **MS–SA E1**–
darkened almost to blackness **SE**

159.10   blow,] **TS1r**– blow and **MS
TS1t**

159.11   father's] **TS1**– fathers **MS**

159.13   her father] **TS1r**– him **MS
TS1t**

159.14   anxious to] **E1**– to **MS–SE**

159.16   old Nelson] **TS1r**– her father
MS TS1t

159.21   quick.] **E1**– quick. She could
not utter a word. **MS–SE**

159.24   black, evil eye] **TS1r**– eye **MS
TS1t**

159.26–35   She did ... excited.] **MS
TS1 SE**– OM **SA**

159.28   one of ... least] **TS1r SE**– one
MS TS1t OM **SA**

159.29a   he were] **TS1r SE**– him **MS
TS1t** OM **SA**

159.29b   off] **TS1r SE**– away **MS TS1t**
OM **SA**

159.34   Nelson] **MS TS1r SE**– Nielsen
TS1t OM **SA**

159.35a   excited] **TS1r SE**– perturbed
MS TS1t OM **SA**

159.35b   you ... tune] **E1**– I heard you
playing **MS–SE**

159.37   nodded] **MS** only nodded
TS1–

160.6   howled, stamping] **TS1r**–
howled. He stamped **MS TS1t**

160.8a   Is his face] **TS1r**– his face's
MS his face is **TS1t**

160.8b   asked] **TS1r**– said **MS TS1t**

160.8c   Nelson. The] **TS1r**– Nelson
and then the **MS** Nelson and the
TS1t

160.9   dawned suddenly] **TS1r**–
dawned **MS TS1t**

160.10   You] **MS** You are **TS1**–

160.11   Lieutenant? Came ... once?]
MS lieutenant? **TS1**–

160.12a   crazy all ... sudden] **TS1r**–
crazy **MS TS1t**

160.12b   in the] **MS–SA E1 A1 E2** at
one **SE** at the **A2**

160.14   got a] **TS1r SA E1**– mad with
MS TS1t SE

160.16   Nelson, beholding this]
TS1r– Nelson. This **MS TS1t**

160.19a   the true] **E1**– another **MS–SE**

160.19b   cause] **E1**– cause for these
symptoms **MS TS1t** cause for such
symptoms **TS1r–SE**

160.19–22   She ... out.] **MS TS1 SE**–
OM **SA**

160.19c   watched] **E1**– had caught **MS
TS1 SE** OM **SA**

160.19–20   Heemskirk's] **TS1r**–
Heemskirk **MS** Heemskirk[ ]s **TS1t**
OM **SA**

160.20–21   herself.] **E1**– herself. She
met it with clear scornful eyes but
she understood **MS TS1t** herself.
She met it with clear, scornful eyes
but she understood the inquiry.
TS1r SE OM **SA**

160.21a   would like] **TS1r SE**– want
MS TS1t OM **SA**

160.21b to be] **MS TS1t SE**– be **TS1r**
OM **SA**

160.22 out. The] **TS1r SE**– out but
the **MS TS1t** The **SA**

160.25–39 "Hurry ... responsible.]
MS–SA E1– OM **SE**

160.27 Heemskirk] **E1**– Heemskirk's
fear of very awkward unpleasantness
being allayed he **MS–SA** OM **SE**

160.29 on the] **SA** the **MS TS1 E1**–
OM **SE**

160.30 Nelson (or Nielsen)] **MS TS1
E1**– Nelson **SA** OM **SE**

160.31 agonizing] **TS1r SA E1**–
horrible **MS TS1t** OM **SE**

160.34a Is ... bad?] **MS TS1r SA E1**–
So bad! **TS1t** OM **SE**

160.34b I used] **E1**– The way I carried
on used **MS** Used **TS1 SA** OM **SE**

160.35 wife sometimes] **E1**– wife
MS–SA OM **SE**

160.35–36 this, Lieutenant?"]
TS1r SA E1– this ... **MS TS1t** OM
SE

160.38 staggering] **TS1r SA E1**–
staggered **MS TS1t** OM **SE**

161.1a Lieutenant," he ... urgently]
TS1r– lieutenant **MS TS1t**

161.1b he] **TS1r SA E1**– Nelson **SE**
OM **MS TS1t**

161.2 you in a minute] **TS1r**– you **MS
TS1t**

161.4 onwards] **MS TS1 SE**– onward
SA

161.11–162.27 Half ... kiss.] **MS TS1
SE**– OM **SA** [*see 162.27–29,
162.30–34, 162.35–163.12,
163.13*]

161.12a faint] **TS1r SE**– faint stiffled
MS TS1t OM **SA**

161.12b mysterious nature] **E1**–
nature **MS TS1 SE** OM **SA**

161.15 and] **TS1 SE**– a **MS** OM **SA**

161.19 had ... in] **TS1r SE**– did not
know much of **MS TS1t** OM **SA**

161.19–20 feminine laughter] **TS1r
SE**– laughter **MS TS1t** OM **SA**

161.21–22 weighty displeasure] **TS1r
SE**– displeasure **MS TS1t** OM **SA**

161.29 it's] **TS1 SE**– its **MS** OM **SA**

161.30 Dogs] **TS1r SE**– Animals,
dogs, **MS TS1t** OM **SA**

161.37a keep] **MS TS1r SE**– keep
him **TS1t** OM **SA**

161.37b Rajah] **MS TS1** rajah **SE**– OM
SA

161.39a took] **MS TS1 E1**– took it **SE**
OM **SA**

161.39b that] **TS1r SE**– that it was **MS
TS1t** OM **SA**

162.1 over him] **TS1r SE**– that **MS
TS1t** OM **SA**

162.3 a not] **MS TS1 E1**– not a **SE** OM
SA

162.8 sustained] **MS TS1r SE**–
sustaining **TS1t** OM **SA**

162.10 these Dutch] **TS1r SE**– them
MS TS1t OM **SA**

162.11 going. He ... officials.] **TS1r
SE**– going. **MS TS1t** OM **SA**

162.14a an inarticulate exclamation]
E1– a sort of articulate sigh **MS TS1
SE** OM **SA**

162.14b If] **SE**– She had said nothing.
If **MS TS1** OM **SA**

162.15–16 him everything, ... now]
TS1r SE– him **MS TS1t** OM **SA**

162.16a It was impossible] **E1**– it was
impossible now. She dared not **MS
TS1t** It was impossible. She dared
not **TS1r SE** OM **SA**

162.16b both out of] **TS1r SE**– either
from **MS TS1t** OM **SA**

162.16c and for] **TS1r SE**– or for **MS**
or **TS1t** OM **SA**

162.19 confessed in a sigh] **TS1r E1**–
confessed **MS TS1t** confessed also
in a sigh **SE** OM **SA**

162.19–20 easier now," ... silence]
TS1r SE– easier **MS TS1t** OM **SA**

162.20 given him] **MS TS1r SE**–
given **TS1t** OM **SA**

162.23 side ... face] **TS1r SE**– cheek
of his **MS TS1t** OM **SA**

162.26a laid] **TS1r SE**– rested **MS
TS1t** OM **SA**

162.26b her] **E1**– them **MS TS1 SE**
OM **SA**

162.26c His] **E1**– Keeping her face
down she felt his **MS TS1 SE** OM **SA**

162.26d   brushed] E1– brush MS TS1 SE OM SA

162.27   a] TS1 SE– a | a MS OM SA

162.27–29   She ... buoyancy.] MS TS1 E1– OM SA SE [*see 161.11–162.27, 162.30–34, 162.35–163.12, 163.13*]

162.30–34   "Flushed! ... began.] MS TS1 SE– OM SA [*see 161.11–162.27, 162.27–29, 162.35–163.12, 163.13*]

162.32   eyelashes] TS1r E1– eyes MS TS1t SE OM SA

162.35–163.12   The mistress ... girl.] MS TS1 E1– OM SA SE [*see 161.11–162.27, 162.27–29, 162.30–34, 163.13*]

162.37a   everything] E1– all MS TS1 OM SA SE

162.37b   exclaimed] TS1r E1– had cried MS TS1t OM SA SE

163.5   an] MS E1– an | an TS1 OM SA SE

163.6   only a] TS1r E1– a MS TS1t OM SA SE

163.7a   the camerista] TS1r E1– she MS TS1t OM SA SE

163.7b   crept] MS TS1r E1– had crept TS1t OM SA SE

163.8   crouch] MS TS1r E1– crouch | crouch TS1t OM SA SE

163.9a   There is] MS There's TS1 E1– OM SA SE

163.9b   run away at once!] TS1r E1– runaway. MS TS1t OM SA SE

163.13   "Never."] E1– To the daughter of old Nelson the planned departure from the bungalow was not a matter of running away. It would be a going forth willed and fixed and appointed, for the sake of Jasper no doubt but also from the conviction that it was the best course to pursue under the circumstances, saving her pride, her consistency affirming her resolution – something courageous, worthy of her deep but governed passion and of her boundless trust in the man ¶ "Get up and plait my hair for the night – come Antonia" she said with gentle decision. MS TS1t To the daughter of old Nelson the planned departure from the bungalow was not a matter of running away. It would be a going forth, willed, and fixed, and appointed, for the sake of Jasper, no doubt, but also from the conviction that it was the best course to pursue under the circumstances, a course saving her pride, her consistency, affirming her resolution – something courageous, worthy of her deep but governed passion and of her boundless trust in the man. ¶ "Get up and plait my hair for the night – come Antonia." she said with gentle decision. TS1r OM SA SE [*see 161.11–162.27, 162.27–29, 162.30–34, 162.35–163.12*]

163.14a   Both] TS1r– But both MS TS1t

163.14b   resolute] TS1r– firm MS TS1t

163.14c   mistress under ... net] TS1r– mistress MS TS1t

163.15   lying curled] TS1r– curled MS TS1t

163.16a   The] E1– A MS–SE

163.16b   that] MS TS1 SE– who SA

163.18–33   Inflaming ... air.] MS TS1 SE– OM SA

163.20a   pretty] MS TS1 E1– creditable SE OM SA

163.20b   this] E1– that MS TS1 SE OM SA

163.20–21   But ... about] E1– It musn't tho' MS TS1t It musn't get about though TS1r It mustn't get about SE OM SA

163.21   outrage] TS1r SE– thing MS TS1t OM SA

163.22   struck] TS1r SE– outraged MS TS1t OM SA

163.23   but another] TS1r SE– another MS TS1t OM SA

163.28a   he ... mind] E1– and that was MS TS1 SE OM SA

163.28b   steal] **MS TS1 E1**– depart **SE**
OM **SA**

163.29   face] **E1**– look at **MS TS1 SE**
OM **SA**

163.30a   out ... fury] **E1**– mad with
rage **MS TS1 SE** OM **SA**

163.30b   thousand] **MS SE**–
thousands **TS1** OM **SA**

163.30–31   devils! I] **TS1r SE**– devils I
MS TS1t OM **SA**

163.31a   the morning] **MS TS1 E1**–
morning! **SE** OM **SA**

163.31b   muttered to himself] **TS1r**
SE– muttered **MS TS1t** OM **SA**

163.32–33   for air] **E1**– like a sea **MS**
TS1 SE OM **SA**

163.34a   He] **E1**– But when he **MS**
TS1 SE When he **SA**

163.34b   at daylight] **E1**– in the
morning **MS–SE**

163.34c   started] **TS1r**– began **MS**
TS1t

163.34–35   door. Faint] **E1**– door he
was checked some faint **MS** door he
was checked by some faint **TS1t**
door he was checked by detecting
some faint **TS1r–SE**

163.35–36   alarmed ... he] **E1**– and
MS–SE

163.36   unexpected sight] **E1**– sight
MS–SE

163.37a   move away from] **E1**– move.
He remained at **MS–SE**

163.37b   crack of the door] **TS1r**–
crack **MS TS1t**

163.38   crack possible] **MS–SA E1**–
possible crack **SE**

163.39a   Freya] **E1**– And Freya
MS–SE

163.39b   that end] **TS1r**– it **MS TS1t**

163.40   wore] **E1**– was in **MS TS1t** was
clad in **TS1r SA** was clad only in **SE**

164.1a   towards] **MS TS1 SE**– toward
SA

164.1b   she] **E1**– she had jumped up
and **MS–SE**

164.1c   ran] **MS–SA E1**– run **SE**

164.2   Heemskirk] **TS1r**– He **MS TS1t**

164.3   looking like] **MS–SA E1**– like
SE

164.5   and with] **TS1r**– with **MS** and
TS1t

164.7a   He] **E1**– He discovered that
he **MS–SE**

164.7b   her at all] **TS1r**– her **MS TS1t**

164.7c   still] **MS–SA E1**– very still **SE**

164.8   door] **TS1r**– nearly closed
door **MS TS1t**

164.9–10   brig already under way,]
E1– brig **MS–SE**

164.10a   Freya] **TS1r** she **MS TS1t SA**–

164.10b   Nelson's] **TS1**– Nelsons **MS**

164.11   dressing gown] **TS1r**– gown
MS TS1t

164.13a   gripping] **E1**– gripped
MS–SE

164.13b   it,] **TS1t E1**– it. He **MS** it,
and **TS1r–SE**

164.15a   And Freya] **TS1r**– Freya **MS**
TS1t

164.15b   her. She knew.] **TS1r**– her.
MS TS1t

164.16   passage.] **E1**– passage. But she
was not to be driven back. **MS–SE**

164.17   triumphant] **E1**– a sort of
triumphant **MS–SE**

164.20   appeared] **TS1r**– looked **MS**
TS1t

164.21   ice] **SE** glass **MS–SA E1**–

164.22   east] **SE**– East **MS–SA**

164.23   his own long] **TS1r**– his **MS**
TS1t

164.25a   that] **TS1**– a that **MS**

164.25b   a supreme] **MS–SE** supreme
E1–

164.26   Jasper's] **TS1**– Jasper **MS**

164.27   held in] **TS1r**– in **MS TS1t**

164.28a   the] **MS TS1t SA**– the the
TS1r

164.28b   burning covetous] **TS1r**–
burning **MS TS1t**

164.36   the brig] **TS1**– brig **MS**

164.37   repeated, passionate] **E1**–
wide repeated **MS–SE**

164.38   hundred again, ... while]
TS1r– hundred while **MS TS1t**

165.1   her white] **MS TS1 SE**– white
SA

165.3a   from] **MS–SA E1**– at **SE**

165.3b   the] **E1**– her **MS–SE**

165.3c　And each time she] **TS1r**– She **MS TS1t**

165.4–5　this ... her] **TS1r**– this ... Her **MS TS1t**

165.5　dipped in response] **TS1r**– dipped **MS TS1t**

165.6　point below] **TS1r**– point **MS TS1t**

165.8a　father's] **TS1**– fathers **MS**

165.8b　her] **MS TS1r**– her with her **TS1t**

165.9　enigmatic] **MS TS1t E1**– enigmatic mocking **TS1r–SE**

165.11–167.2　But ... "poor man!"] **MS TS1 SE**– om **SA**

165.11–12　remained concealed and] **E1**– stopped **MS TS1 SE** om **SA**

165.12　side ... happen] **E1**– side, concealed and watchful **MS** side **TS1** side to see what would happen **SE** om **SA**

165.13　broad, furnished verandah] **E1**– wide furnished verandah **MS TS1** verandah **SE** om **SA**

165.14　came] **E1**– flew **MS TS1t** was pulled **TS1r SE** om **SA**

165.16　gazed] **TS1r SE**– looked **MS TS1t** om **SA**

165.18a　tottering] **SE**– tottering distressed **MS TS1t** laborious **TS1r** om **SA**

165.18b　the] **SE**– a **MS TS1** om **SA**

165.22　sneak off] **TS1r SE**– depart **MS TS1t** om **SA**

165.26　front-rail] **TS1r SE**– front railing **MS TS1t** om **SA**

165.34　love music which] **E1**– music whose passionate utterance **MS TS1 SE** om **SA**

165.36　malice,] **TS1r SE**– malice, and **MS TS1t** om **SA**

166.9　louder] **E1**– rather louder **MS TS1 SE** om **SA**

166.10　Nelson's] **E1**– Nelson's mouth dropped open and his **MS TS1 SE** om **SA**

166.11　open door] **MS TS1 E1**– door **SE** om **SA**

166.14　pierced] **E1**– pierced like a needle **MS TS1 SE** om **SA**

166.16　the boat] **E1**– the a boat **MS** a boat **TS1 SE** om **SA**

166.17　terrific] **TS1r SE**– great **MS TS1t** om **SA**

166.18　but] **MS TS1 SE** for **E1**– om **SA**

166.20　Freya] **MS TS1r SE**– Freya | Freya **TS1t** om **SA**

166.26–27　from neuralgia] **E1**– of pain **MS TS1 SE** om **SA**

166.27　get yourself liked] **E1**– behave **MS TS1 SE** om **SA**

166.27–28　offended with you] **E1**– offended **MS TS1 SE** om **SA**

166.29　now reposed] **E1**– were resting **MS TS1t** now were resting **TS1r SE** om **SA**

166.30　inward discontent] **MS** discontent **TS1 SE**– om **SA**

166.38　friend of ours] **TS1r SE**– friend **MS TS1t** om **SA**

166.39a　something to] **MS TS1r SE**– some- | to **TS1t** om **SA**

166.39b　person] **E1**– man **MS TS1 SE** om **SA**

167.3　V] **TS1r SA E1**– IV **MS** Chapter V. **SE** om **TS1t**

167.4–6　In ... call.] **MS TS1 SE**– om **SA**

167.4　that] **MS TS1 E1**– that it **SE** om **SA**

167.7　infuriated] **E1**– raging **MS–SE**

167.10　steaming] **E1**– gliding **MS–SE**

167.11–14　Old ... indifference.] **MS TS1 SE**– om **SA**

167.13　hard] **MS TS1 E1**– unfeeling **SE** om **SA**

167.14　by her indifference] **E1**– at it **MS TS1 SE** om **SA**

167.17　head] **MS TS1r**– hand **TS1t**

167.20　which] **SE**– though that last **MS TS1** though she **SA**

167.23　Jasper] **TS1r**– He **MS TS1t**

167.24　for a glance] **TS1r**– to look **MS TS1t**

167.28　to] **TS1r**– to behind him **MS TS1t**

167.30　unholy desire] **TS1r**– desire **MS TS1t**

167.32–168.8　That ... piano.] **MS TS1 SE**– om **SA**

167.33   mocked at] **E1**– mocked **MS TS1 SE** OM **SA**

167.37   trader] **E1**– island trader **MS TS1 SE** OM **SA**

167.38   impressions, impressions ... senses,] **MS** impressions, **TS1 SE**– OM **SA**

168.5   to be] **MS–A1 E2 A2b** to **A2a**

168.8   a ghostly] **E1**– an invisible **MS TS1 SE** OM **SA**

168.9a   be recorded] **TS1r**– record **MS TS1t**

168.9b   Lieutenant] **SA**– lieutenant **MS TS1**

168.10   towards] **MS TS1 SE**– toward **SA**

168.12   his arrival] **TS1r**– him **MS TS1t**

168.14a   authority] **MS TS1r**– authorities **TS1t**

168.14b   the permission] **MS** permission **TS1**–

168.16   coast] **MS–SA E1**– shores **SE**

168.17a   straits] **MS TS1 SE**– Straits **SA**

168.17b   a] **MS** the **TS1**–

168.18   phosphorescent] **TS1**– phosphorescent green **MS**

168.19a   deep blue] **E1**– sparkling **MS–SE**

168.19b   day time] **E1**– day time in a level deep blue shot **MS TS1t** daytime – a level of deep blue shot **TS1r–SE**

168.19c   patches over] **E1**– above **MS–SE**

168.20a   reefs.] **E1**– reefs, sown over with bushy round islets, with black heads of rocks set off by beaches of coral sand whiter and more dazzling than patches of snow. **MS–SE**

168.20b   For days the *Neptun*] **TS1r**– She **MS TS1t**

168.20c   moving] **TS1r**– gliding **MS TS1t**

168.21   the shore] **TS1**– shore **MS**

168.22–23   estuaries,] **E1**– estuaries, small and black **MS–SE**

168.23–24   and flooding] **TS1r**– flooding **MS TS1t**

168.25   in] **TS1r**– by **MS TS1t**

168.27   than] **MS SA**– that **TS1**

168.28   * * *] **TS1r SE**– OM **MS TS1t SA**

168.30a   the] **TS1r**– a **MS TS1t**

168.30b   silvery] **E1**– silvered **MS TS1t** silver **TS1r–SE**

168.30c   estuary of ... river] **TS1r**– estuary **MS TS1t**

168.30–31   breath of air] **TS1r**– breath **MS TS1t**

168.33   ghostly ... stealthy] **TS1r**– white and ghostlike **MS TS1t**

168.34   progress;] **SE**– progress. The deep red band of the evening sky extended behind her gave a mournful relief to the black coast, the purple sea, the white beaches of outlying islets away to the southward; **MS TS1t** progress. The deep red band of the evening sky extended behind her gave a mournful relief to the black coast, to the purple sea, to the white beaches of outlying islets away to the southward; **TS1r SA**

168.36   her. The] **TS1r**– her; for the **MS TS1t**

168.39   suave] **MS TS1r**– grave **TS1t**

168.39–169.1   and when ... lightly,] **MS–SA E1**– and **SE**

169.1   the grace ... progress] **TS1r**– in her progress she **MS TS1t**

169.2–3   which ... world] **TS1r**– in her grace **MS TS1t**

169.2   which] **E1**– that **TS1r–SE** VAR **MS TS1t**

169.4–8   Dependent ... conquered.] **MS TS1 SE**– OM **SA**

169.4   vessel –] **E1**– vessel as **MS TS1 SE** OM **SA**

169.5   her] **E1**– his brig **MS TS1 SE** OM **SA**

169.6   love. The ... brig] **TS1r SE**– love and her possession **MS** love and possession **TS1t** OM **SA**

169.7a   appeased] **MS TS1r SE**– appeared **TS1t** OM **SA**

169.7b   in] **E1**– like **MS TS1 SE** OM **SA**

169.7–8   certitude of ... conquered]
TS1r SE– certitude MS TS1t OM SA

169.9   was] E1– was already MS–SE

169.11   shall] MS–A1 E2 will A2

169.12   thought with rapture] TS1r–
thought MS TS1t

169.13   that] MS TS1 SE– this SA

169.19   trading brig] TS1r– brig MS
TS1t

169.20–21   out emerging ... ambush]
TS1r– out MS TS1t

169.21a   of] E1– the man with MS–SE

169.21b   voice] SE– voice and of a
peculiar idiosyncrasy MS–SA

169.21c   given] TS1r– shown MS
TS1t

169.21d   a strange] MS–SA strange
SE–

169.26   of] E1– something about
MS–SE

169.30   miserably] TS1r harshly MS
TS1t SA–

169.31a   But ... fit.] MS TS1 SE– OM SA

169.31b   might] MS SA– might |
might TS1 OM SA

169.33   with me] MS me TS1–

169.36   The] MS TS1r– The | The
TS1t

169.37   and sylph-like] MS TS1r– and
TS1t

169.38   dark spars] TS1r– spars MS
TS1t

170.1   an] MS–SA E1– a SE

170.4–9   In ... smile.] MS–SA E1– OM
SE

170.5   these] TS1r SA E1– her MS
TS1t OM SE

170.7   half-jesting] TS1r SA E1– half
jesting stolen MS TS1t OM SE

170.9–10   Heemskirk ... fashion.] MS
TS1 SE– OM SA [see 170.10,
170.10–19]

170.10   There ... visions.] MS TS1 E1–
OM SA SE [see 170.9–10,
170.10–19]

170.10–19   He ... matched.] MS TS1
SE– OM SA [see 170.9–10, 170.10]

170.13   a] TS1 SE– a | a MS OM SA

170.15   she had] TS1 SE– had MS OM
SA

170.16   That was] TS1r SE– That's MS
TS1t OM SA

170.17a   outraged, struck,] TS1r SE–
outraged, MS TS1t OM SA

170.17b   mocked at] E1– mocked MS
TS1 SE OM SA

170.18a   the] MS SE– the | the TS1
OM SA

170.18b   Seven] MS TS1r– seven TS1t

170.25–28   His ... mica.] MS TS1 SE–
OM SA

170.27   had been] E1– were MS TS1
SE OM SA

170.30   a] TS1– a | a MS

170.31a   he decided] TS1r– resolved
not MS not TS1t

170.31b   neither] TS1r– either MS
TS1t

170.31c   nor] TS1r– or MS TS1t

170.31–32   surprise] TS1r–
astonishment MS TS1t

170.34a   were] E1– were not MS–SE

170.34b   some suspicion] E1– an eye
of favour MS–SE

170.34–35   But ... Nelson.] TS1r SA
E1– OM MS TS1t SE

170.37–171.14   rail as ... forward.] MS
TS1 SE– rail. SA

171.6   sounded] E1– sounded more
MS TS1 SE OM SA

171.10   Schultz] E1– Schultz as if he
were MS TS1 SE OM SA

171.12   a feverish man] TS1r SE– his
mate MS TS1t OM SA

171.13a   actually delirious,] TS1r SE–
delirious MS TS1t OM SA

171.13b   and that] TS1r SE– which
MS TS1t OM SA

171.15   desperately] MS TS1r–
desperate TS1t

171.16   I feel] MS TS1r– feel TS1t

171.19   swung himself] MS TS1 SE–
swung SA

171.20   straddle-legs,] TS1r SE–
straddle-legs, all black MS TS1t
straddle-legged SA

171.21   moonlight,] TS1r– moonlight
and with MS TS1t

171.22–23   something like] TS1r– like
MS TS1t

171.23 chest at ... man] **TS1r**– chest **MS TS1t**

171.24 waited] **E1**– stood **MS–SE**

171.25 Brought ... contact] **TS1r**– Face to face **MS TS1t**

171.26 of their casual meetings] **TS1r**– as in which they treated each other **MS TS1t**

171.29 asked] **TS1r**– said **MS TS1t**

171.30 lieutenant straight away] **TS1r**– lieutenant **MS TS1t**

171.31 the ... that] **TS1r**– these affairs **MS TS1t**

171.32 got] **MS TS1r**– had **TS1t**

171.33a nothing in exchange] **TS1r**– nothing **MS TS1t**

171.33b trade there now] **TS1r**– trade **MS TS1t**

171.36 the rascals] **TS1r**– they **MS TS1t**

171.37 better than to starve] **TS1r**– better **MS TS1t**

172.1 of women] **TS1r**– women **MS TS1t**

172.4–13 They spoke ... large:] **MS TS1 SE**– OM **SA**

172.4 spoke] **TS1r SE**– had spoken **MS TS1t** OM **SA**

172.5 in] **TS1r SE**– or else conversing with **MS TS1t** OM **SA**

172.6 at most, with] **TS1r SE**– with, at most, **MS TS1t** OM **SA**

172.7 object and no more] **TS1r SE**– object **MS TS1t** OM **SA**

172.8 all at once] **TS1r SE**– suddenly **MS TS1t** OM **SA**

172.11–12 lost ... vision] **TS1r SE**– couldn't make a sound or a movement **MS** couldn't make a sound **TS1t** OM **SA**

172.12 absolutely couldn't see Jasper] **TS1r SE**– couldn't even see him **MS** couldn't see him **TS1t** OM **SA**

172.14 detained?"] **TS1r**– detained?" ¶ Jasper had concealed his astonishment and his anger. **MS TS1t**

172.15 Heemskirk made a recovery in a flush of malignant satisfaction:] **MS TS1 SE**– OM **SA**

172.16 take ... tow] **SE**– tow you to Macassar **MS TS1t** take you to Makassar in tow **TS1r SA**

172.17a courts] **MS TS1r**– court **TS1t**

172.17b have to] **TS1r**– soon **MS TS1t**

172.18a aware ... but] **E1**– turning his head away to look at the brig **MS–SA** turning away to look at the brig **SE**

172.18b assumed] **TS1r**– perfectly assumed **MS** perfectly assured **TS1t**

172.22 his ship] **TS1r**– the brig **MS TS1t**

172.23–24 turned away and] **TS1r**– finished his movement and with his back to Heemskirk **MS TS1t**

172.24 answered: "Yes sir."] **TS1r**– answered **MS TS1t**

172.25 receive] **TS1r**– take **MS TS1t**

172.27 What's that] **TS1r**– What **MS TS1t**

172.28 Kindness] **TS1r**– To oblige **MS TS1t**

172.28–29 ironical, ... deliberation] **TS1r**– answered shouting deliberately **MS TS1t**

172.29 "We ... days.] **MS TS1 SE**– OM **SA**

172.29–30 And hospitality.] **TS1r**– OM **MS TS1t**

172.30 invited to stay] **TS1r**– detained **MS TS1t**

172.31 loud] **E1**– short **MS–SE**

172.32 fellow's nerve's] **TS1r**– fellow's **MS TS1t**

172.33a with] **TS1**– with with **MS**

172.33b awakened] **MS–SA** awkward **SE**–

172.34 was] **MS–SA E1**– had **SE**

172.38 stirred ... least] **TS1r**– moved **MS TS1t**

173.2 in his voice] **E1**– of any sort **MS–SE**

173.3 these] **MS TS1** the **SA**–

173.5a towed] **MS TS1r**– taken **TS1t**

173.5b saved] **TS1r**– saved him **MS TS1t**

173.8 must] **TS1r**– shall **MS TS1t**

173.13 apart] **MS–E1 A2 E2** part **A1**

173.15–16   kept ... motionless] **TS1r**– been standing not very far off stock still **MS TS1t**

173.17   fellow] **TS1r**– man **MS TS1t**

173.17–18   approached and ... attention] **TS1r**– approached **MS TS1t**

173.19   that] **MS** the **TS1**–

173.22   giving his orders] **TS1r**– speaking **MS TS1t**

173.23   edification. "You hear?"] **TS1r**– edification. **MS TS1t**

173.27   if] **TS1r**– if he were in a dream in which **MS TS1t**

173.31   China seas] **MS TS1r SA** china seas **TS1t** China Seas **SE**–

173.35   her four years ago] **TS1r**– her **MS TS1t**

173.38–39   Heemskirk to the gunner] **TS1r**– Heemskirk **MS TS1t**

174.1   for? What ... imply!] **TS1r**– aspersion **MS TS1t**

174.6   next thirty hours] **TS1r**– thirty hours which succeeded **MS TS1t**

174.8   was stopped] **TS1r**– stopped **MS TS1t**

174.9   a warrant officer] **E1**– warrant officer **MS–SE**

174.10   his] **SE**– his face remaining lifeless but his **MS–SA**

174.12a   wild blinking] **MS** blinking **TS1**–

174.12b   These two] **TS1r**– They **MS TS1t**

174.13–14   tried ... brig] **TS1r**– inspected his brig anxiously **MS TS1t**

174.14a   common] **E1**– usual **TS1r–SE** VAR **MS TS1t**

174.14b   on board] **SE**– in **TS1r** on **SA** VAR **MS TS1t**

174.15–37   But ... again.] **MS TS1 SE**– OM **SA**

174.17   anybody] **SE**– anybody on board **MS TS1** OM **SA**

174.23a   single] **MS** single one **TS1** **SE**– OM **SA**

174.23b   showed] **TS1r SE**– showed a sign of **MS TS1t** OM **SA**

174.24   rapidly at last] **TS1r SE**– rapidly **MS TS1t** OM **SA**

174.25a   is] **TS1 SE**– is | is **MS** OM **SA**

174.25b   mine] **MS TS1** mein **SE**– OM **SA**

174.26   very funny] **TS1r SE**– funny **MS TS1t** OM **SA**

174.36–37   tongue – that ... smile] **MS TS1r SE**– tongue – **TS1t** OM **SA**

174.36   help] **TS1r SE**– repress **MS** OM **TS1t SA**

174.37a   broad smile] **TS1r SE**– smile **MS** OM **TS1t SA**

174.37b   brig again] **TS1r SE**– brig **MS TS1t** OM **SA**

174.39   united lives] **MS** lives **TS1**–

175.2   world; to see] **TS1r**– world, **MS TS1t**

175.6   chains] **E1**– heavy chains **MS–SE**

175.7–14   Yet ... Freya?] **MS TS1 SE**– OM **SA**

175.7–8   sometimes came] **TS1r** would sometimes come **MS TS1t** **SE**– OM **SA**

175.9   which the] **SE**– the **MS TS1** OM **SA**

175.13   For what evil] **TS1r SE**– What **MS TS1t** OM **SA**

175.16   shall] **MS–A1 E2** will **A2**

175.19   going] **E1**– going in **MS–SE**

175.22   that] **TS1r**– that stronghold, that **MS** that thought fed, that **TS1t**

175.23   like] **MS–A1 E2** as **A2**

175.25   a great] **MS–SA** great **SE**–

175.26–27   the forecastle ... *Bonito*] **E1**– her forecastle **MS TS1t SA SE** the Bonito's forecastle **TS1r**

175.33   Tamissa reef!] **E1**– Tamissa **MS–SE**

175.33–34   yelled with ... lungs] **TS1r** yelled **MS TS1t SA**–

175.35–36   shoulder heavily] **TS1r**– shoulder **MS TS1t**

175.38a   water over ... time.] **TS1r**– water. **MS TS1t**

175.38b   turned about] **TS1r**– spun round **MS TS1t**

176.2–3   cast adrift and shooting] SE–
shot MS shot away TS1t free,
shooting TS1r SA

176.12   spars] SE– spars over MS–SA

176.13   still on the reef] SE– still
MS–SA

176.14   Passage] MS TS1r– passage
TS1t

176.15   ill-omened] MS TS1r– ill –
omened TS1t

176.17   decay] MS TS1r– decoy TS1t

176.18   already] MS TS1r– and TS1t

176.26   the Neptun's] TS1– Neptun's
MS

176.27   Gott ... Hold] MS Gott
for-dam! old TS1t Gott for-dam!
Hold TS1r SA Hold SE–

176.28a   fellow] SE– Englishman
MS–SA

176.28b   for] MS SA– for | for TS1

176.30   hold of] MS of TS1–

176.31   in] SE– in a sort of MS–SA

176.32   widened, clear] TS1r– clear
MS TS1t

176.34   an] MS–A2 a E2

176.35a   had moved neither] SE– had
not moved either MS TS1r SA had
not moved neither TS1t

176.35b   nor] SE– or MS TS1r SA or |
or TS1t

176.35c   by as] MS TS1 as SA–

176.36   breadth] SA– breath MS TS1

176.39–177.7   gangway and ... life.]
MS TS1 SE– gangway. SA

176.39   then moved] TS1r SE– moved
MS TS1t OM SA

176.40   the object ... awed] E1–
watched by covert MS TS1t watched
by many covert TS1r SE OM SA

177.1–2   stared at him] TS1r SE–
stared MS TS1t OM SA

177.3   that infernal girl] TS1r SE– she
MS TS1t OM SA

177.5   Lieutenant] SE– lieutenant MS
TS1 OM SA

177.6   as] MS SE– at TS1 OM SA

177.11   Gone on] MS E1 A1 E2 A2
Gone. On TS1–SE

177.20a   cap] TS1r– uniform cap MS
TS1t

177.20b   towards] MS TS1 SE– toward
SA

177.22   said] TS1r– said in the
vibrating low tone of hate MS TS1t

177.23   VI] TS1r SA E1– Chapter VI.
SE OM MS TS1t

177.24   a] TS1r– some MS TS1t

177.25a   the] TS1r– that MS TS1t

177.25b   perhaps] TS1r– perhaps also
MS TS1t

177.26a   Islands,] MS–A2 islands; E2

177.26b   which however knows] SE–
which knows but MS TS1t but
which knows TS1r SA

177.26c   few] MS TS1r– few events in
the pscychology of at least three
people; even if one of them
lieutenant heemskirk was at that
very moment passing amongst them
on his way to make his verbal
report. No, the minds on the "front"
were not competent for that sort of
invertigation but many hands were
there, brown hands, yellow hands,
white hands were raised to shade
the eyes. The rumour spread
quickly. Chinese shopkeepers came
to their doors, more that once while
merchants rose from his desks to go
to the windowz After all a ship on
Tamissa was not an everyday
occurance the towns in the islands
which knows but few TS1t

177.34   Tamissa] MS TS1r– Tamassa
TS1t

177.34–178.9   That ... shape.] MS TS1
SE– OM SA

177.35   Its] SE– It's MS TS1 OM SA

177.38–178.1   them, Lieutenant] TS1
SE– the lieut: MS OM SA

178.5   eyes gazing ... sea] TS1r– eyes
MS TS1t

178.7   merchant] TS1 SE– merchants
MS OM SA

178.12   "The Bonito. ... What!] TS1r–
The Bonito ... "What! MS TS1t

178.20   for certain] TS1r– right
enough MS TS1t

178.22   has] TS1r– had MS TS1t

178.25   What] MS TS1r– hat TS1t

178.26   impudent] **MS TS1r**–
imprudent **TS1t**

178.28   off these fellows] **MS TS1 SE**–
these fellows off **SA**

178.32a   move her] **MS SA**– move **TS1**

178.32b   sits] **MS** is **TS1**–

178.35   a kind] **TS1**– a **MS**

178.37   fine] **TS1r**– long **MS TS1t**

179.4   much] **SE**– very much **MS–SA**

179.5–11   Well, ... I remember."] **MS
TS1 SE**– OM **SA**

179.5   Well] **MS TS1** ¶ "Well **SE**– OM
SA

179.6a   There was] **TS1r** And **MS
TS1t SE**– OM **SA**

179.6b   He had] **TS1** He **MS** I have
SE– OM **SA**

179.7   has] **TS1r SE**– had **MS TS1t** OM
SA

179.8   very . . . .] **MS TS1** very — " **SE**–
OM **SA**

179.11   fair-headed] **SE**– fair- | haired
MS TS1 OM **SA**

179.12   inner knowledge] **MS**
knowledge **TS1**–

179.15   think] **MS TS1r**– thing **TS1t**

179.18   to] **MS TS1r**– to | to **TS1t**

179.24   the Oranje] **MS** Oranje **TS1**–

179.25   Gomez] **MS TS1r**– Bomez
TS1t

179.26–27   the immediate ... Gomez]
SE– Gomez' immediate attention
MS–SA

179.27   His] **MS TS1r**– is **TS1t**

179.28   brought] **MS** had brought
TS1–

179.29   He] **MS TS1r**– He He **TS1t**

179.32   him] **SE**– him on the [the |
the] verandah of the hotel, **MS–SA**

179.33   table. At ... verandah] **SE**–
table at one end of it; at the other
end **MS–SA**

179.35–36   Two ... too.] **MS TS1 SE**–
OM **SA**

179.37–180.5   On Gomez ... table.]
MS TS1 SE– ¶ Where he wanted to
go? For what purpose? Where he,
perhaps, only imagined himself to
be going, when a sudden impulse
or the sight of a familiar place had

made him turn into Oranje House?
It is impossible to say. He was
steadying himself lightly with the
tips of his fingers on the little table.
¶ On Gomez's coming up to him,
Jasper raised one hand to point at
his own throat. Gomez noted the
somewhat soiled state of his white
clothes, then took one look at his
face and fled away to order the
drink for which he seemed to be
asking. **SA**

179.40   Jasper] **E1**– the gesture **MS** he
TS1–SE

180.9   own eyes] **TS1r**– own **MS TS1t**

180.12a   Allen] **TS1r** him **MS TS1t**
SE– he **SA**

180.12b   wondered, with awe] **TS1r**–
wondered **MS TS1t**

180.16   China] **MS TS1 SE**– Chinese
SA

180.21   the roadstead] **MS SA**–
roadstead **TS1**

180.28   brought] **TS1r**– made **MS
TS1t**

180.29   upon] **TS1r**– round **MS TS1t**

180.32   push] **MS** push on **TS1**–

180.34   very much] **TS1r**– at all **MS
TS1t**

180.40   the Islands] **MS TS1r**– Islands
TS1t

181.2   give] **TS1r**– also give **MS** gave
TS1t

181.7–8   mentioned ... lines of] **MS
TS1 SE**– which enables me to
complete **SA**

181.10   His letter] **TS1r**– It was he
who **MS** t was he who **TS1t**

181.11   Heemskirk's] **TS1**– Heemskirk
MS

181.16   best by ... towrope] **SE**– best
MS–SA

181.19   years'] **MS SA**– years **TS1**

181.19–20   together in the East]
TS1r– together **MS TS1t**

181.20   devoted henchman] **TS1r**–
henchman **MS TS1t**

181.29   secretly] **MS** recently **TS1**–

181.30   this story] **TS1r**– which **MS
TS1t**

181.32   down on] **TS1r**– on **MS TS1t**
181.36   intended by] **E1**– meant in
MS–SE
181.37a   *Bonito* it] **SE**– Bonito **MS–SA**
181.37b   he meant] **E1**– it was **MS–SE**
182.1   the report ... created] **TS1r**–
this looked **MS TS1t**
182.2a   case] **MS TS1r**– case | case
TS1t
182.2b   Allen] **SE**– that Allen **MS–SA**
182.4   brig so much compromised]
TS1r– brig **MS TS1t**
182.5–6   There ... now.] **TS1r**– OM **MS**
TS1t
182.6   disapproved now] **E1**–
disowned **TS1r** discovered **SA SE**
OM **MS TS1t**
182.6–7   And it ... accident.] **TS1r**–
OM **MS TS1t**
182.11a   wait] **MS TS1r**– mark **TS1t**
182.11b   shall] **TS1r**– will **MS TS1t**
182.12a   these] **MS–SA** those **SE**–
182.12b   What tale] **TS1r** Whatever
tale **MS TS1t** When **SA**–
182.13   Heemskirk in the future]
TS1r– Heemskirk **MS TS1t**
182.15   without] **MS** without any **TS1**–
182.20a   that hated] **TS1**– hated **MS**
182.20b   man's] **TS1r** person's **MS**
TS1t SA–
182.25   he talked] **E1**– talked **MS–SE**
182.28   love] **E1**– love for two year **MS**
love for two years **TS1–SE**
182.31   perfectly intoxicated] **TS1r**–
perfect, intoxication **MS** perfect
intoxicated **TS1t**
182.32   a man] **TS1r**– him, **MS TS1t**
182.33   love] **TS1r**– a love **MS TS1t**
182.36   opposite] **TS1r**– opposite to
MS TS1t
182.39   above] **SE**– against **MS–SA**
183.3a   vessel too] **MS TS1 SE**– vessel
SA
183.3b   proceedings] **TS1**–
proceeding **MS**
183.7–8   by ... breast] **TS1r**– to draw
her to his breast by the mere power
of vision **MS TS1t**
183.9–11   All ... how Schultz] **MS TS1**
SE– Schultz **SA**

183.9   friend's] **TS1r TS1t SA**– friends
MS OM **SA**
183.10a   it] **E1**– what **MS TS1 SE** OM
SA
183.10b   appalling] **E1**– appalling was
MS TS1 SE OM **SA**
183.10c   of how] **SE**– how **MS TS1** OM
SA
183.11   Schultz the mate] **TS1r**–
Schultz **MS TS1t**
183.12   he and he] **MS** he **TS1**–
183.13   protested] **E1**– affirmed
MS–SE
183.15   thought that] **MS** thought
TS1–
183.18a   who] **TS1r**– who knew **MS**
who know **TS1t**
183.18b   Schultz's] **SA**– Schultz **TS1t**
Schultz' **MS TS1r**
183.18c   psychology, knew] **TS1r**–
psychology **MS TS1t**
183.19   admit] **E1**– I admit **MS–SE**
183.20   of] **MS SA**– of a of **TS1**
183.20–22   And ... well.] **MS TS1 SE**–
OM **SA**
183.23   seems] **MS–SA** seemed **SE**–
183.24   He says that] **TS1r**– It seems
MS TS1t
183.25   amongst] **MS TS1 SE**– among
SA
183.26a   him] **TS1**– him him **MS**
183.26b   gin one evening] **TS1r**– gin
MS TS1t
183.28–29   as being] **TS1r**– as **MS**
TS1t
183.29   took] **E1**– had **MS–SE**
183.32   piece for them] **TS1r**– piece
MS TS1t
183.33   grief] **E1**– despair **MS–SE**
183.35a   he] **TS1**– he he **MS**
183.35b   felt] **E1**– was **MS–SE**
183.37   by ... life] **TS1r**– that way **MS**
TS1t
183.40   was ... commit] **TS1r**– would
have comitted **MS TS1t**
184.1   it ... order] **TS1r**– he must live
MS TS1t
184.4   sneaking] **E1**– sniggering
MS–SE
184.5   I've] **TS1r**– I **MS TS1t**

184.5–6   tell ... oath] **TS1r**– be sworn **MS TS1t**

184.8a   what] **MS TS1r**– when a **TS1t**

184.8b   once got] **TS1r**– got **MS TS1t**

184.9   would] **MS TS1r**– would never **TS1t**

184.15   lodging] **TS1r**– staying **MS TS1t**

184.16   That] **TS1r SA** ¶ "That **MS TS1t** ¶ That **SE**–

184.17   the] **E1**– that **MS–SE**

184.18   Jasper's] **TS1**– Jaspers **MS**

184.19   have ever] **MS** ever have **TS1**–

184.23–28   He ... jesting.] **MS TS1 SE**– OM **SA**

184.26a   life.] **SE**– life. Well, this was reformation indeed. **MS TS1** OM **SA**

184.26b   that] **MS** the **TS1 SE**– OM **SA**

184.29   manes] **MS TS1r**– names **TS1t**

184.30   looted] **TS1r**– pilfered **MS TS1t**

184.35   a ... sand] **SE**– the point **MS–SA**

184.35–36   had expected] **TS1r**– expected **MS TS1t**

184.37   sign to him] **TS1r**– sign **MS TS1t**

185.1   sullen] **MS TS1r**– sudden **TS1t**

185.2   darkly pained] **SE**– as if darkly pained **MS–SA**

185.3   conveyed] **TS1r**– expressed **MS TS1t**

185.5–16   Then, at ... Rather!] **MS TS1 SE**– OM **SA**

185.7   arriving] **TS1r SE**– coming **MS TS1t** OM **SA**

185.11–12   the Straits] **E1**– Batavia **MS TS1 SE** OM **SA**

185.12   I] **TS1r SE**– Is it true what I **MS TS1t** OM **SA**

185.13a   daughter,] **TS1r SE**– daughter. You know **MS TS1t** OM **SA**

185.13b   that] **MS TS1r SE**– that that **TS1t** OM **SA**

185.17–18   Nelson, at ... he] **MS TS1 SE**– Nelson **SA**

185.18a   flying visit to Makassar] **TS1r SE**– visit **MS TS1t** OM **SA**

185.18b   Mesmans] **TS1r**– Mesman's **MS TS1t**

185.20   Nelson (or Nielsen)] **MS TS1 SE**– Nelson **SA**

185.23   me too] **MS TS1** me **SA**–

185.24   uneasy] **E1**– an uneasy **MS–SE**

185.26   itself out] **TS1r** out **MS TS1t SA**–

185.29   I delayed] **MS TS1r**– delayed **TS1t**

185.32–33   England – to ... Nielsen!] **MS TS1 SE**– England. **SA**

185.32   was] **MS TS1r SE**– was was **TS1t** OM **SA**

185.34   But ... Nielsen)] **MS TS1 SE**– Old Nelson **SA**

185.35   And ... call.] **TS1r**– OM **MS TS1t**

185.36   these] **MS TS1** those **SA**–

185.37   squares, once of leisure] **SE**– squares **MS–SA**

185.39   these] **MS TS1** those **SA**–

185.40a   winter] **MS** wintry **TS1**–

185.40b   devilish elements:] **TS1r**– elements of **MS TS1t**

186.5   Seven Islets] **SE**– Seven islets **MS** seven islets **TS1 SA**

186.6   eye, and] **MS** eye, **TS1**–

186.9   Nelson (or Nielsen)] **MS TS1 SE**– Nelson **SA**

186.10   a shabby] **TS1r**– an old **MS TS1t**

186.12a   of us] **TS1**– of **MS**

186.12b   me] **TS1r**– my **MS TS1t**

186.15–19   His ... marked.] **MS TS1 SE**– OM **SA**

186.17   them;] **TS1r SE**– them and **MS TS1t** OM **SA**

186.18–19   much more marked] **TS1r SE**– more marked **MS** marked **TS1t** OM **SA**

186.19   Like ... senile.] **TS1r SE**– OM **MS TS1t SA**

186.21a   in his] **MS TS1 SE**– his **SA**

186.21b   me] **MS TS1r**– be **TS1t**

186.22   weak,] **MS** weak and **TS1**–

186.23   informed upon ... whatever] **TS1r**– informed **MS TS1t**

186.24   had] **SA**– has **MS TS1**

186.25a   question] **SE**– question from me **MS–SA**

186.25b him going] **MS E1**– him
TS1–SE

186.27 which] **MS TS1r**– which
which **TS1t**

186.27–28 would recall to me] **TS1r**–
I would call of **MS** would call of **TS1t**

186.28a east] **SA**– East **MS TS1**

186.28b verandah of the bungalow]
TS1r Verandah **MS TS1t SA**–

186.28–29 where ... sit] **TS1r**– when
sat there **MS** when he sat there **TS1t**

186.29a quietly] **SE**– quietly with me
MS quietly to me **TS1 SA**

186.29b and ... cheeks in] **TS1r**– in
MS TS1t

186.29c seemed now] **TS1r**– seemed
MS TS1t

186.30–31 He ... tone.] **TS1r**– OM **MS**
TS1t

186.38–39 cries with ... spirit] **TS1r**–
cries **MS TS1t**

186.40 to] **MS SA**– to to **TS1**

187.4a job that] **TS1r**– job **MS TS1t**

187.4b I got] **TS1r**– got **MS TS1t**

187.5a There, doctors] **TS1r**– There
doctors, **MS TS1t**

187.5b Fever] **MS TS1r**– ever **TS1t**

187.8 newspaper] **TS1r**– paper **MS**
paper* **TS1t**

187.13 a long] **TS1**– long **MS**

187.16 up] **SE**– up at me **MS–SA**

187.20a travel] **TS1r**– go **MS TS1t**

187.20b went. She ... go.] **TS1r**–
went. Oh yes. I went. **MS** went. **TS1t**

187.21 Anæmia. Getting ... said.]
TS1r– Anaemia. **MS TS1t**

187.24 him," he] **MS TS1 E1**– him."
He **SA SE**

187.24–25 that ... see him.] **TS1r**– a
reasonable slightly anxious voice.
MS TS1t

187.25–26 I came] **MS TS1r**– came
TS1t

187.27–28 clothes that's ... really.]
TS1r– clothes. **MS TS1t**

187.29 the only live thing] **TS1r**–
alone **MS TS1t**

187.31a in] **MS TS1r**– ** **TS1t**

187.31b grown] **MS TS1r**– rown **TS1t**

187.31c again] **TS1r**– yet **MS TS1t**

187.31–32 stared holding ... hand]
TS1r SE– had his chin in his hand
MS TS1t stared **SA**

187.32 with] **MS SA** and **TS1t** and
with **TS1r SE**–

187.38 Never. Madness.] **TS1r**–
never. **MS TS1t**

187.39a reproach him gently] **TS1r**–
talk to him **MS TS1t**

187.39b by] **SA**– bye **MS TS1**

187.40 you] **SE**– her **MS–SA**

188.3a had belonging to me] **TS1r**–
had **MS TS1t**

188.3b this] **TS1r**– that **MS TS1t**

188.5 shouts] **TS1r**– asks **MS** asked
TS1t

188.6a I shook] **MS TS1r**– shook
TS1t

188.6b Come ... indeed. Anæmia.]
TS1r– OM **MS TS1t**

188.9 to] **TS1**– to to **MS**

188.15 sold then] **E1**– then sold yet
MS–SA then sold **SE**

188.16a it for me] **TS1r**– it **MS TS1t**

188.16b I] **TS1r**– I had **MS** had **TS1t**

188.24a Old Nelson] **TS1r**– He **MS**
TS1t

188.24b I sat] **MS TS1r**– sat **TS1t**

188.24c feeling] **MS TS1 SE**– felt **SA**

188.28a climate they said] **TS1r**–
climate **MS TS1t**

188.28b Oh! these] **TS1r SE–A1 A2a**
These **MS TS1t** Oh! These **SA** Oh,
those **E2 A2b**

188.29 mist] **MS** mists **TS1**–

188.30–31 else had she? ...] **TS1r**–
else ... **MS TS1t**

188.31–34 Sometimes ... moodiness.]
MS TS1 SE– OM **SA**

188.33a looked up] **TS1r SE**– stared
MS TS1t OM **SA**

188.33b strange, childish] **MS**
childish **TS1 SE**– OM **SA**

188.37 would] **MS TS1 SE**– should
SA

189.1–2 know they say anything.]
TS1r– know ... **MS** know **TS1t**

189.3–4 I don't] **MS TS1r**– don't
TS1t

189.4 cries] **MS** cried **TS1**–

189.8   vanquished] **TS1r**– overcome **MS TS1t**

189.9   absurdities, and] **E1**– absurdities **MS–SE**

189.10   me mute] **TS1r** me still **MS** me **TS1t SA**–

189.12   you by name] **TS1r** you **MS TS1t SA**–

189.14a   know] **TS1**– have **MS**

189.14b   A fellow] **MS TS1r**– fellow **TS1t**

189.15   while ....] **TS1**– while she might – **MS**

189.16   a question] **TS1**– question **MS**

189.17   girl. ...] **TS1**– girl. I tell you she was a sensible girl! Love – never. **MS**

189.18   I cried] **MS TS1r**– cried **TS1t**

189.18–19   that she] **TS1**– she **MS**

189.20a   too] **TS1**– too trembling in all his limbs **MS**

189.20b   he] **MS TS1t SE**– He **TS1r SA**

189.20c   doctors.] **TS1**– doctors said **MS**

189.21–22   The ... Pneu ...] **TS1**– Pneumonia. They explained to me. The inflamation of the ... **MS**

189.23a   word] **TS1**– sentence **MS**

189.23b   It ... sob.] **TS1r**– OM **MS TS1t**

189.24   in a ... pretence] **SA**– giving it up in despair **MS** in a gesture of despair, giving it ** **TS1t** in a gesture of despair, **TS1r**

189.25   low, heartrending cry:] **SE**– heartrending cry of a deceived man. **MS** low reproachful cry, the heartrending cry of a bitterly deceived man. **TS1 SA**

189.26   I] **MS TS1r**– I who **TS1t**

EMENDATIONS OF ACCIDENTALS

This list records the present edition's emendations of the accidentals of the copy-texts. A separate list (above) records emendations of substantives. Formal conventions of the documents are, as such, ignored (e.g., Conrad's signatures, the serials' bylines, editorial headings, and instalment statements). Ignored as well are changes in features of typography and styling, including that of ships' names (see the 'Preface', p. xvi, and 'The Texts', pp. 303–4), though such elements may occasionally appear in entries noting other alterations. Also not reported here are corrections of impossible word forms and other obvious errors in the preprinting texts, as when Conrad wrote 'promiment' or 'unnaproachable' or when a typist produced 'baloon', 'prominient', or 'streching'. Numbers below 100 that have been printed as words rather than figures go unreported, as do unambiguous typographical errors (e.g., 'ver yamazed', 'devouruing') in the typescripts that serve as copy-texts. Not listed as well are adjustments to the number and spacing of successive dots that represent suspensions and to the relative positioning of punctuation and closing quotation marks (inverted commas).

Reports on the manuscripts are based on their final readings. Reports on typescripts include not only the text produced by a typist and accepted by Conrad (e.g., TS), but also the typewritten readings underlying and superseded by Conrad's revisions (e.g., TSt), and the text finally created in the course of Conrad's revision (e.g., TSr). Reports on all typescript texts ignore both part-words generated by false starts at the ends of lines (when they do not involve whole words or possible affixes) and characters x-ed out by the typist.

The purpose of this list is not to provide a history of some particular readings in the texts collated, but to report the alterations made by the present editors to the punctuation and word forms of each copy-text and to record the earliest source (whether one of the collated texts or the Cambridge editors) for the emendation. Earlier texts may be assumed to agree, for present purposes, with the copy-text's reading in the absence of a statement to the contrary: if such a text offers a viable alternative to the adopted form, its rejected reading is reported in a separate line together with identifying siglum. Thus the list usually omits recording the readings of the collected editions, and it ordinarily does not record the typewriting errors found in a copy-text typescript and rejected by Conrad while 'correcting' its text.

In each entry the reading of the Cambridge text appears immediately after the page–line citation. It is followed by a bracket, then by a siglum identifying the text in which the emendation first occurs, and then by the rejected reading of the copy-text, which concludes the main statement. When appropriate, reports on alternative readings in intermediate texts follow in the next line. The symbol **ED** identifies readings adopted for the first time in this edition – that is, not present in the texts collated. The swung dash ($\sim$) represents the same word as appears before the bracket; it occurs in records of variants in punctuation or other accidentals associated with that word, when the word itself is not the variant being noted. The inferior caret ($_\wedge$) signals the absence of punctuation. Other conventions of notation conform to those followed in the 'Emendation and Variation' list and explained in its headnote.

The list follows these conventions for both the 'Author's Note' and the tales themselves. Listed in sequence below headings for the preface and for each story are the collated texts relevant to the emendations adopted as well as the sigla used to represent them; those for the book editions of the tales are stated once because for all three they are uniform.

Author's Note

TS1	typescript with holograph revisions (Free Library, Philadelphia Pennsylvania): copy-text
A1	first American edition: *Notes on My Books* (Doubleday, 1921 and Heinemann, 1921)
A2	second American edition: *'Twixt Land and Sea* (Doubleday collected), American (1921–) and British (1923–) issues
E	English edition: *'Twixt Land and Sea* (Heinemann collected, 1921)
S	serial text: 'Five Prefaces', *London Mercury* (March 1921)

5.3	geographical,] **A1** ~ₐ	6.26	The] **A1** the
5.3	scene,] **A1** ~ₐ	6.30	think,] **A1** ~ₐ
5.4	region,] **E** ~ₐ	6.35	"*Narcissus*"] **ED** ₐ~ₐ
5.5	equator,] **ED** ~ₐ	6.36	*Line,*] **A1** ~ₐ
5.12	*'Twixt*] **A1** ₐ~	6.38–39	quality, ... is,] **A1** ~ₐ ... isₐ
5.19	The] **E** the	7.16	story,] **E** ~ₐ
6.9	shipsₐ] **A1** ~,	7.17	book –] **E** ~:
6.22	down stream] **ED** down- | stream	7.19	Freya,] **A1** ~ₐ
		7.19	destiny –] **E** ~,

'TWIXT LAND AND SEA

E1	first English edition (Dent, 1912)
A1	first American edition (Doran (later Doubleday), 1912)
A2	second American edition (Doubleday collected, 1921)
A2a	first state of **A2**, American 'Sun-Dial' (1921) and all British issues (1923–)
A2b	second state of **A2**, Concord and subsequent American issues (1923–)
E2	second English edition (Heinemann collected, 1921)

A Smile of Fortune

MS	holograph manuscript (Berg)
TS1	typescript with holograph revisions (Yale, Berg): copy-text
TS1t	typewritten (unrevised) text of **TS** superseded by revision
TS1r	revised text of **TS** (incorporating Conrad's alterations): copy-text
TS2	typescript (Berg)
S	*London Magazine* (February 1911), 801–36.

13.2–3	sea horizon] **ED** sea-horizon	13.33	horror-struck] **ED** horror struck
13.6	tidings:] **ED** ~: –		
13.7	sir] **TS2** Sir	14.2	deep-seated] **ED** deep seated
13.14	H'm] **ED** Hm'	14.6	encouraging!] **TS2** ~.!
13.25	eastern port)ₐ] **ED** Eastern Port),	14.39	Death,] **ED** ~ₐ
		15.9	sir] **TS2** Sir
13.27	gloomy, little,] **ED** ~ₐ~ₐ	15.13	levelₐ] **ED** ~,
13.30	captain] **ED** Captain	15.26	first-rate] **ED** ~ₐ~ first rate

16.7	"we] **TS2** ∧~	23.3	H —] S H –
16.12	stage,] **ED** ~∧	23.5	married,] **TS2** ~∧
16.13	as,] **TS2** ~∧	23.12	two,] **TS2** ~∧
16.13	cares,] **TS2** ~∧	23.13	eyelids∧... me∧] **MS** ~, ... ~,
16.18	Hallo!",] **ED** ~!"∧	23.15	instructions,] **TS2** ~∧
16.21	haze,] **TS2** ~∧	23.24	leisurely.] **S** ~∧
16.22	bell,] **TS2** ~∧	23.30	etc.,] **S** ~∧∧
16.25	this."] **ED** ~·∧	23.32	you,] **TS2** ~∧
16.35	coast,] **ED** ~∧	23.34	satisfied,] **TS2** ~∧
16.39	mountains,] **ED** ~∧	24.5	scale,] **TS2** ~∧
16.39	low,] **ED** ~∧	24.14	charge,] **TS2** ~∧
17.8	point,] **ED** ~∧	24.18–19	quarter deck] **ED**
17.14	abrupt,] **ED** ~∧		quarter-deck
17.24	empty,] **ED** ~∧	24.22	shipchandlers] **ED**
17.31	sea,] **ED** ~∧		ship-chandlers
17.38	solitary,] **ED** ~∧	24.22	shipchandlers,] **S** ~∧
18.1	was,] **ED** ~∧	24.25	captains] **S** Captains
18.11	sir] **TS2** Sir	25.2	H —] **ED** H∧
18.14	get,] **TS2** ~∧	25.8	Jacobus,] **TS2** ~∧
18.16	morning,] **S** ~∧	25.14	years,] **TS2** ~∧
18.21	tired∧] **MS** ~,	25.17	mention,] **TS2** ~.
18.29	cried.] **MS** ~∧	26.9	seaman] **MS** sea-man
18.35	name,] **ED** ~∧	26.15	sky,] **S** ~∧
18.36	sir,] **TS2** ~∧	26.24	two.] **TS2** ~.:
18.37	loudly,] **S** ~∧	26.27	revolting∧] **TS1t** ~,
19.4	table cloth] **E1** table- | cloth	26.30–31	which, ... merchant,] **S** ~∧... ~∧
19.11	breakfast,] **TS2** ~∧	26.36	reason –] **ED** ~,
19.15	cuddy,] **S** ~∧	26.37	cemetery,] **E2** ~∧
19.25	But,] **S** ~∧	26.38	youngest,] **S** ~;
19.26	mercantile,] **S** ~∧	27.6	he] **S** He
19.33	Jacobus,] **S** ~∧	27.11	business,] **TS2** ~∧
19.38	tale,] **ED** ~∧	27.28	boatman,] **S** ~∧
20.7	stateroom] **MS** state room	27.31	collar∧] **MS** ~,
20.11	thin,] **S** ~∧	28.3	readily:∧] **S** ~: –
20.12	thick,] **S** ~∧	28.10	very∧] **S** ~,
20.29	successfully,] **S** ~∧	28.14	manner∧] **TS1t** ~,
20.38	silent,] **S** ~∧	28.17	splash –] **ED** ~∧
21.4	real,] **S** ~∧	28.19	∧Did] **MS** "~
21.8	Captain,] **TS2** ~∧	28.19	hear ... ∧] **MS** ~. . . . ."
21.10	that,] **TS2** ~∧	28.31	figure-head] **TS2** figure head
21.10	suppose?] **MS** ~.?		
21.29	here,] **ED** ~∧	28.36	Captain] **MS** captain
21.31	that,] **TS2** ~∧	29.2	'Mr Smith,'] **S** "~ ~∧"
21.37	expensive;] **ED** ~∧	29.2	I, 'don't] **TS2** I∧ "Don't
21.39	cutlets,] **ED** ~∧	29.4	figure-head?'] **TS2** figure head?∧
22.2	mutton!] **MS** ~∧		
22.28	captain] **S** Captain	29.7	soberly:] **S** ~.
22.34	H —] S H –	29.9	gilt."] **TS2** ~.∧
22.40	to,] **ED** ~∧	29.14	fiddle head] **ED** fiddle-head
23.27	captains] **S** Captains		
23.2	H —] S H –	29.15	proper."] **MS** ~.∧

29.18 cut water] **MS** cut- | water

29.18 water,] **TS2** ~∧

29.20 animosity:] **S** ~.

29.25 life,] **E2** ~∧

29.37 table,] **E2** ~∧

30.8 port."] **MS** ~.∧

30.11 that,] **TS2** ~∧

30.18 ashore?] **MS** ~∧

30.26 place,] **MS** ~∧

30.28 thunderstruck] **MS**
thunder-struck

30.29 communication,] **S** ~∧

30.31 care?] **MS** ~∧

31.9 like∧] **MS** ~"

31.16 Captain's] **MS** captain's

31.31 flowers,] **S** ~∧

31.33 trouble,] **S** ~∧

31.38 answer:] **ED** ~.

31.40 person,] **S** ~∧

32.3 for?"] **MS** ~?∧

32.7 you,] **S** ~∧

32.17 store] **S** Store

32.19 cheap.∧] **MS** ~."

32.20 some,] **S** ~∧

32.27 as∧] **MS** ~:

32.28 words∧ . . .] **MS** ~" –

32.32 brother,] **E2** ~∧

33.10 wisps] **S** whisps

33.12 light-yellow∧] **MS** ~,

33.14 three-legged] **S** three legged

33.26 simply:] **S** ~.

33.34 say,] **S** ~∧

33.34 loudly.] **MS** ~∧

33.38 in,] **MS** ~.,

34.10 moustache] **MS** mustache

34.21 imperiously:] **S** ~.

34.22 Captain] **S** captain

34.23 deliberately:] **S** ~.

34.31 personally,] **S** ~∧

34.33 me,] **S** ~∧

35.1 body,] **MS** ~∧

35.3 half past three] **ED**
half-past-three

35.4 skipper,] **S** ~∧

35.12 eyelids∧] **MS** ~,

35.14 thick,] **ED** ~∧

35.17 thin,] **S** ~∧

35.22 say∧] **MS** ~:

35.25 Beggarly . . . cheeky . . .] **ED** ~
– ~ –

35.27 upset,] **S** ~∧

35.31 that,] **S** ~∧

35.32 store] **TS1t** Store

35.36 small,] **MS** ~∧

35.37 iron bars] **S** iron- | bars

35.37 windows,] **ED** ~∧

36.1 smart,] **ED** ~∧

36.6 Theirs] **S** Their's

36.10 so?] **MS** ~∧

36.11 goodness."] **S** ~.∧

36.12 good-natured] **MS** good
natured

36.15 meeting,] **S** ~∧

36.16 example.∧] **S** example. –

36.18 "I] **MS** ¶ "~

36.25 doorway:] **MS** ~.

36.26 Captain] **MS** captain

36.27 large,] **E2** ~∧

36.30 steamer-man,] **S** ~∧

36.31 short,] **S** ~∧

36.36 nasal,] **S** ~∧

36.40 Right."] **MS** ~.∧

37.4 now,] **S** ~∧

37.9 Relish,] **S** ~∧

37.10 etc.] **E1** ~∧

37.13 smirking,] **ED** ~∧

37.13 clerk,] **ED** ~∧

37.24 Captain] **MS** captain

37.27 spec.] **S** ~∧

37.30 somewhat:] **MS** ~.

37.31 Captain] **MS** captain

37.40 business."] **S** ~.∧

38.7 beautiful,] **ED** ~∧

38.13 tone:] **S** ~.

38.18 ailing,] **S** ~∧

38.23 doctor,] **ED** ~∧

38.24 manner,] **ED** ~∧

38.24 tone:] **S** ~.

38.28 surprise:] **S** ~.

38.34 said:] **ED** ~.

39.9 visit,] **S** ~∧

39.16 anyone.∧] **MS** ~."

40.8 sisters,] **S** ~∧

40.8 Mary,] **S** ~∧

40.9 spoke∧] **S** ~,

40.9 pre-Revolution] **S**
pre-revolution

40.18 about,] **MS** ~∧

40.20 some day] **MS** someday

40.21 that,] **S** ~∧

40.30 large,] **E2** ~∧

40.38 listened,] **ED** ~∧

41.6 Doctor,] **ED** ~∧

41.9 him,] **S** ~∧

41.11	ship,] **S** ~∧
41.18	him,] **S** ~∧
41.20	circus-woman,] **S** ~∧
41.27	mail-boat . . .∧] **S** ~ . . . . . ."
41.28	perhaps,] **TS1t** ~∧
41.37	*extremis,*] **S** ~∧
41.38	said:] **S** ~∧
41.38	'The] **S** "~
41.39	impenitent.'] **S** ~."
42.6	friend,] **S** ~∧
42.14	only,] **ED** ~∧
42.18	slily:] **S** ~.
42.22	belongs."] **S** ~.∧
42.27	dare say] **MS** daresay
43.1	voice-saving∧] **TS1t** ~,
43.4	kind,] **S** ~∧
43.7	consignees,] **S** ~∧
43.10	old-maidish,] **S** ~∧
43.13	Captain] **MS** captain
43.13	Captain,] **ED** ~∧
43.22	captain's] **MS** Captain's
43.23	store] **MS** Store
43.25	deep,] **S** ~∧
43.29	any one] **MS** any- | one
43.30	store] **MS** Store
43.31	outcast:] **ED** ~.
43.32	Captain] **MS** captain
43.35	business,] **S** ~∧
43.35	amenity,] **S** ~∧
43.39	impulsively:] **MS** ~.
44.1	sleepy,] **S** ~∧
44.3	exclaiming:] **S** ~.
44.4	quarter bags] **S** quarter-bags
44.8–9	quarter bags] **S** quarter-bags
44.12	to . . . . Look] **MS** ~ – look
44.17	soul-shaking] **S** soul shaking
44.18	suddenly:] **S** ~: –
44.19	here,] **S** ~∧
44.26	heavy,] **S** ~∧
44.32	course,] **MS** ~∧
44.34	dare say] **MS** daresay
44.34	not,] **S** ~∧
45.7	street:] **S** ~;
45.15	flower-beds] **MS** flower beds
45.28	Alice,] **S** ~.
45.30	whispering∧] **MS** ~,
45.35	deep,] **S** ~∧
46.2	eyelids,] **S** ~∧
46.6	Make] **MS** make
46.6	long,] **S** ~∧
46.19	young,] **E2** ~∧
46.19	deep,] **E2** ~∧

46.24	chair,] **S** ~∧
46.40	softness,] **S** ~;
47.6	girl; it] **MS** ~. It
47.12	woman,] **ED** ~∧
47.12	large,] **E2** ~∧
47.16	exclaimed:] **MS** ~.
47.18	vanished;] **MS** ~∧
47.24	now,] **S** ~∧
47.29	expression;] **MS** ~,
47.36	verandah,] **S** ~∧
48.1	nightgown] **MS** night-gown
48.1	ancient,] **S** ~∧
48.3	flat,] **E2** ~∧
48.3	brown,] **ED** ~∧
48.4	foot rest] **MS** foot-rest
48.4	rest.] **S** ~∧
48.4	slightly∧] **ED** ~,
48.9	colloquially:] **S** ~.
48.10	to∧] **MS** ~,
48.14	natural,] **ED** ~∧
48.15	pleasure:] **S** ~: –
48.18	whistle:] **ED** ~.
48.25	tone:] **S** ~: –
48.27	him?"] **S** ~?∧
48.31	No,] **S** ~∧
48.36	black,] **MS** ~∧
49.4	shrill:] **S** ~.
49.7	riff raff] **MS** rif-raff
49.14	dummy?] **MS** ~.
49.14	out:] **S** ~.
49.19	accuracy,] **S** ~∧
49.30	when,] **S** ~∧
49.30	attitude,] **S** ~∧
49.37	man,] **S** ~∧
49.37	abruptly,] **S** ~∧
50.3	grave,] **S** ~∧
50.7	me:] **S** ~∧
50.23	Won't ... Shan't] **S** won't ... shan't
50.23	Won't," "Shan't" and "Don't] **ED** won't∧∧ "shan't∧ and ∧ Don't
50.24	dinner,] **E1** ~ –
50.28	which,] **ED** ~∧
50.29	night,] **ED** ~∧
51.3	faint,] **S** ~∧
51.10	S—] **MS** S –
51.15	boatman,] **S** ~∧
51.16	good] **MS** Good
51.19	family,] **ED** ~∧
51.22	large,] **ED** ~∧
51.29	store] **S** Store

51.36	Care] **MS** care
51.36	Care";] **ED** ~ "∧
52.21	dining room] **MS** dining- | room
52.23	Captain] **MS** captain
52.24	Yes!"] **MS** ~!∧
52.29	assurance:] **S** ~.
52.39	see,] **ED** ~∧
53.4	made,] **ED** ~∧
53.6	excitedly:] **S** ~.
53.7	Care] **S** care
53.23	Jacobus:] **S** ~∧
53.30	volubly,] **S** ~∧
54.3	it.] **MS** ~∧
54.4	false,] **S** ~∧
54.16	them,] **S** ~∧
54.17	dining room] **ED** dining-room
54.19	tone,] **S** ~∧
54.23	manner,] **S** ~∧
54.24	manner:] **S** ~.
54.25	fellow.] **ED** ~∧
54.28	instant,] **S** ~∧
54.29	finality:] **S** ~.
54.31	impudence,] **S** ~∧
54.37	Well,] **S** ~∧
54.37	that,] **S** ~∧
54.39	little. The] **S** ~; the
55.3	short:] **ED** ~.
55.6	Captain,] **MS** ~∧
55.22	smile:] **ED** ~.
55.23	Captain,] **S** ~∧
55.27	no,] **S** ~∧
55.27	he's] **MS** He's
55.31	reflections] **S** reflexions
55.31	Jacobus'] **ED** Jacobus's
56.3	captains∧] **MS** ~,
56.5	head clerk] **S** head-clerk
56.17	"You're] **S** —!"~
56.18	chap,] **S** ~∧
56.21	Ocean,] **MS** ~∧
56.24	don't] **MS** Don't
56.27	waistcoat:] **ED** ~∧
56.27	sinner,] **S** ~∧
56.28	jovially,] **S** ~;
56.32	regretfully:] **S** ~.
56.34	S —] **S** ~ -
56.35	D — family.] **MS** D- | family.
56.37	looks –] **ED** ~;

56.37	mocking∧] **MS** ~ –
56.40	town∧] **MS** ~,
57.2	flimsy,] **S** ~∧
57.3	looked,] **S** ~∧
57.10	adornment.] **MS** ~?
57.17	mysterious,] **ED** ~∧
57.19	spell-bound] **ED** spell bound
57.20	dishevelled,] **ED** ~∧
57.25	two.] **MS** ~;
57.25	woman's∧] **ED** ~:
57.30	myself.] **S** ~?
58.6	plump,] **S** ~∧
58.23	captain's] **ED** Captain's
58.23	store] **MS** Store
58.29	murders,] **S** ~∧
58.29	stabbing,] **ED** ~∧
58.38	aristocratic,] **ED** ~∧
58.39	sailors,] **S** ~∧
59.12	End] **S** end
59.12	London;] **ED** ~,
59.16	animosity:] **S** ~.
59.19–20	some day] **S** someday
59.25	tone.] **MS** ~∧
60.11	her∧] **MS** ~,
60.12	full,] **S** ~∧
60.14	straight,] **MS** ~∧
60.23	here,] **ED** ~∧
60.27	good,] **S** ~∧
60.27	air,] **S** ~∧
60.31	shape,] **ED** ~∧
60.31	base,] **S** ~∧
60.36	dingy,] **ED** ~∧
60.37	Oh … never mind …] **ED** ~ - ~ ~ -
61.2	roughly:] **S** ~.
61.4	look,] **S** ~∧
61.5	full,] **S** ~∧
61.5	lips:] **S** ~.
61.11	then."] **S** ~.∧
61.12	viciously:] **S** ~.
61.18	experiment:] **S** ~.
61.26	to-morrow] **S** tomorrow
61.30	hips.] **ED** ~∧
61.31	sensation∧] **MS** ~,
61.39	poison,] **E1** ~∧
62.1	brake,] **S** ~∧
62.5	half-indulgent,] **S** ~∧
62.9	thirst,] **S** ~∧
62.10	voice,] **S** ~∧

62.18	now,] **ED** ~∧		68.12	right,] **MS** ~∧
62.21	inflexion:] **S** ~.		68.12	last.∧] **MS** ~."
62.24	round,] **S** ~∧		68.14	Captain] **MS** captain
62.26	Care?"] **MS** ~.?∧		68.15	breath-saving] **S** breath saving
62.27	violently,] **S** ~∧		68.17	trade,] **S** ~∧
62.28	full,] **S** ~∧		68.22	though] **S** tho'
62.35	hot,] **S** ~∧		68.24	blue,] **S** ~∧
62.36	earth,] **MS** ~∧		68.29	luck!∧] **MS** ~!"
62.36	hopes,] **S** ~∧		68.30	think,] **ED** ~∧
62.38	care." . . .] **ED** ~." –		68.31	meditation,] **ED** ~∧
62.40	words:] **S** ~.		68.32	Captain] **MS** captain
63.10	evidently∧] **ED** ~,		68.36	No!] **MS** ~∧
63.15	death,] **ED** ~∧		68.38	Captain,] **ED** ~∧
63.24	honour," I cried,] **ED** ~∧ " ~ ~∧		69.3	suggestion:∧] **MS** ~: –
64.2	emotion:] **S** ~.		69.6	couldn't,] **S** ~∧
64.5	tone. "I've] **MS** ~." ∧~		69.18	remembered,] **ED** ~ –
64.5	papa] **MS** Papa		69.30	then,] **S** ~∧
64.13	glance,] **S** ~∧		69.33	Captain] **MS** captain
64.19	But,] **MS** ~∧		69.34	shoe∧] **MS** ~,
64.19	animal,] **MS** ~∧		69.37	Captain] **MS** captain
64.26	indolence,] **ED** ~∧		70.6	verandah:] **S** ~.
64.33	crouching,] **S** ~∧		70.12	again,] **S** ~∧
64.36	exasperating,] **S** ~∧		70.29	armchair] **MS** arm chair
64.39	movement,] **ED** ~∧		70.30	contemptuously:] **MS** ~.
65.2	reflection] **MS** reflexion		70.35	subdued,] **MS** ~∧
65.10	me,] **S** ~∧		71.2	quietly:] **MS** ~.
65.13	wide open] **S** wide-open		71.8	shoe,] **S** ~∧
65.20	head,] **MS** ~∧		71.11	Miss] **MS** Mis
65.25	don't!] **S** ~∧		71.11	Care,] **S** ~∧
65.32	undulating,] **S** ~∧		71.11	said,] **S** ~∧
65.32	dive,] **S** ~∧		71.14	strange,] **S** ~∧
66.5	late, alas!] **MS** ~∧ ~∧		71.17	up," I said,] **S** ~∧" I ~∧
66.35	asked∧] **ED** ~:		71.18	fact.∧] **S** ~."
66.35	sort,] **ED** ~∧		71.19	himself,] **S** ~∧
67.1	home,"] **E1** ~∧"		71.20	disreputable] **S** disreptable
67.4	"Oh∧] **MS** "~,		71.21	riff raff] **ED** riff-raff
67.4	you] **MS** You		71.23	you,] **S** ~.
67.4	off,"] **S** ~∧"		71.23	out.∧] **MS** ~."
67.6	Yes,] **S** ~.		71.28	kind,] **S** ~∧
67.13	big,] **S** ~∧		71.29	affirmed:] **S** ~.
67.14	kid,] **S** ~∧		71.32	sea.] **S** ~∧
67.18	Captain,"] **S** ~∧"		71.32	chair.∧ "But] **S** ~." ∧~
67.28	added:] **S** ~∧		72.1	Alice,] **S** ~.
67.33	"No∧] **MS** "No.		72.29	Jacobus'] **MS** Jacobus's
67.33	haven't,] **S** ~∧		72.35	quarter deck] **MS** quarter-deck
67.36	trade.] **MS** ~∧		73.1	Burns – I did,"∧] **MS** ~, ~ ~∧" –
68.2	strange,] **E2** ~∧		73.4	once,] **E1** ~∧
68.3	*me*] **MS** me		73.6	him,] **S** ~∧
68.5	Jacobus,] **S** ~∧			
68.6	consideration –] **S** ~,			

73.6–7	poop ladder] **MS** poop- | ladder	76.6	"I] **S** ∧~
73.7	sky light] **ED** sky- | light	76.6	say∧] **ED** ~,
73.11	till,] **S** ~∧	76.8	potato] **MS** potatoe
73.12	Burns,] **S** ~∧	76.11	office,] **S** ~∧
73.12	longer,] **S** ~∧	76.13	forehead:] **ED** ~.
73.16	Seventeen] **MS** seventeen	76.16	negligently:] **S** ~ –
73.22–23	sir, Rubbish] **ED** ~. ~	76.17	pounds."] **MS** ~..∧
74.3	at,] **S** ~∧	76.25	quarter deck] **MS** quarter-deck
74.8	story,] **ED** ~∧	76.27	hours,] **S** ~∧
74.21	cussedness,] **E2** ~∧	76.32	with,] **MS** ~;
74.25	after hatch] **MS** after-hatch	76.33	you,] **ED** ~∧
74.29	visual –] **MS** ~,	76.35	sir,] **S** ~∧
74.31	eyes∧] **MS** ~,	76.38	Burns,] **S** ~∧
74.34	poop;] **ED** ~,	76.38	exulting,] **S** ~∧
75.16	potato] **MS** potatoe	77.5–6	thought-out] **E1** thought out
75.20	downpour,] **ED** ~∧	77.7	Seas] **MS** seas
75.22	satisfaction∧] **MS** ~,	77.31	Burns,] **S** ~∧
75.25	Pilot,] **MS** ~∧	77.34	it,] **S** ~∧
75.32	Colony,] **MS** ~∧	78.1	Anyhow," he remarked,] **S** ~∧"~ ~∧
75.32	explained,] **MS** ~∧		
75.39	Pilot's] **ED** pilot's	78.4	Burns,] **S** ~∧
76.6	confidentially:∧] **ED** ~."	78.9	luck!] **MS** ~.

The Secret Sharer

MS	holograph manuscript (Berg): copy-text
S	*Harper's Monthly Magazine* (August, September 1910), pp. 349–59, 530–41.

81.4	fences,] **S** ~;	84.13	anchor watch] **ED** anchor-watch
81.10	solid,] **S** ~∧	84.14	incredulously:] **S** incredulously∧
81.23	pagoda,] **S** ~∧	84.15	closed,] **S** ~∧
81.27	them,] **S** ~∧	84.20	nothing,] **S** ~∧
81.28	masts,] **S** ~∧	84.22	people,] **S** ~∧
81.31	here, now there,] **S** ~∧ ~ ~∧	84.30	seas – everything!] **ED** seas. Everything
82.2	stillness,] **S** ~∧	84.30	everything! –] **ED** ~∧ ...
82.27	"Were] **S** ∧~	84.40	teeth,] **S** ~∧
83.6	responsibility,] **S** ~∧	85.8	clear,] **S** ~∧
83.15	say] **ED** say:	85.11	side-ladder,] **S** ~∧~∧
83.16	for"] **ED** ~ –	85.19	established] **S** estabished
83.16	way,] **S** ~∧	85.20	eccentric] **S** excentric
83.28	roadstead.] **S** ~∧	85.35	light,] **S** ~∧
83.29	so,] **S** ~∧	85.37	elusive,] **S** ~∧
83.30	"She] **S** ∧~	85.39	legs,] **S** ~∧
84.6	thereabouts] **S** there abouts	86.6	black-haired] **S** ~∧~
84.8	four,] **S** ~∧		

86.21	"Cramp,"] S ~∧		92.19	it,] S ~∧
86.21	anxious:] ED ~∧		92.30	back –] ED ~,
86.23	to," I said.] S ~∧" " ~∧		92.30	refused,] S ~∧
86.31	tentatively:∧] S ~:–		92.36	chief mate] S chief-mate
86.33	isn't,] S ~∧		93.1	Though] S Tho'
87.18	silent,] S ~∧		93.3	'brand of Cain'] S "~ ~ ~"
87.29	darkness,] S ~∧		93.6	'This] S "~
87.38	features,] ED ~∧		93.7	here.'] S ~∧"
87.39	smooth,] S ~∧		93.7	'So] S "~
88.1	cheeks,] ED ~∧		93.7	won't?'] S ~?"
88.1	well-shaped] S well shaped		93.8	'No!'] ED "~!"
88.8	Yes,] S ~∧		93.8	'Then] ED "~
88.8	warm,] S ~∧		93.8	that,'] S ~∧"
88.10	there,] S ~∧		93.9	'I] S "~
88.12	her...."] S ~"...		93.9	can,'] S ~∧"
88.13	himself:] ED ~∧		93.9	he,] S ~∧
88.13	I] S I		93.12	ago.] S ~;
88.18	man ..."] S ~......∧		93.25	'He's gone!'] S "~ ~∧
88.19	temper,] S ~.		93.26	swimming!'] S swimming∧"
88.24	boy,] S ~∧		93.27	"Certainly] ED ∧~
88.26	boy?"] S ~?∧		93.36	clothes,] S ~∧
88.27	am,] S ~∧		94.7	mile."] S ~.∧
88.40	ill-conditioned] S ill conditioned		94.13	whisper:] S ~∧
88.40	cur ..."] S ~...∧		94.18	thousand-feet] S thousand feet
89.6	brusque,] S ~∧		94.25	ladder ..."] S ~...∧
89.11	running,] ED ~∧		94.26	ship,] ED ~∧
89.19	rat,] S ~∧		94.31	he?"] S ~?∧
89.31	grey∧] S ~,		94.33	answer,] S ~∧
90.1	'Mr] S "~		95.7	himself,] S ~ –
90.3	ship.'] S ~∧∧		95.12	ladder,] ED ~∧
90.7	party,] S ~∧		95.12	"Fancy] ED ∧~
90.19	now,] S ~∧		95.22	me –] S ~,
90.21	in,] S ~∧		95.28	somebody,] S ~.
90.24	yet,] S ~∧		95.29	said –] ED ~...
90.25	much,] S ~∧		95.29	'Fine] S "~
90.29	sir."] S ~.∧		95.29	it?'] S ~?"
90.34	flowers,] S ~∧		95.31	presently?] S ~∧
90.39	use,] S ~∧		95.33	likely,] S ~∧
91.2	stateroom] S state room		95.38	bedplace] ED bed-place
91.4	L.,] ED ~.∧		96.6	safety,] S ~∧
91.7	inside,] S ~∧		96.19	all,] S ~∧
91.8	long∧] S ~,		96.22	quietly:] ED ~∧
91.10	caps,] S ~∧		96.28	thought,] S ~∧
91.15	room,] S ~∧		96.32	here?] S ~∧
91.19	once,] S ~∧		96.33	decks.] S ~∧
91.24	been,] S ~∧		96.34	closed,"] S ~".
91.39	quarter deck] ED quarter-deck		96.36	extraordinary,] S ~∧
92.5	land,] S ~∧		96.38	gentle,] S ~∧
92.12	Anyway] S Any way		97.8	deck,] S ~∧
			97.23	point-blank] S ~∧~

97.26	breakfast.] **S** ~ ₍
97.33	time,] **S** ~ ₍
97.33	myself,] **S** ~ ₍
98.1	mad,] **S** ~ ₍
98.5	far,] **S** ~ ₍
98.6	bathroom."] **S** ~.₍
98.10	dressing,] **S** ~ ₍
98.13	daylight,] **S** ~ ₍
98.14	stern,] **S** ~ ₍
98.21	stateroom] **S** state room
98.26	bath,] **S** ~ ₍
98.26	rights,] **S** ~ ₍
98.26	bang,] **S** ~ ₍
98.26	clatter …] **ED** ~ –
98.27	saloon …] **ED** ~ –
98.27	key …] **ED** ~ –
98.34	stool,] **S** ~ ₍
98.35	together,] **S** ~ ₍
98.40	said:] **S** ~.
99.1	sir!"] **S** ~!₍
99.3	him,] **S** ~ ₍
99.4	sir] **S** Sir
99.13	particular,] **S** ~ ₍
99.14	figure;] **S** ~,
99.28	though] **S** tho'
99.31	fun?] **S** ~ ₍
99.33	No!"] **S** ~!₍
100.1	Disease,] **S** ~ ₍
100.9	shipmaster."] **S** ~.₍
100.10	was,] **S** was
100.20	boy,] **S** ~ ₍
100.22	too.] **S** ~ ₍
100.23	him.] **S** ~ ₍
100.24	think,"₍] **S** ~₍" –
100.24	said,] **S** ~ ₍
100.27	neck.] **S** ~ ₍
100.28	impressively,] **S** impressively₍
100.29	that."] **S** ~.₍
100.35	sight,] **S** ~ ₍
100.35	me,] **S** ~ ₍
100.37	burial.] **S** ~ ₍
100.38	bunting;] **S** ~,
100.39	boots,] **S** ~ ₍
101.4	you,] **S** ~ ₍
101.4	in.] **S** ~ ₍
101.5	did,] **S** ~ ₍
101.7	squalls."] **S** ~.₍
101.8	it …"] **ED** ~ ….₍
101.8	began.] **S** ~ ₍

101.9	"Nothing] **S** ₍~
101.14	subject:] **S** ~.
101.22	*Sephora,*] **S** ~ ₍
101.24	know,] **S** ~ ₍
101.25	feelings,] **S** ~ ₍
101.25	"I] **S** '~
101.27	smart,] **S** ~ ₍
101.29	*Sephora.*"] **S** ~₍₍
101.33	chief mate] **S** chief-mate
101.35	man₍ you] **S** ~" You
101.35	understand,] **S** ~ ₍
101.39	pardon?"] **S** ~?₍
102.2	in.] **S** ~ ₍
102.3	tomorrow,"] **S** ~₍₍
102.9	that.] **S** ~ ₍
102.10	curiosity,] **S** ~ ₍
102.15	ready-made] **S** ready made
102.20	point-blank] **S** point blank
102.23	think,] **S** ~ ₍
102.32	been,] **S** ~ ₍
102.33	step:] **ED** ~.
102.34	ship.₍] **S** ~".
102.36	heat,] **S** ~ ₍
102.36	said.] **S** ~ ₍
103.1	it,] **ED** it₍
103.3	instance,] **S** ~ ₍
103.5	open,] **S** ~ ₍
103.5	bathroom.] **S** ~ ₍
103.7	up,] **S** ~ ₍
103.11	stateroom,] **S** ~ ₍
103.15	part:] **ED** part₍
103.17	comf.…" He] **S** comf …₍he
103.25	quarter deck] **S** quarter-deck
103.28	captain's] **S** Captain's
103.38	point:] **S** ~ ₍
103.39	you …] **S** ~ …
103.39	that …"] **S** ~"….
103.40	loudly:] **E1** ~ ₍
104.1	not.…] **S** ~ ….
104.3	hearing.] **S** ~ ₍
104.11	captain."] **S** Captain.₍
104.12	sir] **S** Sir
104.24	quarter deck] **ED** quarter- | deck
104.26	pursued:] **S** ~.
104.28	'As] **S** "~
104.28	that,'] **S** ~₍"
104.28	'Wouldn't] **S** "~
104.29	hole.'] **S** ~".
104.30	sir?"] **S** ~?₍

104.31	anything.] **S** ~∧
104.33	whatever.] **S** ~∧
104.36	nerve-trying] **S** nerve trying
105.4	dinner,] **S** ~∧
105.9	us∧] **S** ~;
105.16	everything,] ED ~∧
105.18	whisper:] ED whisper.
105.20	foresail:] **S** ~.
105.21	setting.] **S** ~∧
105.24	away,] **S** ~∧
106.1	strung-up] **S** ~∧~
106.6	with∧] ED ~,
106.6	sir∧] ED ~.
106.7	feelings.] **S** ~∧
106.8	up,] **S** ~∧
106.9	directly.] **S** ~∧
106.12	campstool] ED camp-stool
106.14	mysterious,] **S** ~∧
106.18	unalloyed] **S** unnaloyed
106.25	Pagoda,] **S** ~∧
106.28	grave,] **S** ~∧
106.28	though] **S** tho'
106.34	eccentricities] **S** excentrities
106.37	eye.] **S** ~∧
107.10	you?] **S** ~∧
107.10	astonished.] **S** ~∧
107.21	controlled,] **S** ~∧
107.22	invulnerable.] **S** ~∧
107.27	bent,] **S** ~∧
107.36	asparagus,] **S** ~∧
108.7	unavoidable,] **S** ~∧
108.8	dishes,] ED ~∧
108.15	lose.] **S** ~∧
108.16	Steward,] **S** ~∧
108.30	sir.] **S** ~∧
108.31	coming?] **S** ~∧
108.32	sir."] ED ~·∧
108.33	mind."] **S** ~·∧
109.11	Saved,] **S** ~∧
109.14	voice,] **S** ~∧
109.16	deck,] **S** ~∧
109.16	"I] **S** ∧ I
109.18	seedy."] **S** ~·∧
109.19	ago,] **S** ~∧
109.27	coat?"] **S** ~∧∧
109.29	sir."] **S** ~·∧
109.37	be,] **S** ~∧
109.37	myself,] **S** ~∧
109.39	face,] **S** ~∧
109.40	escape!"] **S** ~!∧
110.7	voice∧] ED voice:
110.7	a-lee] ED a lee
110.12	spell,] **S** ~∧
110.17	bath,] **S** ~∧
110.20	that,] **S** ~∧
110.23	Whoever] **S** Who-ever
110.27	again.] **S** ~∧
110.35	tale,] **S** ~∧
110.36	up.] **S** ~∧
111.4	what] **S** *what*
111.4	'Driven] **E1** ~
111.5	earth.'] **E1** ~".
111.6	go."] **S** ~·∧
111.7	can't.] **S** ~∧
111.10	you?"] **S** ~?∧
111.14	night,] **S** ~∧
111.14	"The] **S** ∧~
111.15	offshore] ED off shore
111.16	understand,] **S** ~∧
111.16	"But] **S** ∧~
111.18	purpose.] **S** ~∧
111.38	yet?"] **S** ~?∧
112.3	daylight."] **S** ~∧∧
112.4	solitary,] **S** ~∧
112.6	grey,] **S** ~∧
112.7	bushes, with] **S** ~. With
112.10	geography,] **S** ~∧
112.15	breezes,] **S** ~∧
112.19	said:] **S** ~.
112.20	her."] **S** ~·∧
112.25	sir∧] **S** ~,
112.26	shoals?"] **S** ~∧∧
112.28	one?"] **S** ~?∧
112.30	dreamy,] **S** ~∧
112.34	There,] **S** ~∧
112.39	be.] **S** ~∧
113.12	now,] **S** ~∧
113.13	"Goodness] **S** ∧~
113.13	though] ED tho'
113.15	dark . . ."] **S** ~" . . .
113.16	careful,] **S** ~∧
113.17	future,] **S** ~∧
113.17	fit,] **S** ~∧
113.21	cub] **S** Cub
113.22	out,] **S** ~∧
113.23	ports,] **S** ~∧
113.26	repeat:] **S** ~∧
113.27	quarter-deck] **S** quarter deck
113.27	sir] **E1** Sir
113.34	below –] **S** ~∧

113.35	drunkenness₄] **ED** ~ –	115.34	bareheaded,] **S** ~₄
113.38	surprising,] **S** ~₄	115.34	sun] **S** Sun
114.3	opening,] **S** ~₄	116.4	mind.] **S** ~₄
114.4	out,] **S** ~₄	116.12	voice.] **S** ~₄
114.8	quarter-deck] **S** ~₄~	116.13	weather,] **S** ~₄
114.9	up.₄] **S** ~."	116.14	sir] **S** Sir
114.12	while,] **S** ~₄	116.16	helmsman.] **S** ~₄
114.12	whispered:] **S** ~₄	116.17	full.] **S** ~₄
114.13	understand.] **S** ~₄	116.22	Must!] **ED** ~.
114.14	go,] **S** ~₄	116.24	thump.] **S** ~₄
114.14	"The] **S** ₄~	116.30	sir,] **S** Sir₄
114.22	wet,] **S** ~₄	116.33	warningly.] **S** ~₄
114.23	night,] **S** ~₄	116.34	well,] **S** ~₄
114.23	opaque,] **S** ~₄	116.39	call,] **S** ~₄
114.26	eclipsed.] **S** ~₄	117.2	together:] **S** ~₄
114.30	enough,] **S** ~₄	117.7	Erebus.] **S** ~₄
114.31	level,] **S** ~₄	117.9	thunderstruck₄] **ED** ~,
114.37	sir] **S** Sir	117.12	quiet,] **S** ~₄
114.37	close."] **S** ~.₄	117.14	here?] **S** ~₄
114.38	well,] **S** ~.	117.15	wind.] **S** ~₄
114.38	directly."] **S** directy.₄	117.16	recklessly:] **S** ~₄
114.40	too;] **ED** too₄	117.19	God] **S** god
115.6	Straits."] **S** ~.₄	117.22	already,] **S** ~₄
115.8	it,] **S** ~₄	117.27	forward –] **ED** ~" –
115.8	"No] **S** ₄~	117.27	shake –] **S** ~₄
115.9	what . . ."] **S** ~ . . .₄	117.29	shake."] **S** ~₄₄
115.11	large,] **ED** large₄	117.32	life.] **S** ~₄
115.16	before,] **ED** before₄	117.33	sail-locker] **S** ~₄~
115.17	mingled,] **S** ~₄	118.9	stopped,] **S** ~₄
115.19	Steward.] **S** ~₄	118.11	now?] **S** ~.
115.24	anxiously.] **S** ~₄	118.12	yet?] **S** ~.
115.25	galley."] **S** ~₄₄	118.14	surface.] **S** ~₄
115.26	now.] **S** ~₄	118.22	hat. It] **S** ~ – it
115.27	see.] **S** ~₄	118.24	self,] **S** ~₄
115.29	Now,] **S** ~₄	118.27	hand –] **S** ~ . . .
115.29	saloon –] **S** ~₄	118.34	helm,] **S** ~₄
115.32	door.] **S** ~₄	119.2	seamen.] **S** ~₄

Freya of the Seven Isles

MS   holograph manuscript (Philadelphia)
TS1   typescript (Berg)
  TS1t   typewritten (unrevised) text of **TS** superseded by revision
  TS1r   revised text of **TS1** (incorporating Conrad's alterations): copy-text
SA   *Metropolitan Magazine* (April 1912), 20–29, 51–54
SE   *London Magazine* (July 1912), 649–84

123.1	Seven Isles] **MS** Seven-Isles	123.6	middle-aged,] **MS** middle
123.4–5	fellow-wanderers] **MS** fellow		aged;
	wanderers	123.12	And,] **MS** ~₄
123.5	waters] **MS** Waters	123.12	with,] **MS** ~₄

123.16	East,] **MS** ~ˌ	132.21	side-glances] **MS** ~ˌ~
123.32	respected,] **MS** ~ˌ	132.22	short,] **SE** ~ˌ
124.39	self confidence] **MS** self-confidence	132.22	thick,] **SA** ~ˌ
		132.24	roundˌ] **MS** ~,
125.2	wide open] **MS** wide-open	133.11	here,] **SE** ~ˌ
125.4	Allen] **MS** Allan	133.24	authorities,] **SE** ~ˌ
125.12	there,] **MS** ~ˌ	133.27	did,] **SE** ~ˌ
125.23	dew drop] **MS** dew-drop	134.2	appreciatively:] **SA** ~.
125.23	dew drop] **MS** dew-drop	134.5	unreasonable,] **SA** ~ˌ
125.25	broad,] **SE** ~ˌ	134.9	quiet,] **SA** ~ˌ
126.20	Seven Isles] **MS** Seven-Isles	134.15	blackbeetle] **MS** black beetle
126.26	rattan screens] **MS** rattan-screens	134.15	same,] **SA** ~ˌ
127.8	disgusting, old,] **ED** ~ˌ ~ˌ	134.17	do,] **SA** ~ˌ
127.8	reefs,] **MS** ~ˌ	134.18	Papa] **ED** papa
127.13	said:] **ED** ~ˌ	134.22	better,] **SA** ~ˌ
127.14	remarked:] **ED** ~ˌ	134.30	Heemskirk,] **SA** ~ˌ
127.20	idiot,"] **SA** ~ˌ"	134.34	Nielsen?"] **SE** Nelson?ˌ
127.20	straight,] **MS** ~ˌ	134.35	me:] **MS** ~ˌ
127.21	open,] **MS** ~ˌ	135.15	thick,] **SE** ~ˌ
127.23	that,"] **SA** ~ˌ"	135.20	morose,] **SE** ~ˌ
127.27	bit –] **MS** ~.	136.3	round-eyed] **SE** round eyed
127.35	it,] **MS** ~ˌ	136.4	lean-faced] **SE** lean faced
127.40	Fact. . . .] **E1** Fact.	136.6–7	arrogant,] **SE** ~ˌ
127.40	And] **E1** and	136.14	ill-omened] **MS** illomened
127.40	next,] **MS** next	136.27	accommodation] **SA** accomodation
128.8	though] **SA** tho'		
128.31	feelings –] **MS** ~,	136.36	boy,] **SA** ~ˌ ~ ~ˌ
129.18	come,] **SA** ~ˌ	136.36	said,] **SA** ~ˌ
129.18	cried.] **MS** ~ˌ	137.11	Papa] **E1** papa
129.22	girl,] **SA** ~ˌ	137.33	jokes;] **MS** ~,
129.23	authorities] **MS** Authorities	138.8	days,] **SA** ~ˌ
		138.10	much,] **SA** ~ˌ
129.30	brig,] **MS** ~ˌ	138.21	suppose,] **SA** ~ˌ
130.7	South American] **MS** South-American	138.22	to-day] **MS** to day
		138.25	yesterday,] **SA** ~ˌ
130.10	caballero] **SE** Caballero	138.29	Schultz,] **MS** ~ˌ
130.11	Indeed,] **SE** ~ˌ	138.30	'I] **SE** "~
130.12	caballero] **E1** Caballero	138.30	Captain,'] **SE** ~ˌ"
130.25	and,] **SE** ~ˌ	138.31	his,] **SE** ~ˌ
131.12	capable,] **SA** ~ˌ	138.31	'but] **SE** "but
131.12	self possession] **MS** self-possession	138.33	day.'] **SE** ~."
		138.33	stones!] **MS** ~.!
131.13	voice,] **SA** ~ˌ	138.36	compound,] **SE** ~ˌ
131.24	patience. . . .ˌ] **SA** ~. . . . ."	139.8	Schultz,] **SA** ~ˌ
		139.9	dispassionately,ˌ] **MS** ~,"
132.5	common,] **SA** ~ˌ	139.23	ship,] **MS** ~ˌ
132.9	Seven-Isles] **ED** ~ˌ~	139.23	do,] **MS** ~ˌ
132.17	big,] **SA** ~ˌ	139.29	will,] **SA** ~ˌ
132.17	flat,] **SE** ~ˌ	140.6	all."] **SA** ~.ˌ
132.18	small,] **SE** ~ˌ	140.7	psychology,] **SA** ~ˌ

140.9	think?] **MS** ~.?
140.14	straight."] **E1** ~.ʌ
140.26	Sea] **MS** sea
140.31	yacht,] **ED** ~ʌ
140.32	captain] **MS** Captain
140.32	contemptuously:] **E1** ~ʌ
140.33	pedlar.] **MS** ~ʌ
140.34	say,] **E1** ~ʌ
140.36	impossible,] **SE** ~.
140.38	brig,] **SA** ~ʌ
141.4	suddenly:] **SA** ~.
141.5	is?"] **SA** ~.?ʌ
141.10	know,] **SA** ~ʌ
141.10	on,] **SA** ~ʌ
141.18	eh] **SA** Eh
141.19	beggar,] **SA** ~ʌ
141.27	So] **MS** so
141.31	Cove] **SE** cove
141.37	Freya,] **SE** ~ʌ
141.40	voice:] **ED** ~.
142.2	yes] **MS** Yes
142.6	right,] **SE** ~ʌ
142.27	him,] **ED** ~ʌ
142.40	two,] **E1** ~ʌ
143.5	Ha! ..."] **ED** ~!ʌ"
143.5	And] **MS** and
143.9	looks,] **SE** looksʌ
143.9	spluttered,] **SE** splutteredʌ
143.9	he] **SA** He
143.9	ha! ha! ha!] **MS** Ha! Ha! Ha!
143.14	joke,] **ED** ~ʌ
143.16	up,] **SE** ~ʌ
143.34	policy,] **E1** ~ʌ
143.38	now,] **E1** ~ʌ
144.2	I] **MS** i
144.16	I] **MS** i
144.21	too."] **SA** ~.ʌ
144.24	come.] **SE** ~ʌ
144.26	hollowed,] **SE** ~ʌ
144.27	hours.] **MS** ~ʌ
144.29	moment.] **MS** ~ʌ
144.29	self-reliant] **SE** selfreliant
144.37	room,] **MS** ~ʌ
145.12	times,] **MS** ~ʌ
145.27	I] **MS** i
145.28	it?] **SE** ~ʌ
145.29	here,] **E1** ~ʌ
145.30	us,] **E1** ~ʌ
145.34	imperiousʌ] **E1** ~,
145.34	call:] **E1** ~.
145.37	waited,] **MS** ~ʌ
146.5	mail-boat] **E1** mailboat
146.11	ages,] **E1** ~ʌ
146.15	ages,] **SA** ~ʌ"
146.16	'for ages'] **SA** "~ ~"
146.17	not,] **SA** ~ʌ
147.5	quarter deck] **ED** quarter-deck
147.14	voice:] **MS** ~.
147.22	crop,] **MS** ~ʌ
147.27	authorities] **MS** Authorities
147.33	Allen,] **SE** ~ʌ
147.37	Nielsen),] **SE** ~)ʌ
148.3	vitals:] **SE** ~.
148.14	it,] **SE** ~ʌ
148.14	*do*] **MS** do
148.14	know,] **E1** ~ʌ
148.18	Lieutenant] **ED** lieutenant
148.19	considerably,] **E1** ~ʌ
148.20	moodily.] **MS** ~ʌ
148.26	Lieutenant] **ED** lieutenant
148.37	east] **SA** East
148.37	verandah,] **SE** ~ʌ
148.39	sail cloth] **MS** sail-| cloth
149.8	Freya,] **SA** ~ʌ
149.17	her,] **SA** ~ʌ
149.30	captain] **MS** Cap-short
150.6	short,] **SA** short
150.21	thoughts:] **ED** ~ʌ
150.22	you —] **ED** ~ –
150.25	in,] **SA** ~ʌ
150.25	Jasper,] **SA** ~ʌ
150.26	face,] **E1** face
150.29	Heemskirk,] **SA** ~ʌ
150.32	name.] **SA** ~ʌ
150.33	rivers,] **SA** riverʌ
150.37	kid,] **SA** ~ʌ
150.39	see,] **SA** ~ʌ
151.2	back verandah] **SA** back-verandah
151.3	evening,] **SA** ~ʌ
151.5	west] **SA** West
151.5	light,] **MS** ~ʌ
151.15	"Papa] **SA** ʌ~
151.15	long,] **SA** ~ʌ
151.25	suppose?] **MS** ~.?
151.29	Molluccas,] **SA** ~ʌ
151.34	angrily:] **SA** ~ʌ
151.34	Molluccas,] **SA** ~ʌ
152.4	while,] **SA** ~ʌ
152.12	tiger,] **SA** ~ʌ

152.14	brute,] **SA** ~_∧_	157.7	alarm,] **SA** ~_∧_
152.21	father's] **MS** Father's	157.16	beautifully,] **SA** ~_∧_
152.25	chair,] **SA** ~_∧_	158.10	father,] **SA** ~_∧_
152.26	stomach,] **SA** ~_∧_	158.10	angrily,] **SE** ~_∧_
152.28	girl.] **ED** ~_∧_	158.12	you] **MS** You
152.34	"Psst,] **SA** _∧_~_∧_	158.12	love _∧_] **MS** ~!
152.36	beetle,] **SA** ~_∧_	158.12	hear?] **MS** ~?.
153.5	Papa] **ED** papa	158.13	love. . . .] **ED** ~..
153.6	unreasonable,] **E1** ~.	158.15	stool."] **SA** ~._∧_
153.8	know,] **E1** ~_∧_	158.35	that.] **MS** ~. . . .
153.19	house,] **SA** ~_∧_	159.2	tone:] **SE** ~_∧_
153.22	loitering,] **SA** ~_∧_	159.6	faint,] **SE** ~_∧_
153.24	daylight,] **SA** ~_∧_	159.8	dusky,] **ED** ~_∧_
153.33	stumbling –] **MS** ~-	159.11	rapid,] **SA** ~_∧_
153.38	dark,] **MS** ~_∧_	159.14	music stool] **ED**
154.6	kid,] **SA** ~_∧_		music-stool
154.7	tone:] **SE** ~.	159.25	matter?] **SA** ~_∧_
154.9	"Isn't] **MS** _∧_~	159.32	consistency,] **MS** ~_∧_
154.15	'Here] **SE** _∧_~	159.32	self possession] **ED**
154.16	kid.'] **SE** ~._∧_		self-possession
154.25	tormented,] **MS** ~_∧_	159.34	Nelson,] **MS** Nelson_∧_
154.25	angry,] **MS** ~_∧_	159.39	yes,] **ED** ~_∧_
154.37	thick,] **ED** ~_∧_	160.4	revenge_∧_] **MS** ~,
154.39	ungainly,] **SE** ~_∧_	160.6	O!"] **ED** ~!_∧_
155.8	hussy,] **ED** ~_∧_	160.10	enlightened.] **MS** ~,
155.12	pursed-up] **SE** pursed up	160.11	Lieutenant] **ED** lieutenant
155.17	creature,] **SE** ~_∧_	160.17	glances,] **MS** ~_∧_
155.18	senses,] **SE** ~_∧_	160.21	off,] **ED** off_∧_
155.26	me,] **ED** ~_∧_	160.25	brandy,] **SA** ~_∧_
155.29	do.] **SE** ~_∧_	160.35	this,] **SA** ~_∧_
155.31	ha] **MS** Ha	160.36	Lieutenant] **ED** lieutenant
155.35	Lieutenant] **ED** lieutenant	160.37	short,] **E1** ~_∧_
155.36	dinner,] **E1** ~_∧_	161.1	Lieutenant] **ED** lieutenant
155.37	stars,] **MS** ~_∧_	161.1	Lieutenant,] **SA** ~_∧_
156.1	quarter deck] **MS**	161.1	_∧_he] **SA** "~
	quarter-deck	161.15	Freya,] **SA** ~_∧_
156.2	say:] **ED** ~_∧_	161.16	gown,] **SE** ~_∧_
156.2	'Here] **E1** "here	161.21	unfeeling,] **ED** ~_∧_
156.2	am,'"] **E1** am,"	161.24	funny,] **SE** ~_∧_
156.5	still,] **ED** ~_∧_	161.25	then_∧_] **MS** ~,
156.7	heat lightning] **MS**	161.26	him,] **SE** ~_∧_
	heat-lightning	161.32	mad,] **SE** ~_∧_
156.19	outbreak.] **MS** ~_∧_	162.8	here,] **SE** ~_∧_
156.24	head,] **MS** ~_∧_	162.9	forcibly. "Without] **MS** ~_∧_
156.25–26	half-closed] **SA** half closed		"without
156.28	stay,] **SA** ~_∧_	162.18	much,] **SE** ~_∧_
156.36	flat,] **SA** ~_∧_	162.19	now,] **MS** ~_∧_
156.37	heavy,] **ED** ~_∧_	162.30	flushed,] **ED** ~_∧_
156.40	Papa] **ED** papa	162.37	girl,] **E1** ~_∧_
157.1	me!] **MS** ~.!	162.40	other._∧_] **MS** other."
157.5	him,] **SA** ~_∧_	163.6	night light] **MS** nightlight
157.7	coffee tray] **MS** coffee-tray	163.8	whispers:] **E1** ~.

163.11	away!"] **E1** ~!∧	171.4	end,] **ED** ~∧
163.17	Lieutenant] **SA** lieutenant	171.6	timbre∧] **MS** ~?
163.21	affair!] **MS** ~.	171.8	ill,] **SE** ~∧
163.24	kissing,] **MS** ~∧	171.9	dead,] **ED** ~∧
163.25	purpose,] **SE** ~∧	171.15	harm,] **SA** ~∧
163.27	Some day] **MS** Someday	171.18	opening,] **SA** ~∧
163.28	on:] **E1** on∧	171.21–22	quarter deck] **MS**
163.31	morning,] **ED** ~∧		quarter-deck
163.40	dressing gown] **ED**	171.29	of?] **SE** ~∧
	dressing-gown	171.31	that,] **SA** ~∧
164.4	fair∧] **ED** ~∧,	171.34	I] **MS** i
164.11	dressing gown] **ED**	171.38	know,] **SA** ~∧
	dressing-gown	172.8	*him*] **MS** him
164.18	there,] **SA** ~∧	172.10	spot∧] **SE** ~,
164.22	east] **SE** East	172.13	large:] **SE** ~.
164.32	"You] **SA** ∧~	172.14	detained?"] **MS** ~.?∧
165.31	straddling,] **SE** ~∧	172.15	satisfaction:] **ED** ~.
165.32	shoulder-straps] **SE**	172.17	this,] **SA** ~∧
	shoulderstraps	172.25	towrope] **ED** tow-rope
166.5	him,] **MS** ~∧	172.26	Makassar] **SA** Macassar
166.7	Gone."] **SE** ~∧"	172.28	suppose,] **SA** ~∧
166.11	low,] **MS** ~∧	172.33	pieces,] **SA** ~∧
166.22	board,] **SE** ~∧	172.40	vessel,] **SA** ~∧
166.35	morning,] **MS** ~∧	172.40	Jasper,] **SE** ~∧
166.36	hear,] **SE** ~∧	173.2	passion,] **SA** ~∧
166.37	I] **MS** i	173.7	mad,] **SA** ~∧
167.7	lieutenant,] **SA** ~∧	173.8	Mesman∧] **MS** ~,
167.12	away,] **SE** ~∧	173.12	H'm,] **ED** ~.
167.15	day,] **ED** ~∧	173.13	motionless,] **SA** ~∧
167.16	east] **SA** East	173.14	split∧] **MS** ~,
167.17	eastward] **SA** Eastward	173.20	Ya,] **SA** ~∧
167.18	possessive∧] **MS** ~,	173.21	time,] **SA** ~∧
167.22	*Bonito*,] **MS** ~∧	173.24	Ya,] **MS** ~∧
167.29	meditation,] **MS** ~∧	173.26	Ya,] **MS** ~∧
167.33	outraged,] **SE** ~∧	173.29	tone:] **SE** ~.
168.6	chart-room,] **MS** ~∧	173.38	them,] **SE** ~∧
168.9	Lieutenant] **SA** lieutenant	174.2	monstrous,] **SA** ~∧
168.14	authority,] **MS** ~∧	174.4	go,] **SA** ~∧
168.27	profound∧] **SE** profound,	174.20	left,] **SE** ~∧
168.35	hand,] **SE** ~∧	174.21	officer,] **SE** ~∧
169.12	this,] **SA** ~∧	174.35	funny),] **ED** ~)∧
169.28	aloud:] **SE** ~∧	175.1	calm,] **SA** calm∧
169.32	simply,] **SA** ~∧	175.13	self confidence] **MS**
170.9	quiet,] **SA** quiet		self-confidence
170.13	barefooted] **MS**	175.14	Freya?∧] **MS** ~?"
	bare-footed	175.17	over,] **SA** ~∧
170.17	struck,] **SE** ~∧	175.23–24	mill pond] **MS** millpond
170.18	Isles∧] **MS** ~,	175.24	heavy,] **SA** ~∧
171.1	psychology∧] **MS** ~,	175.29	deep-toned] **SA** ~∧~
171.3	matter?] **SE** ~∧	175.34	lungs.] **ED** ~∧

176.4	fine,] **SE** ~∧	183.23	point,] **SE** ~∧
176.20	him,] **SA** ~∧	184.1	'I] **SA** "~
176.24	him,] **SA** ~∧	184.2	man,'] **SA** ~∧"
176.24	bridge ladder] **MS**	184.3	'You] **SA** "~
	bridge-ladder	184.7	"When] **SE** ∧~
176.27	I∧] **MS** ~:	184.11	handfuls] **MS** handfulls
176.38	sampan,] **SA** ~∧	184.11	'Good] **SE** "~
177.5	Lieutenant] **SE** lieutenant	184.12	gentlemen'] **MS** ~"
177.12	reef,] **ED** reef∧	184.15	half-caste] **SA** half caste
177.14	high-water] **SE** ~∧~	184.16	wreck."] **SE** ~.∧
177.14	tides,] **SA** ~∧	184.17	tender, persuasive,] **SA** ~∧
177.18	top,] **SA** ~∧		~∧
177.22	Englishman,] **SA** ~∧	184.25	mild-eyed,] **SE** ~∧
177.25	Makassar,] **SA** ~∧	184.38	"*Bonito* case"] **MS** "~" ~∧
177.27	front,] **SE** ~∧	185.1	Lieutenant] **SA** lieutenant
178.1	Lieutenant] **SE** lieutenant	185.2	pained∧] **MS** ~,
178.4	hands∧] **MS** ~,	185.6	half a year] **MS** half-a-year
178.28	often∧] **MS** ~,	185.19	London!] **MS** ~.!
178.30	harbour office] **MS**	185.20	Nielsen),] **SE** ~)∧
	harbour-office	185.21	echoless] **MS** ~,
178.31	high-water] **MS** high water	185.29	Notting Hill] **MS**
178.31	power,] **MS** ~∧		Notting-Hill
178.36	clean-shaven] **SA** clean	186.13	I] **MS** i
	shaven	186.17	strangely] **MS** Strangely
178.36	fine,] **SA** ~∧	186.21	round,] **SA** ~∧
178.37	iron-grey] **SA** iron grey	186.28	east] **SA** East
179.3	Freya ∧] **ED** ~,	186.30	reasonable,] **SA** ~∧
179.5	Yes] **MS** yes	186.38	'I] **SA** "~
179.11	A] **MS** a	186.38	him,'] **SA** ~∧"
179.11	I] **MS** i	186.39	'My dear,'] **SA** "~ ~∧"
179.29	boatfare] **MS** boat-fare	186.39	said, 'you] **SA** ~∧ "~
180.1	go –] **SE** ~?	186.40	health?'] **SA** ~?"
180.1	for] **SE** For	187.3	'Do] **SA** "~
180.1	purpose –] **SE** ~?	187.3	Papa,'] **SE** ~∧"
180.1	where] **SE** Where	187.3	Papa] **ED** papa
180.1	he∧] **MS** ~,	187.8	newspaper] **SA** news
180.2	himself∧] **MS** ~,		paper
180.3	House –] **MS** ~?	187.9	'Heemskirk'] **SA** "~"
181.22	firearms] **SE** fire-arms	187.12	day,] **SA** ~∧
181.25	one –] **MS** ~∧	187.12	voice,] **SA** ~∧
182.1	away?] **MS** ~.?	187.17	"'My dear,' I said, 'you] **SE**
182.11	himself:] **MS** ~∧		"~ ~∧" ~ ~∧ "~
182.12	Lieutenant] **SA** lieutenant	187.18	girl.'] **SA** ~."
182.24	keen-faced] **SA** keen faced	187.18	'I] **SA** "~
182.36	coast,] **MS** ~∧	187.18	horrid,'] **SA** ~∧"
182.40	sea horizon] **TS1t**	187.18	'and] **SE** "And
	sea-horizon	187.19	there.'] **SA** ~."
183.13	them,"∧] **SE** ~∧" –	187.21	said."] **SA** ~.∧
183.15	self sacrifice] **MS**	187.23	him,] **SA** ~∧
	self-sacrifice	187.24	him,] **SE** ~∧

187.34	'Is] **SA** "~		188.36	Papa] **ED** papa
187.34	man,'] **ED** ~ₐ"		188.36	Papa.'] **SA** ~."
187.34	that. ₐ] **MS** ~."		188.36	'Of] **SA** "~
187.39	sensible!] **MS** ~.!		188.37	it.'] **SA** ~."
187.40	'Write] **SA** "~		188.37	'I wonder.'] **SA** "~ ~."
188.5	you?'] **SA** ~?"		188.38	'I've] **SA** "~
188.6	Anæmia."] **ED** ~.ₐ		188.38	coward'] **ED** ~"
188.7	"'Aha] **ED** "ₐ~		188.39	'I've] **SA** "~
188.8	ghost,'] **SA** ~ₐ"		188.40	headstrong,] **SA** ~ₐ
188.8	brig."] **ED** ~.ₐ		189.1	afraid ....'] **SA** ~ ...."
188.9	"Mad] **SA** ~ₐ		189.2	said:] **SA** ~ₐ
188.19	'He's mad,' I said, 'and]		189.2	'Yes] **SA** "~
	SA ₐ~ ~ₐ" ~ ~ₐ "~		189.4	know,'] **SA** ~ₐ"
188.20	brig.'"] **ED** ~.ₐ"		189.4	'Draw] **SA** "~
188.21	"'Perhaps,'] **SA** "ₐ~ₐ"		189.4	Papa] **ED** papa
188.21	herself,] **SE** ~ₐ"		189.5	folly.'] **SA** ~.ₐ
188.22	'perhaps] **SA** "Perhaps		189.6	see,] **SA** ~ₐ
188.23	me.'"] **SA** ~.ₐ"		189.11	yourself,] **SA** ~ₐ
188.26	see," he continued,] **SA**		189.18	"Don't] **MS** ₐ~
	~ₐ" ~ ~.		189.20	No!"] **SA** ~!ₐ
188.35	'I] **SA** "~		189.25	low,] **SE** ~ₐ

END-OF-LINE WORD-DIVISION

This list records editorial decisions on the word-division of divisible compounds that are ambiguously hyphenated in the copy-texts. It contains, in the form of the critical text, each compound hyphenated and divided at the ends of the copy-texts lines. The list omits words that have hyphens between capitalized elements (e.g., North-American) and those that are clearly mere syllabication (including syllabication of compound words falling elsewhere than at the point of word-division). Each compound is preceded by a reference to the page and line of the present edition.

A Smile of Fortune

16.18	aloft		38.27	non-|committal
17.21	screw-pile		43.29	any one
22.33	overboard		45.7	grass-grown
29.18	cut water		45.25	wicker-work
29.21	blood-|sucker		47.33	henchwomen
38.19	fellow-shipmaster		54.32	iron-grey

The Secret Sharer

112.24	to-night

Freya of the Seven Isles

187.30	drift-log

APPENDICES

APPENDIX A

PROVENANCE OF THE EARLY DOCUMENTS

THE DOCUMENTARY history of the manuscripts and typescripts for *'Twixt Land and Sea* is unusually complex, partly because the breach between Conrad and his agent, J. B. Pinker, during 1910 and 1911 disrupted the normal processing of both, and partly because these documents were amongst the first that Conrad sold to John Quinn and the routines he eventually followed when preparing documents for sale were still being developed. The essay on 'The Texts' treats the manuscripts and typescripts as part of the generation, revision, and transmission of their texts; the present discussion focusses on the history of the documents themselves and the means by which these physical objects came to be preserved in their present locations.

The Secret Sharer

The Manuscript

HAVING sold the holograph manuscript of 'Freya of the Seven Isles', his latest work, to John Quinn in August 1911, Conrad was within a month offering 'to complete the Freya item' with those of 'The Secret Sharer' and 'A Smile of Fortune' and, later, other stories (*Letters*, IV, 481, 515). The manuscript of 'The Secret Sharer' had apparently been returned to him along with the typescript made from it in the middle of December 1909.[1] By early December 1911, he had posted it to New York (*Letters*, IV, 521).

Now in the Berg Collection of the New York Public Library, the document consists of two kinds of paper stock. The leaves of the principal paper, now cream-white and ruled in a faint blue or grey, exhibit a mock watermark and countermark in various positions. Sometimes faint and difficult to identify with certainty, the watermark is a fancy filigree consisting apparently of three initials, a 'B' followed by an 'L', with a larger 'B' centred and in effect superimposed upon both. This might have been a trademark for the British Bank Linen pads Conrad requested from Pinker in an undated and so far unpublished letter, probably of early August 1909, which he acknowledged (from 'Trosley') having received at Aldington before he left for the Gibbons' home.[2] The countermark, a sort of shield with three lions

---

[1] See the discussion in 'The Texts', pp. 207–9.
[2] *Letters*, IV, 269. The letter of early August is now held in the Berg Collection (Phyllis Goodhart Gordan bequest, 1995) and will be published in the last volume of the *Letters*. The Conrads left their home for the Gibbons' on Saturday 7 August, returning on the 24th.

under which is the arabic number '139', is less informative, but its appearance throughout the document helps confirm that the paper Conrad used was of a single kind.

The document also includes a thick sheet that precedes those containing the text. It is a heavier and coarser stock, now brown, that was probably meant to protect and identify the main document. 'The Secret-Sharer – ' has been inscribed on it in ink.[3] The sheet also includes retrospective notations in the same ink: '(Harpers.)' and the partly erroneous 'Written in Nov. 1909 | published serially | 1910'. Although these words sound like ones Conrad would have written, the ink of these three inscriptions seems different from that seen in the manuscript proper and in most of his other manuscripts. It is now of a brown hue, but this different colour may be owing to its interaction with the coarse paper, whose present condition suggests rapid chemical change over the years. The hand is also smaller than Conrad's normal one, though he is known to have used different hands for different purposes. All these inscriptions are, more likely than not, Conrad's own; if so, they would seem to date from December 1911, when he sent the document to Quinn.

The inscriptions in blue pencil found in the manuscript proper – the head-title, the numeral 'I.' below it, and the two 'SS' notations on later pages – are certainly Conrad's and were probably written at about the same time. As early as August 1911, when preparing to post 'Freya of the Seven Isles' to him, Conrad was inscribing titles at the top of opening pages as a way of identifying and authenticating documents for Quinn's collection. This head-title does both. On the other hand, he probably did not make the 'SS' notations on interior pages for Quinn. That on page 66 occurs on the first or second page which Conrad would have retained after sending the first batch of manuscript to Pinker around 10 December 1909. Although its presence there could be put down to coincidence, it seems likely that when Conrad fastened the leaves together and labelled them, they were still separated into piles that reflected their processing by Pinker's typists. Still, the 'SS' notation on page 21 seems unrelated to the shipment of the manuscript to Pinker and the typing of it. Both notations, however, occur on what were apparently the first leaves of two of the four clutches (fols. 1–20, 21–65, 66–109, 110–125) that were at some time fastened together in their upper left corners. Their function, then, was apparently to identify these clutches of leaves.

These two 'SS' notations, together with the head-title itself, are our best internal evidence for dating the marks in blue pencil. Although none of them can be dated precisely or with absolute certainty, the probabilities can be narrowed considerably, and essentially to late 1909 or late 1911. Like the 'SS' notations, the head-title on the first page of the manuscript proper served partly as a label for its clutch. For Conrad's correspondence with Pinker about the story's alternative titles to have had any plausibility, he could not have inscribed it before he sent the first batch of manuscript to him on 10 December, and thus not until those pages had been returned a few days later (see pp. 208–9).

That inscription might have been simultaneous with the settling of the title in his own mind, if not with Pinker, a few days after his mid-December letter on the subject (*Letters*, IV, 300). That is, the gathering of the document and the blue-pencil inscriptions could have occurred around 20 December – about the time that Conrad had returned the revised typescript without any expectation of further

---

[3] On this title and that inscribed in the manuscript proper, see Appendix B.

revision, that he was therefore free to put the manuscript into Jessie Conrad's hands for safe keeping, and that he was becoming preoccupied with the implications of Pinker's ultimatum of the 18th regarding 'Razumov'.

On the other hand, given Conrad's panic over 'Razumov' by then and his ensuing preoccupation with the novel, it seems more likely that the inscriptions in blue pencil were made when Conrad was preparing the document for posting to Quinn. At that time he and Jessie Conrad were hunting for and sorting through the various documents she had stored away for more than ten years. The 'SS' notations, particularly that on page 21, would have served to identify loose clutches of leaves, rather than batches for Pinker. The head-title, which would have served the same purpose, and the retrospective 'I.' below it, which recalled the subsequent division of the story by *Harper's*, would have also helped authenticate the document for Quinn. Their conformity to the practices he had begun to use when preparing manuscripts for Quinn and would continue to follow throughout that process, and in a more elaborate form when selling documents to T. J. Wise years later, suggests Conrad made these blue-pencil notations in late November or early December 1911.

Further notations help flesh out the subsequent history of the document. The lower left corner of the thick cover sheet contains an inscription '417 / 24' in black pencil (together with the characters 'OESNSN') that does not appear to be Conrad's and was probably associated with the early cataloguing of the document, which was purchased in November 1923 by A. S. W. Rosenbach for $2,400 in the Anderson Galleries' sale of Quinn's collection (item 1855). Similar notations on the document's slipcase, including '$7500' and '$1500', support this conclusion. Although offered to buyers in 1928 and 1931, it remained in the Rosenbach Museum until the last few days of 1955, when it was sold to Sterling McMillan (Cleveland, Ohio) for $1,500. The purchase of it in the early 1980s by Raymond M. Sutton, Jr (Williamsburg, Kentucky), constituted what he considered the 'zenith' of his experience in collecting Conrad. The featured item in the 1985 sale of his collection by David J. Holmes, it was finally purchased by the Berg Collection in 1987 and now bears the accession mark '901334'.[4]

A Smile of Fortune

The Berg Manuscript

LATE in the summer of 1913, Conrad posted to John Quinn the manuscript now in the Berg Collection of the New York Public Library. Its sale, according to Conrad's letters, was delayed by approximately a year because by 1912, when he was selling the bulk of his manuscripts to Quinn, it was no longer in his possession.[5] The identifying inscriptions 'J. Conrad | A Smile of Fortune' in blue pencil on the

---

4 See Holmes's catalogue 9, 'Joseph Conrad: The Raymond M. Sutton, Jr. Collection', 1985, part one, pp. 1–2, 67, part two, pp. 1–2; Gene M. Moore, 'A Descriptive Location Register of Joseph Conrad's Literary Manuscripts', *The Conradian*, 27:2 (2002), 69.

5 See Conrad to Quinn, 12 November 1912, 9 February 1913, 16 March 1913; to Pinker, 28 April 1913, [5 May 1913]; to Quinn, 5 June 1913; to Knopf, 5 September 1913; to Quinn, 25 October 1913, 11 December 1913 (*Letters*, v, 134, 176, 194, 219, 220, 230, 280, 297–8, 313).

first page, the inked line through the original title there, and Conrad's erroneous 'June–Augst | 1911' in ink on the last page, as well as his inscriptions on the shipping envelope, were all presumably made when he was preparing it for Quinn.

Conrad had not sent his original manuscript to J. B. Pinker for typing, because the estrangement between them had changed their working relationship and Conrad, before he could be paid, had to provide Pinker with revised material ready for final typing (see p. 231, n. 3; Karl, p. 683). This change directly affected Conrad's composition of the story (see pp. 231–8). But he apparently did send his manuscript to France for use in a possible translation, a fact that caused his negotiations for its sale to Quinn in 1912 to be protracted. The initial transaction regarding translation is presently undocumented, but it is reasonable to suppose a date either simultaneous with or shortly following a similar venture involving the typescript of 'Freya of the Seven Isles' in spring 1911 (see below; also pp. 261–3).

Both the relatively restrained revision exhibited in the manuscript and its complex relations to the other early documents invite speculation about the originality of the surviving document. The Keating catalogue, for instance, suggests that the manuscript postdated the Beinecke typescript fragment (see below). The difficulties Conrad had beginning the story and his delay in posting the extant document to Quinn could suggest that Conrad's original was in fact a rougher draft, now lost, of which the surviving manuscript was a later fair copy. However, the evidence of the document supports neither suggestion.

The provisional title 'A deal in Potatoes' inscribed at the top of the first page looks very much like Conrad's first thought, as his 17 May letter to Galsworthy (*Letters*, IV, 329) indicates. Working on paper larger than normal, Conrad seems to have been feeling his way back into writing as he varied the placement of page numbers in the early leaves and began dropping the top margins uniformly around page 13, effectively reducing the page size by some six lines, probably to help with estimating the word count. These sorts of adjustment do not fit the notion of a fair copy. Nor is there any evidence, such as might be expected under such circumstances, of layered leaves (the salvaging of some earlier pages) or of the splicing and accommodation of text that would accompany them. Conrad's reference to having written the manuscript in pencil remains something of a mystery, if not a red herring, and might simply represent confused recollection; he had not used pencil as the main medium for a major manuscript since the days of 'Youth' and 'Amy Foster'.[6] The Berg manuscript is the one Conrad described to John Quinn from the first and when finally selling it.

The revisions in the manuscript (see p. 232, n. 1) rule out the more desperate theory that the manuscript is a false document made up by Conrad for Quinn, which the protracted sale of it three years later and the printed texts' frequent use of MS readings, where TS1 has revised ones, might suggest. The nature of the revisions made in MS, including particularly those that were further altered in *TSo* before TS1t was produced, do not support such a theory. When he finally sold the document, Conrad was much too busy revising *Chance* and writing what became *Victory* to have created such a false document. His letters on the subject, especially the first one to Quinn alluding to the original title and the penultimate one describing the document's 'oblong pages', indicate that only one manuscript of the story ever existed, and that the extant document is the genuine original.

---

[6] See Conrad to Galsworthy, 27 August 1910 (*Letters*, IV, 362); to Quinn, 29 July 1912 (*Letters*, V, 89).

Ten years after being sold to Quinn, the document appeared as item 1860 in the catalogue of the Anderson Galleries' 1923 sale of his collection. Purchased by Rosenbach for $2,300 (Moore, p. 72), it was later owned by William T. H. Howe; the Berg Collection acquired it in 1957–8.[7]

The Beinecke Typescript

THIS document, item 158 in the catalogue of the 1925 Hodgson sale of material held by Jessie Conrad and by Richard Curle, appears in the Keating catalogue and was probably bought by him from Heffers (Cambridge), who purchased it in the sale (£18). The Keating description repeats almost verbatim the words of the Hodgson notice, except for its speculation that the typescript fragment represented an ur-version of the story, preceding the manuscript,[8] which must be discounted (see above).

The whereabouts of the document are unclear, once Conrad had sent it to Pinker in the middle of August (see p. 235) in accord with the formal business arrangement between them then in force (see above). That arrangement makes it unlikely that Pinker would, at the time, have returned this first lot of typescript to Conrad any more than he would the second lot or the final fair copy, as he might well have done in earlier and better days when producing typescript for Conrad's further revision (see pp. 238, 246). The exact point at which he did return the material that Jessie Conrad eventually sold in 1925 remains a mystery, but it probably came back to the Conrads after the reconciliation between author and agent, along with the complete but composite typescript now in the Berg Collection, and it was probably treated in the same manner.

The Berg Typescript

ITEM 159 in the 1925 Hodgson sale, this document was first purchased by Maggs (£22) and apparently from them by William T. H. Howe, whose estate sold it in 1940, along with other documents in his vast collection, to Albert A. Berg, whence it came to the Berg Collection.[9] Its history before its sale by Jessie Conrad in 1925 is more problematic. Presumably Paul R. Reynolds showed this composite typescript, received from Pinker in September or October 1910 (see p. 238), to

---

7 See *Dictionary Catalog of the Henry W. and Albert A. Berg Collection of English and American Literature* (1969), I, 624; John Dozier Gordan, 'New in the Berg Collection: 1957–1958', *Bulletin of The New York Public Library*, 63 (1959), 140–41. Its whereabouts between 1940 (when Albert A. Berg acquired Howe's collection from his estate) and 1957 is not entirely clear. See Carl L. Cannon, *American Book Collectors and Collecting* (1941), 237–8.

8 'There are numerous alterations and passages rewritten on every page throughout, entirely in the author's hand, two and one half pages including the first, reproduced on p. 215, being written out by him afresh. It is probable that this typescript predates the complete autograph manuscript.' *A Conrad Memorial Library: The Collection of George T. Keating* (1929), p. 216. The sale ledger records 'Heffer Sons' as buyer (Hodgson Papers, Vol. XI, BL Additional MS 54590). See also Moore, p. 72.

9 Hodgson Papers; *Dictionary Catalog*, I, 624; Cannon, 237–8. The leaf of rough, thick paper kept with the document has the inscription 'Lot 159' in blue pencil.

several New York magazines without success. At some point he must have returned it to England, where it eventually came into Jessie Conrad's possession. An April 1907 letter from Reynolds to Pinker, surviving in Northwestern University's Charles Deering McCormick Library of Special Collections, suggests that Reynolds periodically offered to return unsold stories, but it does not provide sufficient evidence to calculate how regularly or promptly he did so.

Nor is it clear that, had Reynolds returned it before Conrad began selling documents to Quinn, Pinker would have felt obliged to send it on to Conrad, at least until after their reconciliation. Conrad seems to have been unable to lay his hands on the typescript in 1911 when exploring translation in France, for he sent the unhandy and much superseded manuscript (the Pinker typescript that provided copy for the *London Magazine* having by then perished), whereas for 'Freya of the Seven Isles' he sent the revised typescript (see above and below). In 1912, when hunting for manuscripts and typescripts to sell to John Quinn (see *Letters*, v, 143), the Conrads, though able to account for the whereabouts of the manuscript, apparently failed to turn up this typescript. It may well have still been in Reynolds' or Pinker's hands. If Pinker had returned it, Jessie Conrad would probably have deposited it in one of the several deep drawers where she put away such documents, beyond Conrad's, and perhaps her own, ken. Letters to Quinn in 1911 and 1912 suggest that Conrad was dependent on his wife for finding them, somewhat surprised at the amount of material she had stowed away, and for some time oblivious to the fate of his typescripts, as the appearance of so many of them in the Hodgson sale indicates. His failure to retrieve the pages containing the revised (i.e., the typescript) form of the prologue when preparing the tale for book publication reflects this posture.[10]

Freya of the Seven Isles

The Manuscript

THE manuscript is now held in the Rare Book Department of the Free Library of Philadelphia. Identifying it as his 'latest completed' work and commending it for its cleanness, Conrad posted it, along with the manuscript for *An Outcast of the Islands*, to John Quinn in New York on 24 August 1911 (*Letters*, IV, 475). In later correspondence with Quinn, Conrad used the tale as a way of grouping the manuscripts of the other stories he associated with the writing of *Under Western Eyes*, which together apparently brought him about £40.[11]

[10] See *Letters*, v, 131, 145, 146; also p. 246, n. 1. This long-standing attitude and practice were about to change. Up to this time, Conrad had generally failed to make use of manuscripts and typescripts that should have been in his possession when preparing book-edition texts that were to differ significantly from altered magazine texts. His increasingly sophisticated attempts in the next few years to manage the different serial and book texts of 'Freya of the Seven Isles', 'The Partner', and *Chance* contrast strikingly with his recent failures to do so in 'The Secret Sharer' and *Under Western Eyes*, where the serial texts left their marks on the books in ways of which Conrad was both aware and unaware. See S. W. Reid, 'American Markets, Serials, and Conrad's Career', *The Conradian*, 28 (2003), 57–99.
[11] Conrad to Quinn, 23 September 1911 (*Letters*, IV, 481); also 30 September [November] 1911, 11 December 1911 (*Letters*, IV, 515, 521); 28 January 1912, 6 November 1912 (*Letters*, v, 13, 131).

Conrad used black ink to inscribe the title of the story as well as 'J. Conrad' above the section number '1' on the first leaf of the manuscript itself. On the brown envelope housed with the document and used to post it to Quinn, he rewrote the title across the envelope in a decorative manner similar to that found on the first page of the manuscript proper, and in the same ink. Below that title, the beginning and end dates of composition also appear in black ink, as do Conrad's initials, written large and at an angle in the lower left-hand corner of the envelope, and (elsewhere) the abbreviation 'MS.'.

The envelope also contains inscriptions in blue pencil and black (lead) pencil. In the lower right-hand corner, instructions for following numeration are written in blue pencil, in accord with the kind of marking Conrad would often perform when preparing a document for Quinn.[12] This notation coordinates with the consecutive repagination, in the lower right-hand corner of the leaves, of the manuscript itself; they help date those page numbers as well as the blue-pencilled cancellations of blocks of text on pages 145 and 212, which all apparently post-dated Jessie Conrad's use of the manuscript to make the typescript.

The envelope contains still another note, written along the upper left margin in an unidentified hand (possibly Conrad's) and made in lead pencil: 'To go with The Secret Sharer & A Smile of Fortune'. This notation may have been made in connection with Conrad's 25 September 1911 proposal to sell the manuscripts for 'the two companion stories' to Quinn (*Letters*, IV, 481). Two holes in the lower right corner of the envelope confirm that pins were used to hold the leaves of the manuscript together and were presumably inserted when the document was posted. Probably at this time, the flap of the envelope was sealed with red wax.

Also housed with the manuscript and envelope is a sheet containing the verses written by Arthur Symons and printed, with alterations, on the title-pages of the first editions as the epigraph for *'Twixt Land and Sea*.[13] The sheet is blue wove paper, the verses written in black ink. Although the hand of the verses themselves is not Conrad's, instructions to the printer about placement and typography were written and initialled by him and were followed in setting up the first English edition. At his request, this sheet was returned to Conrad, who mailed it to Quinn on 29 July 1912 so he could put it with the manuscript that he had received the previous year (*Letters*, V, 90).

This manuscript and sheet of verse appeared as item 1868 in the catalogue of the Anderson Galleries' sale of Quinn's collection in 1923. It was purchased by the collector James F. Drake for $3,500 (Moore, p. 21). From there, either directly or indirectly, it came into the collection of Richard Gimbel. The Free Library received it from his estate in November 1978.

---

[12] See above, pp. 460–2. Cf. Conrad to Quinn, 12 April 1913 (*Letters*, V, 215): 'I am sending you the MS of Youth, which I have numbered in red and blue pencil. These pages are written on on both sides. First read consecutively the *red* nos then the blue nos (which are on the "verso" of the red numbered pages). . . . The MS [i.e., the typescript] of Freya will be sent to you shortly on agreed price of £25'. Conrad to Quinn, 12 April 1913 (*Letters*, V, 215).

[13] On the leaf containing Symons' verses, an inscrutable line is written under the indication of the author's name as 'A. Symons'; this appears to be a date beginning with the word 'July', though the numbers that follow are illegible, and would confirm the hand as his. On the alterations made to the text, see Appendix I.

The Typescript

THE typescript is housed in the Berg Collection of the New York Public Library, to which it was bequeathed by John Dozier Gordan in 1969.[14] Although Conrad had intended to sell it to John Quinn along with other typescripts, he apparently did not succeed in doing so (*Letters*, v, 131, 143, 215). Soon after Pinker had returned it to him, he had sent it to Warrington Dawson, who was then living in France, for possible publication in a new, and as it proved short-lived, magazine called *Progrès*, where its editor, Mme Adeline de Lano (Conrad's 'Mrs Demachy'), eventually rejected it in favour of de Smet's translation of 'Typhoon', a known commodity.[15] A month later, on 28 March 1911, Conrad wrote to Dawson: 'Would you mind, when you see the lady, asking her to return me the MS of *Freya* if she still has it in her possession. It may be she has given it to Davray who has arranged with her for the *Typhoon*' (*Letters*, IV, 431). On 10 May 1912, Conrad wrote to Davray: 'Avez-vous le "typescript" de ma nouvelle *Freya of the Seven Islands* chez vous?' (*Letters*, v, 61). By this time he had come to realize that Quinn was interested not only in his holograph manuscripts but in his typescripts as well. His April 1913 letter to Quinn promising to send the document at a price of £25 is his last known word on the subject (*Letters*, v, 215).

Certain marks on the document seem to be associated with Conrad's preparation of it for France, rather than for copying by Pinker's typists in London. The most obvious of these are the thirty-four French translations written in fine lead (black) pencil up to page 35. Also in pencil are a dozen stylistic notations Conrad made in English. (For a list of these inscriptions, see Appendix H.) He used black ink to provide a total word count, in French, on the last leaf next to the inked calculation that he had earlier recorded in English for Pinker, which has been cancelled, and to supply the page numbers missing on 44–52.[16] In ink also Conrad has inscribed the title of the story on the first leaf above a rule and his name and in the same decorative style he used on the first page of the manuscript. Here, however, the word 'Isles' was originally written 'Islets', a form which has brief precedence in the manuscript (145.24, 186.5), suggests he was thinking of French readers, and in any case helps confirm that he was writing the title when he was less immediately engaged in composing and revising the tale (see Appendix B). In a few places blue pencil has been used to mark the document. An 'A' appears in the upper right-hand corner of the first page, a 'B' on page 29, a 'C' on page 56, and a 'D' on page 76; the four clutches so defined do not correspond to the evidence that certain pages were at some point pinned together. In one place blue pencil has also been used to supply some of the page numbers omitted during typing (47–50); these numbers were then erased, and rewritten in ink along with others before and after them (see above). Lastly, Conrad apparently used blue pencil as well as black

---

[14] 'John D. Gordan Bequest: A Notable Conrad Archive', *Bulletin of The New York Public Library*, 73 (1969), 145–6.

[15] *Letters*, IV, 417, 413; Dale B. J. Randall, ed., *Joseph Conrad and Warrington Dawson: The Record of a Friendship* (1968), p. 38.

[16] Also inscribed in ink, on the last page, are 'The End' and '1911'; these appear with the original calculation of the total number of words (28,290) based on '123' pages and an average '230' words per page. These inscriptions were likely made at the end of February 1911 in connection with Conrad's appeal to Pinker for extra compensation for so long a story. See 'The Texts', p. 260; also pp. 261–3 on the inscriptions in lead pencil.

ink to reconfirm a cancellation associated with Jessie Conrad's typing error at the beginning of what is now section VI.[17]

All these marks seem to be retrospective, in the sense that they helped order and arrange the document for handling by others, whether a typist, a translator, or an editor. However, the blue-pencil marks defining four clutches do not represent the sort of thing Conrad usually did when sending a document to Pinker and his typists. Like the notes associated with translation into French that he made in lead pencil, these marks and the other marks in blue pencil were probably made when he was preparing the document for France. The few in ink at the top of page 1 and on pages 44–52, as well as the one on the last leaf cancelling the original word count, were likely made on the same occasion and may have been the last ones Conrad made at this time.

Accompanying the typescript is a cover leaf printed with the name and address of Brentano's in New York City. It indicates that the document was once owned by the Rare Books and Autographs department of the bookstore, who in the early twentieth century had a well-known shop in Paris, France, where they could have acquired it. It is not unreasonable to infer that John Gordan bought the document from Brentano's, though its history between Conrad's posting of it to France and Gordan's gift to the Berg Collection remains undocumented.

[17] See 'The Texts', p. 256.

APPENDIX B

The Titles of the Tales

THE TITLES of the three tales found in *'Twixt Land and Sea* are exceptionally variant. The differences are small but sometimes significant. They require separate consideration, both from the larger and often more vexing textual questions in the bodies of these works and from one another, as Conrad seems to have given them no uniform reconsideration when assembling the book.

The Secret Sharer

ALTHOUGH THE story's subtitle quickly became settled and survived until 1912, when Conrad revised it (changing 'Sea' to 'Coast') to fit the tale to the book collection, the title took longer to become established and its precise form remained, and has remained, more uncertain. The only extant preprinting document preserves two forms, one ('The Secret Sharer') on the first page of the manuscript proper, the other ('The Secret-Sharer') on the cover sheet probably prepared by Conrad for sending this manuscript to John Quinn in August 1911 (see p. 207, and Appendix A). The latter appears in *Harper's Monthly Magazine* (1910), but the former in the first editions (1912).

Both the title and the first subtitle were almost certainly in the fair typescript (*TS2*) that served as printer's copy for *Harper's* (S). Although now inscribed in the manuscript (MS) in blue pencil, the title could not have been there, though it may have been in his mind, when Conrad sent the initial manuscript pages to Pinker on 10 December 1909, a full week before he gingerly mooted it upon returning the revised typescript (*TS1*) that derived from them; it must have been added, in the form of a head-title, at the top of page 1 after Pinker had returned those first pages. Nor would the title have been in that revised typescript when Conrad returned it with a letter proposing three alternatives ('*The Secret Self*', '*The other Self*', '*The Secret Sharer*') to the title ('*The Second Self*') that he had suggested (along with the subtitle) when sending the balance of the manuscript a few days earlier. Probably in correspondence following this letter but now lost, Conrad and Pinker settled on a title for the tale, but Pinker may have done as Conrad suggested and chosen the title without further ado.[1] In any case he must have added it and the subtitle to *TS1* or perhaps to *TS2*.

Conrad is likely to have inscribed the head-title on page 1 more or less concurrently with the 'SS' notations that appear on pages 21 and 66. These three inscriptions in blue pencil and the 'I.' below the head-title in that medium were in the document when Conrad sent it to Quinn in December 1911. The manuscript is unlikely to have received any attention between that time and December 1909, when he had put the story and presumably the document itself aside to deal with the crisis over 'Razumov', which was succeeded by the break with Pinker, by his own breakdown, and by subsequent preoccupations. Between Pinker's return of

---

[1] *Letters*, IV, 300, 298. Conrad would refer to the story as 'The other Self' in a letter to Pinker of either 31 December 1909 or 6 January 1910 (*Letters*, IV, 317). See 'The Texts', pp. 208, n. 3, and 215, n. 1.

the second batch of manuscript to Conrad – say, 16 December – and the posting of it to John Quinn in early December 1911, Conrad must have added the 'The Secret Sharer' to the manuscript.[2]

If, as seems more likely, Conrad did so in December 1911, when preparing the document for Quinn, the MS form would represent the one he recorded in the most important spot conceivable and in spite of the form it had meantime taken when published by *Harper's*. If, as seems less likely, he added it in December 1909, the title on the first page of the manuscript would represent the closest thing we have to an artistic decision about its form at the time of the story's composition. In either case 'The Secret Sharer' appears to be the title he used when preparing the tale for book publication in 1912.

Meanwhile, the title had taken a different form on the cover sheet for the manuscript. The inscriptions there in ink were probably but not certainly made by Conrad and served to authenticate the document by reference to the tale's composition (misstated by a year) and its serialization. *Harper's* had printed 'The Secret-Sharer' at the head of both its instalments; the second instance, which lacks the subtitle, would have had no counterpart in its typescript copy, and in this it was presumably like the improvised 'Part II.', which also headed S's second instalment. The hyphen might have been present at the beginning of that typescript (*TS2*), which Conrad never saw (see pp. 213–14), but S's titles, to some extent at least, involved editorial agency.

S's form would be reflected not only in the retrospective and inaccurate statement regarding the story's composition and publication on the cover sheet to the manuscript, but also in Conrad's three letters of 1911 to Quinn about it (*Letters*, IV, 481, 515, 521), though not in that of 1912 (*Letters*, V, 13). Otherwise, however, Conrad's correspondence usually has the MS form found in the head-title at the top of its first page. His letters to Pinker at the times of composition and of preparation for book publication uniformly divide the words (*Letters*, IV, 300, 355, 503, 504, 506; V, 67, 105, 311) except for one instance in late 1911, when Quinn was in view (*Letters*, IV, 500). So do his letters to Henry-D. Davray, Galsworthy, and Garnett (*Letters*, V, 61, 89, 121, 128), again with one exception, in French (*Letters*, V, 153).

When not influenced by *Harper's* during the preparation and authentication of the manuscript for Quinn, Conrad wrote his title in the form 'The Secret Sharer', despite the serial's hyphenated one, which tends to impose a narrower field of reference and meaning. The serial form, along with its two-part division of the text, may well be the most glaring example of the imposition of *Harper's* styling on the story, and even on its author.

A Smile of Fortune

THE MANUSCRIPT contains the title 'A Smile of Fortune', inscribed by Conrad in blue pencil on its first page opposite his rejected provisional title 'A deal in Potatoes', written as well as crossed out in black ink. This title, probably inscribed when the document was prepared for sale to John Quinn, appears in all printed texts. Only the extant complete typescript (TS1) has 'The Smile of Fortune', written by Conrad on the fair holograph that now constitutes its first page and reproduced by the typist in the second typescript. Although the latter is somewhat more

---

[2] For more on these details and dates, see pp. 207–9 and especially Appendix A.

idiomatic and conventional and the former perhaps more ironic, the nuances of the alternatives, if not the distinction between them, might have eluded Conrad, on whom the difference between the definite and indefinite article in English was sometimes lost.

Conrad's letters most often use a short title (*Smile of Fortune* or simply *Smile*) without either article or with 'the' in an ambiguous position where syntax, rather than a precise citation of the title, is at work. At the time of its composition and publication he sometimes wrote 'A Smile of Fortune' but never 'The Smile of Fortune' (*Letters*, IV, 328, 480–81). His letters to Pinker generally contain a short title, but that concerning his recent stories also has 'A Smile of Fortune' in a mocked-up title-page, as does that to John Quinn in a similar context (*Letters*, IV, 506, 480–81). Only in letters of late 1913 – one to Knopf, another to Quinn – does '*The Smile of Fortune*' appear (*Letters*, V, 280, 298).

Although the typescript's more idiomatic title could have received Conrad's close attention, the Captain's statement 'Quite a smile of Fortune [fortune]' (78.4) found in all texts at the end of the tale probably reflects his most considered usage. The definite article in TS1's title may represent an 'improvement' made by Jessie Conrad in her original, now lost typescript (*TSo*)[3] and preserved by Conrad when making a fair copy of the presumably heavily revised pages of TS1 that it replaced, which he must have done before sending the first batch of pages to Pinker in early August 1910. The two instances of 'The' in the letters of 1913 most likely exhibit Conrad's own imprecise usage, comparable to his use of 'Secret-Sharer' in later retrospective and informal contexts.

Freya of the Seven Isles

WHEN PREPARING to send the typescript to France, Conrad first wrote 'Freya of the Seven-Islets' as its title, before changing it to 'Freya of the Seven-Isles'. Like its counterpart 'Freya of the Seven Isles' in the manuscript, this inscription was retrospective, in that it was not made while he was actively engaged in composing and revising the work (see Appendix A). Yet the initial typescript title was also retrospective in another sense, because in the manuscript Conrad had written 'Seven Islets group' early in the story (145.24) and 'Seven islets' at the very end (186.5), as well as hyphenating the form there once in the phrase 'the Seven-Isles group' (185.14), and in the revised typescript at that point and three other times (126.20, 136.29, 145.24) – twice when it did not function as an adjectival phrase.

Although his references to the geographic entity were thus not entirely consistent in the manuscript, and indeed included other forms like 'Seven Group' (136.29, 143.25), the uniform name elsewhere in the revised typescript is 'Seven Isles'. The word 'islets' persists only once, and then (erroneously) as a general reference, not a geographical name (186.5). Conrad also used 'Seven Isles' in his only reference to the complete title in a letter (to Warrington Dawson) contemporary with the tale's composition; later letters (to Pinker, Quinn, Davray) at the end of 1911 and middle of 1912, when they do not refer simply to 'Freya', alternate between '*Freya of the Seven Isles*', '*Freya of the Seven Islands*', and '*Freya of the Islands*' and are sometimes complicated by translation into French, which effaces the

---

[3] Cf. her similar substitution at 78.5c.

distinction and may have occasioned the ambivalence exhibited in the typescript's title.[4]

The question of hyphenation is a bit more problematic because Conrad often had trouble with word-division in English and because in the tale he often used the phrase as an adjectival. Yet as a name and a noun 'Seven Isles' is uniform in both the manuscript and the revised typescript, except for Conrad's hyphenation of its second occurrence in the latter (126.20). The evidence, though not overwhelming, supports the form of the title that appeared in both magazine printings and in the book editions.

[4] To Dawson, 15 February 1911 (*Letters*, IV, 413); to Pinker [12 or 19 November 1911] (*Letters*, IV, 506); to Quinn, 24 August 1911, 29 July 1912 (*Letters*, IV, 475; V, 89); to Davray, 10 May 1912, 29 July 1912 (*Letters*, V, 60–61, 88).

APPENDIX C

THE LONDON MAGAZINE

ORIGINALLY CALLED the *Harmsworth Monthly Pictorial Magazine*, a prosperous illustrated serial, the *London Magazine* had acquired its fourth and final title in late 1903, five years before Conrad's story 'The Black Mate' appeared there.[1] It was one of the many organs of the Amalgamated Press, the publishing empire established by Alfred Charles William Harmsworth (1865–1922), Baron Northcliffe from 1905, and his brother Harold (Lord Rothermere), which included their *Answers to Correspondents* (1888), the London *Evening News* (1894), *Daily Mail* (1896), *Daily Mirror* (1903), and (by 1908) a controlling interest in *The Times*. Conrad's connections with Northcliffe and his empire were frequent, if ambivalent, from 1904 onwards. The *London Magazine* had reprinted 'London's River' and the *Daily Mail* had published three other pieces that became chapters of *The Mirror of the Sea* before 'The Black Mate' appeared in the *London Magazine*,[2] Conrad had apparently begun 'The Secret Sharer' with the *Daily Mail* in mind (see p. 207) and had written four reviews for it while composing 'A Smile of Fortune' (see p. 233) before the *London Magazine* published that story and 'Freya of the Seven Isles'. After 1912 other essays of his appeared in the Harmsworths' newspapers. From 1916 to 1922, Conrad and Lord Northcliffe maintained a private and professional relationship that involved personal visits as well as correspondence.[3]

A souvenir book from the 1910s indicates the breadth of the Harmsworths' Amalgamated Press: 'Fifteen million words are checked in the course of a year by the reading department'.[4] According to William English Carson, the organization sought bright young people who could specialize in writing for, editing, and marketing particular Amalgamated Press publications: 'All his [Northcliffe's] assistants were young men and women – the younger the better – capable of receiving impressions and at the same time ambitious and full of initiative. They were trained in what might be termed the "Harmsworth School of Journalism," and they gradually imbibed the style and spirit of their preceptor. They also became specialists. For instance, a young man would concentrate all his attention on supplying matter for a boys' paper, another would edit a comic sheet, while still another would devote all his thoughts and energies to keeping *Answers* to the front. . . . Thus, in course of time, Alfred Harmsworth gathered about him a staff of highly specialized young

[1] Reginald Pound and Geoffrey Harmsworth, *Northcliffe* (1959), p. 157.
[2] 'London's River', *London Magazine*, July 1906, pp. 481–8, rpt of 'London River: The Great Artery of England', *The World's Work*, December 1904, pp. 19–32 (rpt as 'The Faithful River' in *The Mirror of the Sea*). *Daily Mail*: 'Missing!', 8 March 1904, p. 4; 'Overdue', 16 November 1904, p. 4; 'Stranded', 2 December 1904, p. 6.
[3] See, e.g., *Letters*, v, 614–15, 631. In 1916 Northcliffe wrote from Switzerland to tell Conrad how much he had enjoyed reading *The Nigger of the 'Narcissus'* and 'of seeing other Conrad works in Continental bookshops' (*Portrait in Letters*, p. 109); see also Pound and Harmsworth, p. 504.
[4] William English Carson, *Northcliffe: Britain's Man of Power* (1918), p. 135. The Amalgamated Press was printing fifty periodicals in 1918 (p. 134).

editors and writers who gave such a distinct and personal tone to his publications that whenever a new paper was issued . . . readers knew at once that it would have what they liked – the Harmsworth touch'.[5]

Northcliffe founded his *Harmsworth Monthly Pictorial Magazine* to compete with *The Strand*, which was reaping not only money but 'personal prestige' for its owner, George Newnes.[6] Becoming a 'metropolitan magazine' that was 'edited for a general readership but specialized toward a specific city', focussed on arts and entertainment, 'relatively plush in layout and color', and featuring upper-class society,[7] by 1903 the renamed magazine's ostensible focus was still on fiction, though fiction figured less prominently than in *The Strand*.[8] The issue for February 1911, for instance, contained not only 'complete' stories by Jack London and by authors whose names are now forgotten, but essays on China and Germany, poems on Parliament and the empire, and a piece called 'Starving for Health's Sake' by Upton Sinclair.

Uninterrupted by advertising, which was confined to the end of each number, most fiction and essays appeared in the two columns typical of the sixpenny monthlies of the day (Reed, p. 98) and found in *Blackwood's* or the American *Harper's*. By January 1911, however, the 'complete novel', which had become a standard feature the previous year, was receiving special, book-like treatment; introduced by a section title-page and a full-page illustration, it was printed full measure, as was Ford's *English Review*, for instance. Aside from the editorial matter, photographs, and advertisements that followed, it was the last section of a given number, which usually comprised between 140 and 150 pages. Occupying from 27 to 35 of those pages, the 'complete novel' constituted at least one-sixth and sometimes nearly one quarter of an issue. Its physical fit (perhaps more than its literary) between the other contributions and the editorial matter must have been a major consideration in the planning and production of each number.

In the February 1911 number, where 'A Smile of Fortune' filled this niche, the first page of the column 'Entre Nous' (subtitled 'The Editor's Monthly Chat to His Readers') that followed it was devoted to the story, its author, and the larger question of 'our new feature – the complete novel – and of the class of story' that the magazine was providing its readers. The Editor gave 'a little personal sketch' of Conrad as an 'instance of literary genius', rated him 'head and shoulders above the ruck of contemporary novelists', and compared him as a teller of sea tales to Pierre Loti. Continuing his promotion of this feature, he mentioned past and future fiction by Leonard Merrick, Barry Pain, 'Q.',[9] Morley Roberts, De Vere Stacpole, and Agnes and Egerton Castle, all meant to 'keep up the standard'.

Although the *London Magazine* published three of his stories, Conrad took a consistently dim view of its place in the world of literary publishing. At the time he was preparing 'The Black Mate', he sniped to Pinker: 'It's better for us I think to

---

[5] Carson, p. 118; see also p. 137. A less approving view of the Harmsworth empire than that of Carson and of Pound and Harmsworth may be found in more recent studies: e.g., S. J. Taylor's *The Great Outsiders* (1996), and J. Lee Thompson's *Northcliffe: Press Baron in Politics, 1865–1922* (2000).

[6] Pound and Harmsworth, p. 157.

[7] James L. C. Ford, *Magazines for Millions: The Story of Specialized Publications* (1969), pp. 168–9.

[8] See David Reed, *The Popular Magazine* (1997), pp. 254, 98.

[9] Apparently Arthur Quiller-Couch; see Fred Brittain, *Arthur Quiller-Couch: A Biographical Study of Q* (1948), p. 1.

give them as <u>suitable</u> stuff as possible', and he made similar remarks in connection with 'A Smile of Fortune'.[10] That story comprised 25,773 words and 'Freya of the Seven Isles' 26,157, but both occupied 35 pages when they appeared as the 'complete novel' in their respective issues, a length well exceeding that of others in 1911 and 1912. Both were preceded by a similar section title-page printed within a compartment[11] that consisted of a space for the story's title, author, and earlier titles framed by a port scene, with a wharf and ship's bow at the bottom and top-sails and gulls at the top (see Fig. 9).[12] After this section title came the full-page illustration, for 'A Smile of Fortune' the familiar Beresford portrait with the caption 'Mr. Joseph Conrad: A Character Portrait', and for 'Freya of the Seven Isles' a picture by Gilbert Holiday of the heroine 'Sending a kiss over the sea, as if she wanted to throw her heart along with it' (see Fig. 10).[13] The first pages of text began with a head-title under an identical decorative border, and the last pages concluded with 'The End.'

[10] Conrad to Pinker, [24 January 1908] (*Letters*, IV, 27); see pp. lxxv–lxxvi, 242.

[11] Fredson Bowers, *Principles of Bibliographical Description* (1949), pp. 141–4.

[12] For 'Freya of the Seven Isles' the page also included a dedication to Marris, the wording of which differed slightly from that printed in *'Twixt Land and Sea*: see Appendix I ('The Epigraph and the Dedication').

[13] Holiday (1879–1937), a draughtsman, but best known as a painter of horses, provided illustrations for several stories in the magazine during 1911 and 1912.

APPENDIX D

A SMILE OF FORTUNE

PAGINATION OF THE FIRST TYPESCRIPT FRAGMENT

Section	Blue pencil	Ink	Typewritten
0	one	(one)?	
	2	2	[]
	3	3 & 4	4
	4	[5]	5
	5	6	6
	6	[7]	7
	7	[8]	8
	8	[9 & 10]	10
	9	[]	11
	10	[]	12
	11	13 & 14	14
	12	[]	15
	13	[]	16
	14	[]	17
	15	*9	18
0 / 1	16	18	29
	17	19	30
	18	*10	31
	19	22	32
	20	23	33
	21	24	34
	22	25	35
	23	26	36
	24	27	
	25	28	38
	26	29	39
	27	30	40
	28	31	41
	29	32	42
1 / 2	29A	32A	—
2	29B	32B	—
	30	33	1
	31	34	2
	32	35	3
	33	36	4
	34 over 36	37	5
	35 over 37	38	6
	36	39	7
	37	40	8
	38	41	9
	39	42	10

APPENDIX E

A Smile of Fortune

Correspondence with the *London Magazine*

The Bancroft Library at the University of California, Berkeley, describes one of the documents it holds as follows:

Conrad's copy of three paragraphs of his letter to W. C. Beaumont, the editor of the London Magazine, 2 pages 4to, typewritten with autograph additions and corrections and an autograph postscript at the head of the first page; Capel House, Orlestone, 17 November 1910. Together with a letter from Hubert Filchew of the London Magazine to James B. Pinker, Conrad's friend and literary agent; 2 pages 4to (typewritten) 19 November 1910.

Below are transcriptions of these letters, which bear on Conrad's preparation of the serial version of 'A Smile of Fortune' with its abbreviated prologue and variant ending (see 'Introduction', pp. lxxv–lxxvi, and 'The Texts', pp. 241–4). The second was previously published in *Portrait in Letters*, pp. 74–5.

Conrad to Pinker

This is the copy of the 3 material pars: of my letter to Beaumont. Two (**swering his criticism) are omitted. There was no room for my wife to copy in type the post-script which runs as follows: –

PS In all this I do not in the least blame Mr Pinker's action. He has discretionary powers to deal with my work. Such a point has never arisen before and he was not in possession of my full views on the matter.

> Capel House
> Orlestone.
> Nov. 17th 1910.

I address you directly to make it plain that if you have been led to believe that I would alter my work to suit the tastes, opinion or criticism of any person whatever it has been done without my concurrence and without a shred of authority from me.

I would be inclined to resent strongly such a proposal were I sure it had originated with you. For, pray consider: my work counts in the present-day literature. I am not a casual scribbler. My signature stands for something quite individual and distinctive in the art of expression. How then can I modify my work in its inner texture in accordance with another man's views, and then put it out as my own. for the sake of a few pounds? And if anybody says to me: "Oh, but it's such a trifling matter" – my answer is, that when it comes to a question not of vanity but of honest scruples, no line can be drawn higher or lower, saying: I won't go beyond this. It's simply that one musn't give way at all.

If you had made suggestions of a practical kind I would have given my best consideration to your wishes. I am not an art-crank. For instance, taking into consideration the conditions of serial-reading (when a whole number of a magazine is looked over in a two or three hour's railway journey, perhaps) I think that, what we may call, the preliminaries of the story are a bit too long. The hospital episode (which "establishes" our principal character – gives his "note" as: – impressionable, impulsive, humane) and the descriptive passages – when he is affected by the vision of the Island (which show him susceptible to mystery, imaginative) could be taken out. Altogether 5–6 pages which could be replaced by a paragraph of a few lines making a neat joint. It would impoverish the composition but it wouldn't hurt the story qua story. For the same reason (i.e., hurried reading, a danger to which a tale in a magazine is always exposed,) I think that half a page or so more at the end, giving a greater relief to our man's final feelings, would perhaps be advisable. Or if you had wished to make two instalments – an awkward thing for so "close" a composition, almost fatal – I would have tried to assist by any slight re-arrangement or a few additional lines, to the best of my power.

The *London Magazine* to Pinker

THE LONDON MAGAZINE
154, 156, Temple Chambers,
London, E.C.
November 19, 1910.

Dear Mr. Pinker,

This morning we received a letter from Mr. Conrad in response to one of ours to him, suggesting some slight alterations to and deletions from the complete novel of his which we have had under consideration. After conferring with Mr. Beaumont, I am asked to give you the gist of his remarks.

He says: "if you have been led to believe that I would alter my work to suit the tastes, opinions or criticism of any person whatever it has been done without my concurrence. . . My signature stands for something quite individual and distinctive in the art of expression. How then can I modify my work in its inner texture in accordance with another man's views . . . Taking into consideration the conditions of serial-reading, I think that, what we may call, the preliminaries of the story are a bit too long. The hospital episode (which establishes our principal character – gives his note as: – impressionable, impulsive, humane) and the descriptive passages – when he is affected by the vision of the island could be taken out. Altogether 5–6 pages which could be replaced by a paragraph of a few lines making a neat joint. For the same reason, i.e. hurried reading, a danger to which a tale in a magazine is always exposed, I think that half a page or more at the end, giving a greater relief to our man's final feelings, would perhaps be advisable. . . . These are not essentials. They don't affect the character of the work. However, you don't think the story good enough – and there's an end of it."

Now we did not suggest alterations of such magnitude as to call forth such views from Mr. Conrad. We want to use the story, and are far from "not thinking it good enough". After all we are entitled to give our views of the work of any writer who is in expectation of our accepting his work. We think that Mr. *onrad might have met us in the same spirit in which we approached him – an entirely friendly one.

But will you let us have the MS back first thing on Monday, and we must then discuss with you what to do.

> Believe me,
> Dear Mr. Pinker,
> Yours very truly,
> Hubert Filchew

James B. Pinker Esq.

APPENDIX F

A SMILE OF FORTUNE

THE SERIAL VERSION OF THE PROLOGUE AND ENDING

The serial version of the prologue, which was based on the paragraphs in his original manuscript, was so different from Conrad's revised typescript version that the variants cannot be clearly represented in this volume's main apparatus. (See the discussion in 'The Texts', pp. 243–4.) This is almost as true of the passages at the end of the story that reverted to the MS version when Conrad altered the tale for the *London Magazine* (S). However, briefer differences associated with the two versions are reported in the main apparatus (see 19.28b, 21.16–22, 21.26–28, 25.18–19, 32.29a, 51.19–25, 51.27a, 77.24–78.10).

Below are critical texts, based on MS, of the prologue and of the ending that represent the texts created by Conrad's revisions for S and the book editions. Preceding each is a page–line reference that identifies their counterparts in the text of this edition, which presents the typescript version. The apparatus and notes to these texts follow them immediately and observe the conventions of their counterparts elsewhere in the volume.

The Prologue

[Cf. 13.2–18.14]

MS	holograph manuscript (Berg): copy-text
S	*London Magazine*, February 1911, pp. 801–36
E1	first English edition (Dent, 1912)
A1	first American edition (Doran [later Doubleday], 1912)
A2	second American edition (Doubleday collected, 1921)
A2a	first state of **A2**, American Sun-Dial (1921) and all British issues (1923–)
A2b	second state of **A2**, Concord and subsequent American issues (1923–)
E2	second English edition (Heinemann collected, 1921)

A SMILE OF FORTUNE

A HARBOUR STORY

{tcop}Ever since the sun rose I had
been looking ahead. The ship   1:4   ahead. The] **S**– ahead while the **MS**
glided gently in   1:5   gently in smooth water] **S** smoothly
                                            on a calm sea **MS**
smooth water. After a sixty days   1:6   days] **S**– day's **MS**
passage I was anxious to make my   1:7   to ... and] **E1**– for the sight of our
  landfall,   destination a **MS** to make at last my
a fertile and beautiful   landfall, a fertile and **S**
island of the tropics. The more   1:9   The more enthusiastic] **S**– Some **MS**
  enthusiastic of
its inhabitants delight in describing 1:10 delight ... as] **E1** describe
  it as   it as **MS** delight in calling it **S**
the pearl of the ocean.   1:11a pearl] **MS** Pearl **S**–
                                     1:11b ocean] **MS** Ocean **S**–
   Well – let us call it the Pearl. 1:12b Pearl] **MS** pearl **S**–
It's a good name. A pearl distilling 1:13a It's] **E1**– Its **MS** It is **S**
much sweetness upon the world.
   This is only a way of telling you 1:15   This] **S**– It **MS**
that first rate sugar-cane is
grown there. All the population of   1:17a there. All ... it.] **S**– there. **MS**
  the Pearl lives for it
     and by it. Sugar is their daily 1:17b their] **S**– the **MS**
bread, as it were.   1:18a were.] **S**– were of its people. **MS**
And I was coming to   1:19b And] **S**– They live by it; and **MS**
them for a cargo of
sugar in the hope of the crop
having been good and of the
freights being high.
   Mr Burns, my chief mate   1:24a Mr] **MS E1**– It was Mr. **S**
made out the land first; and very   1:24b made out] **E1**– was the first to make
  soon I became   **MS** who made out **S**
entranced by this blue, pinnacled   2:1   land first; ... pinnacled]
  apparition, almost transparent   **E1**– land. It was an entrancing **MS**
against the light of the   land first; and presently I became
                                            entranced by this blue, pinnacled **S**
                                     2:2   almost] **S**– blue **MS**
                                     2:3   against the light of] **S**– pinnacles
                                            raising up in **MS**
sky, a mere emanation, the astral   2:4   sky, a mere emanation,] **E1**– sky,
  body of an island   **MS** sky, as if it were a mere
                                            emanation, **S**

risen to greet me from afar.	2:5a	risen to greet] **S**– greeting **MS**
It is a rare phenomenon	2:5b	It is a] **S**– A **MS**
this – such a sight of the Pearl	2:5	phenomenon this –] **MS**
		phenomenon, **S**–
at sixty miles off. And I wondered	2:7	wondered half] **S**– wondered **MS**
half		
seriously whether it was a		
good omen, whether what		
would meet me		
in that island would be		
as luckily exceptional as this		
beautiful dreamlike vision so very		
few		
seamen have been privileged		
to behold.		
But horrid thoughts of business		
interfered with my enjoyment		
of an accomplished passage. I		
was anxious for success and I wished	2:19	success and I] **S**– success. I **MS**
too to do justice to the flattering	2:20a	to the flattering latitude of] **S**– to **MS**
latitude of my owners'	2:20b	owners'] **S**– owners **MS**
instructions		
contained in one noble		
phrase. "We leave it to you to		
do the best you can with the		
ship." . . .		
All the world being then given	2:25	then] **MS** thus **S**–
me for a stage my abilities appeared		
to me no bigger than a pin-head.		
Meantime the wind dropped and	3:1	Meantime the] **S**– The **MS**
Mr Burns		
began to make disagreeable		
remarks	3:2	remarks] **S**– remark **MS**
about my usual bad luck. I believe	3:3	my usual bad luck] **S**– the quality of
		my luck **MS**
it was his devotion for me which	3:4a	it was] **S**– that **MS**
made him	3:4b	for] **S**– to **MS**
critically outspoken on every	3:4c	me which] **S**– me **MS**
occasion.		
All the same, I would not have put	3:6	All the same, I] **S**– I **MS**
up with		
his humours if it had not been		
my lot at one time to nurse him	3:8a	my lot] **S**– that **MS**
	3:8b	to nurse] **S**– I had nursed **MS**
through a desperate illness at sea.		
After snatching him out of the	3:10	out of] **S**– from **MS**
jaws of		

death so to speak, it would have
been absurd
to throw away such an efficient
officer. But sometimes I
wished he would dismiss himself.
   We were late in closing in with
the land and had
to anchor outside the harbour till
next day. An unpleasant and
unrestful
night followed. In this roadstead
strange
to us both Burns and I remained
on deck almost all the time. Clouds
swirled down the porphyry crags
under which
we lay. The rising wind made
a great bullying noise amongst
the naked spars with interludes
of sad moaning. I remarked
that we had been in luck to fetch
the
anchorage before dark. It
would have been a nasty, anxious
night to hang off a harbour under
canvass. But my chief mate was
uncompromising in his attitude.
   "Luck you call it, Sir! Aye – our
usual luck. The sort of luck to
thank God it's no
worse."
   And so we fretted through the
dark hours
while I drew on my fund of
philosophy.
Ah! But it was an exasperating,
weary, endless
night to be lying at anchor close
under
that black coast. The agitated
water made snarling sounds all
round
the ship. At times a wild gust
of wind out of a gully high up on
the cliffs struck on
our rigging a harsh and plaintive
note like the wail of a forsaken
soul.

3:11   death so to speak,] **S**– death **MS**

3:13–14 sometimes I wished] **S**– in truth I
often wished that **MS**

3:22   rising] **S**– ***** **MS**

3:26   that ... fetch] **S**– as to our luck in
fetching **MS**

3:27   anchorage] **S**– anchoring ground
MS

4:1a   But my] **S**– My **MS**
4:1b   was] **S**– remained **MS**
4:2   attitude.] **S**– critical attitude. **MS**

4:4   luck. The sort of luck to] **S**– luck –
to **MS**

4:6   we] **MS** he **S**–

4:7   fund] **S**– found **MS**

4:9   under] **S**– under | under **MS**

4:14   harsh] **S**– wild **MS**

. The Ending

[Cf. 77.23–78.10]

MS	holograph manuscript (Berg): copy-text
TS1	typescript (Yale, Berg)
TS1t	typewritten (unrevised) text of **TS** superseded by revision
TS1r	revised text of **TS** (incorporating Conrad's alterations)
S	*London Magazine*, February 1911, pp. 801–36
E1	first English edition (Dent, 1912)
A1	first American edition (Doran (later Doubleday), 1912)
A2	second American edition (Doubleday collected, 1921)
A2a	first state of **A2**, American Sun-Dial (1921) and all British issues (1923–)
A2b	second state of **A2**, Concord and subsequent American issues (1923–)
E2	second English edition (Heinemann collected, 1921)

I dropped the letter and sat
    motionless
for a long time. Then I wrote my
answer (it was a short one) and
    went ashore myself to post it. 138:3   myself ... it.] **TS1**– to post it
                                            myself at the dock gate. **MS**

                              138:4–139:7   But ... slit.] **MS S**– OM **TS1**
But I passed one letter-box, then 138:4   I passed ... and in] **S**– in **MS** OM
    another, and in the end I   **TS1**
    found myself   138:4   found myself going up] **S**– I
going up Collins Street with the   found myself in **MS** OM **TS1**
    letter still in
pocket – against my heart. Collins 138:6   pocket] **MS** my pocket **S**– OM **TS1**
    Street
at four o'clock in the afternoon is
    not exactly
a desert solitude; but I had never 138:8   had ... more] **S**– felt myself
    felt   painfully **MS** OM **TS1**
more isolated from the rest of
    mankind
as when I walked that day its 138:10a   as ... day] **S**– on **MS** OM **TS1**
    crowded pavement,   138:10b   as] **S–A1 A2a E2** than **A2b** VAR
battling desperately with   **MS** OM **TS1**
my thoughts and
feeling already vanquished. 138:12   feeling already vanquished] **S**–
                                            conscious of certain defeat **MS** OM
                                            TS1

There came a moment when 138:14   There ... awful] **S**– At a given
    the awful tenacity of   moment the **MS** OM **TS1**
Jacobus the man of one passion 138:15   of one] **S**– one **MS** OM **TS1**
    and of one idea appeared to
    me almost

heroic. He had not given me up.
  He had gone again to his
odious brother. And then he
  appeared
to me odious himself. Was it for his
  own
sake or for the sake of the poor
  girl? And on
that last supposition the memory
of the kiss which missed
my lips appalled me; for whatever
  he
had seen, or guessed at, or risked,
  he knew nothing of
  that. Unless the girl had told
him. How could I go back to
fan that fatal spark with my cold
breath? No! No! That unexpected
  kiss had to be
paid at its full price.
  At the first letter-box I came to I
  stopped and reaching
  into my breast-pocket I took
out the letter – it was as if I were
  plucking out my very
  heart – and dropped it
  through
the slit. Then I went straight on
  board.
I wondered what dreams I would
  have that night – but
  as it turned
out I did not sleep at all. At
  breakfast I informed Mr
  Burns that I
had resigned my command.
  He dropped his knife and fork
  and looked at me with
  indignation.
  "You have sir! I thought you
  loved the ship."
  "So I do Burns," I said. "But the
  fact is that the Indian
  Ocean and
everything that is in it has lost its
  charm for me. I am going
  home

138:16 heroic. He ... up.] **S**–
  heroic. **MS** OM **TS1**

138:17 to me] **S**– mostrously **MS** OM **TS1**

138:18 poor girl] **S**– girl **MS** OM **TS1**
138:18 And on] **S**– On **MS** OM **TS1**

138:21 missed] **S**– had missed **MS** OM **TS1**
138:22 appalled me] **S**– was appalling **MS**
  OM **TS1**

138:23a seen, ... risked,] **S**– seen **MS** OM **TS1**

138:23b Unless ... him.] **S**–
  Had she told him? **MS** OM **TS1**

139:2 at] **MS** for at **S**– OM **TS1**
139:3 At ... out] **S**—I posted the letter at
  last and went straight on board,
  miserable as though I had dropped
  MS OM **TS1**

139:5 heart – and dropped it] **S**– heart **MS**
  OM **TS1**
139:5 slit. Then ... board.] **S**– slit. **MS** OM
  TS1

as passenger by the Suez Canal." 139:12–13

"Everything that is in it," he 139:14
repeated angrily.
"I've never heard 139:14–15
anybody talk like this. And to tell
you the truth, sir, all the time
139:15
we have been together I've never 140:1a
quite made you out.

What's one 140:1b
ocean more than another?
Charm, indeed!"
He was really devoted to me, 140:3a
I believe. But he cheered up 140:3b
when I
told him that I had recommended 140:4
him for my successor.

"Anyhow," he remarked, "let 140:5
people say what they like, this
Jacobus 140:6a
has served your turn. I must admit 140:6–7
that this potato business has
paid

extremely well. Of course, if only 140:7
you had —"

"Yes Mr Burns," I interrupted. 140:8a
"Quite a smile of
fortune." 140:8b
But I could not tell him that it 140:9a
was driving me out of a 140:9b
ship I
140:9c
had learned to love. 140:10

And as I sat heavy-hearted at that 140:11
parting, seeing all my
plans destroyed, my modest

---

home as passenger] **S**– home **MS TS1**
"Everything that is in] **TS1**– Everything – in **MS**
"I've ... this.] **TS1**– "What sort of talk is it? What's one ocean more than another? **MS**
And to] **TS1**– To **MS**
I've ... out.] **E1**– I haven't made you out. **MS** I've never quite understood you. **TS1 S**
What's ... another?] **TS1**– OM **MS**
He] **TS1**– I believe he **MS**
me, I believe.] **TS1**– me. **MS**
I had recommended him for my successor] **TS1**– he would probably succeed me in the command **MS**
"let ... turn. I must admit that] **TS1**– OM **MS**
admit] **E1**– own **TS1 S** OM **MS**
has paid extremely well.] **E1**– has paid well. **MS** turned out wonderfully." **TS1t TS1r** turned out wonderfully well. **S**
Of course, if only you had — "] **E1**– If only you had ..." **MS** Of course, if you ..." **S** OM **TS1**
interrupted.] **S**– interrupted him. **MS** said. **TS1**
fortune] **MS S**– Fortune **TS1**
could] **MS TS1r**– did **TS1t**
was driving] **MS TS1r**– had driven **TS1t**
a] **MS** the **TS1**–
love.] **S**– love, and endangering my modest future. **MS** love; and he must have wondered at my bitter and ironic tone. **TS1**
And ... attitude.] **S**– And as I sat mute and heavy-hearted he gave up completely for the first time

future endangered – for this
   command was like a foot in
   the stirrup for a young
man – he gave up completely for
   the first time his
   critical attitude.
   "A wonderful piece of luck!" he
   said.
The End.

his critical attitude. **MS** He had
always looked on this affair as a
purely commercial transaction.
TS 1

Note

138:5 **Collins Street** At the time of Conrad's visit, Collins Street was the prime
boulevard of the wealthiest and largest city in Australia. Formally established in
1837 with a street grid of 30-metre main roads and 10-metre lanes, Melbourne
was named after Lord Melbourne, the British Prime Minister, in 1842, and chosen
as the capital of Victoria in 1851. In that year huge deposits of alluvial gold were
found at the foot of the Great Dividing Range to the north, and in thirty years
the ensuing gold rush doubled the population of the city to 258,000. As gold
fever lapsed, a 'land boom' took over between 1881 and 1891 in the form of
frenzied speculation on property, which again doubled the Melbourne population.
The Collins Street that Conrad and his protagonist strolled down in January 1889
ran (and still runs) parallel to the Yarra River, three short blocks south. With
its great business houses to the west, its consultancies of medical specialists to
the east, and the intense animation of its population, Collins Street would have
appeared cosmopolitan indeed after Port Louis. See Graeme Davison, ed., *The
Oxford Companion to Australian History* (1998).

APPENDIX G

FREYA OF THE SEVEN ISLES

THE GARNETT CONTROVERSY

CONRAD'S STRONG language in connection with the misunderstanding that arose with Edward Garnett in 1911 over the composition of 'Freya of the Seven Isles' indicates the importance of the issue to him. Arising while Pinker was trying to place the tale and while Conrad was trying to repair the breach with him that had occurred a year earlier, the misunderstanding's development may be summarized as follows.

1. In early March 1911, the New York literary magazine the *Century* rejects the tale because of its 'overpowering gloom'.
2. In mid-March, Pinker reports this rejection to Conrad, but without identifying the magazine; Conrad infers that it is either the *Century* or *Scribner's*.
3. On 25 March, Conrad replies to Pinker pleading that the treatment of the story's concluding deaths had been 'rather delicate', but that perhaps the writing itself was 'gloomy'.
4. On 18 July, Conrad writes to Garnett congratulating him on his appointment as reader for the *Century*, and responding to his request for copy, states that 'if I am not mistaken' either the *Century* or *Scribner's* had refused 'in March last a very tolerable long-short-story' of his.
5. Around 20 July, perhaps in response to a request from the newly appointed Garnett for new material by Conrad, Pinker sends him the typescript of 'Freya of the Seven Isles'.
6. On 26 July, Garnett returns the tale to Pinker (presumably on the grounds that the *Century* had already seen and rejected it), and remarks, 'the story is undoubtedly very fine. (I remembered reading it years ago.)' and adds: 'I do feel a certain weakness in the manipulation of the tragedy at the end.'
7. On 28 July, Conrad asks Pinker to consider sending the tale to *Blackwood's Magazine*, and tells him that Garnett now reads for the *Century*, and has approached him for material.
8. Around 29 July, Conrad receives a letter from Pinker (presumably written and posted on the 28th), telling him that he had sent the tale to Garnett.
9. On 29 July, Conrad writes to Garnett to say that he has heard from Pinker that he (Pinker) has sent 'Freya of the Seven Isles' to him. He deduces from this that it was *Scribner's*, and not the *Century*, that had rejected the tale in March on the grounds of its 'overpowering gloom', and he 'entreats' Garnett 'to bear up – to react – to be a man!', concluding: 'If only for the sake of the old days don't bring your heaviest guns against the thing. It's but tissue paper after all.'
10. On 3 August, Conrad tells Pinker that he regrets his having sent 'Freya of the Seven Isles' to Garnett, and regrets, too, that Garnett had asked to see it.
11. On 4 August, Conrad writes to Garnett expressing contempt for the preferences of 'american Editors' for '"sunny" endings'. He outlines the origins of the novella. He concludes with an abbreviated account of the efficient cause – Marris's visit.

12. On 7 August, Pinker (presumably informed by Garnett that Conrad is upset) relays to Conrad the contents of Garnett's letter of 26 July.
13. On 9 August, Conrad replies to Pinker, expressing his dismay that Pinker had seen fit to send Garnett a story already rejected by the *Century* ('E.G. could not under the circumstances accept it for publication'), and reviling Garnett for 'the <u>thundering lie</u> . . . that he had seen the story <u>years ago</u>', citing witnesses able to testify that he was writing the story in 'Jan–Febr and March of this present year', and adding: 'Why G. made that monstrous false statement to you I can't imagine.'

Of course Garnett was by no means completely mistaken. The source of his comment was presumably the draft of 'The Rescuer' (later *The Rescue*) he had read in 1898 (see 'Introduction', pp. lix–lx). Garnett's misunderstanding testifies to the intensity of his response to the power of Conrad's narrative, as well as to the tenacity of a memory that had nevertheless magnified a paragraph into a novella.

APPENDIX H

FREYA OF THE SEVEN ISLES

MARKS IN PENCIL ON THE FIRST TYPESCRIPT

Listed below are the words inscribed in lead (black) pencil on the face of the extant typescript (TS1) of 'Freya of the Seven Isles'. These were written by Conrad presumably after the document came back from J. B. Pinker's typists and before he posted it to Warrington Dawson in France for possible magazine publication (see p. 261 and Appendix A). To provide context, the reading of the Cambridge text along with a reference to its page and line (P-L) in the present edition appear in the first two columns. The next column gives the reading of TS1r (i.e., the type-script text sent to Pinker for transcription) which is the subject of the pencilled inscription: when that reading is different from the present text (i.e., has been emended), it is transcribed literally, and when it is identical, a long dash (—) represents that fact. The fourth column records English wording inscribed in pencil, and the fifth French, also in literal transcriptions; blanks in these columns show the absence of pencilled English or French wording at a given point. The last column cites the page and line of the typescript on which the inscription appears.

P-L	Cambridge	TS1r	English	French	TS1
123.19	Eastern Archipelago	—		Archipel Malais	1:19
124.12	Rather	—		Je crois bien	3:2
125.18–19	land from the dinghy	—		debarquer de sa yole	5:4
125.38	upright grand	—		grand piano	6:1
126.5	tackles	—		palans	6:7
126.23	squalls	—		grain	7:5
126.33	nape of her neck	—		nuque	7:14
126.39	Did you ever!	—		Imaginez Vous ça!	8:1
126.39	And mind –	—		Et rappellez vous, que	8:1
127.5	long glass	—		longuevue	8:7
127.8–9	puts the helm down	—		met la barre dessous	8:10
127.9–10	all her sails	all the sails		toutes ses voiles	8:10
127.10	shaking and rattling	—		ralinguant	8:11
127.10	racket	—		vacarme?	8:11
129.8	the Dutch	—	Dutch		12:6
132.2	gunboat	—		canonière	18:8

P-L	Cambridge	TS1r	English	French	TS1
132.22	undress jacket	Cloth undress jacket	undress jacket	petite tenue	19:9
132.32	tiffin	—		déjeuner	20:3
132.34	as	as **	as		20:5
135.31	rounded the reef	—		doublé le récif	25:9
135.32	abreast of	—		par le travers	25:9
135.38	heading east	—		gouvernant a l'Est	25:14
135.38	on the quarter	—		sur la hanché	25:15
136.24	quartermaster	—		timonier	26:19
136.26	gig	—		balánière	27:2
136.29	Seven-Isles group	—	Seven-Isles		27:4
136.31	bridge	—		passerelle	27:7
138.25–26	My mate	—		Mon second	30:14
139.1	mate	—		second	31:8
139.2	to sign him on	—		lui faire signer le rôle	31:9
139.3	to get under way	—		pour appareiller	31:10
139.12	Schultz	Schultz's	Schultz		31:19
139.14	starboard bow	—		bossoir de tribord	32:1
139.14	*Bohemian Girl*	"Bohemian Girl"		Bohé-mienne	32:1
139.30	pull my leg old boy	—		vous moquer de moimon vieux	32:16
140.20	tracks	tracts	tracks		34:5
140.22–23	or lay hove-to	—		ou restait en panne	34:7
140.28	mail-routes	— [routes *above uncancelled* tracks]	— [tracks *crossed out*]		34:12
141.11	beacons	—		balises	35:14
141.15	lowered a boat on purpose	—		met une embarcation a l'eau exprès	35:17
145.22	cove	c**e | cove	cove		43:11 (*cont.*)

P-L	Cambridge	TS1r	English	French	TS1
156.5	but a	a but	but a		62:16
181.3	practical	pratical	practical		109:3
182.20	man's	— [*above uncancelled* person's]	— [person's *crossed out*]		111:12
184.11	handfuls	handfulls	handfuls		114:15
184.33	all along	—	along		115:14
186.28	recall to me	—	recall		119:3

APPENDIX I

THE EPIGRAPH AND THE DEDICATION

HAVING SENT to Pinker printer's copy for Dent's English edition (E1) of the tales themselves in early July, Conrad had 'settled' the title of the volume through direct correspondence with his publisher by the 23rd. No record of their communications about the epigraph and the dedication for the volume is known, but less than a week later Conrad was enclosing in a letter to John Quinn the leaf that had provided copy for the epigraph.[1] Copy for these two bits of text in the preliminaries was probably included in Conrad's letter to Dent's fixing the title.

The dedication had already appeared, in a variant form, in the *London Magazine*'s section title-page to 'Freya of the Seven Isles'. The alterations in wording that appeared in E1 – 'late master' instead of 'formerly master', and 'days of adventure' instead of simply 'days' – added precision (particularly regarding Marris), developed the emotive and exotic effects, and clearly represent Conrad's revisions. These revisions he could have made on the proof of the section title that would have come to him in May as part of the duplicate proofs of the *London Magazine*'s typesetting, which he had eventually used to provide copy of the tale's text for E1 (see pp. 275–8) and which he had forwarded to Pinker along with magazine copy for the other two tales. He could have sent the marked proof of the section title to Dent's, or he might have simply rewritten the text on a piece of stationery. In either case the new text must have been contained in the copy Dent's received because these revisions also appear in A1, which was typeset from a set of E1 proofs that Pinker had posted to New York before Dent's could pull revises based on Conrad's set (see pp. 282–3). There can be no reasonable doubt about the authenticity of the wording found in E1 and A1.

The variants in the epigraph are more important, and the case more complex. The single sheet containing both Symons' verses, apparently in his own hand, and Conrad's instructions to the printer about typography has been kept with the manuscript of 'Freya of the Seven Isles', as Conrad suggested (see Appendix A). Dent's followed Conrad's instructions, but E1's second and third lines are quite different from Symons'. Its text reads:

> Life is a tragic folly
> Let us laugh and be jolly
> Away with melancholy
> Bring me a branch of holly
> Life is a tragic folly

The manuscript leaf has arguably better wording:

> Life is a tragic folly,
> Let us mock at life and be jolly,
> Or droop into melancholy:
> Bring me a branch of holly:
> Life is a tragic folly.

Symons' 'mock at' is a direct echo of Conrad's distinctive phrasing in the account of Heemskirk's ruminations (167.33, 170.17); his 'droop into' is more in tune with the

---

[1] Conrad to Pinker, [6 July], 23 July 1912; to Quinn, 29 July 1912 (*Letters*, v, 83, 87, 90).

final moods of that tale, and his rhythms superior. The juxtaposition between the third line's sentiment and the next line's, which in Symons' version is signalled by a line-end colon, has been obliterated by E1's substitution of the lame 'Away with' and its deletion of that point. E1 in fact eliminates all line-end punctuation, a matter of title-page aesthetics that must be attributed to Dent's agents. Attribution of the changes in wording is slightly more problematic. It could be argued that because E1 exhibits minimal change of wording in the tales, the alterations in the title-page cannot be laid at Dent's door. That would leave Conrad as their source, who would presumably have felt justified in making them because the verses were appearing in his book. However, formidable difficulties with this position immediately arise. The least is the virtual certainty that Dent's, rather than he, intervened when altering the line-end points. Nor is it likely that Conrad would have felt comfortable changing Symons' words, for both professional and personal reasons.[2] Furthermore, E1's variants occur where Symons' inscription is most unclear and likely to have invited misconstruction or outright intervention. Finally, because Conrad did not make these alterations on the face of the extant sheet that served as Dent's copy, the only place he could have done so would have been the proofs he saw in September; yet those proofs must have already contained these alterations, since they appear in A1 as well (see above). It follows that they were generated by Dent's agents and can be confidently dismissed in favour of Symons' superior text.

---

[2] On Conrad's relationship with Symons, who had had severe mental problems, see 1.8n and *Letters*, IV, 150, 184-5, 326, 411-12, 415, 438; *Letters*, V, 10, 90.

NOTES

Topics sufficiently explained in a standard desk dictionary receive no notice. Definitions and similar information often come from the *OED*, which is explicitly cited here in special cases, as when there is uncertainty or dispute. Other sources are, whenever practical, those that Conrad and his first readers could have known. Editorial references to direction aboard ship assume the standpoint of one looking forward from the stern. Citations of maps and figures refer to the illustrations located either at the end of this volume or on pp.190–202.

In notes dealing with alternative readings – whether in the early texts or proposed as emendations, whether adopted here or not – a bracket follows the reading drawn from the text (the lemma) and a statement of variation precedes the commentary. Conventions of notation conform to those followed in the 'Emendation and Variation' list in the 'Apparatus' and explained in its headnote. The sigla for the book texts of the tales and for the earlier texts of each one are listed below their respective headings.

1.8 **A. Symons** Poet, editor, and critic, Arthur Symons (1865–1945) was a member of the notorious 'Rhymers' Club', which grouped together the most creatively 'decadent' (anti-bourgeois) aesthetes and writers of the 1890s. Always hyper-sensitive, he suffered a major mental collapse shortly before Conrad's breakdown. On 15 February 1911, as he was finishing 'Freya of the Seven Isles', Conrad wrote to him a supportive letter in which he told him that 'your *désir de vivre* is your best proof that you deserve to live' (*Letters*, IV, 415). When Symons eventually saw a copy of 'Freya of the Seven Isles', he composed the stanza which Conrad chose as the epigraph for *'Twixt Land and Sea* (see Appendix I, 'The Epigraph and the Dedication').

3.2 **C. M. Marris** Captain Carlos Murrell Marris, a merchant sailor from Conrad's eastern past who was visiting England for his health, called on Conrad in September 1909, just before returning to the Far East, where he died the following year. Conrad indicated that this meeting, which not only resurrected his years of adventure but also revealed to him that his eastern tales were eagerly read in the Archipelago, prompted him to return to writing the kinds of tales that make up *'Twixt Land and Sea*. See *Letters*, IV, 273, 277–8, and 'Introduction', pp. xxxi–xxxii.

AUTHOR'S NOTE

6.1 **the editor of a popular illustrated magazine** W. C. Beaumont, who published the abbreviated text of 'A Smile of Fortune' with illustrations by S. Spurrier in the *London Magazine* of February 1911. See 'Introduction', pp. lxxv–lxxvi, 'The Texts', pp. 241–4, and Appendix C, 'The *London Magazine*'.

6.4–6 **"The Secret Sharer,"** . . . *Harper's Magazine* Subtitled 'An Episode from the Sea', 'The Secret-Sharer' (so titled) was published in two parts in *Harper's Monthly*

Magazine, with illustrations by W. J. Aylward, during August and September 1910. See 'The Texts', pp. 215–17.

6.7–8 **The basic fact of the tale** The killing of a ship's hand by an officer. See 'Introduction', pp. xxxvi–xxxviii.

6.13 **Mr Willis** John ('Jock') Willis, or 'Willis of the White Hat', determined to win the record for the quickest voyage to Anjer, entrance to the Far East, during the waning days of sail, ordered a new ship from the Dumbarton shipyards, from which emerged in 1869 the incomparable *Cutty Sark* (Lubbock, pp. 20–24, 52). After he sold her in 1895, the ship remained in commercial service until the 1920s. Having later served as a training ship at Greenhithe, she was put in dry dock at Greenwich in 1954.

6.19 **New South Dock** Properly called 'The East India South Dock', down river on the right bank of the Thames, it was opened in 1829. *The London Encyclopædia*, ed. Ben Weinreb and Christopher Hibbert (1983).

6.25 **date of the occurrence** According to the 4 August 1882 report of the trial of the alleged murderer printed in *The Times*, the incident took place 'about the 9th or 10th August, 1880'.

6.28–29 **wool fleet** The ultimate feats of speed were performed between 1883 and 1894, when the last generation of clippers found another and final decade of life bringing Australian wool to Britain. See Lubbock, p. 206, for a roll-call of the vessels.

7.4–5 **man in America … angry** Since Conrad 'lost' the letter, the identity of this man cannot be recovered. However, he might be a stalking horse for Edward Garnett, who on 26 July 1911 told J. B. Pinker, Conrad's literary agent, that he found the 'manipulation of the tragedy' at the close of 'Freya of the Seven Isles' unsatisfactory. See *Letters*, IV, 459–66; see also 'Introduction', pp. lvii–lix, and Appendix G, 'The Garnett Controversy'.

'TWIXT LAND AND SEA

E1	first English edition (Dent, 1912)
A1	first American edition (Doran [later Doubleday], 1912)
A2	second American edition (Doubleday collected, 1921)
A2a	first state of **A2**, American Sun-Dial (1921) and all British issues (1923–)
A2b	second state of **A2**, Concord and subsequent American issues (1923–)
E2	second English edition (Heinemann collected, 1921)

A Smile of Fortune

MS	holograph manuscript (Berg)
TS1	typescript (Yale, Berg)
TS1t	typewritten (unrevised) text of **TS** superseded by revision
TS1r	revised text of **TS** (incorporating Conrad's alterations): copy-text
TS2	typescript, partial (Berg)
S	*London Magazine*, February 1911, pp. 801–36

13.1 **A Smile of Fortune** A favour of the Roman goddess Fortuna, or a bit of financial good luck.

13.10 **ventilator** On late nineteenth-century merchant ships it consisted of a tube 15–18 inches in diameter, rising 5 feet above the poop deck, its head curved 90 degrees into a cowl so as to receive the full benefit of a breeze from any quarter. Its location afforded direct communication with the cabin below. See Fig. 5.

13.12 **port bow** To the left of the bow of the ship when facing forward.

13.23 **far above rubies in price** A variation on one or more Biblical phrases, most likely 'Who can find a virtuous woman? for her price is far above rubies' (Proverbs xxxi.10). But see also 'the price of wisdom is above rubies' (Job xxviii.18), 'wisdom is better than rubies' (Proverbs viii.11), and 'pearl of great price' (Matthew xiii.46).

13.33 **Consulate Doctor** The medical officer attached to a consulate in those parts of the world that did not practise European medicine.

14.38–39 **having disputed . . . Pale Death** The unorthodox syntax seeks to communicate the fact that the Captain fought 'Pale Death' all the way for the life of his first mate. The phrase is perhaps apocalyptic (Revelation vi.8).

15.7 **skylight** Horizontal or slightly inclined window or windows raised above the poop deck to bring daylight into the cabin below. See also 31.22n and Fig. 5.

15.15 **known for centuries** No record of indigenous settlement in Mauritius has been discovered, but the world map of the second-century Claudius Ptolemy (a mathematician, astronomer, and geographer) published in 1508 gives Arabic names to what can only be the Mascarene Islands. The Portuguese discovered Mauritius in the first decade of the sixteenth century. The Dutch landed on the island in 1598, naming it after their stadtholder (i.e., governor), Maurice of Nassau, but abandoned it as a supply station in the 1650s for the Cape of Good Hope. The French took possession of the island in 1721 as a staging post for the French East India Company. Finally, the British occupied it in 1810 in their attempts to immobilize Napoleon's navy in the Indian Ocean, receiving it from the Congress of Vienna in 1814 and keeping it as a colony until 1968, when it became an independent state and a member of the Commonwealth. See *Enc. Brit.*, p. 618; Toussaint, pp. 14–26; and Larry W. Bowman, *Mauritius: Democracy and Development in the Indian Ocean* (1991), pp. 8–42.

15.28 **Sugar** The sugar industry was established in Mauritius by the most famous of its French governors, Mahé de Labourdonnais, *ca.* 1740. In 1825 Britain decided to allow imports of Mauritian sugar to enter the country at the same rate of duty as West Indian sugar. As a result, Mauritian sugar production increased tenfold between 1825 and 1855, transforming the island from a strategic sea-port into a plantation colony. See Toussaint, pp. 29–30; see also *Enc. Brit.*, s.v. 'sugar' (esp. pp. 43–8).

15.37–38 **language of signals** 'All well' is a standard signal exchanged by ships crossing at sea. From 1817 British maritime signals took the form of alphabetical flags, codified by the Board of Trade; from 1866, however, the Royal Navy used semaphore and a variation on Morse code transmitted by lights. *Ships and the Sea.*

16.1 **chaffering** Haggling (together perhaps with the bandying of words that sometimes accompanies it), though the term originally meant simply to trade.

16.9 **the Cape** The Cape of Good Hope, at the south-western tip of Africa, so called by the Portuguese navigator Bartholomew Diaz after he discovered it in 1488, when the prospect of reaching India by sea became a reality. *Enc. Brit.*

16.15 **astral body** Astral spirits were formerly believed to live in heavenly bodies, or to be the ethereal counterparts of animal bodies; in Conrad's day they were particularly associated with spiritualism and mysticism. Perhaps Conrad is suggesting that the vision was so 'delicate' that it was as if his Captain saw the spirit rather than the body of the remote island.

16.28 **sailing Directions** The publications titled 'Sailing Directions', commonly known as 'Pilots', were a source of world-wide coastal information that supplemented charts. Each covered a particular area of the coast (for example, 'China Sea Pilot'). After 1884 printed supplements were issued more or less annually. *Ships and the Sea.*

16.38–39 **inland mountains** Port Louis has a semi-circular backdrop of jagged volcanic peaks forming the Pouce range. Mount Pouce ('thumb' in French, for its shape) rises 2,650 feet, while Mount Pieter Botte, still higher at 2,685 feet, is 'a tall obelisk of bare rock, crowned with a globular mass of stone'. *Enc. Brit.* See Map 2.

17.8 **luffed** To luff (the word for the leading edge of a fore-and-aft sail) is an order to the helmsman to bring the ship's head closer to the wind by putting the helm down – i.e., to leeward, a direction *away* from the wind (*Ships and the Sea*). This apparently illogical instruction derives from the way helmsmen handled tillers, which were eventually replaced by wheels; see the comment on 'Hard a-lee' (110.7*n*).

17.19 **harbour well known to ships** Port Louis became a ship-building centre in the eighteenth century, serving as a strategic turntable for the French navy and as an entrepot for its merchant ships. Under the British it lost that role to become a centre for the export of sugar during the nineteenth century, when the export trade grew noticeably: in 1850 the harbour turned round 470 vessels, and eight years later, 825. By the time Conrad called, trade had fallen off. Toussaint, pp. 30, 43, 71–2. See 15.15*n*.

17.20 **cupola** A dome-like lantern or skylight.

17.21 **screw-pile lighthouse** A small, metal, portable lighthouse attached to a foundation pile with a screw at its base – a much more secure attachment than the usual 'driving' (*OED*, s.v. screw). The lighthouse was needed to identify the break in the coral reef surrounding the island which allowed access to the harbour on its north-west coast at the end of a three-quarter-mile channel. See Martine Maurel, *Mauritius* (2000), p. 8.

17.28 **losing her way** Losing the momentum of her progress through the water (*OED*). The ship must come to a standstill for the anchor to set properly; this would have been especially important in a bad holding ground sought to shelter her from the gusting offshore wind.

17.37 **porphyry** A hard purple stone quarried in ancient Egypt. The word was used by the poets of the Romantic movement to evoke the beauty of the polished stone and of enchanted mountains.

18.1 **game** Full of pluck (i.e., having the spirit of a game-cock).

18.5 **roadstead** A place where ships may safely or conveniently lie at anchor near the shore (*OED*); a term for an anchorage only partly sheltered (see 17.28*n*).

18.8 **fetch** To come to, reach, in a nautical sense (*OED*); the term denotes the manner in which the ship reached the roadstead while sailing to windward.

18.17 **the harbour** The Port Louis harbour, built by Labourdonnais (see 15.28*n*) is at the head of a deep inlet, 400 yards broad and 1,200 yards long, leading up to a central dock and quay facing the town's principal avenue, with further docks to the north and south of the quay. In the nineteenth century, without a naval squadron of its own, Port Louis harboured French naval vessels; under the British, dry docks and other installations were created. See Map 2.

18.19 **steward** In the merchant navy, a petty officer who keeps stores, serves the officers' meals, and services their quarters.

18.20 **morning suit** In late Victorian England the extreme formality of the top hat and frock coat in a black-and-white scheme had yielded for day wear to the lounge or 'morning' suit consisting of coat, waistcoat, and trousers of matching material, usually a tweed of some kind. The coat or jacket had small lapels and four buttons closing the collar high up the chest, and was cut to reach the hips rounding away; it also had a broad, darker edging. Doreen Marwood, *English Costume* (1952), p. 213.

18.23 **heave round** A nautical phrase, usually applied to a capstan, denoting exceptional effort. On nineteenth-century sailing ships the anchor was 'weighed' (raised) manually by the crew pushing round the capstan by means of bars slotted into it, which turned it on a vertical axis. See *Nautical Terms*, 11.02.

18.36 **Jacobus** A Dutch name. The Jacobus family proves to be one of the oldest on the island, 'older than the French even' – that is to say, of Dutch origin (58.17–18).

19.3 **cuddy** A familiar name for the 'saloon' or 'cabin' aft, under the poop deck, where the officers (and, in harbour, visitors) took their meals. The term may also be used, more generally, for the whole suite of officers' quarters 'below', including their individual rooms, other common rooms (e.g., the head, the pantry), and even by extension the lobby. See 29.24*n*, 29.34*n* (and also Fig. 20).

19.12 **sixty one days** A satisfactory but not exceptional performance from eastern Australia for a sailing ship.

19.27 **owners'**] **S**– owners **MS** owner's **TS1 TS2** S's changes here and later (23.15) appear correct. Uncertain in the early stages of writing about how many businessmen owned the ship, Conrad seems to have settled on multiple 'owners' (34.34) by the time the Captain meets the other Jacobus and to have returned later to adjust these earlier forms and to correct TS1t's 'owner's' (34.16). Cf. 'my owners' (25.10, 77.5).

19.28 **within ... geographical limits**] **TS1r TS2** in accordance with my own judgment **MS** certain limits geographical limits **TS1t** according to my own judgment **S**–

Both changes, in the lost *TSo* and in the lost Pinker typescript (*TS3*), represent Conrad's revisions. Both were meant to echo the statements in their respective versions of the prologue: the serial version following the owners' 'noble phrase' with 'All the world being then given me for a stage' (see Appendix F, 2:25), the typescript version with 'only one limitation: "but you must not take her beyond the Cape"' (16.8–9). See Fig. 15.

19.33 **charterer** One who hires a vessel under a charter-party (43.15–16), i.e., a 'document embodying a contract between owners and merchants for the hire of a ship and the safe delivery of the cargo' (*OED*). In English law, such a contract goes back to the reign of Richard II: 'A rate what [sic] shall be paid for the freight or portage of the several sorts of merchandises . . .'. *Statutes at Large*, ed. Danby Pickering (1763), v, p. 24.

20.6 **Jackson – or Antrobus** A reassembling of the syllables that make up 'Jacobus' into a commonplace current English name and a fictitious heroic-classical name.

20.18 **companion way** Covered staircase from the poop deck to the cuddy.

20.36–37 **new bee** Short-hand for 'to have a [yet another] bee in the bonnet', i.e., to have an eccentric or obsessive whim.

21.1 **sea breakfast** At the end of a long voyage this would have consisted of coffee or tea, various tinned foods, dried fruit (once the supply of fresh fruit had been exhausted), and ship's biscuit (see 22.15*n*).

21.4 **three weeks . . . potato** Presumably because the supply had run out: on the return voyage the consignment of potatoes from Mauritius (though requiring special care) lasts to Melbourne.

21.24 **little town** In 1888 the population of Port Louis was about 40,000. The town was laid out in a grid pattern before and to the sides of the 'citadelle', a 250-foot hill crowned by a fort. As viewed from the main quay, a palm avenue led eastwards for 200 yards to the French colonial style Government House. The street continued inland with various public buildings and houses on both sides, including a theatre (dating from 1822) that presented plays and occasional operas. It ended on an open space to the south of the citadelle, called the 'Champ de Mars', used as a military parade ground and also as a small race-course. To the right (the south-west) of this axis was the up-market residential area with its balconied houses shadowing the pavements; to its left (the north-east) nearer the harbour was the financial district, with its maritime stores, its sailors' home, and its solid Victorian warehouses. Beyond this area and somewhat inland, the town took on a more run-down, nondescript appearance. See Royston Ellis and Derek Schuurman, *Mauritius, Rodrigues and Réunion* (1988) ch. 13, and, for a less detailed treatment, *Enc. Brit.*, s.v. Mauritius. See Map 2.

21.36 **beef . . . from Madagascar** Stock-rearing had never made any progress in Mauritius because 'it was so easy to get cattle from Madagascar' (Toussaint, p. 77). In the second half of the nineteenth century, the rearing of cattle and the dressing of hides were among the two most important industries of Madagascar, a mere 600 miles due west of Mauritius.

22.15 **ship's biscuit** The daily bread of the mariner: until the introduction of bakeries on ships at the beginning of the twentieth century, it was made from flour mixed with minimal water, force-kneaded into flat cakes, and baked very slowly. Long prone to infestation by black-headed weevils (beetles), in Conrad's time it was packed in weevil-proof tin-lined chests. *Ships and the Sea.*

22.18 **sugar crop** Under the British, Mauritian sugar production increased dramatically in the early nineteenth century (see 15.28n). Based, after the abolition of slavery in British colonies in 1835, on indentured labour from India and conducted under extremely harsh conditions, the growing and harvesting of sugar flourished for much of the century. Only when public opinion in India changed did the system finally become vulnerable – though even after that, race prejudice continued to remain firmly in place. Bowman, pp. 22–3.

22.18 **business houses** These houses, in the very conservative business district (see 21.24n), were generally involved in the import–export trade, especially with India, to which Mauritius sent most of its sugar and from which it imported rice and cotton goods. When gold was discovered in Australia, Mauritius began exporting European goods as well as sugar to Sydney and Melbourne, which led to some trade between the two countries. Conrad's *Otago*, for instance, carried a cargo of fertilizer as well as some soap and tallow to pay for the outward voyage. But Mauritian business inertia ensured that the sugar planters, who needed fertilizer for the sugar-cane plantations which covered most of the island's central plain, continued to import guano-fertilizer from Chile in great quantity and at vast expense. *Enc. Brit.*; Toussaint, p. 72.

22.18–19 **freight market** After 1858 maritime trade gradually declined until the end of the nineteenth century as sailing ships, unable to match the reliability and capacity of steam ships, gave way to them, especially after the opening in 1869 of the Suez Canal (Toussaint, pp. 72–4). By the time Conrad called at Port Louis, sail-freight was in serious difficulties. For his return to Melbourne he was forced to accept his cargo of 500 tons of sugar at the lowest freight rates. See 24.28n.

22.28 **Bay of Bengal** Also called a gulf (as at 28.16), the northern arm of the Indian Ocean, 500 fathoms (or 3,000 feet) in depth, bounded by Ceylon (Sri Lanka) and India to the west, Bengal (Bangladesh) to the north, and Burma (Myanmar) and Siam (Thailand) to the east (*Enc. Brit.*). The *Hilda* serves Mauritius' main markets (see 22.18–19n). See Map 1.

22.32–33 **the Cape – had her decks swept, and the**] S– the Cape – dec*s swept, **TS1t** the Cape – decks swept, **TS1r** the Cape – decks swep* **TS2** VAR **MS** In this further allusion to the Cape of Good Hope (see 16.9n), long known as the 'Cape of Storms', S's alterations elaborate an expansion Conrad had already made in *TSo* and confirmed in TS1r. For S's less fluid phrasing it is difficult to postulate a credible editorial motive. Similar alterations at 40.14–15 suggest that this phrasing represents Conrad's tweaking.

22.35 **cut up** British colloquialism for 'very distressed'.

23.30 **by contract** Under business agreement to supply a ship's needs – which rules out the possibility of shopping around on the part of the customer; hence the dismay of the competitors at 24.19–21.

23.35 **But I was not placated.**] **ED** It was a conciliatory whisper. But I was not placated. **MS** I was angry. **TS1t** I was not mollified. **TS1r TS2** I was not placated. **S–** Although TS1t's 'angry' could simply represent Jessie Conrad's further levelling of Conrad's diction, it finished off the more serious smoothing out of his pointed contrast between Jacobus' tempered (if not oily) demeanour and the Captain's less controlled reaction. The loss of MS's sentence resulted from eyeskip: 'It was a conciliatory whisper. But' occupies the line above 'I was not placated. The confounded' in the manuscript, and the physical similarity of the initial words apparently led her to skip to the second line while typing *TSo*. When thoroughly revising *TSo* Conrad compensated for this error by adding to the end of Jacobus' previous speech the words 'he breathed out quietly', employing what became a trope in the story. His later attempt to restore his negative phrasing when revising TS1 was not as successful. He did recover his adjective while summarily revising *TS3* a few months later, but not the crucial contrasting conjunction recording our Captain's confused reaction, the first, eventually, of three in the paragraph. See 'The Texts', pp. 239, 245.

24.22 **touts** Solicitors of custom. In *Lord Jim* touting for a ship chandler is presented as the worst of all possible employments. Alfred Jacobus does his own (see 23.23–28), which earns him social contempt (including from the Captain at 23.32) but also puts him beyond the competition of his rivals.

24.28 **consignees** As ship-master a captain is formally responsible for the merchandise he carries. His consignees are those to whom his consignment – the cargo entrusted to him – is to be delivered. When the consignees handle outgoing as well as incoming goods, they become the charterers, in which capacity they seek to hire space in ships at the lowest possible rates to themselves (24.35, 43.7–10). The Captain continues to refer casually to his consignees by that term even after they have become his charterers: see, for example, 44.10. See 19.33*n*.

25.32 **cemetery** Between 1769 and 1772 Port Louis's cemetery, which had become a source of infection in the town centre, was relocated to the district of Cassis, immediately west of the harbour. It included the cemeteries of Muslims as well as Christians, and, among the latter, of Anglicans, who had a cathedral in the privileged residential area. Ellis and Schuurman, p. 143.

25.35 **sea-dog** A sailor so conditioned by life on the old sailing ships that land has become foreign territory to him.

26.4 **chick** A term for 'child', often in alliterative combination with it, expressing endearment.

26.12 **that service** The reference is to 'The Order for the Burial of the Dead' of the Church of England's 1853 *Book of Common Prayer*, with excerpt from 1 Corinthians xv.51–5: 'Behold, I shew you a mystery; We shall not all sleep, but we shall all be changed, In a moment, in the twinkling of an eye, at the last trump: . . . O death, where is thy sting? O grave, where is thy victory?' See also 100.37*n*.

26.35 **side-whiskers** Hair on the side of the face, as opposed to the upper lip or the chin, was a Victorian fashion.

27.30–31 **sharp points of his archaic, gladstonian shirt collar** With flaring points rising just beyond the sides of the chin, and worn with a silk scarf or in a bow knot, this comfortable collar was associated for half a century with W. E. Gladstone (1809–98), four times Prime Minister under Queen Victoria. Its hey-day was during his first government, 1868–73. *Enc. Brit.*; R. Turner Wilcox, *Dictionary of Costume* (1969), pp. 80–81.

27.34–35 **panama hat** A wide-brimmed trilby-shaped, soft, pale, straw-coloured hat made of the leaves of the stemless screw-pine of tropical South America – not Panama, as its name suggests. It was much favoured by British planters and merchants east of Suez in the late nineteenth century. It should not be confused with the still more far-flung stiff straw 'boater'. *OED*.

28.2 **barque** Normally a three-masted sailing vessel, square-rigged on the fore and main masts, and fore-and-aft rigged on the mizzen mast. The fore-and-aft rigging (sails in line with the keel as opposed to at right angles with it) permits the barque to sail closer to the wind than the conventional square-rigged ship. Conrad's *Otago* was a small 367-ton barque, 147 by 14 feet, built in Glasgow in 1869 and used as a trading vessel until 1903. *Ships and the Sea*; *CEW*, p. 321. For an illustration, see Fig. 17.

28.8 **his figure-head**] MS the figure-head TS1t the figure-head of his ship TS1r– From the early nineteenth century the figure-head, which until then had represented a whole variety of creatures, became standardized as an ornamental carved and painted female forming a continuation of the stem below the bowsprit. In the early days of sea-going, figure-heads often expressed religious symbolism and the sense of a ship as a living thing. In Conrad's time, female figure-heads, often with bared breasts or arms, were supposed by some to be able to calm a storm at sea (*Ships and the Sea*). When Conrad added the phrase 'of his ship' in TS1, he was attempting to correct one of Jessie Conrad's typical graphic errors (cf. 31.19, 31.26), but the phrase failed to recover fully the sense of personal identification, potential in the symbol and essential to the episode, that he had captured in MS (cf. 28.12–13, 28.28–30).

28.13 **tone**] TS1r– talk MS tale TS1t Although TS1t's reading may be an error that prompted TS1r's alteration, it may also be part of Conrad's developing revision of this passage. The general direction of that revision in *TSo*, TS1, and for S is towards the manner of the speech, rather than its content. MS's 'talk' seems to have been superseded, not lost through a typing error generated partly by anticipation (see 28.13–15) and partly by graphic similarity.

28.28 **How could one care for it? What satisfaction?**] ED Who would care for it? What satisfaction . . . No. MS How could one care for it? TS1t What satisfaction? How could one care for it? TS1r– Although TS1t's 'How could one' presumably represents Conrad's revision in *TSo*, its loss of 'What satisfaction' looks like one of Jessie Conrad's frequent omissions in conjunction with revision. Conrad noticed this when reviewing TS1, but he did not fully recover MS's word order, which puts the emphasis on the *Hilda* captain's personal attachment as the likely reason for rejecting our Captain's suggestion. Cf. 28.8 and 28.8*n*.

28.38 **Procure . . . procure** In this context the idea of procurement acquires sexual overtones, as the reference to Alfred Jacobus as 'that figure-head procuring bloodsucker' (29.21–22) suggests.

29.8 **fiddle head** The stemhead of a vessel lacking a figurehead was often finished off by a curved scroll that resembled the end of a violin, or other bowed instrument (*Ships and the Sea*). The proposal to gild this abstract figurehead underlines its mere ornamentality.

29.18 **cut water** The forward edge of the stem or prow of a ship that divides the water; it often supported the figurehead in a ship fitted with one.

29.22 **old bird** Someone who has become knowing through experience (*OED*), often used playfully or affectionately, though with patronizing overtones.

29.24 **cuddy** Here, apparently, the officers' quarters as a whole. See 19.3*n*.

29.34 **lobby** A small apartment serving here as antechamber to the saloon. (See Fig. 20).

29.36 **togs** Humorous British public-school slang for 'clothes'.

30.2 **dodge** A clever trick or expedient (slang).

30.15 **rupee** The special 'colonial dollar' issued in 1820 by the Colonial Office for Mauritius was replaced in 1860 by the pound sterling which, in its turn, was replaced in 1876, twelve years before Conrad's visit to the island, by the Indian silver rupee on account of Mauritius' exceptionally strong trade links with India. See Toussaint, pp. 67–8.

31.22 **skylight** Rising slightly above the poop deck, the skylight was vulnerable to sea-water, as at 31.33–35. See 15.7*n* and Fig. 5.

31.23 **proper] MS** up **TS1–** The phrase 'fit up' does not occur in Conrad's other manuscripts. It looks like another one of Jessie Conrad's small normalizations (see 31.22).

31.24 **procure] TS1–** procure for **MS** Conrad uses both forms of this important verb, as a more complex instance of revision in TS1r shows (see 51.12). See 'procure you' (28.38*n*) as a foreshadowing of this statement.

32.17 **"store"** That is, his shop or retail outlet, though as will be seen it seems to resemble a small warehouse. The Captain's inverted commas (also at 24.26) signal the term's colonial status.

32.29 **deadly fever] TS1–** serious illness **MS** For Europeans in the tropics, a high temperature often indicated diseases such as typhoid, yellow fever, and malarial fever. TS1's phrase is a revision, made in *TSo*, for the typescript version but perpetuated through all the published texts despite their use of the serial version's opening and closing. The serial opening reverted to the MS phrase 'desperate illness at sea' (3:9); in the typescript's prologue this had become 'bad fever in the hospital' (13.26). Conrad failed to remove the anomaly when shortening the story for S and later did not reconcile the two passages when preparing copy for E1. Cf. 187.15*n*.

32.34–35 **Council . . . authorities** When the British Colonial Office assumed legal responsibility for Mauritius in 1815, it established a Council of Government composed of the Governor, the Chief Justice, the Chief Secretary, the Commanding Officer, and the Controller of Customs. In 1831 this Council was enlarged to include nominated notables from among the principal planters and businessmen. After 1884–5, shortly before Conrad's visit, the Council was divided into an Executive Council under a Prime Minister accountable to the Governor consisting of five officials, two of whom were elected, and a Legislative Council of twenty-seven members comprising eight ex-officio members, nine nominated by the Governor, and ten members elected on a moderate franchise (about 6,000 electors) with two representing Port Louis. The popular Ernest Jacobus who 'made himself objectionable to the authorities' and influenced public opinion (32.34–36) can legitimately be imagined to be one of the two elected Port Louis members. See *Enc. Brit.*; Toussaint, p. 68.

32.36 **A lot**] MS Lots **TS1**– TS1's construction (which may already have had petit-bourgeois associations by his time) appears to be his wife's, not Conrad's, who usually employs that of MS to refer to mankind; in fact, only one instance of his 'lots of people' occurs elsewhere (*The Rover*), whereas there are 'a lot' of people, policemen, and immigrants in, for instance, *Under Western Eyes* alone.

33.7 **business quarter** See 21.24*n*. In Ernest Jacobus, who does very little work and cares nothing for appearances, yet is sought after by the 'good society' that flocks to his week-end country-house parties, Conrad satirizes the extreme provincialism of Mauritius, especially amongst those at the top of an implacably stratified society that under nineteenth-century British rule remained an undisturbed survival from the *ancien régime* and was characterized by social complacency and intellectual stagnation. Conrad affords a glimpse of the effects of such a society (not unlike that of *apartheid* South Africa) on the colonist, but not on the colonized.

33.12 **inky** Ernest Jacobus' clerk might still be using a quill pen and an ink-well, which would explain the ink spots or stains. The 1899 *Notes and Queries* (9th Series, III, 365) records that 'quills as pens remained in use in some houses as the only writing tool up to a dozen to twenty years ago'. Alfred Jacobus' clerk, who carries his pen behind his ear (37.14), must have been using a pen with a steel nib.

33.30 **that boy**] MS this boy **TS1**– TS1t's phrase inappropriately shrinks the narrative distance (cf. 'that lad's' at 35.11) and is unprecedented in Conrad's manuscripts, in contrast to several instances of 'that boy', perhaps the best known occurring in *The Secret Agent* (e.g., 35.4, 50.3, 122.18–19).

33.36 **only gazed**] TS1r S gazed E1–, TS1t VAR OM MS E1's editor responded as Jessie Conrad probably did earlier to Conrad's use of 'only' in this sense (cf. 33.40, 35.26).

34.6–7 **he doubtless had been**] MS and had been clearly **TS1t** he had been doubtless **TS1r**– Conrad tends to place 'doubtless' before verbs and other clauses; TS1t's construction looks like one smoothed out by Jessie Conrad in two respects and corrected by Conrad in only one.

34.31–32 **I don't know him . . . gentleman** A play on the traditional belief that (to cite Shakespeare's formulation) 'the prince of darkness is a gentleman' (*King Lear* III.iv.148).

35.2 **mulatto lad**] S– mulatto MS youth **TS1t** yellow youth **TS1r** In revising the Pinker typescript, Conrad apparently decided to de-emphasize the lad's yellow colouring as such (see also 35.5, 35.18) and reverted to the less graphic description of MS.

35.35 **captain's**] TS1 captains MS captains' S– When not ambiguous as here, MS is uniform in using the singular in this context (24.25–26, 43.22, 58.23). S's forms here and later (43.22, 58.23) represent an editorial attempt, not altogether successful, to regularize the form.

35.39 **earthenware pitcher** In pre-refrigeration days, water was kept cool in slightly porous vessels which permitted evaporation. Conrad's prolonged visit to climatically sub-tropical Mauritius (30 September – 21 November 1888) had ended just as the season of oppressive heat (December to April) was beginning.

36.6 **moored far out** Despite the fact that by 1888 sail was being overtaken by steam, Mauritius adapted its harbour to steam-ships only at the end of the century. This meant that steamers, which displaced a much greater draught of water, could only anchor in the outer harbour, fortunately deep enough to take ships of any size. Toussaint, pp. 74–5.

36.15–16 **winked like a common mortal** A wink inviting or acknowledging con-nivance is regarded as undignified.

36.37 **manilla rope** The best rope was made of the hemp fibre furnished by the 'abaca' plant cultivated in Manila (Philippines). The thickness of the rope was expressed in terms of the size of the rope's circumference: the breaking strain of a 3-inch rope would have been 3 tons. *Ships and the Sea.*

36.39 **shackles** A U-shaped iron piece with the two open ends closed by a threaded pin. Shackles have various uses, including the securing of halyards (ropes for hoist-ing or lowering sails) or of other parts of the standing (i.e., fixed) and running (i.e., moveable) rigging. *Ships and the Sea.*

37.1–2 **fourteen pounds tobacco** An astounding amount for the cabin of a steamer, perhaps suggesting that the shameless purloiner of Jacobus' cigars has a serious addiction problem or is engaging in 'trade' of another kind.

37.7 **Samarang** Java's second port on the central northern coast (also spelled 'Semarang') was then, as now, a major commercial centre of the Dutch East Indies. See Map 4.

37.9 **Yorkshire Relish** A savoury sauce of great ancestry, it was served to travellers in British inns and post-houses as well as on ships.

37.26 **him that**] E1– him **MS** him loftily that **TS1 S** Although TS1's change very probably reflects Conrad's revision in *TSo*, E1's deletion apparently represents his later decision to downplay the Captain's supercilious or superior stance in two rounds of revision, both here when preparing the book texts, and at the end of the episode when revising the Pinker typescript for S (38.36). Despite its diminishing effect on the ironies of the Captain's conversation with the doctor, it more likely reflects Conrad's agency than two interventions by separate editors to the same end.

37.27 **spec.** A contraction of 'speculation' that had become a word in its own right by the early nineteenth century (*OED*).

38.16–17 **medical officer of the Port** Following the 1875 Parliamentary Public Health Act, it became accepted that every major port of the British Empire should have its own medical officer to control the risk of imported infectious diseases, and to attend to the illnesses of merchant seamen. In her autobiographical novel *Ultima Thule* (1929), for example, Henry Handel Richardson depicted her father as a Port Medical Officer in the Australia of the 1870s.

38.24 **prevented** That is, anticipated (from French 'prévenu'), one of many instances of Conrad's use of an English word in its root sense.

38.27 **at this juncture** At this convergence of information (*OED*) – i.e., the narrator's discovery that Jacobus has a daughter living with him, and his recollection of meeting Jacobus' son-in-law earlier.

38.34 **merely said** In the serial version, the narrator notes that Alfred Jacobus has applied the same phrase to his brother at 31.40 – which of course prompts the narrator's 'I found him a very different sort of person' at 38.37–38. See the variant at 38.34.

39.1–2 **beastly habits** Presumably an allusion to the brutal treatment of his half-caste son, though perhaps more generally to his animal behaviour as well.

39.4 **passage** Incident, interchange of communications, or altercation (literal or figurative), the last two senses being derived from the first (the archaic or obsolete) sense of the word. *OED*.

39.8 **A man I knew** 'My friend S—' (56.12), the 'eldest brother' (40.12) of the family that adopts the Captain. See 56.13–18. The family Conrad met in Mauritius was called Schmidt (see 'Introduction', pp. xlv–xlvii).

39.23–24 **old French families** From 1735 the dynamic governor de Labourdonnais introduced into the remote island, which he renamed 'Ile de France', some of the amenities of the *ancien régime*, including eighteenth-century-style architecture, botanical gardens, and cultural events. When, after the fall of Napoleon, the British assumed permanent possession of Mauritius, they allowed the population of French descent to preserve its laws, customs, language, religion, education, and property. This consolidated the cultural, economic, and administrative power of that insular and self-satisfied élite. Toussaint, pp. 29–31.

39.31 **households** The townhouse of the Schmidt family that Conrad knew (39.8*n*) was situated in the best part of Port Louis, on the corner of the rue de la Bourdonnais and the rue Saint-Georges, with a wide balcony overlooking the street. See Jean-Aubry, p. 42; his enquiries suggest that much of what happens in the tale is owed to the transforming powers of memory.

40.4–5 **pantaloons** This term combines the French for 'trousers' ('pantalons') with the English term for the early nineteenth-century trousers with straps passing underneath the boots which superseded knee-breeches (*OED*). It also evokes '*Pantalone*', the lean and doddering old man of Italian stage comedy, a tradition naturalized in French art and drama and familiar to the educated audiences of Conrad's day. 'Freya of the Seven Isles' also draws on this tradition (see, for example, 142.24*n*, 145.20*n*).

40.6 **a tragedy of Racine** The plays of France's greatest tragic dramatist (1639–99) are unrivalled for their fusion of noble elegance and ferocity of feeling.

40.9 **archaic French** The eighteenth-century French population of Mauritius, mostly immigrants from the western coasts of France, received scarcely any replenishment during the Revolutionary and the Napoleonic periods; and the British acquisition of the island after the Congress of Vienna served only to strengthen their insulation. By 1888 Conrad, who had perfected his French in Marseilles between 1874 and 1878, would have found the vernacular of the Mauritians 'quaint' indeed.

40.14 **nodded his head sagely**] TS1– waggled his head **MS** Conrad's 'waggled' would no doubt have occasioned a less happy alteration by Jessie Conrad had not Conrad himself revised it in *TSo*. Nodding and sage behaviour seem to be characteristic of the island's respectable society (e.g., at 41.10, 56.26), and TS1's words appear to be Conrad's, who had recently resorted to much nodding in *Under Western Eyes*.

40.26 **wandering circus** In early October while Conrad was in Mauritius, *Le Progrès Colonial* reported performances of a circus troupe 'de Natal' that included 'Mr and Mrs W. H. Wallett and 9 children', many of them apparently their own. Nineteenth-century circuses were nomadic tent-shows with acrobats, clowns, and trained animals. The most frequent origin of circus tours to the Mascarene Islands would probably have been the Western (Cape) Province of South Africa, to which Alfred Jacobus follows his 'lady-rider' (see 40.31). Popular in South Africa, the earliest and most famous circus, that of W. H. Bell, emerged in the 1870s; by the 1880s Teeley's, Wirth's, Cooke's, Val Simpson's, and Frank Fillis' were touring remote parts of southern Africa and Madagascar. See *The Standard Encyclopedia of South Africa* (1971), III, 239–40.

40.31 **Cape** The Cape Province of South Africa. See 16.9*n*, 40.26*n*.

40.38–40 **love-spell . . . of poems** The Captain is probably alluding to ancient and modern legends of men enslaved by sexual desire, or by magical agency associated with lust of one kind or another, including Homer's *Odyssey* (e.g., the legend of Circe), Shakespeare's *A Midsummer Night's Dream*, Milton's *Comus*, and similar man-beast episodes in Swift's *Gulliver's Travels* and Wells's *The Time Machine* and *The Island of Dr Moreau* (see Cedric Watts, 'The Narrative Enigma of Conrad's "A Smile of Fortune"', *Conradiana*, 17 (1985), 134–6). Perhaps a secondary allusion evokes the incandescent passion of Tristan and Isolde from its legendary origins in Thomas of Britain (*ca.* 1185) and its apogee in Gottfried von Strassburg (*ca.* 1210) to its afterlife in poems by Matthew Arnold (1852) and Swinburne (1882), though in this case the reference to 'moral fables' is unclear. The ultimate post-medieval version was Richard Wagner's 1859 opera, whose music pervades 'Freya of the Seven Isles' (see 'Introduction', p. lxi).

41.27 **mail-boat** In the mid nineteenth century, mail to and from Mauritius was assured by various regular sailings from Southampton to Australia via Cape Town, and in 1872 by the Union Castle Line with four-weekly sailings from Southampton via Cape Town, Colombo, Madagascar, Réunion, and Natal. There were also fortnightly sailings via the Suez Canal from Marseilles. Sir Evelyn Murray, *The Post Office* (1927), ch. 4.

41.35 **Sisters** The hospital they serve is a Roman Catholic foundation which prepares the souls of the dying ('*in extremis*') for salvation.

42.3–4 **put her hair up** In Conrad's day this would still have been said of a girl when she exchanged her 'floating hair or ringlets for the dressed hair of womanhood' (*OED*).

42.9–10 **gouvernante** Governess (French). Cf. 47.9*n*.

42.30 **come forward** Make an offer of marriage. In Alice's case the dowry would have had to be exceptional to attract a respectable suitor.

42.37 **fit in with**] **TS1**– fit with **MS** The phrase in MS is the only example in Conrad's manuscripts. TS1's successive prepositions are characteristic of Conrad, and this particular instance has at least one parallel (*Chance*, p. 308). TS1's reading probably represents a revision in *TSo*.

43.2 **chartered** See 19.33*n*.

43.2–3 **quick round voyage** The more quickly a ship is turned round, the lower the harbour fees and the higher the profits.

43.4–5 **pockete**] **TS1r** pockets **TS1t S**– OM **MS** TS1r's form, which Conrad deliberately substituted for a regularization made by Jessie Conrad that was later repeated by S's editor, suggests a semi-technical term with a French flavour. Although this might be the English word that derived through Anglo-Norman from the French word spelled 'pochette' (*OED*), it probably represents a word he heard in sugar-trading Mauritius – i.e., a French version ('poquettes') of the term used in South African trade for a sack or bag of varying sizes, and for various commodities, that a man could carry on his shoulders. The South African *Grahamstown Journal* of 20 September 1882 mentions '300 pockets sugar'. See William Branford, *A Dictionary of South African English* (1991), s.v. 'pocket'. Cf. *A Comprehensive Etymological Dictionary of the English Language* (1967), s.v. 'pocket'; *OED*, s.v. 'pocket'; *Concise Oxford French Dictionary* (1980), s.v. 'pochette'.

43.15–16 **charter-party** See 19.33*n*.

43.38–39 **Clarkson's Nerve Tonic** A patent medicine with an untraceable name probably as bogus as itself.

43.40 **loading** Cargo; a nautical term signifying 'that which is to be loaded'.

44.4 **quarter bags** A measure of capacity for grain, sugar, etc.; probably the modest capacity referred to in the sugar trade of neighbouring South Africa as 'pockets' (see 43.4–5*n*). The eight British Imperial bushels (an enormous sack) cited in the *OED* could not apply here.

44.12 **hung up** In nautical terms, delayed for an indefinite time.

45.5 **jalousies** This French word for angle-slatted shutters that exclude the sun or rain while admitting the light and the breeze evokes, like many other details of the house, the French legacy in Mauritius.

45.8 **on the latch** A British phrase indicating the door was unlocked; a latch fastens a door (say, against the wind), but allows it to be opened freely from the outside.

45.12–13 **verandah or rather loggia** The distinction between a verandah (Spanish) and a loggia (Italian) is not hard-and-fast; but the loggia usually has rounded arches and tends to serve as an extension to the house rather than as a passage from the house to the garden.

46.14–15 **nothing but to look at** A Gallicism, perhaps induced by the episode's dependence on Maupassant (see pp. xlviii–xlix).

47.9 **the companion, the gouvernante** Cf. 42.9–10*n*. This 'stumpy old woman' (47.12) apparently fills the role of the 'duenna', the elderly lady charged with guarding the chastity of the girls of Spanish families. The duenna is also the crone of folk-tale who functions to bring out by contrast her charge's youth and beauty.

47.25 **posed on** That is, placed on, a Gallicism ('poser sur'); the French phrase would not signal striking a pose.

47.31 **C'est Papa** It's daddy (French).

48.14 **natural, rough wines** An allusion to simple country wines, what the French call 'vin du pays'.

49.20 *that* The reference to Alice as 'that thing' represents an approximation in English of the contemptuous French *ça*.

49.24 **Old sorceress** Literal equivalent of the French colloquialism 'vieille sorcière' ('old witch' or 'old bag'). See 50.1 *n*.

49.26 **the quarrel . . . pot** An English imitation of the French literal rendering of the English proverb 'the pot calling the kettle black'.

50.1 **Look at that now** A literal rendering of 'voyez donc ça' (French). Addressed to Alice, 'that' ('ça') refers contemptuously to the Captain, or to his words, as if he were not present. Perhaps this suggests reaction to a connotation of the word 'bags', used in its contemptuous slang sense, as early as 1880s, for 'women', especially a 'middle-aged or elderly slattern'. See Eric Partridge, *A Dictionary of Slang and Unconventional English* (1970).

50.6 **pretty** Literal equivalent of the French colloquial 'joli', though applied (as often in French) with a touch of irony.

50.8 **my good fellow** Literal translation of the contemptuously patronizing French phrase 'mon bonhomme'.

51.10 **the S— family** See 39.8*n*.

52.1 **blue** Indecent, obscene (colloquial).

52.22–23 **fourteen hundred** The discrepancy with the original 'eleven hundred' (44.4) is probably an authorial slip of no significance.

52.39–40 **something to tell him of** The 'something' remains indefinite throughout the story, consistent with Jacobus' inscrutability; but it hints at 'shady' dealings, perhaps even blackmail, as the last words on the deal (55.27–28) may also suggest.

53.7 **a brick** A public-school term for 'good fellow', suggesting reliability and loyalty.

54.9 **There's plenty of rooms**] TS1t S There's plenty rooms **TS1r** There are plenty of rooms **E1–** OM MS As in both TS1r and in TS1t and S, Conrad uses 'plenty' in colloquial constructions ('plenty of time', 'plenty of money', and 'plenty of room'). TS1r's construction, which results from a deliberate blotting of TS1t's 'of' in a line containing one smaller change, has a few rough parallels elsewhere (e.g., 'An Outpost of Progress', p. 102). In his manuscripts singular verbs, as in TS1t and S, occur in phrases with plural nouns (e.g., *The Nigger of the 'Narcissus'*, p. 108; *The Rescue*, MS, Part I, ch. 2, p. 38, Part II, ch. 5, p. 69), as do of course plural verbs, as in E1 (e.g., *The Rescue*, MS, Part I, ch. 2, p. 60; *The Shadow-Line*, p. 10). The reading of TS1t and S probably represents Conrad's identical revision in both *TSo* and the Pinker typescript, whereas E1's plural is more likely an editorial normalization.

54.24 **piped out** That is, 'piped up': spoke out impudently.

54.32 **parted on the side** Victorian women favoured a middle parting or none at all.

55.6 **murmured]** TS1– muttered **MS** Conrad moved from MS's 'mutter' and other verbs to 'murmur' repeatedly in *TSo* (18.36, 31.31, 36.10; cf. 51.5). The word seems eminently appropriate for Jacobus' placid but tenacious manner: see the reference to his 'mumble' (69.16).

55.35 **I perceived that I]** TS1 S I **MS** E1– This looks like one of the rare instances of substantial error in the typesetting of E1, occasioned by eyeskip and involving a phrase that may have appeared unnecessary. Nonetheless, the phrase is one Conrad added deliberately in *TSo*, perhaps to emphasize the Captain's awareness of his situation (see 'I noticed', 56.2); Conrad's other reversions to MS readings in E1 are not of this nature. See 'The Texts', pp. 248–9.

56.7–8 **niggers on the quays** The stevedores of Port Louis were descendants of the slaves from Africa liberated in 1835 (see 22.18n). The term 'nigger' was a familiar, if not contemptuous, form of 'negro' current throughout the nineteenth century; in nautical and commercial contexts it sometimes indicated hard-working. *OED*.

56.34–35 **S— family . . . D— family** For the former, see 39.8n. The latter, which appears only here, has no identified source.

58.17–18 **older than the French** See 18.36n.

58.19 **the last Dodo** An extinct bird family once found only in the Mascarene islands. The grey dodo, exclusive to Mauritius, was a large flightless bird with feet like a hen, a very large round body, short neck, and massive beak. Having evolved in a benign environment, it had no defences against humans and imported animals, and as a species did not survive the seventeenth century. The neighbouring islands of Réunion and Rodrigues were the habitat, respectively, of the white dodo and of the 'solitaire', shaped like a goose. *Enc. Brit.*; Toussaint, pp. 7–8 and illustrations.

58.30 **Paris and London** Newspapers from these cities, presumably destined for the white élite, arrived in Mauritius regularly, though Jacobus procures those from 'all parts of the world' (35.40–36.1; also 41.27n, 59.11–14). In the early 1830s the colony's first independent newspaper, *Le Cernéen*, founded by an energetic liberal member of the Council (Adrien d'Epinay) who had persuaded the Colonial Office to legislate for press freedom, provided serious local news. See Toussaint, p. 68.

58.35–36 **imported coolie labourers . . . negroes of the town** Under an indenture system (22.18n) in the Mauritius of the 1880s, 'coolies' – the 'name given by Europeans in India and China to a native hired labourer or burden-carrier' and also 'in other countries where these men are employed as cheap labourers' (*OED*) – lived with their families all the year round on the plantations. The 'negroes', descendants of the African slaves that had worked the sugar plantations up to the 1830s, provided cheap labour in the towns, whether as domestic servants, boatmen, or stevedores.

60.17–18 **staring . . . in some far off mirror** To readers of Conrad's time this might have suggested some sort of Arthurian spell, like the enchantment which destroys Tennyson's Lady of Shallott.

61.19 **business** A particular matter demanding attention or a commercial transaction.

62.7 **sallies** Sudden swerves from the bounds of propriety (*OED*); also sorties or attacks, including verbal ones.

64.21 **cynical** In the sense of 'I don't care what *you* think': contemptuous of the conventions of considerateness regulating the social intercourse of human beings.

64.28–29 **from her**] TS1 of her S– OM MS S's form is not Conrad's, who uses 'of' with the phrase 'within a foot' but 'from' with 'less than a foot'.

66.19 **fined down** Purified, refined.

67.7 **gazed persistently at**] MS stared persistently on TS1 S gazed persistently on E1– E1's phrasing is uncharacteristic of Conrad. In his manuscripts he distinguishes between the prepositions he uses with 'gaze' as noun and verb. For the verb the dominant preposition is 'at', along with 'into', 'toward', and so on; virtually never does one gaze 'on' anything, and only rarely 'upon' something. Thus the phrase 'gaze down at' is prevalent, 'gaze down upon' infrequent. On the other hand, for the noun the dominant preposition is 'on', along with 'into', 'toward', and so on; virtually never is a gaze directed 'at' anything, only rarely 'upon' something. This distinction is so stark that we can confidently reject E1's phrase as an erroneous confounding of MS's and of TS1's, which itself probably reflects Jessie Conrad's own wording.

67.14 **glazed kid** Kid-skin leather given a smooth polished finish, in this case dyed grey-blue.

68.16 **without**] E1– but without TS1 S VAR MS The loss of TS1's 'but' with its possible play on the root meaning of 'wink' looks unfortunate, but Conrad's revision of a nearby word in the copy for E1 (see 68.16) suggests he altered this word as well.

68.34 **haven't got**] TS1– haven't MS TS1's phrase is unlikely to be an error of Jessie Conrad's, who rarely adds words or lowers tone. Rather, Conrad seems to be marking the transition from the Captain's previous high tone to the more subservient one appropriate to his growing sense of humiliation.

69.24 **lighter** A flat-bottomed barge used in 'lightening' or unloading (or sometimes loading) ships. In 1888 Port Louis's inner harbour not only had quays, but also berths 'within a long stone's throw from the quay' where the Captain's ship was moored (see 18.17–18). Lighters would therefore be needed to shift the cargo.

71.38–39 **emptiness in all things under heaven** 'I have seen all the works that are done under the sun; and, behold, all is vanity and vexation of spirit' (Ecclesiastes i.14).

73.9 **mountain on the south** Signal Mountain rises to 1,000 feet about one mile south of the harbour.

73.15 **after hatch** The after-hold, accessed through the after-hatchway. The term 'hatch' is used indifferently for the trapdoor and for the opening. *Ships and the Sea.*

73.17 **hoist in** To convey into the hold by means of block and tackle.

73.35 **stern-fasts** Here, ropes (or tackle) by which a vessel's stern is moored. *OED*; *Ships and the Sea.*

73.36 **buoys** A reference either to floating markers showing the course a ship should take, or to mooring buoys to which the stern-fasts led.

73.39 **thwarts** The rowing benches across a boat.

74.23 **with a vengeance** Used (a) as an intensifier, (b) as a means of revenge (by reminding the Captain of his folly).

74.32–33 **satanic refinement . . . smell** One of the Devil's attributes is the stink he emits.

74.34 **poop** The raised after-deck which also forms the 'roof' of the officers' quarters. It is from there that the captain generally runs the ship, since, without losing sight forward, he remains close to the helm, aft of the poop.

74.38 **batten** To fasten down with battens – strips of wood used to hold down the edges of the tarpaulin fixed over the 'hatchways' (see 73.15n) in order to keep out water in bad weather.

75.14 **Port-Philip Heads** The two headlands forming the entrance to Port Phillip Bay, the large enclosed body of water twenty miles across, at the head of which the city of Melbourne is situated.

75.32 **Colony** In 1888–9 the state of Victoria with Melbourne as its capital was still a colony directly under British rule. Confederation of the separate Australian colonies did not come until a constitution, drafted in 1897–8, was approved by the British Parliament in 1901.

75.33 **unparalleled drought** In 1888 New South Wales and Victoria experienced a prolonged drought, 'the worst recorded to date'. On 1 December 1888, the press commented: 'In all directions the long-confirmed dry weather has given rise to apprehension of a scarcity of food products during the next few months. The welcome change will mitigate the alarming character of the future outlook.' The drought, which was most severe in Victoria, broke at the end of November. J. C. Foley, *Droughts in Australia: Review of Records from Earliest Years of Settlement to 1955* (1957), p. 20.

75.34 **root crops** Vegetables, such as beets, parsnips, turnips, radishes, carrots, whose roots are edible.

76.4 **Custom-House galley** This 'galley' was a large open rowing-boat. Formerly used on the Thames by custom-house officials (*OED*), it became the generic name for customs boats in the British colonies directly ruled from London.

76.11 **ship-broker's** Mercantile agent who transacts a ship's business when it is in port.

76.23 **coster** A costermonger: one who sells fruit and vegetables from a barrow.

77.3–4 **extremely unpleasant**] TS1t S– unrefreshing MS extremely pleasant TS1r The affix 'un' is typed at the right margin in TS1, and Conrad has blotted it, as he has several other instances of two such characters on the generally correct assumption that they represent false beginnings of the next words, associated perhaps with the mechanical shortcomings of Jessie Conrad's typewriter. Although this alteration might represent Conrad's conscious decision to create heavy irony, that effect would have been better suited to the Captain's attitude before his humiliation, than to the tone prevalent here. TS1r's change looks like a misguided though half-deliberate mistake that Conrad corrected in S.

77.33 **Suez Canal** Over 100 miles long, Europe's short-cut to the East had been constructed between 1859 and 1869. Until 1888, however, steamers could only proceed during daylight, at 5 miles per hour.

78.4 **Fortune**] **TS1** fortune **MS S**– Although TS1's form might represent Jessie Conrad's amendment of MS's, the typescript's reference to the fickle lady is compatible with its other variant readings in surrounding paragraphs and is probably part of Conrad's revised version of the ending. (See the variants at 78.3, 78.4, 78.6–8.) In the serial version (represented in MS and S), the misunderstanding between the Captain and Burns is shown in the dialogue – in the mate's mistakenly taking the Captain's 'fortune' to mean 'luck' (78.9), and in his speeches on the potato deal. This dialogue undercuts, or at least qualifies, the Captain's assertions in the narrative about the cessation of their disagreements over his luck and his attachment to the ship and the sea – topics not developed in the serial version's truncated prologue. In the shorter, typescript version of the ending, where the mental chasm between Captain and mate is at least as wide, only the narrative reveals Burns's preoccupation with the commercial aspect of the affair, while his response to the Captain's reference to 'Fortune' and his other speeches focus narrowly on the question of luck, without any understanding of the Captain's loss of his romantic hopes and illusions about sea life – issues that are more fully developed in the typescript's revised prologue (see pp. 236–7). Such carefully orchestrated differences between the two versions betray the author's hand.

The Secret Sharer

MS   holograph manuscript (Berg): copy-text
S   *Harper's Monthly Magazine*, August, September 1910,
           pp. 349–59, 530–41

81.2–82.23 **On my right hand . . . poop deck** The spatial organization of this scene remains unaltered until 106.16 – about three-fifths of the tale. The Captain is standing on the deck of his southward-heading ship, facing the sunset (81.11, 82.1–3). His view is unencumbered, so he must be on the starboard rail (82.17–18) of the poop deck (see 82.21–23). Looking to his right (i.e., north) he sees fishing stakes; to his left (south) he sees barren islets resembling ruined fortifications. Looking right again (81.13–14) he sees the disappearing tug-boat, the shore meeting the sea, the trees marking the mouth of the river, and the occasional silvery gleams of its windings. Given his easy visual command of the half-circumference just described, the ship, on a north–south axis, is probably slightly east of the line to the river's mouth (and thus east of the actual, circumscribed anchorage). As the sun sinks below the horizon, the Captain, looking south again, sees the fading light catch 'something' (82.14) behind the islets, which he soon identifies as an anchored ship (82.27).

The relative distances (which vary somewhat from the actual ones) turn out to be much more extensive than a casual reading might suggest. Captain Archbold will inform our Captain that 'the main land is at least seven miles off my anchorage'

(102.7–8) – thus increasing the 'five miles' that Leggatt who, just escaped from a long period under lock and key, will estimate in his conversation with the Captain (93.14). We will also learn that Archbold's ship is at most two miles from the Captain's (the maximum in fact possible): 'I had no more than a two mile pull to your ship' (102.34). By these calculations the Captain's ship would be anchored five miles (actually, over six nautical miles) south of the river-mouth, and about seven (in fact, almost ten) miles from the Paknam pagoda (81.23, 81.33), which would probably have been invisible (Larabee, p. 352). About thirteen miles inland as the crow flies – that is, eighteen miles from the anchored barque – Bangkok is quite out of sight.

81.2 **fishing stakes** Secured on the shallow bottom and fully revealed at low tide, these stakes hold conical or 'gill' nets out of which the trapped fish would be collected at intervals. Stape (p. 5) quotes a guide to Bangkok of 1894 – 'The inner part of the bar commences at about one third of a mile southward of the fishing stakes' – and refers to three other contemporary allusions to them.

81.5 **crazy** Without any discernible order, as in 'crazy quilt'.

81.6 **brown fishermen**] MS fishermen S– That is, fishermen of the eastern seas; cf. Hugh Clifford's *Studies in Brown Humanity* (1898), reviewed by Conrad under the title 'An Observer in Malaya' in *Notes on Life and Letters*, ed. J. H. Stape with Andrew Busza (2004), pp. 50–52. For reasons associated with its negative connotations in America, and actually irrelevant in this context, S's editor deleted a word that Conrad had deliberately added in the margin of MS not only to locate the setting of his story immediately, but also to construct the image of a uniformly 'monotonous' (81.24) landscape, 'half brown, half blue' (81.16–17). Revisions in both MS and the lost typescript, including the rewriting of 'blue sea' (81.10) in MS and deletions for S (81.15, 81.21), suggest the importance of this image to Conrad. It is unlikely he would have cut this opening instance. See 81.6*n*.

81.6 **removed**] MS gone S– The fishermen have changed habitation (US 'moved'), 'abandoned' their home and work-place, cleared out (cf. 'Heart of Darkness', p. 70). Faced with MS's British usage, uncommon in America (according to the *OED*) and in the context likely to confuse most *Harper's* readers, S's editor replaced it with a banal word that Conrad hardly ever uses in this sense, rarely asks to carry this much weight or force, and is unlikely to have substituted here. The probable association of MS's word with 'the Trail of Tears', especially in the presence of 'brown' (81.6*n*), might have been enough to require its excision by S's careful editor, as Gene M. Moore has suggested. Since Andrew Jackson had proclaimed his policy of relocating the Cherokee and other native tribes from America's southeast to its more arid interior, 'remove' and its various forms had recurred as a quasi-technical term in discussions of American Indian policy throughout the nineteenth century; it had appeared even as late as 1906, when it figured prominently in the chapter on 'Indian Affairs' in William MacDonald's *Jacksonian Democracy: 1829–1837*, published by Harpers. See also, for example, Harpers' *A Century of Dishonor*, by H. H. (1881), pp. 14, 284–5.

81.7 **earth**] MS ocean S– Cf. the Biblical echo '"Driven off the face of the earth"' (111.4–5) and the closer references to the 'impassive earth' and 'shadowy earth' (81.29, 82.16–17). The area occupied by the ship and, earlier, the fishermen is a gulf surrounded on three sides by land masses, and on its fourth by islands, not vast open waters. S's word reflects a strange sort of literalism seen elsewhere in its editor's work, here perhaps motivated by the simple notion that fishermen primarily inhabit waters, not land. But his word is not Conrad's, who consistently eschews it, referring to the waters of the area as seas not oceans – a word he generally restricts to proper names (e.g., Indian Ocean, 84.27) or to phrases ('drop in the ocean') and in any case uses sparingly (thirty times less frequently than 'sea') and with particular connotations not appropriate here. Together with its previous substitution (81.6), the magazine's word cancels what is arguably the manuscript's first adumbration of the Cain motif. Conrad did not write it. Cf. the subtitle 'An Episode from the Sea' printed in S, the wording of MS at 87.10–11, and 82.3n.

81.8 **my**] MS the S– S's neutral word is more likely to reflect a typist's misconstruction of MS's indistinct inscription or confusion occasioned by an interlined addition in the lost typescript, rather than a decision by Conrad to scuttle the rhetorical link with the first sentence and to alter, however slightly, narrative perspective.

81.13 **tug** These steam-driven boats towed sailing ships into and out of ports that were difficult for them to reach without assistance. According to Allen (p. 248), they were required for navigating the Meinam, as Conrad would have known from his experience in the *Otago*. See 81.20n. Cf. Port Louis and Port Phillip Bay in 'A Smile of Fortune'.

81.14 **bar** The bank of sand or silt across the mouth of the river, which impeded navigation, had been portrayed in travel accounts and navigational guides since the 1870s as unusually hazardous. See Larabee (p. 351) and Stape (p. 5). See also 81.2n.

81.20 **Meinam** The broad shallow river, known to nineteenth- and early twentieth-century Western merchants and travellers as the Meinam or Menam – the Siamese (Thai) word for 'mother water' or 'main river' – and today as the Chao Phraya, provided navigable access to Bangkok (Krung Thep in Thai). But the way, though broad, was difficult and, with its shifting sands and elaborately winding course, virtually impossible for sizable sailing ships to negotiate (see 81.13n). In his manuscript Conrad identified this river with a similar one, the 'Mekong', which dominates the eastern peninsula framing the gulf where the Captain's ship will languish. See *Enc. Brit.*, s.v. 'Menam'. See Map 4.

81.23 **Paknam pagoda** About three miles up the mouth of the Meinam lay a low mud island, now silted into a peninsula, the site of an impressive Buddhist temple (pagoda), and on the river-bank the village of Paknam together with military fortifications in disrepair. In Siam (Thailand) a pagoda might take various forms, but rarely in the Chinese style of super-imposed roofed stories. To judge from contemporary photographs, the 'Great Pagoda' (81.33) at Paknam, which is still standing, was a dazzling spire broad-set at the base and soaring into a high convex needle. One function of these structures was to represent 'the intersection between the human and upper worlds' (Stape, p. 6).

81.33 **mitre-shaped hill** In most Western churches the bishop's 'mitre' has the form of a tall pointed cleft cap. This bears no resemblance to the pagoda described above. Conrad, however, is evoking the effect of seven miles' distance (see 81.2n), which turns pagoda and grove into 'a larger and loftier mass' (81.22). In fact, the pagoda would probably have been invisible from the actual anchorage south of the Meinam's bar, and no grove surrounded it (see Larabee, pp. 352, 366, n. 20).

81.34 **Gulf of Siam** See Maps 3 and 4.

82.1 **long journey** The return voyage to England is later estimated to last 'three months at the very least' (90.36) and described as a passage 'out through the Malay Archipelago, down the Indian Ocean and up the Atlantic' (84.27–28). The *Sephora*, dogged by various retardations, took 123 days from Cardiff – over four months (83.31–32). See Maps 1 and 4.

82.3 **eastward]** S– East MS The awkward idiom that results from S's change suggests Conrad rather than the precise editor of *Harper's*, who is more likely to have produced something like 'far eastward' instead of the technically redundant compromise it prints. The substitution helps diminish MS's echo of the famous phrase in Genesis iv.16 that concludes the narrative of Cain's banishment, which here Conrad associates not with the ship but with the fishermen that have abandoned their traditional harvest ground (see 81.6–7), though a more important association is to follow.

82.16 **tropical suddenness** Twilight is shorter at the equator, where the sun's descent to the horizon is more vertical than outside the tropics. Nautical twilight ends when the sun is 12 degrees below the horizon and a sextant user can no longer see a line dividing sea and sky. See *Almayer's Folly*, ed. David Leon Higdon and Floyd Eugene Eddleman (1994), 11.11n.

82.39 **hands forward** The ship's crew whose living space is the forecastle, in contrast to that of the officers, which is aft under the poop deck. *Ships and the Sea.*

83.25 **drew too much water** That is, displaced too much water – over twenty feet, we learn at 83.30, and 'a deep ship' according to Leggatt at 89.14 and 92.10 – because she is carrying coal (83.31). The draught of a vessel varies with its size and loading. British merchant ships were equipped with draught figures painted on the sides of the stem and the stern. Maximum draught occurred when, as the loading ship sank into the water, it submerged the 'Plimsoll' mark or line amidships, so-called after the man who drove the 1846 law restraining the practice of overloading through Parliament. See *Ships and the Sea*, s.v. 'deep', and *Literature and the Lore of the Sea*, ed. Patricia Ann Carlson (1986), pp. 75–7.

83.28 **open roadstead** A roadstead is a place where ships may safely and conveniently lie at anchor near shore (*OED*). An 'open' roadstead, unlike a 'protected' one (such as the *Sephora*'s, presumably adjacent to islands), permits unhampered departure as soon as the wind rises. The anchorage at the mouth of Bangkok's Meinam was actually quite restricted and occupied by at least four islands (see Larabee, pp. 352–3).

84.5 **anchor watch** Usually set when there was a chance of the anchor dragging, this watch involved an officer taking compass bearings of objects on shore to determine whether the ship was moving, with a few or more 'hands forward' (82.39) on call to work the anchor. This procedure could deprive at least a quarter of such a ship's company of sleep.

84.8 **turn out** Cf. 'turn in' (84.4).

84.11–12 **Outside the cuddy** The phrase suggests that the second mate's door opens onto a passageway off the saloon, as in the *Cutty Sark*. Conrad's later sketch of the officers' quarters (Fig. 18) can be reconciled with this idea; see the conjectured 'Plan of the Officers' Quarters', Fig. 20.

84.22 **shore**] MS unrelated shore **S**– Although S's addition might be a deliberate repetition on Conrad's part for sonic or thematic effect, it is more likely an instance of recollection from the previous manuscript line by a typist, or by a compositor. The heavy-handed irony seems out of character for the Captain, especially when Conrad is, if anything, toning down disturbing elements (cf. 81.15, 81.21, 81.27, 81.28, 81.30, 84.36n, 85.14) and where he is not otherwise revising.

84.36 **went**] **S**– ran **MS** S's nautical idiom, though possibly traceable to its editor's effort to clarify physical movements aboard ship, indicates that 'went' is probably the first of several substitutions of this kind made by Conrad. MS's word suggests a haste or violence contrary to the air of calm and quiet that Conrad is creating just before the disconcerting arrival of Leggatt (cf. 87.20). It also suggests easy access to the cuddy from the main deck, contrary to the implications of Leggatt's eventual escape route and of readings elsewhere (see 84.38n): no one can literally run below, because he must take steps up to the poop from the main deck and down from it through the companionway into the cuddy. The Captain later rejects a similar scheme at a critical moment on similar grounds (118.17–18).

84.38 **out**] **MS** out again **S**– The Captain has been on the poop (84.25) and in the waist (84.26), but not on the quarter-deck as such except on his way 'below'; there is therefore no reason to be emphatic about his return to the quarter-deck. S's reading is one of its several misguided attempts to clarify movements aboard ship. MS's is much more straightforward, emphasizing the Captain's general tour of the ship, about to be continued as he goes to the 'fore-end' and passes the 'forecastle' (85.1). After Leggatt's arrival Conrad wrote again of the Captain 'coming back on deck' (87.28), having already paused at 'the foot of the stairs' before entering the saloon through the lobby (87.22–23), but he later revised 'out' to 'back' because there the Captain was returning to the spot he had left. Cf. 103.25n and 108.32n.

84.38 **sleeping suit** A two-piece night-wear – as opposed to the night-gown worn by men up to the end of the nineteenth century and beyond. At the end of that century, the Persian word 'pyjama' was correctly reserved for loose drawers or trousers of silk or cotton worn by both sexes in Muslim countries. *OED*.

85.8 **riding light in the forerigging** A ship which displays a white light in its forward rigging announces that it is at anchor ('riding'). At night, a ship's size, status (e.g., sail- or steam-driven), and function (e.g., towing, carrying passengers) is indicated by the position and colour of the lights it displays. *Ships and the Sea*.

85.27 **inboard**] **MS** on board **S**– S's 'on' is probably its normalization of MS's nautically correct form (perhaps transcribed by the typist as two words), for the 'board' in question is the ship's hull and bulwarks, and not, as sometimes supposed, its deck (*OED*). Although the *Sephora*'s captain properly associates 'on board' with persons present 'in ... ship' (100.21–22), the decisive factor here is the context, our Captain's use of 'get ... in' and 'comes in' (85.25, 85.26) to refer to the action and the ladder.

85.37 **summer lightning** Sheet lightning without audible thunder, often seen at sea, and also on land, in hot weather. See 156.6.

85.40 **cadaveric** Cadaverous (Gallicism), alluding to the greenish pallor of a corpse.

86.10 **spare spar** These 'poles' (92.11) were lashed along the quarter or forward decks as potential replacements for rigging supports (e.g., yards, booms) damaged in use. *Ships and the Sea.*

86.21 **I say** An English public-school expression used as an intensifier and denoting social cachet. Leggatt's background is here distinguished, on the one hand, from common local schooling and, on the other, from the even more exclusive 'private' education provided by a live-in tutor. Other instances of prestige vocabulary associated with Leggatt include 'my man' (86.37), 'By Jove' (87.1, 92.23), 'chucked him aside' (92.24), 'old humbug' (92.33), and 'Fancy' (95.12).

87.2 **water**] **MS** the water **S**– The added 'the' seems to be a recollection, by typist or compositor, of the same phrase just above (87.1).

87.6 **induced**] **S**– produced **MS** This change apparently extends a process evidenced in MS, where Conrad first wrote 'affected' before cancelling it and substituting 'produced'. S's word, suggesting the drawing out of something within the Captain, instead of something acting upon him from without, seems to come from Conrad, rather than an editor, who is unlikely to have substituted this less obvious word for MS's. Indeed, the context requires the less usual sense of 'induced' – a sense that has precedence elsewhere in Conrad's manuscripts and typescripts, though the more common usage that takes a person as its object, rather than (as here) a state of feeling, is frequent in Conrad and is indeed the one an editor aiming for comprehensibility would probably have hoped to elicit. See *Nostromo*, p. 152; *The Secret Agent*, 41.19; 'Freya of the Seven Isles', 131.4; *The Rescue*, p. 151.

87.9 **since nine o'clock** The Captain took over the watch around 8 p.m. (84.5–6, 84.13); given the distances involved, Leggatt must have been swimming, on-and-off, about an hour and a half and would therefore have been rescued at about 10:30 p.m. The Captain's account of his own actions implies a briefer time between the commencement of his watch and the discovery of Leggatt.

87.14 **could tell by**] **MS** should have gathered from **S**– Both diction and context suggest that S's phrasing is editorial intrusion. For the paragraph to have any coherence with S's new phrasing, the emphasis must fall on 'gathered', a word Conrad used in this figurative sense only once before he revised 'A Smile of Fortune' (52.15–16) in 1910 and only once thereafter ('Poland Revisited', *Notes on Life and Letters*, 123.9). In his manuscripts, 'gather' in its various forms generally has the literal sense of collecting things together, as with all five instances in *Almayer's Folly* (written 1889–94) and all eleven in *Under Western Eyes* (1908–10). His only use of the word in association with mental activity before 'A Smile of Fortune' was in 1898 ('Heart of Darkness', p. 74), where it has the almost literal sense of collecting impressions, not sorting out a meaning. S's reading indicates the Captain did not instantly perceive that Leggatt was young. However, in MS Conrad temporarily put aside the flat statement 'He was young too' in order to show how the Captain immediately reached this conclusion, not through reason – that is at work in the second clause ('indeed ... issues'), which is retrospective – but by 'intuition', thus making 'it' (87.16) refer to his ability to 'tell'. The point is elaborated in the next sentence and then extended to the following one, which insists on the sympathetic understanding between the two young men and leads naturally into 'I was young too' – phrasing that Conrad had postponed in MS so as to develop the idea of immediate mental identification. Fracturing this seamless argument, S's alteration makes all this nonsensical, shifts the reference of 'it' back to the first sentence ('I felt ... strong soul.'), stresses the Captain's feeling yet dismisses his discernment of Leggatt's 'youth', and thus makes the progression of thought less coherent and the sentence 'I was ... make no comment.' a mere rhetorical flourish. Cf. 105.16 for similar editorial misunderstanding, 95.12 for similar intrusion, and 86.26–27 for another instance of the Captain's intuition, just confirmed.

87.24 **the hook** A long hook and eye would hold a door ajar without its swinging and banging.

87.29 **main hatch** The hatch over the hold that was under the main deck, usually located amidships.

87.30–31 **In a moment he had concealed his damp body**] S– He was clothed in a moment **MS** S's addition particularizes the action in a way it is hard to imagine its editor emphasizing. The image of concealment now anticipates the notion of secrecy which Conrad had begun to develop later in the story when writing the manuscript but which, when he came to revise the typescript, he introduced at this earlier point.

87.33 **right aft** To the wheel and compass at the stern of the vessel. The poop deck, which incorporates the roof over the saloon and other officers' quarters, rises at its forward end about four steps from the quarter-deck and reaches all the way aft, beyond the rear of the cuddy, the binnacle (87.36n), and the wheel, which is linked to the rudder below it. See Figs. 5, 6, 20.

87.36 **binnacle** Housing for the compass, its correctors, and its lighting arrangements. The term is derived from the Italian 'abitacola' (little house) used by the early Portuguese navigators for this housing. *Ships and the Sea.*

88.17 **Thirty nine south** A likely location for the incident is the northern edge of the 'roaring forties', south of the Cape of Good Hope; as we will learn, Leggatt had been under arrest for 'six weeks' (91.25n) when the *Sephora* reached the Sunda Straits (92.15n), and for 'nine weeks' (95.15) by the time she anchored at the head of the Gulf of Siam. Conrad seems to be thinking here of the *Cutty Sark* and the 'manslaughter' (the court's eventual finding against her mate) that occurred in that ship, which like the *Sephora* was loaded with coal from Cardiff, though bound for Yokohama. See Maps 1 and 4, and pp. xxxvi–xxxix.

88.24 *Conway* Founded in 1856 on the wide Mersey waterway as a floating boarding-school, this ship trained boys of, on average, fifteen to seventeen years of age 'to become officers in the Merchant Service'. The Captain-narrator is 'a couple of years older' than Leggatt and had left her before Leggatt joined (88.28–29). This shared history, given the institutional bond generated by student life at what was a version of an English public school, is an element in the feeling of solidarity that develops between the two. The testimonials collected by John Masefield confirm that the ship had the mores of a nineteenth-century boarding-school, except that life was based upon the routines of a sailing ship and 'ran dangers which schoolboys are not called on to face'. The same source adds: 'In the Mersey ... were the splendid ships of our time. . . . In those days the bulk of the world's freight was carried in sailing ships, which had then reached their last, strange, beautiful perfection'. John Masefield, *The Conway* (1933), pp. 3, 103, 118, 120.

88.33 **My father's a parson in Norfolk.** Like Horatio Nelson, though no maritime genius, Leggatt is not bound by a literalist conception of the law. In 1868, of the 123 cadets registered with the *Conway*, 27 were sons of clergymen. This proportion was not unusually high; how many, like Nelson, came from a Norfolk rectory is not recorded. Masefield.

88.33 **You]** **MS** Do you **S–** Although S's conventional phrasing might represent Conrad's revision, it is more likely another instance of editorial correctness. Conrad might have revised in the lost typescript to bring this speech of Leggatt's into accord with his later 'Do you see me' (94.21–22), but the difference between the later one made in the relative security of the Captain's cabin and the earlier made on the poop deck immediately after being rescued from the sea could mark a subtle development in the dialogue. What is more certain is that S's editor frequently smoothed out Leggatt's characteristically 'brusque' expressions (see 'The Texts', pp. 219–20); this one appears to have suffered such treatment.

88.40 **ill-conditioned** Having a bad disposition or temperament.

89.9 **reefed foresail** To reef a sail is to reduce its exposure to the wind by folding or gathering it up. Square sails usually carry two rows of reef points that permit the partial rolling or folding of the sail upwards. Under extreme conditions this task is very difficult but absolutely essential. If in a storm a sail is furled completely (rolled up to the yards) or shredded by being left unreefed, the ship will not be able to maintain headway and will run the danger of being 'pooped' – that is, either being overtaken by following seas and swamped or, running at the same speed as the sea, having its rudder lose its grip, when the risk of serious damage, wallowing, or eventually being rolled over becomes acute. Despite its reefed foresail, the *Sephora* is pooped (89.20–23) because her heavy cargo increases her displacement and slows her down (89.14; 83.25n). Yet the foresail saves her from foundering. See *Ships and the Sea*, s.v. 'poop'.

89.13 **at the sheet** A sheet is a rope or chain used for trimming a sail to the wind. A square sail set on a yard, as here, has two sheets, one for each 'clew', or corner of the sail to which the sheet is secured. *Ships and the Sea*.

89.14 **a deep ship** See 83.25n.

89.15 **funk** Cowering fear.

89.18 **it]** **MS** it coming **S–** Although Conrad revised this phrase in the manuscript and could have been finishing the job in the lost typescript, S's change functions in a characteristically literalist way to pin down the meaning of MS's ambiguous 'it'. The addition probably reflects the disposition of S's editor to clarify nautical events, especially in view of the next alteration to the same sentence (see 89.18n).

89.18 **rigging. I]** **MS** rigging, but I **S–** While Leggatt's account situates the fight within the larger context of the ship's struggle with impending disaster (see 89.20n), S's addition joins the two sentences and thereby makes an explicit contrast. In doing so, it breaches the Captain's statement about Leggatt's 'brusque, disconnected sentences'. Here and elsewhere in this passage (see 89.18*n*, 89.20*n*), S's additions appear to be editorial.

89.20 **fallen**] **MS** fallen on my head **S–** S's additional phrase makes the image explicit, thus blunting the larger connotations of the familiar figure, while making the statement more personal. This focus, similar to S's two previous changes in its effect, seems inappropriate, as the entire passage depicts the scene on ship at large and the altercation in that context. Leggatt's argument is about the situation in which the particular event occurred; the sky falls not just on himself, but on his opponent and the ship, as the next sentence shows. S's editor looks to be active in this paragraph, which recounts a crucial episode in the tale. His changes (e.g., 89.11, 89.18, 89.18) tend to diminish the colloquial and situational aspect of the dialogue, smooth out the narrative, and to that extent deflect the impact of Leggatt's rendition.

89.21 **there was hardly anything**] **MS** hardly anything was **S–** Conrad wrote 'there was' twice in MS, cancelling the first one as he went on to add 'for ten minutes' before the main clause. In the process he interlined 'hardly anything' on a line by itself above deleted 'nothing', and this probably caused the typist to skip 'there' and misinterpret the phrasing.

89.22 **forecastle head** The roof or deck forward, in contrast to the poop aft.

89.25 **forebits** A frame composed of two oak pillars, bolted upright to beams below the deck, to which anchor-cables or mooring hawsers are fastened (*Ships and the Sea*, s.v. 'bitts'). Since the two men were hit by an overtaking wave as they were at a foresail sheet (89.13), they were swept forward against the bits (or 'bitts'), which saved them from being washed overboard.

89.25 **forebits. Not a pretty miracle either.**] **MS S** forebits. **E1–** The sentence, so characteristic of Leggatt's speech and resonant in his account, was written without alteration in MS and survived Conrad's revision in the typescript as well as the supervision of S's editor, who was especially keen on muting such expressions of Leggatt's. Although the literary grounds for its omission in E1 are far from clear, this is apparently a simple if egregious case of compositorial eyeskip, from the end of one word at the beginning of S's type line to the beginning of another at the end.

89.26 **still**] **MS** still when they picked us up **S–** In MS, Conrad deleted 'carried us together aft' to interline 'rushed us aft together', which simply implies the fighters were picked up. The main point is not that they got picked up, as the MS revision indicates, but the general craziness of the crew's reaction and that of the captain, as Conrad's later revision in the typescript shows (89.33–34). S's change again narrows the focus of the narrative (cf. 89.20; also 90.12). Its phrase also anticipates the crew's reaction and changes the sequence of the narrative, which in MS moves from the crew's initial finding, to Leggatt's steadfast grip, to the sailor's black face, and thence to their reaction to these discoveries; in this it resembles another such alteration which upsets Conrad's narrative development (cf. 87.14*n*).

89.40 **on that** over that, on top of that.

90.1 **sou'wester** A large oilskin hat used to protect the head and neck, originally from the south-westerly gales that prevail around the Atlantic coasts of Great Britain.

90.5 **skylight** See 15.7*n* and Fig. 5.

90.12 **his captain double**] MS double S– Although S's omission makes sense and therefore could be either authorial or editorial, it shifts the focus to the mate, whereas the point has to do with the Captain and Leggatt. In MS Conrad struck out his original 'he would think he was seeing double' in order to achieve this focus by adding 'and catch sight of us he would think he was seeing his captain double', but in doing so he interlined the two words omitted in S, and apparently the typist skipped them. Conrad deliberately uses similar phrasing at 91.30, again his second rendition (after cancelling the phrase 'two captains'). Although too far away to have prompted deletion here to avoid repetition, this second instance testifies to the importance of the concept.

90.22–23 **for my relief** That is, the second mate, who was to relieve the Captain (see 84.6–7).

90.31 **ratlines** Lines tied across the shrouds (the ropes used to stay a mast) of a sailing vessel for climbing aloft. *Ships and the Sea.*

90.31–32 **mizen rigging** The rigging of the third, aftermost, mast of a square-rigged sailing ship. *Ships and the Sea.*

90.36 **three months** The estimated time required to reach England (see 82.1*n*).

90.37–38 **rudder casing** The ship's saloon does not extend to the very end of the stern, which has to accommodate the steering mechanism connecting the rudder to the wheel, i.e., 'the rudder stock connecting the rudder blade to the helm' (*Ships and the Sea*). In all but the largest ships this mechanism obtrudes into the saloon and is concealed by a casing. See Fig. 20.

91.3–13 **It . . . saloon.** This description has prompted much discussion. See Figs. 18 and 19 for Conrad's retrospective sketches and Fig. 20 for a conjectural plan.

91.6 **chronometers** Extremely accurate watches, their construction and adjustment required exceptional skill to ensure reliable knowledge of a ship's longitudinal position. The calculation of the 'vertical' longitude, unlike that of the 'horizontal' latitude, depends on an arbitrary meridian. The line running round the poles through Greenwich, chosen by international agreement in 1880 as fixing that meridian, can only be used as a marker at sea on the basis that the earth takes twenty-four hours to rotate. Thus to calculate a ship's longitude, access to the exact time at Greenwich is required for comparison with the time on board, which is determined by astronomical observation. Radio signals and satellite positioning systems have since rendered redundant the two chronometers required to ensure confidence in their accuracy.

91.16 **bulkhead** A vertical partition, fore and aft or athwartships (from side to side), that divides the hull into separate compartments.

91.16 **gimballs** Two concentric metal rings joined in such a way as to counteract the rolling and pitching of a ship, thereby allowing an attached lamp, compass, or chronometer to remain level.

91.25 **something like six**] MS nearly nine S nearly seven E1– S's reading mends, mistakenly, a merely apparent inconsistency: one with the later explicit reference to 'nine weeks' (95.15), another with Leggatt's nearer references to 'six weeks'

(91.37) having passed before the decisive conversation off Java Head (91.36) and 'three weeks' (93.11) since that. The Captain, however, seems to be thinking only of the first statement, as his word 'presently' indicates. Conrad evidently never saw the problem, as he must have been the one who tried to recover the MS estimate when preparing copy for E1 and, once he had noticed something was amiss, would presumably have remembered revising to 'nine' and his reason for doing so. Dent's personnel could not have noticed a problem in S, where the apparent discrepancy had been eliminated. In fact a problem existed only for S's precise editor, who assumed that Leggatt's first statement (91.37) referred strictly to the point in the voyage off Java Head and that another tense was imprecise – that it should have been 'had had' (cf. the precise tense in the previous sentence). On the Captain's (and Leggatt's and Conrad's) terms the whole problem disappears, which it does if we simply restore the MS reading.

91.35 **once**] **ED** after **MS** the *Sephora* after **S** the *Sephora* once **E1**– The reading of MS is conversational, the reference to Leggatt's ship being rather obvious, whereas S's nicety exhibits the sort of fussy editorial interference occurring at this point (cf. 91.25n) and earlier (89.11). E1's substitution, however, appears to be Conrad's, though not predicated on S's literalistic addition.

91.36 **Java Head** The north-west corner of Java; see Map 4.

92.2 **open port** A reference to the port-hole above the bedplace (see also 96.33, 97.7). See Fig. 20.

92.8 **old man** A familiar term for 'master' (abbreviation of 'master mariner') or 'captain' in the English Mercantile Marine; see 92.38n.

92.10–11 **too deep . . . bare poles** That is, too low in the water to be propelled forward by the force of the wind on spars stripped of sail. See 83.25n, 89.9n.

92.15 **Sunda Straits** The channel separating Sumatra from Java and uniting the Indian Ocean with the Java Sea (see Map 4) is fifteen miles broad between the south-east extremity of Sumatra and the port-town of Anjer (or Anger) in Java. The negotiating of this Strait by sailing vessels was not made easier by the presence of an island at the mid-point between Sumatra and Java called Dwars-in-den-Weg (Right-in-the-Way). In the south-western approaches to the Straits lies the larger island of Krakatoa, which in 1883 was partially destroyed by the greatest volcanic explosion in recorded history. *Enc. Brit.*

92.33 **grey headed**] **S**– grey whiskered **MS** Conrad did not establish a physiognomic parallel between the *Sephora*'s second mate and the Captain's first mate in MS, and S's alteration avoids the one that would have resulted from Conrad's decision to alter the first mate's 'moustaches' to 'whiskers' in the lost typescript. Despite its American 'gray' spelling, S's reading almost certainly represents one of Conrad's revisions of this paragraph.

92.38 **skipper**] **S**– old man **MS** S's colloquial word, technically incorrect for the master of so large a ship, is the sort its editor shuns in Leggatt's speech, not reinforces. It emphasizes Leggatt's small estimate of Archbold (see also 89.31) and is adopted by our Captain (99.11). It probably exhibits Conrad altering a phrase he had revised in MS (where 'he' became 'the old man'); in the lost typescript it would have lessened repetition (see 92.8n, 92.32, 92.33, 92.37). 'A Smile of Fortune' (35.4, 35.25) contains similar uses of the term.

93.3 **'brand of Cain'** The fratricidal killer of the innocent Abel, Cain is driven by the Lord 'from the face of the earth'. Cain concludes: 'I shall be a fugitive and a vagabond in the earth; and it shall come to pass, that every one that findeth me shall slay me'. The Lord therefore 'set a mark upon Cain, lest any finding him should kill him' (Genesis iv.14–15). But this did not dispel Europe's dread of him: this 'mark' was popularly converted into a 'brand' – a sign of infamy permanently imprinted on the flesh of criminals by a red-hot iron designed to identify the victim as unfit for contact with human beings.

93.6 **wouldn't**] MS wouldn't listen to me S– Another instance of S's literalisms (unnecessarily and wrongly glossing 'wouldn't'), this addition is quite misguided. The point is that the old man would not do as Leggatt proposed – that is the tenor of the passage, which refers back to 'refused' (92.30) and forward to 'won't' (93.7) – not that he wouldn't listen (be persuaded), which he is literally doing. Although shaken, Archbold is obstinate, as his speeches and Leggatt's account show, in a way that foreshadows his later behaviour.

93.6–7 **I represent the law here** The contractual obligations and duties of a master mariner for the period are defined by the consolidated Merchant Shipping Act of 1854. This consolidation, and the various laws and statutes it brings together, have a history going back to Saxon times, and that history itself rests on 'immemorial custom'. In this perspective, the statement is that of a law-enforcing officer who has the right of arrest but certainly not that of passing sentence. The law in question is not nautical law (pertinent to failure in professional duty, as with the protagonist of *Lord Jim*, who commits only a transgression covered by Admiralty Law, and is judged by a Court of Inquiry accountable to the High Court of Admiralty); it is the law of the land. Transgressions such as theft or homicide fall under Statute Law (enacted by a legislative body) or Common Law (based on judicial decisions and custom). In this context, the deck of a ship flying the Red Ensign (the flag of the British Mercantile Marine) is defined as being a piece of floating Britain, and alleged criminal acts committed on board can be proved and punished only in a British court. This definition is itself legally defined: the 1779 (George III) Offences at Sea Act, for example, established that alleged crimes at sea have to be dealt with as if they were crimes on land.

93.13 **Carimata** An island forty miles off the west coast of the island Borneo in the direction of Bangka. It gives its name to the broad strait dividing Borneo and Sumatra. See Map 4.

93.25 **boat** Probably an ordinary ship's boat which in an emergency would serve as a life-boat. *Ships and the Sea, Nautical Terms.*

93.31 **anchorage** An area, generally off the coast, where ships could safely lie at anchor. See 83.28n.

94.2 **riding light** See 85.8n.

94.4 **glass** Seaman's term for telescope, also called 'spy-glass' in the nineteenth century.

94.20 **round and round** Displacement in a featureless environment without a distant landmark or compass invariably describes a circle.

94.29 **over the rail** That is, above the Captain's cabin, and perhaps directly above the open port (92.2n).

95.8–9 **the eyes of the ship's company**] **S**– their eyes **MS** Although possibly editorial, the wording and construction are probably Conrad's. S's addition amounts to a clarification that expands MS's phrase to include both officers and crew and thus sums up the Captain's sketchy statements. MS's 'their' could have referred either to the 'crew' (95.5) – a word Conrad generally uses to mean the hands as distinguished from the officers (including the petty officers) – or to 'the rest' (95.6), which presumably meant those officers (the two mates and the steward) who are the Captain's chief concern. S's addition exhibits an awareness of the technical problem and covers it without precisely solving it.

95.16 **rudder-chains** These steering chains connected the top of the rudder blade to the wheel. They would offer a perfect hand-hold under the projecting stern to an exhausted swimmer. See Lubbock, illustration facing p. 88, and pp. 95–6.

95.25 **mere impulse**] **S**– sudden fancy **MS** S's editor would almost certainly have eliminated MS's 'fancy' had it been in his copy (see 95.12). However, it seems likely Conrad had already done so in the interest of avoiding repetition, replacing it with 'impulse', a word he frequently uses, notably in *Under Western Eyes*, 'A Smile of Fortune', 'Freya of the Seven Isles', and *Chance*. S's 'mere' could be another matter: producing a phrase not found elsewhere in his manuscripts, it avoids a redundancy for which Conrad exhibits a predilection from *Almayer's Folly* to *The Arrow of Gold*; but 'mere' also avoids overuse of a word that occurs repeatedly in this account (see 93.22, 95.34, 96.16, 96.30) and was probably substituted by Conrad when replacing 'fancy'.

95.38–96.5 **high bedplace . . . drawers underneath . . . serge curtains** This multipurpose space combining bed, storage, ventilation, and privacy would have been more than a bunk and less than a bedroom.

96.12 **fagged out** Colloquialism (originally public-school) for 'exhausted' or 'worn out', as by labour, strain, or toil.

97.2 **unhooked** See 87.24n.

97.12 **companion** The covering, or 'hood', over the hatchway that leads to the staircase or 'companion way' connecting the poop deck to the cuddy. *Ships and the Sea, Nautical Terms.*

97.14–15 **break of the poop . . . ladder** The forward end of the ship's after superstructure, where the poop deck drops to the upper deck, is accessed by two short ladders or steps, one on the port and the other on the starboard side. See Fig. 6.

97.25 **Square . . . braces** The Captain requires the crew to execute a basic task which, under the circumstances, attends to her appearance rather than her performance, though it also allows him to establish his authority. In square-rigged ships the yards are square by the braces when they are at right angles to the fore-and-aft line of the ship, and square by the lifts when they are horizontal. Braces are ropes attached to the ends of yards to allow them to be swung at different angles to the fore-and-aft line (and so make most of the wind); lifts are ropes let down from the mast-heads to the two ends of the corresponding yards in order to support them.

97.32 **after braces** The braces of the after-mast.

97.38 **open**] **MS** own **S**– MS's word directly follows Conrad's introduction of the concept of 'secret self' (97.37). S's alteration counteracts this shift of emphasis from duality and doubling, which lingers (e.g., at 98.22, 99.34), to secret identity and sharing, which predominates from here on, both in the manuscript itself (e.g., 100.12–13) and in subsequent revision (e.g., at 98.12, 98.28, 101.31, 102.25–26). Although MS's 'open' could not easily be mistaken for 'own', the awkwardness of the first character may have put the typist off sufficiently to provoke the substitution of the more familiar and similar sounding word, or S's editor may simply have levelled the startling reading if it survived into the fair typescript (*TS2*) that served as printer's copy.

98.7 **do**] **MS** tidy up **S**– MS's 'do' is clear and businesslike and does not require S's more explicit and domestic phrase (out of keeping aboard ship), as almost identical usage later shows (107.40; see also 107.26). Conrad rarely, if ever, combines 'up' with the simple 'tidy'. Most often he has '(un)tidy' as an adjective, and as a verbal 'tidying'; the three instances of the word with 'up' all function as nouns and appear in the 'Author's Note' to *Notes on Life and Letters* (pp. 3–4), where he writes in quick succession about 'the process [way] of tidying up' his literary remains. Like S's next error (98.8), this one is out of keeping with the Captain's direct tone.

98.16 **there to go back to my room**] **S**– there **MS** The addition is another of Conrad's elaborations in paragraphs that he revised in the first typescript. Although logically the Captain is unlikely to have gone elsewhere than back to his room, the phrase is not the sort of thing that S's editor adds either generally or to clarify movements aboard ship. Cf. 91.15, 98.8, 107.40, 109.9 for references to the relations of the two rooms, and Fig. 20 for a conjectured 'plan of the officers' quarters'.

98.29 **then**] **MS** there **S**– S's word represents a typist's misreading of Conrad's 'then'. The paragraph is organized around a time sequence, not a spatial description, as other words like 'When', 'then', 'day time', and 'Now and then' indicate (98.16, 98.20, 98.32, 98.33), and indeed this structure reflects the entire organizing principle of the narrative.

100.6 **bearings** The captain has 'lost his bearings', i.e., a proper sense of direction, orientation, context, perspective. The figure is drawn from fixing the position of a ship by reference to landmarks, navigation buoys, heavenly bodies, or, in relative terms, to the fore-and-aft line of the ship (*Ships and the Sea, Nautical Terms*). See 106.25*n*.

100.9 **shipmaster** The full and formal title for the position.

100.10 **obviously, densely**] **MS** densely **S**– Without the comma after 'was' added in the present edition, 'obviously' seems clumsy, at best. The cut of an unnecessary modifier which sounds redundant and inappropriate before 'distressed' could be Conrad's, but as such it might just as well have been made by S's editor. The question is whether 'obviously' was to modify 'was', or to join 'densely' in modifying 'distressed'. If the latter, then it plainly had to go, and either editor or author could have managed that. If the former, as seems more likely, then the only problem was whether the word was wanted – and thus the variant becomes almost indifferent. In the lost typescript Conrad made no other revisions in this or immediately surrounding paragraphs, which in MS received only minimal alteration; that fact tilts the balance in favour of retaining MS's word.

100.13 **bulkhead** See 91.16n.

100.32–33 **tongue out** A symptom of strangulation.

100.37 **proper sea burial** The full burial service at sea as set out by the Church of England's *Book of Common Prayer* (1853) would have taken about thirty-five minutes. It is identical to the service on land except for a single short paragraph replacing 'We therefore commit his body to the ground . . . eternal life' with 'We therefore commit his body to the Deep . . . world to come'. The necessarily perfunctory version of the full ceremony would probably have confined itself to that single paragraph. See also 26.12n.

100.38 **bunting** The 'open-made worsted stuff, used for making flags', though the origin of this word is uncertain (*OED*). As a term associated with flags, it is as low down the scale of dignity as 'standard' is up it.

100.39 **oilskins and long boots** The weatherproof oilskin coat and sou'wester hat made of fine canvas had, in the later nineteenth century, replaced the clothes and hats made out of worn canvas sail-cloth, which a liberal application of tar rendered waterproof – hence the name 'tarpaulin' for a sailor's headgear, and of 'tars' for sailors (*Ships and the Sea*). Long boots (usually called 'thigh boots') provided water-proofing up to the top of the thigh.

101.22 **have laid**] S– lay MS Although not one of Conrad's favourite phrases, S's past perfect is apparently his in an area of the text that he revised assiduously. The alteration occurs where there had been revision in MS, and it probably carries on that. The ministrations of the magazine's editor here seem to be confined to the fussy quotation marks around 'countenancing ... sort.' (101.20) – if they are not a proofreader's or compositor's; he did not correct the more apparent lapse at 101.24.

101.24 **went**] MS S went on, E1– E1's added word normalizes peculiar phrasing that is retained in S, that is written in MS in a clear sentence containing no revision, that makes figurative sense on its own, and that resonates more effectively when a different kind of groping occurs later (at 115.38). If Archbold has been exploring his feelings, E1's 'on' is required; but earlier the Captain has probably 'let him go on' talking, not probing his emotions, about the 'terror' overtly 'on him' (101.13). Thus the only reference here would be an indirect one to the complex mixture of 'anxiety' and honour obliquely implied in the preceding sentences (101.19–23). Conrad could have failed to alter this wording when revising the typescript for S, but at that time he had worked over these sentences rather carefully, making some changes that developed Archbold's peculiar tenacity and determination; the awkward phrasing remains consistent with the picture of a man whose speaking and feeling are presented as a single act of self-deception. E1's phrasing, which distinguishes the two and amounts to a coarsening of Conrad's effect, probably represents a not wholly deliberate adjustment made during transmission of a passage Conrad otherwise left unaltered in the tear-sheets of S.

101.26 **on.**] S– on. Our senior partner spoke to me himself. MS Although written without hesitation in MS, the sentence's absence from S is apparently gratuitous and perhaps compensates for the addition at 101.28, which must certainly be Conrad's. See 'The Texts', pp. 211–12.

101.30 **thoughts**] S– thought **MS** If MS means 'consciousness' as a whole rather than particular thoughts, then S's reading could be an error of attraction to 'impressions' or a simple normalization. However, it may be the stuff of consciousness, rather than the entire mental state, that Conrad is driving at here, which would make S's reading appropriate. Conrad used 'thought' in the sense of consciousness as early as 1904 ('Anatole France') and frequently in *The Secret Agent* and *Under Western Eyes*, as well as in 'A Smile of Fortune' and 'Freya of the Seven Isles', but he usually paired singulars with singulars and plurals with plurals in constructions like this (e.g., at 106.6–7). A parallel passage (119.15) suggests that the alteration here is Conrad's revision. Cf. 'the thoughts, the impressions' ('Geography and Explorers', p. 1); 'her thoughts, her feelings' ('The Planter of Malata', p. 36); 'occupied his thoughts, swayed his emotions' ('Heart of Darkness', p. 128); 'joys, struggles, thoughts, sorrows' (*Chance*, p. 208).

102.11 **distrust**] S– suspicion **MS** S's is the less obvious reading and is unlikely to have been substituted by its editor for one that was satisfactory and evoked mystery and suspense. The change avoids repetition later (102.15) that would have amounted to contradiction.

102.13 **felt simply incapable**] **ED** felt **MS** felt utterly incapable **S**– Inadvertently cancelled in his double rewriting of the manuscript draft at this point, Conrad's original words 'simply incapable' were required in order to make simple sense of the sentence. When revising the lost first typescript, he attempted to recover them and the several senses they conveyed, though without consulting the manuscript, and with less than complete success.

103.23 **mates' rooms**] **ED** mate's rooms **MS** mate's room **S**– As Archbold has to see all the quarters, presumably he looks at the rooms of both the mates (see 87.23–25). In MS Conrad interlined 'item' above 'detail' and mis-inscribed 'mate's', not finishing the 'a' before writing the 't' and having to go back and fix it all. This apparently occasioned a lapse, whereas 'rooms' is written distinctly. S's editor spotted a problem but made an erroneous 'correction'.

103.25 **out directly**] **MS** out **S**– The shipmasters move on to the main deck straightaway, without delaying on the poop, having already poked around all the rooms off the saloon. The MS exhibits no hesitation on Conrad's part in writing this passage. S's editor may have removed another anglicism, correctly taking 'directly' in its temporal sense (cf. 102.1, 106.9), or he may have once again attempted to clarify movements aboard ship, taking it in its spatial sense, as he muddled a similar movement earlier (84.38n) and the question of the inspection just above (103.23n). For other Americanizations in S, see 'The Texts', p. 219.

103.30 *Sephoras* **away**] **MS E1 A1** *Sephora*'s away **S A2 E2** Initiating an action which parallels the Captain's escorting of Archbold, the first mate announces that the *Sephora* men are leaving, a statement officially directed at the crew under his command, who properly assemble as their visitors debark, but indirectly at the four men who accompanied their captain on board. The received reading of S and the collected editions represents an easier interpretation – that the mate means 'the boat of the *Sephora* is about to cast off' (let go a rope securing it to the ship), phrasing that could derive from a nautical expression incorporating the homonyms 'away' and 'aweigh' and denoting 'the situation of the anchor at the moment it is broken out of the ground when being "weighed"' (*Ships and the Sea*). In S this rationalization was further prompted by Conrad's imprecision in writing ships' names, which invited clarification of MS's 'Sephoras' by *Harper's* editor, or perhaps by a typist. But the more difficult reading, revived through a deliberate alteration found in the lightly edited E1, must be Conrad's, who also added 'and yelled' (103.30) immediately before this word. Cedric Watts, ed., *Typhoon and Other Tales*, rev. edn (2002), was the first to restore this reading, though with a slightly different interpretation of its significance (p. 230). See Fig. 8.

103.35 **gangway** A portable 'companion ladder' (see 97.12*n*) rigged over the side of a ship when she is at anchor. *Ships and the Sea*.

104.14 **murders in Yankee ships** In the mid nineteenth century, discipline aboard American clippers had become 'famously efficient and notoriously cruel'. This 'notoriety' had become legendary in international waters and continued throughout Conrad's seafaring career. With the discovery of gold in California (1848–9), American clippers abandoned competition with British ships in the Far East in order to supply San Francisco round the Horn. This redirection coincided with a decline in interest in seafaring by Americans in the course of discovering a continent, and recruitment of able seamen became very difficult. Many of the great Californian clippers were obliged to take 'any drunken, broken landlubber', and the completion of a voyage often became a matter of 'mutiny or club the men under'. One notorious master arrived in San Francisco having 'shot several [sailors] from the yards with his pistol to make the others move faster'. Ralph D. Paine, *The Old Merchant Marine: A Chronicle of American Ships and Sailors* (1919), pp. 173–8. See also Basil Lubbock, *Round the Horn* (1902), pp. 32–4.

104.24 **athwart** In a direction across a ship's centre line, or course (in everyday parlance, 'from side to side').

104.24–25 **Not one of the crew**] ED No one of the crew MS– This failure in idiom, retained in all texts, comes from Conrad's revision in MS of 'The men were out of sight', where he retraced 'No' over 'The' before interlining 'one of the crew forward could be seen'. Conrad knew this idiom, his desired sense seems to have remained constant, and the virtual nonsense we have inherited apparently represents a mere slip of the pen.

104.29 **coal hole** A locker, frequently on the main deck amidships, in which the galley's coal is kept. See 115.25*n*.

105.11 **supposed**] MS suppose S– S's change, whatever its occasion, obscures the point. The narrative stream concerns the Captain's (and by implication Leggatt's) view of the situation, which extends beyond this statement, as the tenses in the next sentence and the reference to 'this thought' show. S's reading makes the statement about 'Providence' a retrospective reflection, not one situated in the time and circumstances. It may have been prompted by Conrad's interlineation of 'was, I supposed' over 'was' in MS, but it could also represent a simple memory lapse on the typist's or compositor's part, or a recollection of 104.30–31.

105.24 **main topsail** The second sail on the mainmast, just above the mainsail. Higher sails would have been furled or sent down in preparation for the gale because they would have blown out or overburdened the ship.

105.24–25 **our last hope**] S– it MS While MS's reading is another instance of Leggatt's laconic manner, S's phrase is another of Conrad's expansions, which develops Archbold's weakness. In that sense it carries on an MS revision that had resulted in a repetition. The alteration defines one of the two meanings of MS's 'it': the main-topsail itself (the 'last hope' for survival), rather than the loss of it. The phrase does not sound like wording S's editor would have improvised.

105.32 **boss'en** The 'boatswain' is the officer in charge of the sails, rigging, anchors, and cables, and is responsible for their proper condition. Under the captain and mates he also has direct charge of the work done on deck. Usually a petty officer, he lives with the men in the forecastle. *Ships and the Sea.*

105.37 **coal-waggon** Contemptuous term for a ship carrying coal, which was not prestige cargo.

106.2 **twenty four men** The *Sephora* is a substantial ship, though not quite as large as its model, the *Cutty Sark*, which had twenty-eight (Lubbock, p. 145). Conrad's *Otago* had only nine: the captain, the two mates, and six hands (Najder, p. 105).

106.3 **crushed out**] MS S crushed E1– E1's deletion smoothes out the phrasing Conrad uses when life or existence is the object, and so moderates the force of the Captain's statement. Cf. *Nostromo*, p. 56; *Under Western Eyes*, p. 89.

106.25 **compass bearing of the Pagoda** A bearing in this case would be the horizontal angle between the direction of North and the direction of the object chosen (here the Pagoda, 81.23n), as opposed to a vertical bearing, which would require a sextant. It helps the officer to fix his location on the chart at the moment the bearing is taken. Readings by landmark are, of course, only possible when the landmarks are in sight (see 81.2–82.23n). Here the Captain is concerned not with his overall destination, but with the direction of his first tack (see 108.5n). Faced as he is by a light contrary wind (108.5), he can only make oblique progress against it. For the ship's general direction, see 82.1n.

106.32 **roundness**] MS unusual roundness S– Although S's reading is technically more precise, since all Western eyes may be said to be round and are clearly so to Easterners, its 'unusual' is an addition merely in the interest of explicitness. MS's reading, which simply denotes surprise, is perfectly clear, as a parallel at 83.12 suggests, and Conrad had no trouble writing this passage. Unqualified round-eyed reactions appear in 'Heart of Darkness', *Nostromo*, *The Rescue*, and *The Rover*, and in 'A Smile of Fortune' (34.26) with an intensifier ('very').

107.7 **me**] S– the door MS The reading of S shifts the point of reference from the Steward to the Captain, which is where it belongs. The 'scares' in question (107.4) are not those of the officers and crew but of the Captain, in contrast to the 'self controlled', 'almost invulnerable' Leggatt (107.21–22); the narrative's focus is on what emerges in the dialogue, not the Steward's jumpiness. The shift in S squares with a subtle revision in MS, where this sentence originally continued into the next, which lacked the 'he' and focussed more on the Steward, before Conrad's alterations. S's alteration looks like the result of on-going revision by Conrad.

107.27 **reclined**] S– lay MS Although the verbs seem interchangeable, S's gratuitous alteration occurs in a paragraph Conrad revised heavily. In such contexts neither word is much used by Conrad, but 'reclined' occurs more often than 'lay' in connection with those who are on their sides or not stretched flat out, and it is a word Conrad increasingly favours from 1911 onward.

107.29 **head**] MS hair S– Like the change at 107.29a, this one fails to fix the problem of syntax that arose during Conrad's addition of the clause in MS. Both variants suggest Conrad did not revise this sentence in the typescript, though he noticed something amiss when preparing copy for E1. S's alteration obscures the point about the convict by focussing on the hair, whereas the whole head, in contrast to the body in the sleeping-suit (cf. the beginning of the story), is the point of reference. Cf. 112.32, 115.34.

108.4–5 **east side of the Gulf of Siam** That is, not of the main gulf but of the smaller 'upper gulf', also known as the Bight of Bangkok. The narrative does not concern itself with the larger question of navigating the main gulf, where choice of the eastern or western side was largely determined by the seasons (see Larabee, pp. 357–9). See Map 3.

108.5 **tack for tack** A sailing ship can make progress against a wind blowing from the quarter of the ship's destination only by 'tacking'. To sail directly against a wind is obviously impossible, but what is possible is to advance diagonally against it. This can be managed if the sail is angled sufficiently for the wind to gain purchase on it. Once that happens, movement is imparted to the ship, and it becomes possible to use the rudder to hold the ship on an oblique course towards its destination. For example, to progress southwards against a wind from the south, a ship must take, alternatively, more or less south-west and south-east courses; the progress will be slow, but it will eventually achieve its goal.

As the narrative climax of the tale turns on a change of tack, its force cannot be fully registered without an understanding of what that means. The difficulty is not in keeping the ship on the tack, but in changing tack (e.g., from the south-east to the south-west). A good helmsman on a tack keeps his ship as close to the wind as possible, with sails hardened and just full of wind, but without any shivering or flapping. (The closest tack achievable by a square-rigged ship was about 70 degrees from the direct course, which means shallow zig-zagging and slow progress if the wind is blowing directly from its destination; by contrast, a modern racing rig, for instance, can comfortably manage 40 degrees.) Strictly speaking, however, 'tacking' refers to the change of direction, which involves bringing the head of the ship to the wind (facing it) and across it. This manœuvre, during which the ship is said to be 'coming about' or 'in stays' (see 117.19), requires judgement and decisiveness. The moment this edge is crossed, as it must be if the reverse tack is to be made, the ship will start losing momentum, and if this continues the rudder will quickly cease to function. In those unforgiving moments the sails must be swung across the hull in a certain sequence to await the first purchase of the wind which, for example, having been on the port bow now needs to be on the starboard bow. See *Ships and the Sea*.

108.19–20 **had detected him using ... talking on deck**] E1– had a sight of him once down on the main deck use ... talking MS had caught a sight of him using ... talking on deck S Conrad had a problem with the phrasing in MS, revising from the simple 'had seen him' to 'had a sight of him'. The alterations in S and E1 both represent his continuing effort to improve the wording, especially as the detail of the deck is not just preserved, but moved to later in the sentence, and as the phrasing is still awkward. However, E1's new word suggests the Captain was on the lookout, and it finds precise parallels elsewhere (e.g., *Almayer's Folly*, 54.19;

'Typhoon', p. 29; *Chance*, p. 20). Conrad carried on revision of the passage at 108.21–22.

108.32 **up**] MS up again S– S's addition resembles an earlier one (84.38*n*) in its attempt to make movements on the ship absolutely clear. Here it helps express the Steward's exasperation, but that has already been detailed in the previous paragraph, and the propriety of his actually voicing it is very questionable indeed.

108.34–35 **could hear**] MS would have heard S– S's change for agreement of tense alters the mood in a paragraph Conrad had written in MS without evidence of struggle or hesitation. As a simple positive assertion 'would have' is rare, if not unprecedented, in his manuscripts, where it habitually occurs in negative contexts, as a subjunctive or in conditional clauses where the condition is not fulfilled. S's nicety of consistency appears to be its editor's rather than Conrad's, who, for instance, in revising the typescript with 'could' at 108.21–22, failed to employ such a past tense and left a similar inconsistency.

109.36 **existence**] S– presence MS Although S's alteration is a possible editorial substitution, it carries on revision present in MS, where the phrase is interlined and 'reality' has given way to 'bodily presence'; 'existence' is more precise and its ontological or at least psychological overtones resonate throughout the entire episode (see 109.36, 110.11–12, 110.27).

110.6 **hands going to their stations** That is, taking up their positions for swinging the heavy mainyard and foreyard by means of braces (see 97.25*n*).

110.7 **Hard a-lee** That is, spin the wheel hard to leeward! The lee, as opposed to the windward, is the side of the ship away from the wind (that does not have the wind blowing on it). This command sounds illogical because the direction of a ship's tack is determined by the side of the ship against which the wind is blowing, and the order should therefore be 'hard to windward'. The explanation of this puzzle shows why tradition gets a bad name. When ships were steered by tiller (a bar attached to the head of the rudder turning on a pin fixed in the stern), turning the rudder right meant pushing the tiller left; thus the order 'to starboard' could only be executed by turning the tiller to port. When the wheel replaced the tiller on big ships, it was linked to the rudder so that the steersman could turn it in the same direction as the rudder. However, the habit of centuries had become so engrained that the custom was preserved by transferring it from the mechanism (the tiller) to the human voice (the command). This practice persisted beyond the end of the First World War. See *Ships and the Sea*, s.v. 'helm'.

110.9 **fluttering noise** As the ship turns into the wind, the wind loses its purchase on the sails (see 108.5*n*, 116.34*n*).

110.12 **Mainsail haul** One of several orders, given during the tacking of a square-rigged ship, to 'pull the braces' (the ropes attached to the ends of the yards supporting each sail) so as to adjust the angle of the sail's surface to the ship's new tack. The timing of the orders is vital if the ship is not to be caught 'in stays' (see 108.5*n*). On a barque, with a mizzen rigged fore-and-aft, this would be the last bracing command as the ship completes a successful tack.

110.13–14 **running away with the main brace** The yard from which the main-sail hangs is very heavy, and given its size the arc it has to travel is considerable. It has to be pulled by several hands running over the deck.

110.34 **Cambodie**] MS Cambodje S–A2a E2 Cambodge A2b Conrad's adjectival for 'Cambodia' was apparently misconstrued by a typist and 'corrected' to the proper French name 'Cambodge' only in 1923, for the second American printing of Doubleday's collected edition. Cambodia became a French protectorate in 1863, years before Conrad's appointment to the *Otago*. Its 'shore', even then, properly began many miles south of the spot where the Captain drops Leggatt, but on contemporary maps 'Cambodia' identified the great land mass on the eastern side of the gulf.

111.4–5 **Driven . . . the earth** Genesis iv.14: 'Behold, thou hast driven me out this day from the face of the earth' (Cain to the Lord).

111.8 **Not.**] MS S Can't? E1– E1's substitution seems so obviously necessary to mend an apparent rift in the conversation's continuity that adoption seems required. But MS's word responds to the Captain's 'Impossible!', is a characteristic expression for Leggatt (cf. 'Not it.' at 105.31–32), joins better with the remainder of his speech, and in MS is clearly inscribed in a passage that Conrad wrote very deliberately. Had Conrad revised here, it is unlikely he would have had Leggatt pose a question, even a somewhat rhetorical one. This looks like an intervention by either an editor or compositor performing, though mistakenly, what must have seemed an obvious correction.

111.8 **naked . . . Day of Judgement** 'As he came forth of his mother's womb, naked shall he return to go as he came' (Ecclesiastes v.15); see also Job i.21; Revelation xvi.15. In medieval depictions of the Day of Judgement, souls were often represented as naked babes.

111.15 **offshore tack** That is, taking the ship away from the coast, which lies to the east. Cf. 111.30*n*.

111.18 **on purpose** That is, providentially.

111.22 **talking on**] MS talking S– The idea of continuity is important in MS, where 'remained' is traced over something unreadable and 'on' is added in the margin before the deleted 'this' in such a way as to be construable as crossed out; S's form represents a typist's error or its editor's normalization of Conrad's typical doubling of prepositions.

111.30 **put the ship round** Took the ship onto a new tack, i.e., south-east, towards the coast. See 111.15*n*.

112.2 **If there's any current** The wind is not the only factor that affects the progress of a ship; a current that would drive the ship closer to the islands would make the course steered not the course made good.

112.4–11 **The east side . . . unsolved secret**. Detailed charts of this coast and of the entire Gulf date as far back as 1856, and the one Conrad used to navigate these waters survives (Yale). Although well informed, his description is an impressionist evocation of the area. In striking contrast to the cultivated horizontals of the opening landscape, this underpopulated region of broken islands and challenging escarpments represents a reality beyond the bounds of Western mapping and legal systems. See Larabee, p. 359, and Stape, p. 13.

112.14 **forenoon**] E1– day MS S E1's word clarifies the progress of the ship's course, and Conrad seems to have in mind the progress of the watches on deck when he marks the Captain's decision not to change course (112.17–19). The word is one Conrad uses in such contexts and one Dent's agents are unlikely to have substituted for MS's, which was accepted by S's finicky editor.

112.20 **stand right in** That is, sail or steer directly, hold on course, for the inner waters, with some emphasis on the third word, as the next sentence indicates. Cf. 114.1.

112.24 **land breezes** Evening winds which blow to seaward when the temperature of the land falls below that of the sea, because cool air is heavier than warm (*Ships and the Sea*). Since such breezes can reach out a considerable distance and their strength is affected by several factors, the Captain's argument is questionable, as the first mate's reaction suggests.

112.34 **Koh-ring** The name successfully evokes the region and is possibly based on Koh (Island) Ryn, or Koh Rin (see Stape, pp. 12–14). Given his description, this suggests Conrad was working from charts rather than from direct experience (cf. the tale's opening description); but see *Letters*, VII, 570. See Map 3.

113.3 **Cochin-china** At the southern tip of the great peninsula of Indo-China, Cochin China with its capital Saigon was colonized by the French in 1862 (the eastern part) and 1867 (the western part). To get there Leggatt would have had to travel south-east for 100 miles into Cambodia (a French protectorate from 1863) and continue another 300 miles in the same direction. See 129.13n and Map 4.

113.23 **quarter-deck ports** These openings in the bulwarks on both sides of the quarter-deck served for draining the decks in high seas and to facilitate loading on to the main deck. The order seems senseless to the second mate for, as he points out (113.30–32), being open to all the winds of heaven, it is not in need of ventilation.

114.2 **sail-locker** For its possible location, see Conrad's sketch of the cuddy (Fig. 18), the conjectured plan (Fig. 20), and the next note.

114.6 **give air to the sails** Sails get damp and will rot in unventilated space. Such a hatch opening on to the quarter-deck in the bulkhead that separated the officers' quarters under the poop from the main deck and its seas was apparently not a standard feature of such ships.

114.6 **in stays** See 108.5n.

114.7 **main braces** The braces of the main-mast (see 97.25n).

114.8 **over**] MS get overboard S– Given the major revision in the next sentence (114.9–11), S's addition amounts to a redundancy, an unnecessary elaboration that diminishes the sense of fluid movement described and desired (cf. 'clear road'). Conrad declined to revise earlier in this sentence (leaving 'all the hands'), though much earlier he had supplied a somewhat different 'over' with an object (97.7). Throughout the canon he generally joins 'overboard' with verbs of relatively violent action – 'driving', 'jumped', 'leaping', 'cast', 'flown', 'dumped', 'lost', 'washed' – the weakest being the understated 'go' later in this story (116.6), in contrast to 'fling' and 'throw' (89.35, 118.17). Many of S's other additions involving physical movement on ship are editorial, not authorial, as appears to be the case here.

114.24 **amongst ... outlying**] MS against ... drifting S– S's second word is predicated on its first, which Conrad rejected in MS, whose 'outlying' could quite possibly have been mistaken by the typist as S's more predictable 'drifting'. Together they picture the islands moving against the background of the dark but starry sky, rather than merged and moving within it. But given 'shifting', 'drifting' is redundant (as well as literally misleading) and adds little except emphasis, though it produces an aural echo. MS's 'outlying' emphasizes the contrast between these islands, seemingly merged with the dark sky (cf. the opening description), and Koh-ring, which blots it out and is the main focus of the passage. Conrad could have restored the MS word that he earlier rejected and could have substituted 'drifting' for 'outlying', but if he made any change at all, it would most likely have been to reconcile the preposition with a typist's error. More probably, S's editor is doing the same while eliminating another anglicism.

114.25 **port bow** The left side (when facing forward) of the front part of a vessel is used here to indicate a 'bearing' (see 100.6*n*).

115.3 **sovereigns** One-pound gold coins, one of which in 1889, according to official sources, would have had an equivalent purchasing power in the year 2000 of about £65. For bases of computation, see p. xxxii, n. 1.

115.6 **Sunda Straits** The last area of the region before the ship enters the Indian Ocean. See Map 4.

115.21 **cruet stand** A silver-plated holder of a set of small glass bottles, with stoppers, containing vinegar, oil, and condiments for the table.

115.25 **galley** The ship's kitchen. In ships such as Conrad's *Otago* and *Narcissus*, the galley was situated on the upper deck amidships. It could be part of a larger structure; in the *Narcissus* this included a spare cabin, and in the *Cutty Sark* sleeping quarters for eight hands amidships. In both the *Otago* and the *Narcissus* it was shaped like a capacious sentry box.

115.31 **stairs. A**] MS stairs – through a S E1 A2 E2 stairs – through the A1 Although the dash, rather than S's usual comma, suggests Conrad, S's version makes the movements of the two men more explicit, instead of simply rendering the Captain's impressions. (Cf. 106.5, 115.18–19.) But the subtleties of the passage's entire construction apparently defied the ministrations of S's editor, as they required more than the addition or deletion of a word or two to right them. In the end S does not account very well for the phrasing '. . . a sliding door' (which also has to be attached to 'through', but without the dots, or suspension points, to make the syntactic sense aimed at in this change), nor for the sentence that follows independently in the spirit and flow of MS's version, nor indeed for the whole narrative mode beginning with the previous dash (115.31). S's unsatisfactory reading may well be another instance of *Harper's* editor fiddling to make movements on the ship clearer and more explicit, but not succeeding in this larger context of impressionistic rendering of the haste and tension under which events occur. See Fig. 20.

115.31–32 **tiny . . . passage** Another impressionistic detail, for which see the conjectured plan (Fig. 20).

115.37 **wondered**] ED wonder MS– The context craves the past tense. The Captain's reaction seems to be of the moment, not a retrospective reflection made in his role as narrator, which would be quite intrusive at this point. MS's form evidences the difficulty Conrad had with tenses throughout the story and appears to be one of the few that escaped both his attention and that of his publishers. Cf. 107.18, where he revised to the perfect but typically failed to achieve wholly coherent results.

116.8–9 **leeward . . . on the bow** Away from the wind . . . on the port bow, as the breeze is blowing landward on the south-easterly tack (see 108.5n, 110.7n, 114.25n).

116.11 **me down**] MS me S– The Captain has moved across and thus down the heeled or tilted deck (an inclination normal when sailing close-hauled), while remaining on the poop (cf. 116.8–9n). Conrad interlined 'down' in the manuscript, just as he earlier interlined 'over' in the phrase 'walked over to leeward' (116.8), and it is apparent he was sketching the Captain's movements quite carefully. MS's 'down' must stand in the face of S's omission, which represents either another interlineation skipped by the first typist or the editor's continuing concern with physical movement aboard ship, again misguided.

116.13 **weather** Manage to sail to the windward (of the island). The Captain tells his second mate the ship will get past the island. His unexplained intention to stand in as close as possible for Leggatt's sake and his argument that he needs to do so to pick up a land breeze make this statement far from reassuring. See 108.5n, 110.12n, 112.24n, 114.6–8.

116.16 **the**] S– a MS MS's reading is probably a Polonism in a paragraph that Conrad had no problem writing. Although S's substitution mutes the Captain's sense of isolation from his unruly second mate as well as the tensions between them, which MS's strange word sharpens, a later revision gives 'the helmsman' (117.23–25) a larger part in the drama. Here Conrad may have made the change in the lost typescript as part of this new strategy or simply for consistency (see also 116.34).

116.17 **her good full** Her sails filled with wind (*OED*), by virtue of her course (see 108.5n, 112.20n).

116.19 **sails slept** They were motionless and silent, not fluttering or shaking (because steadily filled with wind).

116.21–22 **too much. ... to shut ... eyes. She ... Must!**] MS too much for me. ... shut ... eyes – because the ship ... She must! S– The first of S's changes, which are of a piece, evidences the literalist tendencies of its editor. The second, possibly traceable to interlineation in the MS, and the third alter the Captain's statements and dilute the impact of the description, making his reasoned anticipation of the future, rather than his immediate shock at the sight before him, the cause of his action. The fourth, exhibiting the fastidious concern for literalness and smoothing out colloquial and clipped speech seen elsewhere in the editor's work, ruins the echo of a parallel passage (116.7). Cf. 89.11, 89.20n.

116.34 **I can't see the sails very well** When on a tack the helmsman has to keep the sails just this side of losing wind. He needs to see them because any loss of wind will first register as a visible fluttering of the sails, and later, if nothing is done, as a flapping sound, a sign of serious loss of headway. See 108.5n, 110.9n, 110.12n, 116.17n.

117.7 **Erebus** In classical mythology, Erebus (Darkness) was the son of Chaos and the father (by his sister Night) of Day. He was identified with the dark passage by which the souls of the dead, ferried in Charon's 'bark', entered the underworld. In 1841 the British explorer James Ross discovered a gigantic volcanic peak in Antarctica, due south of New Zealand, which he called 'Erebus'. Conrad draws on both associations. See *Enc. Brit.*

117.18–19 **weather . . . to stay** That is, never be able to shift tack by turning into the wind (*OED*); see 108.5*n*, 116.13*n*.

117.18–19 **close now**] S– close **MS** Although the addition is not unlike some he makes elsewhere, S's editor is unlikely to have placed 'now' this late in the sentence (cf. 117.40–118.1). Conrad's revision resembles that at 105.2 in its gratuitousness and emphasis on the narrative present. The word stresses the hopelessness of the Captain's present position and course. Logically, 'now' is not needed; but the chief mate, whose instinctive caution transforms the danger into disaster, is far from logical at the moment.

117.19 **stay. She'll drift ashore before she's round.**] S– stay. **MS** There are good reasons for believing S's sentence an editorial interpolation, but they are not in the end decisive. It amounts to a gloss, a near repetition of what the mate has just said in a speech that in MS Conrad wrote without any sign of hesitation or difficulty. 'She'll drift ashore' is virtually equivalent to 'She will never weather' and 'before she's round' to 'you are too close now to stay'. The sentence puts in layman's terms the mate's sailor-speak. In the ship this would be redundant and in such an emergency silly. Had Conrad wished to make this passage plainer for his audience, he could have substituted the new sentence for the old or further modified the original sentence, though the resulting speech would have been less authentic. Nonetheless, these arguments – partly predicated on rational behaviour by a mate who 'was of a painstaking turn of mind' and '"liked to account to himself for" practically everything that came in his way' (83.14–16), and who in the face of potential disaster is as rattled in his own way as was the *Sephora*'s captain – are outweighed by the facts that Conrad apparently revised the previous sentence, that this new one knits so well with the mate's next speech, and that it contains two contractions which S's editor would have normally eschewed. Indeed, it seems unlikely that even the editor of *Harper's*, whose alterations of this kind are often characterized by reductiveness (cf. 89.20, 93.6), would have interpolated such a sentence at this point, even if he had understood Conrad's previous one precisely enough to do so. By and large it looks as if Conrad, who gave these concluding paragraphs inordinate attention when revising the typescript (see, e.g., the substitution at 117.39 and the addition at 117.40–118.2), thought it necessary to make this crucial point more comprehensible and was willing to risk verisimilitude to do so. Cf. the addition at 118.15, which repeats more plainly the statement begun at 118.11.

117.21 **shook it**] S– shook him **MS** S's change literally reconciles this statement with that immediately below (117.26) and keeps the focus on the mate's arm. Although it is hard to conceive of such violent shaking not extending to the whole body rather than merely to the arm, which would be pointless in any case, logic was apparently not the operative factor here. The MS gives no sign of revision or hesitation, but Conrad, who heavily revised this paragraph and the next in the first typescript (cf. 117.18–19*n* and 117.19*n*), seems to have put consistency and immediate comprehension of detail above other considerations.

117.26–27 **Ready about** The order to begin to change tack (*Ships and the Sea*), a general one for the crew, as the previous one was directed to the helmsman, not the chief mate.

117.28–29 **head-sheets . . . overhauled** Ropes attached to the headsails (i.e., to the jibs and staysails) . . . ensured that they will not snag or tangle when the order comes for them to be pulled in or released during the tacking manœuvre. On this whole complex manœuvre – technically, making a sternboard while tacking, and not a complete boxhaul (as some have believed) – see John Harland, *Seamanship in the Age of Sail* (1984), ch. 12, and Frank Scott, *A Square Rig Handbook*, 2nd edn (2001), ch. 3. See also Fig. 21.

117.36 **Hard a-lee** The command to the helmsman to turn the wheel fully so as to bring the ship up into the wind and to keep it turned until the mainsail fills with wind for the new tack (see 108.5*n*, 118.8*n*). This order, which prepares for swinging round the sails, is a paradoxical convention surviving from the days of the tiller (see 110.7*n*). See Fig. 21.

117.40 **coming-to** Responding to the rudder by heading closer into the wind.

118.4 **pivot] S– swing MS** This change in S, along with the previous one (118.3), bears on the reader's orientation and reaches back into the very first paragraphs describing the land and sea and the tug merging in the landscape. S's 'pivot' expresses more precisely the effect the ship's movement has, as if she were stationary and the land revolving – an impression similar to that Conrad carefully crafted earlier when describing the land and the sky (114.24*n*). The revisions here diminish but do not eliminate the alliterative flow of the passage, which is sustained in the next few sentences, though that, too, is diminished later through a revision in E1 (118.15–16).

118.8 **swung the mainyard** Turned the mainsail. Timing of this manœuvre so that the mainsail and rudder counteract whatever drawing power the foresail may have is crucial to avoid both falling off on the same tack (to sure disaster) and making it too difficult to swing all the other yards on the mainmast that have sails set. The Captain, having gotten the ship too close to the land to retain any safety margin, is under double anxiety: he is too new to the ship to know how she will respond, and he lacks a reliable reference point by which to determine how she is moving.

118.11 **taffrail** The after-rail surrounding the stern of the ship.

118.11–12 **way . . . side** For a sailing ship to 'have way' is for it to have movement through the water. If the Captain shifts the helm when the ship is still inching forward, she will fall back on the old tack and go ashore. He steps close to the taffrail on the port side, from which Leggatt has left the ship (and where he loses the 'floppy hat').

118.13–14 **a glassy . . . sleeping] MS** the glassy . . . sleeping **S** the glassy . . . the sleeping **E1–** Although the definite articles make the vision itself more definite, Conrad's weak grasp of the differences between English articles would probably not have led him to revise the first. The second change follows on the first and could be either his or a compositor's patch. Both changes sacrifice alliteration and rhythm for greater definition. But is definition wanted? It appears not: the point, made from the very beginning, is that there is no definition. It seems likely that S's editor substituted 'the' for 'a' to eliminate a perceived idiomatic problem and thus provoked E1's change.

118.27 **the slaying**] MS a slaying S– S's reading reflects a distinction largely lost on Conrad, but in its idiomatic correctness it diminishes the rhetoric and softens the apocalyptic tone. This is probably an editorial intrusion.

118.34 **shift the helm** Move back the wheel – i.e., the direction of the rudder. The order follows from the Captain's first one ('Hard a-lee', 117.36n), so as to produce the turn of the bow to the right (starboard) required for the new tack. See 108.5n.

118.38–39 **break of the poop . . . forebraces** The Captain moves to the front of the poop deck to oversee the main deck, where the hands forward (accompanied by the chief mate) are holding the ropes waiting to rotate the foresail and all the sails set above it, which along with the jibs and staysails will help rotate the ship's bow to complete the change of tack. See 89.9n, 97.14–15n, 97.25n, 110.12n, 119.4n.

118.39 **The**] MS E1– All the S Despite its apparent redundancy, S's repetition of 'all' three times in a row looks like a rhetorical flourish performed by Conrad while touching up his antepenultimate paragraph. However, he apparently reconsidered while revising the next sentence for E1, choosing logical clarity over rhetorical effect.

118.40 **gliding from right to left** Standing on the poop, facing forward, the Captain sees the stars move from right to left and knows his ship's head is moving from left to right, i.e., from port to starboard. See Fig. 21.

119.1 **She's round** See 111.30n. The ship has just passed across the wind and is, much to the crew's relief, now on the new tack and able to gather speed.

119.3 **Let go and haul** The standard order issued when the bow of a square-rigged ship has just come round and is about to 'pay off' – turn away from the wind into the new direction until all her sails are 'full' and 'drawing' (*Ships and the Sea*). 'Let go' refers to the weather braces (the ropes attached to the yard-end facing the wind), and 'haul' refers to the ropes attached to the lee braces (the side away from the wind). Turning a yard requires continuous control over it, with one group of men releasing exactly as the other group draws.

119.4 **foreyards** The yards on the foremast, carrying the 'forecourse' or 'foresail' (the largest sail on that mast) and four or five others above it. See 118.38–39n.

119.11 **taffrail** See 118.11n. The Captain returns from the break of the poop to look out over the stern towards a receding Koh-ring, which the now invisible Leggatt is approaching.

119.13 **catch**] S– have MS Although S eliminates an anglicism where MS exhibits no indecision on Conrad's part about the word, and thus creates a phrase that he uses sparingly – thrice in *Almayer's Folly*, but only once in 'Youth', 'Typhoon', *Under Western Eyes*, and *Victory* – Conrad seems to have revised the typescript here as he did earlier (see 108.19–20n). Such phrasing was present from the beginning (81.30), and even if this first instance gave way to a revision in E1 that helped establish a calm atmosphere before Leggatt's arrival (see 84.36n), other revisions developed rather than diminished the concept (see 90.12n). In the end catching sight and other kinds of catching became so important in the tale that it eventually included this particular phrasing as often as all the rest of Conrad's mature work.

Freya of the Seven Isles

MS	holograph manuscript (Philadelphia)
TS1	typescript (Berg)
TS1t	typewritten (unrevised) text of TS1 superseded by revision
TS1r	revised text of TS1 (incorporating Conrad's alterations): copy-text
SE	*London Magazine*, July 1912, pp. 649–84
SA	*Metropolitan Magazine*, April 1912, pp. 20–29, 51–4

121.1 **Seven Isles** The principal islands in a cluster of some 300 islets, called in Malay *Pulau* (= islands) *Tujuh* (= seven), are located east of central Sumatra on a north–south line between Singapore and 'Banka' (Bangka), about 1 degree south of the equator. See Map 4.

121.2 **Shallow Waters** The seas between mainland Asia and the islands of Sumatra, Borneo, and Java are extremely shallow, 'nowhere more than two hundred feet deep' (Vlekke, p. 2).

123.3 **many years ago** The dating of the action can only be conjectured. Nelson's history, the association of Freya with Wagner's *Ring of the Nibelungen* (first performed complete in 1876), and a very exactly plotted fictional chronology (see 186.29–30n) suggest that the action could plausibly be located in the latter part of the 1880s, when Conrad was himself in the East. See 'Introduction', pp. liii–lv, lxi and 133.31n.

123.4 **a . . . letter** Coming as it does from one of the narrator's 'old chums . . . in Eastern waters', it may recall Captain Marris's letter to Conrad of 18 July 1909. See 'Introduction', pp. liv–lvi.

123.8–9 **specially beloved . . . early** A jocular version of the proverb 'those beloved by the gods die young'.

123.17 **telegraph cables** The cable from Europe was extended from India to Singapore in 1870, the cable linking Singapore to Batavia (Jakarta) via the islands of Mintok (Muntok) and Bangka in 1871 (Turnbull, p. 90). At 146.3 the narrator receives 'cable messages' recalling him to London.

123.17 **had served English firms** By 1867 there were sixty European companies, most of them British, in Singapore, which mainly functioned as entrepot (temporary storage). These firms exported tapioca, coffee, copra, rubber, sugar, cocoa, nutmeg, pepper, tobacco, tin, and oil, especially for petroleum (i.e., paraffin or kerosene) lamps; they imported rice, cotton goods, fertilizers, machines, and tools. See Turnbull, pp. 43–4, 88–92.

123.18 **one of us** A complex and key phrase in *Lord Jim*, here it expresses the sense of solidarity of British traders in the Archipelago.

123.19 **Eastern Archipelago** The Malay Archipelago (known as Indonesia since at least 1857, and also as the independent state of Malaysia since 1949) consists of approximately 13,000 islands extending in a shallow curve along the equator from the Malay Peninsula towards Australia (see Maps 1 and 4). Most of its wealth and population are concentrated in Java with its capital Jakarta (Batavia under the Dutch). By the sixteenth century, Islam, carried by trade to Indonesia from the Near East, had succeeded Hinduism and Buddhism as the dominant religion, while European commercial interests had made their appearance in the region, initially in 1511 with the Portuguese in Malacca, then in 1596 with the Dutch, and in 1600 with the British. The British had confined themselves to India after the Anglo-Dutch conflicts of 1610–23 had secured the interests of the Dutch East India Company in the Archipelago, but the victorious Napoleon liquidated the Company in 1799. British colonial forces under Stamford Raffles (founder of Singapore in 1819) occupied Java and its dependencies between 1811 and 1814. When in 1813 self-government was restored to the Netherlands, the East India Company was not revived, and rule over the Dutch dominions passed to the government. In 1848 the Netherlands adopted a liberal constitution and gradually introduced a liberal economy into the Archipelago, thus greatly accelerating commercial activity during Conrad's maritime years. See Vlekke.

123.21 **eight. For years and years.**] TS1r eight. MS TS1t eight, for years and years. SE E2 eights, for years and years. E1–A2 OM SA TS1r's 'figures of eight. For years and years.' was normalized in SE and corrupted in E1. SE's change reflects an inclination to join fragments to adjacent constructions and clearly counteracts Conrad's deliberate revision in the typescript. The origin of the plural 'eights' in E1 is more problematic, given the near absence of such error and editorial intrusion in E1 as well as the utter lack of precedence for the phrase in Conrad's manuscripts and typescripts. Although it might be a mistake made by Conrad in the course of contending with one and perhaps two errors in SE proofs, 'eights' cannot be adopted with any conviction that it represents Conrad's wording.

123.26–30 **Philippines . . . Inquisition** A possession of the Spanish crown from 1542, these islands, named after the ultra-Catholic Philip II, became notorious for their ungovernability – which only hardened colonial intransigence. In particular, the Moros, a Malay people from the southern Philippines, became ruthless pirates who were finally brought under control only in the middle of the nineteenth century. By then the colonial authority of Spain had been replaced by that of the Jesuits (*Enc. Brit.*). It is possible that the narrator's mockery of 'old Nelson' for frightening himself by reading 'stories of the Inquisition' (such as, perhaps, Edgar Allen Poe's 1843 'The Pit and the Pendulum') may represent a covert joke on Conrad's part. See Map 4.

123.27–28 **dread of . . . authorities** This trait of Nelson's, one of the elements generating the tragic outcome of the tale, is more than individual; it is also a symptom of the effects of cultural displacement, represented by the English name 'Nelson' and the Danish 'Nielsen'. Aggravated after his retirement to 'the very smallest' of the Seven Isles (186.6–7), Nelson's neurosis is not, however, unfounded. In 1870 the Dutch States General enacted the so-called 'Agrarian Law' prohibiting the selling of land owned or used by Indonesians to non-Indonesians and also claiming as government domain those lands, like Nelson's island, to which no Indonesian held claim (see Vlekke, p. 307).

123.32–124.1 **English authorities . . . Dutch . . . Spaniards** These three represent the main colonial authorities in and around the Archipelago at the time. The first controlled the (Malaccan) 'Straits' Settlements (see 141.29n) which from 1826 included Penang, Malacca, and Singapore, and (later) Labuan off N.W. Borneo, and (eventually) a substantial portion of western Borneo. The Dutch controlled formally and informally the great swathe of islands from Sumatra to western New Guinea. The Spanish held the Philippines, until the United States seized them in 1899. See Map 4.

124.8 **cannibals** Cannibalism, in the sense of putting human flesh on the menu, does not seem to have been practised widely in the Archipelago, except in New Guinea. What did take place in other parts of Indonesia, especially in Borneo, was ritualistic headhunting – the strong version of North American 'scalping' – which was thought to initiate youth into maturity and to weaken the enemy. See *Enc. Brit.*; Pamela Brown and Donald Turzin, eds., *The Ethnography of Cannibalism* (1983); and David Gill, 'The Fascination of the Abomination: Conrad and Cannibalism', *The Conradian*, 24 (1999), 15–19.

124.11 **fifty pounds** One pound sterling in 1880 was approximately one week's income on average. This sum would have had the purchasing power of approximately £3,250 in the year 2000. See 115.3n and p. xxxii, n. 1.

124.14–15 **Sultan of . . . the Seven Isles** Although also called 'that Rajah of ours' (161.37–38), these references are not as careless as appears. Historically the Seven Isles had no sultan of their own: they were part of the Residency of Rlouw and without any connection to the large island of Bangka to the south, which possessed its own Residency. Towards the end of the nineteenth century, colonial control, though of course finally unnegotiable, favoured delegation and decentralization. Senior colonial officials were called 'Residents'; they shared authority with native 'Regents' on the principle that as far as possible 'the native population should be left under the immediate government (*bestuur*) of their own headmen' (Furnivall, p. 123). The titles of regents and hereditary chiefs varied regionally: 'sultans' in Sumatra, 'kings' in Bali, 'susuhunans' and 'sultans' in Java, and 'rajahs' collectively. Even in Java, where Dutch rule was concentrated, the principle of shared rule, as opposed to direct rule, was nominally observed. See 129.3n; also Furnivall, pp. 89–92, and Vlekke, pp. 257–8, 263.

124.21 **cultivation** That is, of tobacco (147.22, 167.9). Although tobacco was apparently not grown on the islands between Sumatra and Borneo, it was introduced with spectacular success in near-by eastern Sumatra. Between 1856 and 1885 the value of private exportation rose from 1 million to 20.1 million guilders (Furnivall, p. 169) – roughly the equivalent at the time of £1,654,320 or $8,040,000 (US).

124.24 **Jasper Allen** The surname is English, which politicizes the rivalry with the Dutch Heemskirk, in contrast to the studied ambiguity of Nelson versus Nielsen.

124.28 **alpaca** Llama wool, which by the end of the nineteenth century was second to sheep's wool in the textile trade. *Enc. Brit.*

124.30 **fretful porcupine** As applied to a moustache this phrase, used by the Ghost to describe Hamlet's terror at seeing his father, is mock-heroic. See *Hamlet* I.v.20 ('the fretful porpentine').

125.19 **dinghy** A small open boat, generally a work-boat (Hindi).

125.28 **sailed . . . her parents** For a merchant shipmaster to have his family with him at sea was not uncommon. In Conrad's own work it occurs at least three other times (in 'Falk', 'The Brute', and *Chance*) beyond *Twixt Land and Sea* (see 'A Smile of Fortune', 22.34–35, and 'The Secret Sharer' 92.40–93.1).

125.31 **Singapore** An outpost of European culture and English private education for someone like Freya, Singapore represented for the Dutch a threatening presence. Although indispensable to Dutch trade, it played a material part in the growth of the anti-English feeling that leads to the tragic outcome of Conrad's tale. Founded for the British East India Company in 1819 by Stamford Raffles on a sparsely populated island at the tip of the Malay Peninsula, Singapore quickly transformed its magnificent natural harbour into the trade emporium of the Far East. As such it threatened Dutch interests in the region, especially when, in defiance of the 1824 treaty by which the Netherlands secured its claims to territories south of Singapore, the British did not oppose James Brooke's interventions eastwards in Sarawak (Borneo), though they resisted a similar attempt in Siak, North-East Sumatra. See Vlekke, pp. 297–8. See also Map 4.

125.37 **Steyn and Ebhart's** No such piano maker seems to have been recorded, although several Ebharts are mentioned in *The Pierce Piano Atlas* (8th edn, *ca.* 1975).

126.16–17 ***Bonito* . . . brig** The Spanish 'bonito' (graceful, elegant) is a masculine adjective because the Spanish 'bergantin' (i.e., the original of 'brig') is a masculine noun. These square-rigged, two-masted vessels were known, among other things, for their speed. See 178.13–14, 130.12–23*n*. According to Norman Sherry, 'the *Bonito, Neptun* and the *Bohemian Girl* . . . were names of actual ships which sailed in Eastern waters during Conrad's period of service in the mercantile marine' (*CEW*, pp. 270–71).

126.21 **an] E1**– the usual **MS–SE** E1's substitution might at first suggest the hand of an editor, partly because it removes the contradiction between 'now and again' and 'the usual'. Conrad, however, altered other inconsistencies of this sort (145.34, 166.10, 174.10) and when revising was particularly alert to redundancies like 'the usual', which is not needed once 'now and again' establishes the frequency of the rainstorms.

126.26 **rattan screens** The long, thin pliable stems of this East-Indian climbing plant, split and attached horizontally to hessian strips, can be rolled down as screens that cut light without blocking ventilation (*OED*). See also 125.11 and 148.36.

126.28 **fierce Wagner music** Richard Wagner (1813–83) brought European music to new heights of intoxicating grandeur, largely by dissolving the predictabilities of the diatonic scale and by liberating rhythm from the straitjacket of the bar-line. With a magnificent musical instrument and an echo-chamber consisting of an entire house (see 157.10–12), Freya can compete with tropical thunder and lightning (126.27–29). Wagner's music, which magnifies the self by mythologizing and threatening it, will prove relevant to Conrad's story of love and death at the most literal level. See 'Introduction', p. lxi.

126.34 **cables** Heavy chains or hemp rope attached to the anchor.

127.6–10 **standing on . . . tacking for the anchorage . . . puts the helm down . . . sails shaking** Jasper is approaching the anchorage from the north (presumably from Singapore), which lies below the 'point of land', or peninsula, on which Nelson's house stands, facing west towards Sumatra. See Map 4. Instead of 'standing on' (continuing on the same course) southwards until he can double back at leisure to tack up the safe passage between rocks and land to the anchorage, he impulsively 'puts the helm down' (i.e., to leeward) and, abruptly taking the wind out of the sails, makes them rattle. Cf. 108.5n, 110.7n, 112.20n, 116.34n, 117.36n.

128.30 **mop-headed** The narrator's jocular epithet, echoing the unjudgemental description by Wallace (p. 449) of 'the compact frizzled mop which is the Papuans' pride and glory', undemonizes these cannibals.

129.3 **Governor of Banka** After the discovery of major tin deposits in Bangka (ca. 1709), the Dutch secured sovereignty over the island from Sumatra and introduced direct rule. Vlekke, pp. 201–2.

129.13 **Saïgon** In Conrad's time Saigon was the main port of French Indo-China. Laid out in classical rectilinear style, it was probably the most elegant colonial town in the Far East. See 113.3n.

129.33–34 **Who . . . prison?** Dr Samuel Johnson, as quoted more than once by James Boswell in his *Life of Johnson* (1791), which is, *inter alia*, a diary of Johnson's conversation: for example, 'No man will be a sailor who has contrivance enough to get himself into a jail; for, being in a ship is being in a jail, with the chance of being drowned.'

130.6 **Peruvian** After wresting its independence from Spanish rule in 1821, Peru retained contact with the Spanish Philippines, which face it across the Pacific.

130.9 **"for family reasons"** The invocation of family, source of honour, by a Spanish *caballero* (cavalier, hence gentleman) imposed respect and discretion.

130.12–23 **The brig herself . . . opium smuggler.** In the East, brigs were often associated with the opium trade. During the first decades of the nineteenth century they supplied the drug to ports along the whole of the Chinese coastline. This required them to be exceptionally quick and manœuvrable, for they had to navigate inshore in shallow waters, to outrun pirates and powerful Chinese police junks, and to beat to windward against the summer monsoons. As for the 'opium clippers', these 'tiny, tall-masted, long sparred ships' were the prototypes of the great ocean-going clippers of the later nineteenth century, such as the *Cutty Sark*, associated with 'The Secret Sharer', or the *Torrens*, in which Conrad served as mate on two voyages between England and Australia. See Basil Lubbock, *The Opium Clippers* (1933), pp. 1–29.

131.8 **sword-blade** Cf. 137.28–31n.

131.15–16 **if love begins in imagination** A claim famously defended by Stendhal in *De l'Amour* (1822), where he defined the act of falling in love as 'crystallization', a process in which the lover's imagination transforms the loved being into a creature of perfection much as salt wells cover with glittering crystals anything thrown into them. For Conrad's view of Stendhal, see *Notes on Life and Letters*, p. 12.

131.22 **Heemskirk** The sound of the name (Hayms-kirk in English) may be Dutch, but the spelling, which would require 'kerk', is not.

131.35–36 **the Devil . . . better days** Once a luminary in Heaven, Satan is now 'an archangel ruined' (Milton) – unlike Heemskirk, whose social and naval rank has always been mediocre.

131.35 **had**] MS TS1 has **SE**– OM SA The awkward tense here and in the next phrase (131.36) was changed either by *London Magazine* personnel or more probably by a typist who had trouble reading Conrad's first 'had' and 'corrected' it as well as the second. His habitual difficulty with such matters makes it unlikely that Conrad twice revised both these tenses in SE proofs, one of them a result of revision in the typescript, the other an original reading that survived that revision.

132.2 *Neptun* Military vessels often bore masculine names from classical mythology. 'Neptune' was used for seven major ships of the Royal Navy, 'Agamemnon' for five (Nelson captained the first); at Trafalgar the English had the 'Mars', the 'Achilles', the 'Polyphemus', and so on, while the French had the 'Pluton', the 'Neptune', the 'Achille', and others.

132.4 **to look after the traders** Heemskirk's gun-boat existed because traders such as the narrator and Allen needed protection. Piracy, however defined, had been endemic in the Archipelago. Pirate fleets out of East Borneo, Halmahera (an island between New Guinea and Celebes), the Papuan Islands, and most of all the Sulu islands with their 'Illanos' or 'Moros' (who had fleets of over 100 ships) had ravaged great areas throughout the eighteenth century. Piracy was still rampant in Conrad's time, with punitive expeditions undertaken against the pirates of Tobelo in the Moluccas, the piratical rajahs of Borneo, the Atjenese (Acehnese) of Northern Sumatra, and the Moros of the Sulu Islands. See Vlekke, pp. 206–8, 297–8, 315.

132.9–10 **Mintok . . . Palembang** The first (now Muntok) is the capital of the island Bangka ('Banka'; see 186.34), about seventy miles by sea from the Seven Isles. The second is a major inland town in south-east Sumatra. See Map 4.

132.16–17 **that absurd mistake** The narrator discourages a nationalist or ethnic view of the tale as a struggle between the English and the Dutch.

132.22 **undress** Informal, unceremonial, or ordinary.

132.30 **plantation** An estate in former tropical or sub-tropical colonies which produced cotton, tobacco, coffee, or sugarcane.

132.32 **tiffin** Lunch (Anglo-Indian).

132.36–37 **savage . . . poisoned arrows** Such arrows, or darts, tipped with curare poison, were discharged from a blowpipe; they are apparently still in use in parts of South-East Asia (*Columbia Encyclopaedia*, 5th edn). The implication seems to be that Nelson lacks not physical courage but what might be called 'cultural' or 'moral' courage.

133.19 **for what she was not** That is, presumably, promiscuous.

133.31 **officer of the King** William III; his reign as King of the Netherlands from 1849 to 1890 helps date Conrad's tale, as his successor, Queen Wilhelmina, reigned for nearly sixty years.

134.15 **blackbeetle** The stout cockroach common in the tropics and sub-tropics, not the smaller though equally creepy creature that would have been known to much of Conrad's first audience; the phrase recurs (e.g., at 143.10, 152.36, 153.18, 173.7).

135.2 **holystoned quarter deck** The holystone was a piece of sandstone used for scrubbing (or 'sanding') wooden decks – perhaps so called because one had to kneel to use it, or because the work was usually reserved for Sundays (*Ships and the Sea*). On the 'quarter deck', see 135.38n.

135.4–5 **rake ... spars ... big yards squared** Respectively, angle of the ship's masts in relation to the perpendicular (usually a tilt aft) ... almost any support for sails above the hull ... large spar crossing the masts horizontally.

135.8 **seventh heaven** The location of unqualified rapture in Jewish (and hence Western and Mohammedan) tradition.

135.30 **tropical swiftness** Near the equator the rising as well as the setting sun seems to move more quickly than in temperate zones. See 82.16n and *Almayer's Folly*, 11.11n.

135.38 **on the quarter** Such a wind blows at an angle either on the port or the starboard side (i.e., strikes somewhat behind either the left or the right shoulder of a man facing forward); if at an angle of, say, $25°$ to $65°$, the square sails will be most efficient. The quarters are the two after parts of the ship, on each side of the centre. Cf. 'quarter deck' (135.2n) and 'quartermaster' (136.24n).

135.38–39 **Banjermassin** The capital and main port of South Borneo.

136.3 **Nelson]** E1– Nelson (or Nielsen) MS TS1 SE OM SA Although Conrad was to drop the '(or Nielsen)' figure by the fourth section while he was writing and revising, it remained intermittent in the second and third. Here the phrase came in the middle of a periodic sentence and disrupted its parallelism. The later excision in E1 of this and another phrase (136.5) provided some relief in the extraordinarily long and complex construction.

136.24 **quartermaster** Senior helmsman who takes over when a ship is entering or leaving harbour.

136.26 **gig** A light, narrow ship's boat, built for speed. See also 141.4.

136.31 **on]** MS–SA E1– on to SE The narrator will follow Jasper 'up there' (136.32). SE 'corrected' Conrad's nautical preposition, which he apparently restored in E1 and used again: 'the lieutenant had gone on the bridge' (182.10–11).

137.25–27 **This ... one.** See 125.28n.

137.28–31 **It is ... question.** The nobleman's rapier can prove fragile when confronted with the yokel's cudgel: the intensity of refined love may prove equally so when facing the brutalities of life.

137.38 **twenty-first birthday** The age of legal as well as moral independence in the Britain of Conrad's time.

138.27 **Schultz** Conrad elsewhere associates Germans either with bullying arrogance (e.g., Schomberg in 'Falk', *Lord Jim*, and *Victory*) or with impotent scrupulousness (e.g., Stein in *Lord Jim*).

138.33 **Talk about moving stones** This is the classical trope for eloquence. Orpheus' song 'drew trees, stones' (*The Merchant of Venice* v.i.80) to gather themselves spontaneously into the wall of Thebes; Marc Antony's eloquence was such as to 'move / The stones of Rome to rise and mutiny' (*Julius Cæsar* III.ii.233–4).

138.39 **six white suits** The *Bonito*'s sartorial standards appear to be high. For officers in navies, full uniforms had not been introduced until the mid-eighteenth century, and for petty officers and seamen not until 100 years later; the merchant services followed with various lapses of time (see *Ships and the Sea*, s.v. 'sailors' dress'). It is doubtful that the crews of local independent trading steamers, such as the *Vidar* on which Conrad served as mate, would have worked in white suits.

139.1 **clear the ship** A ship is cleared to sail when all the formalities with the ship's papers at the custom house have been observed. Under Maritime Law, as well as insurance regulations, a ship cannot leave port without an acceptable complement of officers.

139.12–13 **Captain Robinson . . . Chantabun . . . Chinese junk** An example of service gossip, the statement is a mixture of precision and vagueness: the first is a senile adventurer in *Lord Jim* and a person known to Conrad (according to his unpublished outline for *The Rescue*), the second an obscure port on the northeast coast of the Gulf of Siam (Thailand), the third a Chinese sailing ship. More precisely, a junk is a flat-bottomed vessel, high-sterned, with square bows, two or three masts, and four-sided sails made of matting stiffened with battens, which enable it to sail well to windward (*Enc. Brit.*).

139.14 *Bohemian Girl* See 126.16–17n.

139.16 *Nan-shan* A ship of this name sailed in eastern waters during Conrad's career in the mercantile marine, seeing action as late as the First World War. One also appears in 'Typhoon'.

139.17 **brass bearings** Naval brass, also known as 'delta metal', is produced by adding to copper very small amounts of iron and even smaller amounts of zinc, the first making the metal exceptionally hard, the second making it resistant to sea-water corrosion. The brass is used for ships' valves, propellers, and (as here) bearings, which, as their name indicates, support rotating or other moving parts. *Ships and the Sea*.

139.34 **dollars** The common currency of South-East Asia was the Spanish silver dollar, although in some areas, like Singapore, which was subject to the British East India Company's rupee, paper transactions were recorded in that currency. Colonial, as opposed to Company, rule was established in Singapore in 1887, the year in which Conrad was trading out of Singapore, when dollars and cents became the official, as well as the practical, currency. Turnbull, p. 40.

140.22–23 **hove-to**] **E1**– hove-to still **MS TS1** OM **SA SE** To 'heave to' is to lay a sailing ship close to the wind (nearly against the wind), and with some sails working against others, so as to make virtually no headway (see *Ships and the Sea*). Conrad deleted 'still' probably to eliminate a redundancy and because 'like a sleeping sea-bird' sufficiently conveyed the impression of stability. It seems unlikely that a Dent's editor would have excised a word that helped explain a nautical term.

140.26 **Java Sea** The body of water between Java and Borneo. See Map 4; 92.15n.

140.28 **mail-routes** The regular paths or courses taken by ships carrying the mail. In the Archipelago the mail-carrying passenger steamers served only main ports, separated by immense distances. See 41.27n.

141.3 **his business** To deliver rice in North Borneo (147.39, 171.32).

141.8–9 **Palembang . . . Flores . . . Sumbawa** For Palembang, see 132.9–10n. Flores and Sumbawa were part of the Lesser Sunda Islands, which extend east of Java. See Map 4.

141.11 **beacons** The rivers of north-eastern Borneo have very shallow entrances, which make trading with up-river or inland settlements hazardous. As mate of the *Vidar* Conrad had frequent first-hand experience of navigating the River Berau, also known as the Pantai (see *Almayer's Folly*, 5.14n). The entrance to it necessitated finding a channel with the required depth marked by beacons. In *The Outcast of the Islands*, for example, the pioneer Lingard 'had found out and surveyed . . . the entrance to that river' (p. 200). On this river and the beacons required for it, see *CEW*, pp. 123–4. See 168.16–18n.

141.29 **Straits** The territories of Penang, Malacca, and Singapore, on the south-western coast of the Malay peninsula, separated from Sumatra by the Strait of Malacca (see 123.32–124.1n). In 1826 they were unified administratively, initially under the British East India Company and later under the India Office. In view of the extraordinary commercial success of Singapore, 'the Straits' became a short-hand name for that city.

142.8 **heavens] E1–** the heavens **MS TS1 SE** OM **SA** E1's omission reflects Conrad's frequent difficulty with the definite article, rather than compositorial error, as a series of such changes indicates (cf. 131.36, 142.34–35, 145.31); see also his similar deletion in SE (163.31).

142.23 **awnings** These canvas canopies, spread over a deck for protection from the sun, were set over a ridge rope stretched lengthwise and secured to both sides of the deck.

142.24 **A comedy father** Here and elsewhere (e.g., 149.11–12), Nelson is portrayed as the 'guileless comedy father', a stock character drawn from the traditional Italian–French farce to which Molière and Goldoni gave classical status; the tradition also included other stage types. See Robert Henke, *Performance and Literature in the Commedia dell'Arte* (2002), pp. 19–24, for 'Pantalone' (Nelson), 'Innamorata' and 'Innamorato' (Freya and Jasper), 'Franceschina' (Antonia), and 'Capitano' (Heemskirk). Had Conrad required more than what was available to him in the culture of his time, he would have had access to J. A. Symonds' lengthy introduction to his 1890 translation of Carlo Gozzi's *Memorie inutili* (1797). See also 145.20n.

142.34–39 **Somehow or other . . . a few hours later** This refers to the pivotal episode, impersonally recounted by the narrator in section IV from what Nelson tells him in London after events have run their course.

143.17 **why] MS** what **TS1 SE E1–** OM **SA** When Conrad revised his manuscript from 'what on earth have been laughing at' to 'why on earth have we been laughing at', he failed to cancel 'at', a problem Jessie Conrad 'corrected' by reversing his revision.

143.34 **against our declared policy** In 1870 Jakarta (Batavia) enacted a law prohibiting the selling to non-Indonesians of landed property owned or used by

Indonesians, and also retained as government domain those lands to which no Indonesian held claim (Vlekke, pp. 306–7). It is this latter provision, applicable to Nelson's otherwise uninhabited island, that forms the basis of Heemskirk's bullying of Nelson.

145.10 **half-caste Malacca Portuguese** Malacca (see Map 4), which had become a centre of Islamic trade with China, Indonesia, and the Near East, was captured by the Portuguese under Albuquerque in 1511. Following their entry into the area in the early seventeenth century, the Dutch captured Malacca in 1641, keeping it under more or less nominal control as a fortified town until 1795, when the British achieved dominance. By 1818 Malacca had again come under Dutch rule and remained so until the Dutch finally transferred it to the British in 1824. During their 130 years of occupation, the Portuguese freely intermingled with the Malays, creating a mixed-blood community in the Straits. *Enc. Brit.*

145.20 **camerista** The chambermaid was a stock character in the *commedia dell'arte* (see 142.24*n*), where she was often called Columbina and acted as a servant–confidante to Innamorata, the young 'lady in love', on whose behalf she was much given to amorous intrigue. *Commedia dell'arte*, in which Molière went to school, required stage types, virtually open slots, to stimulate improvisation on the part of the comedians.

145.27 **how . . . business** The apparently gratuitous phrase raises interpretative problems. This is not the first time that the narrator archly hints at his own susceptibility. Earlier he interrupts his observation that the powerful Freya as compared to Jasper 'had the more substance of the two' with 'you needn't try any cheap jokes; I am not talking of their weights' (137.32–33). There is more than a suggestion that he is being turned by the *commedia* (see 142.24*n*) into the stock role of the 'susceptible heavy' (an indication that the ostensibly comical situation is ominous with disaster). His comic role would help explain why he quite misinterprets the actions of Antonia who, far from being on the make, is terrified by Heemskirk's brutal handling of her and by his designs on Freya.

146.9 **the city** London's financial district, north of the Thames from half a mile west of St Paul's to the Tower, essentially the area of the medieval walled town.

146.24 **the East . . . out of my life** Despite appearing to drop the narrator's perspective, Conrad scrupulously preserves his function; the only change is that henceforth the narrator's information is no longer first-hand.

146.37 **matters of that sort** The 'matters' in question involve men accosting women, as this episode will show.

147.1–2 **As has been said already . . . Cove** See 142.34–39*n*; see also 187.14–16.

147.21 **drying sheds . . . manipulation** The tobacco-plant, which yields large, coarse leaves, requires the warm climate and well-drained soil provided by Nelson's equatorial promontory. After they have been picked, he has the leaves ventilated in the open air during the day (see 167.9–10) and carried back into 'drying sheds' for the night (148.27–28), where the bundles have to be manipulated into looseness. From 1862 eastern Sumatra took advantage of its volcanic soil and high rainfall to produce high-quality air-cured tobacco. Its commercial success, with dividends at 111 per cent, would have tempted Nelson to grow tobacco in the nearby Seven Isles. *Enc. Brit.*

148.27 **bitters** Often known as Angostura bitters, they give its distinctive wormwood flavour and colour to pink gin, a favourite tipple amongst naval officers since the beginning of the nineteenth century.

150.1 **compound** Derived from the Malay 'campong', which Conrad uses repeatedly in *Almayer's Folly*, the word denotes a living area for workmen or servants adjacent to their work, often enclosed, and somewhat removed from the master's house.

150.11 **to the left** An error, found in all texts, for 'to the right'. (See Fig. 22, Conrad's two sketches of Nelson's bungalow.) This kind of mistake is rare in Conrad's fiction. The bungalow atop its promontory faces west, towards Sumatra (125.21–22) and the setting sun, and overlooks both the anchorage and the steep path that leads up to it (see 127.6–10n). The west verandah with its expensive screens is a reception and dining space, 'the actual drawing room of the bungalow' (126.8–9); the 'back verandah' is Nelson's 'own special nook' (128.3–4), which is also called the 'east verandah' (152.31). Thanks to Heemskirk, it is possible to determine the positioning of the house and its dependencies. Leaving Nelson to finish supervising the storing of his tobacco for the night, he makes for the house 'from the north' (149.26–27). In the north verandah, which is a long secluded balcony blocked up both ends and accessible only from within the bungalow (148.39–149.2), Freya and Jasper are entertaining each other privately. They have set Antonia to keep watch (presumably in case old Nelson returns early); however, she is surprised, and threatened, by Heemskirk, who drags her 'by a circuitous way into the compound' (150.1), where the servants' and workers' bamboo huts are to be found (150.2–3). This compound is east of the house, for Antonia sees Heemskirk enter the house 'at the back' (150.8). We are now told that 'the interior of the bungalow' is divided into four parts 'by two passages crossing each other in the middle' (150.9–10), and that 'at that point Heemskirk, by turning his head slightly to the left as he passed' (150.10–11) sees Freya and Jasper in an embrace, then continues to the west verandah where he collapses into a chair (150.17–19). Thus, had Heemskirk indeed looked 'to the left' –that is to say, to the south, away from the north balcony – Conrad's *commedia dell'arte* would not have ended in revenge, suicide, madness, and death. Conrad does not provide a detailed plan of the bungalow; however, part of its disposition of space can be established. Freya's room opens out on the balcony which she has turned into a 'boudoir' (149.8–10); it must therefore be located on the northern side of the house. Further, it can be entered only from the 'inner passage' of the house (161.11) which, given the fact that the west–east passage connects the front to the back verandahs, must mean that Freya's room occupies either the north-west or the north-east corner of the house – and almost certainly the latter, given the specific impression of privacy (distance from the public space of the west verandah) it conveys (e.g., 161.11–14). As for Nelson's bedroom, it has to be one of the two rooms that open on the front verandah, for Nelson has vacated it for the stricken Heemskirk who, early the next morning, is able to spy diagonally through a very slightly opened door on Freya's uninhibited farewell gestures to the departing Jasper at one of the ends of the west verandah (163.34–39). We can be even more specific, for Freya makes for that end of the verandah from which she will be able to see 'the brig passing the point' (163.39–40) which, as we saw earlier, lies to the north. Nelson's bedroom would, then, occupy the south-west corner of the house.

151.2 **to slip**] TS1r– slip out **MS** slip TS1t Although Conrad incorporated TS1t's error, instead of restoring the MS reading, when making the verb an infinitive, this alteration reflected genuine rethinking. Characteristically, he would have used the word 'out' when describing someone stepping onto the verandah, but in this instance the reader does not actually see Jasper do so.

151.24 **tried to be conversational.**] TS1r– said conversationally **MS** was conversational. TS1t Conrad's revision, though a response to Jessie Conrad's intrusion, changes the nature of the scene by adding an element of tension absent from his MS version as well as hers. As the word 'said' does not occur in the immediate vicinity, his decision does not appear to have been motivated by the need to vary verbs used to signal discourse.

151.29 **Molluccas** The 'spice islands' (Maluku) of eastern Indonesia between Celebes (Sulawesi) and New Guinea, so called because they were the original source of nutmeg and cloves for Renaissance Europe. See Map 4.

151.40 **Tamil boy** 'Tamil', the lingua franca of southern India and northern Ceylon, signified someone living in those parts; 'boy' was a patronizing colonial term for an adult male servant.

151.40 **the lights** In nineteenth-century Indonesia portable lamps, rather than the combustible engine, were one of the first results of the discovery of oil: the story 'of how oil lamps were introduced into all corners of Asia' – and indeed all parts of the then colonial world – 'has often been told, by historians and by novelists' (Vlekke, p. 211). See 123.17n.

153.19 **around**] **MS–SA** round **SE–** SE's change evidences compositorial compression in a tight line of type that needed to include the full-stop and inverted commas. As Conrad uses 'round' more frequently than 'around' in this portion of the tale, the alteration might seem justified, but 'round' might have suggested Heemskirk's 'creeping' not within the house but without it. It seems less likely that Conrad made this change twice, in separate sets of proof for both SE and E1, than that E1 followed a mechanical adjustment made by SE's compositor.

154.35 **outraged**] **MS TS1t SE–** tormented TS1r OM SA SE's reading might be an error of recollection by its compositor or the Pinker typist (see 154.25), but it seems more likely that Conrad restored his MS wording to avoid repetition of a term found only a few sentences earlier.

155.39 **riding lights** White lights displayed in ships' forward rigging announce that they are at anchor ('riding'). See 85.8n.

156.6 **heat lightning** Such illumination from flashes near the horizon, often accompanied by clear skies and thunder too distant to be audible, is frequent in the tropics. See 85.37.

156.21 **the New Guinea coast** The dangers so described are navigational, not from humans (pirates or cannibals). See 132.4n.

157.14 **primed** Filled with liquor.

158.12–14 **Scandinavian goddess . . . devils in disguise** For Heemskirk, Freya is simultaneously divinity and demon, but by virtue of the desire that she provokes in him, not from romantic or religious symbolism. On Freya's association with the Nordic pantheon, see 'Introduction', p. lxi.

158.12 **love do**] **MS** love stop **TS1t** love! Stop! Do **TS1r**– Jessie Conrad's error shifted Conrad's meaning, putting the emphasis on Freya's stopping, rather than extending the notion of her as love goddess (see 158.12–14n). Because Conrad's alteration in TS1r did not solve the problem, his MS wording is here restored.

160.13 **laudanum** A tincture (i.e., alcoholic solution) of opium, used as an analgesic to quiet pain.

160.14 **got a**] **TS1r SA E1**– mad with **MS TS1t SE** Conrad returned to his MS reading in SE and to his later reading in E1. He might have felt that 'mad' was used too often to describe Heemskirk's toothache or that he was pre-empting the later scene in which Nelson and Freya both use the word in different senses.

161.37 **Rajah** See 124.14–15n.

162.32 **eyelashes**] **TS1r E1**– eyes **MS TS1t SE** OM **SA** Although Conrad may have restored MS's 'eyes' in SE, he apparently allowed his TS1r reading to stand for E1. SE's reading could represent an error of the Pinker typist, but this cannot be ascertained because SA omits the entire passage. Images of wet eyelashes appear in *Almayer's Folly* (114.20), *The Nigger of the 'Narcissus'* (p. 8), and *Chance* (p. 45).

165.2 **red ensign** An ensign is the flag carried by a nation's ships. British ships have three: red for the merchant navy, white for Royal Navy warships, and blue for its auxiliary ships. This detail re-ignites the national tensions inherent in the Jasper–Heemskirk rivalry.

165.18 **the last**] **SE**– a last **MS TS1** OM **SA** Although SE's article could be compositorial, Conrad here changed TS1r's 'laborious' to 'tottering', and throughout E1 in particular made other changes to articles, resulting in some odd readings (142.8, 142.34–35, 142.38, 145.31, 163.16, 174.9).

165.38 **ulster** A man's heavy double-breasted overcoat with a belt at the back (so called because it was first produced in Northern Ireland).

167.6 **H.M. the King of the Netherlands** The reference to King William III and the *Neptun*'s full title draws attention to the nationalism inherent in Heemskirk's ruthlessness.

167.16 **Carimata** Trading vessels called regularly at this coal-producing island off south-west Borneo to refuel. See Map 4.

167.19 **long chair** That is, a deck-chair (a Gallicism, from 'chaise longue'), in which it is impossible not to assume a semi-prone posture, thus displaying the physical contrast between the two men.

167.23 **service of love** 'Courtly love', characterized by the lover's 'consecrated' idealization of the beloved, as opposed to the aggressive possessiveness of carnal appetite. Here and elsewhere, the difference between Jasper and Heemskirk is expressed as a contrast between sail and steam. What is new is the invocation of the sacred and the profane in an opposition between Christian salvation (as in the 'elect of Freya' at 175.14) and pagan damnation (as at 167.30–31).

167.27 **chart-room** Small compartment on or near the gunship's bridge normally used to keep sea-charts.

167.30 **Prometheus** For stealing fire from heaven and thus angering Zeus, he was chained to a cliff in the Caucasus where he had his liver devoured daily by a vulture.

168.7 **officer of the watch** Officer in charge of one of the duty periods dividing the twenty-four hours of the seaman's day.

168.10 **Ternate** A small island in the Moluccas south of the Philippines (see 151.29n and Map 4). In the sixteenth century, the Portuguese had turned this island into the spice centre of the world. The Dutch guarded their colonial waters against trespassing rivals and against pirates, to whom the Moluccas were particularly tempting and vulnerable.

168.11 **Makassar** Chief port and city (Ujung Pandang) of Celebes situated at the south-west corner of that octopus-shaped island (see Map 4). It was already a thriving port when the Portuguese reached it in the sixteenth century, and trade continued to flourish after 1667 under the Dutch. In 1848 it was declared a free port (i.e., a port open to all traders). In the later nineteenth century it was a regional military headquarters centred on Fort Rotterdam (see *The Rescue*, p. 101), from which Heemskirk would have obtained official permission to intercept the *Bonito*.

168.16–18 **steamed north . . . virgin forests** The *Neptun* approaches a region of NE Borneo well known to Conrad who, as first mate of the *Vidar*, unloaded and shipped cargo at Dongala in NW Celebes; she crosses to Borneo at Samarinda, passes Tanjong Redeb, thirty miles up the River Berau (Pantai), and steams further north to Tanjong Selor, thirty miles up the River Bulungan. See Map 4; also 141.11n.

169.22–23 **Malay town up the river** Tanjong Redeb, the location of Conrad's first novel, *Almayer's Folly*, a region 'politically disturbed for a couple of years' (170.32–33; see 171.31). In fact, trade feuding between the two rival sultanates, Gunung Tabur (which included Tanjong Redeb) and its neighbour Sambaliung, lasted until 1892. See Jerry Allen, *The Sea Years of Joseph Conrad* (1967), pp. 215–16, quoting respectable authorities. See also Map 4.

169.36–40 **The brig . . . between the two ships** The vulnerability of the brig to the gunboat represents more than Jasper's defencelessness against Heemskirk; it also suggests the disappearance of sail from professional maritime life. Annual statistics of sailing ships and steamships calling at Batavia (Jakarta) describe a remorseless decline: in 1865, 3,077 versus 0; in 1875, 1,773 versus 1,041; in 1900, 184 versus 3,445 (Vlekke, p. 310). See 'Introduction', pp. lv–lvi, lvii.

170.17 **Beak and claws** See 167.30n.

170.22 **Javanese sailors** As a warship, the *Neptun* recruits a crew from a population under Dutch control.

170.23 **warrant officer** In the British and Dutch royal navies, a naval officer appointed not by a commission (a conferment of authority as from the sovereign), but by a warrant deriving from the Admiralty (in the case of Great Britain, the Lord High Admiral). See *Nautical Terms*, 10.02. See also 174.9, 174.21.

173.4–5 **Makassar was ... on his way** The *Bonito* is intercepted at a point considerably north of Macassar. If at the mouth of the River Berau, Jasper's voyage to the Seven Isles would be reduced by about 550 miles.

173.8 **Mesman** Called Mr J. Mesman, and described as 'a colonial-born Dutchman' at 178.35, he is a figure significantly modelled on A. R. Wallace's 'Dutch gentleman, Mr. Mesman' (p. 162).

173.31–32 **At one time . . . defence** Piracy in the China Seas was so aggressive that tea clippers and other trading vessels were armed in the 1860s. According to A. G. Course, *Pirates of the Eastern World* (1966), the Ordinance for the Suppression of Piracy (Hong Kong, 1866) marked the turn in favour of trade when it 'brought within legal restriction the haunts and stores of the receivers and native dealers in marine supplies' (pp. 188, 193).

173.37 **Fore-cabin** A small secure storage cabin in the forward part of the officers' quarters under the poop deck.

174.10 **his**] **SE**– his face remaining lifeless but his **MS–SA** Although SE's reading could be a case of compositorial eyeskip, the omission of TS1r's phrase more likely reflects Conrad's reconsideration of his description of the officer's behaviour. It follows closely 'His immovable fat face looked lifeless' (170.25) and 'a fat man with a lifeless face and glittering little eyes' (173.16–17). Presumably Conrad spotted the double repetition, with its apparent contradiction of the reference to 'the wild blinking of his small eyes' later in the sentence, when revising for both SE and E1.

174.14 **on board**] **SE**– in TS1r on **SA** VAR **MS** TS1t The appearance of 'on' in both SA and SE indicates error introduced by Pinker's typist, who understandably misread Conrad's revision in the typescript, and not an editorial change to avoid the misreading of 'brig' as 'lockup'. In both SE and E1, Conrad inserted 'board' after 'on' and deleted an instance of 'on board' soon after (174.17) – revisions so inextricably bound together that TS1r's reading cannot stand.

175.13–14 **the elect** A theological term for the saved, which once more associates profane and sacred love.

175.15–16 **the sun . . . harbour** Having travelled southwards, they turn east towards Macassar. See Map 4.

175.20–21 **Spermonde . . . Tamissa reef** The Spermonde Archipelago, which lies off the south-western coast of Macassar, consists of four rows of about 100 coral islands, submarine reefs, patch reefs, and fringing reefs. Now known as Sangkarang Archipelago, it covers an area of about 16,000 sq. km. Susan M. Wells, ed., *Coral Reefs of the World*, vol. II (1988), s.v. 'Indian Ocean, Red Sea, and Gulf', p. 122; A. J. Whitton *et al.*, *The Ecology of Sulawesi* (1987), p. 214.

176.27 **Gott fer dam! Hold**] **MS** Gott for-dam! old **TS1t** Gott for-dam! Hold **TS1r SA** Hold **SE**– Although elsewhere Conrad toned down his language for the *London Magazine*, here censorship appears to have produced an early cut, not restored by E1, as part of an editorial intrusiveness that increased as the story's complications grew, instead of diminishing while drawing to an end. Revisions Conrad made elsewhere further elevated Jasper's character and demeaned Heemskirk's (see 150.22, 156.11, 167.30, 175.13); the excision reflected in SE and E1 goes against that trend.

176.36 **cable** Its anchor-chain. Chain cable, replacing hemp rope, first appeared about 1800 in military vessels, then gradually in merchant ships as well.

176.38 **sampan** Chinese for 'boat', applied by Europeans in the East to any small boat of Chinese design. The 'harbour sampan' summoned here has an awning over the centre and after parts and is propelled by a single scull (light oar) over the stern.

177.14 **spring tides** Tides which rise highest and fall lowest from the average tide level, as opposed to neap tides which rise least and fall least. The *Bonito* has been stranded when the water level, now at its highest, will never be able to float her off. Spring tides occur when the pull of the moon and sun act in conjunction, neap tides when they act in opposition.

177.25 **Makassar** See 168.11*n*. The principal source of Conrad's well-focussed description is Wallace, pp. 162–4 (see 'Introduction', p. lx); there is no evidence that Conrad, who navigated regularly through the Macassar Strait between 2 August 1887 and 2 January 1888, ever visited the town. Having thrived first under the Portuguese and then under the Dutch, it became a free port in 1848 and remained a colonial stronghold as imperial rivalries intensified during the rest of the century.

177.36 **900 miles** The direct distance between Macassar and the Seven Isles.

177.38 **at least three people** Although Freya, Heemskirk, and Schultz are the positive agents of the catastrophe, a full analysis of the determinants would have to include Nelson and Jasper (see 189.9*n*).

178.11 **to test a case** Until the discovery that the *Bonito*'s supply of rifles has disappeared, the brig had broken no law. Following the establishment of a liberal economic policy for Indonesia in 1864, the Dutch government confined its role to the maintenance of law and order. However, the government continued to regulate piracy and to prohibit the supply of arms to native states, especially when the states were in armed conflict with each other, as was the case here (see 169.22–23*n*). See Furnivall, pp. 151, 187–90.

178.30 **harbour office** The office from which the harbour's naval traffic is controlled, its regulations policed, and its dues collected.

178.31 **in ballast** That is, laden with ballast only (*OED*). The *Bonito* has dispersed the remainder of her cargo at the last port of call (see 171.31–35). The standard ballast for a vessel of her size would have been stone or gravel in the holds, to stabilize and trim her while sailing empty (*Ships and the Sea*).

179.6 **He had**] **TS1** He **MS** I have **SE**– OM **SA** SE's error, which reflects its increasing intrusiveness and represents a misunderstanding of the complex narrative mode, is predicated on the notion that direct discourse began with 'Well, well' (179.5), where it inserted a new paragraph and inverted commas, which in turn required further 'correction' of 'He had' to 'I have'. In MS Conrad had specifically rejected this alternative by deleting his original quotation marks before 'Well'. The narrator is indirectly reporting an earlier conversation between Mesman and Allen and then directly quoting Mesman's speech during that earlier conversation beginning with '"Mind, when you have happily eloped' (179.9).

179.24 **Oranje House** All free ports (see 168.11n) required at least one established hotel. Conrad plausibly names Macassar's after the ancestral royal house of the Netherlands, even though the Dutch crown had changed hands after 1830.

181.29–30 **a certain person** See 183.25–26, where a 'rascally white man . . . made him drunk'.

184.8–9 **Dutch court . . . explanation** In the last thirty years of the nineteenth century, the second golden age of the European empire builders, the Dutch tightened their grip on the so-called native states from fear that their neglect would offer opportunities for expansion to other European powers, especially Great Britain, which had already taken control of substantial portions of Borneo and were threatening unilaterally to discipline Atjeh (Aceh) 'pirates' in northern Sumatra (see 125.31n). Resentment against the British was further exacerbated by their increasing control of the Indonesian carrying trade as sail yielded to steam. Vlekke, pp. 316–17.

184.16 **That]** TS1r SA ¶"That MS TS1t ¶That SE– SE's paragraph reflects its continuing intrusiveness (cf. 179.6n). TS1r's treatment of internal monologue and its omission of the paragraph break are of a piece and must be accepted together.

184.29 **manes** (Latin, two syllables) For Romans, 'manes' were the spirits of the dead, often revered as minor deities; here, in the singular, the word derives from fourteenth-century Latin and refers to the spirit of a virtuous person.

184.39 **Batavia** Jakarta. See 123.19n.

185.4 **Molluccas** See 151.29n. Heemskirk's posting to a locality at the periphery of the Dutch East Indies not only vulnerable to disorder and piracy, but also permitting greater freedom of action, constitutes a promotion. See Vlekke, p. 315.

185.28 **penny stamp** A comparatively inexpensive course for both sender and recipient. Until 1840, receiving letters through 'posts' established by Cromwell at a rate of over 8 pence for a single sheet had been an exceptional source of government revenue. When the standard rate for the British Isles was fixed at 1 penny, paid by the sender, the service proved to be more of a boon to the public than to the Exchequer. This minimal charge lasted until 1918, when it was raised to $1\frac{1}{2}$ pence.

185.29 **Notting Hill** Also known as North Kensington whose main road, High Street, was in effect an extension of Bayswater Road (185.36n), this London district had begun development in the 1830s and by 1890 had become an area of extreme contrasts, with fine houses and noxious slums existing in close proximity. It was the district where Ford Madox Ford (Conrad's friend and collaborator until 1909) edited the *English Review* from offices near Notting Hill Gate and his first wife ran a 'fantastically gloomy' boarding house at 40 St Luke's Road. The site of the nineteenth-century post-office, probably one of several, seems to have disappeared from the records. See Ben Weinreb and Christopher Hibbert, *The London Encyclopædia* (1983).

185.36 **Bayswater** The southern part of the district of Paddington. In October 1904 Conrad and his wife stayed 'at 10 Prince's Square, in Bayswater – the future whereabouts of old Nelson (or Nielsen)' (Najder, p. 304). Bayswater's main road borders Hyde Park and runs west through Notting Hill to Holland Park, the location of the London home of Conrad's friend John Galsworthy, who had set his novel *The Man of Property* (1906) in Bayswater. It had been developed for the upper-middle-class market from about 1807, and under Victoria had been patronized by the novelist W. M. Thackeray and the philosopher Herbert Spencer; but its large-scale mansions were already deteriorating in the 1880s and were being converted into boarding houses. See *The London Encyclopædia*.

186.2 **unclean garment** The smoke pollution of Victorian London was legendary and remained so until the 1950s.

186.5 **Seven Islets**] SE– Seven islets MS seven islets TS1 SA In the early texts Conrad's references to the islands were variable: 'Seven Isles', 'Seven-Isles group', 'Seven Group' all appear, and here in the manuscript 'Seven islets like minute specks' finds a parallel in the typescript, where he first wrote 'Islets' before revising to 'Isles' when inscribing the title (see Appendix B, 'The Titles of the Tales'). Although plausible, as its retention by SA suggests, the typescript's form is a typing error that Conrad 'corrected' in both SE and E1 by improvising a new form that reflected his varying nomenclature.

186.14 **Hong Kong** The island, on the south coast of China, had been ceded to Great Britain in 1842, after China's defeat in the first opium war, and by 1888 it had become one of the foremost trading cities in the Far East. Although situated on the edge of the tropics, its winters can be severe.

186.29–30 **what seemed now . . . very old days** In fact, about four years. Freya joins her father in the Seven Isles at the age of eighteen. Jasper's brig is destroyed a few weeks before her twenty-first birthday, the appointed date of their elopement. The narrator begins to call at the Seven Isles before the first of these three years (125.38–40). Jasper's first visit to be described by the narrator (128.8–16, 129.27–39) occurs late in that first year. Heemskirk's intrusion occurs early in the second year – at least early enough for his calls to have become regular. The last time the narrator sees 'all those people assembled together' is at the end of the second year (136.1–2). His meeting with Jasper 'a few weeks later' (136.17) in Singapore occurs at the end of the first month of the final year: 'eleven months more [before the elopement]' says Jasper (138.8–9), planning to crowd in three trips before that. At the end of the first of these, the narrator misses him twice – in Singapore (141.29–30), and again at Nelson's Cove (141.31–32). The arrest and destruction of the brig occurs as Jasper prepares to claim Freya, about three weeks thence. Nelson discovers the *Bonito*'s fate 'weeks' later (186.32). Freya is taken for treatment to Singapore, where the full story of Jasper's fate comes out. Nelson's trip to Macassar, where he finds an insane Jasper, consumes another three weeks. On medical advice, he decides to take Freya to Hong Kong (188.27), where she dies of pneumonia. Thus the whole final period – which includes the collapse of Freya's health, Nelson's chance discovery of the news of the *Bonito*'s wreck, Freya's unsuccessful treatment in Singapore, Nelson's trip to Macassar, his daughter's fatal removal to Hong Kong, and his voyage to London to share these disasters with the narrator – would have consumed at least another year. See 'Introduction', pp. lxxxi–lxxxii.

186.34 **Banka** See 132.9–10*n*.

187.5 **Fever** There are cases of 'fever' where the physical cause cannot be detected (*Columbia Encyclopedia*). Cf. 32.29*n*. Freya's fevered death echoes a well-established convention of the nineteenth century seen, for example, in *Wuthering Heights*

(1847), *Uncle Tom's Cabin* (1852), and *Little Women* (1869), and about to be used by Virginia Woolf in *The Voyage Out* (1915).

188.15 **Mahmat** A commonplace Malay name, already used by Conrad in *Almayer's Folly*, 70.12.

189.9 **three men's absurdities** This insistence (see 152.19–20, 156.30–31, 157.1–3, 177.38n) forces even on our narrator what would later be regarded as a feminist perspective.

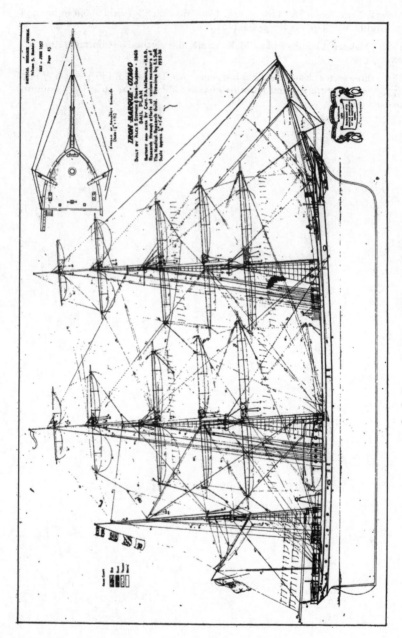

[17] Conrad's *Otago*: a reconstruction.

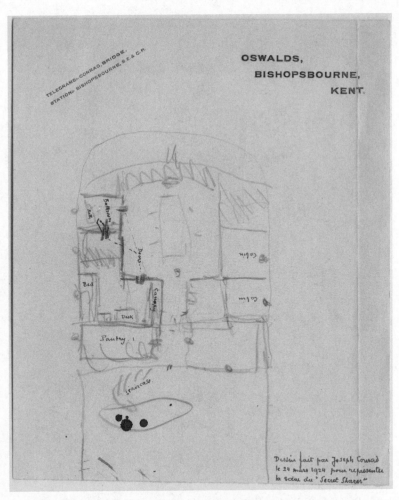

[18] Conrad's sketch of the officers' quarters, 'The Secret Sharer'.

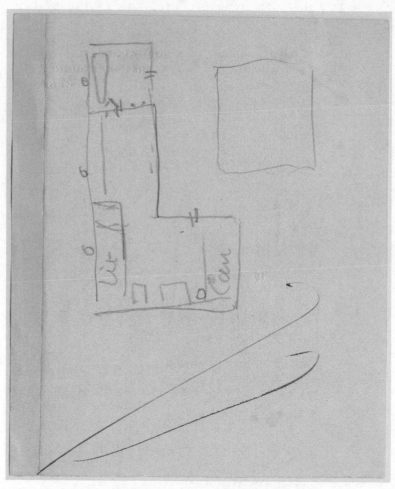

[19] Conrad's sketch of the Captain's cabin, 'The Secret Sharer'.

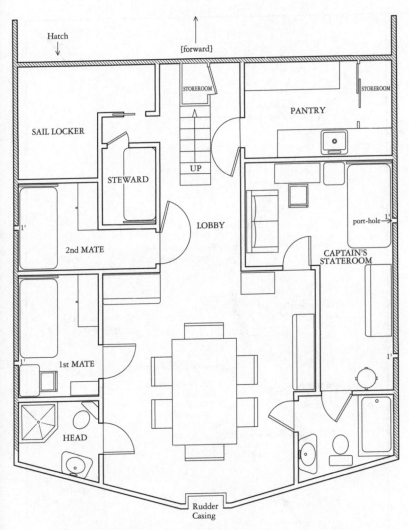

Hatch

[forward]

STOREROOM

SAIL LOCKER

STEWARD

STOREROOM

PANTRY

UP

LOBBY

port-hole 1'

2nd MATE

1'

CAPTAIN'S
STATEROOM

1st MATE

1'

1'

HEAD

Rudder
Casing

[20] Plan of the officers' quarters, 'The Secret Sharer': a
reconstruction.

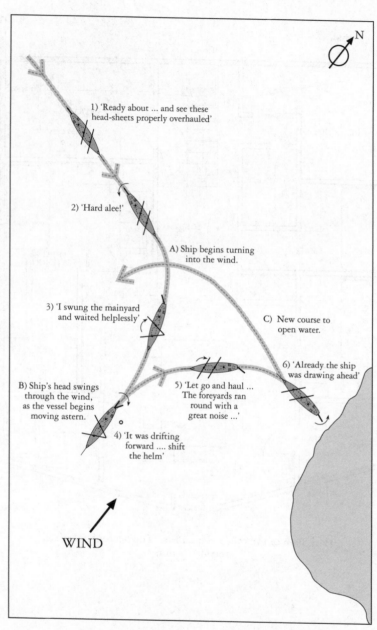

N

1) 'Ready about ... and see these head-sheets properly overhauled'

2) 'Hard alee!'

A) Ship begins turning into the wind.

3) 'I swung the mainyard and waited helplessly'

C) New course to open water.

B) Ship's head swings through the wind, as the vessel begins moving astern.

5) 'Let go and haul ... The foreyards ran round with a great noise ...'

6) 'Already the ship was drawing ahead'

4) 'It was drifting forward .... shift the helm'

WIND

[21] The ship's manœuvre, 'The Secret Sharer': a reconstruction.

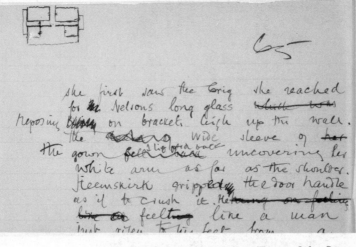

[22] Conrad's two sketches of Nelson's bungalow, 'Freya of the Seven Isles'.

[1] The Eastern Seas.

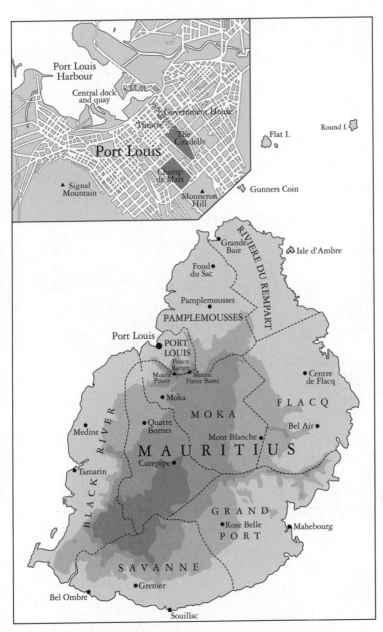

[2] Mauritius, with Port Louis.

537

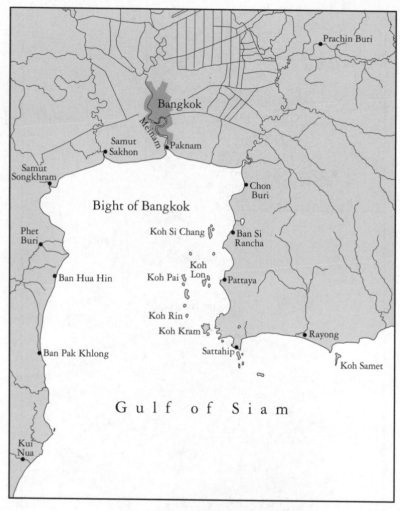

[3] The Bight of Bangkok.

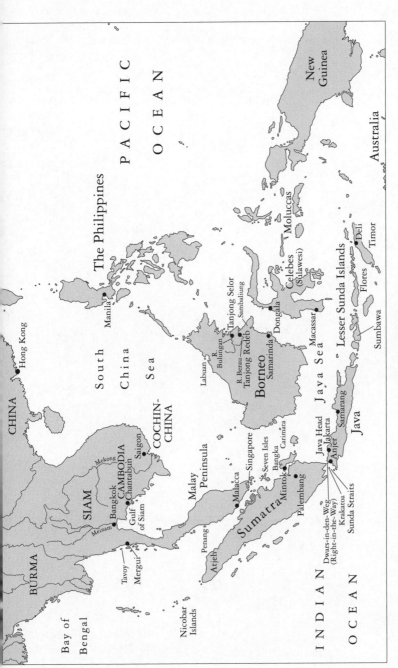

[4] The South China Sea.